LOUIS SULLIVAN

His Life and Work

Other books by Robert Twombly

BLACKS IN WHITE AMERICA
SINCE 1865

FRANK LLOYD WRIGHT:
AN INTERPRETIVE BIOGRAPHY

FRANK LLOYD WRIGHT:
HIS LIFE AND HIS ARCHITECTURE

LOUIS SULLIVAN

His Life and Work

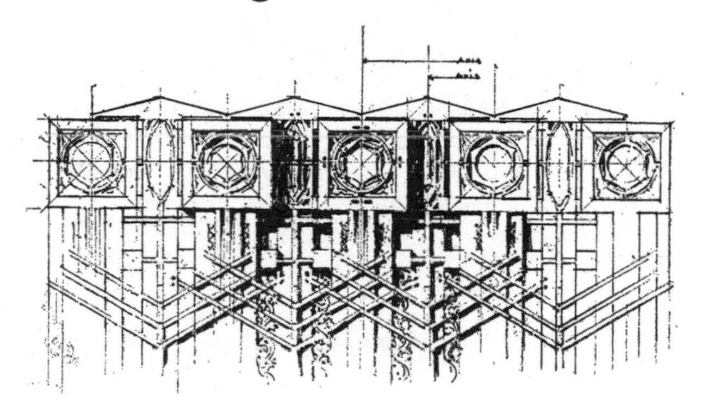

ROBERT TWOMBLY

The
University of Chicago
Press

The University of Chicago Press, Chicago 60637

 Published 1986
University of Chicago Press edition 1987
Printed in the United States of America

96 95 94 93 92 91 90 89 88 87   5 4 3 2 1

Reprinted by arrangement with Viking Penguin Inc.

Library of Congress Cataloging in Publication Data

Twombly, Robert C.
Louis Sullivan: his life and work.

Bibliography: p.
Includes index.
1. Sullivan, Louis H., 1856–1924. 2. Architects—
United States—Biography. I. Title.
[NA737.S9T9 1987]   720'.92'4   86-27279
ISBN 0-226-82006-8 (pbk.)

Preface and Acknowledgments

HAD ANYONE ASKED Louis Sullivan what he was in a word, and had he been willing to answer, he might have said he was a poet, perhaps an artist, but probably not an architect. Louis Sullivan was an artist whose medium was building, a poet whose materials were stone, brick, and mortar. His work was intended to convey messages about life in his times, about democracy, business, selected institutions, human relations, nature and the physical world, but above all about the process of creation. His buildings were, to be sure, calculated solutions for practical problems arising from mundane matters. But they were also the working out of instincts and inspirations about the nature of those problems. Least of all were Louis Sullivan's buildings about themselves.

His preoccupation with issues larger than mere construction carried him to considerable heights of fame and fortune as long as Dankmar Adler, his partner, was content to let him handle the artistry and facade composition of their projects. But without Adler as a buffer between him and the philistines, his career plummeted. Before he was forty, he had passed his peak and was already declining, never in creative or design power, but in his ability to get work. Louis Sullivan's story is one of the great American tragedies: the story of a superior talent rejected at its most productive. His tragedy was that he would not compromise, and could not change when he knew he should. In public he disapproved of those with whom he disagreed, and in private he was guarded, ruminative, and suspicious of what he did not understand. Refusing to reveal himself or let others know who he was inside, he took pains not to let his feelings show, not to let people get too close. When he died in poverty, he was a bundle of nerves.

Discovering what this man was about was not an easy task. Many people assisted in the effort. Since Chicago was his home, it is first of all there that one must look for help. John Zukowsky, Daphne Roloffs, Suzanne Barksdale, Theresa Pruitt, and fellow staff members of the Art Institute; Linda J. Evans, the late Ann Van Zanten, and others at the Chicago Historical Society; Virginia R. Smith and Carolynne A. Sanders of the Chicago Public Library; Daniel Meyer at the University of Chicago Library; and Professor Joan Draper and staff at the University of Illinois at Chicago Circle all contributed to this book. John Vinci, Tim Barton, and Kathleen Roy Cummings, who are laboring to produce *The Complete Work of Adler and Sullivan,* deserve sincere thanks and everyone's support. Irma Strauss bailed me out one day when I ran out of time. Owners, residents, daytime occupiers, and protectors of the few remaining Sullivan buildings in and out of Chicago assisted in various ways: to all of them I am most grateful.

Most of all, in Chicago—or near it, anyway—is Maya Moran: generous, encouraging, supportive, and contributing, Maya Moran literally made this book possible in very tangible ways. She knows how, and I remain in her debt.

Ocean Springs, Mississippi, was Sullivan's winter home for twenty years, and several people there lent their support. Their names will be found elsewhere in these pages. But four people deserve special mention: Mary Ruddiman for showing me her Charnley House; Pat and Phineas Stevens for opening their home for a week to a total stranger, housing him, feeding him, showing him around, and making the research possible; and Courtney Blossman, Sullivanophile to the core, for helping far beyond any reasonable expectation. She, too, made "Southern hospitality" real. Pamela Guren of the Mississippi Department of Archives and History in Jackson found these lovely people for me. For that and other aid, thank you. I do not forget staff members at the Biloxi Public Library and the county courthouse in Pascagoula, and Regina B. Hines, author of *Ocean Springs, 1892,* for her interview.

Some people are so reliable and contribute so much generally that they become organically entwined with the enterprise. David Roessler—architect, student, confidant, chauffeur, and companion—knows more about Louis Sullivan now than he ever wanted to. Answering endless questions and offering regular advice might not get him anything more tangible than a free copy of this book, but I think he had a good time.

Joan Saltzstein of Milwaukee, Dankmar Adler's granddaughter, was more than generous with her time, hospitality, and ideas. Through letters, on the phone, and in person, she demonstrated to me what others already knew: that she is a truly magnificent person.

Distant relatives of Mary Spelman and her husband, Albert, Louis Sullivan's brother, dug up what information they could: Marjorie Devereux Cummins, E. Everett Elsey, Anna W. Burdette, and especially Professor Daniel Wogan of Tulane University.

A number of people assisted on particular areas of Sullivan's life: in Boston, architectural historian John Tucci; Ruth Marshall and R. Eugene Zepp of the Public Library; Joseph M. McDonough, deputy superintendent, Boston School Committee; Kathryn Corcoran of English High School; and most particularly, in Boston, Kevin and Peg Moloney, for putting me up, putting up with me, and opening doors to the archives.

Thanks to Francis T. Bresnahan, Newburyport, Massachusetts, superintendent of schools; Marianne Ventura of the Newburyport Public Library; Elizabeth Roland of the Gloucester, Massachusetts, Lyceum & Sawyer Free Library; Ruth A. Woodbury, Gertrude Stearns, and George Weldon of Wakefield, Massachusetts; Velda M. Model of the Reading, Massachusetts, Public Library, and Miriam O. Barclay of the Reading Antiquarian Society; Garry Shattuck of the Nova Scotia Public Archives; and Ellen Webster of the Halifax Regional Library for clarifying Sullivan's childhood.

Bruce Laverty, Historical Society of Pennsylvania; Joan Haas and Deborah A. Cozort of the Archives, Jeanne Duperreault of the Historical Collections, and Ronald P. Smith, associate registrar, all at the Massachusetts Institute of Technology; F. Giamomoni, sous-directeur, Archives de France; and Theodore Turak of American University, Washington, a William Le Baron Jenney expert, all illuminated Sullivan's early career.

My appreciation, too, to Tony Wrenn, American Institute of Architects archivist, in Washington; photographer William Edmund Barrett; Mary M. Ison of the Library of Congress; Julia M. Young, Bentley Historical Library, University of Michigan; and Thomas Beckman of the Milwaukee Art Museum. Alan K. Lathrop of the Northwest Architectural Archives in Minneapolis forwarded a good deal of valuable information on Margaret Hattabaugh, Louis Sullivan's wife.

At the State Historical Society of Wisconsin in Madison, Barbara Kaiser, Harold L. Miller, Katherine Thompson, and Myrna Williamson gave their aid. Information about Salt Lake City projects was supplied by Karl T. Hagland, Utah Historical Society; Professor Peter L. Goss, University of Utah School of Architecture; and Everett L. Cooley, University of Utah Library. Material on Sullivan's St. Louis work was gathered and clarified by Mary Mewes and Charles E. Brown of the Mercantile Library Association; by Martha Hilligoss of the Public Library, who was especially generous; and by Jack Randall, a former resident and distinguished preservationist now at the Architectural Museum in Buffalo.

Another group of people assisted on specific buildings: Chicago theaters: Charles E. Gregerson; Aurora Watch Company: Patricia J. Caster; Bayard Building: Marvin Shulsky, Ian Smith, Esther Brumberg; Burnet House Hotel project: J. Richard Abell; Carnegie Hall: Jennifer Wade; elevator car: Sally Brazil; Illinois Central Railroad Station, New Orleans: Gay G. Craft, William R. Cullison, Robert W. O'Brien, Mrs. B. S. Foley, Collin B. Hamer, Jr.; Island City project: Ward J. Childs, Sandra L. Tatman, Gail Greenberg, Marianne Promos; Moody's Church: Walter Osborn, Carl H. Johnson; National Farmers' Bank: Kenneth W. Willcox; Opera House, Pueblo: Joanne L. Dodds, Betty M. Carnes, Edward Broadhead, and especially Norman Kaufman; Opera House project, Seattle: Aina Doczi, Herman Pundt; pedestal, Springfield, Illinois: Mark Heyman; Sinai Temple: Rabbi Howard A. Berman; Virginia Hall, Tusculum College: Wayne Dobson.

This book would never have happened without the patience, guidance, and encouragement of Elisabeth Sifton at Viking Penguin, a remarkable editor whose immense personal warmth matched by immense professional skills made the undertaking a pleasure all the way along. So special thanks to her, to Beth Greenfeld for whipping the manuscript into better shape so intelligently, and to Richard Curtis for getting us all together.

Finally and through it all were my sons, David and Jonathan, from whom I took time I hope I can now replace: to them my love and thanks.

Robert Twombly
West Nyack, New York
January 1985

Contents

LOUIS SULLIVAN

His Life and Work

Chapter I

THE HUB OF HIS UNIVERSE
1856-72

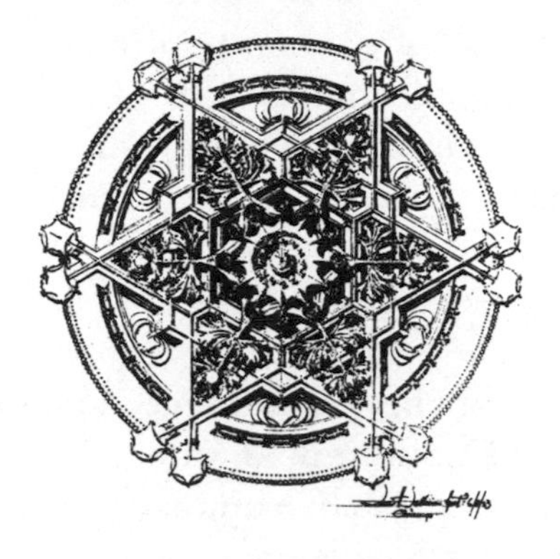

LOUIS H. SULLIVAN began his memoirs in 1922, when he was sixty-six. Writing an autobiography is hardly an unusual undertaking for a prominent person, but Sullivan's was a highly unusual example of the genre. By breaking off the narrative in 1893, when he was thirty-seven, shortly after he became a famous architect, he devoted the bulk of his attention to his childhood and youth, thereby understating, at times even omitting, many of his notable achievements. Ordinary readers unfamiliar with Sullivan's career who approach autobiography for glimpses of greatness might easily ignore a book so full of rumination but so empty of tangible accomplishment. That in itself explains why *The Autobiography of an Idea* was so thoroughly neglected by the general public.[1]

If autobiographies habitually chronicle proud exploits of the famous and fortunate, Sullivan's down-played success to record the evolution of his quite private architectural inspiration. The act of confronting interior feelings and perceptions may account for his inability to write about the last three decades of his life, when he suffered a slow but inexorable decline, less noticeably in physical health, more obviously in professional standing. Recognized abroad in 1893 as one of a handful of important American architects, he would die in 1924, poor and neglected, in a cheap South Side Chicago hotel. Still eager to work, with intellectual and artistic powers as finely honed as ever, he had become a bitter man long before 1922. The pages of his memoir reflect that bitterness, much of it directed toward his father, Patrick, whom he depicted in hateful terms but with whom his relationship was far more complex.

Sullivan described his father as physically repulsive, overly ambitious, much too calculating, and incapable of love. Patrick Sullivan, the architect remembered, "hunger[ed] for Nature's beauty," responded to the "fine art of symmetry, of grace, of rhythm" in the dance, and "revered book-learning and the learned." But "he was no gentleman." He was, in his son's words, "a lackey, a flunkey [and] a social parasite." How strange it was that a man with such "highly virile and sensitive powers" should be "so unlovely in person. His medium size, his too-sloping shoulders, his excessive Irish face, his small repulsive eyes—the eyes of a pig—of nondescript color . . . sunk into his head under rough brows, all seemed unpromising enough . . . until it is remembered," Sullivan admitted, that behind this facade was "the grim will, the instinctive ambition" that had carried Patrick Sullivan "alone and unaided, out of a childhood of poverty."[2]

Louis Sullivan conceded only one thing to his father: that he had pulled himself up by his own bootstraps. That someone "so unlovely" had actually met good fortune may have offended the architect's refined aesthetic notions, but sons do not usually indict parents for lack of physical beauty. Nor is it customary to attach ability so closely to personal appearance. But in 1922, still vain about his looks, his own broken bootstraps having returned him to the poverty Patrick was said to have escaped, Sullivan must have felt the comparison to be onerous indeed. Had he written in 1893, from the height of glory, his feelings about his father might have been altogether different. *The Autobiography of an Idea* is therefore not to be trusted on the subject of Patrick Sullivan, although it must be said that long after the fact, cramped for space in his single room, the architect preserved important family documents, enabling him to reconstruct factual aspects of his story with amazing accuracy.

Only his autobiography records, for example, that Patrick Sullivan sailed from London on July 22, 1847, aboard the five-hundred-ton *Unicorn* bound for Boston, Massachusetts. That seems accurate enough, but it is the apocryphal quality of Patrick's prior life, for which the autobiography is again the only source, that seems so dubious. According to his son, Patrick was the only child of the widower Jeremiah Sullivan,[3] a landscape painter living in a remote Irish town. Their favorite pastime was to visit country fairs, where on one occasion twelve-year-old Patrick got lost in the crowd, never to see his father or his home again. Forced to support himself, the youngster played the violin at village dances, in the process traveling over most of Ireland. After several years as a vagabond musician, he decided on dancing instruction as a career and moved to London, where he "placed himself under the tutelage of the best—most fashionable—masters," eventually to establish an academy of his own. But Patrick had set his sights even higher. Giving up his studio, he left London to take "instruction of the leading masters" in Paris. Louis Sullivan did not record, or was never told, how long Patrick stayed in France or when he returned to England, but he did note that over a period of years on the Continent, his father traveled through much of Switzerland. Finally, captivated by "the lure of America," Patrick set sail, arriving in Boston on September 7, 1847.[4]

A story so full of improbabilities raises a number of intriguing questions. How, for example, could a twelve-year-old boy clever enough to make his way in the world alone not be able to find his home, especially after mastering local geography? How could a teenager fresh from the Irish countryside "place himself under the tutelage of" London's most fashionable dancing masters, particularly in light of English ethnic attitudes? And would it not be considerably more difficult—even with professional experience—for Patrick to have entered Paris's highly rarefied terpsichorean establishment? Sullivan never raised questions like these because it was important for him to imply that Patrick was "successful"—that "he was always successful"—primarily through wile, charm, calculation, and a kind of unseemly determination. If the son in his last years could not retain his standing legitimately by talent and skill, the father was said to have done so only illegitimately by devious means. Patrick's success in America was actually severely limited and tenuous, but his son built him up to tear him down, a way of suggesting that worldly acclaim—which he himself had lost by 1922—was not the best measure of a person's worth.

When Patrick Sullivan arrived in Boston in 1847, he listed his age as thirty, which means he had lived in London for several of the preceding eighteen years.[5] He must have known the city well, and was certainly not without Irish companionship had he wanted it, for in 1841—a year for which figures exist—there were nearly 420,000 Irish-born people permanently residing in England and Scotland, a number that would rapidly increase. Following the appearance of potato rot in 1845, and repeal the next year of corn laws guaranteeing English markets for their agricultural commodities, thousands of Irish farm workers were thrown off the land. In 1847 over 2500 were evicted for inability to pay rent, and by 1850 the number increased to 100,000. Between 1835 and 1865—the great majority after 1847—some 2,500,000 fled their homes, mostly for cities in England, Scotland, and the United States. The Cunard shipping line had successfully captured middle- and upper-class transatlantic passenger traffic by 1842, leaving packet companies to charge low rates to travelers willing to share steerage with cargo. In 1850 it was possible to reach Boston from Liverpool by packet for a mere seventeen to twenty dollars.[6] Presumably, when Patrick sailed from London three years earlier, it had cost about the same.

Patrick Sullivan did not come to America to escape the potato famine or the insensitivity of absentee English landlords, but he found himself swept up in a tidal wave of Irish migration that is traditionally said to have begun the very year he arrived. The number of immigrants to Boston increased from 3936 in 1840 to 28,917 in 1849, and these newcomers, writes historian Oscar Handlin, "were overwhelmingly Irish."[7] In 1845 slightly more than 23 percent of Boston's residents were foreign-born, but by 1850 Irish-Americans alone constituted 26 percent of the city's population, almost 29 percent by 1855. Nearly 50,000 of Boston's 160,000 people that year had been born in Ireland or of Irish-born parents, and from 1856 to 1859, the percentage of Boston children with a least one Irish parent rose from 46.5 to 48.5.[8] The dominant Yankee population responded to these ethnic changes with a distinct lack of civility. But Patrick Sullivan, who lived in Boston for twenty years during its transformation into an Irish stronghold, does not appear to have encountered—at least said nothing about—Yankee racial prejudice.

Patrick may have instinctively taken what steps he could to avoid overt discrimination, not that he had many options. When the Boston-based packet *Unicorn* returned from London in 1847, Patrick Sullivan was accompanied by sixteen other passengers, including four families, all of whom were Irish. Seven of the nine adult males on board, Sullivan among them, listed their occupation as "tailor" on the harbor master's list before they disembarked.[9] Patrick may have learned before sailing or from his fellow passengers that Boston was rapidly becoming the American center of ready-made clothing production.

He could not have known that a single company, George Simmons's Oak Hall, would soon employ three thousand tailors, but he may have heard at the time he arrived that two-thirds of the city's fifteen hundred tailors were Irish.[10] Boston clothing manufacturers paid on average less than half the wages of their New York City competitors, one reason they were able to seize control of the industry. As long as cheap labor remained integral to an expanding economy, Boston would welcome newcomers like Patrick Sullivan claiming to be experienced "tailors."

A second decision he made on arrival was not to settle among his countryfolk. Boston's Irish were concentrating in two neighborhoods in the late 1840s: the North End, the oldest part of town, just above the central business district on the waterfront, defined by Blackstone and Merrimac streets, today a heavily Italian enclave; and the Fort Hill district, the site of seventeenth-century defenses, bordered intown by Milk Street and extending along the harbor's edge into 1830s landfill once known as South Cove. But Patrick managed to escape those areas notorious for offering newcomers some of the worst conditions the New World had to offer.[11] According to the city directory of 1848—the first to list him—Sullivan boarded at 414 Washington Street, in an old residential neighborhood turning commercial as the downtown business district expanded, known then and now as the South End. Washington Street's still-elegant homes were rapidly succumbing to warehouses, retail shops, and working-class flats in the city's southward sprawl toward Roxbury and Dorchester. Although the Irish were moving into the South End, they were still as sparsely clustered there in 1848 as in any other part of town. The city directory listed Sullivan as a "teacher of dancing," with no address other than his residence presumably because he worked where he lived.

Establishing a successful academy was not easily accomplished in Boston during the late 1840s. The city was growing slightly faster than the nation as a whole, but at less than half the rate of American urban areas generally. The fourth largest city in 1830, it would slip to fifth by 1860 despite unprecedented immigration.[12] With fewer than 135,000 residents in 1847—an increasing percentage impoverished as the distribution of wealth grew steadily more unequal—the demand for dancing instruction was not unlimited, especially when the "master" was Irish and his potential clientele largely Yankee. To make matters worse, Patrick had several competitors, the principal being one Count Lorenzo Papanti, a native of Florence, Italy, who had operated an elaborately appointed studio on fashionable Tremont Street for a decade.[13] Sullivan's objective was either to entice students away from Papanti and the other masters or to expand popular demand. He must have succeeded to some extent because by 1851 and possibly sooner, he had opened a studio outside his home at 339 Washington Street, a few blocks nearer downtown and thus more easily accessible. He kept this address until 1856, when he moved even closer, to 323 Washington, where he remained for at least five years. It may have been at his academy or at an evening of musical entertainment at someone's home, as his son believed, that Patrick Sullivan met his future wife.

I.1 *Patrick Sullivan, date uncertain.* Avery Architectural and Fine Arts Library. Columbia University in the City of New York.

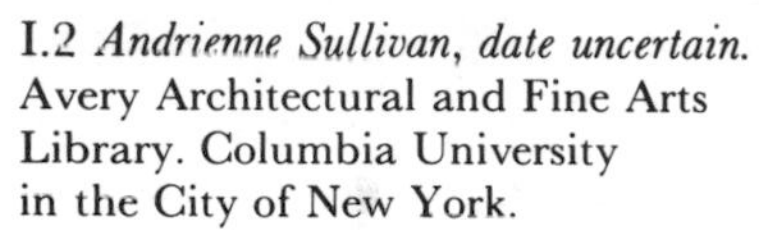

I.2 *Andrienne Sullivan, date uncertain.* Avery Architectural and Fine Arts Library. Columbia University in the City of New York.

Andrienne F. List was fifteen years old when she arrived in Boston with her parents, sister Jennie, and brother Julius from Switzerland in 1850. Her father, Henri List, a Hanoverian German living in Geneva, was in some capacity associated with the university when he met and married her mother, Geneva-born lace-and-linen merchant Anna Mattheus. Family history states that the couple lived sumptuously for a number of years after Andrienne's birth in 1835. Anna List was an accomplished businesswoman, but Henri, who fancied himself something of a skilled financial plunger, listened once too often "to the wiles of a Jew," in his grandson's ill-chosen words, and lost all their money. Anna was able to obtain enough from well-to-do relatives to get the family to Boston, where by 1851 it settled in at 3 Central Court, just off Washington between Bedford and Summer streets in the heart of downtown, a ten-minute walk north from Patrick Sullivan's studio. Henri List found a job teaching French at Chapman Hall School, a private academy on Chapman Place in rear rooms of the Horticultural Society a few blocks from his residence, where he remained until 1861, when the Lists left the city.[14]

A photograph of Andrienne shows her to have been a dignified woman of erect carriage with even features, not beautiful, but clearly proud of her persona. Drawings handed down to her son that are now in public archives and in some instances published reveal her talent as a renderer of natural forms—leaves, trees, and flowers—and her lesser but still noteworthy skill with other subjects. She was an excellent pianist, able to interpret Chopin and Beethoven sensitively but equally at home with current dance music. Immediately captivated when they met, Patrick Sullivan "lost no time in marrying" Andrienne but, says her son, only "as a business asset. She was lovable and he may have loved her. It is possible but hardly probable; for there is nothing in the record to show that he loved others."[15] Louis Sullivan's "record"—his own memory in 1922—was hardly unbiased. The reality is that Andrienne and Patrick parented two sons, lived together more than thirty years through good times and bad, shared many mutual interests, and were never far apart.

Their attraction led them on August 14, 1852, with Patrick thirty-four and Andrienne seventeen, to marry in Boston in a civil ceremony. Flush with the optimism of new beginnings, possibly more candid than usual about his true self-image, or perhaps just eager to impress his young bride, Patrick gave his occupation on the wedding certificate as "artist."[16] That he chose not to call himself a "dancing master," as he was officially listed everywhere else, is revealing. Like his father, Jeremiah, he too drew, as well as Andrienne, and, after all, he had made his living for years as a musician and dancing teacher. But to use the more general and prestigious title "artist" was to declare his aspiration and to elevate his status. After the wedding Patrick took Andrienne to his new quarters at 11 Hayward Place, which ran from Harrison Avenue into Washington Street near his academy at number 339. There a year later Andrienne delivered a stillborn baby girl. This terrible disappointment at the beginning of married life, coupled with a financial squeeze serious enough to force them out of their apartment, may explain their move to New York City sometime in 1854.

If their intention was to make a fresh start in a new setting untainted by depressing associations, they were apparently unsuccessful. Their stay in New York was brief, wedged between the March 1854 and 1855 compilations of Boston city directories, both of which listed Patrick's name, which did not appear, on the other hand, in New York tax or business records or its county census of June 1855. The only remaining trace of the Sullivan's visit to New York City is a birth record dated September 17, 1854, for Albert Walter Sullivan, their firstborn son, ushered into the world by R. Girandon, M.D.[17] Their home at the time was a flat at 9 Jay Street, running east-west between the river and Hudson Street in a commercial and Irish working-class district on the west side of lower Manhattan. If Andrienne's second pregnancy had prompted the Sullivans' move to New York for its financial possibilities, Patrick would have established an academy, but it must have been so short-lived or unprofitable that he decided to return to Boston no later than March 1855.

Patrick reopened his academy at its old address but boarded with his wife and infant son in rooms at 85 Bedford Street, in the central business district two blocks from his in-laws, the Lists, at 3 Central Court. Here they remained through the rest of the year until May 1856, when, undoubtedly with help from Andrienne's parents, Patrick purchased a house on Bennet Place, at the corner of South Bennet Street, off Washington in the South End, in roughly the same neighborhood he had lived and worked in since 1847. Buying a house was a major accomplishment for so recent an immigrant, a measure of success available to few newcomers. Jesse Chickering, a statistician for the city of Boston, wrote in 1851 that "those who come from other places bring with them no capital; . . . the only idea of *success* in their vocabulary, is the acquisition of property. . . . Of those who resort to cities to better their condition, very few succeed."[18]

Between 1850 and 1860, only 43 percent of Boston's taxpayers owned real estate, while a mere 11 percent of the working population owned any landed property at all.[19] By this standard Patrick Sullivan entered a somewhat select group, having achieved a degree of upward mobility denied to most. But his success was more symbolic than real, as the city's financial records disclose.

Patrick Sullivan's two-story brick house rested on a forty-three-by-eighteen-foot corner lot, sharing a party wall with the dwelling next door. Of the $5425 purchase price, Sullivan paid $2000 in cash, taking out a $3425 mortgage with the seller, Stillman Willis. Patrick agreed, in keeping with home-financing practices at mid-nineteenth century, to repay the loan in one lump sum after five years at 6 percent interest due semiannually, that is, in two $102.75 installments totaling $205.50 yearly. Patrick was also responsible for taxes and insurance and for keeping the premises in repair, but he had the right to rent. According to the deed and to prevailing legal procedures, Andrienne Sullivan was denied joint ownership.[20] The house was assessed at $5300 in 1856 but declined to $5000 in 1859, where it remained as long as Sullivan owned it. This drop occurred at precisely the time Boston real estate values were rising, from an average per-property assessment of $9210 in 1850 to $24,470 in 1860. Not only was Patrick's dwelling losing value while the city's as a whole was climbing, an indication of the changing nature of his neighborhood, but its worth was also considerably below average for the time he bought it. Thus he had reached only a very low rung on the upward-mobility ladder.

To make matters worse, his tax rate rose over the years, from $42.40 on a $5300 house in 1856 to $52.50 on $5000 in 1862, a 23 percent increase on a dwelling worth 6 percent less. When he sold his house to David Greenough in July 1862, Patrick still owed $3000 on the mortage he was supposed to have retired fourteen months before. Having paid only $425 plus his original $2000, with Greenough giving him a mere $1250, Sullivan suffered an appreciable loss of $1175 on his first and last venture into real estate. And by paying Willis his $3000 mortgage and Sullivan his $1250, Greenough picked up a $5000 dwelling for only $4250.[21] Patrick must have been desperate to sell, a common-enough situation when nineteenth-century working people were caught trying to effect upward mobility through property ownership beyond their means.

The decision to purchase in the first place must have involved serious family deliberation, because Patrick could not afford it alone. The $2000 down payment most likely came from Anna's Geneva relatives, who had helped finance the List voyage to America in 1850. There was no other source of money in the family; neither List nor

Sullivan could have saved that amount in less than a decade on their meager incomes. When it came time to occupy the tiny dwelling in 1856, seven people moved in: Anna, Henri, Jennie, and Julius List, and the three Sullivans, further indication the Lists had helped secure the premises. The motivations for this move were undoubtedly complex. Andrienne and her relatives were not so far removed from their Geneva affluence to have given up hope of regaining its trappings. Home ownership—even on a small scale—symbolized for them their rightful place, for Patrick his social progress, and for interested bystanders another American success story. If Patrick was reluctant to live with his in-laws, he presumably considered the trade-off—a happier Andrienne and access to financial resources—to have been worth it. Thus he followed the route of many aspiring immigrants: doubling up for necessity and appearances. So in the summer of 1856, everyone moved into the tiny back-street home to prepare for another reason they had purchased it: the arrival of Andrienne's second child.

According to Boston birth records, "Henry Louis" Sullivan was born at 22 South Bennet Street on September 3, 1856. The listing was most likely a mistake—considering that "Andrienne" was misspelled in the documents—since the boy was always called Louis Henry, but it would have been like his mother to insist that one of her sons be named after her father.[22] With two boys the family was now complete, and for the next five years, the Sullivan-Lists shared cramped but comfortable quarters. The architect recorded no complaints from anyone, at least not in his autobiography. Throughout his life he expressed great love and affection for his grandparents, remembering them in the context of a warm and happy extended family atmosphere. Sullivan described his early years, in fact, largely in terms of his mother's love, his grandmother's attention, Henri List's grandfatherly indulgence, and of fun and petting from his youthful aunt and uncle. Even if his father was the unattractive person Sullivan later claimed, young Louis was too small to know it. And even if the family was not terribly affluent, home life appears to have been all that a young preschool child could want.

During those five years on South Bennet Street, Patrick Sullivan walked daily to his dancing academy a few blocks away, Henri List continued to teach French at Chapman Hall, and teenage Uncle Julius grew old enough to take a clerk's position at 60 Franklin Street downtown, while Anna, Andrienne, and Jennie—who turned nineteen in 1856—stayed home with the two small boys. (Anna may have tutored French as well.) Louis retained a number of strong impressions from those early years, events of great significance to a wide-eyed young boy if to no one else. Standing at the window for hours at a time watching "a large world" go by, he especially remembered the day that teams of men and horses—"the Pageant of Labor," he later called it—marched down his block to clean the street. He was captivated by nature, recalling his fascination with the

1.3 *Photograph of Louis and Albert Sullivan, date uncertain.* Gift of George Elmslie.

moon and passing clouds, the swirling snow, and wind in the trees. He remembered his intense emotions when his mother's piano playing seemed to generate great outpourings of love. Finally he recalled little Alice Look, the girl his own age next door, who called him "Papa" when they played in her walled-in backyard. Dynamic relationships between people and things impressed him greatly before the age of five.

Alice Look's "sacred dwelling" was Sullivan's metaphor for a happy life on South Bennet Street. So he must have been disturbed when Patrick Sullivan sold the house in 1862, packed up his family, and left. Inability to pay the mortgage was the ostensible reason for the sale, but the move may have been prompted by more delicate considerations, which city tax records again suggest. In addition to real estate levies, Boston homeowners were also assessed on their "personal estates," that is, on household and private possessions. In 1856 and 1857, Patrick Sullivan paid about $5 annually on $600 "personal estate," only $100 higher than average for working people in the city at the time. But in 1858 his assessment suddenly shot up to $6000, and in 1860 to $7000, where it remained through 1862, on which he paid taxes of $51 in 1858, $62 by 1861, and $73 in 1862.[23] The most plausible explanation for this unexpected jump in personal wealth is a gift or an inheritance and, since Patrick had no known relatives of his own, it likely came from Andrienne's well-to-do Geneva family, possibly in the form of jewelry or small heirlooms, which, unlike money, would have been detected by port authorities on arrival and thus reported to the city's tax collectors. Since prevailing property laws conveyed a wife's possessions to her husband, Patrick was the owner of record. But if the estate was actually Andrienne's, neither she nor the Lists would apparently permit Sullivan to liquidate even part of it to save the house.

This could easily have become a source of friction in the family, prompting the Lists to consider leaving and Patrick to concur. And if Andrienne gave the income to the Lists or if it was actually theirs in the first place, it would account for Henri's ability to purchase four pieces of real estate in South Reading, Massachusetts, in November 1861 for $4750 in cash.[24] It may have taken several years after 1858 for the Lists to find the property they wanted, or they may have been reluctant to leave their grandchildren and daughter in the company of a man unable to support them in a manner promised by the acquisition of a house. If this was true, the last three years of their stay at South Bennet Street might not have been as congenial as the first two. But young Louis knew nothing of this. He knew only that at the end of 1861, when he was five, all four Lists moved away, ending his familiar, comfortable life. Without his in-laws to help him, Patrick sold the house at a loss less than a year later, taking the scanty proceeds and his family to Folly Cove in Gloucester, Massachusetts, a farming and fishing settlement on the Rockport line north of Boston. Here, in a rented farmhouse on land spilling down to a sheltered, rock-bound inlet of the sea, the Sullivans spent the rest of the 1862 summer clearing their memories of an unhappy separation from Boston and the Lists.

Not privy to these matters, Louis exulted in the sea at Folly Cove, exploring the rocky coast and its rolling hills, learning the lore of boats, and discovering with amazement that when people sailed toward the horizon, they seemed to be swallowed up. He walked and talked and fished with his father, disclosing in his autobiography the pleasure he took in their companionship. On one occasion Louis fell into a well, but was quickly rescued by a farmhand. As he stood naked before giggling playmates to be rubbed down with rough towels in front of a roaring fire, he felt his first hint of sexual awakening, "a new world . . . gestating in the depths," he recalled. Eighteen sixty-two was his first of many country summers, and he loved every bit of it. Little wonder he was unwilling to leave the Cove to start school in the fall.

When the family returned to the city in September, Louis entered the same primary school his brother had attended in 1861. In the spring of 1862, Albert had advanced to the Brimmer School, on Common Street between Washington and Tremont, for the March-to-June term and was registered for readmittance in the fall. But just as school was about to resume in September, its records show that Albert was "discharged."[25] The reason for this is probably that when Louis began school, he rebelled so strongly against it that his parents consented to let him stay with his grandparents to study in South Reading. Although Louis did not mention Albert when he later wrote about the experience, his brother probably went with him, relieving the financial burden on Patrick and Andrienne. Unfortunately, Louis found the West Ward Grammar School equally boring and, though only six, played a good deal of hookey with the complicity of his grandfather, who, despite his own years of teaching, had little patience with formal public instruction. With the wonders of Folly Cove countryside fresh in his mind, and rote classroom learning dreadfully dull, Louis found it much better to explore neighboring farms, following his boyish inclinations. Grandfather answered the many questions raised by his outdoor discoveries, while all the Lists provided him and his brother with plenty of love and comfort. From these and similar experiences, the architect later developed the view that learning was best accomplished outside the classroom by the study of nature and by taking instinct to the level of intellectual inquiry, not excluding the Socratic method, an educational philosophy he would advocate in his mature writings. Sporadic attendance during his first school year, coupled with indulgent but responsive adults, and large chunks of nature study added up to an unusual educational episode, but one that proved to be a precedent, in fact, for an entirely unusual educational career.

Patrick and Andrienne's address at this time is unknown. Sullivan was not listed in the city directory for 1863, nor is there any other clue to his whereabouts. But toward the end of the academic year, while Louis was languishing "in misery" during those infrequent occasions he actually attended the West Ward School, word came that Patrick had opened a summer dancing academy in Newburyport, on Massachusetts's northern shore, his first attempt to capitalize on the cultural proclivities of vacationing Bostonians. Andrienne arrived at South Reading in June to bring Louis and Albert to their father by the sea.

While the family boarded at a "dingy" hotel, Louis resumed his countryside rambles, this time not so entirely on his own. Believing the Lists had been "too soft" on Louis, had "pampered him outrageously," Patrick decided "it was high time his son was brought to him, that he might establish in him a sense of respect, order, discipline [and] obedience." Patrick undertook the job in a way six-year-old Louis immediately liked and would emulate later on: with a regimen of strenuous, programmed, physical exercises. Arousing his son each morning at five, Patrick put Louis through the paces of calisthenics, swimming, diving, and fence vaulting. The two ran races, threw stones at targets, and pumped well water. "And the child worked with gusto; it became play," Sullivan later admitted, "for the father did all these things with him jointly." This and similar activities at Folly Cove and elsewhere demonstrate that as a boy Louis did not hate his father at all.

The training was intensive, but there was plenty of time for relaxation. There were trips along the Merrimack River, where the boys played while Patrick and Andrienne sketched; there were fishing and boating holidays. Louis fell in love with a nearby suspension bridge, which lost some of its mystery when Patrick explained how chains and towers worked in tandem to hold up the roadway. At the Newburyport shipyards, Louis entered "seventh heaven" watching "the workers—his idols"—swing adzes, pour tar, bore holes, and hammer planks. Men organized to build things, and the objects of their efforts, became as fascinating to young Louis as the outdoors, especially when he remembered the wonderful street-cleaning crews on South Bennet Street. But this good thing, too, came to an end, and shortly after his seventh birthday, it was time to return to school. When Patrick closed the academy, the family left for Boston.[26]

But Louis's worst apprehensions did not come true. Patrick decided to try his luck elsewhere, and apparently on the spur of the moment, after a very brief stay in Boston or South Reading, moved his family to Halifax, Nova Scotia, in September 1863. Patrick opened another academy, installing Andrienne and the children in a residential hotel. Louis had not even had time to register for school in Boston, and if he studied in Halifax, it must have been privately, since public instruction did not begin there until 1864.[27] The physical-exercise program continued; but in sub-zero weather, he did not find it much to his liking. Andrienne recovered from a bout of diphtheria, "but her illness," her son remembered, "was prophetic of change." From everyone's point of view, the Halifax interlude was a mistake, probably the reason Sullivan devoted so little space to it in his autobiography. After six months he seemed quite happy to leave in March of 1864, since he was scheduled to return to his beloved grandparents at South Reading, where even the prospect of several weeks at the West Ward School did not diminish his enthusiasm. Patrick and Andrienne moved into a boardinghouse at 846 Washington Street, deeper into Boston's South End, farther removed from downtown, where rents were cheap but business probably dear. Patrick gave no separate address for his business, so he must have taught dancing at home.

I.4 *Patrick Sullivan's sketch of Newburyport bridge, 1868.* Avery Architectural and Fine Arts Library. Columbia University in the City of New York.

Louis returned to Boston in the fall to enter the twenty-year-old Brimmer School, a four-story, fourteen-room establishment for boys he immediately found "vile." It was "unspeakably gloomy," he wrote, "a filthy prison for children." He hated everything about the place, said he learned nothing at all, and passed the winter "yearning for a *teacher*." So began the repetitive process of the next five years. Each summer Patrick set up in Newburyport, leaving Louis (and presumably Albert, who is never mentioned in the autobiography) with his grandparents. In the fall Patrick would return to 846 Washington Street, gather up his sons, and send them back to school. There are grammar-school records for Albert, age ten, from the 1864–65 academic year, and for Louis, age nine, for 1865–66. Drawings of the Newburyport suspension bridge signed and dated by Patrick and Andrienne establish their whereabouts for 1867 and 1868.[28] Sometime in the intervening months, Patrick again changed the family residence, this time to a boardinghouse at 3 Acton, a newly created street located even deeper into the South End district toward Roxbury. In the fall of 1866, after two years at the Brimmer School, Louis was promoted to the Rice Grammar School, a three-story, ten-room structure built in 1848 at 1119 Washington Street. The following September he and his classmates moved to temporary quarters on Concord Street, and then in 1868 into the new Rice School, just opened on Dartmouth Street in the Back Bay district.

Louis found the old Rice building as "gloomy" as the Brimmer School, and again claimed to have learned nothing in the classroom. When he was transferred in 1868 to the new structure—"up to date in all respects"—he expected better things, and to a certain extent his hopes were fulfilled. He found his teachers' methods and ideas quite conventional, and often disagreed with their racial and artistic opinions. He got in trouble once for reciting "Old Ironsides" with too much sarcastic enthusiasm and too little patriotic respect. He would have been dreadfully bored had he not retreated into his own thoughts and fantasies, which ironically were sometimes inspired by the very textbooks his teachers made so tiresome. But he studied and learned and performed well, despite prevailing pedagogical practices. In June 1870, at the age of thirteen, Louis graduated from the Rice School with the first and only diploma of his life.[29]

Outside the classroom things were much more interesting, especially when he discovered in Beadle's Dime Novels a wonderful new world of romance, action, and manliness. He did not particularly care for the perpetually eighteen-year-old, ravishingly beautiful heroines, he remembered, but he was tolerant of the villains, and worshiped the "magnificent, man-god heroes" for whom no obstacle was too great to overcome. He also became "citified" during his years at the Rice School, wandering through Boston's dock and commercial neighborhoods, ferreting out every alley and blind court he could find, even hiking to outlying villages. With his father he took long walks into undeveloped sections of the city, and with both parents attended Handel and Haydn Society concerts. But his attempt to learn the piano bored him completely, even though he loved to listen to his mother play. And when he tried to copy a lithographic plate, he found he "detested drawing."

It had not yet occurred to young Louis Sullivan that he would have to learn to draw if he wanted to be an architect. But one day after school, when he was eleven, exploring the streets as usual, it dawned on him that he had been intrigued by buildings for some time without realizing it. Even then he did not understand that his interest most likely stemmed from his favorite Newburyport bridge his mother and father had so carefully sketched and from his own fascination with men making things. So his realization seemed to come as a bolt from the blue, and was associated in his mind with a particular structure he had probably watched go up: Merrill G. Wheelock's Masonic Temple, built in 1867 on the corner of Tremont and Boylston streets downtown, a florid Gothic Revival edifice long since demolished.[30] To Louis, the Temple was incredibly exciting, much more so than Charles Bulfinch's dignified State House from the 1790s that everyone praised, even more than Alexander Parris's Faneuil Hall (1740–42), Peter Banner's handsome 1809 Park Street Church, or any of the other architectural landmarks Louis had seen and admired. For him, there was only the Temple:

> How it gleamed and glistened in the afternoon sunlight. How beautiful were its arches, how dainty its pinnacles; how graceful the tourelle on the corner, rising as if by itself, higher and higher, like a lily stem, to burst at last into a wondrous cluster of flowering pinnacles and a lovely pointed finial.[31]

In retrospect, Louis Sullivan recognized the Masonic Temple for the mediocrity it was, but at the time "he raved."

He was still raving when one day he noticed a particularly dignified and distinguished man come out of a doorway, call for his carriage, and signal his coachman to drive away. From a workman he learned that the gentleman was an architect, that many structures had architects, and, when he inquired as to what architects did, came away with the notion that they invented buildings in their heads and bossed everyone else on the job. What a revelation this must have been to a boy so attracted to men collaborating at work and to romantic heroes of dime novels able to cope with improbable challenges. Here was undoubtedly the unseen man buried deep in Louis's subconscious who had directed "his idols" at South Bennet Street and Newburyport. Right then and there he made up his mind.

I.5 *Merrill G. Wheelock, Masonic Temple, 1867.* Courtesy Bostonian Society.

When he confided his "heart's desire" to become an architect, Patrick encouraged him by saying he could remain in school until age twenty-one if he wished, but urged him to consider agricultural college, believing with good reason that Louis's fondness for nature and the outdoors indicated an obvious career choice. But the young man insisted. He would settle for nothing less. In the end, after much discussion, the issue was resolved: he would finish his general education, attend a technical school, and someday study abroad.

With his goal of becoming an architect firmly in mind, Louis was better positioned to confront probably the most significant event of his young life. During the winter of 1867–68, Andrienne experienced her fifth annual bout with diphtheria since attacks began at Halifax in 1863. Believing coastal northeast winds debilitated her thoroughly enough to account for her susceptibility, the family in conference decided that for Andrienne's health the Sullivans would move to Chicago. Possibly with List support, but certainly without Andrienne's, Louis persuaded his father to let him stay behind, convinced that "The Hub of the Universe," as Bostonians like to regard their city, offered better educational opportunities than Chicago. Patrick,

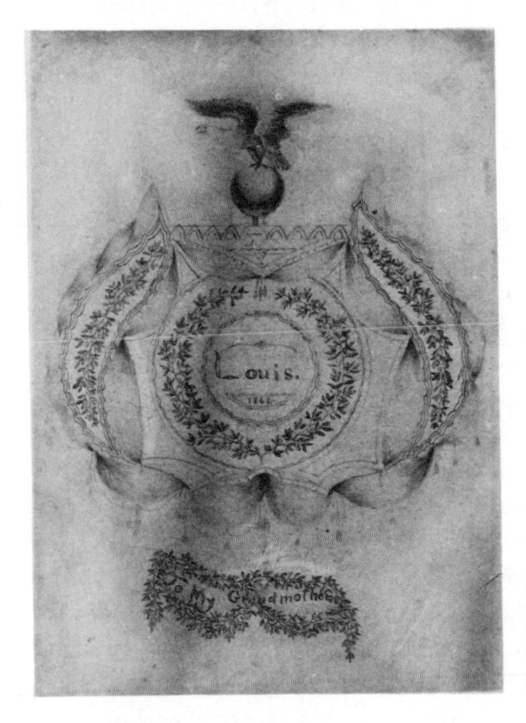

I.6 *Louis Sullivan's 1867 "To My Grandmother." Pencil on paper.* © The Art Institute of Chicago, all rights reserved.

Andrienne, and Albert departed for the Midwest at summer's end in 1868, leaving Louis with his grandparents in their South Reading home. Certainly he was shaken to see Andrienne leave, especially in such poor health, but wrote only that when the day came, he "sobbed on his mother's shoulder." About Patrick's departure he professed no regrets: "He was much relieved," he insisted half a century later, "to say to his father: Good-bye! Now he was free!" About Albert, he wrote nothing.

Louis had just turned twelve when his family left Boston, a crucial age in the development of any young man. Even though his grandparents could offer him a loving and supportive home atmosphere, he must have experienced a certain anxiety at his parents' departure. His autobiography contains few hints of trauma or distress, but that may have been the result of Sullivan's insistence on stressing his boyhood maturity. One unrecorded consequence of 1868 may have been the beginning of Louis's negative feelings toward Patrick. But in retrospect, there is much to be said on his father's behalf: he had struggled to provide for his family, had been a willing companion and teacher for Louis, and had always been available when needed. In his autobiography Sullivan was unable to offer anything factual, no event or series of actions, could cite nothing specific—other than Patrick's ambition and "unloveliness," for which the evidence seems somewhat manufactured—to explain his antipathy. When he wrote that Patrick's leaving had set him "free!" Sullivan conveniently ignored the exceptional parental leniency that had allowed him as much physical and mental freedom as any young boy could want.

Perhaps there are other explanations for Louis's dissatisfaction with Patrick. Louis's boyhood was characterized by a series of close encounters with adult males, first Patrick Sullivan and Henri List, of course, then dime novel heroes, and finally two other men—Moses Woolson and John A. Tompson—soon to be discussed. But Patrick was the crucial figure. If the boy was unusually dependent on adult male relationships, needing that kind of intimate contact for his own sense of security, then the loss of someone *so* close, largely at Louis's own insistence, might have sparked a feeling of guilt that for his own psychic protection he could not accept. Perhaps the architect, lonely and dispirited in 1922 when he recalled these events, had come to regret the loss of his family but, unable to accept the responsibility, projected onto Patrick what he would not admit about himself: that in the final analysis, he, not his father, had put career ahead of loved ones, that he, not his father, had let ambition transcend all else. Louis stayed behind in 1868 for himself, for himself alone, but when he came to regret it as an old and lonely man, he could not face facts and therefore transferred to Patrick his own unendearing characteristics. Eighteen sixty-eight was the year Louis Sullivan's childhood ended. From then on, beginning at the age of twelve, he was more adult than boy.

With his parents gone, Louis continued at the Rice School, commuting the twenty miles round trip by train each day from South Reading to the city. The arrangement was that he would go on to Boston's English High School—his parents preferred the Latin School, but Louis wished to make his own decision—and then to a technical college. He followed this agenda faithfully, never missing a day of classes, and apparently dedicating himself to schoolwork much more happily than his autobiography indicated. Late in 1869 Anna List wrote to Albert that Louis, still at the Rice School, "has taste for study and strong perseverance in addition to his great desire to learn. . . . He can't stop to write, not to mention having very little time for it."[32] This and other evidence suggest that Louis was unusually independent, self-reliant, and single-minded for his age. He had a goal in mind, he knew what he wanted in life, and nothing, not his parents' move or anything else, would be allowed to interfere.

Louis's character, his determination to succeed coupled with a strong sense of self, may be attributed to growing up in a flexible extended family, actually two families, with their multiple role models and range of adult influences. At South Bennet Street, he had, so to speak, two mothers and fathers, three if Uncle Julius and Aunt Jennie are included. With several adults having significant input into his socialization, Louis became attached to them all, proof being his autobiography, where he recorded as much affection for Anna and Henri List as for his mother, strong feelings for his aunt and uncle, and understated but nonetheless real pleasure in his father's company. Home life offered him a much greater variety of experiences and attitudes than most young boys of his social class could anticipate. Languages spoken at home included French and German, and if not Gaelic, at least he had his father's lovingly told Irish legends. Religious views ranged from his grandfather's outspoken atheism through Patrick's unacknowledged agnosticism and Andrienne's insistent Protestantism of some unnamed variety to his grandmother's dedicated Mennonism tinged with Baptism. His family valued education, individuals differing only over the necessity of school attendance. Arts were important in the home, nature was revered, and travel was a fact of life. Louis was given a loose rein but also as much love, guidance, and attention as he wanted. Other advantages of having two families were more obvious: when he grew tired of school, there was always his grandparents' farmland; as he got older and demanded more from life than South Reading could offer, there was always Boston. His family atmosphere was culturally rich without being demanding, varied without being frenetic. He had maximum freedom to develop at his own pace in his own direction. That he became as strong-willed and fiercely independent as others in his household should have come as no surprise.

In 1868, when he moved in with the Lists, Louis's adopted hometown separated from Reading to become the independent village of Wakefield, with a population of some six thousand farmers and small-business people, ten miles north of his old South End neighborhood. Henri List still owned his four properties: an eleven-and-one-half-acre pasture; a three-acre meadow; a four-hundred-by-one-hundred-foot lot in the northeast corner of town on Prospect Street, the road leading to Woburn; and on a larger lot a two-story white frame

I.7 *Henri List, date uncertain.* Avery Architectural and Fine Arts Library. Columbia University in the City of New York.

house, with attic and basement, a barn, and other outbuildings, at 106 Prospect on the corner of Chestnut—all offering Louis plenty of roaming space even if he never left the family land. Next door to the Lists, at what is now 98 Prospect, was the home of John A. Tompson, a Boston businessman, whose son George had been Louis's good friend since 1862. About a mile down Prospect Street, in the opposite direction from Woburn, was the West Ward Primary School, site of gloomy associations for Louis.[33] For two years, beginning in the fall of 1868, Louis's life consisted primarily of commuting to the new Rice School every day, roaming Boston's streets in search of architectural discoveries before going home at night, and spending weekends with George Tompson in the Wakefield countryside.

During the summer of 1870, Henri List decided to visit his daughter Jennie, who in 1862 had married Walter Whittlesey, a farmer and railway engineer from Lyons Falls, New York, near Utica.[34] When Louis arrived with his grandfather, he met eighteen-year-old Minnie, Whittlesey's niece by a previous marriage, who was spending the summer with Jennie studying French. They quickly became like brother and sister, Louis recalled. During their long walks and talks together, Minnie guided Louis on an imaginary tour of faraway places: her boarding school, her brother's life at Yale, their comings and goings in Utica society, and her recent trip to the capitals of Europe, meanwhile introducing him to Byron, Tennyson, James Fenimore Cooper, and other unfamiliar writers. From the safety of her four-year age advantage, Minnie flirted outrageously with Louis, who sensed but did not quite recognize what was happening, although he responded with great waves of emotion. Their encounter was brief, only a few weeks one summer, but Louis fondly remembered Minnie fifty years later for opening to him vistas of great literature and distant cities, new horizons of experience she assured him he could reach if he continued to study and to cultivate his talents. Hers was also the first hint that Paris was a place he should someday visit.

Louis returned to Wakefield that fall to prepare for entrance examinations to Boston's English High School. "He was accustomed" by then, he wrote, "to thinking and acting for himself, seldom asking advice," and had thus chosen English over its rival because the study of Latin was "suitable only to those who might have use for it in afterlife." Boston Latin, the oldest high school in the nation, was founded in 1636 to prepare aspiring ministers for entrance to Harvard College. Almost two and one-half centuries later, it was still regarded as Boston's "leading school among those which fitted boys for the university." But when the city established primary schools in 1818, a need was immediately felt for "a school of higher grade, which should afford to the youth of the town not intending to enter college," although in later years many would. In 1821, therefore, the English Classical School opened for boys twelve and over who after "suitable examination" would study for three years under university-trained teachers to enter the worlds of trade and manufacturing.

Although the name was later changed to English High School, the course of studies hardly differed in the 1870s from its original curriculum. In the entering or Third Class—sophomore year, in today's terminology—all the boys studied English language and literature, ancient history, algebra, bookkeeping, botany, music, drawing, and their choice of French, German, or Latin. Second-year subjects included English, medieval history, a foreign language, plane geometry, physiology and zoology, music and drawing. Third-year studies were still more advanced, and by the time Louis entered, there was an optional fourth year devoted to college preparation. The school was not yet divided into departments, each instructor being responsible for all subjects except a few specialties.

By 1870 English High had moved to its third location, on Bedford Street—where Andrienne and Patrick had lived before purchasing their home—in a building shared with Latin. Erected in 1844, its three stories with Greek attic, pilasters, and frieze, twelve rooms, two halls, and observatory, must have been terribly cramped considering that the seven rooms and hall assigned to English High housed 475 students, a headmaster, thirty-five instructors and assistants, including specialists in French, mechanical and regular drawing, and music.[35] Louis's "division" of the entering Third Class had thirty-six boys, all of whom studied the same subjects, except for foreign languages, in the same room. His favorites were mathematics, French, and botany.

English High records still exist from the 1870s, but only for the first of Louis's two years there, when his instructor was Moses Woolson, about whom he wrote so favorably in his autobiography. According to the complicated numerical grading system Woolson employed to chart student performance, Louis, like most of the boys, was never absent or tardy, even though he commuted from Wakefield. With a few others, he received the highest possible marks for deportment and for military drill, a Civil War leftover still part of the instructional routine. He also ranked at the top of his class in drawing, having developed a new and more favorable attitude toward the subject. Louis took one of Woolson's lowest grades in penmanship, and in verb declension was among the poorest performers. His above-average English compositions won sixteen of a possible twenty points, and in 156 recitations on all subjects, which Woolson graded on a scale of First, Second, Third, and Bad, Louis got 136 Firsts and only four Bads; just ten students did better. At the end of the 1870–71 year, he had accumulated 798 points, the highest total being 842, the lowest 738, placing him thirteenth in his division of thirty-six. But on a separate page on which Woolson wrote one-word evaluations for each student, he described Louis as one of eight "excellent" scholars in his charge.[36]

Moses Woolson was the teacher Louis had been looking for since the Brimmer School. Loving literature, science, nature, and poetry, Woolson was skillful and energetic enough to convey a contagious enthusiasm for learning to his pupils. He insisted on discipline and attention in the classroom, not for their own sakes, but to facilitate reflection, observation, and discrimination. Each day ran on roughly the same schedule: a testing period on the previous night's homework was followed by recitations on all subjects, recess, nature study from Asa Gray's *School and Field Book of Botany,* and Woolson's closing lecture, which Louis remembered as stimulating and delightful.

Woolson brought in Professor Gray himself from Harvard on several occasions, introduced his class to Hippolyte Taine, advocated "women's rights," and all in all thoroughly impressed the young would-be architect. Louis came to think of Woolson as a complete and wonderful man, combining the best qualities of teacher, poet, scientist, and naturalist. Although he did not specifically say so, he seems to have regarded Woolson if not as a substitute father, then certainly as a model of what a father should be. "By the end of the year," Sullivan later concluded, "Moses Woolson through genius as a teacher, had turned a crudely promising boy into, so to speak, a mental athlete." The pages devoted to Woolson in his autobiography ring as a memorial to a valuable and good man who otherwise would be lost to history.[37]

Eighteen seventy-one was the high point of Louis's high school, indeed, of his entire educational, career. His second-year teacher, a Mr. Hale, was pedestrian, and Louis did little more than put in his time. He probably took his studies seriously, as his grandmother had reported to Albert, but his heart was not in school. The loss of Woolson was minor, however, compared with a second, very personal, loss that year. Late in the winter, Anna List was suddenly taken seriously ill for the first time in her life with a liver ailment. Pneumonia developed and within a matter of days she died, on April 2, 1871. Louis was crushed, and in his autobiography recorded his considerable remorse. Henri List, his daughter ten years removed to upstate New York, his son, Julius, recently gone to Philadelphia for work, and himself unable to remain in Wakefield without his wife, decided to sell the family properties. In June fellow townsman Edward Walton agreed to purchase the four List parcels for $7000, and in December, after securing a bank mortgage, took possession. Henri List left to join his son.[38]

For the second time in three years, Louis watched part of his beloved family move away. But he was now fifteen, exceptionally mature, and even better able to cope with personal loss than when Patrick and Andrienne moved away in 1868. Although Louis was now the last of his family in New England, he apparently gave no thought to joining his parents in Chicago, where by 1871 Patrick had established a home and academy at 85 Twenty-third Street, on the near South Side.[39] Instead, "Louis found welcome and shelter with the next door neighbors," his friends "the John A. Tompsons, whose son George for years had been his playmate." Someone, the Chicago Sullivans or the Philadelphia Lists, must have reimbursed the Tompsons for Louis's care, since there is no record of his working. With the Tompsons acting as a surrogate family, he finished the year at English—his standing slipping only slightly after his grandmother's death in the spring term—went on to complete the Second Class, and continued to live for an additional year at 98 Prospect Street, only a few feet away from the List family home.

John A. Tompson, a shipping-register publisher in Boston, became a significant influence in Louis's life from 1871 to 1873. It is therefore worthwhile to reproduce in full the delightful description Sullivan later inserted in his autobiography. Every evening, he wrote,

> John A. Tompson returned from Boston at an exact hour, removed his hat, walked to a glass cabinet, took exactly one stiff swig of Bourbon straight, smacked his lips, twinkled his eyes, sank into an easy chair which had remained in the same place for exactly how many years no one knows, dozed off for exactly ten minutes, arose, stretched his short muscular body, smiled widely, displaying false teeth, a fine high forehead and dark fine eyes with as merry a twinkle as one could wish; then he went forth to see if each cultivated tree and shrub and bush and vine were exactly where they were in the morning.[40]

The next two years passed easily and well. Tompson took a keen interest in Louis, a boy he had watched mature, instructing him in the techniques of botany and music, for which he was now developing an appreciation. Without intending to be, Tompson was an instinctively excellent teacher, as much by example as with words. His orderly and economical movement of hand impressed Louis so much that he began to pay attention to everything Tompson did. If Moses Woolson had encouraged Louis to appreciate work of quality, Tompson showed him how to do it.

Toward the end of his second and less satisfying year at English High School, George Tompson, then in the Third Class studying railway engineering at the Massachusetts Institute of Technology, suggested Louis take the entrance examinations for "Boston Tech," as everyone called it. Assuming he needed a diploma before he could apply, the notion of early entrance had never occurred to him. But for young Sullivan, bored with high school and impatient to begin architectural training, George's assurance to the contrary was welcome news. Perhaps Louis had intended to go to "Tech" right along, for he gave no thought to alternatives, not to another college, and not to apprenticing with an architect, the usual way to train for the profession in the 1870s. So in June and again in September, he took two-day batteries of examinations in arithmetic, algebra, plane and solid geometry, French and English grammar, composition, and geography, which he passed with flying colors. On October 7, 1872, just turned sixteen, Louis Sullivan entered the Massachusetts Institute of Technology to begin formal training for his life's work.[41]

I.8 *John Tompson house.*
Courtesy Gertrude Stearns.

I.9 *Mr. and Mrs. John Tompson, date uncertain.*
Courtesy Ruth Woodbury.

Chapter II

ITINERANT STUDENT 1872-74

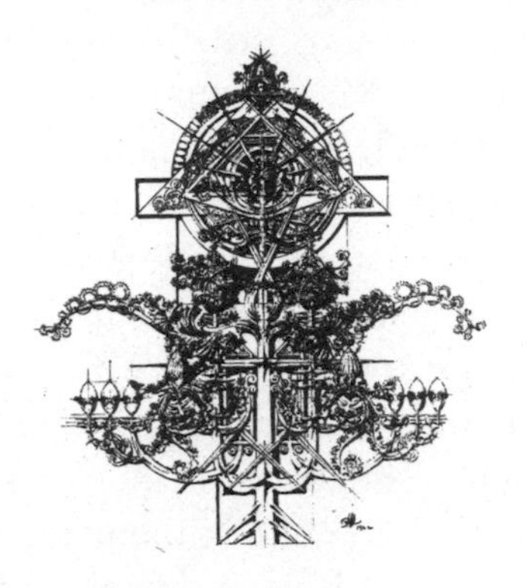

LOUIS SULLIVAN at sixteen would have quaffed an "instant architect" potion if he could, for the young man was in a terrible hurry. As it was he took the fastest possible route to his objective, using every available opportunity to shorten his period of training. His friend George Tompson had shown him how to skip his senior year in high school. When he discovered that by passing certain examinations he could also by-pass his first two years in college, plus a host of required courses, he enrolled directly in MIT's Class of 1874 as a third-year special student in "Building and Architecture." It was not unusual to enter MIT at the age of sixteen, but to do so as a junior was comparatively rare. If all went well, he could be looking for work before his eighteenth birthday.

The Massachusetts Institute of Technology was still in its adolescence when Louis Sullivan arrived in October 1872. Incorporated by an act of the state legislature in April 1861, its first building was designed and built two years later by Boston architect William G. Preston. Named after the school founder, William Barton Rogers Hall was located in the Back Bay on Boylston Street between Berkeley and Clarendon next to the Society of Natural History, another Preston structure from 1863, today a Bonwit Teller Company store. Both were early examples of a new French style just beginning to penetrate the city. Since Rogers Hall was near the Rice School, Louis had probably passed it in his boyhood wanderings, and since at the time it was the westernmost edifice on Boylston Street, he might also have seen it en route to the undeveloped sections of town he and his father had liked to explore. In any event, young Louis Sullivan was certainly aware of MIT long before he actually went there, perhaps from the very moment he decided to be an architect.

During its first half century, before moving to majestic neoclassical quarters across the Charles River in Cambridge, "Boston Tech" acquired a national reputation for its training in mechanical and civil engineering, chemistry, geology and mining, general science, and in the many specialities available to students within those broad rubrics. Classes at the Institute had hardly begun, when in 1865 its administrators decided to add a course in architecture, calling on the promising young Boston practitioner William Robert Ware to organize and direct it. In 1868, with four students, MIT opened the first professional architecture school in the United States. By the time Louis Sullivan enrolled, the program had grown to include some twenty-seven students, all of whom studied under Ware and his earnest young assistant, Eugene Letang, a recent graduate of the Ecole des Beaux-Arts in Paris.[1]

II.1 *Rogers Hall, Massachusetts Institute of Technology.* Courtesy Bostonian Society.

William R. Ware (1832–1915) was born into a prosperous Cambridge family of Congregational and Unitarian ministers who had taught at Harvard Divinity School. After attending Phillips Exeter Academy, Harvard College, and the Lawrence Scientific School at Harvard University, in 1856 Ware entered the architectural office of another old-line Bostonian, William Cabot. Two years earlier Jonathan Preston, father of MIT's architect William G. Preston, had assisted Cabot on the Boston Theatre, one of the great mid-nineteenth-century American opera houses, and may have still been associated with the firm when Ware arrived. To cite these peripheral connections is not to make idle note of coincidence because the Boston Theatre was one of the earliest and finest examples of French-influenced architecture in the city.[2] Because he knew this and was attracted to the style, Ware left Cabot in 1859 for the New York office of the leading American exponent of French classicism, the first American to attend the Ecole des Beaux-Arts, Richard Morris Hunt.

Soon to touch Louis Sullivan's life tangentially, Hunt (1827–95) had studied at the Ecole off and on from 1846 to 1854 and had worked for a Paris architect before returning to America late in 1855. The Studio Building he designed in 1858 for his own offices on West Tenth Street attracted as tenants some of the best-known painters and writers of the day: John La Farge, William M. Hart, and Thomas Bailey Aldrich among them. His own assistants in the closest thing to an Ecole atelier America would ever know included several young men who would gain architectural fame: Charles D. Gambrill, early partner of Henry Hobson Richardson; George B. Post, architect of the City College and Stock Exchange in New York and of many other substantial projects; Frank Furness, whose works included the Pennsylvania Academy of Fine Arts, the University of Pennsylvania Fine Arts Building, and numerous other commissions; Henry Van Brunt, Ware's partner; and Ware himself, who stayed through four years of thorough indoctrination in Hunt's Beaux-Arts methods. In 1863 Ware returned to Boston to begin a twenty-year association with Van Brunt, whose many buildings around the country, several in New England, included their most famous, the 1874–78 Memorial Hall at Harvard. Ware also published a number of books, the most influential being *The American Vignola,* a technical manual on the classical orders that ran through at least five editions between 1902 and 1906, plus several essays and speeches, two of which from the 1860s explained his philosophy of architectural education.[3]

In *The American Vignola,* Ware extolled the classical style, but with Van Brunt he designed mostly in Gothic. MIT's Rogers Hall, where he taught, and its next-door neighbor, the Natural History Museum—both by the younger Preston—had already set a "standard of excellence," says an authority on Boston architecture, for a "restrained French Classicism reminiscent of the Place de la Concorde,"

II.2 *William R. Ware.* Avery Architectural and Fine Arts Library. Columbia University in the City of New York.

which by the early seventies could be seen all over town in "numerous and important" new buildings.[4] Ware and Van Brunt contributed their share, which Louis Sullivan undoubtedly saw. The hall in which he would study, his beloved Masonic Temple, and his entire course of instruction at MIT reflected the French academic tradition. "Everything that has been done at the Institute," Ware later wrote, "has followed . . . the whole scheme of the Ecole."[5] It would have been impossible for Louis not to have absorbed the look and the philosophy of the latest Parisian work.

In his speeches and essays, Ware contended that the quality of recent American building had declined drastically. Earlier, when contractors and builders had followed Giacomo Barozzi da Vignola's *Rules for the Five Orders of Architecture* (1562), a kind of handbook of Greek and Roman styles readily available in popular English translations, buildings were "comely and decent," he said. But after the Civil War, architects began to apply newly introduced English, French, German, and Italian styles and their innumerable combinations and permutations without knowing the proper occasions for their use. As a result, "the rules of professional procedure became corrupted and lost," he insisted, "artistic work pretty much unknown, and even the traditions of professional etiquette and the old-fashioned way of doing business . . . fell into abeyance and were forgotten," creating architectural anarchy in which bad taste and unscrupulous practices abounded. At MIT Ware hoped to remedy this situation by "leaving matters that can be learned in offices to be learned there, and not encumbering the student with useless and irrevelant lore." Fundamentals would therefore receive "systematic and theoretical discussion for their proper comprehension" by thorough grounding in the mathematics, physics, chemistry, engineering, mechanics, and modern language courses everyone at the Institute was required to take.[6]

Students specializing in architecture would also study traditional styles within general surveys of their cultures so as not to apply them incorrectly. In practice this meant the repeated execution of assigned projects in competitions and for occasional prizes, moving from less to more complicated work during the last two years of the four-year curriculum. Further in keeping with the French method, Professor Ware stressed the importance of floor plans, believing that a handsome building would inevitably result from a well-conceived and articulated program. Drawing skills were to be cultivated by starting with tracing, then moving through copying, original composition, and perspective to outdoor sketching in connection with instruction in the appropriate uses of pencil, pen, and brush. Ware's objectives were technical proficiency and cultural enrichment, for he was certain that only as polished gentlemen well versed in European traditions—in his circles most men were—would architects know how best to operate, when to use what style. But since his entire pedagogy was firmly based on knowledge of the five orders—Greek Ionic and Doric, Roman Corinthian, Tuscan, and the Composite—he must have felt that when in doubt architects could always fall back on the ancients. Or as Louis Sullivan was told: "These orders were 'Classic,' which implied an arrival at the goal of Platonic perfection."[7]

Tuition at the Institute was $200, a $125 installment in October and $75 in February, plus a $200 refundable bond "to pay all charges accruing under the Regulations of the School." Students selected their fields of concentration, in Louis's case "Building and Architecture," upon successful completion of the sophomore year, and could expect a bachelor of science degree if they passed "a satisfactory examination in all the prescribed studies and exercises of the course in the third and fourth years, and in all the studies of the previous years in which [they have] not already passed a satisfactory examination." Having sailed through this second batch of tests before entering, Louis would graduate from MIT when he submitted "an original architectural design accompanied by an explanatory memoir."[8]

Professor Ware insisted his students devote "their time exclusively to the school, . . . pursuing a stated curriculum within it."[9] Louis entered MIT on much his own terms as a third-year special student, but he was nevertheless required to take a first- and second-year course in military drill in one of the Institute battalion's two companies. Mandated by a Civil War Act of Congress on July 2, 1862, that had never been repealed, MIT still taught tactics to all its students with arms and equipment loaned by the state of Massachusetts.[10] Louis did not mind that excuses for absence were rarely given because he "liked the exercise, the neat evolutions and the compact team work." Although he loathed war "as the wild dream of madmen who stood safely behind the evil," he considered military training to be "discipline in play." Perhaps as he marched around the streets of Boston, he mentally compared the drill with the organization of street cleaners he so fondly remembered from South Bennet Street or with the exercise programs he and his father had so carefully followed.

The training may have buoyed his confidence when the MIT battalion was assigned to patrol Boston's streets after the horrible fire of November 9 and 10, 1872. From a wooden building at Kingston and Summer streets during the night of the ninth, the fire raged north over a sixty-acre portion of the central business and residential district bounded by the waterfront, Washington, Summer, Milk, and Oliver streets, destroying Trinity Church and 775 other buildings, causing $60,000,000 in damage, and leaving twenty thousand people homeless. "Clad in full uniform with Springfield rifle and fixed bayonet," Louis walked a beat for hours but did not see "a soul." After two weary and boring nights on the lookout for nonexistent looters, he was glad to return to his studies. Like Frank Lloyd Wright, who never forgot the partial collapse of the Wisconsin Capitol in November 1883, Louis may have received his own youthful object lesson on the importance of safe, fireproof construction. A more certain consequence of the Boston conflagration was that after 1872 that part of town would never again be a residential area.[11]

Aside from military drill, Louis's other subjects were dictated by a rigid third-year curriculum with no free electives. Far from being the "atmosphere of *Laissez-faire,* of a new sort of freedom . . . with no special regularity of hours or of attendance" he said had impressed him when he arrived, his program of studies filled almost every minute of every weekday from nine to four-thirty plus Saturdays till one. In the first semester, from October 1872 through January 1873, Louis began his mornings at nine with Institute president John D. Runkle's calculus course, except for Wednesdays, when he went next door to the museum for natural history, and Saturdays, when he studied English composition and literature. At ten o'clock on Monday, Louis took drawing (plans, elevations, sections, detail, ornament, and sketching from buildings) taught by E. Edward Warren, and from Tuesday through Saturday German, drawing again, formal logic, French, and physical manipulation (drill). At eleven his courses were natural history, French, formal logic, German, stereotomy (shades and shadows, perspectives, and elements of machine construction), and drawing; and at twelve o'clock, depending on the day, drawing, perspectives, and drill. There were no classes from one to two-thirty—he must have appreciated that—after which he studied either drawing, architectural practice, or architectural design for the rest of the afternoon.

During the second semester, from February into June 1873, Professor Runkle's mechanics course replaced calculus at nine o'clock except on Wednesdays, when drawing replaced natural history, and Saturdays, when Louis took drill instead of English. Ten o'clock during the week was occupied with geology, French, drawing, the constitutional history of England and the United States, taught by William P. Atkinson, French again, and drill, which ran every Saturday until one. At eleven from Monday through Friday, there was stereotomy, German, history, stereotomy again, and drawing, followed at twelve by more stereotomy, geology, drill, drawing, and German. And, finally, from two-thirty to four-thirty, architectural drawing, architectural practice, civil engineering twice, and drawing on Fridays closed out his weekday afternoons. Louis's other instructors were E. C. F. Krauss for German, Jules Levy for French, Thomas Sterry Hunt for geology, George H. Howison for logic, and Gaetano Lanza, an assistant in mechanics and calculus, none of whom he ever mentioned in his writings. In the mechanics course, Louis learned about stress, stability, strength, and stiffness—perhaps called the "Four S's"—and in architectural design about the elements and principles of composition by analyzing executed buildings. Lectures in architectural design and practice were given by Ware, while his assistant Eugene Letang supervised student drawing projects.[12]

Louis began this rigorous schedule with high hopes, attending classes as faithfully as in high school, even though he still commuted the twenty miles round trip each day from Wakefield, a time-consuming and uncomfortable journey by train. After a few weeks, he purchased a handsome 217-page leather-bound "Records" book, and on the inside of the cover boldly inscribed "Louis H. Sullivan, Mass. Institute of Technology, Boston. Nov. 23rd, 1872," before transferring to it the "Notes on Proffessor [*sic*] Ware's Lectures on Architecture" he had taken down on loose pieces of paper. Lecture One, the "Introductory," began in strict conformity with Ware's objectives for the school: "In offices we get that training which experience *alone* can furnish," Louis wrote. But in "school we become acquainted with the *science* of architecture." In the margin he added notes to himself, emphasizing Ware's contention that colleges and firms taught very different things. By examining and comparing various methods of construction and works by the great masters, Ware and Louis continued, students acquired "that aesthetical and poetic taste and refinement, which it is impossible to obtain in offices."[13]

Having reminded his listeners of their raison d'être at the Institute, Ware continued his "Introductory" by launching directly into the classic. First he defined an architectural order (pedestal, column, entablature), a wall and its parts (which Louis illustrated in the margin by a tiny section drawing), and then explained how walls were connected to roofs. The rest of the lecture was filled with what might easily have been left to after-class reading: definitions and descriptions of architraves, taeniae, coronae, friezes, abaci, echnia, and on and on about classical elements. Anal compulsives might have been fascinated, but other beginning students must have been bored silly.

Louis was clearly more bored than fascinated. There is no way of knowing how many lectures he copied into his book, for pages three to twenty-two have been ripped out, beginning with the final portion of Ware's "Introductory." Perhaps he took no more notes at all, or failed to transfer them to his "Records," for twenty-two pages seems hardly sufficient for a semester's work. But since he used the book regularly from 1876 to 1880 as a sort of diary, and kept it near at hand for the rest of his life, Sullivan might have subsequently decided that Ware's lectures were inconsequential or incompatible with his later "Records," and thrown them away. It would be helpful to know when—and why he retained the first two pages.

His autobiography has more to say about MIT—for instance, that Ware was not a compelling lecturer. Other evidence indicates he was capable of humor,[14] but apparently in class he was serious to a fault; students reacted by occasionally throwing spitballs around the room, which Ware studiously ignored. Sometimes a good idea or two got through to Louis, but Ware, teaching by the book, stressing the ancients and especially the Greeks, dissecting the important historic styles, seemed to be imparting only facts. Despite his stated intentions, Ware did not analyze fully enough for Louis the social and cultural values informing design. Gradually, as he sat in the classroom dodging missiles and letting his mind wander, he began to realize there was more to the study of architecture than the recitation of technicalities. Perhaps from Eugene Letang, who liked to recall his Ecole mentor, Joseph Auguste Emile Vaudremer, runner-up winner of the prestigious Grand Prix de Rome in 1854,[15] or even from Ware's own references to Hunt's atelier, Louis began to understand that MIT "was but a pale reflection of the Ecole des Beaux Arts," concluding that he himself should go to the source, so to speak, "to learn if what was preached *there* as a gospel, really signified glad tidings." So probably with a certain disappointment, perhaps with the feeling of having been cheated, Louis decided to leave "Tech" at the end of the year. It simply was not as good for him as he thought it would be.

But all was not a total loss. Faithfully going about his studies, he learned "not only to draw but to draw very well," he said. Work in his hand from 1873 and 1874 confirms his assertion.[16] He also picked up important technical information, a basic vocabulary of the architect's language. Outside classes, prowling the streets as always, he was singularly impressed with the Brattle Square Church, designed and built between 1870 and 1872 on the corner of Commonwealth Avenue and Clarendon Street near MIT by "the mighty" Henry Richardson. Sullivan did not mention it, but he must have also observed the beginning stages of Richardson's masterpiece, the new Trinity Church, on Copley Square, a block from the Institute, where construction began in April 1873. Louis was mightily impressed indeed with Richardson, whose Marshall Field Wholesale Store (1885–87) in Chicago would later be such an inspiration to his work. He also made good use of the school library, where he found in architecture books pictures of intriguing buildings that by seeming to contradict Ware's ideas reinforced Louis's feeling of inadequate classroom instruction.

Years later Sullivan recalled that his third- and fourth-year classmates included George B. Ferry (1851–1913) of Springfield, Massachusetts, later a prominent Milwaukee architect; William Rotch Ware (1848–1917), the professor's nephew from Milton, for over thirty years editor of *The American Architect & Building News,* the first professional magazine in the country; and Arthur Rotch (1850–94, not "Roche" as Sullivan wrote), for whom the American Institute of Architects' Traveling Scholarship Fund was named. It is noteworthy that the three he remembered were the only ones prominent enough for listings in Henry and Elsie Withey's *Biographical Dictionary of American Architects* (1956). Although he made a number of friends among his twenty-three other classmates, he chose in his 1922 autobiography not to mention their names lest his own obscurity, perhaps, be underlined by theirs. He did, however, attempt to emulate their collective student style. Louis took to wearing fashionable clothes, tried to induce growth in his side whiskers, and injected a bit of swagger into his walk. He wore his black hair neatly parted in the middle, and for a photograph three years later posed with a pearl-studded white shirt and a black suit of the latest material and cut, all befitting a polished young college man about town.[17]

His best friend at school was his oldest friend, George Tompson, who more than likely commuted with him from Wakefield every day in pursuit of his engineering degree. Father John A. Tompson's attitude toward the rapid maturation of his young charge is unrecorded but was undoubtedly favorable because Louis remembered his last year in the household warmly. The major development at this time was his interest in music, not just in the oratorios that were the senior Tompson's joy, but also in Strauss waltzes and other popular melodies. Tompson was versed in theories and techniques of composition, and although he may never have compared music to architecture, like Victor Hugo, he cultivated that inchoate appreciation Louis's mother, Andrienne, had tried to nurture. Louis eagerly attended several concerts while at MIT, from then on seeking out the best performances wherever he went.

The *Autobiography* barely hints at the many serious discussions on all manner of subjects he assuredly had with Tompson during his college year. Louis "had now definitely entered the cultured world," he remembered, "the world of intellectual dissection, surgery, and therapeutics" where "Instinct and Intellect" roamed freely, a recollection made not in connection with MIT but in reference to Tompson. As a role model and a man of practical wisdom, he clearly made a greater impression on Louis than Professor Ware or anyone else at college. Perhaps it was at Tompson's suggestion that Louis decided that when he left MIT he would not head immediately for the Ecole but would work a year in an architect's office to learn "concrete preparations and results; how, in effect, an actual building was brought about." This would have been typical of Tompson: to stress technique, to get down to basics, to learn the "how" of things, in short, to let theory develop from process. So this became his "program," as Louis put it: to "see what architecture might be like in practice."

The way he told the story, what happened next was casual and unplanned. Saying good-bye to Boston, to his "dear Wakefield," to his friends, and certainly with regret to John A. Tompson, whom he would never see again,[18] he made his way to New York to meet "the dean of the profession," Richard Morris Hunt, whose assistant Sidney Stratton told him to apply for work in Philadelphia with Frank Furness. "But this was not Louis' way of doing [things]," he wrote. Arriving in the City of Brotherly Love, "where he was to find his uncle and grandpa"—as if by accident, it seems—he prowled the streets until a residence on South Broad "caught his eye like a flower by the roadside," so "fresh and fair" it was. When coincidentally it turned out to be a Furness building, Louis applied for and got work with the firm. This makes a good story, surprisingly like the one in Frank Lloyd Wright's autobiography, first published ten years after Sullivan's, in 1932.[19]

Playing fast and loose with the facts, Wright recalled that, disgusted with it all, not caring about a diploma, he had dropped out of college in his senior year to look for a job in Chicago, but refused to approach architect J. L. Silsbee, who had worked for his family. Instead, he called around at various firms without success and finally, in desperation, went to Silsbee, who, unaware of his family connections, hired him strictly on the basis of his excellent drawings. What really happened was somewhat different. Wright quit college after his first, not during his fourth, year and went directly to Silsbee, who had employed him the previous summer and knew him well. It was all a matter of image: unwilling to admit he had exploited family connections, Wright insisted he had made it by talent alone. And so with Sullivan. Avoiding any mention of personal contacts, he said he sweet-talked Furness into hiring him for a week, but then extended the job by outstanding performance.

Probably he did do a good job, but more than likely the truth was something else. There were two good reasons for going to Philadelphia: far from "finding" his uncle and grandfather there, Louis knew Julius and Henri List would give him a place to live, while Professor Ware, a former Furness associate in Hunt's office, could use his influence to get him a job. Ware might even have written a letter of introduction to Hunt, a busy and somewhat haughty man whom one would hardly drop in on unannounced, as Sullivan said he did. Armed with an epistolatory entrée, Louis stopped at Hunt's, but finding no work went to the next name on his list. If Furness also turned him down, he could at least be assured of food and shelter until something came along. Given his great admiration, it is instructive that Louis did not apply at Richardson's lower-Broadway office during his stop in New York. The reason may have been that he had no introduction.

He did manage to see Hunt long enough to outline his plans. No doubt as a favor to Ware, Hunt took a few minutes to regale his young visitor with stories of his student days at the Ecole, patting him on the head, so to speak, before turning him over to Stratton, who added his own recollections of the good life in Paris. Stratton was more interested in Louis and more encouraging than Hunt, urging him to stick to his plans for further education, to keep in touch, and to stop by on his way to France. Louis was mightily impressed by two such respectable men giving him their valuable time. "Proud and inflated," he wrote, he went on his way, taking careful note before he left, however, of New York's high energy level, its people's rapid speech, and its rough and arrogant way of life. Arriving at his destination a few days later, he went directly to his relatives at 3224 Chestnut Street in West Philadelphia. Now sixty-eight, Henri had long since retired from teaching, and thirty-three-year-old Julius, an importer during his first years in town, was now a salesman and a commission merchant about to open a dry goods store downtown at 312 Chestnut Street.[20] Assured of bed and board, Louis went off the next day to get his job.

As it turned out, Ware and Stratton could not have suggested a better employer. Frank Furness (1839–1912), something of a wild man in American design, was the first significant architectural influ-

II.3 *Frank Furness, 1880s.* Courtesy George Woods Furness.

ence on Louis's career. A Philadelphia native, he was the son of William Henry Furness, a Harvard-educated Unitarian minister, lifelong friend of Ralph Waldo Emerson, and abolitionist who had turned his cellar into a station on the Underground Railroad and had opened his home to antislavery stalwarts like William Ellery Channing, William Lloyd Garrison, and Wendell Phillips. He was also an excellent draftsman—on one occasion he addressed the American Institute of Architects—and was exceptionally conversant with English and German literature. Frank's oldest brother, William Henry, junior, became a renowned portrait painter, while another brother, Horace Howard, earned a national reputation for his Shakespearean scholarship while a professor at the University of Pennsylvania. With this intellectual and artistic family background,

Frank Furness studied architecture in a Philadelphia office before joining Richard Morris Hunt from 1859 to 1861. After service in the Union cavalry, he returned to Hunt for a year or so, but by 1866 was back at home beginning his own architectural career.[21]

Although his work was praised by contemporaries after his first executed commission in 1867, and although he turned out more than 360 structures for many prestigious clients, Furness fell from critical favor at the turn of the twentieth century, in part because his buildings were hard to understand, quite personal, idiosyncratic, and difficult to categorize. Furness was always something of a loner, in old age a "sharp-tongued curmudgeon," his latest biographer notes.[22] Philadelphia architect Albert Kelsey, a longtime friend and colleague, wrote that

> he was one of the most picturesque personalities I have ever known. . . . He could swear like a trooper. . . . [W]ith his shoulders squared, head erect, swinging soldierly stride, and a devil-may-care attitude, . . . [he] was a man who neither gave nor asked for quarter. . . . [I]n his dress he always wore the loudest and biggest plaids that he could find. . . . [H]e wore his hat with a rakish tilt over his eye. . . . In his . . . office he was a severe and strict disciplinarian but as ready in kindly counsel and friendly aid as he was quick to wrath and explosive anger over any exhibition of indifference or stupidity.[23]

When Louis met him in June or July 1873, Furness was, true to form, sporting plaids, a "marvelous red beard" sprouting "fanlike" from a face as "gnarled and homely as an English bulldog's," and was spouting "a string of oaths yards long." Louis loved it.

For two years Furness had been partners with George W. Hewitt on the top floor of the four-story Franklin Telegraph Company Building near the corner of Third and Chestnut, devoting much of his time to designing the Pennsylvania Academy of Fine Arts (1871–75). He had as many as twelve buildings in planning or construction in 1873 on which Louis could have worked, although he mentioned only one. In addition to the Fine Arts Academy, Furness and Hewitt had four or five houses under way, including the residence Louis found so "fresh and fair"—now known to have been the B. H. Moore residence (1872–74) at 510 South Broad, since demolished—and alterations on Furness's own home at 711 Locust. Work was also proceeding on the Jewish Hospital, the Philadelphia Warehouse Company, St. Peter's Episcopal Church, the Mercantile Library, St. Timothy's Church and Parish House, and the Guarantee Trust and Safe Deposit Company, all downtown or in outlying districts. Finally, there was the Union Bank Building at 310 Chestnut, next door to the structure that would soon house Uncle Julius's dry goods store. Louis remembered retracing the bank plans "so systematically and in so short a time that he won his spurs at once," for which he thanked Moses Woolson's training in accuracy and speed but not, be it noted, his instruction at MIT. Union Bank was the only Furness project on which he recalled working.

Louis admired George Hewitt's drafting ability but otherwise thought him overly bookish and pedestrian. With Furness, on the other hand, he was "infatuated." In keeping with his boyhood beliefs about architects, he attributed to Furness the ability to make "buildings out of his head," remembering him as an "extraordinary freehand draftsman" who kept Louis "hypnotized" by drawing and swearing at the same time. Furness was also an exceptionally talented ornamentalist after the manner of Owen Jones, whose *Grammar of Ornament* (London, 1856) became for many the bible of the subject. Louis's own floral drawings from 1873 and 1874 were clearly influenced by Jones filtered through Furness, resembling decorations over the front windows on the Fine Arts Academy. There is little doubt that Sullivan's professional interest—"passion" is more accurate—in foliated ornament had its origins in Furness's office in the summer of 1873, although his mother's drawings and his instruction at MIT may have also played their parts.

Furness influenced his new assistant in other less direct but equally important ways. His bold building forms—some French, others Greek, some amalgams, others virtually unprecedented—were often executed in the polychromatics most notably advocated by the English architect and critic John Ruskin; his first building of national reputation, the Pennsylvania Academy of Fine Arts, is a case in point. Its stair hall, enhanced by exquisite floral patterns on railings and walls, is one of the finest ever built in America. The home for Aged and Infirm Israelites at the Jewish Hospital (1871–73), now the Einstein Medical Center, was similarly massed, with a three-story pavilion receding into a mansarded attic flanked by two-story wings capped in the same manner. Both were strikingly detailed in contrasting stone and brickwork. Many Furness buildings, in fact,

II.4 *Louis Sullivan drawing, 1873.*
Avery Architectural and Fine Arts Library. Columbia University in the City of New York.

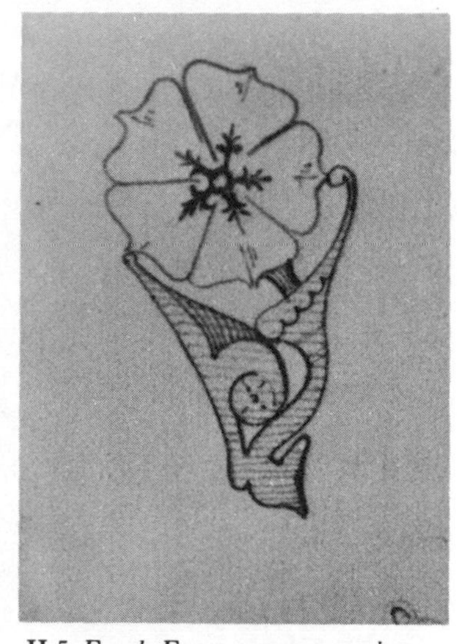

II.5 *Frank Furness, ornamental study, 1870s.*
Furness sketchbook.

were characteristically rugged, with powerful individual elements bursting from strongly massed backgrounds. They were colorful, picturesque, obviously different, and clearly one man's personal statement. (Critics agree that Furness, not Hewitt, conceived the designs.) Furness himself was vain, iconoclastic, and ribald; he chafed at convention and ridiculed the philistines. But he was also a disciplined and demanding employer, permitting no nonsense when it came to work. Furness undoubtedly reinforced Louis's own inclinations toward self-assertiveness. The younger man already admired people who, like himself, went their own way. Furness's style in person and in buildings was, like Richardson's, recognizably unique. Much the same would be said later on about Louis Sullivan, too.

Hewitt's younger brother William (mistakenly remembered as "John" in the *Autobiography*) was another important influence on Louis. As the shop foreman, he freely gave his time and advice helping the youngster with his sketching (which might mean that Louis did preliminary or detail drawings as well as tracing for Furness). "It was not long before he made of Louis a draftsman of the upper Crust," Sullivan later wrote, and for this "his heart went out." Looking back on his stint with Furness after fifty years of experience, Sullivan gave thanks at his "great fortune to have made his entry into the practical world in an office where standards were so high—where talent was so manifestly taken for granted, and . . . where craftsmanship was paramount and personal," strong praise indeed for any employer.

Although little is known and likely to be found out about Louis's actual tasks, he worked "very hard" he recalled, "day and night,"

II.6 *Frank Furness, Guarantee Trust and Safe Deposit Company, 1873.* Lithograph by Bunk and McFetridge.

but not necessarily on office business. The reason he left his uncle's and grandfather's home for a still-unknown address, he explained, was to burn the midnight oil reading and studying, certainly in keeping with his previous scholarly habits and his impatience to advance. He also wanted to be nearer downtown; the walk from West Philadelphia across the Schuylkill River to work was several long, hot miles. So with wages undoubtedly higher than the ten dollars a week at which he had started, Louis took a room nearer the office from which after hours he could more easily explore the city. He remembered the "comfort and surcease" of his many Sunday-afternoon rambles through Wissahickon Valley in Fairmount Park and the cherished *Lohengrin* performance he heard one night at the Academy of Music. But he was probably more permanently influenced by buildings he encountered on his daily walks.

Architectural historians Henry-Russell Hitchcock and Winston Weismann have separately noted important similarities between commercial buildings in Philadelphia Louis would have seen during the summer and fall of 1873 and structures he designed more than a decade later. A number of local architects, especially William L. Johnston, Stephen D. Button, Joseph C. Hoxie, and Napoleon Le Brun, now called the "Philadelphia functionalists," began in the late 1840s to emphasize the structure, height, and purposes of their load-bearing, stone-walled buildings by projecting piers forward of their facade planes. The effect was to embrace verticality and to advertise structural technique. The best-known example of this "Philadelphia system" was Johnston's Jayne Building (1849) on Chestnut not far from Furness's office near the corner of Third. Button's Leland Building at 37–39 South Third and another at 723–727 Chestnut (1853), as well as work by his contemporaries, were also in the neighborhood. Their "new vertical formula of design for commercial facades," says Hitchcock, featured "narrow granite piers in the form of clustered colonnettes [rising] the full height of the building." Louis Sullivan, he adds, probably saw and admired these structures in the seventies; "certainly they are very premonitory of his characteristic work of the eighties and even the nineties."[24]

Louis's experience with Furness and Philadelphia taught him a good deal and, since he suggested nothing contrary, was entirely enjoyable. Given his great affection for his uncle and grandfather, however, the peculiar thing is that he wrote so little about them beyond moving into their house and later leaving it. Perhaps in retrospect he felt their influence over him should properly have ended years before in Wakefield, or perhaps he left West Philadelphia for reasons other than stated. Possibly they were too "parental," unwilling to allow him the freedom he was used to as a headstrong and independent sixteen-year-old. Unfortunately, there is no evidence to substantiate conjecture. Nor is there any telling how long he would have remained in town were it not for circumstances far beyond his control: the financial panic of September 1873. Louis remembered one very hot day hearing from Furness's open windows first a murmur, then a shout, and then when he went to look, seeing a "solid black mass of frantic men . . . jammed from wall to wall" in the street. Word came upstairs that Jay Cooke and Company had gone into bankruptcy, touching off widespread hysteria. Credit dried up, businesses folded and, eventually, architectural work slackened. Furness had enough jobs to keep going until one November day when he summoned Louis to inform him he was sorry but "the jig is up." He praised the bewildered young man's work, told him he liked him, that he wished he could stay on, but that as the last hired, it was only fair he be the first fired. Thanks to speculative chicanery, Louis Sullivan's short employment with Frank Furness came to an abrupt end.[25]

He stayed in town about a week longer, possibly looking for work,

II.7 *William L. Johnston, Jayne Building, 1849.*

but, without success and another place to go, decided to head for Chicago. Perhaps because he could not return to the Lists, he contacted his parents, who encouraged him to join them. He had just turned seventeen, was not yet ready for Paris, wanted additional office experience, and knew he could get it in Chicago, still rebuilding from the 1871 fire. No doubt he wanted to see his family, too. As his train headed west, Louis thrilled to the scenery, but when he reached his destination, he was overwhelmed, not by the city's size and activity, as one might expect, so much as by the dirt, the ugliness, and the endless devastation remaining from two years before. But he loved it, and as he stepped to the platform "raised his hand and cried in full voice: THIS IS THE PLACE FOR ME!" That was the day before Thanksgiving, 1873.

His family welcomed him home like a prodigal son for a sumptuous Thanksgiving feast and a week's relaxation before he went job hunting. Patrick Sullivan, now fifty-six, was in the midst of the longest period of stability in his life. When they moved to Chicago late in 1868, he, Andrienne, and Albert had settled in a rented house at 85 Twenty-third Street,[26] about two miles south of the Loop in an area of one- and two-story frame houses for working and middle-class people near Lake Michigan. The Sullivans would keep that address for eight years, until 1877, their longest tenure in any one place. Patrick had presumably taught dancing at home, for he did not open an academy until 1873, at 147 Twenty-second Street, one block north and west of his residence, which he retained two years. Albert had meanwhile turned nineteen shortly before his reunion with Louis. After graduation from high school, he took a job with the Illinois Central Railroad as an apprentice machinist in 1872 and was still living at home.[27] With two incomes the small Sullivan family was probably in its best financial shape ever.

After Thanksgiving Louis set out to examine the city and the two monumental construction jobs making it easier to find work. The first was the municipal street-regrading program. As originally platted in 1830, Chicago was barely above the water level of Lake Michigan and the Chicago River. In common with most other American cities at the time, its generally unpaved streets turned to quagmire every time it rained, but Chicago's exceptionally high water table caused frequent floods, rendering pumps and drains inoperable. The resulting sewage and sanitation problems were staggering, not to mention the damage done to buildings. On their boggy, mosquito-ridden site, citizens sarcastically debated whether the name "Chicago" came from the native American "Chickagou" meaning "garlic," or from "Shegagh" meaning "skunk," but all reluctantly agreed that it was indeed "the place of the evil smell."[28] Olfactory and other inconveniences had gotten so horrendous after twenty-five years of settlement that the city council decided in 1855 simply to raise the city three feet higher. Every structure was either jacked up and reinforced, torn down, or relocated. This Olympian task was nearing completion in 1873, but it was still under way.

The second undertaking was equally monumental: reconstruction following the catastrophic fire of October 1871, started, so legend has it, when Mrs. Patrick O'Leary's fabled cow kicked over a lantern in its barn behind the family cottage on De Koven Street. The fire raged through the night of October 9 and all the next day, destroying everything in its path. By the time it was spent, it had consumed 1688 acres from Twelfth Street north to Fullerton, and from Halsted east to the lake, an area about four miles by two-thirds of a mile embracing most of the central business district. The fire had missed the Sullivans by a mile and a half, but had left one-third of the city's 300,000 inhabitants homeless, had reduced eighteen thousand buildings to rubble, and, according to the local board of trade, had caused some $200,000,000 in property damage, an almost inconceivable amount at the time.[29] The suffering was immense, but not for everyone. Added to the regrading program, the fire attracted architects to Chicago like bees to pollen. Several of the city's leading firms opened their doors immediately afterward or during the next year. With such massive work to be done, Louis Sullivan had no trouble finding a job.

This time he seems to have gone about it the way he said he did in Philadelphia—although there is an alternative possibility—by walking around until he saw a building he liked, learning the name of the architect, and knocking on his door. The edifice he picked was the brand-new seven-story Portland Block at Dearborn and Washington streets, whose architect, William Le Baron Jenney (1832–1907), is best known today for his contributions to the structural development of the high-rise building. Jenney has been named by some, in fact, as the "inventor" of the skyscraper, mostly on the basis of his ten-story Home Insurance Office Building (1885) at La Salle and Adams, which made early extensive use of fireproof metal members. He is also remembered, though not as well, as a planning collaborator with Frederick Law Olmsted and Calvert Vaux, and as the principal executor of Riverside, Illinois (1869), the most famous nineteenth-century American "romantic" suburb, where Jenney designed several houses including his own. He was also appointed chief architect and planner in 1869 of Chicago's extensive West Park system, in which he designed the Douglas, Humboldt, and Garfield facilities.[30]

Jenney was born in 1832, the same year as William R. Ware, in Fairhaven, Massachusetts, and like Ware attended Phillips Exeter Academy and the Lawrence Scientific School, graduating in 1853.

(It is therefore conceivable the two knew each other well enough for Ware to recommend Louis for work.) After completing his training at the Ecole Centrale des Arts et Manufactures in Paris in 1856, Jenney worked in France and the United States until 1861, when he joined the Union Army, eventually to attain the rank of major. After the war he moved to Chicago, to open an architectural office in 1869. Jenney's early buildings were in a French-inspired romantic style suitable for suburban Riverside, where in addition to houses, he designed a hotel, its refectory, and a water tower. Although he produced dwelling and park facilities throughout his entire career, he had begun by 1873 to do commercial structures and may have been working on the six-story Lakeside Building at Clark and Adams when Louis Sullivan entered his employ.

II.8 *William Le Baron Jenney.*

Though greatly impressed with the Portland Block, Louis had little respect for Jenney—as an architect. He applauded Jenney for being one of the few Chicagoans in 1873 "who were intelligently conscientious in the interests of their clients" but he insisted that "the Major" was "not an architect except by courtesy of terms. His true profession was that of engineer." Writing this in 1922, Sullivan probably meant that Jenney was more interested in structure than in composition or aesthetics, a distinction that would increasingly matter to Louis as he matured. In fact, he continued in his autobiography, Jenney was even less an engineer than "a *bon vivant,* a gourmet." The Major knew his wines, cheeses, and sauces thoroughly, and was frequently observed passing through his office on the way home with a brace or two of wild duck for one of his many dinner parties. Louis was as impressed by this as by Jenney's ability as a raconteur to raise storytelling to the level of dramatic acting: he was "a really and truly funny man," he remembered. Louis genuinely liked the Major, but in his youthful intensity seems to have mistakenly believed him blasé about his work. He was equally impatient with Jenney's physical characteristics. "He was monstrously pop-eyed," Sullivan later exaggerated, "with hanging mobile features. . . . He spoke French with an accent so atrocious that it jarred Louis's teeth, while his English speech jerked about as though it had St. Vitus's dance." During his frequent absences from the office, of which Louis disapproved, Jenney left matters in charge of his foreman, a young man who would have an important impact on Louis's life, twenty-four-year-old John Edelmann.[31]

Were it not for the architect's autobiograhy, Edelmann, like Moses Woolson, might be lost in history. Born in Cleveland in 1849, he worked as a draftsman before moving to Chicago in 1872 to take a job with the newly formed partnership of Edward Burling and Dankmar Adler, who would soon be even more vital in Louis Sullivan's life. After a very brief period, Edelmann switched into Jenney's employ in Room 29 of the Portland Block late in 1872 or early in 1873. Although he did not remain long—in 1874 he formed his own partnership with Joseph S. Johnston at 182 Clark Street—and would leave Chicago from 1877 to 1879 before departing for good by 1881, he and Louis formed a friendship that survived his absences from town and implanted itself indelibly on Louis's memory.

Louis was first attracted to Edelmann's clowning. As soon as the Major left the office, Edelmann would mount a table to "make a howling stump speech on greenback currency, or single tax," or another political issue, inspiring Louis to launch into an oratorio, usually his favorite, "Why Do the Nations So Furiously Rage Together?" from *The Messiah,* which he had first heard with his parents as a small boy at Boston's Handel and Haydn Society. Bedlam would follow until the office lookout—possibly Martin Roche (1855–1927), soon to be a famous Chicago architect in his own right—signaled the Major's return. Then all would be quiet as work

II.9 *Louis Sullivan's 1880 sketch of John Edelmann.*

resumed, apparently to Jenney's satisfaction, for he seemed never to complain. But more important to Louis than Edelmann's antics were his intellect, his self-assurance, his artistic persona, his gregariousness, and his physical dexterity, all of which Louis tried to cultivate himself. Edelmann saturated his young admirer with German metaphysics, the latest political and psychological theories, and with Richard Wagner's music at Sunday-afternoon concerts conducted by Hans Balatka in the North Side Turner's Hall. Edelmann was in no way profound, but he was clever and well informed—fifty years later he would have been thought Bohemian or avant-garde—a perfect cultural and intellectual mentor for an eager young man anxious to explore new realms of experience.

His major impact on Louis at this time came outside the office in the Lotus Club, a group of amateur athletes who met each weekend from March to November on the banks of the Calumet River, about fifteen miles south of the Loop in the vicinity of Indiana Avenue and 134th Place at the Chicago-suburban Riverdale line. Their principal activities were spirited swimming, running, jumping, weight throwing, and sculling contests, but they also gave attention to mental self-improvement. As a group they competed in meets with similar clubs as far away as New York City, under the leadership of their founder, thirty-seven-year-old William B. Curtis, an athlete whose impressive skills had won him considerable renown. With his permission Edelmann brought Louis into the club, and Louis in turn enlisted his brother, Albert. For several years, Louis, Albert, Edelmann, Curtis, and a handful of other friends periodically enjoyed the weekend world of the suburban outdoors.[32]

Athletic activity was nothing new to the Sullivan brothers, although Lotus Club dedication to self-improvement surpassed anything they had previously experienced. When the boys returned from their weekends on the Calumet, they must have reported to Patrick, whose own exercises ten years before at Newburyport had launched his sons on their athletic careers. But after a lengthy absence from systematic physical training, Louis was eager to participate, and if judgment can be made on the basis of his autobiography, was far more enthusiastic about running and jumping than Jenney's architecture. Since the club suspended activities with the first snowfall, ordinarily around Thanksgiving, Louis and Albert did not get involved until the spring of 1874. From then on they and the others spent two nights each weekend at Curtis's boathouse on the far South Side.

Louis was the youngest member and the Lotus was the first club he had ever joined. Both facts were important to him. Flattered to have been admitted, he threw himself joyously into the program, not as the best performer, but neither as the worst. Soon he was working strenuously to develop his abilities and his body, prompted in part by an emerging realization that intellectual and physical dexterity were mutually dependent. But he was also motivated by an awakening interest in male anatomy, to which he had never paid particular attention. So when Bill Curtis, whose physique was the best developed among them by far, "walked the pier for a plunge, he was a sight for the Greeks, and Louis," the architect recalled, "was enraptured at the play of light and shade." The extent to which his enjoyment was sexual, aesthetic, or a combination of both is impossible to determine. As a member of this club during the first half of 1874 and again from 1875 through 1877, he made male athletic bonding an important part of his activities. And never in his life would he draw or write about the physical attributes of women with the same pleasure he derived from watching Bill Curtis.

Sullivan completely excluded his brother, Albert, from the pages of his autobiography—their falling-out will be discussed later on—

but it is clear from correspondence and from his MIT "Records" book, soon to be a Lotus Club ledger of sorts, that there was no shortage of brotherly love in the 1870s. Living in the same house on Twenty-third Street and sharing weekend outings, they had ample opportunity for reacquaintance and to strengthen fraternal ties. Possibly at Louis's suggestion, Albert decided to go into architecture; later in the year he would list himself as a "draughtsman" in the city directory for 1874–75. Louis's relationship with Patrick also seemed settled. Despite his hostility in later years, there is nothing to indicate that in 1874 he had anything but good feelings for either parent. He spent his weekends away from home not to avoid Patrick and Andrienne but to enjoy the company of new friends, an entirely appropriate sentiment for an independent-minded adolescent.

If Sullivan had little to say about his parents at this time, he wrote at greater length about Major Jenney, but even that was brief. Beyond describing his physical features, eating habits, personality, and pranks in his office, Sullivan left no record of what he did there, the buildings he worked on, or even what Jenney was designing at the time. This does not mean that his seven months with the Major, from December 1873 to June 1874, were unimportant. Louis added to his skills in tracing and sketching, since those were most likely his jobs; he could not have helped but absorb other practical lessons working for a leading firm, and he may have made additional contacts to serve him later on. But the specifics he could have picked up anywhere were not the Major's principal legacy, for as a recent student of his career has observed, Jenney made important contributions to the emergence of modern architecture not only with the skeletal construction for which he is best remembered, but also "by preaching functionalism, embracing romanticism, and damning mindless eclecticism."[33]

Jenney's early houses, the ones Sullivan would have known in 1874, were not so different from the picturesque cottages and villas advocated before the Civil War by Calvert Vaux, Andrew Jackson Downing, and others who had urged the straightforward expression of seemingly simple structure. Less formal, more aesthetically accessible to working- and middle-class people than the classic, with plans apt to follow function rather than preconceived formats, Jenney's picturesque or romantic architecture made servicing actual client needs as high a priority as fulfilling prescribed academic canons. People associated romantic houses with individualism, closeness to nature, the virtues of a stable family, and other culturally important late-nineteenth-century values. Within this tradition Jenney's residential work can be seen as a prelude to the prairie style that thirty years later expressed similar notions and helped usher in the modern movement.[34] Without being a great architect or an original thinker, Jenney presented Louis with a down-to-earth alternative to, and an implied criticism of, the more abstract, scholastic approach to design he had encountered at MIT.

II.10 *William Le Baron Jenney residence, c. 1870.* From *Riverside,* 1871.

From Jenney, Furness, and the "Philadelphia functionalists," Louis developed an appreciation for color, ornament, originality, boldness, and for the expression of structure and function. But valuable as his experiences were, he was yet incapable of incorporating them into designs hc could call his own. Lacking an architectural overview, a set of principles to organize his knowledge, he felt by the middle of 1874 that it was now more urgent than ever to finish his half-completed "program," to develop the theory that so far eluded him. French classicism, he knew, was an increasingly important influence on the American architectural scene. Louis found its traces in MIT, Furness, Jenney, and everywhere else he looked. And now that greater numbers of Americans were attending the Ecole, the acknowledged center of advanced architectural thought and practice, it make good sense for Louis to go there too.

In retrospect, it is difficult to see how he could have avoided the Ecole des Beaux-Arts. From his French-speaking mother and grandparents, his father's stories of life on the Continent, and his cousin Minnie Whittlesey's romantic descriptions of Paris, Louis had learned to appreciate France. To this were added the French-inspired Boston buildings he had admired, the Francophile Ware and his Parisian assistant Eugene Letang, the entire curriculum at MIT, Hunt's and Stratton's Ecole stories, and Jenney's recollections, no doubt eagerly repeated by the noted raconteur, of his student and early practicing days. Everyone important with whom he had come in contact except Furness—and he had studied in Hunt's atelier—was a dedicated admirer of the French way. It was almost as if there were no choice, as if it were Louis's destiny to attend the Ecole. And so, without objection from his parents—who six years earlier had endorsed his desire to study abroad and who could not have dissuaded him in any case—perhaps with modest savings from a year of working, Louis took the train to New York. On July 11, 1874, he sailed aboard the White Star Line's steamship *Britannic,* bound for Cork and Liverpool en route to London, Paris, and the Ecole des Beaux-Arts, repeating in reverse his father's more extended journey twenty-seven years before.[35]

Chapter III

LONDON, PARIS, AND ROME

1874-75

LOUIS SULLIVAN embarked for Paris with the same high hopes he had taken to MIT. Eager to begin his career, to develop a theory of design, and to visit Old World monuments he had seen only in books, he looked to the Ecole des Beaux-Arts as a font of architectural wisdom and inspiration that would shape his randomly gathered experiences into a program for action. But balancing his optimism about the Ecole was the same hard-nosed practicality that as a teenager had gotten him positions in the prominent firms of Furness and Jenney. So before he sailed from New York, he returned to Richard Morris Hunt's for another chat with Sidney Stratton, who from personal experience told him what to do in Paris. There was no use arriving at the Ecole unprepared.

On the "disappointing and stupid" ten-day voyage to England, Louis apparently spoke to no one, saw nothing memorable overboard and only machinery and crew on board to hold his interest. Deeply depressed by the endless monotony of the sea, he rejoiced when the *Britannic* finally anchored at Cork. But that and the coast was all he saw of his father's native Ireland. Liverpool was next, but eager to get to the capital, he stayed only a day or two, and wrote nothing about it. Arriving in London by train, his first impression was frightening as he walked through Euston Station fearing the heavy roof would fall in upon him. But when he rushed to the street for safety, he liked what he saw enough to linger in London two weeks examining everything he found.[1]

Like many a nineteenth-century American traveler, Louis Sullivan was simultaneously attracted to and repelled by the Old World. During the two-hundred-mile train ride through the countryside from Liverpool to London, he felt a mixture of joy and discomfort. "Surely it was a finished land," he wrote of rural England, "beautifully finished, sturdy, vigorous, solid, [and] set." Overwhelmed by the charming villages, he marveled at their precisely arranged plots, at the beauty of their landscape, and at the manifest ubiquity of their traditions, concluding that everything must have been as it was for centuries. Compared to England, he decided, America was hastily settled and flimsily made. Yet there was about the countryside a self-consciousness and a self-centeredness he found vaguely oppressive. In London he thrilled to Big Ben's boom, was awed by the Houses of Parliament and St. Paul's Cathedral, and wandered happily around Hyde Park and the Thames Embankment. But, on the other hand, he was shocked by Haymarket poverty, appalled by the rudeness of store "clarks," and "astonished" by the "brilliance of the [Music Hall] demi-monde." There was in London the attraction of the old, typified for Louis by its architecture, and the repulsion of the new, embodied in the "cold reserve," the "dismal hardness," and the "selfish push" of the people. It was as if England had learned to cope with life only grudgingly. Louis enjoyed his fortnight there but never expressed a desire to return.

During the first week in August 1874, he sailed from Dover to Dieppe, taking the train through Normandy, to be stunned by Rouen cathedral before finally reaching Paris, aglow with nighttime lights when he arrived. Probably at Stratton's suggestion, he hailed a cab for the Hotel St-Honoré on the Right Bank, near the Tuileries and the Louvre, where he stayed until he found permanent quarters in the seventh-floor attic of a rooming house at 17, rue Racine, on the southeast corner of rue Monsieur-le-Prince in the Latin Quarter on the Left Bank.[2] Rue Racine was only two blocks long but well situated for Louis's purposes. It began to the east of Number 17, at boulevard St-Michel, about a thousand meters south of the Seine from the Palais de Justice and Notre-Dame; to the west it ended at the Théâtre National in Place de l'Odéon, diagonally across rue de Vaugirard from the Sénat in the Jardins du Luxembourg. From the windows of his boardinghouse, which rose above the other buildings in the neighborhood, he could see the lycée St-Louis down the block and beyond that the Sorbonne. Walking north on rue Monsieur-le-Prince, Louis would pass the Académie de Médecine on the opposite side of rue Racine, then enter rue de l'Odéon where it met boulevard St-Germain. If he turned left to Place St-Germain, then right into rue Bonaparte, he would pass the Société de Géographie, the Société de la Charité, and the Académie de Médecine before reaching the left bank of the Seine where, about 1500 meters from his room, was the Ecole des Beaux-Arts.

Its official name is the Ecole Nationale et Spéciale des Beaux-Arts, recognizing an 1807 union of the School of Architecture and the School of Painting and Sculpture.[3] In 1816 the Ecole was granted the site of the former Petits-Augustins monastery, upon which was built in 1794 the Musée des Antiquités et Monuments Français, a revolutionary-era museum the Bourbons suppressed after their restoration. The physical plant was remodeled and expanded over the years until architect Félix Duban designed the "new" Ecole, facing quai Malaquais on the Seine, between 1860 and 1862, thus completing the structure awaiting Louis Sullivan in 1874. Its history as an institution, however, was much longer. The Ecole des Beaux-Arts traced its roots to 1671, with the establishment by Louis XIV's finance minister, Jean-Baptiste Colbert, of the Académie Royale d'Architecture, a lecture forum that, under the king's auspices, gradually evolved into the first school devoted solely to the training of architects. Its design concepts were in large part based on the Italian Renaissance and through it to classical antiquity, meaning that the origins of the French academicism Louis Sullivan had first encountered in Boston and had come to Paris to study went almost as far back as the beginnings of formalized western art and ideas.

The Ecole's history had at times been tortuous. Closed during the Revolution, its most recent upheaval occurred when the noted Gothic revivalist Eugène-Emmanuel Viollet-le-Duc (1814–79) persuaded Emperor Napoleon III to reform the Ecole in 1863. In keeping with Napoleon III's general policy of centralizing political power, his twelve-part decree of November 13 required that the Ecole's director be selected by the emperor rather than the faculty, that professors be appointed by the imperial minister, and that new design studios—*ateliers intérieurs*—be established within the Ecole under the charge of professors chosen by imperially approved administrators to compete with *ateliers extérieurs* located outside the school. One of

III.1 *17, rue Racine, Paris, Louis Sullivan's student residence.*
Photo by Robert Twombly.

III.2 *Library (1856–62) with entrance to the Gaillon Chateau, Ecole des Beaux-Arts, Paris.* Photo by Lucien Mercier, 1890s. Courtesy Roger-Viollet, Paris.

the nine other parts of the 1863 reorganization appointing Viollet-le-Duc professor of art history and aesthetics proved especially troublesome because almost all five hundred students opposed his medievalism and the fact that his courses were required. They saw the reforms as an attempt by Napoleon III to seize control of the Ecole and to supplant its traditional classicism with the Romanesque and Gothic principles that had recently attracted attention in Paris.

Among the many arrested during the student protest was Henry Hobson Richardson, then in the fourth year of his six-year stay at the Ecole (from 1859 to 1865, when, after Richard Morris Hunt, he was the second American to attend). Forced to resign after a very short tenure, Viollet-le-Duc was replaced by the noted art historian Hippolyte Taine (1828–93), who retained the post until 1883. Since Louis had been impressed by Taine's writings in high school, thanks to Moses Woolson, it is possible he attended his lectures. All the other 1863 reforms remained in place.

Like the Ecole, the Paris Louis discovered in 1874 had also been reshaped by Napoleon III, whose Second Empire (1852–70) embodied the last and most ambitious of the monarchical construction programs, beside which those of his predecessors appeared haphazard and incidental. Under the direction of Baron Georges-Eugène Haussmann (1809–91), prefect of the Seine from 1853 to 1870, Paris was in large part rebuilt. The basis of Haussmann's plan was a boulevard system, incorporating existing avenues into a new network defined by two concentric rings. Grand interior boulevards circled north and south from Place de la Bastille on the east to Place de la Concorde on the west. Outside this ring exterior boulevards connected Place de la Nation with Place de l'Etoile (site of the Arc de Triomphe), including on its southern arc the boulevard St-Germain Louis Sullivan took to the Ecole each day. Major east-west, north-south axes and diagonal boulevards tied the inner and outer rings together, the entire network resembling the spokes and rims of overlapping wheels. The visual significance of boulevard terminations and intersections made them appropriate sites for major public monuments and buildings, while the 125-foot-wide thoroughfares themselves became prestigious addresses for the rising bourgeoisie, whose five-to-seven-story Second Empire row buildings created an exceptionally harmonious streetscape, for which Paris became renowned.[4]

Although Haussmann concentrated his efforts on the center of the city, paying less attention to outlying *arrondissements,* he did not limit his constructions to the street system. Modern boulevards were certainly important for facilitating the distribution of goods and services in an expanding market economy, and for speedy troop movement, given fearful monarchical memories of the 1789, 1830, and 1848 revolutions. But in addition Haussmann also supervised a network of gas street lighting, a modern water supply, the building of numerous parks and gardens, the planting of over 100,000 trees, the siting of imposing monuments, and the erection of at least three military barracks. The prefect merged the fifteen omnibus companies into one, in 1860 extending new lines to the city limits. And not the least of his achievements was the construction of spectacular new public buildings.

Of these, the Paris Opéra is perhaps best known, today considered the great showpiece of Second Empire architecture,[5] the symbol of Napoleon III's official style. Designed by the talented young Charles Garnier, its High Renaissance facade was regarded as somewhat avant-garde and slightly distasteful by the Ecole establishment. The new Louvre was built between 1852 and 1868, in the interval accompanied by two state theaters in Place du Châtelet, the Tribunal de Commerce, an addition to the Palais de Justice, the Halles Centrales market, the Gare du Nord, the Palais de l'Industrie, the expansion of the Bibliothèque Nationale, the Docks de St-Ouen, and in the private sector, innumerable grand residences, shops, and hotels for the *haute bourgeoisie.* Although Haussmann did not control private building, his broad new boulevards and handsome public structures stimulated and helped direct its growth. Large-scale construction projects, on the other hand, displaced thousands of Parisian workers during the 1860s, contributing to the popular unrest that began to bubble up against the emperor. As part of an effort to undermine domestic discontent, but for diplomatic reasons as well, Napoleon III, like many another politician before and since, created an external diversion by declaring an ill-advised war against Prussia in July 1870. In less than six short weeks, in early September, he was forced to surrender to William I, in the process losing an eighty-thousand-man army.

Two days after Napoleon's capture at Sedan, a French provisional government, declaring the formation of the Third Republic, prepared to meet the Prussian invaders. But after four and one-half months of fruitless fighting, during which Paris was put under siege, the Republic capitulated at the end of January 1871. The armistice provided for a brief, symbolic Prussian occupation of Paris beginning March 1. But Parisian workers, long resentful of Napoleon III, frustrated by the incompetence of the Third Republic, angered by its choice of Versailles as the national capital, and furious at the thought of Germans marching through their city, formed a revolutionary municipal government on March 18 known to history as the Paris Commune. With Prussian approval regular French troops invaded on May 21, bringing the Commune to an end on May 28. So fell the first proletarian government in modern history.[6]

As the Communard position became increasingly tenuous in May, workers began to destroy what one writer calls "the city's architectural monuments," although it is equally accurate to say that in their desperation, and in retaliation for the incredible brutality leveled against them—some thirty thousand were shot and forty-five thousand more arrested after May 21 by government forces—the Communards sacked symbols of a state authority that had repeatedly oppressed them. First to go was the column in Place Vendôme, with its statue of Napoleon Bonaparte. The Tuileries Palace was next, followed by a large portion of the Palais Royale, the Préfecture de Police, the Ministère de Finance, the Cour de Comptes, and one of their command headquarters, the Hôtel de Ville. "The clouds of smoke hanging over Paris," an authority notes, "inspired comparisons with the eruption of Vesuvius and the fall of Babylon."[7] All this occurred little more than three years before Louis Sullivan arrived. But in his memoirs he mentioned none of it, even though many of the architectural casualties were restored during his stay in Paris, and traces of the Communard struggle could be seen at every turn. Nor did he mention Haussmann's boulevards, Second Empire buildings, the 1863 reorganization, or any other aspect of the recent history whose legacy affected his every Paris move.

Even though he had looked forward to seeing it since at least 1870, when his cousin Minnie Whittlesey told him about the wonders of the Continent, Sullivan gave Paris only two of the twenty-one pages in his autobiography devoted to his European sojourn. But he actually liked the city very much. He took immense pleasure from its architectural monuments, happy children, and the public parks, especially the Luxembourg Gardens, near enough to his room for him to visit them regularly. He delighted in window shopping on the Grand Boulevards, in the museums, and in midnight mass at Notre-Dame. His drawings indicate that he spent a good deal of time sketching at sidewalk cafés. Obviously, he took advantage of what Paris had to offer, but he described it years later in a flat, matter-of-fact tone. Perhaps he came to associate the city with his ultimate disillusionment at the Ecole, or with his discovery that he was less impressed with its architecture than with the Italian landmarks he would soon visit.

Sullivan ignored Paris in his memoirs to concentrate on himself, particularly on the ordeal of studying for and passing his Ecole entrance examinations. When he called at the American Legation, as Sidney Stratton had advised, after spending a few days casually inspecting the city, he discovered to his dismay he had but six short weeks to prepare and that he was woefully unfamiliar with the subject matter. (So says his autobiography, at any rate.) In a flurry of activity, he engaged three tutors of conversational French (the first two did not work out), a mathematics instructor named Clopet, and burned the midnight oil reading history. His principal memory of Clopet was an important one, that upon inspecting the textbook Louis had been advised to acquire, he abruptly dismissed it, saying: "Observe: Here is a problem with five exceptions or special cases; here . . . three . . . another nine, and so on and on, a procession of exceptions and special cases. I suggest you place the book in the waste basket; we shall not [have] need of it here; *for here our demonstration shall be so broad as to admit of* NO EXCEPTION!"[8] What a revelation Sullivan said this was. If it were true in mathemetics, he wondered, then why not in architecture? So on the spot he resolved to discover a principle he was convinced existed but that no one had heretofore addressed: a design theory that could fit all occasions without exception. This, Sullivan wrote in the 1920s, came to him in a flash in the summer of 1874 to guide his life ever after. So after six weeks of intensive study followed by grueling examinations in history, mathematics, drawing, and design that he passed with flying colors, he was then able to make "his *entrée* into the *atelier* of Monsieur Emil [*sic*] Vaudremer, practicing architect."

The examination arrangements, however, together with Sullivan's Ecole dossier, establish that his first weeks in France were somewhat different from his autobiographical version. What actually happened was typical for incomng students: Arriving early in August, probably with full knowledge of the examination schedule, his first and most important step was to call on Emile Vaudremer, director of an *atelier extérieur* and former instructor of Eugene Letang, William R. Ware's assistant at MIT, who had supervised Louis's drawing classes. Perhaps he had secured letters of introduction from his former college teachers (or from Hunt or Stratton), since Vaudremer would have required some basis other than personal impression to sponsor a young unknown. Attendance at the Ecole was free, but since it was limited to thirty new students between the ages of fifteen and twenty-five, admittance was highly competitive. In order even to apply to take the entrance exams, a prospective student needed a patron, a practicing architect and atelier director whose job it was to help screen almost three hundred hopefuls. This was accomplished by interview followed by observation in the atelier during the weeks of preparation for the exams. Like Richard Morris Hunt before him, Louis more than likely proceeded under his patron's watchful eye. It may even have been Vaudremer, not the American Legation, as Sullivan claimed, who suggested he hire mathematics tutor M. Clopet, who, it turns out, was an adjunct instructor at the Ecole.[9] Benefiting from the very best supervision, Louis progressed so satisfactorily that on September 11, 1874, Vaudremer wrote out the following form letter:

> I am honored to present to the Director of the Select Imperial School of Fine Arts M. Louis Sullivan residing at 17 Rue Racine, an architecture student. I ask that the above cited student be admitted as a student and certify that he is willing and able to take his entrance examinations.

Having secured the necessary sponsorship of a patron who, to protect his own reputation, would not have endorsed anyone without ample observation, Louis then called at the American Legation to obtain the second required letter of introduction. On September 17, temporary chargé d'affaires Wickham Hoffman wrote to the French minister of education and fine arts:

> I am honored to support the application of my fellow citizen Mr. (Louis) Sullivan for admission to the National School of Fine Arts in the Department of Architecture.
>
> Mr. Sullivan is 18 years old and comes from a very fine family living in Chicago.
>
> Please accept, M. Minister, my most profound respects.[10]

Hoffman would hardly support Louis's application without evidence of merit, in this case Vaudremer's endorsement. So Sullivan did not simply walk into the examination room after six weeks of private study, as he implied in his memoirs, but followed instead the normal procedures, subjecting himself to a month or more of careful scrutiny by Ecole faculty before submitting to the rigorous oral and written testing that began in late September.

Entrance examinations were spread over several weeks, with little change in format from Hunt's experience in 1845 to that of architect Ernest Flagg (1857–1947) in the 1880s. Since Louis's in 1874 fell between the others, of which there are detailed accounts, it is useful to supplement his memories with theirs.[11] The architectural examinations always came first, followed by descriptive and plane geometry, algebra, general mathematics, and history. Sullivan wrote offhandedly that "the free hand drawing, the mechanical drawing, and an *esquisse en loge* [literally: a sketch in a stall] of a simple architectural project, went smoothly enough for Louis. . . . [T]he real test for him would [be the rest]." What he did not say was that the drawing exams were eight hours each and that the *esquisse,* also a grueling affair, had many characteristics of a latter-day "happening."

When the moment for the architectural examinations arrived, *aspirants* were let into a large room, thirty feet wide and much longer, on the fifth floor of an Ecole building. Down the center ran a long series of drafting tables and along the walls "a row of stalls, for all the world," remembered Flagg, "like those of a stable," called *loges.* At the door each aspirant received a set of instructions for a plan, section, and elevation of a prescribed building with dimensions and other specifications set forth. To be completed in one continuous twelve-hour session, the project would be judged the following day at an exhibition of all the work. After receiving instructions, aspirants rushed to get stalls because of their shelves and windows; latecomers worked at center tables where the light was poor. Applicants were allowed to talk, roam about, bring food and candles, and by Flagg's day to go out to eat. A number who had previously tried and failed were old hands at the affair. Dressed in outrageous costumes and carrying wine bottles, they greeted each other loudly with shouts back and forth. The din was at first terrific, but as the twelve-hour deadline approached, the carnival-like atmosphere turned deadly serious as one of the fundamental instructional techniques at the school came into play: the requirement that the esquisse, or freehand preliminary sketch of the project, be the recognizable basis of the final presentation. Students were therefore judged on how well the plan, section, and elevation served each other, met the specifications of the design program, and fulfilled the promise of the initial esquisse.

Having cleared the several drawing hurdles, to which he devoted only a single sentence in his memoirs, Louis then confronted his historical and mathematical obstacles, described in detail for four and onc-half pages, on the face of it, a surprising imbalance in his account. According to Ernest Flagg, exams were weighted by their professional significance: the applicant's score in architectural composition, for example, was multiplied by twelve, in mathematics by five, and in history by one. The least relevant as far as the Ecole was concerned were to Sullivan the most important, at least in retrospect. Asked to discourse orally for one-half hour each on the history of the Hebrew people, the ten emperors of Rome, and the era of Francis I, Louis faced his most difficult challenge, so he cherished forever his examiners' exuberant praise. "I felicitate you, Monsieur Sullivan," said one. "You have the mathematical imagination which is rather rare." The history professor gave him "the highest rating," adding his certainty that one day Louis would make "a contribution to the knowledge of mankind." On October 22, 1874, Louis Sullivan was formally admitted into the Ecole des Beaux-Arts as a "Second Class" (beginning) student after two and one-half months of intensive study and punishing tests.[12]

One might suppose that Sullivan would have described his esquisse en loge and other drawing exams at length, giving short shrift to mathematics and history, which, after all, were not his primary interests. But precisely the opposite was true. In his autobiography he pictured himself as an inadequately prepared novice surviving a historical and mathematical trial by fire to emerge triumphant. Perhaps, as historian Sherman Paul speculates, Sullivan was unconsciously attempting in his memoirs to upstage Henry Richardson, whose success at the Ecole was public knowledge but who had initially failed the exams.[13] Perhaps he was comparing himself favorably with Hunt, later known as the "dean" of American architecture, who tried twice before passing the crucial esquisse en loge that Louis had breezed through. Certainly his success was a tribute to his physical stamina—"Great God," he told his brother, Albert, two months afterward, "it makes me weak to think of them"[14]—always a matter of importance to him, to the training he had received from Moses Woolson and John A. Tompson, to the program at MIT, and to the drafting ability he had acquired in Philadelphia and Chicago. Or perhaps he stressed his nonarchitectural achievements because in later years, as an outspoken critic of academic training, he could not very comfortably associate himself with it. To have done well in the enemy's camp, so to speak, would have been a dubious victory.

Once enrolled in the Ecole, Louis and his classmates were each assigned a project by the director to be completed in a specified number of months after producing a twenty-four-hour esquisse filed as a brief. Like the other students, Louis could work on his own schedule but was required to garner enough points from periodic competitions in both architectural projects and academic subjects for promotion to the First (or upper) Class, a process the best performers completed in two to four years. No one was obliged to attend lectures, the only stipulation being that everyone enter at least one competition annually. The architectural projects usually demanded that within two or three months, the student design a plan, section, and elevation of a prescribed building utilizing the esquisse technique of the entrance exams. Developed under periodic supervision of atelier patrons, the projects then formed the basis of competitive exhibitions. Since advancement and ultimately certification were in large part the result of accumulated points, student rivalry at these affairs was intense.[15]

Although few attended, Second Class lectures were offered in architectural history, theory, and perspective, in elements of construction, and in mathematics by professors who were generally distinguished architects. Important and enlightening as the lectures might have been, however, the backbone of the teaching system was the atelier. There was no necessary connection between classroom instruction and design work, but all Ecole ateliers used the same esquisse method. Once the students received their project assignments, the design process proceeded through three stages. First, the esquisse, a rapid, considered, preliminary sketch of the structure, was done freehand, kept on file, and referred to periodically. Conceived as an inspiration or instinct made permanent, it was followed by large, carefully detailed studies of various parts of the building. In the final stage, the studies were brought into an ink drawing synthesis in no vital way departing from the esquisse. Atelier patrons gave advice at every stage of the design process, but since students proceeded at their own pace, seeking assistance as needed, supervision was informal and relatively unstructured.

The twenty or so students in most ateliers paid the patron a fee, purchased firewood, candles, and other necessities, and were responsible for maintenance. Taking charge of day-to-day operations, advanced students claimed the right to order newcomers to fetch coffee and food, tend the fire, run errands, and in general handle all the trivial dirty work. Like most of the other patrons, Louis's had distinguished himself in the competition for the Grand Prix de Rome, the Ecole's highest student award, placing second in 1854 with his "Edifice for the Burial Place of the Rulers of a Great Empire," just the sort of monumental design project typical of the curriculum.[16] Forty-five years old when Louis met him, Emile Vaudremer's executed works included the church of St-Pierre-de-Montrouge and the Prison de la Santé. His studio on a courtyard giving off rue du Bac, a bit west of the Ecole and about a kilometer and one-half from Louis's room, normally rang with noise, conversation, and horseplay except at competition time, when it was deathly still and very crowded. Vaudremer visited two or three times a week to review the work and offer suggestions. Louis never described the project he drew under Vaudremer's supervision, and wrote very little about the man himself, but he did seem to respect him. His criticisms, Sullivan recalled, "were clear, clean-cut, constructive, and personal to each student. . . . Always, however, he was [a] disciplinarian, and one felt the steady pressure." Louis's easy mastery of the language—thanks in large measure to his family background and his English High courses—won the approval of his French-speaking fellows, freeing him from the onerous duties of wood hauling and cleanup reserved for new arrivals, while his occasional use of street argot, he remembered, raised him to the level of a comrade. He fondly recalled immersing himself in the congenial atelier atmosphere, where a spirit of community and friendly discourse prevailed (except at competition time), "so much so that he became rather more absorbed in the work of others than in his own."

Unfortunately, there is no record of his atelier activities, of the project he drew to satisfy Ecole requirements. For years it was assumed—largely because Frank Lloyd Wright said so[17]—that several fresco studies he dated in Paris in November 1874 and April 1875 were part of his Ecole assignment. But since the school did not normally set beginning students to work on interior detailing, this seems unlikely. Louis wrote his brother, Albert, on December 7, 1874, that he was "crawling slowly at the atelier": "I am working along steadily on my project, which is to be finished on the 28th inst." (of December), a two-month assignment, following admittance on October 22, not three months, as he later wrote. "I shall begin on the [remainder] of my plan tomorrow," he added; "it is to cover two sheets of 'double-capping.' "[18] Whatever its nature it was surely historical, in keeping with Ecole policy, and probably it was this that stimulated him, in January and February 1875, when he had time, to read René Menard's histories of ancient, medieval, and modern art. Work on

III.3 *Joseph Auguste Emile Vaudremer, Edifice for the Burial Place of the Rulers of a Great Empire, 1854.* From Armand Guerinet, *Les Grands Prix de Rome d'architecture.*

his project or possibly Hippolyte Taine's lectures may have prompted him to read the professor's volumes on the philosophy of art in Italy and Greece.[19] However it happened, Louis's introduction to Michelangelo would soon have enormous consequences for his future.

Although the young man labored diligently at the atelier, all was not all work without play. In the one remaining letter from his Paris student days, Louis described the "first masquerade ball of the season" he attended with a friend to celebrate Thanksgiving, presumably thrown by the handful of Americans in residence. The costumes "were as grotesque and outlandish as could be imagined," he wrote Albert, "and to see them dance the cancan in such rigs was . . . exceedingly amusing." After the party broke up at 4:30 a.m., he fell into bed exhausted to sleep for twelve hours. Occasions like these were probably infrequent, but he apparently reveled in them when he could. Not so the chill and damp of the Paris winter; his chest cold in November led to diarrhea, which sapped all his strength, "and you can imagine," he wrote, "the way I am cussing and swearing is enough to make hell shiver." Even his new "inch-thick" overcoat did not keep him warm enough. Aside from attending parties in his spare time Louis reflected on Lotus Club sporting events, mentioning to Albert his concern with keeping in condition—a losing battle, he believed—and asked for news about his friends' athletic activities.[20]

However enjoyable, diversions like these took him away from his main business in Paris, but never very far. Having completed his atelier project by the end of 1874, he turned his attention not only to art history, but also to resuming work on an architectural exercise that would shortly take him home. His December letter to Albert disclosed that in addition to keeping up with family and Lotus Club affairs, he had also remained abreast of John Edelmann's career. During Louis's absence from Chicago, his friend had resigned his position with William Le Baron Jenney to form a partnership late in 1874 with Joseph S. Johnston that would last until 1876 at offices in Suite 18, 182 Clark Street. Two of their jobs in short order involved Louis Sullivan. The first, Sinai Synagogue, at Indiana Avenue and Twenty-first Street, was designed by Edelmann's former employers Edward Burling and Dankmar Adler, who subcontracted the interior decoration to Johnston & Edelmann probably soon after they formed their partnership, since construction on the building began May 1, 1875.[21] Work on the second, evangelist Dwight L. Moody's Tabernacle, at Chicago Avenue and La Salle Street, was began in August 1873, stalled during the decade's depression with only its basement and a temporary roof completed, and resumed in August 1875 with Johnston & Edelmann the new architects.[22] Both structures required elaborate interior frescoing, and by April 1875—possibly even as early as November 1874—Louis was making decorative studies in his rue Racine quarters.

A purple-ink drawing on tracing paper of a bird flanked by stylized flowers was the essence of a "Fresco-border on ceiling to correspond with centerpiece and frieze" signed by "Louis H. Sullivan to John H. Edelmann, Paris, Nov. 29th, 1874." With it is an unsigned drawing of the same motif, folded and glued into four quadrants labeled "center-piece." Five months later he composed at least three delicate ink studies of quite different stylized flowers, one a "Centerpiece in fresco," another a "Fresco-border," both signed "Louis H. Sullivan to John H. Edelman [*sic*], Paris, April 1st, 1875."[23] Whether one set was for Sinai Synagogue and the other for Moody Tabernacle, whether both were for the same building or simply samples for Edelmann's consideration, is impossible to determine conclusively since the two structures have long since been demolished and so far no visual record of their original interior decoration has come to light. But lengthy descriptions in contemporary newspapers establish that the motifs of all the Sullivan drawings closely resemble the executed Moody frescoes, which in turn, one reporter noticed, had "a considerable correspondence of theme" to those at Sinai.[24] It is therefore virtually certain that Sullivan's studies were drawn on commission, not as gifts to Edelmann, as some have thought. In late November 1874, Louis was struggling through his project in Atelier Vaudremer, and would hardly have taken on the extra commitment unless highly motivated. But afterward, until the first of April 1875, when the second drawings were completed, he had both the time and the inclination to do other things.

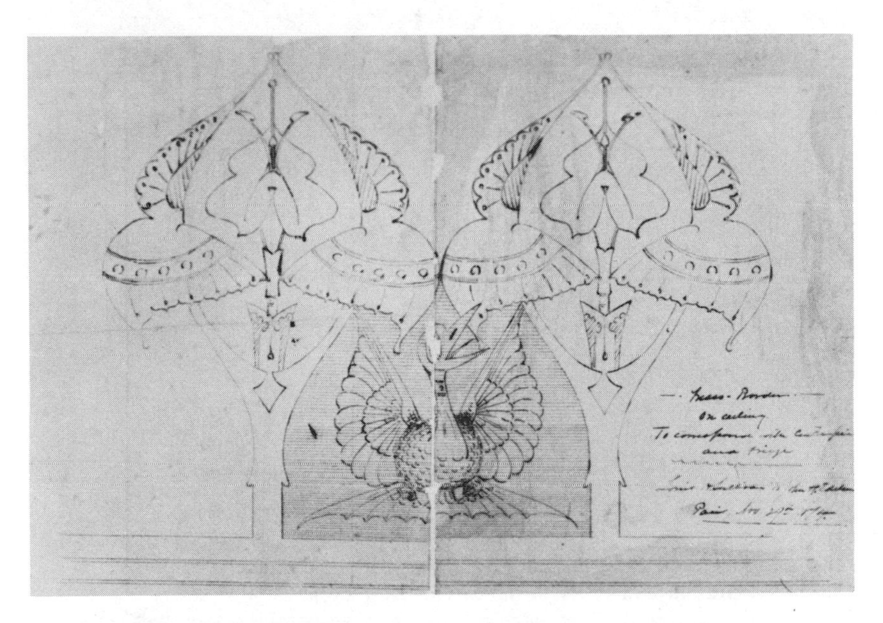

III.4 *Louis Sullivan, fresco design, 1874.* Avery Architectural and Fine Arts Library. Columbia University in the City of New York.

And one other thing he could no longer delay was a pilgrimage to Rome. The first reason for going was simply to get away from the scene of months of arduous labor. Another was to visit the classical architecture his instructors praised so highly. But the immediate motivation, Sullivan recalled, was Taine's contention that Michelangelo's *Last Judgment* in the Sistine Chapel was executed *en momentum,* on the spur of the moment without detailed planning. (Actually,

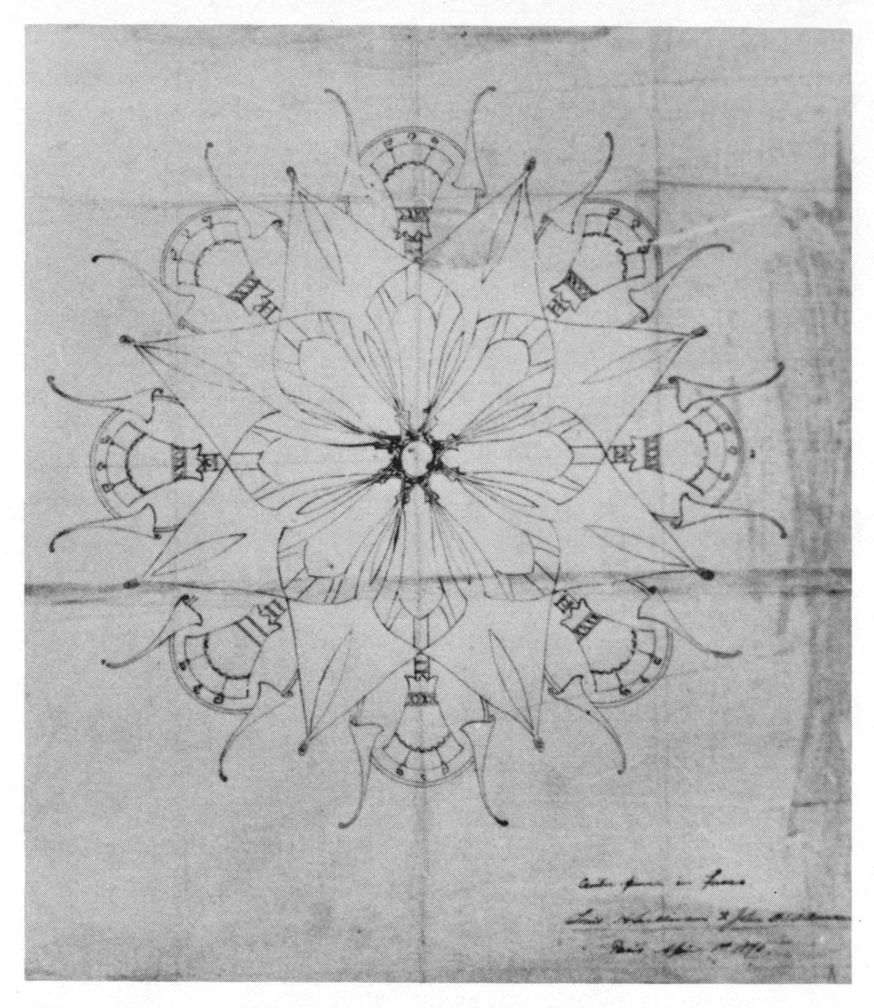

III.5 *Louis Sullivan, fresco design, 1875.* Avery Architectural and Fine Arts Library. Columbia University in the City of New York.

Taine does not make the assertion in his writings; Sullivan may have confused it with something else he read.) Was Michelangelo's method so obvious that Taine could say it was "self-evident"? If so, then Louis had entirely misread the painting. Doubting his own perceptions, he decided to inspect it firsthand, in April 1875.

Once in Rome the classical monuments he had learned to respect, indeed, everything else in the city, paled in comparison to the Sistine Chapel ceiling. After two days staring at it, a kind of epiphany for Louis, he concluded, somewhat arrogantly perhaps, that Taine was wrong about *momentum,* that he—Louis—could detect and understand as much if not more about art than the mighty professor, and that "he could see everything that eye could see." But this discovery about himself was considerably less revelatory than his confrontation with Michelangelo. Here, he waxed ecstatically in his writing, was "a Super-Man," "a great Free Spirit," the "first great Adventurer," "the first mighty man of Courage. The first man with a Great Voice. The first whose speech was Elemental. The first whose will would not be denied. . . . The man, the man of super-power, the glorified man, of whom he had dreamed in his childhood. . . ."[25]

In Michelangelo, Louis found Power, Life, Courage, and Imagination: capitalized. All his youthful heroes—street cleaners, shipyard workers, dime novel protagonists, Moses Woolson, John A. Tompson, even architects—all were surpassed, humbled, by this one great man. In Michelangelo's work Louis detected human possibility developed to its fullest, human achievement surpassing all previous achievement, human creativity completely unshackled. But most important of all, he realized his life's purpose: to be another Michelangelo, to develop his own Power—now an operative concept—and from it his art. So after three days in Rome, two in the Sistine Chapel, he left, without a word about anything else he may have seen. After Michelangelo it was all anticlimactic. He traveled on to Florence, loving it so much he said he stayed six weeks, but after the Sistine Chapel no single object there—not even Michelangelo's *David*—was worthy of his pen. Proceeding north along the Riviera to Nice, he recorded in his mind the beauty of the Mediterranean, but nothing about the city before returning to Paris, in body if not in spirit. Weeks of exposure to Italian art—especially Michelangelo's—made it impossible for him to continue at the Ecole.

Surviving records indicate that Louis took a vacation from reading and drawing from March through May 1875, except for a few Paris sketches completed by April 1, the date on his second set of fresco studies.[26] On May 24, 1875, *The New York Times* listed "Louis H. Sullivan" among the "Passengers Arrived" that day on the *Britannic* from Liverpool via Cork.[27] So it is reasonable to suppose that Louis's pilgrimage to Italy, beginning sometime in April, ended no later than early or mid-May, after which he immediately prepared to leave France. His autobiography gives a contrary impression, that after Italy and the south of France he returned to rue Racine and Atelier Vaudremer for an indeterminate but substantial period. Sullivan was never precise about the length of his stay at the Ecole, going so far later on as to leave associates with the impression it had been almost two years,[28] suggesting perhaps, in light of his subsequent criticisms, that he had indeed given it every chance to meet his needs. But if Louis visited the atelier after returning from Italy, it was only to say good-bye. Since the Ecole exhausted all the academic possibilities, formal studies were now beside the point. With Michelangelo as a model and a job waiting for him in Chicago, there was no reason to stay.

Louis's architectural education had turned out to be a backwards tracing of academic ideological development. MIT had been a pale carbon copy of the Ecole, so Louis went to the original. But in Paris he discovered the Ecole to be a modern outpost of ancient and Renaissance design. So Louis went to Italy to experience personally what he had only glimpsed from afar. After that, there was no place else to go, no deeper well of architectural nourishment from which to drink. In the process of following Western architecture back to its source, Louis unexpectedly discovered that the monumental accomplishments of classicism were in his own day put to improper use. Despite exacting historicism and intelligent instructional methods, the Ecole had bogged down in a quagmire of abstract, "local and specific" rules lacking inspiration, freshness, and real creativity. The freedom and power of Michelangelo had in Paris been transformed over the years into moribund formulas and technique. Both Louis and the school looked to the ancient masters for guidance, but whereas the institution had elevated Michelangelo's principles de facto to timeless truths universally applicable, Louis found him to be the a priori embodiment of innovation, rule breaking, and independent thought. For the Ecole, Michelangelo's oeuvre was a static entity to be copied, but for Louis he was a dynamic man to be emulated in spirit, not in form. At the Sistine Chapel, Louis learned to value the process of creativity as much as its products; he learned that he alone could determine the methods and forms most suitable to his own art. So Louis decided the Ecole had no more to offer. He would return home as a modern-day Michelangelo, not to design classical buildings—although classical vocabularies appeared from time to time in his mature work—but to turn his intellect, emotions, and instinct loose in search of new and personal paths to architectural expression. The truth and the source of art for him, he had concluded, were not in books, but within himself.

Despite his ultimate dissatisfaction, Louis's short-lived association with the Ecole was beneficial. Writing to architect Claude Bragdon in 1904, Sullivan claimed that "because of the teachings of the school . . . there entered my mind . . . the germ of that law which later, after much observation of nature's processes, I formulated in the phrase, 'Form follows Function.' It was at the school, also, that I first grasped the concrete value of logical thinking."[29] Elsewhere, he praised the Ecole's insistence on the primacy of plan, that is, on the importance of determining the ground plan of a building before working out its elevation, section, or facade features, a method of design he seems to have retained throughout his entire career. Sullivan also utilized the esquisse technique for the rest of his life. Many of his mature buildings, one authority notes, reveal "a remarkable similarity between conception and execution"[30] or, as it would have been stated in Paris, corresponded closely when built to their preliminary drawings. As Sullivan himself recalled: "Louis thought the exigent condition that one hold to the original sketch in its essentials, to be discipline, of an inspired sort," much like holding "firmly to a thesis."[31] By this he did not mean to advocate close-mindedness, only to insist that architects follow their inspirations and instincts. This is what he had in mind when he paid his ultimate tribute to the Ecole: "My work has consistently shown . . . that I *absorbed* the real principles that the school *envelopes.*"[32]

How much of this came from the Ecole—certainly the theories of plan and esquisse did—how much from other sources or from within himself is difficult to determine. Historian Sherman Paul notes that from his mathematics tutor, M. Clopet, Louis learned to begin a demonstration with a personal assertion ("I say . . ."), a device for enhancing the appearance of authority that became the method of explanation in his posthumous book, *Kindergarten Chats,* first published as a series of articles in 1901 and 1902. Clopet also taught him to beware of untested abstractions and logical rigidities, and to delight in disciplined imagination. And from Clopet he also discovered the architectural objective of finding a law so "broad as to admit of no exception!" From his examination studies, his design project, his reading and possibly lectures, Louis seems to have acquired a taste for history, especially the history of art. He absorbed valuable if immediately intangible lessons from continental architecture, and observed the low life as well as the high (depicted in a number of his drawings). And of course there was Michelangelo, the most important learning experience of them all.

So Louis's ten months in London, Paris, and Rome were hardly a waste of time, but were in fact an immensely liberating period. No longer searching for a font of wisdom, knowing that the source of architectural power was within himself, he left the Ecole and academic studies forever at the age of eighteen in May 1875. With the promise of work from John Edelmann, a firm belief in his own abilities, and the objective of finding a rule to admit of no exception, Louis returned to Chicago ready to begin his life's adventure.

III.6 *Louis Sullivan, a Paris sketch, 1875.*
The Michigan Historical Collections.

Chapter IV

JUNIOR PARTNER

1875-83

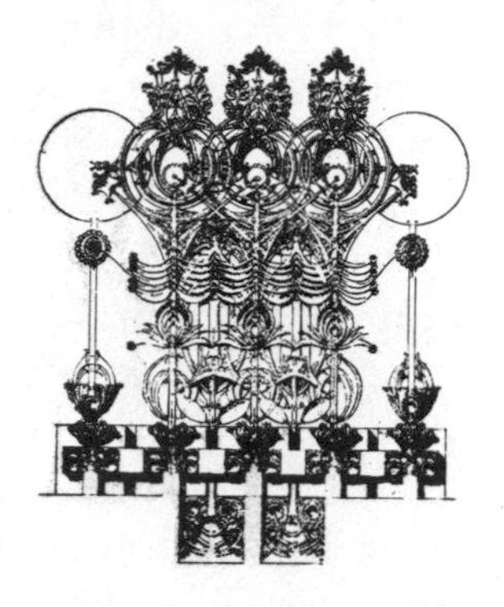

THE "GARDEN CITY," as Louis Sullivan called Chicago, was coming "into its own" in 1875, when he returned from Paris. Perhaps the blooming of summer was his metaphor for changes within himself, for during the next few years, he, too, would blossom into the architect he had wanted to be. But the process was not without struggle. Just as the Chicago of 1875 had three vast shantytowns "where no gardens grew," he recalled, so his new architectural roots required lengthy germination in the relatively unproductive ground of office assistant before springing to life as a full-grown professional.

In mid-1875, with the city's building industry not yet fully recovered from depression following the financial panic two years earlier, Louis prowled Chicago twenty miles on foot each day, he said, until "he knew every nook and corner." He also had time to continue his reading. From Francis Parkman's narrative histories of French explorers in the American West, he learned about Chicago's original settlers. Fully aware of its vast stretches of commercial ugliness, he also developed from Parkman an appreciation for the romance, the courage, and the "power" of its pioneers. Personal power—the ability to accomplish great things—seemed to him to flourish in his chosen city. So in 1875 he reaffirmed that this burgeoning metropolis, this "hog butcher to the world," as Carl Sandburg would later dub it (also from affection), was *"the Place for me!"*[1]

While Louis was abroad, his father, Patrick, had moved his dancing studio farther west, from 147 to 159 Twenty-second Street near State, retaining his home at 85 Twenty-third Street. Andrienne presumably continued to assist, playing piano while Patrick gave instruction, possibly to the young women of Dearborn Academy, a fashionable finishing school nearby. Louis's brother, Albert, about to turn twenty-one in September, apparently still lived at home but, unlisted in city directories for 1875 and 1876, may have had doubts about his future. In 1870 he had hired on as an apprentice in the Illinois Central Railroad locomotive works. Four years later, possibly influenced by Louis's career goals, Albert declared himself a draftsman, with offices in his father's dancing studio. But in 1877 he returned to the ICRR at the rank of machinist, although within a year he left that job to enter the administrative offices as a clerk, from which he would rise to positions of considerable authority over the next thirty-five years. But in 1875 Albert was probably much as Louis had left him, a young man still more interested in athletics than in romance, just beginning to make his way in the world. In that regard the Sullivan brothers had much in common.[2]

Of interest to both was the Lotus Club, the Riverdale athletic group Louis and Albert had initially joined in the spring of 1874. In

IV.1 *Albert Sullivan at age thirty-six, 1890.* Photo by Max Platz. © The Art Institute of Chicago, all rights reserved.

his brother's absence, Albert had regularly participated in its activities, including the match it had recently lost to the fledgling New York Athletic Club. His specialty was the hundred-yard dash, at which he had beaten Louis on one occasion by six yards. Although Louis had written from Paris in December of his eagerness to return to the club, had asked to be kept "well posted in athletic and general news,"[3] and worked out during the summer of 1875, he entered no contests, perhaps feeling the need of additional time to regain his former peak condition. Albert, on the other hand, was a tireless competitor. In the club "Records," Louis's old MIT notebook,[4] he recorded his own best efforts in the one-, three-, seven-, and twenty-mile walks, the latter accomplished in four and one-half hours, only three minutes slower than Charles J. Williams and leader Bill Curtis. Albert faithfully logged his running times for every furlong (220 yards or one-eighth of a mile), quarter-, half-, mile, and three-mile race; in swimming for four different events; in weight throwing his distances for the hammer, the put, and even the fifty-six-pounder. Albert attempted every one of the twenty kinds of contests in which the club engaged.

Louis seems to have devoted more time to reading during the 1875 season than to athletics, continuing the rigorous exercise in intellectual self-improvement he had begun in Paris. There he had gone through several volumes of art history by Hippolyte Taine and René Menard, Camille Selden's *Etudes de Mendelssohn* and Agathe Audley's study of Beethoven. He had read Walter Scott's *The Pirate* and had so delighted in the satirical Petroleum V. Nasby *Papers* by David Ross Locke that he went on to read more of his works. Locke seems to have interested Louis in American authors. Soon he had consumed Bret Harte's sketches and poems, Mark Twain's *Celebrated Jumping Frog of Calaveras County*, and James Russell Lowell's *Bigelow Papers*. In Chicago, under the tutelage now of John Edelmann, who organized the Lotus Club library, Louis read *Our Girls* and *Our Digestion* ("Talks about People's Stomachs," he called it) by Dr. Dio Lewis, James Parton's *Smoking and Drinking*, W. C. Tyler's *Brownville Papers,* the first volume of Charles Darwin's *Descent of Man,* John Tyndall's *Fragments of Science,* and much more, totaling from January through October 1875 some twenty-eight titles, several quite dense for any eighteen-year-old. Aware of his son's intellectual hunger, Patrick gave him a copy of John William Draper's *History of the Intellectual Development of Europe* for Christmas 1876, the year the book was published.[5] Draper contrasted ages of faith with ages of reason, the one reinforcing a stultifying feudalism, the other stimulating a liberating democracy, for which science was a major agent of fulfillment. Draper seemed to confirm a pet theory of Edelmann's, his notion of "suppressed functions." Feudalism, according to Louis's reading of Draper filtered through Edelmann, by repressing humanity's creative spirit, had bound architecture to tradition. The functions of buildings were obscured by their forms, quashing humanity's aspirations toward free expression with antiquated architectural precedents. But a democratic architecture would promote human liberation by directly stating the functions for which it was designed.

As these ideas developed slowly within Louis, nurtured by reading and conversations with Edelmann, he devoted more time in 1876 to the club's athletic program. Over the years its members developed a strong sense of camaraderie. When Louis met him in 1874, their leader, William B. Curtis, was a cashier for his father, Henry, an agent for C. S. Maltby oyster and fish wholesalers. At the age of thirty-six or thirty-seven, Bill Curtis in 1875 finally left the family home at 661 Wabash Avenue for rooms at 475 North Franklin Street, just below the point at which the South Branch of the Chicago River breaks away from the main channel in the heart of today's downtown business district, at the same time becoming a "paper-ruler," inking lines on blank stock. In 1876 he took on a second job as a cashier, no doubt to finance the maintenance of a second residence, in Riverdale, the boathouse in which the club met and in which he lived part-time. But the responsibility for two dwellings might have been too burdensome in a financially troubled period, for in 1877 Curtis gave up (or lost) both the cashier's job and the Riverdale building to move to Hurlburt Street in the far northwest Norwood Park district. Eighteen seventy-eight found him back in his old neighborhood on Larrabee Street, but the next year he returned to North Franklin, a house or two away from his earlier address.

All the other members of the Lotus Club listed in the city directories lived near Franklin Street, which may have prompted Curtis to return to the vicinity. Charles A. Billings, an agent for the Cleveland Rolling Mill Company, at first resided in the 1000 block of South Wabash but then moved to 243 Michigan Avenue, sharing rooms in 1878 with Charles S. Downs, a salesman, who had previously boarded with Curtis and his father. Charles J. Williams, a bookkeeper, lived close by at 251 Michigan. With one or two excep-

IV.2 *Louis Sullivan at age 20, 1876.* Avery Architectural and Fine Arts Library. Courtesy Columbia University in the City of New York.

tions, the several address changes of these four men between 1875 and 1880 fell within a compact area bordered by the main channel and South Branch of the Chicago River to the north and west, Michigan Avenue on the east, and Congress on the south. All of them worked on the fringes of this district, sometimes lived in the same quarters or on the same block, and must therefore have seen a good deal of each other outside their club. Their bachelor male bonding is illustrated by Louis's and Edelmann's reaction to the marriage of one of their members (or another unnamed friend). Under a profile sketch in the "Records" book of a rather androgynous person with eyes sublimely uplifted appeared this statement dated May 26, 1876, in Louis's hand: Matrimony—"That holy state, in which they will have a legal right to hate each other as much as they please." To which, four pages later, Edelmann added under his drawing of a knight on horseback: "I am not married nor have I any thoughts that way; but if I had, it would not be for a woman's fortune but her character. . . . [P]ublic reputation is the life of a lady's virtue, and the outward appearance of modesty is . . . as good as the reality, since a private sin is not as prejudicial in this world as a public indecency." Whether these comments represented their actual attitudes toward the institution or their assessment of the actors involved, they indicate that marriage was not something these comrades approved of or anticipated.

Observations like these notwithstanding, the principal business of the Lotus Place Athletic Club, as its members now called it, was just that: athletics. Assuming the notebook to be an accurate guide, it appears that the club was most active from 1876 through 1878, with Albert the most dedicated member and the most enthusiastic participant. He recorded his weight religiously at the same time each year, carefully measured out the distances for walks and runs, listed every Lotus event, and read voraciously on physical development. He was also the most consistent performer. In the Graeco-Roman wrestling matches of June and July 1876, Albert won fourteen contests, losing only two. Curtis was not defeated at all but wrestled only twice. Louis's performance was respectable—second best, in fact, with a record of four and two—while Edelmann came in last, winning only one of thirteen bouts. Most of his matches were against Albert, with whom a vaguely unpleasant rivalry seems to have developed. Louis had once found it necessary to chide his brother about his "supercilious tone" after "some little fuss" between him and John.[6] Trying desperately to improve his showing, Edelmann made careful note of a new system for throwing seven- to ten-pound hammers he had perfected, recording with a not-too-carefully disguised satisfaction that in their July 4 match to celebrate the nation's centennial he actually beat Albert for the first time, tossing an eight-pound weight one hundred feet. The following week, when Albert and John wrestled and Louis took on Charles Williams, no results were listed.

Albert, Curtis, and Williams kept careful track of body measurements from June to September 1876. For the club's walking tournament in October and November, Albert made an elaborate record of each participant's time, down to the seconds, at every quarter mile of their one-, three-, seven-, and twenty-mile walks along the Illinois Central Railroad tracks. Louis did not take part. In October Albert lifted eight hundred pounds on the Riley machine in a gymnasium and by April 1877 had improved to half a ton. Not only was he training at another club on specialized equipment, but he was also the first to get outdoors at the start of the Lotus season in 1877. Only a week after he marked off a walking course on February 11, Albert began rowing, throwing weights and hammers, and, obsessive as it may appear, "plunged in river, temperature of water 35°." The "Records" notebook lists hammer throws and sculling distances for the summer of 1877 and the opening of the 1878 season, which had been pushed back to February for the benefit of Albert, Curtis, Downs, and Billings, the most dedicated members. December and January were now the only months they stayed inside. But by 1878 Louis no longer joined in the Lotus athletic program, his last participation having been in June 1877, when he finished third, fourth, and fifth in running competitions. His high point of involvement was actually 1876, the last year John Edelmann attended before ending his partnership with Joseph Johnston and moving to Cleveland.[7]

Louis was much more gifted than Edelmann—"John certainly did not make a very brilliant showing in the athletic line," he had written earlier—and might have been even better had he exercised consistently. Even in 1876 he preferred Edelmann's company to the rigors of bodybuilding, however much pride he took in physical fitness. The "Records" book for that year is, in fact, a kind of dialogue in graphic and literary form between the two young architects, with Edelmann assuming the role of mentor. On more than one occasion after Louis entered a musing, Edelmann would reply. (Their com-

IV.3 *John Edelmann sketches of E. Bates House.* Lotus Club Notebook.

ments on marriage are one example.) "I believe," Louis wrote, "that the object of and aim of distemper decoration is to produce a combination of colors, which shall be harmonious in itself, and with its surroundings, forming a unity, of which the primary function is general effect." Edelmann replied, also using Louis's new method of first-person assertion acquired from M. Clopet, his Ecole mathematics tutor, that "I believe the object of all *decoration* to be the pleasure to be derived from looking at it," and then proceeded to write an essay on the evolution of art from cave people to its acquisition of formal religious content. Edelmann clearly assumed the posture of Louis's instructor, the senior partner in their ongoing dialogue, leading his charge to levels of analysis not previously considered. Elsewhere in the "Records" are what seem to be the opening paragraphs of a lecture on art, possibly dictated by Edelmann to Louis and much corrected, as if meant for a wider audience. "Art is noble thought nobly expressed," Edelmann contended; "ideas . . . give permanent value to an art production—Technical skill," he added, as if to warn his young colleague away from self-congratulation, "is not art itself but merely [its] servant."

In addition to instructing Louis in the theory of art, Edelmann also organized a program of reading for him and the rest of the club. As "Librarian," with the two Sullivans and Ralph Cleveland sharing the "board of directors," Edelmann catalogued their books under the headings of poetry, fiction, science, and miscellaneous. Spenser, Longfellow, and Harte appeared among the poets; Cervantes and Thackeray among the novelists (along with Joseph L. Worcester's *Elements of History*, either misplaced or judged to be fictitious); books on water power, locomotives, and money as a medium of exchange were in the science section; while miscellaneous included *Robert's Rules of Order* and a dictionary.

The notebook also contained a number of architectural studies, some of them commissions Edelmann and his partner were designing or hoped to get. The Sinai Temple, for example, on which Edelmann and Sullivan were working at the time, was depicted in a "spandrel for synagogue" sketch. Others were drawings of earlier Edelmann projects: general and detail views, plus a plan for a three-story Chicago mansion for E. Bates, built when Edelmann worked for Burling and Adler, and sketches of an unexecuted 1869 country house like the Bates residence in Gothic Revival. A "Design of City Hall for Chicago," a study for a suburban church in Englewood, Ohio, and "A Cathedral for the Diocese of Cleveland" were all drawn in anticipation of commissions unobtained, accompanied by Gothic details of arches, windows, and towers. Partly for Louis's edification and partly for his own discipline, Edelmann wrote on one occasion that "the chief difficulty in designing a [city hall] tower so large is 1st to cut it up enough to avoid dwarfing the features of the build[ing and] 2nd to keep it simple . . . the great temptation being to—for us at least—to use the buttresses, pinnacles, etc. of church towers." Not to mix architectural metaphors by putting religious touches on secular buildings was a lesson Louis had already learned but one that Edelmann never really did. Nevertheless, the drawings seem intended to illustrate one or another point in their running design seminar.

Finally, the Lotus Club "Records" book contained a number of pencil and purple-ink nonarchitectural drawings by the two young men. Several depicted club activities: men running, jumping hurdles, and diving. Edelmann drew horses and wrestlers, Louis pencil sketches of a woman's face, possible the "Madame Girard" who cooked for the club.[8] Although somewhat uncomplimentary to the subject, they were clearly the work of a talented artist. Of the fifty or so other nonarchitectural sketches by young Sullivan between 1875 and 1881 not found in the notebook but surviving in archives,[9] most are explorations of the medium: academic nudes, grotesque heads, human muscles, and real-life faces, some of them clearly drawn at the clubhouse from available subjects, others taken from books, possibly Asa Gray's, or done in a modeling class. Overall, they are extraordinarily good, showing a real feeling for the shading and texture of surfaces, for capturing motion, and for distilling a subject into its essence. As a group the drawings devote much more attention to the human form—perhaps as a result of studying Michelangelo—than to the botanical for which Sullivan would be applauded later on. Acting as a leavening for his precise symmetrical fresco studies, demonstrating in grotesquerie a cultured sense of humor, serving perhaps as a socially acceptable outlet for sexual expression, these freehand drawings indicate that Sullivan—like Edward Hopper—could easily have made a living as a commercial or graphic artist had he not chosen another field.

It is difficult to know to what extent—if at all—John Edelmann instructed Louis in the art of drawing. The authors of the only scholarly study of Edelmann conclude he was "at least Sullivan's equal as architectural renderer and even his superior as freehand artist."[10] Clearly, the two drew similar subjects—men in motion—at the club, and Edelmann would surely have been inclined to give his junior partner pointers, as he did with everything else. But this is speculation. What is certain is that Edelmann made a profound impact on the younger man. His own preference for Gothic Revival further enticed Louis away from the French academic style he had imbibed since childhood. His notion of "suppressed functions" guided Louis in his gropings toward an architecture that would reveal itself for what it was. Edelmann instructed Louis in the endless niceties of de-

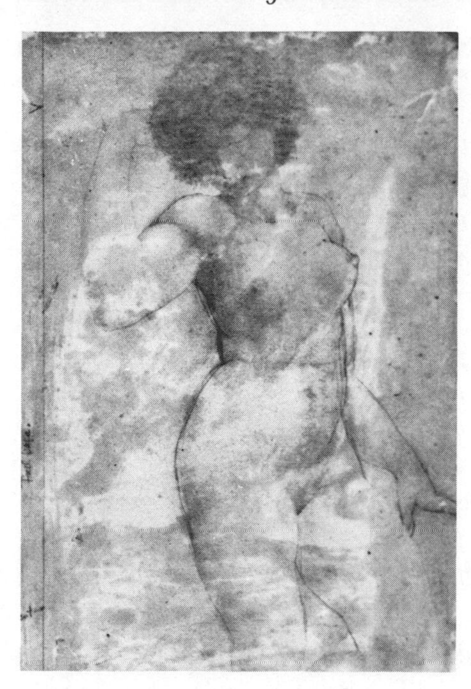

IV.4 *Louis Sullivan nude figure, 1880. Pencil on paper.*

sign technicalities, talked with him about the meaning of decoration, put him in touch with authors to reinforce his thinking, befriended him, encouraged him, and in general was a perfect mentor. John "is one of the smartest and most honorable boys I have ever met," Louis had told his brother; "my reputation as an architect," he added ironically, given subsequent history, "will always be inferior to his."[11] So it must have been a blow to Louis when Edelmann decided to leave Chicago, probably in pursuit of the million-dollar cathedral commission in Cleveland. With an inflated sense of his own talent, no doubt due in part to Louis's admiration, Edelmann thought he had a chance to get it, but ended up a draftsman in someone else's office. After he left, Louis began to drift away from the Lotus Club, not the same place without John. But even in absentia, Edelmann's impact lasted primarily because he had given Sullivan his first two commissions, in a real sense starting him out on his architectural career. Without John Edelmann, Louis Sullivan might not have been the force he came to be.

Sullivan's frescoes for Sinai Synagogue and Moody Tabernacle are important in themselves and for the boost they gave his career. There are no detailed descriptions of the Sinai work, but in the May 21,

1876, issue the Chicago *Times* art critic wrote his judgment of both structures. After finding Moody's Tabernacle a smashing success, the reviewer concluded by noting that

> there is only one other building in this portion of the country in which the frescoing belongs to the same school—the new Jewish Synagogue on Indiana Avenue and Twenty-first Street. The interior of this edifice is well worth going to see for its rare beauty and the delightful harmony which characterizes its brilliant and unique ornament; but the design, which is similar in principle [to Moody Tabernacle's], with a considerable correspondence in theme, is on a much smaller scale. . . .
>
> The decorator of both the Sinai Synagogue and Moody Tabernacle is a young architect, Mr. Louis H. Sullivan.

The reviewer for the *Chicago Tribune* on the occasion of Sinai's dedication in April had said only that "the internal decoration is quite elegant, and is a departure from the ordinary."[12]

The *Tribune* also noticed Moody Tabernacle, and on June 2 published a full-column article almost as long as the *Times*'s. The reason for this exceptional notoriety was that the building was Dwight L. Moody's, and Dwight L. Moody, flamboyant evangelist, attracted attention whatever he did. But a second reason was that when the frescoes went up, they caused a sensation within the congregation. Anticipating traditional religious motifs, several Moody followers found Sullivan's offerings much too secular. Others, complaining that the colors were overly bright and varied, demanded modifications. Sullivan refused, pointing out that changes would destroy the coherence of the overall conception already partly in place, and kept working while his opponents waited for Moody himself to make the final decision on whether or not the frescoes would stay. But Moody said nothing until the work was nearly completed, prompting one irate woman to take matters in hand by scrawling on the building in chalk: "This is the most disgraceful coloring that ever defaced the walls of a church." Noting that the "unique style" of the frescoes "has occasioned various words of comment," a *Daily Inter-Ocean* reporter solicited the views of Edelmann's partner, Joseph S. Johnston. "Not knowing just what it was to be, some of the people were inclined to make trouble about the style before the scaffold had been taken down, but the majority of them now agree that the frescoing is all right. Mr. L. H. Sullivan, the artist," he added in his employee's defense, "did not spare his colors, and they harmonize perfectly, to my mind."[13]

A few days before the building's dedication early in June, the evangelist had his say. "There seems to be considerable difference of opinion among the congregation as to the character of the frescoing," a Chicago *Times* reporter prompted Moody. "It's a fine job. The artist has done his job well," was the reply. "But the principal objection seems to be that it is too 'loud,' " the reporter persisted. "What is your opinion?" "I don't think so," Moody intoned. "It is peculiar, but I don't see anything out of the way in it. If I had been directing it I might have had something different, but then no doubt just as many would have objected to my style as do to this. Why that work has cost already $2,200, and it would be a shame to throw all that money away. I think the frescoing is in keeping with the rest of the building. This thing of working for and trying to please the public is an ungrateful task."[14] Whether Moody endorsed Sullivan because he liked the frescoes, was annoyed at his followers, or because he had already spent the money will never be known.

The controversy attracted reporters and art critics from the city's largest newspapers. Three mentioned Sullivan by name, but all of them recognized his work to be original and unique. Three papers praised it openly while another, the *Inter-Ocean,* preferred to remain neutral. All the accounts noted Sullivan's use of rich colors, his botanical motifs, and the "scientific" way he brought out the building's structural characteristics in the decoration.[15] Since the Moody frescoes were one of Sullivan's two earliest works (the Tabernacle was completed after the Synagogue, but it is impossible to determine which frescoes were designed first), it is worthwhile to quote at length from the most extensive description of them, in the *Tribune:*

> To the visitor the effect of the ceiling is startling. The apparent intricate design, or rather absence of design, the loud and to all appearances utterly inharmonious intermingling of colors strike the eye painfully. But a study of the work developes a simplicity wonderful when compared with the first impression. The work is merely a surface flower painting, without perspective, and the flowers and leaves, not at all relieved, combine with a most artistic background to deceive the careless eye into a contempt for the whole. The flowers are magnificent specimens of botanical

imaginings, and yet are not entirely without the range of botanical possibilities. The severe simplicity, coupled with the absence of perspective, gives an ancient, or perhaps a cabalistic, cast to the whole, yet when the puzzle is solved it astonishes the beholder with the very lack of what at first seems most prominent. It is like the landscapes of which the attraction is the man shooting at the rabbit, but which must be carefully studied before the student learns that the man, the gun and the game are artistically formed by the combination of branches and leaves. When you see it, it is alright, but until you do see it it don't amount to much.

Radiating from the skylight 36 feet in diameter are a series of sprigs, executed in glass and cast-iron, in green, yellow, blue, and white. Bounding this is an outer circle of rosettes of white glass with blue center. Outside this circle is a wide band of maroon with gold beads. If left here the result would be a perfect architectural design. Then comes the cove, passing at the bottom into an octagonal lintel. The problem then became the unity of the two features, solved by the introduction of huge plant forms starting from the columns, and throwing out from each two leaves, 16 feet long, crossing each other and extending to the skylight. This formation leaves a triangular space between the edge of the maroon band and the point of intersection of the two leaves. The triangles, eight in number, are filled each with an immense flower, 7 feet 6 inches across the top, resting on a gold background. From the opening of the flower arise four stamen and one pistil. The calyx is blue and the corella white. The flower springs from a rudimentary spathe of maroon. The effect of the eight flowered triangles is an octagonal star, losing its corners in the crossing leaves. The spaces between the large plants, which make the real field of the cove, is deep cobalt blue, and bear minor designs of large leaves, falling opposite, and giving birth to two lateral and one central flower. Between the cove and the gallery ceiling the heavy lintel, supported by thirteen columns, is of maroon, with a gold bead. The design of the gallery ceiling serves a dual purpose, affording a distinct border for each classroom, and still preserving the whole effect. The field is cobalt-blue, traversed at equal distances by maroon bands, which sustain elaborate borders in red, brown, pink, and white. While the borders have the appearance of perplexing complications, they are really exquisitely simple and refined. The design is a series of botanical forms, connected by a running-root stalk. A casual glance fails to disconnect the field from the leaves, but study evolves a plant of rare beauty unfolding graceful leaves, and supporting a white flower. The tops of the flowers produce a long, broken white band, while the droop of the leaves lets the blue of the centres in to meet the red of the field, producing striking effects of shape and harmonious blending of color. A change in the scheme of division into apartments has militated against elaborate decoration of the walls, which are treated with great simplicity.

The chancel follows the same design. The central window is the presentation of an open flower in a square, the corners filled with rosettes. The square border is of gold, enriched with large flowers and leaves. Either side of the square is another of deeper pattern, which completes the chancel.

The gallery front presents the most interesting study of all. It is the harmonizing of two different plants, each bearing a flower, and each inverting the colors of the other. The field is dark blue, the stalks are light blue, and the flowers are pink and white. The intermediate design is a pink stalk, and a green and white flower.[16]

The author of another long article, in the *Times,* wound down his equally flattering piece with a brief biography of Sullivan he could only have gotten from an interview. Sullivan described his Boston and Paris training, his stint with Furness, and then, in a burst of exaggerated self-advertising, told how he had "obtained the important advantages arising from a professional residence in the several capitals of art on the continent." In conclusion the reviewer praised Sullivan's culture, taste, and artistic imagination. "Leading architects of the city," he revealed, "have bestowed upon his work the highest encomium, and some of them characterize his invention and power as wonderful." Another public comment on Moody Tabernacle appeared on June 3, when the local *Real Estate & Building Journal,* quoting the *Alliance,* a religious publication, noted that "the usual frescoings appear in the rear of the pulpit, which are perhaps more striking than beautiful."[17]

Aside from this brief demur, the unusual amount of overwhelmingly positive attention paid to Sullivan's frescoes must have been heady stuff for a nineteen-year-old at work for less than a year. Sullivan got much more press than Edelmann and Johnston, the architects, although peculiarly enough he mentioned none of it—and nothing about the frescoes—in his autobiography. But others were beginning to take notice, as the *Times* account suggested, for Sullivan recalled that "he worked briefly now and then, at intervals, in the office of this or that architect, until he had nearly covered the field." Drawing perhaps on Edelmann and Johnston's connections, and citing his completed work, he went free-lance, for the first time in the 1877 city directory listing his occupation as an "architect." Three years later he more realistically changed his entry to "draughtsman" and the next year to "designer." In 1879 he asked Sinai's directors for an open letter of endorsement he could show prospective employers, but the request was tabled as contrary to temple policy.[18] But he plugged on. "He had made a reputation as a worker," he claimed, even without Sinai's help, "and consorted now with a small aristocratic group of the highest paid draftsmen. They met at lunch at a certain favored restaurant [Kinsley's on Adams near Michigan,[19] and] talked shop." The names of his new friends are still a mystery, but as to the architects he worked for there was first of all Johnston & Edelmann. Since this firm never had many commissions, however, Sullivan may have begun to free-lance even before the partnership ended in 1876. He was also employed by architect William Strippelman in 1880,[20] but what he did, for how long, and what happened during the four years between remain unknown, except for the fact that, as he wrote, "he was now looking out for himself."

This was true in several ways. First of all, his mentor John Edelmann left town after completing Moody Tabernacle by mid-1876. With his best friend and employer gone, Sullivan was more than ever forced to rely on his own resources. At almost the same time, brother Albert, twenty-two years old in September of that year, and working his way up the rungs of the Illinois Central administrative ladder, decided to strike out on his own by moving into the City Hotel at the corner of State and Sixteenth streets, not far from home. Changing his address frequently as his fortunes improved, Albert did not remain in one place for more than a year until 1884. Some sort of financial difficulties, furthermore, may have overtaken Patrick and Andrienne in 1878. Unlisted in the city directory for the first time since 1871, Patrick reappeared in 1879 in a boardinghouse at 806 Wabash Avenue and seems to have temporarily lost his dancing academy. Beginning in 1880 and for the next four years until his death in 1884, Patrick kept a studio at 137 Twenty-second Street, close to his former establishment at Number 159, but he never again had a separate residential address. Presumably, he resumed his former Boston practice of working where he lived, a necessity in his earlier days. If this was again true after 1878, Patrick Sullivan may have ended life as he began it: struggling to survive.

Another explanation for the senior Sullivan's move is that with the family shrinking, it simply needed less space. The year after Albert left, when Patrick disappeared from the city directory, was also the year Louis moved out, to a boardinghouse at 396 East Chicago Avenue, where he remained until 1883. At twenty-one, in 1878, he must have felt it time to follow his brother's example. In business for himself but still unable to afford an office, he, like Patrick, was forced to work at home. So with Edelmann and Albert heading in their separate directions, and the Lotus Club consequently losing much of its appeal, with a growing résumé of work completed and under way, Sullivan was indeed "looking out for himself. His success in this regard made him proud," he recalled. "He was now a man, and he knew it. He knew he was equipped to hold his own in the world." As a free-lance draftsman/designer, he clearly had enough jobs to support himself, although no one knows what they were. But he did leave a record of what he read, and in the late 1870s, he was strongly attracted to engineering.

He often talked at length with German-born Frederick Baumann, whose 1873 essay, "A Theory of Isolated Pier Foundations," introducing a system of footings capable of supporting heavy loads on the local spongy soil, became immensely important in Chicago building history. He pored over and devoured John C. Trautwine's *Civil Engineer's Pocket-Book* (1872), and in the weekly *Railway Gazette* followed the progress of the great cantilever bridge (1876–77) designed by Charles Shaler Smith and L. F. G. Bouscaren to span the Kentucky River at Dixville for the Cincinnati Southern Railway. He also remembered reading at the same time about engineer James B. Eads's triple-arch bridge over the Mississippi River at St. Louis, but that was completed in 1874, before Louis went to Paris. Nevertheless, the engineer now personified for Sullivan the "Creative Dreamer" with "the power of vision needed to harness Imagination, to harness the intellect, to make science do his will." Hearkening back to dime-novel heroes who could do anything, the engineer became in his mind the modern-day Michelangelo, utilizing science "to make the emotions serve him—for without emotion nothing." To express emotion in architecture and at the same time reveal structure functionally was becoming Sullivan's professional objective.

But to do that it would be necessary to control the design process, which meant something more than free-lance drafting. So Sullivan developed a plan—he always had a plan, it seems: "in due time to select a middle-aged architect of standing and established practice, with the right sort of clientele: to enter such an office, and through his speed, alertness and quick ambitious wit, make himself so indispensable that partnership would naturally follow."[21] If that architect was also an accomplished engineer, so much the better. Though in no particular hurry, he claimed, events moved faster than anticipated.

Central to Sullivan's story once again was his friend John Edelmann. In his memoirs he recalled that "early in 1879," before leaving his job with Dankmar Adler to form a "partnership with a man named Johnson [*sic*]," Edelmann took him to meet his boss. (A previous meeting arranged by Edelmann some years before had come to nothing.) "Timid in making advances," but needing someone to "take charge" of his office when Edelmann left, Sullivan wrote, Adler hired him on the spot after a brief but congenial interview. So impressed was he by Sullivan's subsequent performance that within a few months Adler gave him one-third interest in the firm with the understanding that a year later, on May 1, 1881, he would become full partner. And so he did.[22] Told this way the story not only makes Sullivan rather young—less than twenty-five years of age—when he became the design partner of one of the most respected architects in the city, but it was also quite inaccurate.

On the subject of John Edelmann, for example, Sullivan's account is particularly unreliable. After leaving the city in 1876 to work briefly as a Cleveland draftsman, Edelmann took up horse farming in Ohio or Wisconsin (accounts differ), developing an interest in radical politics—the Greenback and single tax movements—that would lead him later on through socialism to anarchism. Returning to Chicago sometime between July 1879 and June 1880, he set up as an architect in his suburban Oak Park home. There is no indication of his working for Adler before his final departure from town early in 1881. "Early in 1879," therefore, when Sullivan claimed to have replaced him in Adler's office, Edelmann was still horse farming, his partnership with Joseph S. Johnston three years behind him. And by the latter half of 1881, furthermore, which contrary to his memoirs was the earliest Sullivan could have actually joined Adler full time, Edelmann had left the area. Why Sullivan gave Edelmann so much more credit for his success than he deserved remains an enigma.

Sullivan's arrival at Adler's can be determined from other sources. Having ended his eight-year association with Edward Burling in

IV.5 *Dankmar Adler.* From *Inland Architect,* 1885.

1879, "Dankmar Adler, architect," Room 21, 133 La Salle Street received a permit in September 1880 to build the John Borden offices at Randolph and Dearborn.[23] By June of 1881, after Edelmann left Chicago and when the city directory for that year was fully compiled and published, Adler had moved into Room 58 of that newly completed structure. "Louis H. Sullivan, designer," had meanwhile opened his first business office at 135 La Salle Street, next door to the premises Adler had just vacated. Not until a year later, in June 1882, was he listed in the directory at 58 Borden Block, working for "Dankmar Adler & Company, Architects," the phrasing of which indicated the presence of a junior partner: "Louis H. Sullivan," in parentheses. In the 1883 directory, when the name "Adler & Sullivan" appeared for the first time, the new "copartnership" had already been announced on the front page of the *Chicago Tribune.* "The business heretofore carried on under the firm name of D. Adler & Company, Architects," the May 1 issue read, "will be continued by the same parties under the name of Adler & Sullivan." So it was not "early in 1879" but late in 1881 or early in 1882 that the two men joined forces, and not in 1881 but in 1883 that they became full partners.

For the next fourteen years, until the dissolution of the partnership in 1895—and in some respects for longer than that—Dankmar Adler was the most important person in Louis Sullivan's life. Born July 3, 1844, in Stadt Lengsfeld, a town of some two thousand residents in Saxe-Weimar, Germany, Adler was named (Dank—German for "thanks"; Mar—Hebrew for "bitter") by his father, Liebman, the local rabbi and cantor, when his twenty-three-year-old mother died six days after his delivery. But Liebman soon remarried, and the boy grew up in a rambunctious family of thirteen siblings and half-siblings. When Dankmar was ten, the Adlers migrated to Detroit, where Liebman became rabbi of Temple Beth El. During the next seven years, Dankmar developed an interest in and facility for architecture, working in the office of an E. Willard Smith, who laid the foundation for Adler's practical knowledge in the field. In 1861 Rabbi Adler moved his family to Chicago when called to the Kehilath Anshe Ma'ariv Temple, where he remained as a reader, preacher, and distinguished emeritus until his death almost forty years later. Dankmar found work with German-born architect and engineer Augustus Bauer, who had assisted on New York City's Crystal Palace, but on his birthday in 1862 joined the Union Army.

After seeing a good deal of combat, Adler was assigned during his last nine months of enlistment to the Topographical Engineers Office, where he received the equivalent of college training under the guidance of the noted Milo Burke. He returned to Chicago in 1865 for a short stint in Bauer's office before entering the firm of O. S. Kinney, a church, school, and courthouse architect. After Kinney's untimely death, Adler joined his son Ashley J. Kinney in partnership, but little is known about their work completing the senior Kinney's projects. Here he remained until 1871, when he formed a new partnership with carpenter-builder Edward Burling at the time of the Chicago fire. Neither had had formal architectural training, but the fire created so much opportunity that the new firm counted its commissions "by the miles of frontage," Adler recalled.[24] Near the end of the decade, Burling was indicted (but subsequently acquitted) for professional malpractices. Wealthy promoters of the Central Music Hall, fearing the taint of Burling's name, offered the commission to Adler, who promptly dissolved the partnership to go into business for himself in 1879.[25] During the intervening eight years, the two had been responsible for the First National Bank, the Chicago Tribune Building, the Methodist Church Block, Sinai Temple, and many other highly regarded commercial, residential, religious, and theatrical structures.

For many years after his death in 1900, Adler was principally remembered as the engineering and business partner of Louis Sullivan, as the acoustical and structural expert who got the commissions for Sullivan to mold into architectural masterpieces. At times both Adler and Sullivan appeared to confirm this notion. "Of late years," Adler wrote in his still unpublished autobiography, "owing to the preeminence in the artistic field of my partner Mr. Sullivan, I have devoted my efforts to the study and solution of the engineering problems which are so important . . . in the design of modern buildings." Sullivan maintained that "Adler was essentially a technician, an engineer, a conscientious administrator . . . the sturdy wheel-horse of a tandem team of which Louis did the prancing. . . . Adler lacked sufficient imagination," Sullivan contended, to be a "dreamer."[26] So it was long assumed that Adler, as "in-house" engineer and client procurer, was, first, not much of an architect who, second, played a minor role as a designer. Neither of these assumptions is true.

Sullivan would never have signed on with Adler in the first place had he not respected his work. John Root, one of the premier architects in the country at the time, confirmed Adler's worth in 1891: Of late he "has passed the artistic crayon to Mr. Sullivan," Root explained, "but work designed by him in the earlier days . . . shows a strength, simplicity, and straightforwardness together with a certain refinement which reveals the true architect." And a recent student of Adler's sadly neglected career has added that "if the elements of his designs are not fresh and new, the context in which they are found is." Specifically, she argues, Adler's interest in the wall as a plane, his manipulation of texture and contrasting colors for decoration, and his emphasis on structural members as potential aesthetic features are "characteristic of the best that the Chicago School produced."[27] Although Adler could not be considered as one of the city's most outstanding architects, he was very highly regarded in his day, and despite his association with Sullivan would have been remembered as a major contributor to Chicago commercial and theatrical design in the late nineteenth century.

Since it has generally been assumed that Sullivan entered Adler's office early in 1879 (rather than late 1881 or early 1882), a number of buildings Adler designed by himself have been attributed to the subsequent partnership. Among these was the Central Music Hall at Randolph and State streets, a nineteen-hundred-seat structure dedicated on December 4, 1879. Backed by some of the wealthiest capitalists in the city—including George M. Pullman, Marshall Field, Martin Ryerson, and Ferdinand Peck—the hall soon attracted "the best musical performances." On opening night the *Chicago Tribune* declared the efforts of "Mr. Adler [to] have been crowned with success," an opinion shared by the architect. Central Music Hall was one of the most financially "successful buildings ever erected in Chicago," he proudly recalled, "which I shall always consider the foundation of whatever professional standing I may have acquired."[28] Sullivan said the Hall was still unfinished when he started with Adler, which was, of course, simply not true. In fact, Sullivan arrived as a full-time employee nearly two years after it opened, and probably had nothing to do with its design, but several authorities have nevertheless given him partial credit for it, necessarily at Adler's expense.[29] Through no fault of their own—except perhaps Adler's unfailing modesty and Sullivan's literary exaggerations—history has often concluded that were it not for the younger man, the senior partner would merit little more than footnotes in its pages.

Central Music Hall did indeed bring Adler "into the mainstream" of Chicago architecture, as one writer put it,[30] helping solidify his reputation as an architect and acoustical engineer and leading to other commissions from which he and his partner would benefit. Among these were three buildings of confusing architectural authorship: the 1880 reconstruction of Hamlin's Theatre into the Grand Opera House owned by William Borden, whose father, John, hired Adler for the other two, his office block (1880) already mentioned, and his residence (1880) at 3949 Lake Park Avenue. Sullivan listed the "three large orders" as the first to come into the office "soon" after he started in 1879. The designing actually occurred in 1880, so there is no great difficulty with Sullivan's dating. But there is a two-part problem regarding authorship: in 1880 Sullivan had still not arrived at Adler's, nor is there reliable information that he ever worked at Adler's La Salle Street address, where his replacement office, in the Borden Block, was designed. Sullivan's claim to have "put through" these buildings might therefore be dismissed were it not for convincing visual evidence and for Adler's autobiographical recollection that he worked "in conjunction with" Sullivan on the Opera House and the Borden Block. The most reasonable reconciliation of this discrepancy is to assume that Sullivan's 1875 to 1881 free-lance stints "in the office of this or that architect" included several with Adler. Neither of the two confirmed this, but the assumption accords with their probable meeting on the Sinai Synagogue project in 1875 or 1876, and accounts for Sullivan's claim to have been with Adler before Central Music Hall—on which he presumably did some decorations—was finished at year's end in 1879. Success on "his first fine opportunity," as he called the three 1880 commissions, and not Edelmann's alleged intervention, probably convinced Adler to hire him full-time.

When it opened on September 4, 1880, the Grand Opera House was immediately acclaimed. The old Hamlin's Theatre had been virtually gutted. One exterior wall was strengthened by "enormous buttresses," but the other walls, the ceiling, roof, almost all interior partitions, most of the floors, all the stairs, and practically everything else inside were torn out and rebuilt. The auditorium was entirely redesigned and elaborately reappointed.[31] In two lengthy descriptions, the *Daily Inter-Ocean* lavished compliments on its carved walnut woodwork, its rich colors, its luxurious ambiance, and its acoustical triumphs, all "reflecting great credit upon the designing skill of the architect, Mr. Adler."[32] At an informal reception for "representa-

IV.6 *John Borden Block, 1880.* Courtesy Chicago Historical Society.

tives of the city press, prominent architects, artists, and musical celebrities," the *Times* reported, "on all sides there was great praise sounded for the treatment, architectural, decorative, and managerial, of the new house."[33] Especially noteworthy were the frescoes, custom wallpapers, gold gilding, and other details, "as well in keeping as the parts of a perfect picture." The decorators, singled out by one critic for particular approval, "have left an evidence of their ability that will command the admiration of hundreds long after the novelty has worn off the theatre. . . . Nothing but commendation can be bestowed upon them":[34] J. B. Sullivan & Brother, 266 North Clark Street.[35] *Louis* Sullivan was not mentioned in any of the several contemporary accounts of the Grand Opera House, making it difficult to determine his role on the job. He had obviously not been hired as the principal decorator.

Both the Borden Block and residence, however, reveal Sullivan's presence, although both are very much in keeping with Adler's own style. The office building was a six-story-plus-attic, brick-and-stone corner structure, one of the first to depart from solid-wall construction by narrowing the piers to lengthen the bay span for increased light. Although articulated in horizontal layers separated by projecting cornices at the third-, fifth-, sixth-floor, and attic sills, its prominent piers and mullions gave it the vertical quality Sullivan had observed in Philadelphia office buildings that later become a trademark of his work. Sullivan's ornament appeared in attic lunettes and in panels at window and column tops. On the other hand, the mixture of colors, textures, and materials, as well as the horizontal layering, were quintessential Adler. The Borden Block is thus something of a synthesis between Adler's already developed style and ideas Sullivan had been formulating for several years. It also shows how well the two men could mesh their individual design personalities.[36]

In several ways John Borden's home was strikingly like his office. In keeping with Adler's style, both featured alternating bands of red-brick plane and white-stone trim. Narrow high-rising chimneys, moreover, and (for a residence) noticeably narrow windows directly above one another, gave portions of the facade a vertical appearance, especially when clustered in the south side pavilion or continued upward through the mansard roof. Ornamental panels over second-story windows recalling the office building and a heavy-handed decorative outburst on an attic dormer were pure Sullivan. The house was intentionally massive and compact, the architects' way of expressing the "dignified solidity"[37] befitting the public image of a late-nineteenth-century entrepreneur. If this dwelling is more Adler than Sullivan, the junior partner (still a free-lance designer) had nevertheless made his abilities known on both Borden buildings.

Additional opportunities came quickly. From January 1881

IV.7 *John Borden residence, 1880. Chicago Daily News* photo.

through April 1883, Dankmar Adler "Architect" and "Company" received at least fifteen commissions, all but two after Sullivan's full-time employment began. The Rothschild Building on Monroe Street and the five Rosenfeld three-story flats at Halsted and Meridian came in earlier, receiving building permits in January and June 1881 respectively,[38] but Sullivan helped design them as a free-lance. "Adler & Sullivan" announced thirteen additional commissions in 1883, after May 1, when he became full partner but some—how many cannot be determined—were undoubtedly received before then. Of the twenty-eight Adler (& Sullivan) projects from 1881 through 1883 that are known, thirteen were totally or partially residential (five single and eight multiple-family dwellings), three were office or store buildings or both in combination, six were manufacturing plants, three were theaters, and there was one school, one library, and one warehouse. (These and additional structures through 1886 will be discussed in the next chapter.) Although Sullivan's style would not fully emerge for a number of years, he now had a stage on which to work out his architectural theories.

Chapter V

RISING HIGHER 1879-86

FROM 1879, with Louis Sullivan occasionally at work free-lance in Dankmar Adler's office, through July 1895, when the latter announced his retirement from the architectural profession, thereby dissolving the partnership, Adler & Sullivan, under its three firm names, received at least 180 commissions. Of these, sixty, or one-third of the total, were single and multiple residences, thirty-three (18 percent) were commercial buildings (principally offices and stores), twenty-seven (15 percent) were for manufacturing, seventeen (9 percent) were theaters, music halls, and auditoriums, and eleven (6 percent) were warehouses. The remaining thirty-one, some 17 percent of their decade-and-one-half output, were an assortment of clubhouses, schools, railroad stations, hotels, burial vaults, religious structures, recreational buildings, stables, decorative work, an orphanage, a library, and an infirmary.[1]

Perhaps the single edifice for which Adler & Sullivan were and remain best known is the Auditorium Building, the $3,200,000 complex containing 136 offices and stores, four hundred rooms and other hotel facilities, a forty-two-hundred-seat theater, and a five-hundred-seat recital hall, at the southern end of the block bordered by Congress Street, Michigan and Wabash avenues in Chicago, today the home of Roosevelt University. From December 1886, when the commission came in, until early 1890, when its last details were finished, Adler & Sullivan devoted the bulk of their time and attention to this world-famous building, thereby changing the pattern of their work load. During the five-year period from 1882, when Sullivan was employed full-time, through 1886, when planning for the Auditorium began just before the end of the year, Adler & Sullivan received an average of sixteen commissions annually. But from 1887 through 1889, they accepted barely ten a year; only seven in 1888, when Auditorium activity was most intense. After its completion, in 1890 and 1891 the partnership's output returned to an average of sixteen buildings, before dropping to eight in 1892 and during the subsequent depression years.

Adler & Sullivan's success with the Auditorium changed the nature of their practice. Through 1886, forty-four of their ninety-two buildings (47 percent) were residential, but during the three years of hectic Auditorium work (1887–89), the figure fell to eight of thirty-one (25.8 percent), further declining during the remainder of their association to eight out of fifty-seven commissions (14 percent). In part this drop in residential work from almost half their early output to about one-seventh followed the professional pattern of establishing a reputation with dwellings, then moving on to more lucrative opportunities. But in this case neither partner particularly enjoyed designing houses (unlike Frank Lloyd Wright, for example, whose vast majority of buildings even late in his seventy-two-year career were residential), and after 1886 they did not energetically seek the work.

Fewer residential commissions enabled them to concentrate on other kinds of buildings. Commercial structures rose steadily from less than one-fifth of their total before the Auditorium to over 30 percent afterward. Factories and other manufacturing buildings peaked at 19 percent during the Auditorium years before dropping in the 1890s to slightly less than the 14 percent level of the early 1880s. Although theaters and auditoriums fell from 13 percent before to 5 percent after 1886, warehouses—the fifth largest specific category for Adler & Sullivan—rose from 6 to 8 percent. And if all the remaining buildings are lumped together, the category "miscellaneous" rises from almost nothing to more then 25 percent during and after Auditorium construction.

This monumental structure was therefore a decisive turning point in the partnership's history. At the end of 1886, Adler & Sullivan had designed 73 percent of all the houses they would ever do, 87 percent by 1889. After the Auditorium they were best known for large business buildings: offices, warehouses, factories, and stores constituted over half their output, up from just over one-third before 1887. On a percentage basis, Adler & Sullivan did much less residential work and fewer cultural facilities during the 1890s than before. But, at the same time, their output in other categories increased dramatically. Therefore, while they tended to concentrate on business structures after the Auditorium, they also diversified into previously untried or little-explored areas: "skyscrapers," hotels, and mausoleums among them. Lucrative commissions generated by the Auditorium's success gave them the opportunity and confidence to do new things.

Raw percentages do not reflect the amount of time and thought the partners gave to particular types of buildings. That 47 percent of Adler & Sullivan's commissions from 1880 to 1886 was residential does not mean that houses took up 47 percent of their time or generated 47 percent of their income. Compared to the huge simple spaces of factories or warehouses, for example, or the repetitive nature of multi-storied office buildings, dwellings yielded fewer dollars in fees per hours of work. Preferring to design commercial and other nonresidential structures, Sullivan, whose principal office responsibility was ornament and facade composition,[2] was undoubtedly obliged to devote more time to houses than he would have wanted. But he knew the professional ropes: dwellings meant income and bigger commissions later on. With so much of their work in the residential field, Adler & Sullivan was a much different firm in the early 1880s than it would become.

Analysis of partnership buildings must therefore begin with houses. Although a complete list of Dankmar Adler's commissions before Sullivan's arrival has not yet been compiled, he appears to have had limited interest in residential work.[3] In this his partner concurred. Design challenges were greater elsewhere, especially at a time when experiments in home style and format were of relatively low priority. Yet, in the period under discussion, the firm turned out at least forty-four dwelling places, forty after 1881, or eight a year on average from 1882 to 1886. Ten of their twenty commissions in 1884, eleven of their eighteen in 1885, and, excluding the Auditorium, nine of their eighteen in 1886 were residential, meaning that in the last three pre-Auditorium years, thirty of their fifty-six buildings—over 50 percent—were houses. As Adler's facade designer, Louis Sullivan may have been especially interested in working out an aesthetic for commercial architecture, but he was forced to spend more time than he wanted on what he found least stimulating and rewarding.

Thirty-one of the forty-three residential buildings between 1880 and 1886 were on Chicago's South Side (Adler & Sullivan received no out-of-town house commissions), almost all between Sixteenth and Thirty-sixth streets, from Wabash Avenue to the lake. Within that area their twenty-seven single- and four multiple-family dwellings were even more clustered. There were four, for example, in the 1700 and 1800 blocks of South Michigan Avenue (then called Michigan Boulevard), and four farther south between Twenty-fifth and Twenty-eighth streets, up to a block east or west. Immediately east of today's Illinois Institute of Technology, in the neighborhood bordered by Michigan and Calumet avenues, Thirty-first and Thirty-third streets, Adler & Sullivan built seven homes, some of them only one street away from two others on Wabash. Still farther south were another four in the 3500 block of Ellis Avenue.

This residential clustering was hardly accidental. Of all the city's districts, the South Side was one of the best served by new forms of public transportation. The Illinois Central Railroad ran down the lakefront, where at Thirty-ninth and Forty-third streets, Adler & Sullivan built commuter stations in 1886 and 1888. The city's first cable-car line opened along State Street from Madison to Twenty-first in 1882 before pushing farther south to its Sixty-third Street terminus in 1887, the same year a second cable line built during the 1880s on Cottage Grove Avenue reached Sixty-seventh Street. State and Cottage Grove were pretty much the east-west boundaries of the district in which Adler & Sullivan's clients lived. Since both lines began downtown, anticipating the Loop of another day, easy access to work stimulated South Side settlement. Traveling twelve miles an hour in residential neighborhoods and six to eight in business districts, cable cars were considerably faster than their predecessors, the horse-drawn lines, which seldom reached one-half the slower speed.[4]

Wherever cables went, land appreciated, another incentive for settlement. Secretary H. F. Windsor of the Chicago City Railway maintained that within six months of conversion from horse to cable power, "property along these lines rose in value from thirty to one hundred percent, and on adjoining and contiguous streets in amounts proportionate to the distance from the cable lines." With this stimulus, write two authorities on Chicago history, "the new mode of transit facilitated the outward movement of the population."[5] Since Thirty-sixth Street, the outer reaches for Adler & Sullivan clients, was only three miles from downtown, they could look forward not only to a mere half-hour commute at most, but also to the long-term benefits of wise real estate investments.

The area was also characterized in the 1880s by "the continued drift southward of the city's elite."[6] One of the favorite locations for local business magnates was Michigan Boulevard, from Jackson to Thirty-fifth streets, as well as Prairie Avenue—two bocks east—spreading from a node at Eighteenth. Parallel thoroughfares were also desirable, but Prairie and Michigan were most prestigious of all. Marshall Field, George Pullman, Philip Armour, financier Ferdinand Peck (the principal force behind the Auditorium), piano manufacturer W. W. Kimball, International Harvester director John J. Glessner, Chicago Title and Trust Company founder Fernando Jones, and many other plutocrats and aspirants to their ranks hired prominent architects like Richard Morris Hunt, William Le Baron Jenney, Solon S. Beman, and Henry Hobson Richardson to design palatial homes from the 1700s to the 1900s of Prairie and Michigan. Although most conspicuous at certain intersections and in particular blocks, residential wealth stretched for miles. Charles Brega, member of the Chicago Board of Trade and the Chicago Real Estate Board, built a Beman stone mansion at 2816 Michigan, while John Cudahy, later ambassador to Belgium and major second-generation power in his father Patrick's meat-packing company, erected a $200,000 residence—impressive even for "Millionaires' Row"—at Michigan and Thirty-second.[7] From 1873, when Marshall Field began the trend by moving to a Hunt mansion at 1905 Prairie Avenue—then "little more than a cow path running through sand dunes"[8]—to the depression of the 1890s, "Millionaires' Row" as far south as Hyde Park was one of *the* places to live.

Adler & Sullivan designed no $200,000 homes, but many of their solidly upper-middle-class clients thought it best to rub residential elbows with the likes of Field, Pullman, and Armour. Nine of them, in fact, built along the most desirable stretch of Michigan Boulevard between 1600 and 3200 south. Three others lived on Prairie, another on Indiana in between, another on Calumet, two blocks east of Prairie, and four more on Wabash, one street west of Michigan. Their most expensive commission was probably for the self-described "capitalist" Marx Wineman, an $80,000 house with stable on a $40,000 lot at 2544 Michigan built in 1882.[9] Next was the $45,000 dwelling designed that year for 22 East Ontario Street (on the North Side), owned by Charles P. Kimball, carriage manufacturer and later consul-general in Stuttgart,[10] followed by the $28,000 (1883) residence for boot-and-shoe manufacturer Morris Selz at 1717 Michigan.[11] But these were exceptional. Of the twenty-six private houses for which approximate construction costs are known, seventeen fell into the $12,000-to-$25,000 range. The cheapest six went up for $5000 to $10,000 each. All twenty-six were erected for roughly $481,000, an average of $18,500 per house, $14,700 if the three most expensive (for Wineman, Kimball, and Selz) are omitted. Although with price tags like these they did not qualify for Chicago aristocracy, Adler & Sullivan's clients were for the most part substantial upper-middle-class businessmen in prestigious neighborhoods showing every sign of steady upward mobility.

If convenient transportation and good investment plus the desire to live in socially correct places help explain the residential clustering of Adler & Sullivan's early clients, equally important were business, ethnic, and family connections. Adler was himself a member of the group for which he designed, and several early commissions were the result of family ties.[12] In 1885, for example, when he and Sullivan planned three contiguous row houses on Ellis Avenue, Adler's own at 3543 was flanked by similar homes at 3541 for his mother-in-law, the widowed Fanny Kohn, and at 3545 for family lawyer Eli B. Felsenthal, son of Bernhard Felsenthal, former rabbi of Sinai Congregation, for which Adler (with his partner Edward Burling employing Sullivan as frescoist) had designed the 1875 synagogue. Across the street at 3538 Ellis was the 1886 home for Adler's maternal uncle, Levi A. Eliel, law partner of his relative by marriage Charles W. Holzheimer, whose family also lived there long enough to be mistakenly identified as the clients.[13] Eliel's brother Gustave, an insurance broker, commissioned Adler & Sullivan in 1886 to design his house, six blocks south at 4122 Ellis.[14] Charles H. Schwab, another relative of the Eliels, who as chairman of Sinai Temple's building committee in 1875 had paid Adler's fee, hired him in 1883 to design his home at 1709 Michigan, abutting number 1717, residence of his business partner, Morris Selz, who married Hannah, twin sister of Adler's wife, Dila.[15]

A number of other clients were Adler family friends, members of the large and very close upper-middle-class South Side Jewish com-

V.1 *Kohn, Adler, and Felsenthal residences, 1886.*
From *Building Budget,* 1886.

munity. Hugo Goodman's 1886 house at 3333 Wabash was next door to the 1884 residence of another Eliel relative, Abraham Strauss, his partner in an apparel factory.[16] Strauss's brother Leopold, also a clothing manufacturer, commissioned an 1884 Adler & Sullivan dwelling at 1838 Michigan, one block south of Selz and Schwab, who lived next door to their mutual friend Hannah Horner, widow of wholesale grocer Henry Horner, residing with her brother-in-law Isaac, her late husband's partner, in an 1886 house at number 1705.[17] The Stern brothers were also in the clothing business when they hired Adler & Sullivan to do 1885 homes for Henry at 2915 and Samuel at 2963 Prairie Avenue.[18] Of the remaining residential clients for whom information is available, Leopold Schlesinger, in his 1884 house at 2805 Michigan, was partner with Daniel Mayer in a well-known Chicago dry goods firm.[19] The profits from Benjamin Lindauer's four-hundred-employee clothing factory enabled him to purchase an 1885 home at 3312 Wabash, across the street from Hugo Goodman.[20] Henry Leopold (1882 home) at 2516 Indiana, Martin Barbe (1884) at 3157 Prairie, and Adler relative Abraham Kuh

(1885) at 3141 Michigan were all in the garment business;[21] Sigmund Hyman (1882), 2624 Wabash, was a well-known downtown jeweler; Lewis E. Frank (1884) at 3219 Michigan was a salesman; M. C. Stearns (1885), 29 Douglas Avenue (at Thirty-fifth Street east of Cottage Grove), developed real estate; Joseph Deimal (1886), 3141 Calumet, owned a furniture factory with his brother Rudolph, who went to Adler & Sullivan in 1887 for a house at Calumet and Twenty-second. On the West Side Reuben Rubel (1884) at 237 South Ashland sold livestock.[22]

Most if not all the South Siders were children of German Jewish immigrants, members of either the Reform Sinai Congregation established in 1861, or of its parent temple, Kehilath Anshe Ma'arav ("Congregation of the Men of the West"), where Adler's father had been rabbi, where he was a member himself, and for which he would help design new quarters in 1889. As successful business associates or in the same lines of work—predominantly clothing manufacture and other kinds of wholesaling—they knew each other well enough to recognize the social discrimination they all met as both Jews and Germans. Eager to maintain kin and ethnic ties, and from a mutual sense of the need for protection, they clustered near each other resi-

V.2 *Leon Mannheimer residence, 1884.* Photo by Robert Twombly.

V.3 *Benjamin Lindauer residence, 1885.*
Photo by R. M. Line.

dentially. As businessmen they hoped the benefits of wise real estate investments in desirable locales would generate a measure of social acceptance by the wealthy Gentile elite toward which they gravitated.

Once the partners, in conference with clients, determined the materials and internal requirements for their houses, Adler worked out the technology, Sullivan the aesthetics. This is what he was hired to do and what he preferred. Adler soon learned to trust him implicitly, since their design personalities meshed so well. Their social objective in residential work was to create emblems of dignity, material well-being, and permanence befitting the accomplishments and ambitions of the upper middle class. Never departing far from popular architectural styles, Adler & Sullivan performed this function well. Since aspirants to higher social circles tend to adopt the values of others already in, Adler & Sullivan's residential message was as appropriate for the upwardly mobile as for those already on top. Using conventional architectural language, the dwellings declared their inhabitants to be doing very well indeed.

As a group their houses were not remarkable, but they successfully appealed to prevailing architectural tastes of late-nineteenth-century aspirants to the *haute bourgeoisie.* Adler & Sullivan did not devote their major intellectual efforts to residential work, but they depended heavily upon it for income and were certainly skillful enough to design competently within popular idioms. Out of a sense of loyalty, but also because they liked their homes, several clients (the Deimals, Selz and Schwab, Levi Eliel, Leopold Schlesinger, and others) returned to Adler & Sullivan for commercial facilities later on. Contrary to prevailing opinion, more clients hired them to do houses first and business buildings later than the other way around. And it is certainly obvious that the professionally well-established and socially well-connected Adler, not the unknown Sullivan, brought in the bulk of the work. Many of their designs were two-story, with basement, attached dwellings faced in smooth-surfaced, sharp-edged "pressed" brick and stone trim, often featuring a

V.4 *Samuel Stern residence, 1885, door panel.* From Southern Illinois University architectural ornament collection.

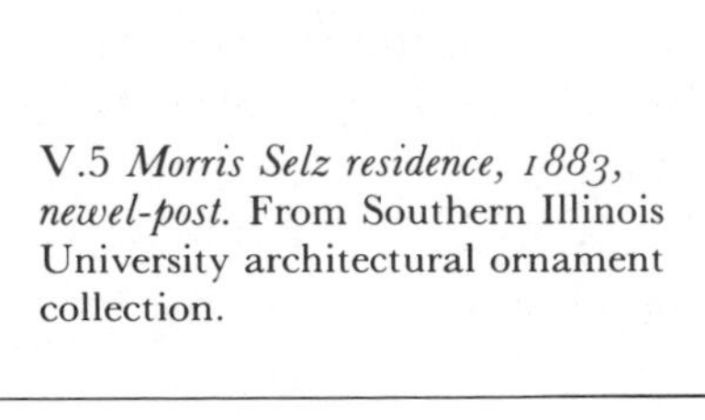

V.5 *Morris Selz residence, 1883, newel-post.* From Southern Illinois University architectural ornament collection.

mansard roof to accommodate servants in an abbreviated third story, on twenty-five-foot lots. After 1885 their larger, detached homes were more likely done in vaguely Richardsonian Romanesque with rusticated brownstone and brick facades on lots of up to fifty-foot frontage. Inside, the partners offered a typical program of public rooms downstairs, bedrooms above, and children or servants in the mansarded attic.

Authorities agree that Adler & Sullivan houses by and large fall into predictable Victorian picturesque categories. Principal roof massings, sometimes embellished by corner towers or prominent dormers, were generally gabled, pyramidal, or the truncated pyramids formed by mansards. Elaborate capitals, heavily ornamented spiky cornices, tall, thin chimneys, even quasi-balustrades, on occasion further enlivened jagged roof lines. Projecting sill courses across facades,

V.6 *Benjamin Lindauer residence, 1885, stringcourse.* From Southern Illinois University architectural ornament collection.

V.7 *Martin Barbe residence, 1885, panel.* From Southern Illinois University architectural ornament collection.

sometimes in combination with horizontal bands of light-colored stone, clearly delineated the stories, although by 1885 piers between doors and windows were beginning to receive vertical treatment up the elevations. Nor was there any shortage of Sullivan-designed ornament or of Adler's preference for constrasting color, although the trend over time was to use these devices more discreetly. The 1883 Selz and Schwab houses, for example, displayed exuberant ornamental panels on the upper stories, lavish cornices, capitals, and vigorously decorated lunettes. Schwab's intricate moldings and stained glass and Selz's fantastic roof crest poking through the cornice above a three-story bay window made the facades rather spirited, to say the least, a bit excessive, if the truth be known. But by the time of the Stern brothers and Benjamin Lindauer houses of 1885, and the Goodman home the next year, the ratio of ornament to mass and surface was considerably reduced. Relying more now on rusticated stone for surface or trim and on the interplay of stone with brick, Sullivan apparently began to examine the self-decorating possibilities inherent in the contrasts and textures of plain materials. Although his work was beginning to show "a marked sobering," in Hugh Morrison's words,[23] at the same time taking on its own personality, his use of ornament was itself an unquestioned Victorian convention.

Some of Sullivan's best performances were inside the houses, where, according to Victorian preference, any surface or object was grist for the decorator's mill. Sullivan designed newel-posts, door and wall panels, ornamental bandings, column capitals, between-room screens, balusters, handrails, leaded glass, window-frame and fireplace trim, ceiling medallions, decorative hardware, and many other items, taking his motifs from animals and plants, including snail shells, snakelike forms, leaves, and flowers. Some of his ornament was precisely symmetrical, on Samuel Stern's doors, for example, where rich panels of leaves and flowers were contained by simple squares. But as Sullivan developed his confidence and skill, new methods of organization appeared. Morris Selz's asymmetrical newel-post was held in balance only by the harmony of its proportions. The leaves in Martin Barbe's paneling burst out of their square frames, while at the Lindauer House the chimney string course revealed a decidedly lateral movement. By the mid-1880s, Sullivan's ornament was richer and more complex, increasingly three-dimensional, with greater *trompe l'oeil* effect, but as he brought it under control, it appeared to

V.8 *Henry Richardson, John J. Glessner residence, 1885.*

be simpler and more harmonious. As heavy, chunky, separately articulated forms gradually gave way after 1885 to subtle interweavings, the work acquired an energy, a sense of direction and movement. At first Sullivan had tried to inject power into decoration by employing bold, emphatic, but self-contained images. By the middle of the decade, he began to associate power with dynamic, plastic flow. Instead of designing brooches, so to speak, placed singly here or lined up side by side there, he was entwining his imagery like links in a bracelet.[24]

Morrison was quite correct to say that by 1885 Sullivan's work was quieter and more coherent. Facade simplification may have been due in part to the influence of Henry Richardson, a Sullivan hero since his Boston boyhood. Richardson received three Chicago commissions in 1885, on which construction began before his untimely death in April the following year. Sullivan later acknowledged his admiration for the Marshall Field Wholesale Store, but it is the two houses he probably saw published before they were built that are pertinent here: for John J. Glessner (May 1885), at Prairie Avenue and Eighteenth Street, and for Franklin MacVeagh (July 1885), on Lake Shore Drive. Though completed by Shepley, Rutan, and Coolidge after Richardson's death, they both display the master's touch. As simple, solid masses of rough gray granite, they were almost entirely undecorated except for the intrinsic texture of stone and for rhythmic groups of openings serving as doors, windows, and galleries. Compared with its granite neighbors down the block, the MacVeagh house was bold, powerful, and straightforward, while at the L-shaped Glessner house facades were reduced to barrierlike containers. Sullivan had begun to employ arches over doors, windows, and as pediments before 1884, but the next year he designed strong Richardsonian entries for the Adler, Kohn, Felsenthal, and Samuel Stern houses, among others, and rough, relatively unadorned granite facades for a number of other homes. By incorporating only selected Richardson elements, Sullivan's residential work after 1885 in no way approached the older man's standard of excellence or his level of innovation, but it was clearly influenced by his mannerisms.

It was for less-expensive commissions, however, that Sullivan, out of budgetary necessity, reduced facades to their simplest, developing modes of expression with a strong family resemblance to some of his nonresidential work. At a time when homeowners announced their social standing with elaborate ornament and exteriors, simplicity was interpreted to mean either limited resources or personal eccentricity. But more than once Sullivan transformed financial limita-

V.9 *Solomon Blumenfeld flats, 1884.* Photo by Joseph Barron.

V.10 *Ann Halsted flats, 1884–85.* Photo by Robert Twombly.

tions into occasions for unusually prophetic work. Particularly for flats in respectable but less-fashionable neighborhoods than his single-family clients chose for themselves, he produced remarkably modern alternatives to standard facade treatments.

The 1884 Solomon Blumenfeld flats building on a twenty-five-foot lot at 8 West Chicago Avenue was striking for its time. Its narrow smoothed-stone facade was divided into two vertical sections. To the right, columns on either side of the entrance rose past second- and third-story windows almost directly to a comparatively plain cornice, by Victorian standards, culminating in a flat roof, a rather unusual treatment during the heyday of fanciful building tops. In the wider portion at the left of the facade, three windows on each story with ornamental spandrel panels were recessed behind exceptionally thin clustered colonnettes serving as mullions—reminiscent of Philadelphia "functionalism"—supporting a narrow third-floor balcony. Except for the slight interruptions of balcony and shed-roof entry, piers rose straight from the street, pushing lightly decorated capitals through the cornice. Medallionlike facade ornament was also minimal, compared with his other dwellings. At the Blumenfeld flats, Sullivan almost but not quite captured the same feeling of verticality appropriate to its proportions he was struggling to achieve in his commercial buildings.[25]

The five 1884–85 row houses for Ann Halsted, at 1826–34 Lincoln Park West on the North Side, were in some ways similar. Together they formed a symmetrical composition end to end, but each was separately articulated. Wide decorative bands across the top at roof line projected neither vertically nor horizontally and the ornament was noticeably restrained. Even with a second-story sill forming a continuous string course the length of the block, the brick facades were exceptionally spare. The first, third, and fifth buildings featured arched double windows and rectangularly framed entrances at first floor below a row of arched windows above. All openings in the second and fourth houses by contrast were rectangular, with the strongest facade ornament on any of the buildings confined to their second-story pilasters. Although the relative absence of adornment on the Halsted houses correctly suggested modest social standing and low budgets, they nevertheless achieved a quiet elegance by their very simplicity.[26]

Arches alternating with rectangles had appeared the year before in the Max M. Rothschild flats at 3201–05 Indiana Avenue. Here, the second and third stories formed a single plane divided from street level by the usual sill course, but united by a continuous bracketed cornice. Sullivan achieved horizontal flow and rhythm down the block by grouping two windows per floor below a rounded triple window at the top from which the center mullion was removed, alternating these apparent three-story arches with rectangular entrances underneath tiers of similarly shaped single windows, in the manner of the Blumenfeld house. Aside from three small arched panels of ornament over second-story windows, the buildings were almost undecorated, achieving planar continuity up and across except for the second-story sill.[27] The low-budget Blumenfeld, Halsted, and Rothschild flats, more so than Sullivan's other rental housing for higher-income groups, approached the facade simplicity and integration of his factory buildings.

As a group Sullivan's facades embodied another important Victorian convention, the conscious expression of class. Social statements made by relatively stripped-down multiple-family houses were not to be confused with the image of genteel individualism his wealthy residential clients demanded for themselves. As landlords, their class-determined reluctance to provide spatial and aesthetic amenities for renters beyond an acceptable minimum found its architectural expression in facade simplicity, which doubled as a reference to the

V.11 *Max M. Rothschild flats, c. 1883*. Photo by Joseph Barron.

workplace. Since bourgeois landlords believed that employee ability to perform only rountine tasks was reflected in a mindlessly simple life-style at home, they had few compunctions about owning working-class dwellings that resembled factories. To their way of thinking, the visual repetitiveness of multiple housing akin to repetitive factory facades made perfect sense when the interchangeability of laborers at office or mill paralleled their interchangeability as apartment renters. Early mill housing in England and New England had established the precedent anyway. On the other hand, the individuality and sophisticated living patterns expressed by upper-income housing had their counterpart in office buildings—daytime homes for male members of the bourgeoisie—where artful, elegant facades indicated variety of function and superior social standing. Sullivan had little difficulty with multiple housing and factories, giving them dignity and quiet distinction quite beyond the norm, in fact. Single-family dwellings did not much interest him, but office buildings, which did, confused him for the first decade of his career.

The 1880 Borden Block was something of a landmark in Chicago construction history because it addressed two clusters of problems raised by the emergence of high-rise commercial buildings. Before 1880 the typical office structure had been three or four stories tall. But escalating ground rents in central cities plus unrelenting demand for space encouraged greater height. In self-supporting masonry architecture, however, vertical growth meant thicker load-bearing walls, up to three feet at the base, for example, in a four-story building. The tallest masonry-supported offices ever erected in America, Burnham and Root's Monadnock Building (1891) in Chicago, required twelve-foot walls at street level to carry its sixteen stories, substantially reducing rentable floor space, interior light, and air. As iron became an acceptable substitute for masonry, and buildings got taller, other problems arose. One set was technical: how to minimize weight, how to anchor high-rises in Chicago's watery soil, and how to provide light, air, and services over great vertical distances. The second problem was aesthetic: how to articulate or properly express this historically new building form. Adler & Sullivan were uniquely suited to accept the challenge: Adler was intrigued with the technical, Sullivan with the aesthetic, side of high-rise construction.

Authorities think the Borden Block may have been the first masonry building to break away from solid-wall construction with narrow piers to permit wider intervening bays and thus more window space to increase available light and air. Cast-iron I-beam lintels tied the piers together, carried carved stone spandrels, and supported thin nonstructural mullions separating the paired windows within each bay. The logic of this system rendered a continuous foundation unnecessary. To carry the piers—and interior columns—Adler introduced nine-foot-deep isolated stone footings, apparently the first in commercial architecture. Sullivan's aesthetic treatment of Adler's engineering was simultaneously new and old-fashioned. Most architects confronted the problem of articulating the high-rise by, in effect, piling a number of small structures on top of each other, that is, by dividing the building into several horizontal layers of grouped floors defined by entablatures, heavy cornices, or prominent sills. But at the Borden Block, Sullivan took rectangular piers straight from street to cornice, alternating them with thin mullions running to the bottom of the attic, where within each bay a lunette or semicircular panel capped their upward thrust. Since spandrels and other horizontals were recessed behind the piers, the Borden was potentially

V.12 *Max M. Rothschild store, 1881.* From Hugh Morrison, *Louis Sullivan.*

V.13 *Jewelers' Building, 1881–82.* Photo by Kaufmann & Fabry Company.

vertical, but Sullivan compromised this tendency with Adlerian bands of light stone trim and with heavy cornices and courses wrapped around the piers on four of the seven stories. What might have been a path-breaking vertical treatment ended up a hesitant compromise between verticals and horizontals, but the Borden Block was nonetheless aesthetically somewhat novel and structurally quite innovative for its time.[28]

If the Borden Block of 1880 was confusing on its facade, so, too, were Sullivan's next several structures, taken collectively. The $75,000 six-story store for Emanuel Rothschild & Brothers (Max M. and Abraham), clothing manufacturers and wholesale distributors, at 210 West Monroe Street, was designed in 1880 but built the next year. The building shows two developments: a marked increase of glass and of vertical organization. Divided into two twenty-foot bays, its three continuous masonry piers are forward of all other elements including the thin "Philadelphia-style" cast-iron mullions dividing the windows. All the verticals, moreover, rise uninterruptedly from the second floor to the top, marking Sullivan's first use of the "vertical system" of construction he would repeatedly return to in his later work. Had he left the composition there, the Rothschild would have been a clear step forward from the Borden Block. The trouble, however, was with decoration, one of several instances when Sullivan's two fundamental interests—expressing height and developing ornament—canceled each other out. "The efflorescence of cast-iron ornament at the top," Hugh Morrison observed, "is arresting." Another writer used the same word but was nearer the truth when he noted that the "arresting clutter . . . was diversionary."[29] Roof crests at the center of each bay, along with heavy capitals dripping decoration down their columns and across fourth-story lintels to encase the fifth floor like a gilt picture frame, made the structure so top-heavy, detracted so from the otherwise strong facade, that its virtually all-glass front—far in advance of its time—was compositionally a wasted effort.

The $90,000 five-story Jewelers' Building for Martin A. Ryerson at 15–19 South Wabash was simpler but without an orderly pattern. Piers for the two narrow bays flanking a wider central bay were again broken by string courses. Second-story windows with projecting frames contradicted others recessed behind the facade plane, creating organizational confusion. Although the ornament was much more restrained than the Rothschild Building's, Ryerson's interplay of line and surface was vague and indecisive.[30] A second building for the same client, designed in 1881 but not completed until 1883 at the northeast corner of Wabash and Adams, was known by the name of its original tenant, the Alexander H. Revell Furniture Company. At $320,000, it was the costliest of Adler & Sullivan's early works, and at six stories and 116 by 172 feet was one of the largest. The Revell Building was Sullivan's first use of false piers, the aesthetic deployment of vertical members that appear to but do not support horizontal members, one of several devices he later used to suggest verticality. But if that was his purpose here, it was compromised by horizontal polychrome similar to the Borden Block's. Its jagged roof line, complicated facade divisions, and fussy combinations of ornament and color further revealed Sullivan's lack of a fixed idea for exterior composition.[31]

Between 1881 and 1883, John M. Brunswick and Julius Balke, "Sole Manufacturers and Patentees of the Monarch and Nonpareil Novelty Billiard Tables," commissioned Adler & Sullivan to design their factory, warehouse, and lumber-drying plant at Orleans, Huron, Superior, and Sedgwick streets for a total of $168,000. Com-

V.14 *Revell Building, 1881–83.* Courtesy Chicago Historical Society.

V.15 *Brunswick, Balke factory, 1881–83.* Photo by Robert Twombly.

pared with high-rises—indeed, with almost everything else around at the time—the five- and six-story brick buildings were simple and unadorned except for bracketed cornice, low-arched lintels above the first floor, and protruding sills.[32] Similar arches and sills, this time interrupted by a stone string course above the first floor, characterized the three-story $100,000 Aurora Watch Company factory, dial, and boiler works at Aurora, Illinois, designed in 1883, with two years' anticipated construction time. Adler & Sullivan's original plans called for a four-story cupolaed tower with pyramidal corner turrets bisecting the main building, and for deeply recessed windows set behind strongly articulated piers rising to a gabled roof. This would have been Sullivan's most consistently vertical facade composition but ironically was not well suited to the problem. With the tower removed, the 320-foot machine shop as built was more appropriately organized horizontally, with wide shallow piers and a continuous string course.[33] In the F. A. Kennedy Bakery on Desplaines Street, for which Adler & Sullivan did a $20,000 addition in 1883 and a $50,000 building the next year, Sullivan took the brick piers straight to the top but projected them only slightly—not as conspicuously as at Aurora—in front of the wall plane, a "simplified and refined vernacular essay" he immediately repeated for the five-story 1884 Knisely factory building on West Monroe. "This when completed," *Inland*

Architect decided, after contemplating Kennedy's system of mixing flour on the top or sixth floor before sending it through several processing stages to the six 240-ton ovens three stories below, "will be one of the most perfect bakeries in the country."[34] Perfect or not, in the Kennedy, Aurora, Knisely, and Brunswick & Balke factories, Sullivan developed a simple aesthetic he was not prepared to apply to other kinds of commercial buildings.

A case in point is the contemporary Ryerson Building, designed in 1884 but erected in 1885 for over $150,000 at 16–20 East Randolph across from Adler's Central Music Hall. "Every effort is being made," Boston's *American Architect & Building News* reported, "to construct without excessive cost a business building, the contents of which may burn without destroying the building itself," in other words, a reliably fireproof edifice.[35] Adler & Sullivan's solution was to use a Bedford (Indiana) limestone, cast-iron, and plate-glass facade, iron posts and girders sheathed in porous terra-cotta, and wire plastering cloth on metal furring strips dropped two inches from the joists. The six-story building may have been safe, but it was not attractive. Arranged in three bays, its almost entirely glass facade bowed out slightly from the second to the fourth floors to capture more light. But above that the three windows per bay abruptly increased to four, rectangular mullions suddenly switched to rounded colonnettes in the attic, fifth-floor windows were recessed to contradict the bow, and at street level squat circular columns were carved to resemble grotesque totems. Egyptoid ornamental motifs and a haphazard facade were steps backward from Sullivan's elegantly simple factory buildings, even from the preceding office blocks, again revealing the inconclusive results of his ongoing experiments in high-rise composition.[36]

The six-story building for Brunswick & Balke officer A. F. Troescher at 15–19 South Market Street (now Wacker Drive), between Madison and Monroe, costing over $90,000 in 1884, was a much clearer statement of structure, probably Sullivan's best effort among his pre-Auditorium high-rises. From a base of five lightly rusticated stone columns, plain piers rose to the top of the fifth floor almost flush with broad expanses of window and unadorned spandrels (except on the second story). Left at this, Troescher would have been a clean, successful composition of geometrical relationships, startlingly advanced for its time. But by referring to the street level at the top with two large center bay arches capping ornamented

V.16 *Troescher Building, 1884*. From *Inland Architect*, 1884.

lunettes, flanked by two smaller arches over similarly adorned panels, Sullivan weakened the effect. Variations on pier capitals from the Selz, Schwab, and Blumenfeld houses and other buildings, in combination with a spiky cornice and circular colonnettes, made the top even more jarring; not as awkward as the Rothschild and Revell buildings, to be sure, but a disruption of the overall composition nonetheless.[37]

One more commercial building warrants attention to illustrate Sullivan's developing ideas for business aesthetics: the $50,000 five-story factory at Washington and Desplaines streets for James W. Scoville. The commission involved altering an older Adler structure to make it fit with a new, much larger addition. Adler & Sullivan's approach was to strip the cornice from the 1877 factory, add a fifth floor matching those below, replicate that facade on new buildings at the other end of the block, then infill with four bays tying it all together. The duplicate sections terminating the block were capped with lunettes above the old-style, widely spaced single windows from 1877, ornamental panels were applied above fourth-story windows, and light-toned lintels were stretched into string courses on the floors below. In between, Adler & Sullivan reverted to their more modern structural and aesthetic vocabularies, namely, by clustering windows in threes between each pier taken straight to the top from the second floor, and by reducing ornament to relatively inconspicuous panels below the cornice. String courses from the older building and all its other horizontals were brought across to unify the entire composition. Masonry piers alternating with cast-iron window spacers (mullions) were equally innovative but by now familiar in their work. The Scoville Building had "a strong and monumental" character, its historian concludes. It was "a well-articulated and handsomely proportioned building [serving] both as an ordinary factory and as a visual adornment to the street."[38]

Adler & Sullivan designed at least a dozen other commercial structures before the Auditorium, incorporating some or all of their emerging design strategies. Adler's ingenious structural and programmatic contributions should be apparent from the Borden and Scoville blocks alone. His aesthetic preferences were still evident in Sullivan's work as late as the 1885 flanking portions of the Scoville Building, where conditions imposed by the 1877 structure account for the polychrome reminiscent of his pre-Sullivan years. Sullivan's design direction was more certain on factories than on "high-rise" offices. On these three- to six-story brick buildings, he had begun to set continuous piers a few inches beyond the wall plane, on occasion supplementing their verticality with alternating tiers of cast-iron mullions. Trim was minimal, sometimes little more than the pattern of repetitive windows and verticals, other times combinations of simple ornamental panels, slight arches, modest sill lines and courses. Aesthetics suggested by structural elements and intrinsic rhythms had been anticipated in Adler's earlier work and in the Philadelphia Sullivan knew in 1873, but with less assurance. The reductionism of his residential facades after 1885, due perhaps to Richardson's influence, and of his multiple houses generally, was most apparent in his factories, where simplicity resulted from custom, owner social attitudes, and practical considerations.

Office buildings, however, were another matter. Here, the organization of shops, lobbies, handsome facilities for owners or managers, spare clerical space, and multiple rental units did not suggest immediate or obvious facade solutions. If in a factory rationalized manufacturing processes and the placement of machinery were best served by large open floors inside an unadorned box, the potential variety and multiplicity of functions in office buildings demanded something else. Nonmanufacturing activity seemed more suitably treated with elaborate ornament and facades analogous to upper-class residences than with the aesthetic simplicity associated with making things in mills. These social and practical considerations made it doubly difficult for Sullivan and other architects of his day to shape an appropriate aesthetic for this new kind of edifice. Below their attics, the Troescher and Rothschild buildings were comparatively straightforward statements about structure, in retrospect pointing the way toward twentieth-century design, but their ornament and fanciful tops muddied their clarity as architectural essays. The Ryerson Building of 1884 was less convincing than the Borden Block of 1880 even with its Adlerian trademarks. Sullivan's objective was clearly to develop a high-rise aesthetic, but by 1886 he had made little progress, was still inconsistent from building to building. Adler, on the other hand, advanced within his field of responsibility by helping solve the related problems of support, using isolated footings, and of light and air, by narrowing piers to widen bays for more window space, although he had not gone as far as William Le Baron Jenney, say, in the use of steel frames. Elaborately ornamented, highly individualistic for each client, still in the picturesque tradition, Sullivan's high-rise facades before 1887 did not point the way toward a typology of form. Had his career ended then, he would never be considered a "prophet of modern architecture."[39]

His writing was decidedly more prophetic than his architecture. Sullivan outlined his philosophical and social objectives in his very first speech for a professional audience, apparently the first formal address he ever gave. "Characteristics and Tendencies of American Architecture," read in October 1885 to the second annual convention of the Western Association of Architects in St. Louis, was well enough received to be published in *Building* magazine and in Chicago's own *Inland Architect.*[40] Discussing an issue that had troubled American observers for decades, Sullivan argued that the long-awaited "distinctly American" style would not emerge quickly but only after a slow, gradual "assimilation of nutriment and a struggle against obstacles" supported by "a spontaneous architectural feeling arising in sympathy with the emotions . . . in our people." Everywhere, he found average citizens shaping their surroundings to match their desires, sometimes with impressive results. Certain that these germs of "spontaneous and characteristic feeling" would be the basis of an authentically national architecture someday, Sullivan had little patience with calls for an official style based on European precedent.

If one were to look at American literature, "the only phase of our national art that has been accorded serious recognition, at home and abroad," he offered by analogy, one would find "exquisite, but not virile" writing, "too much a matter of heart and fingers . . . too little an offspring of brain and soul." American literature, he believed, was painfully self-conscious, timid, and embarrassed by the "delineation of all but the well-behaved and docile emotions." When dealing with real passion, it offered only "tacit fiction," the consequences of a still-tentative and provisional national culture. The first step toward a new order of things for both literature and architecture, he asserted, was the gathering of fresh impressions to cope with contemporary problems, a kind of natural receptivity he found buried even in old-fashioned literary attitudes. Underneath the "curious *melange* of super-sentimentalisms . . . offensive simplicity . . . [and] highly wrought charlatanisms" of American romanticism, he detected a stubborn common sense informed by a "marvelous instinct." Once developed, this instinct toward a "more rational and organic mode of expression" would yield up "a plastic alphabet"—a flexible set of artistic techniques—Americans could use to identify and articulate their beliefs.

Architects, Sullivan chided his listeners, had not taken the lead in developing a basic vocabulary of national expression. But there was among the citizenry one "shining example which we have often ignored." Knowing how to channel power to productive use, businessmen and financiers had followed a simple, "congenial" notion—making money and goods—to its obvious, manifold, and logical conclusions. Power "in one class of our people," he contended, "augurs well" for the rest of us, even though its "ability to develop elementary ideas organically" had initially been "so crude and harsh as to be revolting to a refined taste. But once subtlized, flushed with emotions and guided by clear insight," personal power could work miracles, forcing nature to divulge her poetic secret: "the germ of artistic greatness."

Sullivan believed Americans had as much poetic feeling, idealism, and love for beauty as any other people, but criticized his country for substituting sentiment for creative thinking, as in the case of architects, who generally found it more "expedient to maintain the traditions of their culture than to promulgate vitalizing thought." So Sullivan advocated a professional posture similar to that of the Italian Marxist philosopher Antonio Gramsci (1891–1937) forty years later. Too often, he reflected, architects had tried "to lead the public, when we more wisely should have followed it; and have, as a body, often followed, when . . . we could have led," for "no architectural style can become a finality, that runs counter to popular feeling." Architects were skilled technicians, the executors of buildings, to be sure, but "the shaping and controlling process is mainly in the hands of the public who are constantly keeping us within our bounds." Since "the public itself can only partially and imperfectly state its wants," however, it required experts to articulate "its conceptions of the beautiful and the useful." Like Gramsci's "Modern Prince," architects should listen to the people, build for their wants and needs, learn from popular reaction, then adjust their work in light of public response. Through this process of educating and being educated by dialogue with the citizenry, architects would construct "a fund [of buildings] representing our growth in emotional and spiritual wealth." The development of a national style would therefore take generations, Sullivan concluded, "and need be of little practical concern to us of today," but conversation with the people in the meantime should be the profession's *modus operandi.*

Forthrightly rejecting enterpreneurial greed and shoddy ethics, Sullivan nevertheless respected businessmen's ability to take simple ideas organically and logically to their myriad conclusions. But far from applauding plutocracy, Sullivan urged the spread of democracy. He did not question America's commitment to "free" enterprise, its choice of businessmen as cultural heroes. Since their energy fueled the engine of the nation, it was only fitting that their buildings be the occasion for a new architecture. Understanding the high-rise to be the characteristic edifice of the era, as Europeans were beginning to realize about American design, Sullivan felt that by working out its aesthetics, he could make a real contribution toward an American style. But just as business power was best deployed by social appropriation, so its architecture would acquire real meaning when broadened into a national mode of expression. As a self-styled interpreter of the people's will, Sullivan would undertake the task himself.

He was drawn to commercial architecture, therefore, not from a sense of identification with business leaders, as some have suggested, but for more profound ideological reasons. Neither he nor Adler neglected other kinds of buildings, however, nor could they, with such an important cultural mission at stake. Aside from houses, during their early partnership they also designed the 1882 Hammond Library for the Chicago Theological Seminary and a small schoolhouse in 1883 for Marengo, Illinois.[41] In the busy year of 1884, Sullivan fashioned a bronze elevator car built by Chicago's R. T. Crane Company for the Bank of Manhattan (now Chase Manhattan) Building in New York; a stable for Mandel Brothers, a large local dry goods firm; and a $75,000 headquarters and apartment house for the Lakeside Club on Forest Avenue.[42] Next year came Zion Temple at Washington and Ogden Avenue, and the 95-by-160-foot pavilion at Seventy-ninth Street and Lake Michigan for the Chiltenham Improvement Company, a $235,000 complex of verandas, dining-, club-, and ballrooms, bar, bathing facilities, and support services, constructed in fifty-six days during May and June.[43] This is by no means a complete list. Adler & Sullivan's theaters and music halls will be described in chapter 6.

An additional commission in 1886 probably came about through

V.17 *Zion Temple, 1885.* From *Inland Architect,* 1885.

the influence of Louis's brother, Albert Sullivan, who, having risen to assistant superintendent of the Illinois Central Railroad's Machinery Department, was now living in a rented house in Kenwood, an up-and-coming South Side neighborhood. The sixty-by-ninety-foot stone-and-pressed-brick commuter station at Thirty-ninth Street did not depart far from convention, with its twin gabled waiting and baggage rooms facing the tracks and its bayed ticket window jutting into the canopied platform. It was, nevertheless, a "handsome" structure, at least according to the newspaper reporter who examined the plans while construction was still under way: "patrons will be astonished at the sight of one of the prettiest depots in the city," he concluded.[44] But he failed to notice that the ornament on side dormers was exactly the same as Sullivan had used at his West Chicago Clubhouse erected the same year on Throop Street, another instance of not letting a good idea go to waste.

Sullivan was also drawn to the fashionable South Side during these busy and prosperous years of the middle 1880s. Leaving his Chicago Avenue flat in 1883 for another at 409 Dearborn Street, near work, he moved again in 1884 to Kenwood, where he may have shared a house with Albert—whose exact address was unlisted—at 4805 Hyde Park Avenue, near the lake. Renting a house may have been prompted by the decline of their father, Patrick. But if the intention was to be near him, to take him in, or to assist their mother, Andrienne, they failed, for Patrick died on June 15, 1884, at the age of sixty-six. With her sons busy at successful careers, Andrienne closed the dancing academy to join her sister Jennie Whittlesey in Lyons Falls, the small farming community in upstate New York. Still young, not yet fifty years old in 1885, Andrienne probably realized that vicarious participation in her sons' affairs would not satisfy her desire for a full life. By October 1885 she had moved back East, there to remain the rest of her life.[45]

There is absolutely no evidence to suggest that Patrick died on bad terms with either of his sons, despite the tone of Louis Sullivan's autobiography many years later. Ambitious himself, he was probably as proud of Louis, swamped with work as partner in a prominent architectural firm, as he was of Albert, a divisional assistant superintendent on a major railroad. But in recent years the sons had been too busy to spend as much time with their parents as they might have liked. Albert had also dropped out of the now-defunct Lotus Athletic Club sometime after Louis, signaling an end for both to leisurely days free from the obligations of work. As the boys matured into men, building substantial career niches for themselves by 1884, Patrick might have died happy in the knowledge that he had contributed to their well-being in the best way he knew.

With his father buried in Chicago's Graceland Cemetery, his mother safely ensconced with his aunt and uncle in Lyons Falls, and his brother traveling for the railroad, Louis Sullivan may have been free of familial obligation, but he had no loved ones nearby to rely upon in time of need. Perhaps it did not matter. Always independent as a boy and young man, he now threw himself furiously into work, helping to design fifty-six projects from 1884 to 1886. With little time for anything else, he became in today's parlance a "workaholic," much to his misfortune later on. But he was clearly making his mark. Reading a paper to the Western Association of Architects, a sure sign of recognition, provided the backdrop for an equally illuminating indication of his rising professional stature.

During the annual banquet on the eve of his presentation, Sullivan had been wandering around the St. Louis hotel, perhaps rehearsing his speech to himself. While the architects were happily toasting each other after dinner, Sullivan slipped quietly into the banquet hall, but had no sooner sat down than he was called upon to respond to the toast, "We are all jolly good fellows." Recorded by a diligent if necessarily sober secretary, Sullivan's remarks are revealing. Obviously nervous, he could not permit, or did not know how to allow, his awkward attempts at humor to moderate his unswerving seriousness, even on this lighthearted occasion. "I kept away from the banquet hall until about five minutes ago," he began,

> when I opened the door about two inches or three-eights of an inch, I think possibly it was five-eighths, and I heard a voice in the corner there. . . . I came in and very modestly sat down at the end of the table, where I thought I was perfectly safe. I never made a speech in my life [his first would be the next day], and I think I don't know how to do it; I don't know what I am going to do. I have not the ease of diction of my predecessor. I wish I had. I wish I had the faculty of weaving the ideas as gracefully and beautifully. . . . I cannot even get any inspiration from my theme [that we are all jolly good fellows]. . . . For jollity, I think, that is found rather in private and smaller gatherings. . . . I think, however, the future is full of promise in the matter of jol-

> lity. I think there is more jollity here than there was a year ago. I think another year will bring about still further increase. I think if certain results of our labor in this convention prove successful in bringing about the fruits which we expect, we will then have occasion for being manifestly jolly. (Applause ended the banquet.)[46]

With Dankmar Adler smiling approvingly from another table, Sullivan might have been talking about himself, not the Western Association. At twenty-nine years of age, he was well on his way, with greater opportunities just ahead. Of course, he did not know that the Auditorium would soon make him famous, or even that he would have the chance to design it. But he had many other reasons to be optimistic. And the next few years were indeed professionally jolly times for him and his partner.

Chapter VI

DRAMATIC BREAKTHROUGH 1879-87

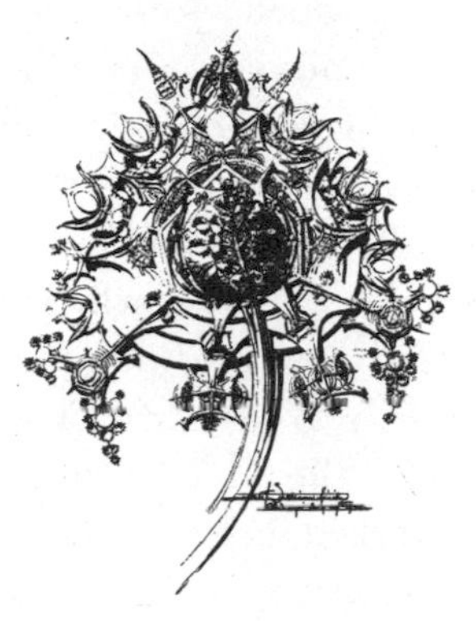

ONE OF THE many idiosyncrasies in Louis Sullivan's memoirs is his disinclination to identify his early buildings, although he was careful to suggest their larger, collective importance. In the early 1880s, he recalled, writing as usual in the third person, "a series of mercantile structures came into the office, each one of which he treated experimentally, feeling his way toward a basic process, a grammar of his own." (His self-evaluation was so far correct.) In those days the problem was to increase daylight to the maximum, leading "him"—no mention of Dankmar Adler here—to use slender masonry-faced iron piers. These "beginnings of a vertical system . . . upset all precedent," he maintained, with a certain exaggeration, since other architects were also attending to the high-rise problem, "and led Louis's contemporaries to regard him as . . . a revolutionary, which was true enough." He realized that only "slowly" did a "corresponding system of artistic expression" infiltrate his designs, appealing to some as novel but repelling others by "its total disregard of accepted notions." To all objections he nevertheless turned a deaf ear: "if a thousand proclaimed him wrong, the thousand could not change his course."[1] In retrospect, Louis Sullivan saw himself an embattled warrior for architectural change, but in the 1880s, mostly because of theaters and concert halls, his pathway to fame was generously paved with ringing endorsements.

Whatever his reason for neglecting specifics in his autobiography, Sullivan had not failed to name his commissions seven years earlier at a 1916 memorial to Adler, when he recounted his version of recent Chicago building history. To the Illinois Chapter of the American Institute of Architects, he described innovations at the Borden Block (including isolated footings pioneered by his friend Frederick Bauman), Adler's acoustical triumphs at the Grand Opera House, and their "solidly built, well equipped" John Borden residence. Claiming the Revell as "the first [fireproof commercial] building," he said it was such "a marked improvement on anything existing at that time" that it led Martin Ryerson to commission six additional structures between 1881 and 1884.[2] By then, he remembered, "I was developing a little technical knowledge myself," which came in handy on the theaters he and Adler renovated and designed. The only one he discussed at length, however, was McVicker's, where he made "a little innovation of my own": "the first decorative use of the electric lamp," which Sullivan worked into ornamental backgrounds instead of using clustered exposed fixures, this despite exceedingly primitive generator-powered electrical circuits of wires embedded in plaster without conduit. Sullivan also remembered inaccurately that Adler put in two stories of offices carried on trusses over the theater space—"the first time that thing was done"—and installed unusual ventilation at the outrageous cost, according to J. H. McVicker, of $6,000.[3]

Before his peers in 1916 Sullivan proudly discussed the technicalities of his early designs, but he did not do so when it came to his autobiography, intended for a larger audience. And in 1916—at a tribute to Adler, to be sure—he emphasized his partner's contributions, but was more reticent later on. Perhaps it became too painful to share the credit later in life when, further down on his luck, he might have been more inclined to embellish the historic significance of his own professional career. But with the one project that really mattered, he was scrupulously fair. On both literary occasions, in 1916 and again in the 1920s, he was careful to report that the commission for his greatest theater of all, the monumental Chicago Auditorium (1886–90), came about because of Adler's previous accomplishments, particularly the "temporary audience room" for the 1885 Opera Festival installed in the old Interstate Exposition Building on Michigan Avenue in Grant Park. Sullivan was actually quite modest about his own rather considerable reputation as a decorator

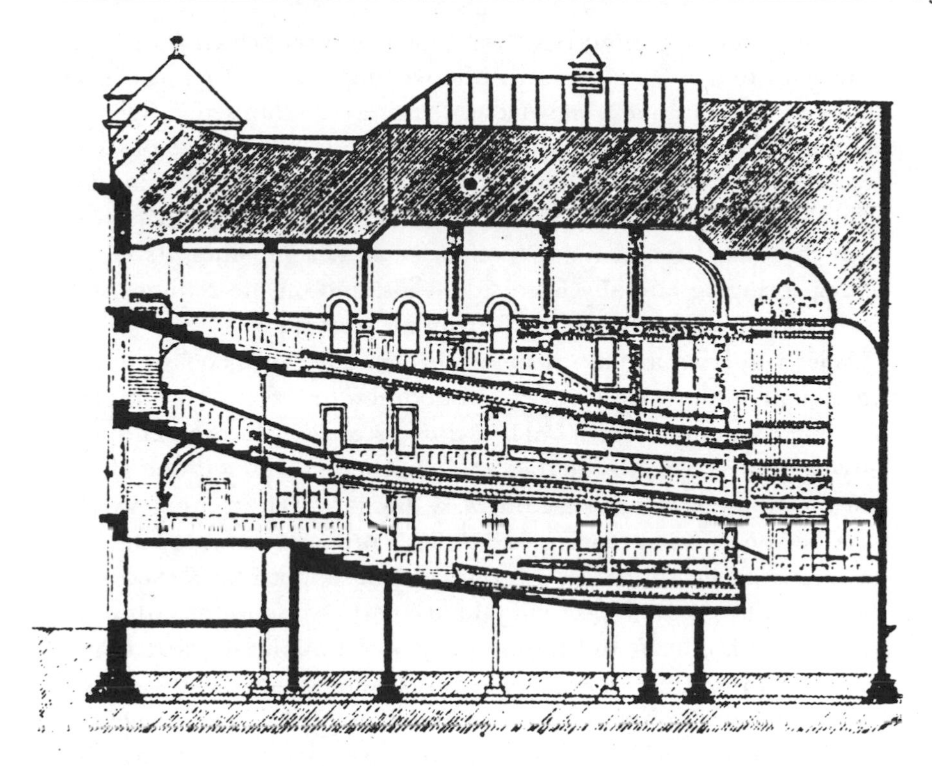

VI.1 *Central Music Hall, 1879, section.* From *Engineering Magazine,* 1894.

in 1886, but as if to establish his credentials for the Auditorium—de facto raising himself to an authority in Adler's own area of expertise—he recounted in 1916 how "we" completed Central Music Hall in 1879 and how the next year "I" absorbed "very quickly" everything Adler knew about acoustics at the Grand Opera House. History shows that largely due to the Auditorium, Sullivan had no need to pad his résumé, but in his last difficult years, he had no idea it would be remembered at all.

With Sullivan occasionally on board as a free-lance draftsman, Adler's first important theater projects were, in fact, Central Music Hall and the Grand Opera House, already discussed in chapter 4. But a few additional words are necessary here. Adler's artistry on both jobs was heartily praised, but their acoustics elevated his standing even more. Central Music Hall became "nationally famous," says an authority on Chicago construction, giving Adler the reputation of the "leading acoustical 'engineer' of his time." "Engineer" requires quotation marks because, as Sullivan biographer Hugh

Morrison observed, acoustics "was not a subject which had been dealt with to any extent in scientific writings," so Adler must have obtained his "unique" knowledge "entirely by himself." Specific sources of his expertise cannot be fully determined, but acoustical excellence at the nineteen-hundred-seat Music Hall stemmed in part from three innovations: the upward curve of the orchestra floor away from the stage beyond requirements for clear sight lines; its coved ceiling springing laterally from side walls; and on the ceiling itself, transverse projections carrying furring for trusses.[4]

Adler's interior arrangement of this unique, $210,000 structure was equally innovative for 1879. In addition to the auditorium, the building contained a recital hall, a dozen street-level stores, and seventy-five offices around the theater's periphery, making it one of the first mixed-use commercial edifices, a dramatic venture that would have been even more daring had Adler's proposal for carrying two floors above the auditorium without column supports been executed. Years later he recalled specifying three eighty-two-foot iron trusses to span the hall, but "found the timidity of the public so great that I abandoned the upper [floor]." Adler also claimed that Central Music Hall was the first business block to have more than one passenger elevator.[5] The historical consensus, moreover, is that its unusually large number of windows not only foreshadowed a distinguishing characteristic of turn-of-the-century Chicago architecture, but were also deployed harmoniously, even though Adler was forced to articulate them differently on the two main facades, one on State Street, the other around the corner on Randolph. His ability to maintain design clarity in difficult situations is only now being recognized as another of Adler's many strengths.

Contemporary observers were thoroughly pleased. The *Chicago Tribune* reported that the longer people studied the building, the more they appreciated its importance. Goodspeed Publishers, whose *Industrial Chicago* (1891) was an accurate barometer of local commercial opinion, praised its "airy and well arranged" offices but also detected its historic significance. This "modern building . . . pointed out at once a change in style and the return of good times after six years of depression. It outlines . . . the utilitarian ideas which architects were forced to follow . . . and forms the link or divide between the columnated or pilastered store fronts of former days and the gigantic brick fronts of later days." The decade between 1879 and 1889, when a city emerged from the ruins of a village, *Industrial Chi-*

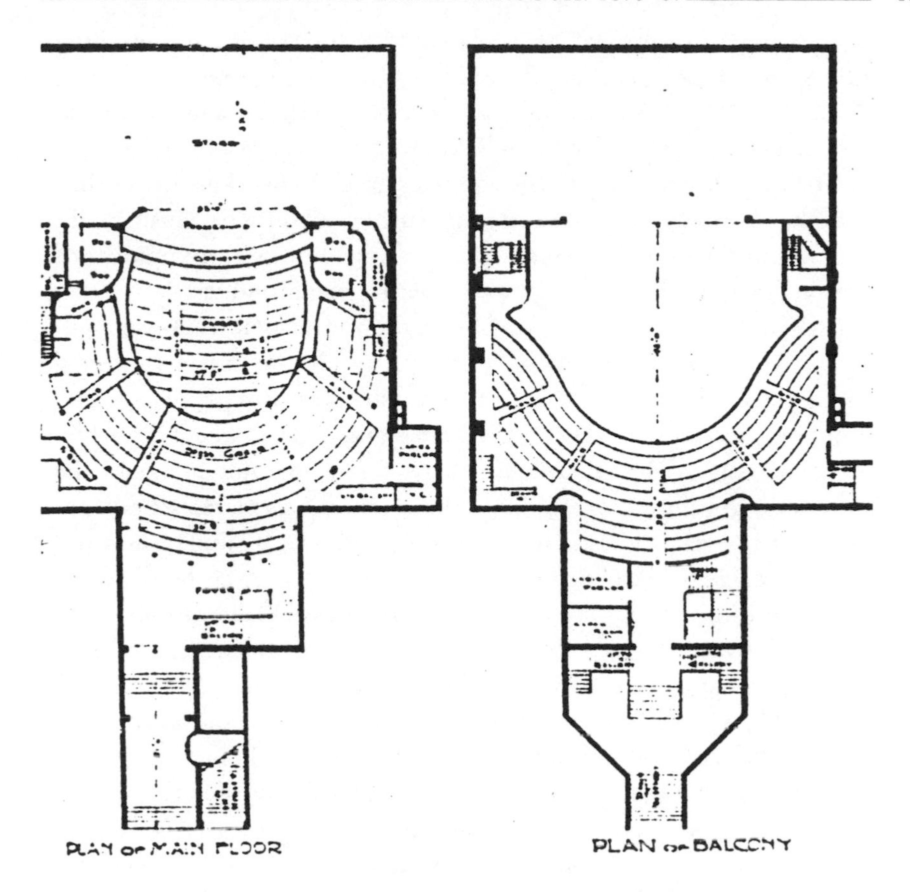

VI.2 *Grand Opera House, 1880, plans.* From *Engineering Record,* 1894.

cago boasted, was also a distinct period in local architecture, marked at one end by Central Music Hall and the other by the Auditorium. As Goodspeed's choice of examples suggests, Adler & Sullivan played a key role in this urban transformation. The Music Hall was, in fact, an "ancestor or prototype of a long series of theatres designed by" them, says one critic, the forerunner, adds another, of the Auditorium itself.[6]

After the Music Hall, Adler recalled, when I "found myself so overcrowded with work as to be unable to discharge my duties to my clients [I] . . . began my business connection with Mr. Louis H. Sullivan" on such projects as the Grand Opera House.[7] Reconstructed from the old Hamlin's Theatre in 1880 at a cost of $55,000 and elaborately reappointed, its new interior was wholeheartedly applauded, favorably compared by the *Daily Inter-Ocean* newspaper with "the exquisite beauty of McVicker's Theatre as now ornamented. The Grand Opera House will fully equal . . . this remarkably well decorated house. There will be nothing to the disadvantage of the latter [*sic*] in a comparison of the two." Although absence of visual records for the demolished Opera House makes analysis of its acoustics difficult, they were apparently based on features similar to the Music Hall's. Describing the "remote ceiling, with its huge but beautifying beams, forming sectional squares," a newspaper reporter inadvertently noted Adler's projecting sound baffles.[8] Sullivan was himself impressed with "what Mr. Adler knew about acoustics. . . . It was not a matter of mathematics, nor a matter of science, [but had to with his] perception [and] instinct. . . . Mr. Adler had a grasp of . . . acoustics which he could not have gained from study, for it was not in books. He must have gotten it by feeling. . . . The Grand Opera House was immediately a great success," according to Sullivan. "It was quite a luxurious theatre for that day and quite a wonder in architecture."[9]

Acclaim for the Music Hall and Opera House undoubtedly led to Adler's first out-of-town theater commission, his first designed with Louis Sullivan, the Academy of Music in Kalamazoo, Michigan. In June 1881, when two stockholders in the local opera company visited Chicago "to consult with leading architects," they wasted little time selecting Adler to prepare and submit plans. Construction of the $58,000, 1250-seat edifice began in July; by February 1882 the roof was on, and the grand opening took place May 8. The three-story, and attic, red-brick, white-stone, and slate-roof building featured two stores with plate-glass facades and recessed entries flanking the main entrance in the center bay, which had a second-floor balcony and a mansard tower with a portholed dormer and corner pinnacles topped by finials. Since the Academy was wider than it was high, its vigorous horizontal stone bands across slightly projecting piers were appropriate, and Sullivan capped the resulting recessed walls with brick corbeling supporting an ornamented cornice. Its four windows per floor in the side bays flanking three per floor at the center were to culminate in the attic with decorative arched lunettes that, perhaps for economy reasons, since the building went over budget, were never executed. Although it has been compared with Solon S. Beman's 1881 Arcade Building at Pullman, Illinois, the Academy's polychromatics, prominent piers wrapped with stone trim, and its window arrangements were familiar Adler & Company touches.

Unlike the flat rectangular floor of the Arcade Theatre, the Acad-

VI.3 *Academy of Music, 1882, Kalamazoo, Michigan.*
From *King's Handbook of the United States.*

emy's rose fanlike from the stage. "Sectional squares" formed by transverse and longitudinal ceiling projections curved laterally at the cove to become wall tops. Unlike the Chicago Auditorium and most of Adler & Sullivan's later theaters, the proscenium opening was higher than it was wide. Sullivan's decorative hand was seen not only on the exterior but also over side boxes inside the auditorium, where circular floral patterns contained by rectangles recalled his Paris studies for John Edelmann as well as drawings by Frank Furness and the Welsh ornamentalist Owen Jones. Since the Kalamazoo Academy was probably Sullivan's first auditorium after Sinai Temple and Moody Tabernacle in 1876, it is not surprising he referred to his early successes. The rest of the interior, including wallpaper, paintings, wood carving, and other ornamental art, however, seems to have been someone else's responsibility. Although the Kalamazoo commission received little notice out of town, and was only recently rediscovered as an Adler & Company opus, the local *Daily Telegraph,* presumably speaking for the community, judged the "magnificent" theater to be "comfortable and conveniently arranged."[10]

"Wanted—A Music Hall," Chicago's *Real Estate & Building Journal* demanded in April 1882. Central Music Hall was "good enough in its way" but "its space, cut into small offices and halls"—the very features so widely applauded three years before but now considered shortcomings by the *Journal*—were "suitable only for society meetings." "We want a building with a stage in it capable of seating five or six hundred" and "an auditorium for six thousand more," not the puny 1900 Adler had provided for in 1879. True to form for local boosters like this magazine, Chicago could not build big enough fast enough: yesterday's wonder was today's albatross. Far from taking offense at this backhanded journalistic slight,[11] Adler with Sullivan renovated five theaters in Chicago during the next four years and assisted on another out of town. However successful they may have been, only the greatest—the Auditorium—more than satisfied the *Journal*'s demand.

Their next Chicago theater was the first in which Louis Sullivan's work was publicly scrutinized independently of Adler's. "Old, gray" Hooley's at the northeast corner of Randolph and La Salle streets was regarded as the last "Quaker prim," rigidly simple, inflexibly plain "amusement temple" in town. But in a speedy "top to bottom" renovation in July and August 1882, Adler and Sullivan waved their "fairy wand" for a complete transformation. Critics agreed that the six-foot-wider stage and proscenium, generous exits, bright lights, and modern dressing rooms were "real glories," but saved their warmest praise for Sullivan's decorations. Six stepped-up boxes on each side, the floor of those in the rear only two feet above heads in the lowest, were treated as open, projecting loges at the front of curving balconies. Faced with three square panels of "remarkably delicate tracings and moldings of floral study," each box was bronzed in "so exquisite . . . so delicate" a manner "it seems incredible that the parts are castings." Ceilings and walls were fully repapered, painted, frescoed, and gilded, but the proscenium received the most acclaim. On the inner side of the braces against the flat ceiling were thirty-four gas burners reflecting on the bronzed arch top as a rich, soft offset to the footlights. "This completes as handsome a stage front as was ever given a theatre in this country," one reviewer raved, while another agreed that managerial hopes for perfect detailing had at "each point . . . been fully met." From a decorative standpoint, this critic added, "visitors [will] long remember their first hour in this beautiful temple of Thespius."

"Mr. Louis H. Sullivan, of the firm of D. Adler & Co[mpany]," a Chicago *Inter-Ocean* columnist revealed, "was the master spirit directing and shaping the creation." Mr. Sullivan is a "pleasant gentleman, but somewhat troubled with large ideas tending to metaphysics." Much to the interviewer's consternation, the young architect explained his work in terms of Herbert "Spencer's first principles and [Charles] Darwin's doctrine of evolution." Pressed to "classify" his admittedly unique decorations "within the orders of architectural exactness"—Gothic, Moorish, Renaissance, and Japanese sprang to mind—Sullivan would not cooperate. "I have no terms to characterize what you see," he declared. "I have not given study to the nomenclature of the peculiar art forms developed in these boxes or carried out in that proscenium crown," indescribable anyway, he insisted, in "stock" phrases. Then how do you define your work "in words"? he was asked. "I cannot," he replied. "I prefer that you speak of it as the successful solution of a problem. The vaguer you are in such matters the better I shall be pleased," particularly since Chicago people "are not prepared" for "a discursive consideration of art in architecture" partly because "we have no appreciative art criticism here." Not yet twenty-six years of age, Sullivan's assertions could be dismissed as youthful arrogance when he claimed exemption from conventional critical standards. His interviewer tended to adopt this view. But Sullivan was suggesting something profoundly more important, having to do with the way he functioned as an artist. Uninterested in labels, categories, in "nomenclature" or styles, he was most of all concerned with the creative process. Art solved problems and was an exercise in problem solving, different in every situation. Predigested solutions from the library, that is, historical styles, might be acceptable for critics who praised tradition to the public, he intimated. But for him style was not so much chosen as arrived at spontaneously, by instinct. However odd or unprecedented this may have seemed, the reporter nevertheless concluded that "the envious eye of criticism looks about [Hooley's] only to soften into commendation."[12]

Even before the Hooley success, impresario J. H. Haverly had anticipated the *Real Estate and Building Journal*'s call for magnificence by hiring architect Oscar Cobb in 1881 to design "the most thoroughly appointed theatre in the West" at the intersection of Dearborn and Monroe. Quick to applaud his intentions, the *Journal* believed that Haverly's observations during a recent European tour would result in a facility "better than anything [else] in the country." But no sooner had it opened than the disappointed magazine declared it unsafe, a firetrap with too few exits incorrectly situated.[13] A year or so later, Haverly made facade changes, lighting and ventilation improvements, but apparently still dissatisfied called on Adler & Sullivan in the spring of 1884 to bail him out. Their partial renovation was another feather in their caps. Small art galleries on either side of a new entrance and ticket booth opened through a "glittering vestibule" to the auditorium, where the rearranged orchestra was the city's largest and the proscenium and boxes were completely redecorated. Haverly purchased an adjacent building to give him space for a half dozen more exits, "perhaps the most significant alteration that has been made in this house," one reviewer remarked, clearly aware of its previous flaws.[14] Everyone thrilled to the architects' most eye-catching innovation, the 325 electric lights that transformed the entrance, vestibule, and proscenium into glowing jewels the likes of which they had never seen before. Equally striking was Sullivan's high-relief, papier-mâché wall and ceiling ornament—"an imitation of wood-carving at one-quarter the cost," its supplier said—tinted to resemble gold, bronze, and hammered copper, "so harmoniously blended in tone that no one hue is predominant."[15]

When the new Haverly's opened in August, it caused a minor sensation, the first of a series of concert hall tours de force culminating in the Auditorium. Even critics with reservations were lavish in their praise. "Beneath the radiance of electric lights," one wrote, "it is gorgeous in spots." The portions not renovated by Adler & Sullivan, the "dull and dreary" auditorium seating area, for example, suffered in comparison to those that were, especially the "golden" entrance and "flaring" colors of boxes and arch. How peculiar, furthermore, that the ticket booth should overshadow the art galleries in splendor, as if "a vision of beauty was trampled to death in a rough-and-tumble fight" with moneymaking. However disappointing the "tout ensemble of the gorgeous chaos," another observer concluded that "the spirit of the undertaking can scarcely be too highly commended."[16] But a traveling English journalist saw the matter somewhat differently. Sullivan's decorations were probably "the best in the world!" he flat-out declared. From the street, brightly lit stained-glass windows had a "dazzling, jewel-like quality," forecasting the brilliant lobby where illuminated papier-mâché "produces an effect of richness without gaudiness, to which a plain description can do but scant justice." The box office and foyer doors of gilt-framed beveled mirrors arabesqued in black were as striking as the metallic-lined reliefs, the chandeliers, and the "clusters of Edison's incandescent burners flood[ing] the interior with their radiance." Not to be upstaged by foreign enthusiasts, the local *Inland Architect* judged the new entrance the best of any in Chicago.[17] Even those for whom Sullivan's decorations were too "flashy" and complicated could not refrain from praising his overall conception. Haverly's was the first Chicago theater jointly designed by Adler and Sullivan as partners. Sullivan's lighting—a very early theatrical use of electric lamps—and his ornament made an enormous impression, becoming with Adler's acoustics two of the firm's most characteristic trademarks.

The next opportunity came when merchant philanthropist Ferdinand Peck, soap manufacturer Nathaniel K. Fairbank, pipe miller Richard T. Crane, and other prominent businessmen, lacking a home for their recently organized Chicago Opera Festival, decided late in 1884 to renovate the Interstate Exposition Building, designed in 1873 by William W. Boyington, a prolific if undistinguished local architect known mostly for railroad stations. Sullivan's Haverly accolades, Adler's unparalleled reputation for theatrical acoustics, plus his work fitting up the Exposition Building for the 1884 Democratic National Convention,[18] made the partners a logical choice to remodel the northern half of the mammoth facility for the Festival's April 1885 season. Agreeing with the sponsors that a temporary wooden structure seating sixty-two hundred could be inserted into the existing shell, Adler & Sullivan prepared plans in February for a furious construction schedule.

The March renovation was another dramatic demonstration of their skill. The 40-by-60-foot proscenium arch fronted an 80-by-120 stage with full-height drops. Flanked by eleven unusually large dressing rooms, the stage opened at the back to company assembly areas in a seventy-five-foot semicircle. Out front the auditorium fanned to a width of 140 feet. The stage protruded twenty feet beyond the curtain into the twenty-two-hundred-seat parquet, which rose five feet to its rear at a twelve-foot aisle, where a fifteen-hundred-seat dress circle beginning three feet higher than the last parquet row climbed another thirty. Projecting the same distance over the dress circle and rising to the rear wall 250 feet from the proscenium, the balcony for eighteen hundred wrapped around the sides of the hall until it descended in flanking series of unusual stepped boxes to the stage. The vaulted ceiling was divided by arched trusses into occasions for ornamental panels and friezes, acting in the megaphone-shaped room to distribute sound evenly. One reporter marveled at the "astonishingly perfect" acoustics, "the slightest sound being heard from the stage in every part of the house." The curved fronts of Sullivan's richly ornamented boxes were an acoustical element of the proscenium, which opened like a funnel into the parquet some sixty feet on either side of the arch to the legs of the first truss. Breaking up this large expanse visually, helping make it "an immense sounding board," the boxes featured color decorations and "plastic" forms in papier-mâché. "The effect," Sullivan remembered, "was thrilling." Sixty-two hundred people could see without obstruction and hear every note—no mean achievement at that time—

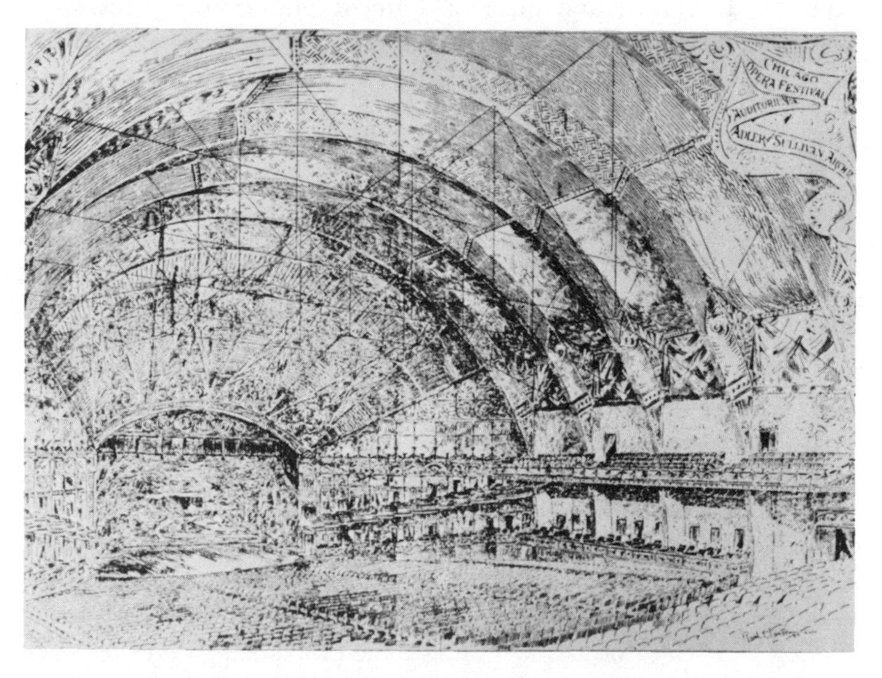

VI.4 *Interstate Exposition Building auditorium, 1885.* From *Inland Architect,* 1885.

"even to the faintest pianissimo. No reverberation, no echo,—the clear untarnished tone, of voice and instrument, reached all. The inference was obvious," he added, referring to the momentous opportunity that would soon be his: "A great permanent hall housed within a monumental structure must follow."[19]

The $60,000 renovation, never intended as a permanent home for the Opera Festival, was demolished with its building in 1892 to make way for the Art Institute on Michigan at Adams. But Adler & Sullivan designed a monument nonetheless. "All the appointments of a first-class opera house are arranged for," one observer noted, and "care has been taken to secure stability of construction and [an] agreeable and harmonious interior." Patrons applauded the seven thousand brilliant gas lamps, the superabundance of exits, wide corridors and staircases, and the spacious promenades, salons, and vestibules—far beyond the ordinary in contemporary concert halls—with excellent climate control offering a profound sense of safety and comfort. Recognized to be the aesthetic consequence of Adler's acoustical requirements, Sullivan's decorations were widely praised: the place was so beautiful, the *Chicago Tribune* intoned, the audience felt "privileged to leave seats between acts" to stroll in the grand promenade and mingle in the salons. Instead of the makeshift everyone had expected, the public was given a building "as elegant in its decorations and as attractive to the eyes as if it were a permanent structure devoted to the lyric art." Its success made everyone realize, according to a newspaper editorial, how much Chicago needed a splendid new facility.[20]

The Festival opened the same day construction began on another of Adler & Sullivan's heralded renovations, at McVicker's, Chicago's premier theater, 78–84 Madison Street. Erected in 1857, its exceptionally tortured history began with its destruction in the great 1871 fire, five days after a $90,000 remodeling was finished. Rebuilt the next year, it was reconstructed in the early 1880s, but apparently unsatisfied with the results, its owner hired Adler & Sullivan for further alterations in the spring of 1883. Inexplicable delays forced them to revise their plans in the fall of 1884 for work beginning April 1, 1885, with a grand opening the first of July. Everything seemed fine until January 1888, when a well-known Chicago interior decorator who had assisted on the renovation publicly charged the architects with, in effect, stealing his ideas, claiming authorship of the interior design scheme. In August 1890 McVicker's was again destroyed by fire. Called in to provide the replacement, Adler & Sullivan's second effort served until demolished in 1925.[21]

Like their previous theaters and concert halls, the 1885 McVicker's was very highly regarded. The $75,000-to-$100,000 commission called for regrouping seventy-six offices around and over the remodeled auditorium, modern climate control and lighting systems, and new decorations, entrance, exits, stage, and seats. In short, McVicker's was "practically rebuilt," a local building magazine announced, "so that a new theatre now replaces the old one." After several plan revisions, Adler & Sullivan ended up placing mechanical systems and storage in a new but contiguous four-story building, and a photo gallery and most of the offices on the old fifth and a new sixth floor of the main edifice with its own street entrance. In the theater itself, every aisle led directly to one of twenty-six exits, and for additional safety sliding iron doors in fireproof walls separated the auditorium and lobby from the stage and its service rooms on the one hand, and from the offices on the other. Patrons in the 1950 seats and 12 proscenium boxes were delighted by the 1235 electric lights, while J. H. McVicker reveled in his own personal pride and joy, an innovative ventilation system. From intakes on the roof, "fresh" air was fan-forced through a chamber for filtering, icing in summer and steam heating in winter, before introduction to the hall through a complex network of pipes. Stale air was drawn out through one thousand return vents hidden on the floor beneath the seats.[22] "The cooling apparatus for hot weather works like a charm," one observer noted, "and the heating and ventilating is so perfect that the house is filled with fresh air continually," every fifteen minutes, in fact.

Sullivan's work at McVicker's in 1885 generated even more interest than either Adler's highly praised structural and mechanical successes or their joint accomplishment at Haverly's the year before. "In magnificent decoration, and in elegance of appearance and beauty of finish in all its details, it is the model theatre of our times," one critic contended, "typical of the position, prestige, progress and promise of the city it represents." The theater was so luxurious that it "equals, if not surpasses," according to a second critic, "the parlor and drawing-room appointments of most costly residences. . . . The boxes are perfect gems."[23] C. H. Blackall, traveling correspondent for New York's *American Architect & Building News,* the most influential professional magazine in the country during the 1880s, was impressed enough to write a glowing account worthy of partial reproduction as one of the few comprehensive contemporary descriptions. Others had discussed the beautiful "automatic folding spring seat sofa chairs, with gold plated castings and gold nails" in the parquet and dress circle, the spheroidal curve of the proscenium leaving room for a large sounding board, and the heavily draped drop curtain with its running brook–rustic bridge–distant woodlands motif.[24] "It is, however, the decoration of the interior which attracts the most attention," Blackall wrote:

> The general effect of the color is salmon and dull bronze. The tones of the wall start from the bottom with a decided salmon tint as a ground, fading out as it rises, until in the center of the ceiling it becomes a delicate buff. Over this is a large pattern formed in relief with heavy rosettes like the centre of a sunflower, and lines of long, spikey leaves, touched up with strong, red bronze, the pale salmon, however, remaining the principal color. This decoration is carried over nearly all surfaces, no distinction being made between walls, beams and ceiling, except by accentuated lines, rosettes or varied ornament in relief, or by using slightly deeper tones of the general color. The columns and girders under the galleries are of a deep bronze or rather brass tone. The corridors are finished with a very effective combination of pale blue and bronze, and the openings . . . into the auditorium are hung with heavy peacock-blue curtains. . . . The upholstery of the seats is all in deep red plush. The proscenium arch, the private boxes, and the portion of the ceiling within the outline of the boxes, which is flared down toward the rather low proscenium opening are all finished in woodwork . . . ; but the designers did not commit the error of attempting to enrich the immediate surroundings of the stage by obtrusive gilding or pronounced decorations. The tones are rather subdued about the proscenium.

The walls above the upper gallery, Blackall continued, flared into a wide cove ceiling sparingly decorated with a geometrical flower pattern. The ceiling itself was nearly plain except for a faint diaper (of facing bricks arranged with contrasting headers in a diamond pattern). "There is no chandelier, an innovation which every theatergoer is ready to applaud," Blackall pointedly remarked, echoing the general opinion. Instead, incandescent lights worked into the design at the center of the ceiling were "festooned" about the periphery and down the walls. "It helps out the decoration amazingly to see those luminous spots shine out from the dark tones" of their holes deep in plaster, he observed, where "little balls of fire peep out most happily from amid clumps of the spikey foliage or in the rosettes of the gallery front." The entire interior was, in fact, "exceedingly harmonious. . . . Everything is in thorough good taste." As far as Blackall was concerned, McVicker's was not only the most "successful" theater in Chicago, but was also "the best," a verdict done one better by another critic who claimed that "the general plan of decoration [was] designed and executed in a style superior to anything heretofore seen in any public building in this country."[25]

Most interested Chicagoans agreed. On the July 1 opening night, one local newspaper labeled McVicker's "an architectural success [but] a dramatic failure," referring to the performance, before concluding in a second long feature article that "the beautiful transformation" of a once-gloomy theater into a "perfect remodeling . . . has placed this firm of architects far beyond all competitors."[26] *Real Estate & Building Journal* followed its own flattering appraisal with an assessment of Adler & Sullivan's skyrocketing reputation. Their work, it declared, "is the best certificate of premiership in their profession." Their other theaters, "first class" public buildings, and private homes were uniformly marked by originality, common sense adaptation of means to ends (the correct materials for the job, for example), and by skillful execution. The results of their "motto"—"Let there be light"—could be seen all over town by the abundance of illumination in their buildings, "far greater than is usually obtained by other architects." Moving unconventionally along new paths guided by study, observation, and experience, by the "genii of necessity, use and beauty," Adler & Sullivan were receiving "abounding orders from confiding patrons." An authority on heavy construction, the *Journal* added, Adler was always consulted, presumably by other architects, when strong materials were required and heavy pressure had to be sustained. "Mr. Sullivan's speciality," on the other hand, "is in the artistic department, and he has won the laurels in ornamental architecture," not excluding this magazine's for this building.[27]

But as Sullivan might have predicted by now, had he chanced to recall the 1876 Moody Tabernacle incident, professional acclaim was sometimes accompanied by petty sniping. In response to Blackall's enthusiastic review, Joseph Twyman (1842–1904), a Chicago furniture designer, lecturer, and interior decorator, informed *American Architect* that "the decoration of McVicker's theatre . . . was executed under my charge and dictation and was my own conception without control of architect or owner." Adler & Sullivan immediately replied, eliciting further response from Twyman. The illuminating exchange[28] clarified little for readers—"as the statements are clearly irreconcilable," the editors declared, "we must . . . leave the matter an open question"—but it enabled the architects to outline their design philosophy. Twyman claimed total credit for McVicker's color and decorative schemes, including reliefs, draperies, and upholstered dado, 278 electric lights, the selection of wallpaper and stained-glass windows. The architects had designed only the proscenium, boxes, vestibules, and the arrangement of a few lights, he insisted, in effect saying that after planning McVicker's general organization and some major decorations, Adler & Sullivan had left the rest to him.

The architects noted that at the time of the job, Twyman, a salesman in charge of interior decorations for John J. McGrath's wallpaper company in Chicago, the major supplier for McVicker's, had been chosen by them to select color and paper for the flat portion of the main ceiling, for ceilings under the gallery and balcony, and for foyers and retiring rooms "which are small." Not only had he settled on wallpaper previously designed by Sullivan (Twyman admitted this), but he had also been bound at all times, according to the architects, by their overall decorative conception, itself a consequence of the theater's construction and acoustics. Elaboration of this assertion was the most valuable part of their letter.

The decorations, they began (the letter was signed jointly, but since the issue was chiefly Sullivan's concern, he probably wrote it), were determined by McVicker's interior shapes. Ornamental motifs had been worked out geometrically to fit the subdivisions of ceilings and walls dictated by Adler's structural and acoustical calculations. Sullivan, the design partner, then developed the geometry through increasingly complex stages until it finally evolved or rose into foliated, efflorescent patterns conditioned by their original geometric boundaries. Within this ornamental system, he arranged the lights to enhance his floral motifs. After completing the general scheme, Sullivan fashioned full-scale details executed in plaster models. The problem then became to find color values for the structural, geometrical, and foliated parts of exposed surfaces that would harmonize with their relative solid values, lest incorrect accentuation obliterate the "simple" idea or impulse informing the entire conception. His solution was to unite the three parts by blending close, only subtly different, family-related colors characteristic of the material (the wooden beams, for example) or of the depicted foliage, suggesting all the while the mutual dependency of parts by gradually and smoothly merging colors into each other as the structural, geometrical, and efflorescent parts themselves merged. This blending conception, he wrote, determined the selection of paint and paper elsewhere in the building, including subsidiary portions supervised by Twyman and other decorators. Therefore, even if Twyman had made independent choices, he was always bound by the guiding scheme and could not truthfully claim to have conceived any part of the finished work. The most important point in this discourse on McVicker's decoration was the architect's contention that ornament was an interpretation of structure, one implication being that it could never simply be applied, for example, as tattoos to skin, without regard for context.

Like the commercial buildings discussed in chapter 5, McVicker's also revealed that in 1885 Sullivan's facade compositions did not approach the sophistication of his interiors, his ornament, or of his design theories. Rising vigorously from second story to roof, exterior columns at McVicker's were infilled almost entirely with glass, an excellent example of the "let there be light" philosophy so admired by a previously quoted reviewer. But each of the six stories was heavily outlined with cornices, compromising McVicker's vertical potential. Peculiar wedge-shaped, third-to-fifth-story indentations formed unorthodox "bay" windows flush with the facade plane, but with Sullivan's by now familiar arched windows on top, sprightly cornice, jagged roof line, and rather ambiguous treatment of structural supports at street level, the front was highly confused. Nevertheless, the firm's acoustical and decorative achievements brought considerable notoriety, solidifying their reputation as leading concert-hall and theatrical designers, indeed, as one of the premier architectural firms in the country.

After completing the Haverly, Interstate, and McVicker renovations, plus a lot of other work during a very busy two years, Adler visited Salt Lake City late in 1885 to inspect sound properties at Mormon Tabernacle.[29] There he saw how the balcony, suspended a few feet from the rear wall of the open "turtle-backed" hall with no division between auditorium and foyer, facilitated an unimpaired flow of sound waves. These observations corroborated his own theories, which were by now so highly regarded that early in 1886 he was invited to upgrade two major structures. One was the Milwaukee Exposition Building—designed in 1880 by local architect Edward Townshend Mix—which the city's Musical Society decided to renovate for the National Sangerfest, an annual German festival three years in the planning. By installing an immense overhead sounding board half the length of the hall, Adler precluded "all chance of echoes," according to the *Milwaukee Sentinel.* He arranged the chorus into tiers, the topmost "at quite a giddy height," while raking the audience seats from halfway back, every one of the 5174 "commanding a good view." The first rehearsal removed all doubts

VI.5 *McVicker's Theater, 1885.* From *Inland Architect,* 1885.

about sound reaching "remote corners" in the barnlike edifice. "Prominent members of the musical profession," according to one source, "pronounced it to be superior, as to acoustic quality, arrangement, and convenience, to any great concert room they have ever seen." Adler supervised the installation of four thousand gas-jet lights, the conversion of art galleries into press rooms and dining rooms into company quarters, and the speedy provision of postal and telegraph offices, barber shops and baths. There was no suggestion of Sullivan's involvement in this mammoth three-month undertaking, probably because its brief life did not warrant extensive decorations. After a mere two weeks, the *Sentinel* disclosed, a large crew "will remove every vestige of the work done for the Sangerfest" to prepare for an exposition. Adler's "vast" effort and "the great expenses incurred in preparing the building, will therefore be utilized for this one occasion only."[30]

But Sullivan was certainly involved in the other major renovation coming into the office almost simultaneously. For years Chicagoans had anticipated the opening of Henry Ives Cobb and Charles S. Frost's Opera House Block at the southwest corner of Clark and Washington streets. Built in 1884 and 1885, it stood until 1912 as one of the many successful Chicago buildings—like Central Music Hall and McVicker's—with a shell of offices surrounding a theater. Despite the growing demand for a large, permanent operatic room, however, observers were strangely quiet as its August 18 opening neared, as if sensing the Opera House would not live up to expectations. Everyone acknowledged that the first season was highly creditable from a musical standpoint, but even before it ended, managerial dissatisfaction with sight lines and ventilation prompted the hiring of Adler & Sullivan in April 1886 for a major remodeling. During the next five months, they arched the previously square proscenium, raised the roof at the rear for acoustically better proportions and sight lines, and deepened the gallery for more reserved seating in front. Twenty-two boxes of a lighter color increased the original number by ten while brightening the stage area. Observers seemed to think that when the hall reopened in September, its sight-line and ventilation problems had been completely solved. The only "event of dramatic interest during the dull week just over," the *Tribune*'s theater critic reported, "was the re-opening of the Chicago Opera-House. . . . The theatre itself, which has been practically rebuilt, and which is richly decorated, excited considerable comment on all sides," unhappily not recorded. "The occasion . . . was pleasantly auspicious in every way." Perhaps in deference to Cobb and Frost, who were popular, well known, highly regarded, and no doubt embarrassed by the need to renovate, the press said little about it, but those in the know understood that Adler & Sullivan had done it again.[31]

By September 1886, when Louis Sullivan turned thirty, two months after Adler's forty-second birthday, he and his partner were famous. One remarkable theater renovation after another brought them extensive publicity as far away as East Coast publications like *American Architect.* Although their residences were respected and their commercial buildings praised, their theaters and concert halls established their reputation more than anything else, enabling critics, furthermore, to discern more clearly their separate contributions. Adler's superior engineering and his acoustical pyrotechnics were by now taken for granted, while Sullivan—known only to a small circle of professionals when he joined the firm five years earlier—had come to be regarded as one of the most talented ornamentalists on the architectural scene. His imaginative use of color and unusual naturalistic forms, but especially his innovations with artificial light, made him a designer of distinction who brought as much luster to the partnership by 1886 as Adler did himself.

The general understanding that Adler & Sullivan's 1885 Interstate Exposition renovation for the Opera Festival led directly to their selection in 1886 as architects for the Chicago Auditorium is accurate only in the sense that both projects had some of the same influential backers. When in response to growing public clamor and to Ferdinand Peck's personal vision of a permanent opera company housed in a great new hall—both in large measure stimulated by the Festival's success—the Chicago Auditorium Association was incorporated on December 8, 1886, several of its officers did, in fact, know Adler & Sullivan well. Peck was himself elected president; Nathaniel K. Fairbank, another Festival organizer and close financial associate of George B. Carpenter on Central Music Hall, was a vice-president; and frequent Adler & Sullivan client Martin A. Ryerson served on the board of directors. But other officers and stockholders, who were also among the city's wealthiest and most powerful men, undoubtedly had ideas of their own. Marshall Field, for example, who had hired the late Henry Richardson in 1885 to design his instantly famous wholesale store, might easily have lobbied for his professional heirs, the firm of Shepley, Rutan, and Coolidge. Similarly, George Pullman had virtually his own in-house architect, Solon S. Beman. Most of the principal investors, in fact, had comparable connections, in many cases the designers of their South Side mansions. Such a prestigious and expensive commission, furthermore, initially projected at more than $2,000,000 in December 1886, was a plum every architect in town and many from outside desperately wanted. So Adler & Sullivan's selection was probably not a foregone conclusion, and certainly did not rest on something as unremarkable as success or the contacts they made on a single edifice. Rather it was the persuasiveness of their cumulative work since Central Music Hall that got them the job. Well-placed clients certainly helped their chances, but their acknowledged mastery of the concert hall genre—as their able renovation of Cobb and Frost's Opera House had so graphically demonstrated—plus their well-known individual talents, made them a logical choice, but one made with considerable trepidation by some Auditorium sponsors.[32]

Once determined, however, their selection was a popular one. Because their "practical knowledge . . . both in facilities for seating large audiences and for securing perfect acoustic properties, is exceptional," a Chicago building magazine had declared in 1885, Adler & Sullivan had an "almost national reputation."[33] The tone may have been boosterish, but the assessment was proven correct when in 1887 Adler was invited to discuss "The Paramount Requirements of a Large Opera House" at the Twenty-first Annual Convention of the American Institute of Architects meeting in Chicago in October. Written during the early stages of Auditorium construction, Adler's paper is a reliable guide to his (and his partner's) approach to that particular commission as well as the most advanced and comprehensive thinking on the general subject then available.[34] Concentrating on the "essentials and peculiarities" of an American concert hall capable of seating three thousand or more that could also be used for conventions, Adler first of all considered siting. "Our building should be an open square surrounded by broad streets" on at least three sides and constructed of the most solid and enduring fireproof materials, as monumental as can be—although he did not use that word—disregarding the possibility that its environment might someday deteriorate. "By making permanence and stability of structure paramount considerations," he suggested, "the ever-changing conditions of desirability so characteristic of American cities" might be altered. Subsequent Auditorium history seems to have borne him out.

Recognizing that in America the absence of government support for the arts meant the facility would be built by private capital, which would demand continuous profit even during long intervals between performances, Adler recommended commercial space on the ground floor, particularly at street front, even though this inevitably created difficulties in planning the theater's lobby, corridors, and foyers. Whatever the needs of commercial clients, he insisted, "there should always be lobby space enough to hold almost the entire audience." Similarly, the stage must be large enough for performances "far grander" than in ordinary houses lest there be no justification for this sort of building, but, in the absence of government subsidy, not so large as to compromise commercial requirements. There would therefore need to be "a reasonable proportion" between concert production costs and the size of the anticipated audience. As to set storage and movement, "nothing is more annoying to American audiences" than the exceptionally long waits between acts that invariably characterize operatic performances. To remedy this, Adler suggested relatively small moving accessories changeable vertically, meaning the width of the stage could be minimized, although great depth below and height above were necessary.

Light should be partly natural to save costs during cleaning and rehearsal, but must be blocked out during productions. Artificial light should be evenly distributed without glare, shadow, or interference with sight lines, should be spread over several circuits to avoid total blackout in emergencies, and should be backed up by "oil lamps and wax candles." Ingress and egress must be ample, no less than three to four feet in width for each two hundred persons per aisle, door, or stairway. Many narrow aisles were preferable to a few wide ones and should lead as directly as possible to exits, corridors, lobbies, and stairs, with frequent landings capable of handling at least one-half the audience at any one moment. Heating and ventilation should be independent of doors and windows. Since forced air was necessary in such a large space, care must be given to drafts, and for acoustical purposes it was best to direct all air currents from the stage outward. Fresh air should enter the hall from the top in greatest volume near the stage, and stale air be removed through or close to the floors in increasing capacity toward the rear. One-third of the ducts must open on stage to remove smoke and other theatrical detritus at the prompter's direction. Galleries should be disengaged from the rear wall to permit air and sound flow (like the Mormon Tabernacle, which modern fire codes would now ban), there should be a least four sets of doors between main lobbies and the street for warmth, air must be cooled and washed before entering the auditorium, and provision be made for only moderate heating during rehearsal and cleaning. Adler also discussed the many provisions that might be taken against "conflagration."

All this "will be as naught," he continued, "unless the acoustical properties" are outstanding. His audience probably picked up its collective ears. In the construction of banks and seats, he began, "Scott Russell's isacoustic curve should be adhered to as far as practicable." John Scott Russell (1808–82), a Scottish civil engineer, first described the curve as that line or surface connecting points in a room with the same acoustical property, particularly in relation to intensity of sound issuing from a fixed point. In an auditorium it is achieved when the curvature of a bowled floor is so designed that the elevation of each person's head above the person in front as viewed by the speaker is apparently the same. Adler discussed how modifications in the isacoustic curve should be used for banking the seats, emphasizing that the "nearer the approach to these conditions the easier will be the sight-lines for all the occupants of the house." In addition, he advocated resonant materials for construction and facing; avoiding large, hard, smooth surfaces; breaking ceilings and walls into small reflecting units; increasing house width and height in proportion to distance from the stage; and comparatively low but neither excessively wide proscenium arches. The purpose of these features was threefold: to reduce to a minimum air set in motion by people on stage, to direct sound waves toward the audience, and to prevent the dissipation in space of air currents. If one hundred years later Adler's ideas seem routine, they were not at the time. Acoustical disasters in prestigious concert halls have recently revealed persistent mysteries in the science, demonstrating by contrast that Adler, who never had a failure, was far ahead of his day.

By the time of this speech, in October 1887, the Auditorium was well under way, a graphic demonstration of the principles Adler stressed. Its story will be told in the following pages.

Chapter VII

TOWERING SUCCESS

1886-90

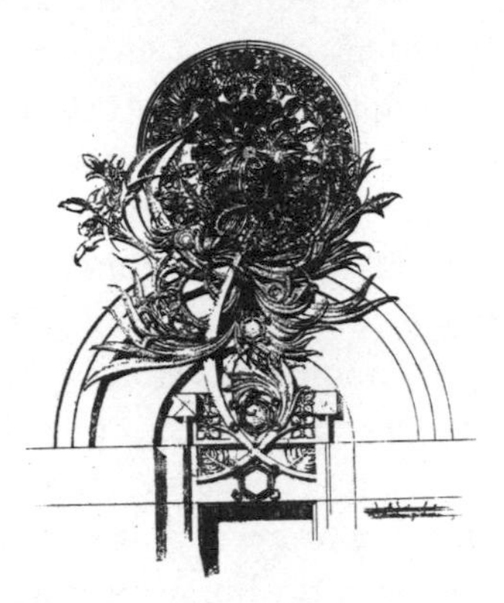

THE AUDITORIUM BUILDING was the biggest thing to hit Chicago since the 1871 fire. Three and one-half years in the making, from the autumn of 1886, when Louis Sullivan began preliminary sketches, to February 1890, when the last details were done, it finally costed out at $3,200,000, the most expensive edifice in the city, ten times more so than any previous Adler & Sullivan commission. It was also by far the largest. At 270 feet above sea level, its seventeen-story tower made it the tallest building in town, and at 110,000 tons, it was the heaviest and most massive in the world. Its frontage of 187 feet on Michigan Boulevard continued along an entire 362-foot block of Congress Street, then turned a second corner for another 162 feet on Wabash Avenue for 63,350 square feet in plan, over an acre and a half, which, multiplied by ten stories plus seven more in the forty-by-seventy-foot tower, yielded 8,737,000 cubic feet of volume. This huge space was divided into a four-hundred-room hotel on Michigan and partway down Congress, a business section for 136 offices and stores on Wabash and in the tower and, with its entrance on Congress Street, a forty-two-hundred-seat theater together with support facilities occupying half the total area and one-third the volume of the entire structure, the largest permanent concert hall ever built at the time. No wonder Chicago, as easily impressed by size as by beauty, reeled at the achievement, and no wonder its leading newspaper devoted its entire first three pages to the theater's dedication on December 9, 1889. Not since the great fire decimated downtown had Chicago paid so much attention to a single event.[1]

The man behind it all was Ferdinand Wythe Peck (1848–1924), once a lawyer, but by 1885 estate manager for his late father, Philip F. W. Peck, an early Chicago settler who made a fortune in trade. An art and music lover, the younger Peck sponsored a host of cultural activities, served as president of the Opera Festival when Adler & Sullivan renovated the Interstate Exposition Building in 1885, and in response to the enthusiasm for that event organized the Chicago Auditorium Association in 1886. As much as anything else, it was Peck's dedication to the arts, his vision for Chicago's musical future, persistence in the face of formidable obstacles, and his clout with the city's business elite that brought the Auditorium project to fruition.

The 1885 Festival had been a smashing success. During its two-week run in April, some ninety thousand people witnessed twelve different operas, demonstrating to Peck that Chicago not only thirsted for the best in music but could also sustain a permanent facility—

VII.1 *Auditorium Building, 1886–90, from Grant Park.* Photo by Robert Twombly.

VII.2 *Ferdinand Peck.* From *The Auditorium Building.*

under the right conditions. Agreeing with Adler that a mammoth concert hall would not be financially viable by itself, Peck insisted on linking it to a hotel and sufficient commercial space to underwrite expensive artistic productions. Once committed to the project, he was not one to waste time. Only six weeks after the Festival, a rumor circulated that a Peck-led business syndicate had secured options on property at Michigan and Monroe for a large opera house, but that legal complications with the title were bound to subvert the plan. A few months later, another story made the rounds: the effort to build a grand hotel at the northwest corner of Michigan and Congress (the Auditorium site) was beset with so "many difficulties . . . it is not likely to be undertaken in the near future." But Peck could not be so easily deterred.[2]

By May of 1886, his behind-the-scenes efforts began to yield significant results when his friend Wirt D. Dexter took control of the old Scammon property, 160 feet deep along the north side of Congress, and promptly offered a sixty-day option to the newly formed Auditorium Association. The site contained the Brunswick Hotel, a florist's shop, a private home, and a skating rink, but speaking that month to the prestigious Commercial Club, Peck outlined his plans for their replacement: a three-hundred-room

European hotel on Michigan and a ninety-six-foot-deep business block on Wabash flanking a 125-by-125-foot, five-thousand-seat auditorium with a 70-by-120 stage entered from Congress. Persuasively arguing that the city needed this facility at that location, Peck secured the club's endorsement, a necessary prerequisite for opening fat Chicago wallets. By September his "indefatigable" efforts sowing $100 "Grand Auditorium Association" shares had reaped promises of $30,000 from Marshall Field, $25,000 each from C. R. Cummings, Martin Ryerson, and the Chicago City Railway, and $10,000 from Charles Hutchinson, Nathaniel K. Fairbank, and Edson Keith among others, while many more, including Charles Schwab and George Pullman, were expected soon to subscribe. By the end of November, Peck had pledges in hand for three-quarters of a million dollars from wealthy individuals who were already asserting their right to scrutinize the design, not only to insure it be "an ornament to the city," they said, but also because it would inevitably reflect on the "good taste of its citizens," that is, them. Some, in fact, had even announced that dissatisfaction with the building's front depicted in Louis Sullivan's preliminary drawings would prompt them to make "suggestions" at the December 4 stockholders meeting for formally organizing the association and electing its officers.[3]

That conclave, with Marshall Field presiding, selected a board of directors. The Chicago Auditorium Association was officially incorporated at Springfield, the state capital, on December 8, 1886, and three days later, at its first session, the board chose Peck president, Edson Keith and Nathaniel K. Fairbank first and second vice-presidents, and Charles Hutchinson treasurer, all to serve with Martin Ryerson as the executive committee. With the bandwagon gathering speed, Peck announced that pledges had now reached $2,000,000 (plenty for the job, it was thought), that the site had been leased for ninety-nine years, that demolition would begin December 13, and ground most likely broken January 1, 1887. The building, Peck revealed, would be ten stories high, with a three-hundred-foot tower over the Congress Street entrance to a five-thousand-seat theater capable of handling eight thousand at conventions. With three thousand seats on the main floor, two galleries, fifty-one boxes, and a 70-by-120-foot stage, the concert hall as presently conceived would be second in size only to Milan's La Scala. Its vast, elaborately decorated, carved stone facade relieved by bowed bays running from the top of the second story to the flat roof would be on an ornamental scale, he said, heretofore attempted in Chicago only at Solon S. Beman's Pullman Building (1883) at Michigan and Adams, "but good critics," one newspaper assured its readers, "say it will be highly commendable from an artistic and utilitarian point of view." Photographs in the possession of stockholders, the *Chicago Tribune* reported on December 10, show the "design of the building [as it] has been fixed."[4]

Unfortunately for Adler & Sullivan, the design had not been "fixed," nor would it be for quite some time. Nor for that matter had they or any other architects actually been hired. Sullivan had forwarded at least two proposals by December, but the board of directors, skeptical of his youth and comparative lack of experience, guarding their own reputations, and reluctant to adopt a design without an expert second opinion, was not convinced. And with good reason, for the Auditorium as finally erected was a vast improvement over Sullivan's early ideas, preserved in two renderings showing its evolution. One depicts a two-story stone base for six brick floors plus a double-height, pitched-roof, gabled attic enlivened by chimneys, cupolas, pediments, and arches. With a steep slope, a large dormer, and a cupola on top, the tower did not rise far above the main roof line, but its window arrangements made it look like a separate edifice bisecting the rest of the building. Two- and three-story oriels increasing to six at bulging corners with pointy towers made the facade exceedingly picturesque. The second version added a tenth story under a flat roof and a higher square tower with a tall blank pyramid on top. Although Sullivan had simplified the facade, his huge Congress Street oriels flanking a loggia were, in Hugh Morrison's apt judgment, "a Gargantuan conceit."[5] Both versions contained elements of the final building: a Congress Street tower signaling the triple-arched auditorium entrance, a similar entry under a loggia on Michigan for the hotel, a two-story base supporting a superstructure of horizontally articulated clusters of floors, and tiers of windows arched on top. But with their elaborate, highly ornate exteriors, both versions were hardly superior to other buildings of the period except in scale.

Hungry for news about the mammoth project, local papers gobbled up every scrap of information they could find, reporting on December 19, 1886, for example, that although the architects and plans "were about decided upon . . . there was a chance that there would be a radical change in both." (In fact, however, no other firms were

VII.3 *Auditorium Building, preliminary scheme, 1886.*

ever mentioned or apparently ever asked for proposals.) During the coming week, this anonymous source continued, "the matter would be definitely settled, probably in favor of the gentlemen whose names have frequently been mentioned in connection with the enterprise,"[6] that is, Adler & Sullivan, who were officially hired on December 22, despite directorial doubts about Sullivan, his soaring reputation and Adler's strong assurances notwithstanding. Disregarding Sullivan's already extensive labor, therefore, the board went over its architects' heads. Perhaps it was only happy coincidence, or perhaps it was through Sullivan's (or Adler's) shrewd maneuvering, that William R. Ware, his old MIT professor, now director of Columbia University's Department of Architecture, was chosen to judge his latest plan. Writing to his brother, Albert, who had for a short time been living in Cairo, Illinois, Sullivan recorded his version of Ware's visit to Chicago.

"The professor has come and gone," he began on January 20, 1887, leaving in a closely argued five-page analysis "a very strong and sound endorsement." His only suggestions were for minor changes in detail: that the tower be more forthright, that the sequence of stories be expressed a bit differently. During his appearance before the Auditorium board, Ware was asked if he would have

VII.4 *Auditorium Building, preliminary scheme, 1886.*

produced the same result had he designed the building. Probably not, was his reply, "but if I had reached such a result, I should consider it the inspiration of my life." The board was "electrified," according to Sullivan, "and stared at each other." Peck was "completely knocked out. A & S stock rose into the hundreds," he exclaimed, "and I am considered an artist, it seems. Poor fools!" Although it is not at all clear which version of the building Ware so resoundingly endorsed—one of the two discussed above or another modification—making it impossible to determine if the tower pyramid or the "Gargantuan" oriels were his suggestions later removed by Sullivan or the architect's ideas stripped away by Ware, it is certain his recommendation gave Adler & Sullivan a tremendous boost. Collecting his $1000 fee, Ware returned to New York, agreeing to a final review later, and the board paid its architects a welcome $10,000 on account.[7]

After Ware's performance the directors adopted Adler & Sullivan's plans "in the main," but withheld approval of particulars. Meeting on January 29, they agreed to certain unspecified details but announced that its design would more than likely change even as the structure progressed so that no one could tell what the building would look like until the roof was on. Appearances will speak louder than words, Peck seemed to say, as if to stir up enthusiasm for a project that had already captured the public's fancy. All he could add was that alterations were proceeding "in the direction of severe treatment."[8] Dankmar Adler himself, not one to complain about clients, especially his friends, lamented their interference in this instance, particularly their rejection of external ornament and their indecision about program. "Not once, but a score of times," he wrote somewhat bitterly in 1892, the architects produced "a complete and well-rounded design," expressed on one occasion by nearly two hundred plans and diagrams, only to learn that new commercial considerations made "months of arduous labor" totally useless. Even during construction new requirements repeatedly forced them to scrap their drawings and begin all over again. The Auditorium might have been even better, Adler implied, "had the final intentions and resources of its owners been known to its architects at the outset." He especially regretted the facade's "severe simplicity," which he attributed to an unfortunate coincidence of three factors: uncertainty over the financial policy and changing commercial considerations of the sponsors, the architects' own shift from the "highly decorative effects" of their previous work, and "the deep impression made by [Henry] Richardson's 'Marshall Field Building' on the Directory of the Auditorium Association."[9]

VII.5 *Henry Richardson, Marshall Field Store, 1885.*

Marshall Field's Wholesale Store (sometimes called the Warehouse) made as deep an impression on Sullivan as it did on his clients, a fact Adler neglected to mention. Richardson's aesthetic simplifications and powerful massings had already crept into Sullivan's emerging style, but in 1886 his inescapable influence launched Sullivan on what was surely a Richardsonian rite-of-passage until he found his own métier in the skyscraper at the close of the decade. Designed early in 1885, the Field Building began to rise late the same year, prior to Richardson's premature death in 1886, and was nearly complete by early 1887, when Sullivan finally resolved the Auditorium facade. Like the lower portions of the latter, the seven-story Field Building was granite, with generous piers rising straight from street to flat roof. Both were of load-bearing, solid-wall, masonry construction, among the finest of the genre prior to universal adoption of the steel frame. Above its high base, the Field had a tier of windows in each bay, two separated by heavy mullions and lintels on the second and third floors, one tripartite window on the fourth arched to unite the whole. At the top of the next two-story section, every window was arched so that each pair halved the arch below it, doubling again on the seventh floor, this time to four rectangular windows per bay below the cornice, the sequence of stories from bottom to top being 1-3-2-1.

Sullivan did not need Marshall Field, the Auditorium's most generous backer, to call his attention to Richardson. Nor is it likely that Field used his clout with the board of directors to "influence" Sullivan to quote his wholesale store. The architect would have certainly bristled against that kind of interference. Still feeling his way with facades in 1887, however, he acknowledged his admiration for Richardson, whose work would help him find his own architectural language during the next few years. The taller Auditorium, Sullivan's most spectacular Richardsonian essay, is in many ways similar to the Field Building, especially on the exterior, even though the organization is 3-4-3, with minor horizontal divisions making it 1-2-4-2-1, in either case perfectly symmetrical. Above the three-story base, Sullivan stretched Richardson's large arches from three floors to four, keeping the arrangement of two windows per bay except, like Richardson, at the seventh story (the Field's fourth), where he emphasized the mullions even more. Next came two stories with two small arches (on the ninth) for each larger one below, and finally a top or tenth floor of rectangular windows, in this case three per bay instead of Richardson's four. In its floor sequence and fenestration rhythms, the Auditorium's facade practically duplicated the Field's on a larger scale, but in many particulars was necessarily quite different. The very presence of a seven-story tower, for example, clearly distinguished the two. Set off from the rest of the building by a simple but strong tenth-story cornice, it featured arched tiers of windows, compact loggia, and a small boxlike penthouse (a tiny eighteenth story) added to the design in 1889 as a United States Signal Service Station. Below the tower on Congress Street, a triple arch announced the theater, like another for the hotel entrance on Michigan, with a protruding loggia centered above it similar to its more conventional counterpart over the business entry on Wabash. Three additional doorway arches flanked by large windows on Congress Street and at the corners completed Sullivan's treatment of the commercial ground floor. When he met Peck in New York to get Ware's approval of the revised plans, as agreed, in February 1887, the exterior was substantially complete.[10] Sullivan could now turn inside, to the even more time-consuming ornamental work that for three years would test his energies and skill as they had not been tested before.

Work at the site had meanwhile begun. Demolition of the old buildings and excavations for the new started almost simultaneously in January 1887, signaling the speed with which the entire project was pushed from beginning to end. The first shovelful of dirt was removed on the twenty-fourth as two hundred men with thirty teams of horses, periodically huddling near barrel fires for warmth, hacked at the frozen ground and hauled away debris. All except the old Brunswick Hotel, its guests safe until the lease expired May 1, were dismantled by the first week in February, and by the twenty-fourth foundation borings were under way to determine the nature of the subsoil. Adler and Sullivan continued to plan—the one for a monumental engineering job, the other for incredibly extensive and intricate decorations, both for the disposition of interior space—to take estimates from the many builders hungering for a piece of the lucrative action, and began in the spring to award contracts for exterior and structural work. At the end of May, architects and sponsors agreed on the building material, a rose-tinted, coarse-grained granite that cut easily and took a high polish. Thanks to a new railroad line to Lake Superior from quarries at Hinsdale, Minnesota, about eighty miles from Duluth, the stone was available in Chicago for the first time.[11]

Originally to be used as facing over brick for all external walls, it was decided early in 1888 that to prevent the possibility of gloominess, the rusticated (rough-cut) darker Minnesota granite would give way at the fourth story to ashlar (smooth-cut) Indiana limestone in buff gray. With foundation excavations completed near the end of May, a $700 building permit secured on June 25, and subsurface construction begun July 1, the cornerstone laying and its inevitable ceremony took place on October 5, 1887, when Adler & Sullivan let contracts for hardwood finish, painting, elevators, and other interior work. By this time, according to *Building Budget,* a Chicago real estate magazine, "over 150 of the richest and best of our citizens have made handsome subscriptions to the stock." But even they could not prevent delays in delivery of the supposedly "inexhaustible" Minnesota granite, which soon proved insufficient in quantity for the entire building anyway. Stonemasons fell behind bricklayers and iron men who labored day and night under electric lights, another first for local building history. After working three months at a cost of $15,000 wages, twelve men completed scaffolding for the theater ceiling toward the end of the year. Long before all its huge arches were fixed in March 1888, roof tiles were being laid between those that were, providing partial shelter for workmen and their fires on the floor below. Construction sped through the winter, even on outside walls when weather permitted, so that by Christmas 1887 Auditorium spokesmen announced that after initial doubts the theater would surely be ready for the Democratic and Republican national conventions the next summer.[12]

Chicago wooed them both, but the Democrats demurred in favor of St. Louis. To get the hall ready for the Republicans on June 19, Auditorium promoters adopted the concept of erecting one building inside another. Adler & Sullivan had done this before, at the Interstate Exposition site in 1885, but here it was another irksome example of midstream client course changing so annoying to Adler. Given delays in granite delivery, the decision actually made sense, but of course the overriding concern was to placate the GOP, regardless of construction schedules or architect grumbling. At least two significant consequences followed: the hall was to be finished sooner than expected, before the outer walls, putting greater pressure on Sullivan, and to speed up delivery the sponsors decided to purchase the Minnesota quarries, reorganizing its work force. By the end of March 1888, the ceiling, its arches, the walls, and masonry work of the auditorium proper—all to be deep inside the larger building—were done. Stone arrived faster in the spring, so that at the end of June, the granite and limestone walls reached five stories, hiding most of the theater from view. Even in the rush to accommodate Republican conventioneers, however, there were no structural compromises or unnecessary additions. In the theater delegates saw the same walls, ceiling, balcony, galleries, stage, and proscenium arch that others would see eighteen months later when the room was dedicated. Only a few wooden partitions and temporary floors, a large sounding board, seating on the stage, the platform, and framework for red, white, and blue patriotic bunting were installed especially for the occasion.

Enclosed in an otherwise completed facility, the delegates were almost unaware of the noisy work outside the scene of their deliberations. The consensus was that the Auditorium theater was just about as magnificent a space as any Republican had ever witnessed. And elaborate efforts had indeed been made on their behalf. Every square inch of the 120-by-260-foot space was carefully utilized. Seventy-six hundred opera chairs, supplemented by standing room for fourteen hundred, were arranged on the floor, balcony, galleries, and for special guests onstage overlooking the platform in the orchestra. The electrical systems were tested and ready, and the ceiling studded with lights in the shape of stars. The cloth and paper decorations—not Sullivan's, of course—supervised by the Republican National Committee were deemed more than worthy.[13] And once again, as in Adler's previous buildings, the acoustics were perfect, amazingly so. Accompanying a group of political dignitaries on a June 8 tour, Adler climbed to the highest seat to speak to the rest of the party 180 feet away on stage. "With our voices pitched a little above the conversational tone," one of them exclaimed, "we could distinctly understand him and he us."

The sight lines were also a cause for celebration. "They are so perfect," another functionary remarked, "that the space for the delegates may be seen from any seat in the building. This fact, together with the splendid acoustical properties," he added, "makes [every] seat as nearly as desirable as [any other]."[14] Since this was virtually the first time anyone other than Auditorium personnel and workmen had gotten a close look at the long-awaited theater, Chicagoans could hardly be denied their own inspection, especially after out-of-towners had had their say. And once inside, local luminaries set new standards for boosterish hyperbole. Republican Sam Adams surveyed the hall from a gallery with unconcealed pride. "Biggest thing in the world," he boasted. Recalling his recent tour of Milan's La Scala, Naples's San Carlo, and Venice's Pergola, Adams asked his companions: "What are they to this? Mere molehills," was his own reply. "Europe can't build theatres. Europe has lost the art. Chicago overtops them all. Look at the people [down there] on the floor," he proclaimed. "What pygmies they appear."[15]

The biggest and the best—that was Chicago. Already the Auditorium had become *the* symbol of municipal progress, and if Sam Adams's assessment of European opera houses demonstrated his own and his city's chauvinism, clearer heads prevailed in other parts of town, among them Dankmar Adler's. Partly for vacation but mostly to gather information, Adler visited several of the same concert halls in July and August 1888, paying special attention to the Budapest Opera House, reopened in 1884 after a serious fire with the first fully equipped hydraulic stage in the world.[16] Sullivan stayed home to work on the seemingly endless interior decorations, a staggering job requiring additional staff, more than thirty in all by the end of the year. One of the early newcomers was twenty-one-year-old Frank Lloyd Wright, hired away from architect Joseph L. Silsbee, probably early in 1888, to develop Sullivan's rough sketches of ornament into working drawings. A year or so later, Sullivan again tapped Silsbee, this time for teenager George Elmslie (1871–1952), who would be his invaluable assistant for more than twenty years until he opened his own office in 1909. Adler returned to find the Auditorium's backers determined to raise the tower from sixteen to seventeen stories, adding eighteen feet in height and twelve hundred tons in weight, another mid-course change, in this case causing problems for the foundations. Otherwise, things were progressing nicely. The architects let the $44,000 organ contract to Roosevelt's of New York in August. Except for the top floor, the Wabash Avenue front was completed on schedule in September amid hopes the entire business wing would be ready for May 1889 rentals, thereby generating income well before the hotel and theater openings projected for the fall—if all went well. It was not so much that the backers were financially hard-pressed, only that the total cost of the building was now acknowledged to be approaching $3,000,000.[17]

Even at this stage of the Auditorium's history, its impact on the city was profound. As with other large building projects, like the recently opened Brooklyn Bridge, it was hazardous for laboring men. At the end of March 1888, after a workman was seriously injured in a fall from the fourth story to the basement, it was disclosed there had been so many accidents already that to avoid labor unrest, contractors had taken the unusual steps of insuring each worker's life for $2,000 and paying two-thirds wages during layoffs due to job-related disability.[18] At the other end of the class spectrum were the more fortunate real estate speculators. Auditorium second vice-president Nathaniel Fairbank, for instance, had bought up property all around the immediate neighborhood. "Plans are maturing for . . . several new shops in the vicinity," the *Tribune* reported in March 1888, while older buildings were sprucing up for an anticipated upsurge in retail trade. Shortly after Fairbank acquired this third Wabash Avenue property in May, a large new structure was projected for a corner of Congress across from the Auditorium, and during the next few months, wholesale furniture firms began clustering nearby. "Undoubtedly the erection of the Auditorium building was the prime cause of the transactions," the *Tribune* observed in August, "that structure now being looked upon as the center of a new business district." It was safe to assume that Fairbank's and other "holdings will soon have an enhanced value."[19]

By February 1889 *The Economist,* a local commercial and real estate magazine, no longer looked to the future. Noting the rapidity with which the Auditorium was renting and nearby enterprise increasing, it concluded that "an important new business center . . . has already been established." It therefore endorsed the proposal by a number of prominent Chicagoans to widen Congress Street from sixty-six to one hundred feet, the better to accommodate large numbers of carriages at theater performances, to provide a "little room for display of the great facade," and, perhaps most salient of all, to increase the value of surrounding property. It had long been considered unfortunate "that so magnificent a structure . . . should front on so narrow a street," *The Economist* noted, speaking for the promoters who had contemplated the change for some time. Secured with the support of other interested parties, a city ordinance in February 1889 added thirty-four feet to Congress Street's south side.[20] The Auditorium Association had already completed another transaction with potentially important implications, the construction of an oil tank on the lakeshore connected by pipeline to the building's engine room. In order to keep as little flammable fuel on the premises as possible, oil would be shipped by rail to the tank for storage, but would eventually come directly from outside the city by underground pipes. Businessmen watched the experiment as carefully as they shopped for property in the Auditorium vicinity.[21]

Accompanied by Senator Chauncey Depew, Cornelius Vanderbilt visited the Auditorium in October 1888. "Wonderful! Wonderful!" he declared after his tour. "The most impressive structure in the world," echoed his friend Depew. Such unrestrained enthusiasm from prominent New York capitalists was hardly a disincentive for potential Second City tenants eyeing the Auditorium tower. "In these days of rapid elevators," a real estate journal explained, "so far as light, ventilation and quiet are concerned the higher the better. Merely in the matter of freedom from noise such quarters possess great advantage over lower stories."[22] By March 1889 it was further reported that investors had underestimated the Auditorium's earning capacity. Wabash Avenue frontage was renting at double the anticipated rates, while the hotel owners—almost a year before entertaining any guests—were said to have offered a "bonus" of $100,000 to secure their lease. In April investors announced their continued satisfaction with rapid rentals, and on May 1, as if giving their ultimate imprimatur to the project, Adler & Sullivan moved into temporary tenth-floor offices prior to occupying their permanent sixteenth-story suite shortly after July 1.[23]

As more details fell into place, citizen anticipation rose, stimulated periodically by tantalizing reports from Auditorium officials. When Adler and Sullivan escorted Peck, the city's mayor, and a party of businessmen through the nearly completed structure in June 1889, Italian artisans were laying marble mosaic—some of the twenty-five thousand square feet in the building—on the Michigan Avenue loggia floor, while other workmen installed hydraulic lifts that would soon enable stagehands, Peck proudly explained, to set up one scene even while another was in place. To considerable fanfare, the first official tenants arrived in July, the four-year-old Chicago Conservatory of Music and Dramatic Art, occupying the entire specially designed Wabash Avenue ninth floor, with additional eighth-floor studio space. By the end of September, the signal station atop the tower was ready, as were most of the building's "unique" decorations, and that month the *Tribune* devoted more than half its front page to the history of "The Great Auditorium," announcing that on October 2 the copestone—the topmost and final piece of masonry on the seventeenth floor—would at last be set in place.[24]

On that happy occasion, the Grand Lodge of Free and Accepted Masons, hundreds of white-aproned men, marched through downtown streets to the intersection of Congress and Wabash, where for the first time in Illinois history, before thousands of enthusiastic spectators, they publicly performed the ceremony of topping out a building. Seated on the platform, Ferdinand Peck, Martin Ryerson, other Auditorium sponsors, the mayor of Chicago, and Louis Sullivan learned that when the stone was set in place at the southwest corner of the tower, it would bear two copper plates inscribed with the date, and names of Masonic officials, the Auditorium's board of directors, and the architects. To climax the ceremony, Grand Master Pearson introduced Sullivan, who responded, according to ritual:

> Most worshipful Grand Master: Having been entrusted with the duty of designing this edifice and of supervising and directing the workmen in its erection, and having been enabled to witness its completion, I now, with due respect present to you for inspection and approval the last stone that enters into its composition, and with it the implements of operative Masonry, there being no further occasion for their use.

Sullivan handed three tools of the trade to the grand master, who, with his deputy and the senior and junior grand wardens, reported that the stone was indeed square, level, and plumb. Turning to the architect, he said: "Mr. Sullivan: From you, as the architect of this building, I accept the work, assuring you of my hearty approval, and will forthwith consecrate it according to ancient usage."[25] Ten days later, on October 12, the five-hundred-seat seventh-floor recital hall was dedicated, again to enthusiastic popular acclaim.

But the best, as often happens, came last. On Monday night, December 9, 1889, at a performance by America's operatic idol Mme. Adelina Patti, the Auditorium theater was dedicated before a splendidly bedecked throng, including President Benjamin Harrison and Vice-President Levi Morton—returning to the site of their nominations eighteen months before—the governor of Illinois, the mayor of Chicago, other public officials, the Auditorium's financial backers, and the city's most elite citizens. Every paper in town recorded every detail of that fabulous night. Dignitaries outdid each other bestowing encomiums, but even President Harrison was something of a warm-up for the hero of the hour, Ferdinand Peck, who recounted highlights of the Herculean building task to rounds of applause and huzzahs every time he mentioned the magnificent hall. A thousand special guests on stage and in the boxes and four thousand others in regular seats listened happily as speaker after speaker praised Chicago's achievement. When Mme Patti at last arose for the evening's finale, she did not wax operatic; that could wait for her Tuesday-night debut as prima donna in *Romeo and Juliet.* ("The Auditorium is perfect," she would announce in Wednesday's papers. "The acoustics are simply perfect." How did it measure up to the Metropolitan Opera House? "Why, there's simply no comparison at all. The Met is a beautiful place, but one might as well try to sing in a balloon.") Instead, as a fitting climax to a magical evening, Patti sang "Home Sweet Home" and, in response to thunderous applause, encored with "Swiss Echo Song." After more than three years of anticipation, Chicagoans were already sentimental about their new opera house. The city, at least large parts of it that night, literally rejoiced at its good fortune.[26]

Louis Sullivan and Dankmar Adler were there that night, of course. One can only imagine their thoughts and feelings as they listened to superlatives lavished over their work, the finest building in Chicago, maybe in America, everyone agreed. Sullivan may have felt most comfortable leaning against his magnificent hotel bar, as one writer believed, imbibing an endless flow of the evening's good spirits.[27] But it is no conjecture that in all the fancy speeches and flowery praise that evening, Adler and Sullivan were never mentioned by name. They were alluded to at times, and in his remarks Peck referred to "the talented architects," but on that historic occasion nothing, not one word, was said about "the men," as one observer put it the following day, "who have worked as few men work on a building they are constructing." The oversight was probably not intentional. Swept along by the fervor, those who could take the credit for paying the bills claimed the night failing, unlike the Masons, to share the limelight with the architects. Perhaps it was simply carelessness, or as one person implied, a lack of local civility that tarnished for Adler and Sullivan their finest hour.

In a letter of protest to the *Tribune*'s editor the next morning, "one of the contractors" attempted to remedy the situation by emphasizing that "Mr. Sullivan was the guiding spirit, everywhere and all over, attending to the smallest details, giving up a great deal more time than his health warranted, until, in fact, his nervous force gave way, and he was some weeks in recovering. Had such an event as the opening of this building occurred in Paris or in any large city in England," the writer continued, "the architects would have been among the first called before the people and publicly thanked upon the stage. It is their due, and I am surprised that the citizens of Chicago should neglect to give the full measure of praise to whom it belongs."[28] Sullivan could not have said it better. If he was bitter about the slight, if that is what it was, neither he nor Adler complained. Nor did they neglect their final duties. For another month or more, they supervised the last details in the rest of the building, principally the hotel, which opened in January, until in February 1890 the largest and most expensive edifice in America built by private capital was done. By then Louis Sullivan had left town for a well-deserved vacation.

The building he left behind was a masterpiece. Together and independently he and his partner surmounted huge obstacles to create a monument to themselves and for their city. Adler's engineering, first of all, was brilliant. The three main parts of the Auditorium—business block, hotel, and theater—were separated inside by load-bearing brick walls faced in masonry resting on continuous concrete foundations reinforced by heavy timbers in the deeper courses underneath steel rails. Nonstructural loads fell on pyramidal isolated footings on a concrete bed strengthened by one to three courses of railroad bars. The various foundations were further connected by sand- and rubble-filled trenches designed with the help of other devices to prevent rot by keeping the timbers constantly immersed in water. Although the foundations were able to transfer four thousand pounds per square foot to the soil, the heavier tower presented a major difficulty. Weighing almost sixteen thousand tons above the tenth story, it delivered 480 pounds per square foot more pressure than the rest of the building. So Adler carried it on a kind of floating solid raft, sixty-seven and one-half by one hundred by seven feet thick (its 6750 square feet extending beyond the tower's 2800), comprised of two layers of timber, three each of steel rails, twelve- and fifteen-inch I-beams "crossing each other," Adler reported, "as to distribute the weight over the entire surface."[29]

But even trickier than distribution was the settlement problem,

VII.6 *Auditorium Hotel Bar.* From *Architectural Record,* 1892.

which Adler solved most ingeniously, "a regular Columbus egg stunt," Sullivan recalled in admiration,[30] referring to the fifteenth-century game whose trick required creative thinking to figure out. Foundations would normally settle uniformly as the walls rose and weight increased, but under the tower they were designed to carry a heavier load. If its walls were built up at the same rate as those adjacent, its foundations would settle more slowly than those next to it, and the walls would tear and crack. But if, on the other hand, the tower was built independently, it would be virtually impossible to bond it to adjoining walls or achieve level courses. So after much deliberation, Adler improvised "what amounted to a kind of crude prestressing of the supporting soil," one historian wrote. By piling vast quantities of pig iron and brick in the basement and lower stories, he artificially increased the load on the foundations as the tower rose toward the tenth story (the height of the main building), all the while maintaining an exact mathematical ratio between the weight of the tower to its foundation capacity and the weight of adjacent walls to their foundation capacities. In this manner full settlement for the entire building was achieved when it reached the tenth story.

Above that point the artificial load had to be translated into real

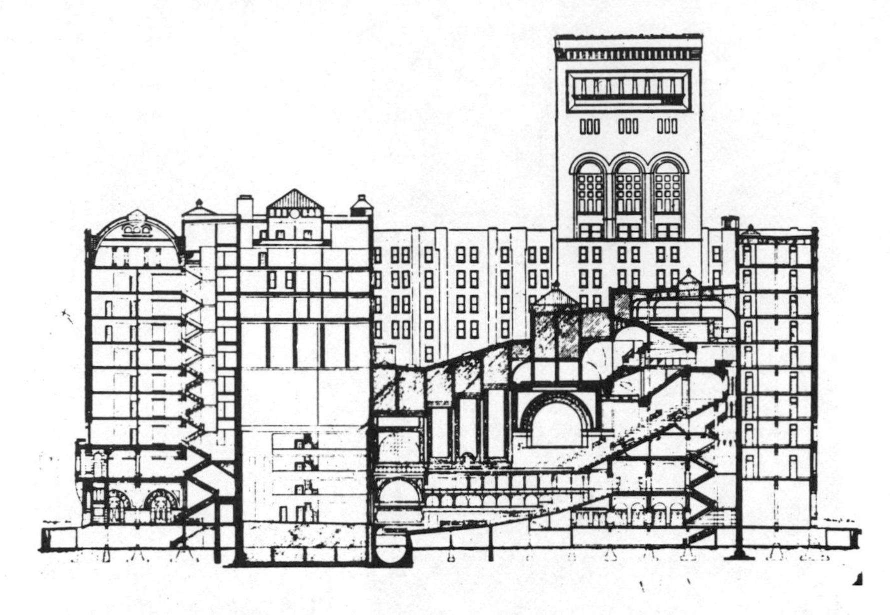

VII.7 *Auditorium Building, section.* From *Architectural Record,* 1892.

load, accomplished by removing pig iron and bricks in proportion to further increase in the tower's weight as it was built up. When it topped out at ninety-five feet above the main roof line, all the artificial weight was gone and the total was the same as at the tenth story. (When Adler introduced caisson foundations going to bedrock at the 1893 Chicago Stock Exchange, this sort of Herculean effort was no longer required.) The total settlement was eighteen inches, necessitating lead connections to absorb strain on iron pipe and conduit. This was somewhat more than originally anticipated, due to additions during construction, among them the twelve-hundred-ton seventeenth story a year after foundations were in. Adler nevertheless insisted his method proved that equal loading per unit of soil, even with different adjacent foundations on Chicago clay, would produce equal settlement.[31]

The tower was not the only, although it was the most serious, of Adler's concerns that led to pioneering solutions. The exceptional amount of mechanical theater equipment, for instance, required an especially deep basement, twenty feet below grade under the stage—and here was the difficulty—placing it seven feet below the mean water level of Lake Michigan. The problem was not so much sealing concrete—that had been done before—as doing it against unprecedented pressure. Adler's novel solution was a laminated floor built up in alternating layers of concrete, asphalt, and asphalt-saturated felt weighted down by more concrete and steel rails to offset the presure of underground water. Adler was particularly pleased with his solutions for other, more minor, difficulties; the need to take some weight from the adjacent Studebaker Building, for example, by methods he carefully illustrated in *Inland Architect* or, when he found it necessary to make such small foundations for columns bearing nominal loads that they settled too slowly, his use of screws that could be periodically tightened to insure equal settlement. For these and other problems discussed below, Adler demonstrated time and again that mix of ingenuity, pragmatism, and sheer genius that made him a giant among structural engineers.[32]

Like Central Music Hall ten years earlier, the Auditorium Building was a shell of commercial space on three sides (south, west, and east) surrounding the theater, which at no point touched the street. Determined by lighting requirements in the hotel and office block, the fenestration was therefore modeled by Sullivan into a facade expressing the power and simplicity of monumental masonry construction and the efficiency of American entrepreneurialism. Most of the 136 offices were in the Wabash Avenue wing, where a series of arched

VII.8 *Auditorium tower detail.* Photo by Robert Twombly.

and rectangularly framed doorways under a five-bay second-story loggia gave access to shops and lobby. Less ceremoniously stated than the hotel and theater entrances, this one was nevertheless a dramatic addition to the avenue, in part because it served as an auxiliary exit for theater galleries connected to the sixth-floor corridor by bridges and doors. The seventh-floor recital hall over the galleries was also entered from the business wing. Except for the Chicago Conservatory of Music and Dramatic Art on the two stories above that, the rest of the wing was devoted to conventional office requirements.

The more prestigious offices in the tower were reached by elevator from the Congress Street lobby. Of greatest interest here was Adler & Sullivan's Suite 1600, occupying the entire sixteenth and seventeenth floors. Visitors emerged from two elevators in the southwest corner of

VII.9 *Auditorium Building from Wabash Avenue.* Photo by J. W. Taylor.

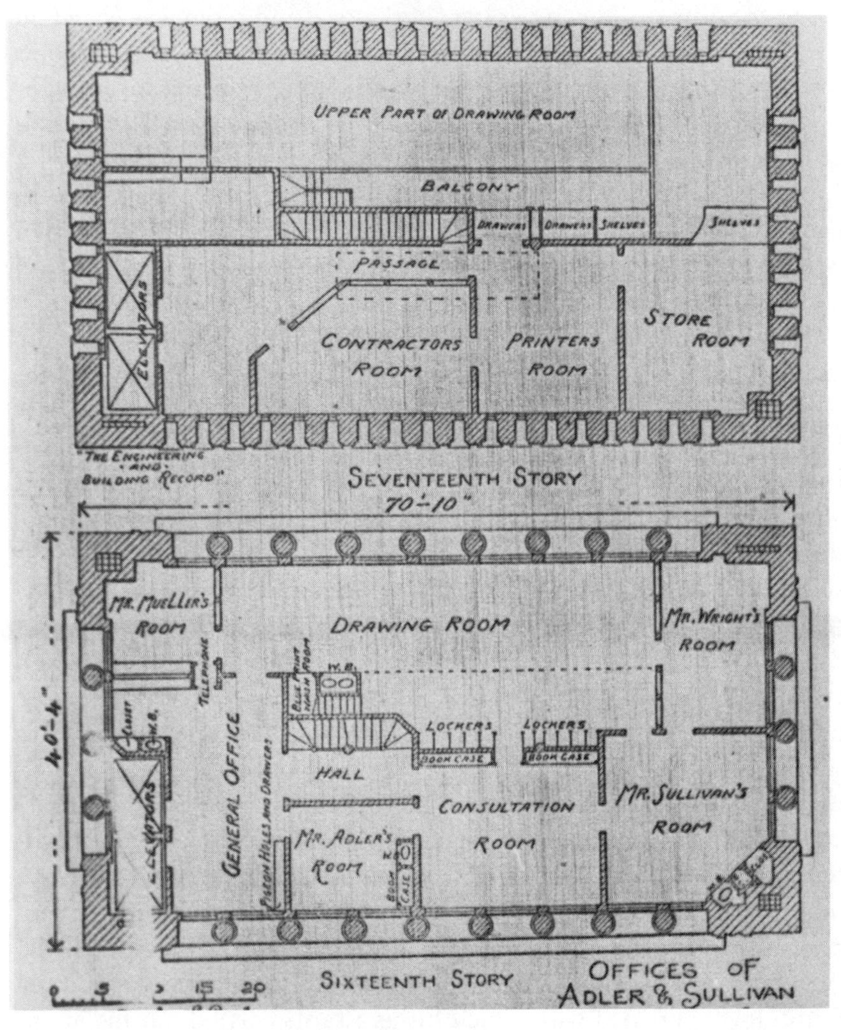

VII.10 *Adler & Sullivan office plans.* From *Engineering & Building Record,* 1890.

the reception area and waiting room next to Dankmar Adler's office—he handled clients—which was separated by a conference room from Louis Sullivan's larger office, tucked away in the southeast corner. From there, one door opened to the room assigned to Frank Lloyd Wright, by 1890 Sullivan's principal assistant, another to the two-story drafting room running approximately forty-five feet along the north wall, connected at one end to Wright and at the other to the office of Paul Mueller, for years a structural engineer with

Adler & Sullivan. The upper part of the drafting room was edged on the seventeenth floor by a storage balcony on the south next to rooms for contractors, printers, and additional storage. From larger windows behind the sixteenth-story colonnade and from smaller rectangular openings above, the suite was awash with light.[33] In his quiet corner, Louis Sullivan could shut himself off from office bustle to confer with Wright, or from his perch high above the city look down Michigan Boulevard toward the burgeoning South Side, where several of his residences were within his view.

Here it was that Sullivan did some of finest work, including the last drawings for the Auditorium itself. His method of design had not changed much over the years, nor departed very far from techniques he had learned at the Ecole des Beaux-Arts. One scholar believes that as many as four types of drawings for each piece of ornament were produced in this office: a small-scale summary sketch, a more detailed larger sketch, a working drawing at fixed scale, and a full-sized working drawing. While it is impossible to prove that any particular ornament was taken through all four steps, drawings in Sullivan's hand show that, at one time or another, he produced each type. Sullivan ordinarily directed an assistant, often Wright, before he left the office in 1893, or George Elmslie afterward, to ready his summary sketches under careful supervision for the modeler or carver. When he was particularly enamored, or if the firm was especially rushed—as a drawing signed on Christmas Day, 1890, attests—Sullivan might do the working drawings himself. But no matter the development process, his ornament and architecture generally show little modification from original sketch to executed work, suggesting both the persistence of his training in the esquisse, and the faithfulness and skill with which his assistants carried out his intentions. Sullivan seems to have considered mechanical instruments—T square, compass, and ruler—encumbrances to the creative process, preferring to draw freehand, although this is not absolutely certain.[34] It does appear, however, that day or night, no matter the hour, hidden away in his sixteenth-floor garret, which may have reminded him of his attic room in Paris, Sullivan devoted much more time to work than to anything else in life. Certainly from 1886 to 1890 he had to because the Auditorium, not the only major project during these years by any means, was an incredibly demanding job.

His decorative achievements were best revealed in the hotel and concert hall. The L-shaped Auditorium Hotel fronted on Michigan

Boulevard but continued around the corner along Congress to the east line of the tower. Flanking the theater on two sides, it was only forty-five feet deep on average, but by an ingenious organization contained four hundred generous guest rooms, 275 facing the street, 90 with private baths, a large lobby and reception area, a magnificent bar, a dining room, banquet hall, café, parlors, kitchens, barbershop, and other service rooms. From the triple-arched entry, hotel guests walked into the sumptuous lobby through Sullivan's ornamented colonnade and across his marble mosaic floor to the desk in the right of three more arches. Overhead were Sullivan's geometric stencils between the ceiling's beams, and his gilded plaster reliefs in the archivolts, friezes, and on the upper walls. To the left of the desk facing the entry from the larger central arch was the magnificent grand staircase, expansive, majestic, and yet another engineering challenge for Adler because its thirty-two-foot opening required huge girders to carry the upper stories. But, once registered, most hotel guests were unaware of this as they climbed the stairs past Sullivan's floral balusters, decorated strings, and ornate riser backs en route to the second-floor reception room.

Here, they encountered a stunning view of Lake Michigan through the originally open, later glassed-in, loggia projecting over

VII.11 *Auditorium Hotel lobby.* From *Architectural Record,* 1892.

VII.12 *Auditorium Hotel grand staircase.* From *Architectural Record,* 1892.

the hotel entrance. The reception room was in gold-accented greens with highly patterned Wilton carpeting, claret draperies, and a large fireplace and stained-glass windows on the north wall, plus ceiling medallions with sprays of electric lights, column capitals and brackets, wall panels, and balusters on the private staircase to the guest rooms above, some of the hundreds of striking decorative effects Sullivan fashioned for the building. When they returned to the lobby, hotel patrons might turn right at the foot of the grand staircase to the café in the southeast corner of the ground floor, again observing Sullivan's ornament in the arched entrances, over the beams, and in bands at wall tops. Connected to the west end of the café, farther along Congress Street, was the Auditorium Bar, its elegant oak counter set between richly carved columns at either end. The long, narrow room was in several shades of brown, complemented by a random mosaic floor, rectangular inlaid wall panels, richly ornamented friezes in bronze, and octagonal light posts subdividing the space. "One of the most beautiful bar rooms in architectural history" quickly became a favorite watering hole for well-heeled Chicagoans but, like so many other landmarks that once graced the city, was lost along with the café in 1952 when an arcade was cut through the south end of the building to widen Congress Street.

The main dining room was placed on the tenth floor only after the architects convinced management that its building-long view of Michigan Boulevard and the lake would enrich the gustatory experience. Considered by many the finest public space in the hotel, its barrel-vault ceiling sprang directly from the floor and was separated at either end from smaller dining areas by a row of polygonal mahogany columns under wide friezes of ornamental plaster surmounted by picturesque murals. Divided into panels by five trusses supporting a portion of the building's roof, the ceiling was richly stenciled in dull gold on white ground and the arches faced with soffit panels of plaster relief centering on electric lights. Connected to this room by bridges, the structurally independent four-story kitchens plus theater machinery, together weighing 2500 tons, were carried on 110-foot wrought-iron trusses spanning the auditorium's stage. The 660-ton banquet hall and ballroom was also supported by trusses, a span of 118 feet, because it, too, was planned and added after the theater's bearing walls on which it rested were completed in 1888. Although improvised products of necessity, both truss systems were further examples, as if any more were needed, of Adler's daring engineering.

VII.13 *Auditorium Hotel main dining room.* From *Architectural Record,* 1892.

Like the main dining room, the banquet hall was elaborately ornamented with stenciling, stained glass, decorative lights, and plaster relief on beams, columns, and arches. Tables and chairs could be lowered into an opening at one end to clear the floor for dancing. Two rows of unusual chandeliers hanging from ceiling panels were additional indications of Sullivan's imaginative treatment of light fixtures and, probably of interest to many guests at the time, demonstrated that the Auditorium was one of the first buildings wired for electricity at construction. Adler wrote in praise of his partner that the banquet hall was "at once aggressively unconventional and original and still extremely delicate and refined . . . the culmination of the boldness, originality, and refinement which are characteristic of the decoration of this building." Hugh Morrison judged the main dining room, on the other hand, to be "one of the most beautiful rooms which Sullivan designed," adding that if nothing else were to survive from all his work, the two rooms alone "would establish Sullivan as a great architect."[35]

Everything in the Auditorium Building, including this array of artistic and engineering brilliance, was in a sense incidental to the the-

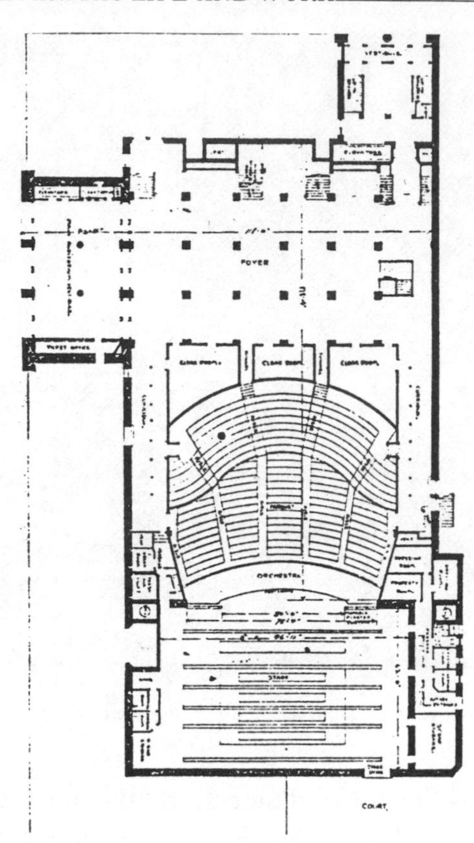

VII.14 *Auditorium Theater, first-floor plan.* From *Engineering Magazine*, 1894.

ater, the centerpiece and raison d'être for the entire undertaking, and Sullivan's greatest achievement, not that Adler's was inconsiderable. The box office lobby under the Congress Street tower led through six doors to a ground-floor, 80-by-118-foot foyer with tunnels opening to the orchestra. A main foyer above led to the rear of the parquet, and more tunnels and foyers to the balcony and galleries at various levels. The hall's general dimensions of 118 by 246 feet, an area of almost thirty thousand square feet, did not include parlors, dressing rooms, elevator shafts, entrances, exits, and the like, some of which, in Adler's words, "encroach and penetrate the surrounding business and hotel buildings, some in one story only, others through from two to six stories."[36] The main floor rose seventeen feet from the orchestra front following the lines of Scott Russell's isacoustic curve to seat fourteen hundred persons. The eighty-foot-deep elliptical balcony tapering to narrow sides sat over sixteen hundred, above that two galleries held another five hundred each, and the forty boxes an ad-

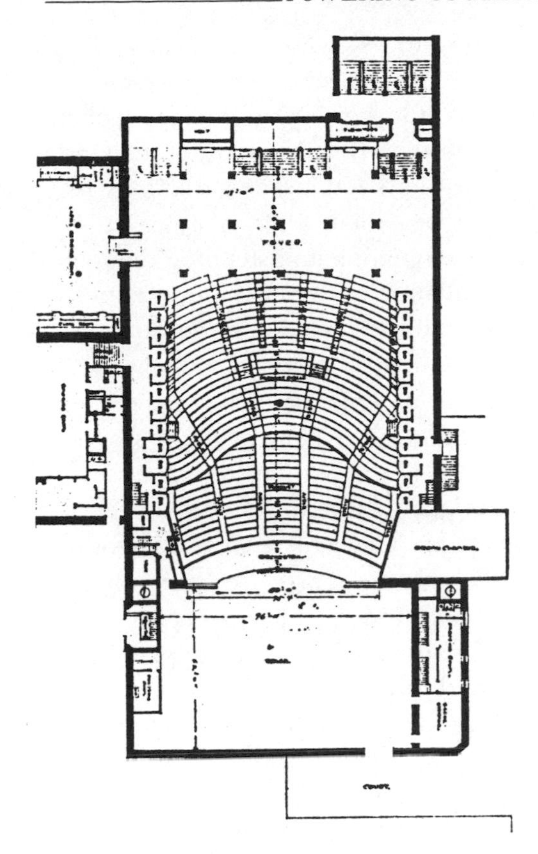

VII.15 *Auditorium Theater, second-floor plan.* From *Engineering Magazine,* 1894.

ditional two hundred, for a total of slightly over forty-two hundred, twelve hundred more than the Metropolitan Opera House in New York, previously America's largest concert hall. The boxes were arranged in two tiers on each side of the parquet, the lower a curving arcade of arches supporting the second. Together they were notably more open and airy than those in most other theaters.

After consulting with concert artists and structural experts, Adler devised a system for reducing the seating when circumstances required. The coved ceiling over the second gallery could be lowered with chains and hinges to block it off completely. Similarly, the underside of its floor could swing down to screen out the lower gallery. Both these hinged ceilings weighed twenty tons but were counterbalanced so effectively that six men could raise or lower them in twenty minutes. Each was received by custom-made fittings on the gallery railings, and in either case, up or down, Sullivan ornamented them to fit perfectly with the architectural scheme of the hall. The rear portion of the balcony, furthermore, could be curtained off across the row of columns supporting the lower gallery. By these devices the theater's seating capacity could be reduced to 2574 (which some still considered too big for certain events). If, on the other hand, more and different space were required for larger gatherings like conventions or society balls, Adler provided other alternatives. By lifting the reducing curtain from the opening and stepping the stage from front to rear with hydraulic lifts, more than five hundred seats could be added to the room. The parquet could also be expanded into its foyer, the boxes reseated, and their corridors utilized for a total capacity of seven thousand. The stage could be cleared for dancing, and a hardwood floor ordinarily stored away in sections laid over the orchestra and front half of the parquet to make a ballroom, a convention hall for up to eight thousand persons, or even an indoor sports stadium when "soft" or "Chicago" ball, among other games, was played during the 1890s. No matter its size, any audience could leave through numerous exits in less than five minutes.

The 70-by-110-foot stage (with a 95-foot loft for rigging) was divided into eleven sections raised and lowered by the same hydraulic system that operated the building's thirteen elevators. Variegated terrain, wavelike and rocking motions, disappearances, and a complete range of dramatic effects were therefore possible. An endless canvas roll on a track around the sides and rear of the stage was painted the colors of the sky in every season of the year and every weather condition, the rigging loft held eighty tons of miscellaneous apparatus, and an electrical screen controlled 5000 houselights, 150 footlights, six borders with 165 lights each, and an artificial moon, stars, and lightning. There were transparent clouds to play against the endless horizon and three curtains weighing sixteen tons each. This and more of the most modern equipment provided every kind of theatrical option in space ample enough for elaborate productions—Wagnerian opera was popular among Chicago's large German population—with enormous casts. All personnel was comfortably accommodated in a musicians' room for a hundred-piece orchestra, thirty fully equipped dressing rooms, six larger ones for principals, and a stage reception area. When it opened, the Chicago Auditorium Theater was immediately deemed one of the finest in the country, if not the world.

Sullivan's work in it was quickly recognized as a masterpiece of decorative art. Adler's acoustical requirements again formed the pa-

VII.16 *Auditorium Theater, view from stage.* From *Architectural Record,* 1892.

VII.17 *Auditorium Theater, view toward stage.* From *Architectural Record,* 1892.

rameters of his inspiration. At its maximum opening, the stage was seventy-five feet wide by forty feet high. From a point six feet back of the apron's lip the room flared outward and upward with wall and ceiling surfaces well broken. With their faces and soffits ornamented in gold relief, four elliptical arches, each wider and higher toward the rear, divided the ceiling into smooth ivory panels of the most delicate, lacelike tracery acting as sound reflectors. Hung from iron trusses carrying the 600-ton banquet room above, the arches were not structural, though they appeared to be, but Sullivan made them the basis of his decorative scheme. Their repeated curves are strongly rhythmical and grandly majestic, framing the stage as they determine the hall's ambiance. Chevron moldings divide their faces into hexagons enclosing foliated designs that flower into electric lights, into grilled bosses (like beehives) hiding air inlets, and into smaller triangles with additional foliage. Like jewels sparkling against an old-gold background, the lights run down the arches across the box tops like an illuminated necklace, tiara perhaps, for the entire room. To the rear of the arches, where the coved ceiling leaps dramatically to give sight lines to the galleries, Sullivan placed an immense skylight in stained glass. The proscenium wings and reducing curtain in luxuriously patterned gold leaf and the full-width mural atop the arch made the view of the stage unforgettable, but hardly less so than the vista back toward the rear of the hall. Rich but simple ornament everywhere added up to a Sullivan showcase. Even paintings on side walls referred to "Inspiration," the prose poem he read to the Western Association of Architects in December 1886. If the banquet hall and main dining room established Sullivan as a great architect, the Auditorium Theater won him a place in the annals of art, *Interior Design* magazine decided eighty years later, equal to Picasso and Chagall.[37]

Earlier critics were just as impressed. "In the interior of the great hall itself," *American Architect* declared, "the sight is one of the most remarkable of its kind in the world," not so much because of the decoration, "for that is comparatively simple, but it is almost entirely the result of the splendid architectural lines and the vast sweep that one gets." The editors of *Industrial Chicago* added that "a volume might be devoted to the glories of this one room and yet not be a complete description of all it presents." Speaking of the building as a whole, the authors of *King's Handbook of the United States* claimed the Auditorium as "one of the high culminating points of American" life, "the 'Parthenon' of modern civilization." Agreeing with this assessment, the *Daily Inter-Ocean* called it "the most splendid tribute to the genius of art on the American continent. . . . It was builded to the ages, and it will endure with the nation, and only fall into ruin when the great principles upon which this government is based have been overwhelmed by the folly and degeneracy of man," that is, probably never.[38] Writing a bit later, in the four-year-old *Architectural Record*, by 1895 the most influential professional magazine in the country, the prominent critic Montgomery Schuyler was rhetorically more dignified but just as complimentary. To Adler and to Sullivan, his words of approval were probably the most welcome of all, since they appeared in the forty-five-page second installment of his Great American Architects series. What he said, and their very inclusion in the series, was the highest form of praise they could have received.[39]

Schuyler's thoughts about the exterior, first of all, would inform critical judgment for the next century. Acknowledging at the outset his immense regard for the building, he then pointed out what he thought were its flaws: the Congress Street arches were too "huddled," not nearly as impressive as the hotel entrance, when it should have been the other way around. "Probably a single great opening at the base of the tower would have conveyed the sense of [largeness] more forcibly than the three." The tower itself, moreover, was not sufficiently emphasized below its tenth-floor cornice, which looked like a belt interrupting its top-to-bottom unity. But Schuyler's major complaint was with the principal ten-story wall, especially the middle portion of the 3-4-3 division he found too nearly equal. Had this four-story section been elongated to six and been set off more decisively from the top floors, and had the horizontal members received greater emphasis, he believed, the facade would have been stronger and more monumental. For the base of the building and the tower above the tenth-floor cornice, however, he had nothing but praise.

The success of the theater, on the other hand, "is striking and unchallenged." With its general forms "determined . . . entirely by acoustical considerations," it was "a most impressive and quite unique interior." The concentric elliptical arches framing the stage for the spectators brought all parts of the auditorium, "huge as it is," into much closer intimacy with the performers than in smaller, more conventional theaters, and did so with "a very noble largeness and simplicity, which the designer has been careful not to impair by his detail, rich and intricate as this often is, or by his color-decoration." This "great and simple" space with expanding arches above and expanding "terraces"—widening plateaus of seats—below, offering equal hospitality to all regardless of location or ticket price in contrast to "royal" or "imperial" opera houses, was "a new kind of art," he contended, "an art of democracy." Schuyler disagreed with "some of his professional brethren" who, because of "Mr. Sullivan's singular endowment as a decorator, . . . describe him as a decorator only." The Auditorium alone, he thought, "would suffice to refute that unjust limitation." Finding the general scheme of the theater, the lakefront balcony, the "crowning" tower, the banquet hall, and the main dining room "eminently 'architectonic,' " he concluded his review by proclaiming Sullivan "one of the most striking and interesting individualities among living architects."

The Chicago Auditorium prospered for almost two decades until rising costs and taxes made it unprofitable after the turn of the twentieth century. As times and tastes changed, management entertained a variety of schemes to expand its appeal by updating its contents, calling upon Dankmar Adler in 1898 to design a roof garden, and Louis Sullivan in 1908 and 1909 to convert the entire edifice into a hotel, then into an office block. None of these plans materialized.[40] Financier Samuel Insull subsidized the building for years by supporting the Chicago Opera Company, which used the theater from 1889 to 1928, when it moved to new facilities on Wacker Drive over the protest of many preferring Sullivan's ambiance and Adler's acoustics. In 1927 Insull was prepared to tear it down, but the cost, especially once the Depression began, would have been more than the land was worth. After the Auditorium Association went bankrupt, the landowners continued minimal operations, including sporadic stage performances—making cosmetic hotel improvements in 1933 for visitors to the Century of Progress Exposition—until World War II. Although the building was by now in desperate straits, the city of Chicago took it over as a servicepersons' center when estimates showed it was still too costly to demolish. "The first floor of the hotel now boasts a 150 foot canteen counter for hot dogs," an architectural magazine lamented in 1942, "while bowling alleys have been built over the main floor of the once magnificent theater."[41] Other parts of the building were abandoned and rotting away. Adler & Sullivan's masterpiece had reached rock bottom.

In 1946 two-year-old Roosevelt University purchased a badly deteriorated physical plant, made minimal alterations to satisfy municipal codes, and moved in the next year. Offices and guest rooms were turned into class and faculty rooms, the dining room became the library and its kitchens the book stacks, and hotel parlors were transformed into student lounges. Intensive fund-raising campaigns enabled the university to restore some of the architecturally most significant spaces between 1953 and 1975, including the ladies' parlor (now the Louis Sullivan Room), the second-floor reception area, the banquet hall, men's smoking lounge, and the Michigan Avenue lobby. After years of painstaking rehabilitation, the theater was carefully restored to its former glory for a $3,000,000 price tag—the cost of the entire building in 1890—opening amidst great fanfare for public performances in 1967. Five years later the university converted the tower, after three decades of virtual neglect, into faculty offices and the Walter E. Heller College of Business Administration.

On a wall in a sixteenth- (now seventeenth-) floor hallway, a plaque hangs to mark the spot where once upon a time Adler & Sullivan's offices bustled. The tower's interior is much different now: ceilings have been dropped to add another floor, narrow corridors have been inserted and windows divided, and the spacious suite where American architecture made history has dissolved into cubicles. In this claustrophobic rabbit warren, a modern quick-fix in a nineteenth-century masterpiece, no physical trace of Sullivan's hand remains. But when school is out of session and the tower eerily quiet, the solitary visitor can still feel his presence. After charging the atmosphere for twenty-five years, Sullivan's energy survives the purge of his old surroundings.

VIII.1 *Louis Sullivan, 1891.* Avery Architectural and Fine Arts Library. Columbia University in the City of New York.

Chapter VIII

THE ORGANISM IN ITS SURROUNDINGS 1880s-1890s

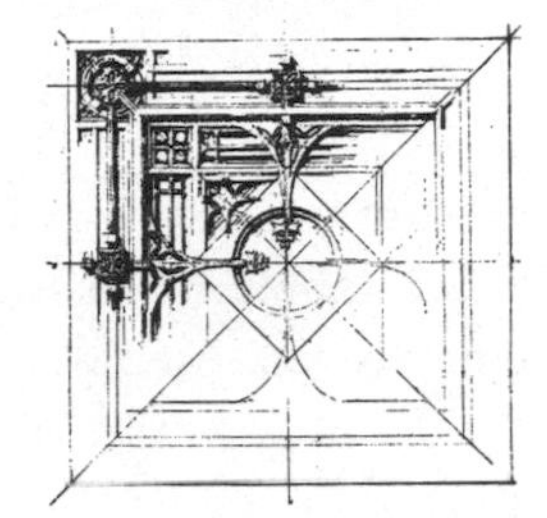

STRONG AND HEALTHY though he was, the "unremitting strain" of Auditorium work eventually took its toll on the thirty-three-year-old architect. Major new commissions plus a dozen papers and reports for professional meetings taxed Louis Sullivan's stamina until he finally succumbed to nervous exhaustion in the summer of 1889. For several weeks he was completely unable to work. His partner was also affected adversely. Dankmar Adler "did not collapse at the end as Louis did," Sullivan remembered, but "the effect was deadly and constitutional [enough to] doubtless shorten his life." So in January 1890, while the last touches were being put to the Auditorium Hotel, Sullivan left Chicago with "utter weariness" on his first vacation since touring northern Italy in 1875.[1]

He had taken that trip as an Ecole student to inspect the heritage of the Italian Renaissance, enjoying himself immensely in Florence and in Rome, but never giving himself entirely to play, for to Sullivan study was pleasure enough. Fifteen years later he was still unable to separate work from recreation. According to a sometimes unreliable biographer, Sullivan left Chicago in 1890 on partnership business, but finding himself completely "enervated," decided on the spur of the moment to take a mid-winter holiday.[2] Although this is not confirmed by his own account, it would have been like him to believe that all he needed was a change of scene. Auditorium publicity had already generated several new commissions that could have taken him to far geographical fields. As early as January 1889, Adler & Sullivan's preliminary plans for the Pueblo, Colorado, Opera House were nearly done; between March and May 1890, they reported progress on three major new projects: the Wainwright office building in St. Louis, the Opera House Block in Seattle, and the Ontario Hotel in Salt Lake City; and in November announced that plans were proceeding for the Dooly commercial building, also in Salt Lake City.[3] Any or all could have called the partners out of town early in the year. On the pages immediately following the autobiographical account of his 1890 trip, Sullivan wrote that "as Adler did not much care for travel," but since Louis "retained his boyhood delight in it," he was pleased that business eventually took him to every part of the country except Oklahoma, Delaware, and northern New England. So it is possible he visited Pueblo to check on Opera House progress, as biographer Willard Connely claimed, or conferred in other cities with new or potential clients. But it is more likely he did so later on.

Sullivan said his first stop was somewhere in central California, but "irritated" by the damp climate, he soon left to visit friends in San Diego. Even though the rainy weather there was equally objectionable, he stayed until he learned what a " 'slight' earthquake" was like. So perhaps at the suggestion of his brother, Albert, whose new job as a divisional superintendent on the Illinois Central Railroad took him to New Orleans, Sullivan went South. But "that filthy town, as it then was, disillusioned him" as well. By chance, he met Chicago friends, Helen and James Charnley, who took him to Ocean Springs, Mississippi, a quiet beach community of less than two thousand people on Biloxi Bay about ninety miles east of New Orleans. In this sleepy village "sheltered by ancient live oaks," Sullivan found "peace, and the joy of comrades, and lovely nights of sea breeze. . . . Here in this haven, this peaceful quiescence, Louis's nerves, long taut with insomnia, yielded and renewed their life. In two weeks, he was well and sound."[4]

After fifteen years of mostly work and precious little play building a career, the last three and one-half particularly demanding, Sullivan had his first real rest. This is not to say he never relaxed. During his early days as a free-lance draftsman, perhaps including his first years with Adler, he and his young colleagues met regularly for late-evening dinners, but even then convivial conversation ordinarily turned to work. As the demands of business grew, he had less time for even these kinds of simple pleasures. Never so dedicated to fitness as brother Albert or Bill Curtis, Louis nevertheless kept himself in reasonable condition, principally by walking, one of his favorite pastimes. Even before moving to Kenwood on the South Side in 1884, he preferred to be close to Lake Michigan. Without exception, no matter where he lived in Chicago from his first days until his last, he was either in sight of the lake, or no more than a five- or six-block walk away. For a man who had grown up in Boston, summering on the Atlantic Coast, where he had learned to love the sea, it was hardly surprising—almost a subliminal impulse, perhaps—for him to gravitate toward water. At the beaches and shoreline parks of Chicago—urban nature preserves, of a sort—he found his most refreshing interludes.

Hence the appeal of Ocean Springs, in 1890 a newly discovered vacation retreat for wealthy Chicagoans, in large part due to its location on one of the closest ocean beaches to the city. The village was best reached by taking the Illinois Central some 920 miles south to New Orleans, a twenty-one-hour trip on the fastest Pullmans, then heading east on the Louisville & Nashville three hours more to Ocean Springs, four miles past Biloxi. In February 1890 one H. H. Curtis surveyed and platted his twelve hundred acres on the eastern edge of town for a real estate development he named Alto Park. Curtis was a good salesman and his land was very appealing, for in July 1892 the New Orleans *Daily Picayune* reported that Alto Park, which now extended beyond the original survey, was entirely owned by "Chicago men" who had embellished their properties with fruit trees and roses. One of the most attractive was the "charming winter home" of Mr. Louis Sullivan.[5]

When he first arrived, he had no intention of buying land but fell so in love with the place he could not resist. Nor could James and Helen Charnley. On March 1, 1890, Helen purchased twenty-one acres of beachfront property just south of the Alto Park development—in 1892 she transferred title to her husband—from Newcomb Clark, former speaker of the Michigan House of Representatives, who had retired to Ocean Springs to speculate in land. On March 7 Sullivan bought six acres with 260 feet of beachfront adjacent to the Charnleys on the west from Florence and Florian Shaffter of New Orleans for $800. Three days later, for one dollar, on the condition that he plan a home for them, Sullivan acquired five of the Charnleys' twenty-one acres abutting his own to make a total of eleven. He must have gotten down to work immediately, since he remembered that on March 12 he and the Charnleys returned "light-heartedly" to Chicago, leaving his plans for his house and theirs with a local carpenter to construct before their next visit.[6]

Back in Chicago Sullivan's enthusiasm for Ocean Springs was apparently contagious because in April 1890, the very next month, Albert Sullivan purchased nine acres from Newcomb Clark with 198 feet of beach bordering Charnley on the east for $850. Beginning the next February, Albert, as general superintendent for the entire Illinois Central Chicago-to-New Orleans division, periodically commandeered a private railroad car to visit his property. Although he never built a house in Ocean Springs, he shunned the attractive local hotel to live for days at a time in his luxurious car parked on a spur a few hundred yards north of his land. Albert bought another two and one-half acres on the eastern edge of his holdings in December 1892 from Horace Williston of Duluth for $88. The strip was quite long, some 850 feet, and very narrow, only twenty-two feet wide, but he now had 220 feet of uninterrupted beach. In the meantime brother Louis made a $5500 acquisition in April, his only one from Newcomb Clark, a forty-one-and-one-half-acre tract running 852½ feet along the shore, separated from Albert's land by the Williston strip. With this purchase the Charnleys and Sullivans would have controlled almost 1800 feet of continuous beachfront on seventy-nine acres. But only four months later, in August 1892, Sullivan sold his large parcel for the same price he paid for it to Williston, who later conveyed the two and one-half acres to Albert. If Sullivan had bought the land for speculation, he failed to hold it long enough for it to appreciate. If he bought it to create a vacation colony for like-minded people, or to provide himself with enough space for total privacy, his reason for selling—obviously not for profit—is anybody's guess. Or he may simply have purchased it as a favor to Williston.[7]

For twenty years, until 1910, Sullivan went south whenever he could, usually during the coldest part of Chicago's winter until Ocean Springs began to heat up in late spring, staying a few weeks at a time, occasionally returning for a second visit. For the first few years, he rode down with his brother in the private car, which was sometimes at his service when Albert was not around.[8] By the winter of 1890–91, his house, and the Charnleys' some three hundred feet to the east, were finished, both quite similar in plan. Facing the sea in the distance, the one-story, shingled, fairly steep-roofed, T-shaped bungalows were fronted by deep, full-breadth verandas. The front door at the Sullivan house opened directly on a spacious living room with ample bookshelves, a large fireplace, and tongue-and groove paneling in local curly pine, put up vertically between three-foot bands of horizontal courses top and bottom continued on the ceiling. Large enough for casually scattered furniture arrangements and a dining table in the rear alcove, the living area was flanked on the left by two guest rooms and bath and by similar facilities for Sullivan on the right. All these rooms faced the veranda and, terminating in triple-windowed bays at either end of the main axis, were sufficiently cross-ventilated to help cool the house in the hottest weather. At the back of the living area, a passage dividing left and right service rooms led to the kitchen, behind which was a series of walk-in storage and utility closets. To their rear at the end of the passage and the stem of the T was an octagonal water tower that housed a holding tank until Sullivan sank an artesian well later in the decade. Like the front portion of the house, the back wing also opened through numerous windows to broad flanking verandas. With their sweeping front and side porches, generous dead-air spaces overhead, their sun-blocking far-overhanging eaves, and their openness within and to the outdoors, the Sullivan and Charnley "cottages" are neglected milestones in the history of American environmental design.

Sullivan reserved most of his famous ornament for the showpieces of his place, the rose gardens and other landscaping. His eleven acres formed a rectangle more than twice as long as it was wide, within which he laid out a magnificent ensemble of drives, walking paths, gardens, and outbuildings. To reach his house from the lightly trafficked white shell road on a bluff slightly above the beach, Sullivan provided three options: the first was through the west gates along a curving carriage drive to a parking circle in front of servants' quarters at the side of and slightly behind the main dwelling. A good distance farther back were the stables with a handsomely arched vehicular entrance, hayloft, and additional guest rooms. Near the east end of the grounds, a second pair of gates opened on a footpath that immediately split into two routes through the gardens. The central entrance was more formal, leading directly to a three-foot-deep, thirty-foot pool encircled by a walkway, arbors, small summerhouses, and seats worked into flower beds. An artesian well–fed jet discharged its water at the center of the pool, which fed into a basin

VIII.2 *Louis Sullivan residence, 1890, Ocean Springs, Mississippi.* From *Architectural Record,* 1905.

curving toward the parking area. Along a direct axis from the jet to the front steps was the center of Sullivan's spectacular main rose garden, which he developed through a series of concentric circles of beds and paths into an ellipsis about 160 feet long parallel to the house. A similar but smaller rose garden at its west rear obscured in the distance a vegetable or kitchen garden, also in concentric circles with a center fountain terraced down from a broad double pathway bordered by flower beds. Farther back still Sullivan had a chicken yard, a fishpond stocked with Gulf crabs—one of his favorite delicacies—and a bridge leading off his property into the woods. Water was pumped over the grounds through buried pipes with surface taps, house sewage to the natural salt marsh running from Biloxi Bay to the extreme rear of his land.

Carefully planned and landscaped under Sullivan's quite-specific directions, the grounds were completed by 1905. An ardent student of nature since his boyhood rambles in Wakefield, Massachusetts, Sullivan as an adult developed a particular affection for roses. He studied them extensively, owned a number of books on the subject, tended them lovingly hour after hour, and carefully photographed his dozens of varieties, some of which were initially developed in his gardens. His roses bloomed from early spring to Christmas in a riot of colors and scents that gave him as much pleasure as anything else in life. But his horticultural expertise was hardly limited to his favorite flower. The entire estate, planned with a distinct philosophy, revealed his skill as a landscape architect. Front to rear, the place changed from formal to functional, from decorative to utilitarian. Near the beach Sullivan cut down a small number of trees to open framed vistas of Biloxi Bay toward Deer Island, a natural breakwater twelve miles offshore. Closer to the house, under a canopy of tall gums, live oaks, pines, and hickories, he scattered shorter indigenous dogwoods, magnolias, catalpas, and other flowering trees whose colors he carried gently to earth by integrating them with banks of azaleas, wild honeysuckles, and numerous other shrubs arranged as patterns in a green grass carpet. Near the beach the grounds were like a ceremonial garden or park approach to a grand estate, but as the land rose toward the house and the forest behind, it made a smooth transition to a more relaxed and natural setting—except for the gardens—befitting a vacation retreat in a semitropical wilderness. According to a friend, Sullivan left his gates open to all "visitors and lovers of nature" without any "No Trespassing" signs. In this lovely oasis of his own making, he "did his purest, finest thinking," he recalled, in the peace he periodically needed to rejuvenate his spirits.[9]

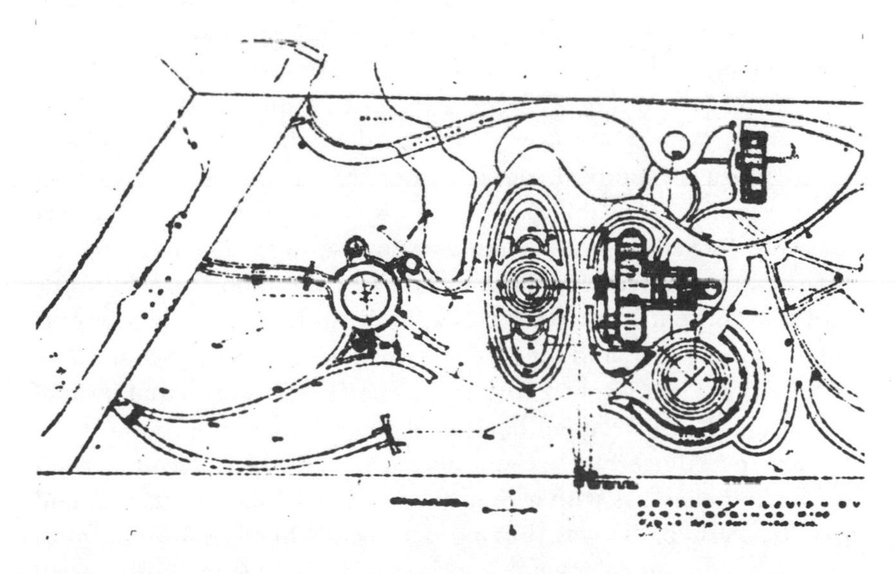

VIII.3 *A portion of Sullivan's estate plan showing* (left to right) *circular pool with fountain, eliptical rose garden, T-shaped residence with kitchen garden, and servants/guest house.* From *Architectural Record,* 1905.

VIII.4 *Louis Sullivan residence, stables.* Photo by The Chicago Architectural Photographing Company.

It was fundamentally the setting, not its people, that attracted Sullivan to Ocean Springs. Over the years his practice was to send ahead to local shopkeepers the lists of provisions and supplies he expected to be waiting when he arrived. Infrequently appearing in the village, he kept mostly to his gardens, nearby beaches, and woods. With a bountiful supply of oysters just outside his gates, a well-stocked pond of his favorite crabs, a large vegetable garden, chickens, fuel and water supplies, and sewage disposal, he approached self-sufficiency. Leaving much of the labor to a full-time gardener and part-time work crews, Sullivan tended his roses, read, did some designing, and prowled the woods and beaches communing with nature, a source of creative inspiration and his principal form of relaxation. Little wonder he stayed near home, not because he disliked the village but because he did not need it. Ocean Springs lore nevertheless has it that Sullivan was personable, outgoing, and friendly. Perhaps he was. But no one recalls his entertaining local people or coming to town on social calls. In business and casual encounters, he was cordial and polite. But he rarely went out of his way to make friends. If he ran across people with similar interests,

Bobby Davidson Smith's shopkeeper parents, for example, who were conversant in the arts, Sullivan might be perfectly charming while he stopped to chat. But he normally kept to himself, preferring to bring his Chicago friends to Ocean Springs, rather than make new ones there.[10]

Among those closest to him in the 1880s and 1890s was his most frequent Ocean Springs guest, I. Giles Lewis. Born eight years before Sullivan in 1848, Lewis was a salesman at the time for Robert Stevenson & Company, a wholesale drug firm at 92 Lake Street, Chicago. Sullivan knew Lewis, his wife, and his mother (who later lived with them) well enough by 1887—when he designed a cover for Stevenson's catalogue—to mourn the passing of their Angora kitten, the only household pet he seems ever to have liked. Eight years later Lewis brought Sullivan a second commission on behalf of the University of Michigan Alumni Association, the 1895 winner's medal for the annual competition sponsored by the Northern Oratorical League. But the best measure of their friendship was recorded in the *Chicago Blue Book of Selected Names,* a kind of lesser Social Register listing Sullivan by virtue of his Auditorium fame when it began publication in 1890. When he moved to 220 Forty-sixth Street that year, Mr. and Mrs. Lewis moved in with him. For the next decade, wherever Sullivan lived, so did the Lewises, at 4575 Lake Park Avenue, from 1892 until 1896, when Lewis began to give his winter address as Ocean Springs, then at 4853 Kimbark and at the Hotel Windermere, 125 East Fifty-sixth Street, from 1897 to 1899, when Sullivan also placed his winter home in city directory columns. A check of Jackson County, Mississippi, deed records reveals, however, that Lewis never owned property in Ocean Springs. This means that his "home" there was actually Sullivan's, and that the two must have been particularly close if he could "borrow" his friend's address. Yet, in all his writings, the architect never mentioned Lewis anywhere, leaving not the slightest hint of their relationship. It was common at the time for single individuals to live with married couples. Only when Sullivan got married himself in 1899 would he and the Lewises go their separate residential ways. But if they were still close, it was nowhere recorded.[11]

With the winter cottage finished and its landscaping under way, the Sullivan brothers agreed to build a home for their mother, Andrienne, who had been living since the year after her husband's death in 1884 with her sister Jennie Whittlesey, in Lyons Falls, New

VIII.5 *Louis Sullivan residence, pool.* From *Architectural Record,* 1905.

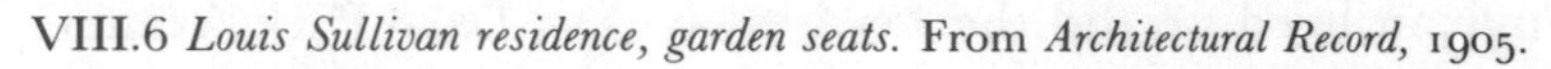

VIII.6 *Louis Sullivan residence, garden seats.* From *Architectural Record,* 1905.

York. At fifty-six years of age in 1891, Andrienne had been in dubious health for years, and her sons probably wanted her as near to them as possible now that they could afford to support her. So in November construction began on an unusual house at 4575 Lake Park Avenue in Chicago's South Side.[12] On a twenty-six-by-one-hundred-foot lot, its two stories and raised basement were wedged between adjacent homes. The bracketed flat cornice and the second-story bay were as highly decorated as the arched panel over the front door. To its right a broad modified "Chicago" window (a plate-glass center flanked by sash) behind two columns doubling as mullions would give Andrienne a clear view of the street. Despite its rich ornament, the Sullivan house was remarkably unpicturesque, with its flat roof and smooth stonework. Albert paid for it, Louis's firm designed it, but Andrienne never saw it. On May 15, 1892, she died of an atrophied liver and was brought back to be buried with her husband in Chicago's Graceland Cemetery. Reluctant to occupy the house himself but needing larger quarters, Albert moved from 3030 Lake Park Avenue to 4830 Kimbark, leaving the new house for Louis Sullivan and the Lewises to inhabit right away.

The brothers had seen a lot of each other during the preceding fifteen years. Lately, they had traveled together to and from Ocean Springs, where in 1891 Louis worked on plans for the Illinois Central Railroad Station in New Orleans, the third commission received through Albert's influence. As a divisional superintendent, Albert was important at both ends of the line. In New Orleans, he had regular business dealings with Mark Rolla Spelman, a transplanted New Yorker, now general agent for the Illinois Central. Spelman's twenty-five-year-old daughter, Mary, was fifteen years younger than Albert when they fell in love, but as that seemed no obstacle to anyone, they were married in the New Orleans family residence on February 6, 1893, moving to Albert's Chicago home after their honeymoon. In February 1896 their daughter was born, named Andrienne Françoise after her paternal grandmother, followed two years later by their son, Mark Rolla, junior. Needing more living space, they took over the Sullivan house late in 1896. Louis was forced to leave, the Lewises with him, for 4853 Kimbark, almost across the street from the residence Albert and Mary had just vacated.

The elder brother's career was meanwhile quite spectacular. Having rapidly climbed the rungs of his company's managerial ladder, he rose to assistant second vice-president of the Illinois Central around 1900. During the next four years, he was thrice elected president of the American Railway Association, held the same office for the American Section of the International Railway Congress, and later served in various executive positions with the American Railway Engineering and Maintenance of Way Association. At the St. Louis Exposition in 1904, the Illinois Central won an award for a steel-frame, side-door suburban car Albert designed in 1900 that remained in service until 1929. Perhaps more on the strength of this achievement than his many others, he moved to St. Louis in 1904 as

VIII.7 *Albert Sullivan residence, 1891.* Photo by The Chicago Architectural Photographing Company.

vice-president and general manager of the Missouri Pacific Railroad, where he directed its forty-five-thousand-employee Operating Department. After his retirement on January 1, 1912, Albert Sullivan lived in Poughkeepsie, New York, until his death in 1938 at age eighty-four, occasionally dabbling in local politics, city planning, and national railroad affairs. When he built a neocolonial home for his wife and children in 1912, the architect he hired was not his brother, for the two had severed their ties.[13]

They had always been close, never allowing distance to separate them in any other way. Helping each other's careers, sharing friends and social activities, they had lived in close proximity on Chicago's South Side and even owned vacation property in the same remote Mississippi town. But when Mary Spelman came on the scene, their tightly knit bond began to unravel. Louis Sullivan's relations with her family were "somewhat chilly," according to a distant relative. Mary's genteel unbringing was more attuned to Albert's corporate milieu than to Louis's solitary life-style, which she and her parents considered "bohemian," therefore rather suspect. When she married in 1893, Adler & Sullivan was one of the top architectural firms in the country, and with Louis himself at the very peak of his fame, Mary could overlook the personal idiosyncrasies she found so disturbing. But by 1896, when her daughter was born, with the partnership dissolved and a depression in full swing, Louis Sullivan began to feel the financial pinch. Things were bad enough by August 1897 for him to mortgage his beloved Ocean Springs property to Joseph B. Rose of Chicago to secure a $3000 loan. Although he paid if off by March 1898 and took his title back,[14] Mary may have already decided that his difficulties were evidence of some sort of character flaw. Eager to provide for the needs of his family and the wants of his wife, Albert agreed—reluctantly, perhaps—to claim the house he had paid for, and in so doing permanently alienated his brother.

To make its painful associations even worse, Louis's removal from the Sullivan residence came at a psychologically most inopportune time. Since leaving Bennet Street in Boston at the age of five, he had never lived in or owned his own home except for his recently acquired Ocean Springs retreat. Nor had he ever again remained in one place as long as his five years there. During the three decades from 1862, when his father sold the family dwelling, to 1892, when he took over the Lake Park Avenue property, Sullivan had lived in some twenty different rooms, flats, and homes of friends and relatives. It would probably have given him little comfort to know that he moved only slightly more often than the national average, for during the last four years, as he approached the age of forty in his own home, he may have grown accustomed to residential stability, to the security of having roots for the first time in adult life. With room to work, his books and friends around him, and enough space to stretch out in the neighborhood he most preferred, he could easily have grown attached to his surroundings, especially in the absence of a family. Having created an idyllic situation in Ocean Springs, moreover, he may have been inclined to make his urban environment equally ideal. And what better place than the house—the nest—he had prepared for his own mother? To move at his age with all his accumulated possessions and emotional investments would surely be more difficult and disruptive than ever before. So when Mary pressured him to leave and Albert reminded him who really owned the place, Louis must have been terribly hurt. After 1896 he had less and less to do with his brother, never saw Albert again once he moved to St. Louis in 1904, and in his autobiography almost two decades later failed to mention him at all.

Albert married Mary less than three months before Frank Lloyd Wright left Adler & Sullivan, around May 1893, to open his own office. Together with impressions left by George Elmslie, by William Gray Purcell (1880–1965), who assisted Sullivan briefly in 1903 before forming a partnership with Elmslie in 1909, and by a handful of others, Wright's recollections give a partial picture of his employer.[15] None of these descriptions are entirely trustworthy, however. Elmslie and Purcell became virtual hero-worshipers, inclined to dismiss anything unflattering about Sullivan. Wright was sometimes gratuitously critical, as if chipping his "lieber meister" down to size in order to surpass him. But their accounts are important because Elmslie and Wright in particular knew Sullivan, or thought they did, about as well as anyone. Not that that was especially easy. Throughout his life Sullivan seemed intent upon revealing almost nothing personal about himself, either in print or in public. Even in his autobiography, which superficially seems quite revealing, where he freely discussed ideas and feelings, he wrote only in the third person, raising his experience to an abstraction, to a case study in human development. Mostly discussing his childhood and youth—as if they were someone else's, be it noted—he never emerged from behind the "Louis" persona. His seemingly candid self-analysis was, in fact, a kind of scrim through which the real man was only vaguely perceived. The result was to build a protective barrier between himself and the outside world. Shrouding his essential self in autobiographical psychologizing, shrinking in real life from the spotlight except on professional occasions, Louis Sullivan was an exceptionally guarded and private person.

But of course he would not hide everything, least of all his physical presence. He was, as everyone could see, of medium height but "powerfully built [and] broad-chested" with a tendency to put on weight if he was not careful, explaining perhaps his interest in physical fitness and why he joined the Chicago Athletic Club in 1896. His close-cropped, dark-brown hair, parted in the middle, was already thinning when he posed for a photograph in 1885 just after his twenty-ninth birthday. As it receded and grew silvery in his fifties, he would part it on the left, brushing it across his head to minimize its loss. In the 1880s and 1890s, he sported a neatly trimmed full beard and mustache, by 1909 only a mustache, and later on no facial hair at all. "His outstanding feature," Wright thought when they first met in 1887 or 1888, was "his amazing brown eyes" that "took me in at a glance." However penetrating his stare, his eyes were soft, warm, and almost sad in his middle years, becoming somewhat cold and humorless as he grew older, looking at the world through small rimless glasses. His fingers were unusually long and sensuous, his thumb bent back like a modeler's, Purcell recalled, forming "remarkable hands," which he described as extensions of Sullivan's mind. Even at rest his fingers were "potentially dynamic," "his hands appear[ing] tremendously ready to do . . . with a skill, dexterity and economy of motion that gave me an entirely new perception." His posture was erect, confident, his stride brisk, "a firm springy step," one assistant remembered. Wright thought it too long for his short legs, dangerously close "to a strut." But to another draftsman he simply "held his handsome head high." Everyone agreed that Sullivan appeared to be exceptionally self-assured.

He also took considerable pride in his appearance. Always immaculately groomed, with never a hair out of place, he was, in a word, vain about his looks. His preferences ran to brown three-piece suits, his necktie precisely knotted over his vest, his collar starched and spotless. Even in the more casual atmosphere of Ocean Springs, his short-brimmed fisherman's cap, bow tie, pleated linen shirt, highly polished shoes, and summer whites conveyed an air of gentility "of which any old Bourbon might have been proud," one employee suggested, an image never compromised by photographs that in his maturity were always carefully composed with Sullivan studiedly postured. If his seemingly aristocratic demeanor was a way of compensating for poor Irish roots, only Frank Lloyd Wright thought him "haughty." "He could be arrogant," Elmslie admitted, "and a bit prone to give advice where not needed." "But we had a great respect for him," another employee maintained, "and a great admiration for his vigorous personality."

In the workplace most agreed he was firm but fair, permitting no nonsense on the job, more like his former boss Frank Furness than William Le Baron Jenney. Once again Wright's impression was somewhat harsher than the others. "I could see the cringing fear of him wherever he went" in the office, he wrote. Wright claimed that Sullivan more than once told him he "had no respect whatever for a draughtsman," intimating that he bullied his office staff unmercifully. Purcell's view was almost the opposite. Sullivan had a friendly good-morning for everyone, he remembered, a moment with each of them during the day, and an amiable good-bye at night. William L. Steele (1875–1949), a Sullivan employee from 1902 to 1905, took the middle ground. When the draftsmen heard Sullivan coming, he recalled, "we instantly subsided into graven images of unremitting toil." But he was not so much a tyrant as a man insisting on serious purpose: "He did not care how much time was consumed in the drafting-room," Steele continued, "as long as the work was done up to his exacting taste. . . . His method was to stride up and down dictating eloquently and copiously. His specifications were models of clarity and precision." Purcell remembered that Sullivan scrutinized his staff's work carefully but always complimented individuality. Contrary to Wright's view, which may have been a projection of his own authoritarian manner, Sullivan at work was simply a demanding perfectionist, for himself and for those he employed.

Architect John Root thought him "one of the most individualistic personalities" in Chicago, "cultivated in many directions, with a bold, alert, vigorous and imaginative mind bending its energies into many channels. . . . Self-confident and enthusiastic," he was an ideal complement to Adler. "Sullivan has accomplished much admirable work," Root maintained in 1891, "and will achieve even more. [His buildings] attest the boldness, freshness and ingenuity of his mind." If he had a criticism, it was that Sullivan concentrated so much on "delicacy, beauty, and significance of detail that he sometimes neglected mass, the play of light and shade, and differences in materials." (Montgomery Schuyler, for one, would have certainly disagreed.) Nevertheless, Root thought, Sullivan was "the author of some of the most characteristic work" in town.

Outside the office Sullivan "liked to be alone," Elmslie recorded. He "was a bit of a recluse . . . a solitary man in most ways and constitutionally averse to social display of any kind." Preferring not to attract attention, he willingly gave interviews but said nothing per-

VIII.8 *Louis Sullivan in Ocean Springs, date uncertain.*

sonal. Mostly he avoided public situations in which anything but art or architecture was likely to be discussed. Yet he loved to talk with individuals or with handfuls of friends; small groups were his forte. Words such as "fascinating," "compelling," and "inspiring" appear again and again in descriptions of his conversation. He was "an extraordinary talker," Elmslie wrote. "Wherever he sat was the head of the table." "Sometimes he would keep on talking . . . until late at night," Wright remembered, "to express his own feelings and thoughts, regardless, forgetting me often," in more a monologue than an exchange. Other observers confirmed this impression. Sculptor Karl Bitter first met Sullivan by chance on the street. After "a friendly drink at a nearby place," they went up to the Auditorium tower, where "this interesting man read to me aloud and with splendid pathos his prose poems on art and architecture, which, compelling the most serious and admiring attention, were a rare treat to me. The man fairly fascinated me; I confess that I was surrendered to him in ecstasy."[16]

Sullivan was notoriously intense and compulsively serious. In private he might swear and joke, and did not resent being the object of humor, but in public he was completely business. His pleasures were equally determined. Late-night conversations on art and architecture, long walks in the city to look at buildings, contemplation of nature—his play was invariably didactic. An exceptionally well-informed man, Sullivan read widely and eclectically. Aside from architectural publications, his library when inventoried in 1909 included books on history, precious stones, music, horticulture, physical fitness, language, religion and philosphy, the sciences, art, and several other subjects. He owned multivolume sets of Mark Twain, Lafcadio Hearn, Ibsen, Shakespeare, Victor Hugo, Molière, Chaucer, and Kipling, but his real passions were Richard Wagner's music, Herbert Spencer's philosophy, and Walt Whitman, especially the *Leaves of Grass* poem "Sea-Drift," the section entitled "As I Ebb'd With the Ocean of Life," which he edited more to his liking in his own 1882 edition. In February 1887, just as he received final approval of his Auditorium proposals after months of directorial indecision, Sullivan wrote a combination soul-search and fan letter to Whitman, whom he had not met. "I, too, 'have sweated through fog with linguists and contenders,' " he confided, undoubtedly with his clients in mind. "I, too, 'have pried through the strata, analyzed to a hair,' reaching for the basis of a virile and indigenous art." Enclosing a copy of his poetic essay "Inspiration," "because it is your opinion above all other opinions that I should most highly value," he asked for Whitman's advice and understanding. Although he may not have replied, the poet cherished the letter. Believing that as a fellow artist Whitman was pursuing the same objectives but in a different field, Sullivan had found a distant soul mate.[17]

Most of Sullivan's friends were, in fact, safely distant, if not in miles then in age or situation. Beginning as a youngster with his attraction for older men—Moses Woolson, John Tompson, John Edelmann, Bill Curtis—and continuing into maturity with Giles Lewis, Dankmar Adler, Chicago interior decorators Thomas Healy and Louis J. Millet (whom he met at the Ecole), the Charnleys, and a handful of others, the people Sullivan liked and admired most were either older or married, with commitments and priorities of which he could not be fully part. If this was a way of protecting himself from others, of guarding himself from too close an intimacy that might because of his own doing unravel as had his childhood family, then Sullivan would be forced always to go it alone. Even with younger men, Sullivan talked shop, not self. Frank Lloyd Wright claimed a certain priviness, but their conversations were less personal than professional, less dialogues than Sullivan musings. Lest error be interpreted as some kind of personal vulnerability, Sullivan held his convictions tenaciously. Even George Elmslie said he was sometimes too decisive, as if certain issues were simply off limits for debate. Sullivan was not the easiest man to know. Inflexible and uncompromising on occasion, he could be socially graceful but was always, first and foremost, bound up with himself, which may explain why he married so late and why that marriage was so unsuccessful.

With little rootedness in his life, Sullivan spent a good deal of time outside his Chicago home—especially after 1896, when he left Lake Park Avenue—working, traveling, in restaurants, and in his clubs. In addition to the Athletic Club, where he periodically boxed after 1896, he was also admitted to the Union League in 1890, along with Adler and his brother, Albert, and to the prestigious Chicago Club, where he lived occasionally from 1898 to 1909. Later, he would have a desk at Cliff Dwellers, an association of writers and artists. Although he made a considerable amount of money before the 1890s depression—how much is impossible to calculate—he did not live extravagantly. "In his way of life, his mode of dress, his manner of speech," he was "an aristocrat," according to one observer. To some he may have been "a fine raconteur and bon vivant"[18] (shades of Major Jenney!), but he generally lived quietly and tastefully, even primly. His late hours, impulsive flow of ideas, reported fondness for alcohol, explosive temper (ordinarily held well in check), and artistic sensibilities may have been so foreign to his sister-in-law and her family, so one historian thinks, they did not want him around. But not many others seem to have reacted so negatively. There was in his life no hint of scandal, nothing to excess (except work), no womanizing—far from it—to sully his reputation. If he was not the kind of person other people immediately warmed to, he was nevertheless liked by some and respected by most. He was, in short, with a few notable exceptions, a stern Victorian gentleman of the old school, an obvious credit to his profession.

Which is one reason why, just as he was beginning to build a reputation, his profession put him to such good use. Sullivan was eager and able to work long hours for the organizations he affiliated with, using them to disseminate his ideas and to advance the professionalization of his craft, which was very much on his agenda in the 1880s and 1890s. The Chicago Architectural Club, founded in February 1885 as the Chicago Architectural Sketch Club, was an association of draftsmen, artists, mechanics, architects, and occasional representatives of the building trades dedicated, said a later secretary, Herman V. von Holst, to "the development of an unaffected school of modern architecture in America." Considering itself a forum for advanced ideas, the club opened its doors (after 1892 in the new Art Institute building) to members and nonmembers alike. Its activities included exhibitions of renderings and photographs (often of Sullivan's work), the yearly publication of a catalogue after 1894, periodic competitions in drawing and design, regular meetings with featured speakers, and an annual banquet. The exhibitions came to be important events, attracting close to six hundred entries by the 1890s, and with thirty to forty functions a year by 1898, the club enrolled several important architects, although youthful practitioners were the majority. Sullivan never joined, but by 1886 he was a regular participant in its activities, was an honorary member in the 1890s, and by 1900 an honorary patron, perhaps even something of a patron saint.[19]

Dankmar Adler was also involved, speaking now and again on structural matters. Adler occasionally supplied the humor for which Sullivan was not especially noted. "In a characteristic speech which sparkled with wit," a local building magazine reported in 1892, he responded to a toast by concluding, " 'The Client: may he live long with a full purse.' "[20] Sullivan's principal interest was to encourage architects to abandon historic styles, rethink design problems without relying on precedent, and develop a poetic sensitivity toward life itself. To this end he was a regular competition judge, earning a reputation for disinterested honesty and serious purpose. From 1886 through 1889, with his friend John Root and his former employer Jenney, he established the criteria for and evaluated the entries to the annual drawing shows, in 1888 awarding first place for an eight-room frame house to T. O. Fraenkel (second place went to William B. Mundie, Jenney's partner after 1891), and for a park fountain to Charles Whittlesey. In other years the subjects varied from twelve-foot wrought-iron gates with stone posts to a public library in a rich suburb to carved Indian panels for front-hall seats. Never sparing in his criticism, he found the 1889 entries, for example, so "very poor and lean and lacking that delicacy of significance characteristic of Indian work," that he could not recommend a winner.[21]

The substance of his critiques apparently negated whatever hostility words like these might have generated. Speaking to the club's annual awards banquet in 1888, Sullivan praised the competitors' efforts but chided them for treating exhibition drawings as mere recreational labor. *Every* design, he insisted, was a serious occasion with a definite purpose. Leaning on his Ecole training, he urged draftsmen to formulate each project in their minds before drawing a single line. Architectural work, he said, should always be critical of life in a constructive way, and should be based on a thorough study of the sources of design including the five classical orders.[22] In his speech "Style," read to the club in April the same year, he discussed the difficulties of creativity. By studying common, ordinary things, he insisted, the architect would discover new and deeper meanings in life. Any pine, he offered by example, expressed the "peculiar nature or identity of this kind of tree," and in a general way "sums up its style." But since there were several species of pine, each with its own nature, and since "one pine-tree is not precisely like another," the style of a pine "is the resultant of its identity and its surroundings." Therefore, he asked his audience by way of analogy, "is it not equally and especially true that the style of an artist is in its essence and form the resultant of his identity and his experiences?" His answer was that "style is ever thus the response of the organism to the surroundings." As he often did in speeches, Sullivan left the major point unstated. But his obvious message was that when designing, his architect and draftsmen listeners should attempt to translate their own personal experiences and the present circumstances (the architectural opportunity at hand, he meant) into an historically unprecedented solution with a style of its own.[23]

A year and one-half later, he developed these ideas further in "Artistic Use of the Imagination," read to the club in October 1889. The artist receives impressions and transmits them to permanent forms having *his own* characteristics, he explained. More a creature of instinct than of reason, the true artist was actually a poet, and therefore as a student of natural, real, everyday things—learning their essence—was able to convey irreducible realities to others. An artist understands that within him reside certain thoughts, feelings, and emotions, but does not know how they got there. He prefers to remain unquestioning, neither rejecting nor dismissing any of these realities as improper. Instinct discovers them, and reflection later turns the object of instinct into art. Were I to look at your drawings, he told the assembled audience whose work he had, in fact, looked at many times, I would see not so much the subject matter as "the man." "It is, of course, the man that I hold in my hand in each case and look secretly into." How do you suppose I am sizing you up? "What do you think is my estimate of your experiences and your faculties? Do I understand that my poetic web has caught your practical fly?" Inspiration and imagination preceded thought in the creative process, he insisted. Since they, not reason, were the measure of the man, architecture was, or should be, autobiographical. If Sullivan's identification of the sources of architecture with emotional instinct rather than with historical precedent was rather unconventional, his remarks were nevertheless "based on the most practical common sense," *Inland Architect* concluded, and "made a deep impression upon the club members. The meeting was the largest in attendance of the year."[24] Due to the pressure of business in the 1890s, however, Sullivan withdrew from club affairs, although his work was periodically exhibited and his ideas continued to influence the club's philosophy.

Sullivan was even more active in the Illinois State Association of Architects he helped organize in January 1885 as the local chapter of the Western Association of Architects. From the beginning his impact was substantial, his ideas influential. At the founders' meeting, he complained that twenty-five dollars annual dues would be too high but opposed admitting charter members like himself free. Since in-town members by virtue of their location would be shaping policy by doing most of the work in the new organization and would also have lower travel expenses, he favored higher dues for them, eventually agreeing to twenty-five dollars a year for Chicagoans, ten dollars for down-staters. The motive for associating, he believed, should be to define and restrict the position of architects: "This is not to be a mere society," he proclaimed; "it is to be organic and vital; it is to be the voice of our profession here." As a founder with a willingness to work, Sullivan was elected to the executive committee every year from 1885 to 1891, serving as its secretary in 1886 and 1888. (In October 1887 he received six votes in his only bid for chapter president but lost to Samuel A. Treat's ten.) He also gave time to several ad hoc committees examining technical matters, the architect's liability for complications arising from party wall footings, for example, or the association's position on adding passenger elevators to a new city ordinance requiring brick facing on freight elevator shafts.[25]

Over the years Sullivan involved himself in a wide range of association issues, no matter how big or how small. He was instrumental in selecting permanent meeting rooms, advocated with fellow officer Dankmar Adler a standardized examination for applicants to the profession, recommended a permanent association library, a regular luncheon for ongoing exchange of ideas, and the formation of study groups based on design specialities that would report periodically to the larger body. As chairman of the executive committee in 1887, he proposed that a code of ethics be drawn up and administered by a national architectural congress so that individual legal difficulties might immediately become collective causes. In June of 1888 Sullivan called for a "Protective League" to defend architects against vexatious litigation brought by unprincipled clients, agreeing to draft a proposal that, approved by the executive committee, was sent to six hundred architects around the nation for consideration that summer.[26]

His August 1 circular letter noted that rules governing the financial obligation of architects for actual construction costs were impossibly vague. Building was now so complex and the courts so inexperienced in this matter that architects through fear of expensive litigation, powerful opposition, and reckless cross-examination in lower courts often waived their rights, suffering undue hardship "in some cases amount[ing] practically to confiscation." Most situations arose when clients sued purely out of "sharp-practice," but even when the suit was legitimate, Sullivan pointed out, there were no standards for determining liability if something went wrong with the job. The annual loss to the profession, he claimed, far exceeded the sum necessary to establish a fund for common protection with sufficient means to appeal to the highest courts.

Although architects had only recently begun to form professional associations, he reminded his colleagues, it was proper to believe that the interest of one was the interest of all, especially since "we have gradually drifted into a tacit assumption of responsibilities so vague that the developments of a day may prove such assumptions to have been reckless." He therefore offered his Protective League as a way of taking "typical," universally significant cases all the way to the highest court of appeal if necessary. In his scheme individual architects could rely on the backing of a powerful organization when unscrupulous or even well-intentioned clients threatened lawsuits, frequently a way of forcing compliance with outrageous demands. The league would be composed of all members of the profession organized by states with a national executive committee employing legal counsel. Any party seeking aid could transfer his rights by power of attorney to the executive committee, which would act in the name of the league, after determining if the individual grievance was vital to the profession as a whole. State chapters would decide matters like frequency and location of meetings and elections, the cost of dues, procedures for record keeping, and the like. All those interested in forming such an organization, Sullivan concluded his letter, could contact the Illinois State Association of Architects, whose executive committee intended at once to set up a Protective League of its own.[27]

By December 17, 1888, the committee received 172 replies from ninety-one localities in twenty-eight states and territories. Thirty-six respondents said they had not received the original circular, but of the 136 remaining, 104 were favorably inclined. Eleven wanted state organizations only, another eleven liked the idea but did not presently feel able to join. Two architects opposed the plan because it smacked of "trade unionism," which was "so far from the idea . . . of the circular that your committee [for the Protective League] hardly feel that such objectors have carefully examined the manuscript." Sullivan and the committee (on which he did not serve) pressed the

VIII.9 *Louis Sullivan* (second step, third from left) *at the Western Association of Architects Convention, St. Louis, November 18, 1885. Dankmar Adler is in first row center.* From *Inland Architect,* 1885.

Illinois architects to organize immediately. Dankmar Adler thought there were already too many associations and did not want another, even though he had proposed the resolution requesting Sullivan to prepare the circular letter. The project did not go forward because a movement had already begun to merge the Western Association, parent body of the Illinois State Association of Architects, with the American Institute of Architects (AIA). The feeling was that the new and more powerful national organization would be better equipped to handle the matter.[28]

Sullivan had also been a founding member of the Western Association of Architects in November 1884. He faithfully attended all the national conventions, participating energetically in discussions of procedural matters—dues, expenses, what rule book to use, what to call members, and so forth—generally advocating that such a new kind of organization should best adopt a flexible posture. Let's try things out for a year and see how they go was the gist of his repeated advice. At the second convention, in 1885, he urged the association to pay travel expenses of the board of directors, to which he had been elected in 1884, and strongly opposed displaying manufacturers' wares at meetings. At one point in the proceedings, he rose to say that unless architects strove for "something higher than merely drawing lines on paper, there is very little use in forming an organization," an indication of the elevated—almost spiritual—role he claimed for his profession. When someone knowing Sullivan's dedication to architecture as art, perhaps also inferring an unfriendly attitude toward the business community, asked in jest: "But suppose my friend, Mr. Sullivan, was president of a bank?" John Root shot back to general laughter: "That is too violent a supposition."

In 1886 Sullivan was defeated thirty-nine to thirty-five when he ran for secretary of the association—perhaps because some perceived him as too artistic, too high-toned—but was appointed to the Committee on Standard of Professional Requirement for Members, where he pushed the organization to consider a general code of ethics. The original raison d'être for the committee had been to propose admission requirements for the Western Association, but Sullivan argued at the 1887 convention that rather than try to judge an applicant's record, skill, or whether he would live by his pledge to sustain a sound standard of professionalism, the organization "should *itself* declare the standard which it is willing should govern its *own* course [italics added]." The time was ripe, he resolved, to promulgate a code of ethics defining an optimum relationship of members to each other and to the larger body. Once the association got its own ethical house in order, so to speak, it could then judge who its residents should be. After adopting his resolution, the convention through its chairman appointed a Code of Ethics Committee of three members from each state with Sullivan as general chairman.[29]

The plan was that members from the several states would constitute subcommittees, each with a chairman to report to Sullivan, who would revise and return their proposals for a code prior to the 1888 annual convention. "I have allowed things to take their natural course," he reported that November, with the result that nobody did anything. But in thinking about the matter, he had decided the following: that a code of ethics should define exactly *when* an architect was engaged in business with a client so that others could avoid unprofessional interference. It should prevent one member of the association from competing with another, and clearly indicate the parameters of all client relations, the first duty of the architect always being the protection of the public. Sullivan pushed for a code so strongly because he believed that as a group architects functioned entirely too randomly. Believing strongly in standards, in minimum rules of the game, both for the protection of his colleagues and the public and as a democratic indication of equal access to professional advantage, Sullivan hoped that if the Western Association adopted a code before the proposed merger with AIA, it could influence the new body's course of action. The 1888 convention agreed, putting itself on record in favor of the idea by appointing Sullivan a committee of one to draw up a professional code of ethics for either the Western Association or its replacement to consider.[30]

Sullivan endorsed the consolidation of the two bodies, believing it would enhance the power and unity of architects generally. As an elected associate member of AIA since October 1887,[31] he had no particular reason to oppose a merger until it was suggested that all Western Architects be assigned a secondary designation in the new union as "associates" not "fellows," regardless of previous status or accomplishment. "I have given the subject considerable thought," he told the fifth and final meeting of the Western Association in 1888, "and I am deeply impressed that it is a scheme . . . fraught with danger." There should be absolute democracy in architectural organizations, he insisted. "No man should be placed above his fellows any more than his own individuality will place him. . . . I believe that a favored or special class is dangerous to any party, or government, or country. . . . I think that a man can do better work when he feels that he is an equal with others who claim no higher standing by reason of some official action. . . . I truly desire this consolidation, but I feel that the proposition to effect two grades of membership is insurmountable to the uniting of the two bodies."[32] Sullivan's position, also that of Adler, who had been conspicuous in the debates in both organizations, ultimately carried the day. In November 1889 at the twenty-third AIA convention in Cincinnati, the Western Association disappeared as an autonomous body. Adler was elected to the new board of directors, beginning with Sullivan an active involvement throughout the 1890s.

In 1890, as a result of his previous efforts, Sullivan was appointed chairman of AIA's Committee on a Code of Professional Ethics, agreeing to serve simultaneously on another committee to meet with representatives of the National Board of Fire Engineers to discuss matters of mutual interest.[33] In August 1893 he delivered "Polychromatic Treatment of Architecture" to the AIA-sponsored World Congress of Architects at the Columbian Exposition in Chicago, a topic prompted by his "Golden Doorway" for the fair's Transportation Building. When asked to submit a copy of the paper for publication in AIA's *Proceedings,* he replied that it had really been an informal talk from notes, and in any case would be meaningless without the lantern illustrations, which were impossible to reproduce. Accordingly, only Sullivan's speech at the World Congress has been lost to history.[34] At the 1894 annual convention, he was elected to a three-year term on the board of directors, expiring December 31, 1897. In 1895, his most active year in AIA affairs, he was appointed to the board's executive committee for a one-year term during which he helped adjudicate a dispute between the city of Milwaukee and the architects of its new Library and Municipal Building, served on a committee to suggest improvements in the design and construction of federal buildings, and helped devise a method of electing members to the board of directors that would more fairly reflect state representation.[35] Partly because nothing further was done on the matter of a code of ethics, Sullivan began to reduce his activity in AIA at the end of his term of office. He continued to pay his ten, later fifteen, dollar a year dues through 1908 and was carried as a member until 1913. After 1900 he occasionally spoke to the Illinois Chapter of AIA (created by an 1890 Sullivan-supported merger of the Illinois State Association of Architects and the Chicago Chapter of AIA), but after the formation of the Architectural League of America in 1899, he was virtually inactive in the national affairs of the parent body.[36]

Sullivan used professional organizations as debating societies and as fora for spreading his ideas. His first speech to the Western Association, "Characteristics and Tendencies in American Architecture," delivered in 1885 when he pointed out the power of businessmen to effect change, was typical of all his presentations. Sullivan preferred to argue by indirection. He spoke of artists and poets, for example, but rarely architects, of nature and creativity, but not of the design process, leaving it to listeners to extract the message, to apply the lessons to themselves. Representative of his method but much more ethereal than most was the "Essay on Inspiration," read to the Western Architects' 1886 Chicago convention, a long prose poem about nature's cycles, about the rhythms of life itself. Originally entitled "Growth and Decadence," the essay, according to *American Architect*'s reporter, was "an allegorical and poetical production which commanded close attention" for thirty minutes. Sullivan prefaced the reading by saying that inspiration was like eyesight: everyone knew what it was but no one could define it. So he did not try to either, "but treated the subject in the language of metaphor. He divided the essay into three parts, being a direct appeal to nature, whence all our emotion and all our inspiration must come, taking nature to its most impressive and deepest phases—the phase of growth, . . . of decadence, and the inscrutable cause underlying both of these. Part first was "Growth, a Spring Song," part second, "Decadence, Autumn Reverie," part third, "The Infinite, a Song of the Depths."

In "Inspiration," says Sherman Paul, Sullivan "first expressed his awareness of the rhythm that was the basis—and the most profound meaning of his art in building, ornament, and writing." Life and death, growth and decay, death as the condition of life, were the challenges to humanity. To be bold, that is to create, in the face of death—humanity's fate—was the source of artistic energy. Art was the fruit of inspiration that comes from understanding life, from the serenity achieved by knowing that death is itself a form of recreativity. Spontaneous and vital art, Sullivan said, "must come from nature" not from scholarship, logic, or taste. "Inspiration" was a difficult, obscure, and esoteric essay, and although his listeners were duly impressed—some observers thought them completely mystified—Sullivan was not invited to speak to the Western Association again during its last three years of existence.[37]

In March 1887, at a regular monthly meeting of the Illinois State Association, during a forum on "the present tendencies of American architecture," Sullivan disagreed when John Root argued that the nation would need to develop a distinctive character before it could have its own style. "I think we are starting at the wrong end entirely," Sullivan replied. Style comes from within the self, from thinking, reflecting, observing, and assimilating. "The eventual outcome of our American architecture will be the emanation of what is going on inside of us at present." Were he to predict what American style might be, he would look to the living generation, not to the past. To be good stylists, we must be good observers first, then good draftsmen. When Root responded in disagreement that to design properly one should search history for inspiration, Sullivan said that would mean imitation: "The use of any historic motive, which once had a special significance, now seems rather thin and hollow when used in our designs."[38]

At the next meeting in April, when Sullivan spoke to the question "What Is the Just Subordination, in Architectural Design, of Detail to Mass?" he admitted being "at a loss for a precise answer." Just what is the proper ratio of leaves and branches on a tree? he asked. "For my part, I find their thousand ways all charming and fruitful in suggestion. I graciously permit them to grow as they will." Architecture ought not to be so different, "for I insist strenuously, that a building should live with intense, if quiescent, life, because it is sprung from the life of an architect. On no other basis are results of permanent value likely to be attained." As to the question specifically? "For the moment [this was just after his "simplified" Auditorium plans were approved] it suits me to favor a very simple outline, particularly at the roof." Mass should be divided into detail only for practical purposes, only when utility dictated. The form of details should be determined by the materials as a rule and "above all," he emphasized, "there shall effuse from the completed structure *a single sentiment* [emphasis added] which shall be the spiritual result of a prior and perfect understanding and assimilation of all the data." Here in a single sentence Sullivan carried his Ecole training to a mature conclusion: the purpose of architecture was to express simply and boldly the life of the architect—"the organism in its surroundings"—acting for society.[39]

Seven years later, in 1894, Sullivan again dealt with the relationship of style to the creative process when he delivered one of his most famous speeches, "Emotional Architecture as Compared with Classical," to AIA.[40] By taking inspiration (a product of "touch"—openness to experience—and intuition), honing it with thought, and perfecting a mode of expression based on the two, Sullivan argued, "then, and not till then, shall we possess, individually and as a people, the necessary elements of a great *Style.*" Subjectivity, the soul of the artist, and objectivity, the expression thereof, must always be complementary and harmonious. The intellectual and the emotional, in other words, lie at the very heart of creativity as they do in nature itself. But architecture schools, Sullivan lamented, taught only the "objective aspects and forms of architecture." The student learns that

> architecture is a fixed, a real, a specific, a definite thing, that it's all done, that it's all known, arranged, tabulated, and put away neatly in handy packages called books. . . . [W]hen his turn comes, if he wishes to make some architecture . . . he can dip it out of his books [like] a grocer dipping beans out of a bin. . . . He has been taught many cold and dead things, but the one warm living thing that he has not been taught [is] that architecture, wherever it has appeared and reached a spontaneous culmination, is not at all what we so stupidly call reality, but, on the contrary, is a most complex, a glowing and gloriously wrought metaphor, embodying as no other form of language under the sun . . . the pure, clean and deep inspiration of the [human] race flowing as a stream of living water from its well-spring to the sea. . . . This seeking for a natural expression of our lives, of our thoughts, our meditations, our feelings, is the architectural art as I understand it.

America would someday "possess a most interesting, varied, characteristic, and beautiful architecture," he was sure, but only when the young rejected "the benumbing influence of an instruction that insulates them from the vitalizing currents of nature, . . . [from] a full, a rich, a chaste development of the emotions."

Classical architecture, especially Greek, Sullivan continued, "was almost exclusively intellectual," the Gothic likewise "one-sided and incomplete . . . because of the almost total absence of mentality," that is, it was overly emotional. Architectural art in general was thus far incompletely developed because it had not harmoniously united emotion with intellect: "it does not yet respond to the poet's touch." The Greeks knew the statics, the Goths the dynamics, of the art, but neither suspected its mobile equilibrium because neither understood the simultaneous movement and stability of nature, therefore of building. Too much emphasis on the one or the other yielded imperfect expression. Only imaginative freedom conditioned by thought would generate a mode of expression suitable to the life of the times; architects must combine emotional (the Gothic) with intellectual (the classic)—not their forms but their attitudes—before they could arrive at their own styles. Sullivan's call for a new architecture based on autobiography and the study of society was beginning to make an impact on many in the younger generation by 1894, when he gave this speech, among them Frank Lloyd Wright. By the end of the decade, Sullivan's own work, some of his contemporaries', and his followers', seeking to put "progress before precedent," had pushed Chicago architecture to the frontiers of world design.

Sullivan was an "organization man" in the 1880s and 1890s, somewhat against his personal inclinations. Preferring his solitude and the company of small groups of friends, he nevertheless joined associations in order to raise professional standards and to campaign for a modern indigenous architecture. He understood that in the late nineteenth century, architects needed the power of organization to survive the age of giant corporations. He would rather have been at his drafting table, at his writing desk, or in his study, but as a realist who knew that in unity there was strength, he was active in organizations from 1884 to 1900, not just to make speeches but also to assist with down-to-earth, very practical matters. He did not particularly relish this work—except the speeches he learned to deliver quite eloquently—nor did he especially dislike it. He saw it as the necessary obligation of a responsible professional.

Sullivan showed considerable disdain for categories and labels, but if pressed to describe himself in a word, he certainly thought of himself first and foremost as an "artist" or a "poet" and secondly as an "architect." He was an artist whose medium happened to be design. Tradition has it that because Adler was such a good businessman, Sullivan could concentrate exclusively on architecture and philosophy. But in point of fact he was as active as his partner in day-to-day associational work. From their office in the Auditorium tower, the man at the top of his profession was also helping to lay its foundations.

Chapter IX

BUILDING GREATNESS 1887-94

FROM JANUARY 1887 through the end of their business association in mid-1895, Dankmar Adler and Louis Sullivan received some eighty-eight commissions, about ten a year, peaking at thirty-two in 1890–91. Before the Auditorium they had designed approximately ninety-two buildings, or more than thirteen each year from 1880 to 1886, almost seventeen annually during the hectic forty-eight months beginning in January 1883. Although there was more of it in terms of numbers, the early work was generally smaller and less expensive than their later jobs, for example, their forty-four pre-1887 houses (73 percent of their total of sixty). Before the Auditorium, houses constituted well over 40 percent of their output, but during and afterward, only 18 percent. Only nine of their sixteen dwellings after 1886 were designed in the 1890s—all but two multiple residences were done by 1891—and two of these were for Louis Sullivan's own use. Beginning in 1887, and especially by the time the Auditorium was completed, Adler & Sullivan received larger, more substantial, and costlier work distributed farther afield geographically with different kinds of problems than they had hitherto encountered.

Leaving skyscrapers to be treated separately in the next chapter, their mature work can be assigned to a few simple categories. The handful of residences are important as hints at new directions in Sullivan's design, but mostly for their role in the emergence of Frank Lloyd Wright. There were six important theaters and concert halls through 1894, thirty-six warehouses, factories, and other commercial buildings, three synagogue projects, four hotels, three tombs, one of their most famous structures—the Transportation Building at the 1893 Columbian World's Fair—and a scattering of other work, some of which reveals Sullivan's dependence on Henry Richardson in the late 1880s and then his movement away later on. The partners designed only seventeen projects after the onset of the depression in 1893, which got so severe during the next two years that five were never executed, the highest proportion in their history. In 1895 no new jobs came their way. By 1894 their most important undertakings were skyscrapers, so with that exception, for all intents and purposes, their most creative period came to an end six months to a year before they parted company.

Except for the unexecuted 1894 Eliel apartment project and the Herman Braunstein store and flats, their sixteen post-Auditorium residences were designed between 1887 and 1891. Three of the remaining fourteen were flats buildings, for contractor Victor Falkenau (frequently employed by Adler & Sullivan) and builder

IX.1 *Victor Falkenau flats, 1888, drawn by Frank Lloyd Wright.* From *Inland Architect,* 1888.

Patrick Farrell, both on South Wabash, and for the Loeb Brothers, Adolph and William, at Elizabeth and Randolph. One of the eleven single-family residences was an unexecuted interior alteration and addition to Wirt Dexter's house on Prairie Avenue, two were for Sullivan himself (already discussed), and two were for James Charnley, one in Ocean Springs, another on Chicago's near North Side in Astor Street.

Sullivan's last few dwelling places looked entirely different from his pre-1890 work (in the absence of early floor plans, extensive interior comparisons cannot be made); certainly, the four Sullivan and Charnley houses from 1890 and 1891—one for each in Chicago and Ocean Springs—were something completely new. To explain this sudden break with the past, historian Grant Manson introduced Frank Lloyd Wright, arguing that the Victor Falkenau flats on which Wright worked signaled the beginning of a new phase in Adler & Sullivan's residential work.[1] The architect himself seemed to confirm this. "Adler and Sullivan refused to build residences during all the time I was with them [1888 to 1893]," Wright recalled. "The few that were imperative, owing to social obligations to important clients, fell to my lot out of office hours."[2] Since Falkenau's building was designed no later than February 1888,[3] at just the moment Wright entered the firm, not in June, as Manson thought, the logic of this scholarly contention combined with the sense of Wright's memoirs is that the newcomer was the creative force behind the new Adler & Sullivan look. Although Wright actually claimed to have designed only the Sullivan and Charnley dwellings, Manson accepted the larger implication, fortified by the visual evidence of the Falkenau flats, that Adler & Sullivan's new residential aesthetic began in 1888, not in 1890 or 1891, and that it was basically Wright's doing.

But there are several difficulties with this view, the first being Sullivan's quite explicit statement that in 1890 he designed the Ocean Springs cottages himself. A second difficulty involves the Falkenau building itself. That one of the published drawings bore Wright's signature (another had a different employee's) does not verify him as the designer, since it was common at the time for renderers to sign their employers' work. The "surprisingly clean" facade, "styleless" ornamentation, and "quiet horizontality" detected by Manson as evidence of Wright, furthermore, could as easily be traced to Henry Richardson's influence on Sullivan's hand, especially in light of his new commercial structures, particularly the Walker Warehouse and the Dooly Block (see below), with which Falkenau shared a family resemblance, bearing in mind as well that he had previously designed multiple housing with imagery similar to business edifices. Not for another thirteen years, moreover, would Wright's work consistently reveal the properties seen at the Falkenau flats by Manson, who may have prematurely judged them according to a later aesthetic standard.

A third difficulty with the Manson interpretation is the hazard of accepting Wright's insistence that "social obligations to important clients" gave him the opportunity to design on his own.[4] Only two of the 1888 to 1893 residential customers had hired Adler & Sullivan before: the Loebs and Wirt Dexter, whose houses Wright did not mention doing. Of the rest, contractor Falkenau was a close business associate, builder Patrick Farrell may have been, and James Charnley was Sullivan's good friend. These people plus Sullivan himself accounted for nine of the firm's eleven houses during Wright's tenure. The other two, for George M. Harvey (1888) and Dr. J. G. Berry (1891), averaged $11,000. Neither was an indication of unusual social standing, they did not lead to further commissions, the Harvey House did not look particularly "Wrightian" or new, and Wright did not remember designing them anyway. It is unlikely, moreover, that even under the pressure of Auditorium work, Sullivan would have entrusted houses for friends and business associates to one so young and inexperienced as Wright was before 1890. Even if he did, his assistant's autobiographical recollections were surely exaggerated, his assertion, for example, that neither Adler nor Sullivan "ever saw (the [Ira] Heath House),"[5] a truly remarkable claim considering that Heath was Adler's friend and that both partners ran a very tight ship.

But around this time office responsibilities seem to have been somewhat reallocated. In June 1890 the floor plan of Adler & Sullivan's new suite atop the Auditorium (occupied during the latter half of 1889 or early the next year) showed Wright with his own office—actually shared with George Elmslie—indicating that he had recently been promoted. Having proved his abilities with house renderings for previous employer Joseph L. Silsbee, by planning and constructing two residential buildings—one in 1887 for his aunts at their Wisconsin boarding school, the other for himself in Oak Park, Illinois, in 1889—and by developing Sullivan's rough sketches for Auditorium ornament into working drawings, perhaps even designing small portions of the building himself,[6] Wright became Sullivan's principal assistant, charged with, among other things, planning at least one of the firm's 1891 dwellings. Most authorities accept his claim to have been the actual architect of the $25,000 Charnley house at 1365 Astor Street, designed in June 1891, a brilliant building, remarkably clean and straightforward for its day, with smooth, skinlike, taut brick walls, an early landmark of the modern movement. It is not Richardsonian and not like earlier Sullivan houses, although certain details like the front-door window and the porch's balusters and frieze reveal either Wright's mastery of his employer's ornament or the employer's hand itself.

The contemporary Sullivan house on Lake Park Avenue, on the other hand, is not so easily attributed, even though the two have strong conceptual similarities. Both rest on high, smooth, stone bases with deeply inset rectangular windows punched through. Both have flat roofs with heavily decorated fascia (a new Sullivan trademark), the deep frieze at the Sullivan house approximating in proportion the reduced third story above the horizontal course at the Charnley residence. Immediately below are overscaled projections, the porch at the one house, the oriel at the other. In each case the windows are deeply recessed and each sports a conspicuously placed colonnade, of sorts. Neither is anything like Sullivan's earlier residences, up to and including work as late as 1888. On the other hand, the two are also conceptually quite different, the small home for Andrienne Sullivan being a narrow, vertical row house, the larger building for Charnley a detached, horizontal townhouse with a much more spacious, open interior at twice the cost. The ornament at Lake Park Avenue further confuses the matter of attribution. Over the entrance, on the capitals and front door, it is Sullivan, but since elsewhere it could be Wright's version of Sullivan, resembling as it does the work at Astor Street, a case could be made for either as the principal architect. Wright certainly designed the Charnley house, and most likely assisted at Lake Park Avenue, but there is little evidence to suggest that before 1891 his employers' dwellings were his responsibility.[7]

Since there were only three in 1891 and none after that for his remaining year and one-half with the firm, Wright got his residential experience in other ways. His success on the Charnley house may in fact have prompted him to take rather drastic action. In his autobiography he confessed that to pay for his Oak Park home, built in part with money borrowed from Sullivan, he "accepted several houses on my own account"—he named three—designing them "out

IX.2 *Frank Lloyd Wright, c. 1889.* Courtesy Frank Lloyd Wright Home and Studio Foundation.

of office hours, [but] not secretly." (In a word, he was "moonlighting.") When Sullivan learned that his assistant had broken the terms of his five-year contract by taking his own commissions, he was offended enough to delay signing over the deed for the Oak Park residence Wright had since paid off. "Your sole interest is here, while your contract lasts," he was reported as saying. "I won't tolerate division under any circumstances." Wright appealed to Adler, but Sullivan was adamant, so a few months before his contract was to have expired, no later than May 1893, as other sources reveal,[8] Wright quit. After more than five years together, Sullivan and his protégé parted, not to speak to each other until the end of the decade.

Wright identified only three "bootlegged" houses, as he later called them, for Warren McArthur and George Blossom, next door to each other at Forty-ninth Street and Kenwood Avenue, and for Dr. Allison Harlan, on Greenwood. Historians have alleged as many as ten distributed over the period from 1890 to 1893, but recent, more exhaustive, research has reduced the number to six, five of which were designed in 1892, when the sixth, from 1891, was built.[9] For reasons of interest to both Wright and his employer, 1892 was a particularly important year, the first in their decade-old partnership that Adler & Sullivan had no residential commissions, leaving Wright with none to do. Assuming that with at least three houses (his own, his aunts', and the Charnleys') behind him, he enjoyed this kind of work (as his subsequent career amply demonstrates), and was bitten by the residential bug, that he was short of money (chronically the case), and was already thinking of striking out on his own, then 1892, possibly even halfway through 1891, was the logical time for Wright to seek his own jobs. In addition to the three in Chicago, the six bootlegs were for Thomas Gale and R. P. Parker in Oak Park, and Robert Emmond in La Grange. Their location is as important as their date.

Wright never mentioned the three suburban homes because for good reason they were less important to him than the Chicago bootlegs. The Harlan house, at 4414 Greenwood Avenue, designed in July 1891 (one month after Charnley) , was located less than two and one-half blocks northwest of the Lake Park Avenue dwelling Sullivan occupied early in 1892, directly in view down Forty-fourth Place along his everyday route to the Forty-third Street railroad station, where he caught the train to work. The McArthur and Blossom

IX.3 *James Charnley residence, 1891, Chicago.*

IX.4 *Two "bootlegged" houses by Frank Lloyd Wright, 1890: Blossom* (left) *and McArthur.* Photo by Robert Twombly.

houses, designed and erected in 1892 on Kenwood at the corner of Forty-ninth, were almost as close to Sullivan, just four blocks south and a little east at numbers 4852 and 4858, easily seen from the rear of 4830 Kimbark, the next avenue over, where Albert Sullivan lived in 1892, frequently entertaining his brother before his marriage the following February. Knowing one of Sullivan's greatest pleasures was walking, that he would be curious about new construction in his neighborhood, especially if it were somewhat different, like the Harlan house, Wright tried to hide the three Chicago jobs from his employer, contrary to what he wrote in his memoirs.

But had Sullivan read the local building magazines or glanced at the real estate column in the *Sunday Tribune,* he would surely have seen the following. In July 1891 the press reported that

> C. S. Corwin has completed drawings for a two story, basement and attic residence to be erected on Greenwood avenue, for Dr. A. W. Harlan. It will have a basement of stone and pressed brick and above this will be frame, the interior to be finished in hardwood. The cost will be about $15,000.

Eleven months later, in June 1892, another notice appeared:

> C. S. Corwin is preparing plans for two two-story basement and attic frame residences to be erected on Forty-ninth street and Kenwood avenue for George Blossom and W. McArthur. They will have pressed brick basements and cost $8,000 each.[10]

"C. S. Corwin," an architect, was none other than Cecil Corwin, Wright's best friend, whose name he "borrowed" to disguise his business affairs. He omitted the three suburban houses from his memoirs because in the 1890s he had not announced them under Corwin's name. Knowing Sullivan would probably never see them, in fact, Wright never bothered to announce them at all. The only reason for publicly attributing the Chicago bootlegs to Corwin, rather than ignoring them altogether, was to deceive Sullivan, to forestall his asking workmen the architect's name, which he probably would have, had he simply come upon the houses on the street. The ploy apparently worked for a while. Sullivan did not discover the actual architect for several months. When he did, and told Wright to stop taking outside work as his contract stipulated, his assistant refused, and quit. His ethically questionable tactics were made even more painful by the fact that Corwin had also been a Sullivan employee. So when the two young architects joined forces in 1893 to open an office together—in Sullivan's 1891 Schiller Building, be it noted, perhaps as a kind of repentance—they shared more than the same address. They also shared the knowledge that they had offended the one man who had inspired them most. More than three decades later, when Wright described this affair in his autobiography, first drafted in the fall of 1926, he did not mention using Corwin's name as a cover-up. But his insistence on identifying the three bootlegs for all the world to know may have indicated a lingering guilt, made all the more disturbing by Sullivan's death two and one-half years before and by the two eloquent tributes he penned about his "lieber meister" in the following months.[11]

Despite the historic significance of this business, houses were hardly the most important aspect of Adler & Sullivan's work, particularly after 1886. In terms of numbers, the three years before the Auditorium were the busiest in the firm's history, with fifty-six commissions averaging over eighteen annually. During the Auditorium's construction, the partners took on only thirty new jobs—just ten a year, little more than half their previous output—although a few were more substantial than anything they had done earlier. Many of their clients from 1886 to 1889 were personal friends, had employed them before, were business connections, or were prominent members of the Chicago Jewish community, obligating them to take the work, perhaps, despite the Auditorium. But in 1889, as the end of their labors neared and their practice returned to a more normal equilibrium, they began to consider large and important commissions from new clients and other parts of the country. Only then did Sullivan find his own architectural language, beyond the influence of Henry Richardson, in a new kind of edifice, the skyscraper. But in the meantime his work was a series of explorations in several building types, the most important of which are now described.

The Standard Club for socially prominent Jewish men was founded in 1869 by early Adler & Sullivan clients Charles Schwab and Morris Selz, among others. Emanuel Frankenthal, Simon and Emanuel Mandel, Marx Wineman, and Levi Rosenfeld, each a member said to be worth upwards of a half million dollars, had also hired the firm. So early in 1886, when the club purchased a 70-by-185-foot lot on the southwest corner of Twenty-fourth Street and

IX.5 *Standard Club, 1887.* Photo by The Chicago Architectural Photographing Company.

Michigan Avenue, it knew where to look for architects. Construction was anticipated that summer, but the planning was inexplicably deferred until 1887, when the first contracts were let in July. Except for interior details that took until the next February, the clubhouse was finished at the end of 1888 for more than $100,000.

Its four stories in Romanesque detail were faced with rusticated limestone blocks, diminishing in size toward the flat, uncorniced roof. Its windows were treated as alternating tiers and rows of arched and flat-headed openings with emphatic single-piece sills, lintels, and mullions. The only obvious ornament were buff terra-cotta panels under the third-story windows. String courses over the first and third floors divided the elevation into a 1-2-1 format compatible with the horizontal cut of the stone. *American Architect* disliked almost everything about the building except "the generous arch with a fine sweep" that served as the main entrance, but the *Chicago Tribune*'s critic, correctly perceiving "that it is of the Richardson type . . . like the Marshall Field warehouse," was impressed by the interior's rich decorative work, especially Sullivan's "decidedly original mantels." Despite Richardsonian references, its base of arched and rectangular doors and windows more closely resembled Sullivan's recently de-

IX.6 *Wirt Dexter Building, 1887.* Photo by Kaufmann & Fabry Company.

signed Auditorium than it did the wholesale store. Everyone agreed the Standard Club was massive, bold, and imposing, though not necessarily one of Sullivan's finest efforts.[12]

Two highly regarded non-Richardsonian Chicago buildings from May 1887 are now considered landmarks in their genres. The six-story, $100,000 Wirt Dexter store and warehouse on Wabash and Panorama Place, "a logical outgrowth of [Sullivan's 1884] Troescher Building," according to Hugh Morrison, was "the end-point of the style development of the early and middle eighties." Rising smoothly from its rusticated granite base in virtually unornamented ashlar, its plain facade served its masonry and iron materials in Sullivan's first mature deployment of a "system of vertical construction." Unencumbered by the capricious ornament of his earlier high-rises, the Dexter Building anticipated the aesthetics of the steel frame, its clear, realistic expression of structure forming a link in the retrospectively selective chain from the 1881 Rothschild Store and the Troescher Building to his genuine skyscrapers of the 1890s. The $75,000 Selz, Schwab boot-and-shoe factory at Superior and Roberts streets, built for a mere five and one-half cents per cubic foot, was, according to one historian, "one of the few architecturally worthwhile factories of the latter part of the nineteenth century." Recalling his 1884 Kennedy and Knisely buildings, Sullivan took the piers without a break from sidewalk to rooftop parapet, recessing the windows and all the horizontals. He relieved the potential starkness of this noticeably architectonic and rhythmical composition with slightly tapering piers, gently curving window heads, and white stone sills. Selz, Schwab was Sullivan's best factory—simple and austere, yet graceful, powerful, and self-assured.[13]

Since Sullivan had been designing factories and high-rises for several years, the Dexter and Selz, Schwab buildings of 1887 can be used to measure his progress. At the Dexter Building, Sullivan reduced the high-rise facade to its essentials: a straightforward, unadorned expression of vertical superordinate supports and subordinate horizontal ties, creating visual interest in and of itself, a kind of clean slate, Morrison suggested, ready to accept the steel frame. With only the slightest historical references, the Dexter Building went beyond its contemporaries in asserting the relationships among aesthetics, structure, and form. Selz, Schwab, on the other hand, was Sullivan's equally sophisticated contribution to the art of factory building. Its strong rhythms, clear statement of support systems, and

IX.7 *Selz, Schwab factory, 1887.*

IX.8 *Martin Ryerson Tomb, 1887.* Photo by Robert Twombly.

treatment of the outer wall as nothing more than enclosing skin (like the Dexters', as well) culminated several years of experiment. In these two design categories that had especially interested Sullivan, he did not need Richardson or anyone else to help him. But in other areas, clubhouses, for example, where he was less experienced, the Bostonian's influence was greater, but only until Sullivan developed his own architectural systems as the next decade opened.

Although Martin A. Ryerson's was his first tomb, Sullivan did not turn to Richardson's Romanesque. The Chicago client died in 1887, and by November Sullivan had completed his design for a Graceland Cemetery site. Composed of dark Quincy (Massachusetts) granite and polished blue Bedford (Indiana) limestone, its sloping central mass with a severely rectangular door and tiny clerestory windows was capped by a four-course pyramid and flanked with concave wings flared at the base. The tomb was massive enough to suggest eternity, but its curving sides and soaring shape could easily symbolize regeneration, the renewal of life in the earth from which the structure seemed to grow. The eternity alluded to here seemed not to be everlasting death, however, but the perpetual cycle of life—as expressed in his essay "Inspiration" the year before—seen when the highly polished stone reflected passing clouds, changing tints of sky, and gently swaying trees, the same natural forms that had captured his boyhood imagination at his Bennet Street window. Death, Sullivan appeared to be saying, was but a part of life, not an end in itself.[14]

As if to confirm the notion, Ryerson's death interrupted but did not stop Sullivan's intention to build a warehouse at the southwest corner of Market and Adams, planned on and off from January 1887 to early 1888, with construction beginning that July for an October 1889 opening. Built for $300,000 to $400,000 from smooth ashlar masonry instead of the originally anticipated pressed brick and stone, it was the closest contemporary to the Auditorium, which in many ways it resembled, although some think it an even better example of Richardsonian Romanesque. Known as the James H. Walker Warehouse, after its first tenant, a furniture wholesaler, it was clearly influenced by the Marshall Field Store, even if in some ways it improved upon it. Its seven floors were divided into a two-story base, a middle four-story section with deeply inset windows arched at the top (like the Field and Auditorium buildings) in two tiers for each of the four bays, and an attic. The Walker Warehouse is essentially a study in geometry wherein Sullivan developed a perfectly rectangular plan into a three-dimensional essay in volume. By using smooth instead of his usual rusticated stone and emphasizing the openings so emphatically, Sullivan again expressed the wall as skin rather than solid mass. The corner piers rose straight from sidewalk to shallow cornice, the building was virtually unornamented, the overlarge twenty-four- and twenty-seven-and-one-half-foot double arches at street level were not for entry but for composition, and the deep reveals formed a play of light and shadow suggesting enclosure rather than density. The harmony of rectangles and arches teamed with the brilliant balance of verticals and horizontals to make one of Sullivan's most successful facades. The Walker Warehouse was powerful, simple, crisp, and clean, an experiment in the possibilities of masonry and iron construction that was a step beyond Dexter and Selz, Schwab toward his skyscrapers of the 1890s.[15]

His next major building was the Opera House Block in Pueblo, Colorado, at $400,000 Adler & Sullivan's costliest out-of-town work to date. Hired on June 12, 1888, Adler visited Pueblo with Sullivan's preliminary sketches less than three weeks later, on the thirtieth.

IX.9 *Walker Warehouse, 1888.*

IX.10 *Pueblo Opera House Block, 1889.* From *Inland Architect,* 1893.

Plans were submitted on September 1, returned to the architects for revision in November, and finished in January 1889. Problems with the foundations, perhaps with other matters, too, delayed construction for a year until excavation began in February 1890, after which Adler & Sullivan assistant Henry W. French supervised the work until completed in October. The four story block fronting 120 feet on Main Street, 190 on Fourth, was composed of rusticated Manitou (Minnesota) red stone on an eight-foot base of gray granite. The first-floor front offered three arches (the center somewhat larger) as the theater entrance, two more as bank windows, and a framed rectangular door to the bank replicated around the corner on Fourth Street, where it introduced a line of nine arched windows, five preceding and four to the rear of the rectangular auxiliary doorway for the music hall. Four shops on Fourth and two more inside off the vestibule increased the block's commercial potential, while over the large Main Street arch, a small, slightly projecting loggia also recalled the Chicago Auditorium. On the two business facades, second- and third-floor offices were treated with simple rectangular windows, but at the fourth floor, recessed galleries were fronted by thin columns under six-foot eaves. Flush with the Main Street elevation but cut off at its base by these roof projections, again like the Auditorium, on which its entire program was modeled, was a 131-foot tower with an observation platform sheltered by a far-reaching overhang. On the roof back of the tower forming a fifth story over the theater were two thirty-seven-by-eighty-four-foot "penthouses"—one for stage rigging, the other a "summer garden"—both capped with conical lanterns, one with an additional steep-roofed, step-gabled turret for exhaust vents.

The auditorium at Pueblo was one of Adler & Sullivan's more imaginative. Accommodating eleven hundred chairs, it was seventy-eight feet wide by eighty-five deep. Its balcony curved toward the stage in a shallow C, flaring a bit at the far sides in a well-established pattern Adler & Sullivan had used at the Grand Opera House (1880), McVicker's Theater (1885), and elsewhere. The rear gallery above was the first in America not supported by columns. Massive arches at the side walls underscored a cross-vaulted ceiling dropped at stage end to form a sounding board. Rising to the rear, the floor fanned out like a scallop shell through the parquet and circle in front of a colonnade designating the vestibule that wrapped the room until terminating at four boxes on either side, each stepped down one foot to the first, placed slightly below stage level. The thirty-two-by-thirty-foot-high proscenium arch fronted a forty-by-ninety-foot stage with seventy-five feet of loft space for platforms and mechanical equipment. There were twenty sinks, traps, and bridges on the floor, the stage was lit by seven hundred electric lights arranged in red, white and green groups, performers were given fourteen dressing rooms, and the scenery was housed in a separate building reached by a bridge.

Sullivan's highly praised decorations were another indication of his preeminence in concert hall design. The gold-leafed proscenium arch, placed within the shortened end of a crossing vault, corresponding to the chancel of a cathedral, was divided into rectangular panels with floral motifs on fascia and soffits. The cove ceiling high over the gallery (clinging to the rear wall well above the balcony) was left undecorated, the flat main ceiling in front was heavily ribbed, and the vaulted portion nearest the stage lightly ribbed into

IX.11 *Pueblo Opera House auditorium.* From *Pueblo Chieftain,* October 10, 1890.

panels with medallions and various geometric shapes painted salmon with gray-blue accents. The side arches and the gallery and balcony balusters in ivory with gold leaf were studded with five hundred electric lights worked into the ornament, a Sullivan trademark since McVicker's. In the spaces separating the outer double-glazing for energy conservation from the inner art-glass windows, Sullivan placed lights to accentuate his ornamental work, additionally evident in the large grates he designed to disguise air vents. Local reviewers applauded the decorations, congratulating the architects additionally on the theater's excellent sight lines and outstanding acoustics.

The Opera House Block burned down in 1922. Before and after that, perhaps because of its western location, it was the least known and appreciated of Adler & Sullivan's theaters. But its cross-axial vaulted ceiling, forming a sounding board and containing the proscenium arch, was as pleasing as it was unique and functionally successful. The Pueblo Opera House was also the first occasion on which the architects placed boxes below stage level—they would do it again at McVicker's renovation in 1891—or housed rigging in a rooftop penthouse that was, in effect, a separate building, or suspended the gallery without post supports. Although the main floor of the facade was Romanesque, the eaves, loggia, and tower suggested a Florentine inspiration. Designed during the last year of Auditorium construction, it was in many conceptual ways a direct offspring of the parent building, but by moving outside the Romanesque and with their innovative interior, Adler & Sullivan brought new solutions to a familiar design problem. The influence of Richardson was waning, but not yet gone.[16]

The second major building of 1889 was the Kehilath Anshe Ma'ariv Synagogue for the Adler family congregation at Thirty-third Street and Indiana Avenue. The first set of plans from the spring of 1889 envisioned a monumental structure of polychromatic limestone ashlar with deeply raked joints making a noticeably textured skin. A steeply pitched, pyramidal-roofed clerestory would have projected through the hip roof of the main massing. But in May 1890 the original battered wall substructure was redesigned for rusticated Joliet stone with an ornamentally stamped sheet-metal clerestory. The arched entrance of receding concentric rings, soon to reappear in more majestic form at the World's Fair Transportation Building, the Schiller Theatre, and elsewhere, was a Romanesque touch, like the arched third-story windows capping tiers formed by rectangular openings below. Although Anshe Ma'ariv can be classified as another of Sullivan's Richardsonian efforts, it also resembled Ryerson's Tomb in general shape. The visual effect of the executed structure was jarring because the two materials clashed and the clerestory, without benefit of a hip roof on the main mass, sat like a lump on its different-colored base. The reason generally given for this unfortunate result is insufficient funds to carry the stonework all the way through, even though the estimate for the original scheme was $50,000; for the second, double that. One contemporary observer believed that if the bottom portion was Romanesque, the top was Venetian, "and never before was a Venetian form so out of place."

After the second version was dedicated in June 1891, the Jewish publication *Reform Advocate* congratulated Kehilath Anshe Ma'ariv for erecting "so noble and beautiful a structure which will ever be looked upon as a masterwork of architectural genius." Hopefully, it had the interior in mind. Occupying the second and third stories, the sanctuary rose in an oak-paneled barrel vault into the clerestory with

IX.12 *Kehilath Anshe Ma'ariv Synagogue as built, 1890.* From *Inland Architect,* 1891.

windows on three sides. Receiving transverse ribs, the curved panel at the front of the vault held Sullivan's richly decorated arch framing the ark and organ loft. A gallery around the back and sides looked down at floor seating in a four-part segmental arch. The terra-cotta lower and ivory upper walls were embellished by floral and geometrical entwined ornament on the gallery front, the foot of the vault, and within the arch, some of the finest and most luxuriant Sullivan ever designed. To accommodate a gallery, the elevated barrel vault was structurally different from Adler's other auditoria, but the acoustics were reportedly excellent nonetheless. Sympathetic viewers felt the interior to be "warm, rich, and yet subdued."[17]

It was also in 1889 that the firm of Adler & Sullivan, but apparently only Adler, was hired to assist New York architect William B. Tuthill with the acoustics of Carnegie Hall, although to this day the extent of his contribution is unknown. Tuthill sought the advice of prominent musicians, was himself an accomplished cellist, made many acoustical experiments for the project, studied dozens of concert halls around the world, and as secretary of the Oratorio Society, a sponsoring organization, was amply qualified to undertake the task. Officials have searched Carnegie Hall's every nook and cranny for documentation of Tuthill's ideas and Adler's role in the planning but without success. Nor have records so far surfaced in any other place. Tuthill saw to it, however, that when "Adler & Sullivan" was inadvertently omitted from the published drawings in 1890, a correction was quickly made, thereby observing a professional courtesy, perhaps also acknowledging Adler's indispensable

IX.13 *Kehilath Anshe Ma'ariv Synagogue, auditorium.* From *Inland Architect,* 1891.

IX.14 *Chicago Cold Storage Exchange Warehouse, 1890.* From *Inland Architect,* 1890.

role, but otherwise he made no statement about his associate. Carnegie Hall, as Serge Koussevitzky once said, "is one among the very few best auditoriums, acoustically." But the extent Adler helped Tuthill make it so may never be fully understood.[18]

Eighteen-ninety was a particularly productive year for Adler & Sullivan. Their enormous Chicago Cold Storage Exchange Warehouse at Lake, Randolph, and West Water streets, designed in April and May, but only partially executed, would have contained over 6,500,000 cubic feet, almost half for wholesale food storage, the rest for brokers' and commission offices and for three large stores. Two parallel ten-story wings, 382 feet long, one 82 feet wide, the other 70, were divided in plan at Chicago River level by railroad tracks. Above, at the street, a broad terrace functioned as a waterside promenade, the roof for transport spaces, and the foreground for the thirty-six-foot-wide "West Water Street Arcade" of offices separating the wings under a hipped, clerestoried canopy. A series of arched entrances spreading across the main facade at terrace level continued around the corner on the river as truncated third-story windows in the form of lunettes. The five storage floors under the cornice were given only narrow slotted openings arranged in tiers, the spandrels recessed to form pencil-thin continuous vertical arches. Recalling the Walker Warehouse, Sullivan treated the surface, in this case where no windows of consequence were necessary, as a planar indicator of volume, which was, in fact, the essence of the two giant boxes. But at almost $2,000,000 these rather expensive boxes were to contain refrigeration equipment sufficient to dispose of six hundred tons of ice a day. With its massive, clifflike walls, elegant detailing at the roof line, impressive entrance arcade, overall handsomeness, and efficient disposition of river, rail, and street traffic, the Exchange was one of several 1890 projects demonstrating to the few remaining skeptics—and there were some—that the recently completed Auditorium was not a fluke.[19]

With the warehouse still on the drawing boards, Adler & Sullivan was hired in May to remodel the thirty-year-old Grand Opera House in Milwaukee, purchased by Captain Fred Pabst for $125,000 in February 1890 as the new home for the Stadt Company, a German theatrical group he helped support. By the time it reopened in September, nothing remained of the original hall except the stage floor, a few brick partitions, and a portion of the gallery. By pushing the rear wall out eighteen feet, Adler & Sullivan added almost two hundred seats for a total of twelve hundred, including eight boxes, and expanded the stage by one thousand square feet to twenty-four hundred. Published plans show an arc-shaped orchestra, a three-part scallop shell parquet and a four-part parquet circle, the latter under the deeply curved balcony with a rectangular gallery above that. Their new ceiling was arched as usual, every section of the theater had its own enlarged exit, the curtains (including one of iron) were electrically operated, fan-driven heating and ventilation systems were improved, hydrants for fire protection were increased, and everything was illuminated by fourteen hundred incandescent lights of sixteen candlepower each. Little is known of Sullivan's ornament except that walls were white and gold, the boxes draped and stuccoed in "Renaissance style"—according to a press account—and the curtain with allegorical scenes of the Muses and a partial view of Milwaukee was painted by a well-known New York artist, Otto von Ernst. Opening night, the *Journal* reported on September 18, "was one of the most pleasing events in the history of Milwaukee." When Fred Pabst contemplated renovating the entire Opera House Block in November, he may have considered returning to Adler & Sullivan, but nothing further was done before the building burned down in 1893.[20]

Another project in May 1890 was the $300,000 Ontario Hotel for Salt Lake City, which, like the Cold Storage Exchange, consisted of two parallel blocks, here six stories high and seven bays long, under a

IX.15 *Ontario Hotel project, first version, 1890.* From *Inland Architect,* 1891.

broadly eaved hip roof. The major axes were connected by four-story arcades with two floors of open galleries (later reduced to one) over a triple-arched entry (one door, two windows) at the street, reminiscent of an Italian Renaissance palazzo. The galleries continued into the main masses as slightly bowed balconies in each of three open arches (later filled in), rising from the third to the fifth floor. The long facade around the corner featured two broad oriels turning into open porches under the eaves, and a rectangular reception canopy stretching across the sidewalk. With its red stone base flowing up the corners as quoins (removed in the second version), then crossing under the attic sill to frame the lightly tinted facade, and with handsome enfoliated trim on oriels, galleries, and attic, the Ontario Hotel was another example of Sullivan's increasing mastery of surface organization. Whether hotel, warehouse, religious edifice, or office block, he had learned by 1890 to treat each situation individually, to find a mode of expression suitable to the nature of the particular case, to the solution of the particular problem. The horizontal, elongated, and harmoniously integrated Ontario Hotel was, like several of his recent buildings, almost pure in form, with simple shapes elegantly handled. Sullivan could now state the essence of the project in richly embellished but fundamentally reductionist terms. In November 1890 contracts were let for the foundations, and Frank Lloyd Wright reported they were "laid," but the hotel was "never built—one of the office tragedies," he correctly surmised.[21]

Another office tragedy was the burning of McVicker's—"the pride of the city . . . the model theatre of the country"—that Adler & Sullivan had so carefully reconstructed in 1885. On August 4, 1890, the night watchman's report of thwarting attempted arson was dismissed as alcoholic delusion, until three weeks later, near midnight of the twenty-fifth, when he extinguished a small blaze at the main entrance. The real fire started around 3:15 a.m. on the twenty-sixth in the smoking room at the west end of the stage, causing $80,000 to $100,000 damages, including the roof, the boxes and top gallery, portions of the lower gallery, the entire parquet, stage, and many of the decorations. The inside and outside walls remained standing; indeed, the fireproof partition between the theater and the offices withstood the test perfectly. The proscenium arch was also spared, as was most of the substage machinery. Undaunted by the setback, J. H. McVicker announced early in September that he would incorporate to sell $200,000 worth of capital stock for an entirely new facility. Adler & Sullivan was immediately hired for the reconstruction, began letting contracts that month, plans were finished in October, and on March 30, 1891, the new McVicker's opened to an eagerly awaiting public.[22]

Better fireproofing and expanded office space were the architects' principal objectives. To accommodate the latter, Adler spanned the auditorium with six steel trusses supported at their ends by latticed wrought-steel columns rising directly from footings independent of the old walls. The trusses carried twenty-four offices on two stories connected to the business front of the building. To ensure adequate fire protection, each piece of steel was encased in porous terra-cotta tile, the same material as the floors, ceilings, partitions, and roof. Applauded as these features were, the new auditorium provoked the most discussion. "The effect on entering" one observer wrote, "is startling."

> There seems to be no parts to the theater; it appeals in its unity. The prevailing shades in the decorations seem formulated on the same body. In reality there are several browns, terra-cotta pink, and mahogany red, but their combined effect is the inde-

> scribable luster on the surface of freshly broken brown earth. All the decorations are brought out and toned by gold-leaf in bands, and no other shade. All the usual kaleidoscope colors and effects that dazzle for a moment and then disgust with their tawdry finery have no place in the new playhouse.
>
> The proscenium arch starts almost in the center of the ceiling. It is in six diminishing sections, each section being a different part of a component whole. The arch is of filigree work and canopies the orchestra and part of the parquet.[23]

Instead of balcony boxes, Sullivan deployed sixteen-foot murals depicting scenes from Illinois history. Beneath these, three boxes on each side of the room were divided by Doric columns and ornamented pilasters. There were fifteen perforated pendant ceiling lights of seven lamps each, and ninety-six hooded lights on each balcony balustrade. "It would be hard to conceive of better taste than that exhibited in the interior of McVicker's theater," a *Chicago Tribune* reviewer concluded. "Costliness of materials is combined with simplicity of design and there is a warmth of tone without a visible primary tint of color." A leading building magazine had applauded the decision to retain Adler & Sullivan because "from their hands we may expect a structure worthy of the position which it is destined to occupy in progressive Chicago." When the results were in, another journal noted that though the new McVicker's was similar to the old, it was "much more beautiful."[24]

The unexecuted Seattle, Washington, Opera House was the third office tragedy of 1890. The $325,000 auditorium and commercial edifice for the intersection of Second and University streets was to have been six stories high with a tower capped by an observation deck under a steep roof high above the triple-arched, emphatically framed theater entrance. This section's twelve stories were divided above the entrance into a group of four with an oriel, and a second group of four with slim inset windows leading to the lavishly decorated platform. With its projecting deck and high roof, however, the tower was too top-heavy. Related to the office block in its lower floors but articulated differently as it soared smoothly above the main roof line, it fought against itself; like the Chicago Auditorium, which was more happily resolved, it appeared to be either an extension of the principal mass or an independent high-rise. Sullivan seemed unable to decide.

Planning began during the summer of 1890, with excavation and site grading following by the middle of August, when it was announced that within six weeks "Architect Sullivan . . . will have completed the designs [for] one of the most imposing structures in the West" to be built in gray stone, 180 feet long by 108 feet deep. On September 8 the architects telegraphed Judge Thomas Burke, one of the project's backers, that the "general plan . . . as sketched by Mr. Sullivan in Seattle [was] pretty well matured," its only modification being the extension of Second Street stores back underneath the theater. Steam heating, the electric-light plant, and stage equipment were in the hands of "our experts," one of whom, a Mr. Rebb, would leave for Seattle in ten days to supervise the start of construction on the concert hall portion. The architects asked for further instructions once the backers had time to examine the "general sketches," except that "the opera house part of it will not be advisable to change and we shall push the working drawings right along. We shall nominate" a stage mechanic, Adler & Sullivan continued, who should begin work as soon as the building was roofed over. Six days later, on September 14, they sent the floor plans, but even though the project was taken this far, it fell through, apparently for lack of funds.[25]

The last of Sullivan's major Richardsonian buildings was the $300,000 Dooly office block, designed late in 1890 and built the next year in Salt Lake City, immediately adjacent to the site of the ill-fated Ontario Hotel. Like the Walker Warehouse, it is a study in the possibilities of almost unornamented post, lintel, and arch construction. The Dooly was also seven stories tall with strong corner piers rising from sidewalk to cornice and four-story tiers of windows arched on top. But since it contained both stores and offices, Sullivan separated the two functions with a cornice over the first floor, inserting large plates of glass at street level. And since its attic housed mechanical equipment, its tiny windows near the roof were a further departure from Walker. But the major difference was the roof itself, in Salt Lake City a flat projecting lid with rich fascia ornament, the same treatment Sullivan gave to the Wainwright Building (his first "skyscraper"), designed at the same time for St. Louis. As a descendant of the Walker Warehouse, the Dooly Block was both an end and a continuation for Sullivan. It was, on the one hand, his last important Richardson Romanesque design. Compared with the Walker Warehouse, its higher glass-to-masonry ratio, flattened mullions and piers, smoother, more monochromatic ashlar surface, and

IX.16 *Seattle, Washington, Opera House project, 1890.*
From Hugh Morrison, *Louis Sullivan.*

its shallower reveals combined even more clearly to suggest airy volume as opposed to heavy density, with skinlike thinner walls rather than massively thick enclosures. Despite its comparatively low scale and its extruded Romanesque arches, indeed, because of the arches perhaps, the Dooly Block gave the impression of moving energy—as the eye was drawn to the roof lid—rather than of earthbound power. Sullivan successfully transformed the arch, a Romanesque symbol of muscular compression, into an altogether different image of upward thrust, actually a rather Gothic objective. Thus it was that the Dooly Block was also a continuation, the final link in the preskyscraper chain, of his search for a way to create a "system of vertical construction." Although the Dooly was neither a high-rise (by the standards of 1890) nor had a skeletal steel frame, even more than the Walker Warehouse it anticipated Sullivan's next, most significant phase of development.[26]

The tomb for Carrie Eliza Getty in Graceland Cemetery is the last important edifice of 1890. Above the third course, its gray Bedford limestone blocks were delicately carved in octagonal motifs embracing the arched entrance with its superb bronze gates and companion lunettes with sloping sills and inset decorations. Its four-piece stone plinth and modest entrance step projected slightly farther than the roof, which was composed of three stone slabs gracefully scalloped at their edges. Like the Dooly and Wainwright buildings, the cornice fascia was intricately trimmed with floral carvings compatible with its other ornament. Faces of the wedge-shaped entrance voussoirs were scored with decorative lines and bands that Montgomery Schuyler thought were too literally derived from the porch of Austin Hall at Harvard Law School. Sullivan had on several occasions taken "valuable suggestions from the works of Richardson, which he has carried out in his own way and stamped with his own personality," Schuyler observed, but in this case much too directly. Nevertheless, he thought the arch "a very interesting and effective piece of design," and the tomb as a whole "very successful." Only because its author "is entitled to be held to higher than the current standards," he explained, had he criticized him at all. Schuyler's reservations did not in this case appreciably compromise the general consensus that Getty's ornament is even more exquisite than Austin Hall's, which was one of Richardson's best, and that the tomb itself is one of Sullivan's most sensitive and masterly compositions. As Moorish as it is Romanesque, it is fundamentally a eulogy in stone to perpetual serenity and in delicate artistry to eternal creation.[27]

Eighteen ninety-one was every bit as active as 1890, with the partners landing at least eighteen commissions, about three more than the busy preceding year. The new nonskyscraper work was less diverse, however, than in 1890, which prompted discussion of eleven buildings in this and the previous chapter. Designing no tombs or hotels, Adler & Sullivan (with Wright) produced three private residences (already mentioned), the same as the year before, and another warehouse. Their four factories—basic bread-and-butter jobs—two more than in 1890, are assumed in the absence of visual evidence and contemporary commentary not to have surpassed the high standard set by the Selz, Schwab Building. Nevertheless, at least three of the

1891 commissions are especially memorable: Sullivan's historic contribution to the Chicago World's Fair, the remodeling of an early Adler synagogue with some especially spectacular ornament, and their only major railroad station.

The story of the World's Columbian Exposition, or the Chicago World's Fair, would require a book in itself. There have been, in fact, many books about the "White City," that 633-acre ensemble of landscaped architecture, fine art, eclectic buildings, tawdry arcades, and "neoclassicism" at Jackson Park on Lake Michigan's South Side shore, dedicated in October 1892 and opened in May 1893 to commemorate the four-hundredth anniversary of Christopher Columbus's arrival in North America. More than twenty-one million visitors—the equivalent of almost one-third the entire United States population—were so impressed by the fair until its October 1893 closing that they would have probably agreed with sculptor Augustus Saint-Gaudens, who reputedly told his fellow exposition designers that "not since the Renaissance has a comparable group been brought together for an enterprise like this," an assertion many think less arrogant than accurate. Directed by chief of construction Daniel

IX.17 *Carrie Eliza Getty Tomb, 1890.* Photo by David Roessler.

H. Burnham, ten of America's leading design firms—some say *the* ten—five from Chicago, five from elsewhere, created the landmarks of a dazzling architectural array millions would remember for years.

Once the site was chosen, Burnham, his partner John Root, and a panel of consultants began the delicate process of picking the ten-firm board of architects and assigning major buildings. After a good deal of wrangling based on political considerations and regional jealousies, they decided in December 1890 on Chicagoans Adler & Sullivan, William Le Baron Jenney, Henry Ives Cobb, Charles S. Frost, and Burling & Whitehouse, along with New Yorkers Richard Morris Hunt, George B. Post, and McKim, Mead & White, Peabody & Stearns of Boston, and Ware & Van Brunt of Kansas City. Because of their acoustical and decorative expertise, Adler & Sullivan were at first assigned the relatively small, peripherally placed Music Hall, which, Burnham argued, would duplicate and therefore win them as much acclaim as the Chicago Auditorium. Dubious about this and objecting that the Music Hall would—like most of the other fair buildings—be a temporary structure, Adler & Sullivan demurred. Next they were offered the Art Building, which was to be permanent, but again they hesitated and the project went to Charles B. Atwood of Boston and New York. By January 15, 1891, with all the major assignments given, Adler & Sullivan still had nothing. But after further discussions between January 12 and 24, when Sullivan suggested the transportation exhibits be removed from the Machinery Hall to one of their own, the partners consented to do a transportation building. The board of architects agreed to abide by a uniform cornice height of sixty-five feet—the only significant design restriction they imposed on themselves—and to prepare only elevations, sections, floor plans, and ornamental details. Since the Department of Construction under Burnham would furnish working drawings and structural specifications for every edifice, Adler's usual rolc in the design process was usurped. The Transportation Building was therefore unlike any other in the partners' history. With outsiders giving technical assistance, Sullivan did the building by himself, and was finished with it, or thought so, in less than a month, sometime before February 10, 1891.[28]

The Transportation Building took the form of a giant train shed, 256 by 960 feet, fronting a 425-by-900 annex, altogether over fourteen acres, costing $370,000. Facing Post's much larger Manufacturers Hall across the southern end of a lagoon, it stood behind and

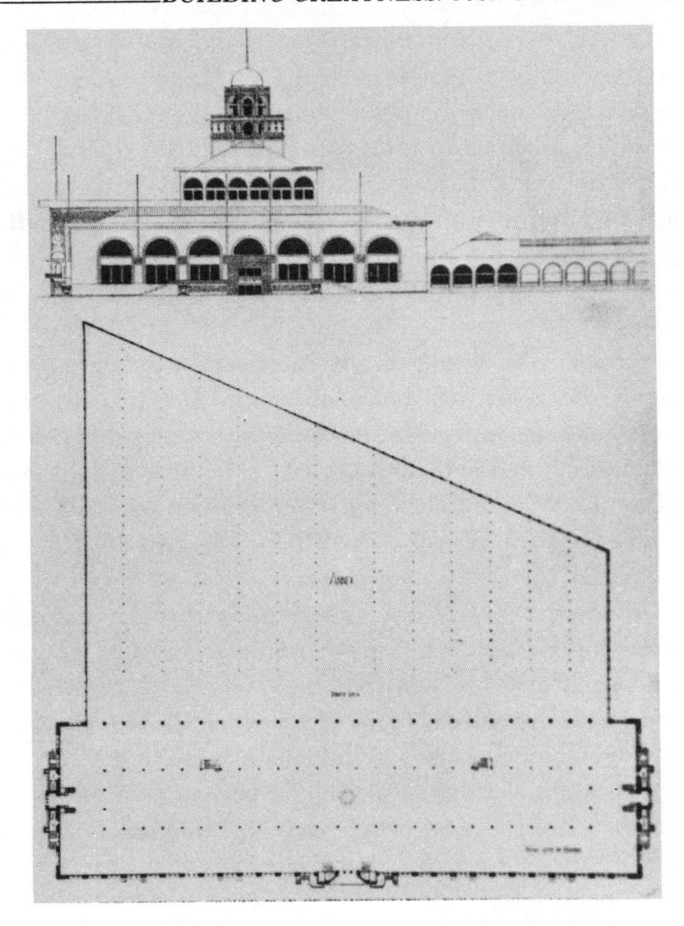

IX.18 *Transportation Building, 1891, plan and north elevation.* From *Inland Architect,* 1891.

IX.19 *Transportation Building, 1891.* From *Inland Architect,* 1891.

slightly north of the buildings grouped around the Basin, the centerpiece and focal point of the entire fair. Here at the Court of Honor, Easterners decided on classical and Renaissance treatments in formal arrangement. Elsewhere on the grounds, architects had greater leeway to let their imaginations wander, but of the larger structures only Sullivan's building and Cobb's Fisheries departed significantly from the "neoclassical" format. And herein lay a problem. Sullivan initially specified two main entrances facing the lagoon, with supplementary doors at either end of the hall. But after pondering this proposal, Burnham, who was mightily impressed with the formalistic treatment of the Court of Honor and worried that Sullivan's entrances could not accommodate an anticipated thirty thousand people an hour, suggested a major change. "The best possible method for handling the axis trouble we discovered the other day," he wrote Sullivan on February 11, 1891, "will be for you to have one grand entrance toward the east . . . much richer than either of the others you had proposed, . . . [o]n the axis running through the center of the Manufacturers Building. It's the natural place for an entrance anyway. . . . I am sure," he continued, "that the effect of your building will be much finer than by the old method of two entrances . . . neither of which could be so fine and effective as the one central feature."[29] Far from objecting, Sullivan seized the opportunity to create a mammoth "Golden Doorway," one of the most remarkable achievements of the fair and of his entire career. But for Daniel Burnham's "neoclassicism," Sullivan might never have done it.

His revisions were essentially complete by February 25, when in a statement signed by both Adler and Sullivan he outlined the design. "The Transportation Building is simple in architectural treatment," he began,

> although . . . very rich and elaborate in detail. In style it is somewhat Romanesque, although to the initiated the manner in which it is designed on axial lines, and the solicitude shown for good proportions and subtle relation of parts to each other, will at once suggest the methods of composition followed at the *Ecole des Beaux Arts*. . . . The main entrance . . . consists of an immense single arch enriched with carvings, bas-reliefs, and mural paintings; the entire feature forms a rich and beautiful yet quiet color climax, for it is treated entirely in gold-leaf and called the golden door. The remainder of the architectural composition

falls into a just relation of contrast with the highly wrought entrance, and is duly quiet and modest, although very broad in treatment. It consists of a continuous arcade with subordinated colonnade and entablature [divided into thirteen arched bays on either side of the Golden Doorway]. Numerous minor entrances are . . . pierced in the walls, and with them are grouped terraces, seats, drinking-fountains, and statues.

The interior . . . is treated much after the manner of a Roman basilica, with broad nave and aisles. The roof is therefore in three divisions. The middle one rises much higher . . . and its walls are pierced to form a beautiful arcaded clerestory [topped with an observation cupola reaching 166 feet, served by eight elevators].

Not the least interesting feature is the beautiful scheme of polychromatic decoration. . . . To treat the building externally in many colors was the original thought of the architects in the first conception of their design. The architecture of the building, therefore, has been carefully prepared throughout with reference to the ultimate application of color, and many large plain surfaces have been left to receive the final polychrome treatment. The ornamental designs for this work in color are of great and intricate delicacy; the patterns, interweaving with each other, produce an effect almost as fine as embroidery. . . . [T]he colors themselves . . . comprise nearly the whole galaxy, there being not less than thirty different shades. . . . These, however, are so delicately and softly blended and so nicely balanced . . . that the final effect suggests . . . a single beautiful painting.

The general scheme of the color treatment starts with a delicate light-red tone for the base of the building. This is kept entirely simple and free from ornament in order to serve . . . the more elaborate work above. The culmination of high color effect will be found in the spandrels above the main arches. Here the work is carried to a high pitch of intensity of color, and reliance is placed on the main cornice . . . very simply treated, to act as a balancing and quieting effect in the general composition. In the center of the spandrels is placed a beautiful winged figure [an angel, most believed] representing the idea of transportation . . . painted in light colors [with] a background of gold-leaf.

The color scheme of the building as a whole, of course, culminates in the great golden doorway. The entire entrance, 100 feet

> wide and 70 feet high, which is encrusted over its entire surface with delicate designs in relief, is covered . . . with gold, and colors in small quantities are worked in between the designs and reliefs so as to give the whole a wonderfully affective aspect.[30]

Along with his paper at the fair's World's Congress of Architects in August, this statement clearly establishes Sullivan's strong interest in polychrome. He was, in fact, the only prominent architect at the Exposition to experiment with color, employing dozens of tints, principally oranges and yellows to accent the predominantly red exterior, a dull ocher on the inside, and silver and greens to highlight the golden entryway. The Transportation Building was indeed a decorative and color tour de force, but without Adler to guide him, perhaps, Sullivan did not do as well with the exhibition space.

Construction began around July 1891 and was finished in October 1892 in time for the dedication. Frank Lloyd Wright remembered that the Transportation Building cost Sullivan the "most trouble of anything he ever did"—not the "great doorway," which he got "straight away," "but the rest [which] hung fire." One of the most serious problems stemmed from the basilica format dividing the interior into a long high "nave" rising through the clerestory to a trussed roof flanked by aisles under galleries supported by colonnades, an arrangement with unfortunate consequences for the display. Not only did the columns impede vista and take up valuable space, but they also, as the fair's director-general George Davis reported to the *Chicago Tribune,* made "proper installation exceedingly difficult." Because the main room and access to it through the columns were so restricted, "it was impracticable to place the largest exhibits under the highest roof, and many of the most important and in every way most attractive exhibits, must be relegated to the least desirable portions of the annex." The space-intensive post-and-beam construction was also, as several observers have since noted, rather reactionary for its time in this situation. Sullivan did not employ the lightweight metal-and-glass roof that by the 1890s was commonplace in train sheds and exhibition and market halls. Cantilevers or vaulting would have cleared the way for a vast, open interior, the kind of room he and Adler had placed in the Exposition Building in 1885. Nor was the luxurious exterior ornament carried inside, as several disappointed critics pointed out. All in all the Transportation Building did not work well as an exhibition hall. In Wright's understated words: "It was no masterful solution of a practical problem."[31]

Even the exterior played to mixed reviews. Montgomery Schuyler applauded it as "a perfectly legitimate attempt" to create a "plaster architecture," "the most ambitious of all the great buildings" because "there is no such thing as an exterior architecture of plaster in the world." Sullivan, furthermore, was the only fair architect to "treat the material of which all the buildings are composed." The ample cornice was therefore necessary to protect the walls and the ornament was properly molded, not chiseled. But Schuyler criticized the use of masonry moldings on a plaster building, the too-bare facade, and even the Golden Doorway as an "isolated fragment, entirely unrelated to the general scheme." Architect Peter B. Wight judged the "festive" Transportation Building in light of its location as "the first to break from the formal arrangement of the central group," the Court of Honor, that is, at that point on the grounds where "styles of architecture change and the utmost variety in design prevails." Wight would have accepted Schuyler's contention that by not being part of an ensemble, it could be idiosyncratic. But Henry Van Brunt, the partner of Sullivan's former teacher William R. Ware, "barely concealed his distaste . . . beneath circumlocutions and ironies," according to one historian, in an essay for *Century* magazine.

Judging by heavy doses of ripe prose and strained metaphysical explanations, the Transportation Building seems to have generated stronger emotions than any other structure. In "Sights of the Fair" for *Century,* critic Gustave Kobbe burlesqued the winged "angels," wondering if they symbolized the many railroad and streetcar fatalities who had been "transported" to heaven. In *World's Fair Studies* Denton Snider argued that the stiff, lifeless, mechanical angels were supposed to be that way, to represent flying mechanisms—"what else is Transportation with its locomotive speeding over the land?" he asked. More so than the stationary engines in Machinery Hall, the angels suggested the "heavy world of matter taking the pinions of thought and flying." Snider congratulated himself for "beholding their celestial and not their diabolical element." In *The Dream City: A Portfolio of Photographic Views of the World's Columbian Exposition,* Halsey C. Ives thought the angels "bizarre," though "creditably relieved by the commanding beauty of the Golden Door."[32]

Two additional reactions illustrate the range of emotions and criticisms Sullivan's work engendered. The Chicago correspondent for New York's *American Architect* thought the building "one of the most interesting in point of detail, [but] one of the least successful in general outline," a not uncommon appraisal. The dignity of the main entrance, which unfortunately stood out too aggressively from the whole, was "much lessened by . . . two curious *kiosks* on either side, semi-Moorish in character," reached by short flights of stairs. Perhaps their purpose, he mused, was "for the benefit of the few faithful followers of Mahomed who may happen to journey to the Fair, that they may in their seclusion send up their prayers to Allah." His general impression of the ornament was that while individual elements were admirable, showing "more original thought and careful study than those of any other building on the grounds," the overall composition with its out-of-scale Golden Doorway was objectionable.[33]

The *Melbourne* (Australia) *Argus* inflated its dislike to an emotional outcry of rage. "The Transportation Building is the worst of all," its correspondent believed,

> and a doubt may well be held whether it has not purposefully been made as hideous as possible in order to be a foil to the others. It is really nothing but a shed . . . but the architect has tried to make it present externally some new and original type of architecture, with a result that can only be described as a nightmare of bad taste and wasted ingenuity. It is painted dark red, with scrolls and twirligigs in all sorts of other colors, and this *bizarre* effect is aggravated instead of relieved by huge figures of flat and lanky females with wings, plastered on the walls at regular intervals, all exactly alike, as if done with a stencil-plate, and each bearing in her pallid hands a tablet inscribed with the name of somebody or other, who is supposed to have furthered the art of transportation. The entrance consists of an enormously heavy archway, surmounted by a kind of slab or cap, the object of which is a mystery; the whole arabesqued in a bewildering pattern, and entirely covered with very brassy-looking silver. I have never met anybody who could explain what it all means, or how such a sanguinary-looking blot was allowed to be placed in the White City. I believe it is a piece of native Chicago talent; but every Chicago man I have ever spoken to about it either laughs at it or swears at it, so there is reason to hope it by

no means represents the Western-American architecture of the future. Luckily, it is not very conspicuous, and nothing but willful malice could make anyone condemn the whole World's Fair on account of that one shocking example of what American architecture ought not to be.[34]

The French reaction was altogether different. Observing the fair for *Revue des Arts Décoratifs,* organ of the Union Centrale des Arts Décoratifs, André Bouilhet was particularly struck by the Tiffany

IX.20 *"The Golden Doorway," Transportation Building, 1891.*
Photo by Chicago Architectural Photographing Company.

Glass exhibition and by the Golden Doorway. Partly because Sullivan's ideas seemed compatible with Art Nouveau and with those of symbolist painters, the most avant-garde art theories in the French capital at the time, Bouilhet sought the architect out for a meeting, read his essays, visited his other Chicago buildings, particularly noting the Auditorium, and, in his published review, praised only Sullivan of the World's Fair architects. Probably without too much difficulty, he also persuaded Sullivan to lend examples of his work to the Union Centrale's Musée des Arts Décoratifs for display. Sullivan responded by donating casts of Transportation Building ornament and the Wainwright Memorial doors (see below), and a model of the Getty Tomb. In appreciation of his gifts and "as a tribute to the[ir] beauty and artistic merit," the Union awarded Sullivan a gold, a silver, and a bronze medal in 1894, installing the pieces in a special "Louis H. Sullivan Section" of the museum. In an official letter informing him of these awards early in 1895, the Union enclosed a request to reproduce the work from the director of the Russian School of Applied Arts in Moscow, asking Sullivan in addition to make his permission sufficiently general to allow others the same privilege. There had been "so much admiring comment among artists" during the few months the pieces had been exhibited, it was reported, "that other art schools on the continent were almost certain to repeat the request of the Russians."[35] Evidence of further European exhibitions has not yet come to light, but it is nonetheless clear that the Golden Doorway elevated Louis Sullivan's (but not Dankmar Adler's) international reputation.

Functionally, the Transportation Building was less than successful in part because structurally it was antiquated, but compositionally it worked well (certainly for latter-day and in some cases contemporary tastes) and as an experiment in an unusual material it was innovative. To praise it for not being neoclassical, as many in retrospect have, is pointless; because many buildings outside the Court of Honor were not in that style, it was not unique in that regard. But as a straightforward statement of its mundane purposes and material, it was in a sense more honest than the fair's architectural norm: this is what bothered so many of the critics. Viewed from a distance, as the facade particulars receded into texture, the Transportation Building dissolved into a rhythmically harmonious composition, simple and handsome enough for lay appreciation. Though not the largest structure at the fair, it was still so immense that the Golden Doorway, looked at head-on or in perspective from afar, lost its overwhelming sense to become a kind of linchpin tying the facade together at a point of central focus; matching the height of all its other arches, the Golden Door was secured into the main mass by its cornice, so that if up close it seemed poised to float away, from farther back it resolved and relieved the entire arrangement.

But even up close, the seventy-by-one-hundred-foot portal achieved human proportions. Its terrace was fronted by thick octagonal columns with ornate capitals separating three rectangular double doors of normal height flanked by murals that slanted inward from the building line to recess the actual entrance, which was thereby reduced to manageable scale. Over the lintel reading "Transportation Exhibit," a semicircular mural depicting horses was wrapped by a broad band of intersecting circles and vegetation. Around this, five concentric arches, each with a different ornamental pattern, projected forward from the smallest until the largest was flush with the building line at the end of the doorway murals. All this was framed by a plain rectangular border enclosing the "twirligigs" that might have been abstract lightning bolts inside a broader rectangular band of circles and leaves capped by a heavy projecting cornice doubling as the balustrade for the observation deck on the portal roof. The color and form of the framed concentric arches was by all accounts an unforgettable image. Its ornamental patterns varied from ring to ring, but each contained at least one motif similar enough to the next for the whole to "bleed" visually together into a composition so beautiful, so striking, that the most often asked question at the fair, according to several reports, was, "Have you seen the Golden Doorway?" And precisely because it was such a tour de force, in an ornamental style only the French and a few American critics were prepared to accept, many people reacted emotionally, some in hostile disbelief. As a fragment and as a compositional linkage, the doorway was one of Sullivan's greatest accomplishments. The Transportation Building "was not architecture in its highest sense," Frank Lloyd Wright recalled years later, "except as a great theme suggested, an idea of violent changes in scale exemplified, [and] noble contrasts effected. . . . It was a holiday circumstance and superb entertainment," he insisted, making a telling point that has generally been neglected, "which is what it was intended to be."[36] Sullivan thought enough of the doorway to quote it several times over, beginning with Temple Sinai a few months later.

The original temple at Indiana Avenue and Twenty-first Street was designed in 1875 by Dankmar Adler and his early partner, Edward Burling, but erected in 1876 by Louis Sullivan's first employers, John Edelmann and Joseph Johnston, who had put him in charge of the auditorium's frescoes, one of his first two commissions as a young decorator, which, with those at Dwight Moody's church, had brought him so much notoriety. With close personal ties to prominent members of the congregation, Adler was retained with Sullivan in 1884 to supervise some $15,000 worth of alterations to the building and the rabbi's home, including painting, roof repair, glazing, ventilation improvement, and decorative refurbishing. Although Simon B. Eisendrath, another well-known Jewish architect, pursued the commission when the congregation decided to expand its facilities in 1891, Adler & Sullivan got the $50,000 job by June, in part because of Adler's long-standing connection but also because of Sullivan's towering reputation as an architectural decorator. The partners' widely discussed temples for the Zion Congregation at Washington Boulevard and Ogden Avenue in 1884 and for Kehilath Anshe Ma'ariv in 1889–90 also made them a logical choice.

In his treatment of the facade, Sullivan left most of Adler's original Romanesque composition intact. The tall entrance pavilion on Indiana Avenue, culminating in a square convex dome flanked by similar but shorter service pavilions, remained the same. But westward along Twenty-first Street, Adler & Sullivan removed the rear domes to deepen the building from four to seven bays, adding a large receding-arch entry set within a rectangular frame with a projecting cornice much like the Transportation Building designed shortly before. True to its Romanesque parent, the addition was incorporated unobtrusively into the whole, not out of allegiance to Richardson but because the situation called for careful replication. Inside, however, Sullivan let his controlled fancy take flight.

Here, a narrow barrel-vaulted ceiling arch followed the center aisle to the platform where against the rear wall it stretched into a half ellipse pointing heavenward. On either side of the arch, the ceiling flattened into a ribbed row of coffers with light-emitting, stained-glass disks, then coved down to form the upper walls, where one rose window per bay backlit the balcony that was stepped down near the platform. Facing the center aisle behind the pulpit, four columns framing three arches supported a highly decorated rectangular proscenium angled back from the sides and top as a sounding board, much like the entry at the Transportation Building. Immediately above this, an ornate balustrade fronted a seven-arch organ-and-choir loft outlined by another frame of rectangular ornamental panels that reached the ceiling and almost touched the balconies as it descended to the floor as a border for the entire ensemble. Within the elliptical arch above all this, a myriad of intersecting circles and ovals screened the organ pipes. Panels on the balcony front and a row of ball-shaped electric-light clusters suspended from the center of the arch carried the decorative work into the room, at the same time drawing the eye toward the breathtaking auditorium front.

Counting the colonnade on the stage floor, there were six major ornamental motifs stacked behind the pulpit. From bottom to top, dominant ellipses gradually gave way to circles contained below by rectangles and above by squares, although near the top the framing receded into the background altogether. Mostly geometrical forms accented organically, they were bolder around the proscenium, but in the arch were transformed especially from a distance into a delicate filigree. Used practically to disguise light fixtures and air vents, they sparkled in gold and tinted plaster to form a series of motifs—and from afar one powerful composition—revealing the energy and finesse of which Sullivan was capable. Temple Sinai and a number of its contemporaries showed the hand of a master, an unsurpassed ornamentalist who had reached the height of his substantial powers.[37]

By August 1891 Adler & Sullivan completed planning an entirely different kind of edifice, the Illinois Central Railroad Station and General Offices at Rampart and Delord streets in New Orleans. Resembling the familiar shedlike depot descended from the horse-and-buggy stable more than the majestic portals gracing several major American cities, Sullivan's design was deemed "not quite as grand as [others] . . . the traveler might mention," but still the "best New Orleans has ever had." Its two stories of pine and pressed brick fronted 180 feet by 72 deep on Rampart with a 100-by-30-foot baggage wing to the rear. Eight tracks terminated within the resulting "L" under a

IX.21 *Illinois Central Passenger Terminal, New Orleans, 1891.*
From *Inland Architect*, 1891.

triple-arched iron-and-glass roof cantilevered widely at its sides. Between the two porte-cochere-like elements spanning the sidewalk at either end of the front facade, Sullivan placed an eight-column colonnade supporting a canopy that doubled as a gallery for second-story offices. These twenty fifteen-by-twenty-four-foot rooms were double-loaded on a wide hall lit from above through the windows of a rooftop cupola. Some had tiled hearths, even though the building was steam heated. The four corner offices were nine feet high, but over the central sixteen rooms the roof soared to a thirty-five-foot arch. Five wood-encased steel beams spanning this space received nine-foot partitions separating ceilingless offices, and each supported three posts that converged on the beam but then fanned out where they met the roof. Unlike those at the corners with openings in both walls, the other sixteen offices each had two sash windows, shared the light from small dormers, and were protected by six-foot overhanging eaves. Sullivan supposedly said that the long hip roof with dormers and gallery was inspired by Creole plantation houses he saw from the train. If so, then his Ocean Springs cottages might have had a similar derivation. On the other hand, the station's overall appearance resembled the facade of the Transportation Building. Whatever their motivation, all three southern buildings were intelligent confrontations with hot, humid local climates.

When Sullivan visited New Orleans in April 1892, the depot was two months from completion. The main floor contained a ninety-by-fifty-six-foot waiting room for whites, a thirty-by-fifty-six-foot counterpart for "colored" travelers, a ladies' parlor, men's smoking room, a lunch counter, telegraph office, and other normal railroad station facilities. Beams and girders upstairs and down were left exposed but boxed in by ornamental scrollwork in various designs. The brown brick walls in the waiting rooms were trimmed with six courses of flecked blue brick beginning twenty-two courses above the red quarry-tile floor. The wood on the job was long-leaf yellow Mississippi pine planed smooth to enhance the grain and given several coats of oil and varnish. The arched street-side windows set several feet behind the curb-side colonnade, the balustrade on the second-story porch, the fenestration behind that, and the long hip roof, all continuous in rhythm, unified the building horizontally. Its long, low lines, the consequence of compositional, environmental, and traffic considerations, anticipated by a decade or more a visually similar unity of practical and aesthetic characteristics that Frank Lloyd

Wright—who as Sullivan's principal assistant probably worked on the building in some capacity—and his contemporaries made famous as the prairie style.

Local observers never quite knew what to make of the terminal. Sensing there was something different going on but objecting it was not monumental enough, *The Daily Picayune* concluded in 1892 that "it is not the finest depot in America, but it is a comfortable, ornamental building." The next day it decided that "altogether," it was "the prettiest passenger station New Orleans has had," but in a third story reverted to its original uncertainty: although it was handsome, it was not grand enough, but still "one of the prettiest depots in the south." The rival *Times Democrat* thought it "new and magnificent" with woodwork "in a very modern style," presenting "a strikingly handsome appearance." At its demolition in 1954, a reporter for the *New Orleans States,* quoting the *Times Democrat*'s sixty-two-year-old assessment scornfully, looked down the tracks to the "gleaming" chrome, steel, black marble, white stone, and brilliant fluorescent lighting of the new Union Passenger Terminal. "Its clean straight lines and functional design," he wrote, "contrasted sharply with the old, squat structure capped by the ridiculous cupola and picketwork of chimneys." Perhaps even in doubt, nineteenth-century New Orleanians had the inside track on aesthetic acuity.[38]

Four of Adler & Sullivan's eight most substantial commissions in 1892 were for St. Louis, where their 1890 Wainwright Building was the first of ten projects, more than anyplace else but Chicago. Aside from the $50,000 addition to the Standard Club, featuring two remodeled private homes connected to a new three-story rear wing in the same style as the original, their other major Chicago structure that year was the seven-story, $250,000 wholesale store at the southwest corner of Van Buren and Franklin streets for the estate of William Mayer. Rediscovered by Hugh Morrison while preparing his 1935 biography of Louis Sullivan, the Mayer Building had even then been altered, possibly before construction, so that photographs show something quite different from the architects' intention.

As originally published in April 1892, the 120-by-168-foot edifice featured an inset wall of plate glass at street level broken by columns with ornate capitals supporting an unornamented lintel sweeping across both street facades. Five stories of rectangular windows (in two tiers per bay) were capped by another broad unornamented band tying in cleanly with corner piers rising from the sidewalk to a slightly canted decorative cornice that was also separated by a plain band from the continuous strip of small attic windows. The only ornament on the chocolate-brown terra-cotta exterior aside from the capitals and cornice were small medallions on the pier faces at the second-story sill line and the contrast created by the heavy moldings of each bay. In the 1887–88 Walker Warehouse, Sullivan established a similar relationship between corner piers and the clear planes holding attic fenestration, and at the 1890 Dooly Block, he emphatically articulated the plate-glass street floor with a cornice of its own. But in this 1892 steel-frame building, he eliminated the second-story cornice, squared his familiar rounded arches at bay tops, accentuated sidewalk showcase glass, expressed the attic as a continuous window strip, and softened the roof line. Although the columns, piers, and moldings suggested verticality, the repetitive fenestration, the cornice, and the facade bands were insistently horizontal. Since neither impulse took particular priority, Sullivan very neatly accomplished two things. First, he stated the character of the building, a broad, relatively low structure—with an expansive but uncomplicated interior—where height was not a notable feature, and, second,

IX.22 *Mayer Building as originally conceived, 1892.* From *Inland Architect,* 1892.

IX.23 *Victoria Hotel, 1892.* From *Inland Architect,* 1893.

he expressed the character of steel framing, amounting to a cage of interconnected vertical posts and horizontal beams, neither being structurally or visually more important, cladding it all, furthermore, in a colorful but simple skin. More than other architects, by 1892 Sullivan was able to make a mundane business building beautiful by handling its structural system and everyday materials without pretense, explaining perhaps why he and his partner declared the design one of the handsomest in town. The clients liked it because it was cheap, but to Sullivan the Mayer Building was an honest revelation of basic architecture.[39]

The $75,000 Victoria Hotel in Chicago Heights was designed in the summer of 1892. Its three stories and basement contained some 105 guest rooms, seven shops and a bank, a rotunda, and a billiard room and bar within a roughly 110-by-125-foot perimeter. The two bottom floors of red brick sported arched shop entrances and windows, the third floor of yellow stucco some striking geometric surface ornament attributed to Frank Lloyd Wright. The ornament reappeared at the top of the five-story clock tower that signaled a main entrance reminiscent of the Transportation Building's rectangularly framed arch. Capped with wide overhangs, the tower descended cleanly to the street through a gap in the main roof, a more satisfactory resolution than at the Pueblo Opera House (on which the Victoria was modeled), where the tower was cut in two by the principal cornice. Flanking second-story oriels, a recessed porch or loggia around the corner on the same floor, a slightly projecting side bay, octagonal dormers, and a gently canted base rising some four feet from the sidewalk completed the architectural treatment of this elegant small hotel. The Victoria's overhanging eaves, hip roofs, textured top floor, and horizontal impulse not only bore a family resemblance to the Pueblo Opera House, the Transportation Building, the Ocean Springs cottages, the New Orleans station, and the Ontario Hotel project, but they also anticipated some of Frank Lloyd Wright's early work.[40]

Adler & Sullivan's last hotel—also named the Victoria briefly, before construction—was designed by November 1892. Built by Henry and Lucy Semple Ames for $750,000 at the northwest corner of Locust and Eighth streets in downtown St. Louis, the St. Nicholas Hotel was 92 by 130 feet, 129 feet tall, and had 120 guest rooms in eight stories. Planned in association with St. Louis architect Charles K. Ramsey, who, as a dabbler in local real estate probably handled municipal red tape, functioning more as a front man than as a designer, the St. Nicholas began to rise in February 1893 and was ready for occupancy by the end of the year. Since the basement contained a café, barber shop, saloon, and kitchens, the main floor was six feet above grade, explaining its sidewalk-level windows. On the main floor were the women's and men's restaurants, private dining, a writing room, reception, and other facilities, above which were five stories of guest rooms with public and private baths so designed that each floor could be rearranged into suites. The *pièce de résistance* and motive for the unique upper facade was a banquet hall–ballroom rising from the seventh into the eighth story. Served by a second large kitchen, a men's smoking room, a ladies' parlor, and two elevators, the "noble apartment" was finished in oiled hardwoods with birch wainscoting and white maple flooring. A trussed roof opened the space internally for a broad vista that spilled outside through generous doors and windows to a seventh-story loggia and balcony. Here on hot summer evenings under cooling awnings amidst moist plants, a local observer predicted, "substantial St. Louis citizens . . . will sit and eat superb viands and enjoy their cigars away from the noise and heat of the streets" in surroundings so luxurious that even New York's "Four Hundred" at "Sherry's famous white and gold ballroom in Fifth Avenue" would probably be envious. St. Louisians had waited years for a first-class hotel, so when it came they were prepared to make the most of it.[41]

IX.24 *St. Nicholas Hotel, 1892.* From *American Architect & Building News,* 1895.

If local opinion seemed a mite boosterish, it was nevertheless shared by at least one New Yorker, *Architectural Record* critic Montgomery Schuyler, who admired the hotel very much indeed. Ten years ago an eight-story building would have been tall, he pointed out in 1895, but now structures twice as high presented "no difficulties." "Every educated designer," he believed, "would adopt, without question," Adler & Sullivan's hotel scheme in a similar situation: a one- or two-story base, a series of virtually identical floors he called the "superstructure," and an "enriched attic of a single story." He recognized that the large banquet hall–ballroom provided the motive for the sumptuously decorated overhanging balcony under the steeply pitched red slate roof. Elsewhere, the lower four of the five guest floors featured oriels with intricate designs on buff terra-cotta spandrels and projecting flat roofs creating sixth-floor balconies tucked away under the seventh-story overhang. The large arched entry and double-height arched windows at the street indicated the two-story commercial base treated as an arcade in brown sandstone. "The unquestionable success of the building is purely 'architectonic,' " Schuyler observed. The striking individuality resulting from the banquet hall revealed the "skill with which the designer has followed the indications supplied by the facts of the case." The functions of the building, in other words, dictated its form.[42]

Schuyler's insight might have been applied to Sullivan's work in general by 1892. The phrase he later coined to summarize his architectural method, "form follows function," was reduced over the years to strict functionalist dogma. To many it came to mean that architecture should have no ornament and minimal contrasting color, should incorporate mechanical and structural systems into design, be nothing but utilitarian, and employ aesthetics compatible with a technological era. But Sullivan meant something altogether different. By the time he completed the Auditorium, if not earlier than that, he believed that the requirements of a commission could be distilled into a single "idea," a governing motive, possibly metaphysical, suggesting the essential form the building would take. Thus the St. Nicholas Hotel "idea" hung on the banquet hall, the Ryerson Tomb was meant to address the eternal cycle of life, and the Transportation Building was intended to express "holiday" excitement in mammoth juxtapositions of scale. However reductionist his approach may have been, it left ample room for architectural flourish, for Sullivan was careful to create mosaics of textured detail rendering all these structures visually rich. If motive, technology, and detail could be harmoniously resolved, he believed that the viewer, the client, and the user would benefit, spiritually and practically. Sullivan's work was modern because it found new forms for old and new needs, but unlike "modernism" later on, it did not reject history. Sullivan was no historicist, no dutiful copier or adapter of ancient styles. But as a student of history, he did not disguise his architectural references to the Gothic, the Romanesque, to Florentine and North African design, and to other great epochs of the past. Like all artists, Sullivan borrowed ideas, feelings, even actual fragments, to work into new syntheses. Art is rarely created entirely in a vacuum. It tends instead to rearrange, to put together familiar things in new ways through personal visions that define creativity, which is exactly what Sullivan did by the 1890s with startling consistency.

One final building from the Adler & Sullivan partnership, the last to be discussed in this chapter, illustrates the point. Charlotte Dickson Wainwright's Memorial in St. Louis's Bellefontaine Cemetery was probably designed shortly before it was occupied late in the fall of 1893, well after her death in April 1891. The main massing is a twenty-foot square in Bedford buff limestone outside, dark blue Carrara marble inside. On the roof back of the ten-foot walls rises a shallow stepped circular base for a two-foot dome, the interior of which has a gold star at its crown. All the walls are decorated outside by bands of rich, exquisite ornament along the top, down the corners to the parapet in front and the sills on the sides, then across the facades to rise over the door and windows, returning on itself in an endless chain. In front the parapets enclose seats at the ends of the porch, which extends four feet on either side beyond the central block reached by four broad, low steps. The double-door entry is framed by a fifth ornamental band; no two bands are alike. Hugh Morrison thought the Wainwright Memorial "unmatched in quality by any known tomb. Altogether it is one of Sullivan's masterpieces." Montgomery Schuyler, after declaring that there is "no worthier ex-

IX.25 *Charlotte Dickson Wainwright Tomb, c. 1892.* From *Inland Architect,* 1892.

ample . . . of Mr. Sullivan's power of decorative design," went on to praise his "structural instinct, or the reasoned engineering knowledge of mechanical relations, whichever you please, which presides over the placing, the magnitude, and the forms of his masses." Sullivan's achievement put Schuyler "at a loss to name any other American architect whose perception of these things is more unerring." Almost all reviewers detected the Oriental "quality" or "suggestion" in this work, but it was historians Dimitri Tselos and Narciso Menocal who pointed out that the Wainwright Memorial was adapted from the tomb of an Arab saint, a *qubba* in Blidah, Algeria, that might well have been depicted in Sullivan's own books on ancient ornament and sepulture. He certainly saw it somewhere, for there is no mistaking the similarity. Had Sullivan simply copied this tomb, he would have accomplished nothing. But by incorporating its essence into an entirely different context treated in a manner all its own, he produced one of his most beautiful structures.[43]

Of the seventeen known Adler & Sullivan projects from 1893 and 1894, at least five went unbuilt, in large part because of the economic depression that by the latter half of 1893 settled in to stay for the next five years. With commissions disappearing, the partners were able to erect only three warehouses, a tannery, the conversion of an armory to an amusement park, a shop-and-flats building, a stable, and additions or alterations to an eye-and-ear infirmary and two stores, mostly workaday jobs that paid the bills but did not turn critical heads. Two that did, the Chicago Stock Exchange and the Guaranty Building in Buffalo, under construction in 1894 and 1895, also helped them keep financially afloat, but not well enough to offset the absence of new work. In 1873, when he was laid off by Frank Furness under similar circumstances, Sullivan fell back on his parents. But twenty-two years later, with no one to help him, no family, no work, and Adler anxious about his own wife and children, the situation was a good deal bleaker. In the intervening decades, Sullivan had succeeded at building greatness, and if nothing else, had his reputation to sustain him. "Nobody who really pays attention to his work," Montgomery Schuyler wrote in 1895, "can imagine that he has said his last word."[44]

Chapter X

PROUD, SOARING, AND ALONE 1890-96

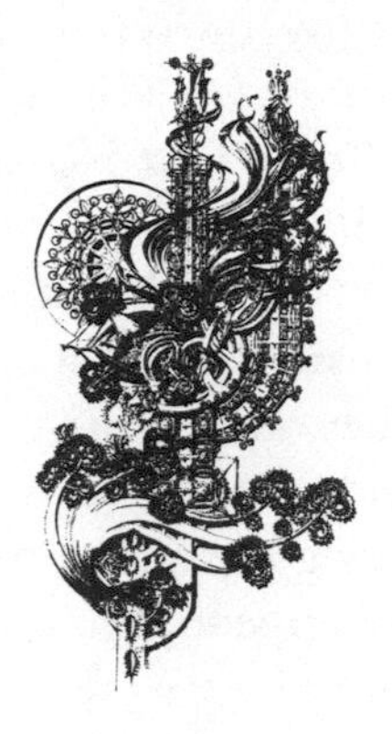

LOUIS SULLIVAN, of course, had not said his last. In March 1895 the Chicago-based *Inland Architect* published a two-page rendering of the Guaranty Building in Buffalo, considered by many—but not by the thirty-eight-year-old architect himself—to be his finest and most perfect skyscraper. Sullivan was hardly new to the genre by then. The Guaranty, something like his eleventh or twelfth skyscraper design, counting from the first in 1890, was the fifth to be erected, the third outside Chicago. Of his seven steel-frame high-rises actually constructed during the 1890s, four were located in other cities, helping to crystallize his national reputation and to spread his message about their proper form.

In the 1980s everyone knows what a skyscraper is. If "high-rise" can designate a towering apartment house, a skyscraper usually means a very tall office building. When pushed for precision, people might agree that, yes, there are sometimes shops and restaurants, flats and parking garages, even saunas and schools, to complicate the matter, but still and all, when it comes right down to it, a skyscraper is a very tall edifice—how tall is a matter of opinion—mostly filled with offices, which soars above the average, unless it is hidden by similar giants. Something like this seems to be definition enough, even for specialists. When a *New York Times* columnist published a history in 1981 called simply *The Skyscraper,* he felt no obligation to define it, presumably because everyone knew what he meant.[1]

So it was in the 1880s, when the name was coined, although "great," "high," "tall," "grand," or "skeletal" building was preferred until the next decade. One hundred years ago, people on the street agreed, like today, that a skyscraper was a very tall office building, allowances being made, of course, for different perceptions of height. Today, few are impressed by thirty, even forty, stories, but in the 1880s ten made front-page news. The popular understanding of a skyscraper as an office building that rose above its neighbors, in the nineteenth century more than likely not blocked by others, was good enough for contemporary critics. If Montgomery Schuyler, Barr Ferree, or local reviewers discussing the first one in their towns bothered with a definition at all, they were ordinarily rather imprecise.

Enter modern critics and scholars. To reconstruct its history, they have raised an array of very good questions to complicate in a tangle of uncertainties what once appeared so obvious. Popular definitions simply will not do. If height alone were sufficient—if "very tall" was enough to make a skyscraper—then the Washington Monument, Irish round towers, Italian campaniles, and the Brooklyn Bridge would qualify. In 1894 Barr Ferree wrote that "vertical architecture would be impossible . . . without the elevator,"[2] but since sprawling shopping malls, grain silos, and the Eiffel Tower have them, elevators, even coupled with height, are not definition enough. Perhaps steel framing could be added. But then the question lingers: How much height is required? Six, eight, ten floors? And what happens to Burnham and Root's 1891 Monadnock Building in Chicago, that sleek sixteen-story pile everyone knows is a skyscraper but lacks a steel frame? Problems like these have driven historians to great lengths for accuracy's sake, in one case to the point of dividing its evolution into seven phases, a worthy effort yielding an instructive "view of skyscraper history," but not a working definition.[3]

Perhaps all this has limited importance; the public still knows what a skyscraper is. But other questions persist. When, for example, was the first one built, who designed it, and is there any such thing as a "first" one anyway? Competing claims to the earliest skyscrapers—perhaps "preskyscrapers" would be more accurate, or maybe even buildings with features that skyscrapers would later employ—have been made for Boston, Philadelphia, New York, Chicago, and other cities. It is said that the first was designed by William Le Baron Jenney, Leroy S. Buffington, Holabird & Roche, Louis Sullivan, any number of lesser figures, some anonymous, or perhaps it was someone else, and was either the Tacoma, the Home Insurance, the Wainwright, or the Leiter Building, if not another. If metal construction is a defining characteristic, then to be a skyscraper, did a building have to be entirely supported by steel, or would iron or steel in combination with masonry suffice? And what if it had metal columns but not a metal frame?

Then there are aesthetic questions. Did a steel-frame building have to look the part, or could it be legitimately disguised as masonry-supported? Conversely, if it was very tall and looked like a steel-frame building but was not, what then? What if it was vertical in form but articulated horizontally? What if it was very tall but part of something shorter, like the seventeen-story Auditorium Tower? Or what if it had all the right structural and aesthetic components but was of dubious height, like Adler & Sullivan's seven-story Mayer Building? When it comes right down to it, thanks to modern scholarship, it is very hard to know what a skyscraper is, or was. But a hundred years ago architects were less perplexed by these kinds of uncertainties.

Absence of agreement, however, had one consequence Louis Sullivan found especially troublesome. No one, it seemed, knew how to express this historically new form logically, or to put it another way, everyone knew but no one agreed. Some thought the skyscraper to be like a classical column with a monumental base, a repetitive shaft, and an elaborate capital, like George B. Post's Union Trust Building (1889–90) in New York. Others tried to deny its height altogether by piling several layers of horizontally articulated floors on top of each other, in effect making a stack of small buildings, separated by heavy cornices, entablatures, sills, or moldings. Post's St. Paul Building (1898) and Robert Robertson's Park Row Building (1896) in New York typified this approach. Sometimes architects had no sense of proportion at all, like Bradford Gilbert in his 1888 Tower Building in Manhattan, while others loaded their work with as much ornament and as many historical references as it could carry. Leroy Buffington designed an almost featureless stick for his 1888 proposal for a twenty-eight-story office edifice, while two years later, in his Sun Building scheme, Bruce Price was one of many to fashion a tower after Italian campaniles. Although many architects embraced the skyscraper enthusiastically as an artistic challenge, few attempted to develop its design implications. Either they applied familiar rules from traditional styles and the closest architectural analogies they could find, or they let fancy fly without thinking through the new aesthetic possibilities. The result was not uncharming—somewhat akin to the random eclecticism of "postmodernism"—but Louis Sullivan believed that no one understood the skyscraper sufficiently well to develop it as a generic type.

Except for him, of course. In 1890 Sullivan decided he knew what skyscrapers ought to be, and within a few years clearly understood that his first one opened the most important phase of his career, marking a significant moment in architectural history. "As to my buildings," he wrote in 1903 to architect Claude Bragdon, a young admirer, "those that interest me date from the Wainwright Bldg. [1890] in St. Louis. . . . It was a sudden and volcanic design (made literally in three minutes) and marks the beginning of a logical and poetic expression of the metallic frame construction. . . . All my commercial buildings since the Wainwright are conceived in the same general spirit. . . . The structures prior to the Wainwright were in my 'masonry' period [from which] the Auditorium Bldg. and the Walker [Warehouse], Chicago, are the best. . . ." It was with the Wainwright Building, he added, "that I 'broke' (see K. C. Chat 'The Tulip')."[4]

"The Tulip" was installment twenty-two of *Kindergarten Chats,* fifty-two architectural dialogues between a master and his pupil, that Sullivan published serially in 1901 and 1902 in Cleveland's *Interstate Architect & Builder.* In it he explained that the tulip grower could not propagate new varieties from roots, buds, offshoots, or cuttings. The only way was from seed, carefully fertilized into shoots, then thinned, cultivated, and set outdoors in beds when strong enough. Despite this lavish attention, they nevertheless bloomed "a common grayish blossom" year after year, Sullivan wrote, "showing reversion to the early tulip type. And so they live along, a dull and stupid brood, without apparent promise, until suddenly . . . one of them 'breaks' . . . into a gorgeous, stately flower, and lo!—a new variety, a tulip of tulips . . . a new thing of beauty born of untoward surroundings [bursts] into a needy world. . . . After five, six, seven years," he noted further along, "if there be no 'break,' the seedling tulip never breaks. There is a moment in our lives," he added to emphasize his major point, "when we burst our bonds or fail to burst them," like that "tide in the affairs of men" that Brutus pondered in *Julius Caesar,* "which, taken at the flood, leads on to fortune."[5]

So when Sullivan wrote to Bragdon that he "broke" on the Wainwright Building, he meant he had seen the light, had achieved a higher level of understanding enabling him to supplant his "common grayish" older designs with "a new variety . . . a new thing of beauty." This interpretation relegates his pre-1890 work to comparative unimportance. It suggests that some of his first commercial buildings were not attempts—however tentative or disorganized—to work out a high-rise aesthetic, as previous chapters and other authors maintain. And it claims the Wainwright as a spontaneous breakthrough without precedent in his or any other corpus, a kind of design epiphany transforming him from a masonry Saul of Tarsus to a skyscraper Saint Paul. But if, on the other hand, Sullivan meant Bragdon to read his three-minute "sudden and volcanic" achievement in light of the "five, six, seven" year gestation of the tulip, which in his own life would have begun around the 1884 Troescher Building, seen by many as an important early step toward the skyscraper, then for consistency's sake he might have acknowledged the Wainwright as the culmination of a much longer process.

Only the immediate results of the process, but not the "break" itself, were observed by others. One story has it that after inspecting the Wainwright site, Sullivan returned to Chicago with a kind of designer's block. He could not draw a line. So taking the advice he sometimes gave his staff, he went for a walk up Michigan Avenue to commune "far away from paper and pencil." Suddenly, it came in a flash. He ran back to the office and "literally in three minutes" tore off a preliminary sketch. Frank Lloyd Wright recalled that day, not the Michigan Avenue walk or the three-minute torrent but the point at which Sullivan burst into his room with part of the facade "stretched" on a board and threw it on the table. "I was perfectly aware of what had happened," he remembered. "This was Louis Sullivan's greatest moment—his greatest effort. The 'skyscraper' as a new thing under the sun, an entity with . . . beauty all its own, was born."[6] Not yet thirty-four years old in the summer of 1890, Sullivan produced what may be his historically most important building.

As a kind of absentee godfather to the birth, Ellis Wainwright was an especially sympathetic client. A beer manufacturer, president of the St. Louis Brewing Association, and a respected community leader, he combined hard-nosed entrepreneurial pragmatism with an aesthetic sensibility nurtured by his avid art collecting. When he discussed his objectives for the project, a speculative rental venture attracting over twenty realty agents as tenants long before it opened, he said he wanted the latest and best skyscraper technology within the most beautiful commercial facade in town. The thinking of Wainwright, his mother, Catherine (a partner in the development), Louis Sullivan, and Dankmar Adler, with his vast structural expertise, must have been exceptionally well aligned.

The endeavor began in cloak-and-dagger fashion. On May 29, 1890, a 114-by-127½-foot lot on the northwest corner of Chestnut and Seventh streets, locally known as the Jay Gould property, was sold for $130,000 to a "secret" buyer "known to be a non-resident westerner." A day later it developed that the seller had made a handsome $40,000 profit on an eight-month turnover, and on the thirty-first that "another grand building, to compare with the city's finest," would soon rise on the site. The "non-resident" buyer proved to be Ellis Wainwright, who, acting through an intermediary, intended at first to erect an eight-story building with ground-floor offices, saloons, billiard rooms, and a pool hall surrounding a twenty-five-foot court opening on a rear alley. The disposition of the upper seven floors was not decided, but Wainwright said he wanted more than the usual number of windows, plus a glass roof, for as much natural light as possible. Although the architects had not begun their plans, two suites had already been engaged.[7]

In mid-September the *Post-Dispatch* reported that architectural "plans for this improvement are ready and have been submitted," making the Wainwright an almost exact contemporary of the Dooly Block in Salt Lake City, in many ways a similar edifice, which Adler & Sullivan completed in December. When St. Louis construction began by early November, the program had changed somewhat. Though they complemented the character of neighborhood backstreet life, the alley saloons and pool room were no longer compatible with Wainwright's upgraded vision of a fashionable commercial district. By now his building had grown to nine stories and taken its ultimate U shape. In order to capture as much light with as little wasted space as possible, "the architect [*sic*] has arranged the building in the form of a double L." A thirty-two-by-sixty-five-foot central court extending into the building as a skylit corridor from the first floor rear to a line forty-nine feet from the Chestnut Street facade corresponded in depth to a nine-foot offset light shaft on the north side. With two alleys and streets bordering its corner site, the Wainwright stood free, its court giving outside exposure to every office but

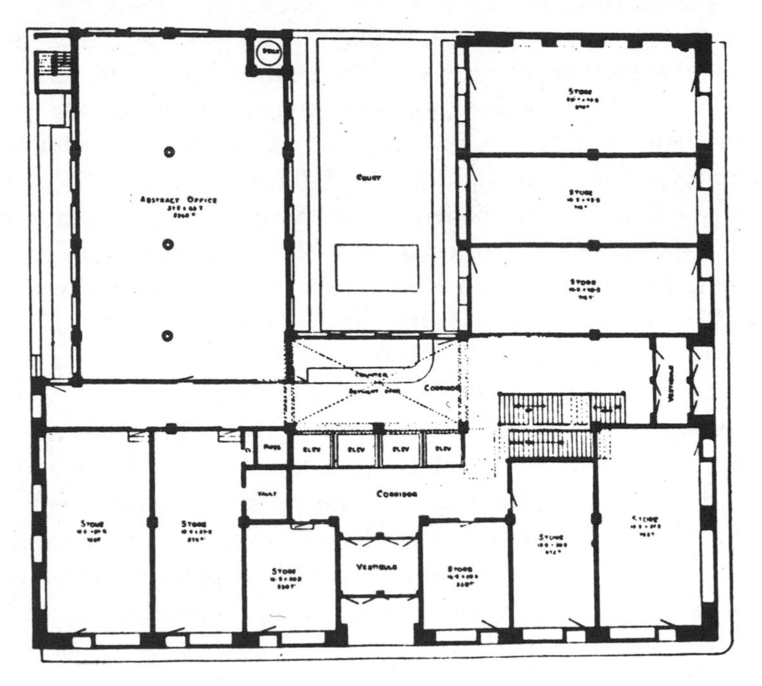

X.1 *Wainwright Building, 1890, first-floor plan.*

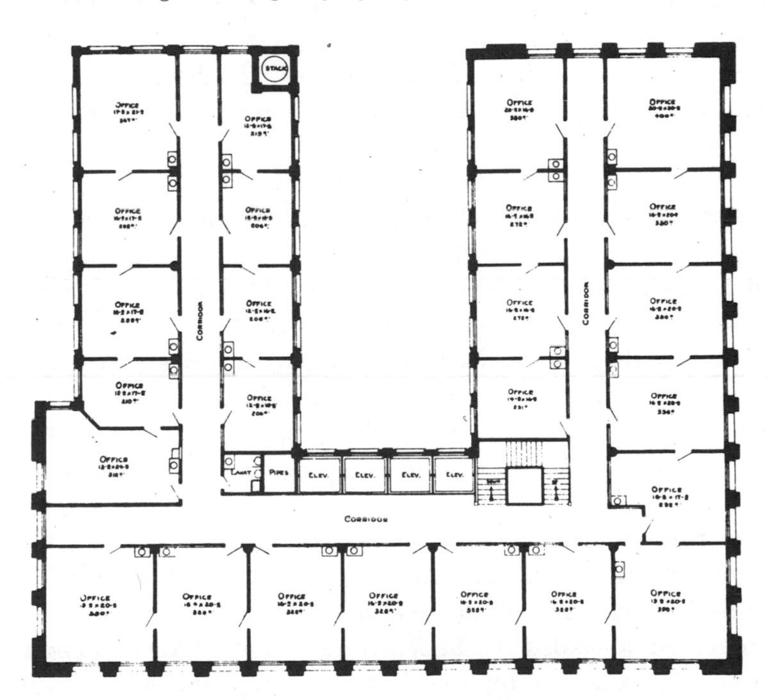

X.2 *Wainwright Building, 1890, typical floor plan (ninth floor).*

taking up less than 20 percent of the ground space. A typical floor plan had twenty-five offices, a U-shaped corridor, a public lavatory, two utility stacks, a stairwell, four elevator shafts with ornate gates, and the light court, leaving an efficient 53 percent of the lot area available for rental. At slightly over $560,000 for 225 offices,[8] the ten-story edifice as built costed out at twenty-five cents per cubic foot, a respectable figure when compared, for example, with thirty-two cents for Burnham and Root's Rookery (1888), forty-two and one-half at their Monadnock Building (1891), and fifty-eight for Burnham's Masonic Temple (1892).[9]

Although the 135-foot Wainwright was not structurally or spatially innovative, it utilized the most advanced building technology, demonstrating that Adler & Sullivan, in their first steel-frame high-rise, had kept pace with a decade of major Chicago construction developments. The foundation of reinforced-concrete isolated footings taken to sixteen (one source says thirty) feet supported braced and riveted steel columns and girders encased in fireproof tile. Exterior walls were carried on steel spandrel shelves at every story and non-bearing interior partitions could be easily rearranged according to tenant need. To maximize outside exposure for street shops, the architects filled each bay with glass: one large plate (some with a recessed entry to the side) and three clerestories. Above that the broad single windows between each column were one-over-one double-hung sash. The building weighed two and one-half tons per cubic foot, but by 1893 had settled only a quarter of an inch.

Interior arrangements are of special interest in light of Sullivan's facade composition and his well-known 1896 thesis on office buildings discussed below. The finished basement took up the entire lot, not with the Turkish baths at first envisioned, but with storage, lavatories for the ground floor, and with an electrical plant, pumps, engines, and a boiler under the light court for access to coaling from the back alley. The first floor had nine shops of varying size, three on Seventh Street behind the side entrance, three each flanking the main entry on Chestnut. Passage through the front vestibule continued at the right of the elevator bank to a crossing corridor leading past the skylight to a large office, over sixty by thirty feet, in the northwest corner. The second to ninth floors all had exactly the same plan, a double-loaded, U-shaped corridor with larger rooms along the outside walls. The top-story attic with skylights and small porthole windows contained additional lavatories for the offices, a barber shop, mechanical systems, and large steam mains. The vestibules, elevator waiting areas, and lavatories had mosaic pavings and Italian marble wainscoting, while the remaining floors were quartered oak at street level, red oak in upstairs side halls, and maple in the rooms. "In general," one observer believed, these conveniences and improvements were "superior to other office buildings previously erected."[10]

Sullivan's facade objective was threefold: to indicate a range of functions and the nature of the structural system, and to express verticality—to his way of thinking, the essential characteristic of this kind of edifice—not literally but poetically and by suggestion after the method of his speeches and writings. Sullivan had isolated three principal functions of most office buildings, including this one, each requiring different facade treatment: first, a mixed-use ground floor (or two) for shopping and sometimes offices, ingress and egress, waiting and meeting, and other occasional activities warranting outside display windows, simple but stately articulation, and a clear relationship to street concerns such as locating the address and entrance, and enhancing neighborhood beauty and pedestrian vista; second, a sequence of floors, in this case from the second to the ninth, ordinarily treated identically because of identical—at least similar—office functions; and, third, an attic for service and maintenance facilities not found elsewhere decisively terminating the elevation. Although Sullivan handled each part differently, he did not depict interior events exactly. Had he done so, the red Missouri granite and brown sandstone ashlar of the Wainwright base would have been one story instead of two because the second floor, for offices, was functionally the same as the next seven, not an extension of the ground floor, as the facade seemed to indicate at first glance. From a strictly functionalist standpoint, this "lie" about the interior made the second floor appear to be something it was not. But since Sullivan was not a strict functionalist, he may simply have decided that in a 1-8-1 composition, the base would not adequately sustain the superstructure. Nevertheless, the size of the windows, their reveals, and the space between them exactly matching those above the second floor, gave more than a hint of its purpose. Sullivan would rather demonstrate the presence of different functions than specify their exact location.

At the Wainwright's corners, seven-foot angle piers soar without interruption from the sidewalk to the top of the ninth floor. Beginning at the third-floor sill shelf, thin bearing columns and nonbearing mullions, looking exactly alike, also rise straight to the attic, causing some (lapsed) modernists like Philip Johnson to complain that disguising the support system showed "Sullivan's interest was not in structure, but design."[11] This exaggeration misses the point, which is that Sullivan was interested in both or, put another way, was concerned with how to express—not reveal—structure through design. The Wainwright's thin columns were obviously not masonry and its recessed spandrels not load bearing: no dishonesty there. Since the intermediate mullions were discontinued below the second floor, Sullivan was hardly "lying" but indicating rather clearly that every other "column" was not a column. These "false piers," as they came to be called, emphasized height and drew the eye upward, accentuating the rhythm and vertical lift of the facade. If the Wainwright Building had been given thinner, recessed, or broken mullions, revealing the true width of the bays, the resulting flatter planes and wider spans would have diluted Sullivan's "system of vertical construction," that is, the *look* of verticality, as much a matter of design as of structure. Doubling the uprights made the building appear taller than it was, at the same time repeating vertically the horizontal sequence of the office floors behind. What Johnson failed to see was that with Sullivan, design was an interpretation of structure.

Over the tenth-story attic, the edges of Sullivan's outward-projecting cornice were decorated with interlocking circles, a stylized version of the leafy garlands playing down the walls in a rich frieze surrounding the portholes. Clearly indicating a functional difference between the attic and lower floors, perhaps acting as a unifying capital for all the columns, the frieze was nevertheless tied to the rest of the facade with related ornamental patterns on the spandrels (different on all six levels), on third-floor sills, around the entrances, and at the base and capital of individual mullions, in other words, at the major horizontals, at obvious points of visual inspection (the doorways), and at directional inducements for the eye (the upright tops and bottoms pointing up and down). Organic ornament also served to soften or humanize what might otherwise have been angular and hard. Sullivan seemed intuitively to understand that as buildings inevitably got taller and bulkier, they could become intimidating, inside and out. Even with the rich attic frieze, the Wainwright's ornament was restrained but still able to negate the potentially threatening quality of a large, impersonal pile. Carefully placed ornament, "false" piers, shifts in material, and other visual effects were

X.3 *Wainwright Building, 1890.* From *Architectural Record,* 1925.

Sullivan's devices for interpreting structure, function, and essence poetically, as opposed to stating them literally. Portraying the character of the office edifice as he saw it more clearly than the content, Sullivan fashioned the Wainwright Building into a brilliant first essay about the modern skyscraper.

It was not, of course, completely without precedent in his work. Among other things, his early "high-rises" also demonstrated a consuming interest in the aesthetics of verticality and structure, compromised at the 1880 Borden Block and the 1881–82 Revell Building, for example, by Adlerian polychrome, wrapping cornices and sills, and unsystematic ornament. At the Rothschild Store of 1881, the window heads varied in shape and the top exploded in a frenzied flourish to negate the clear structural statement of the lower stories. Three years later the Ryerson Building's totemlike columns, jagged bay windows, ersatz attic colonnade, and horizontally layered floors overpowered the facade's innate simplicity. His best early effort, the 1884 Troescher Building, showed what might have happened had he failed to emphasize the Wainwright's mullions: the facade had a clean but flat quality lacking visual interest and a clear sense of direction. Only in his series of cheap and simple factories, from 1884 to 1887, did he find a satisfactory synthesis between recessed horizontals and soaring verticals, but since they were so much broader than high, and were used for seemingly pedestrian purposes, Sullivan did not think to apply this resolution to more prestigious buildings.

Despite these early inconsistencies, he had grappled with the problem of expressing high-rise structure more resolutely than any other architect, and in the late 1880s made real progress. At the 1887 Wirt Dexter Building, only a rusticated base, thin sills of contrasting color, and a slightly inset central bay with protruding cast-iron mullions detracted from an otherwise straightforward integration of structure and form. At the 1887–88 Walker Warehouse, the Wainwright's unobstructed corner piers made their first appearance, along with early versions of the third-story sill and attic molding. And in the extruded arches of the 1890 Dooly Block, Sullivan recessed the spandrels, taking the piers almost straight from top to bottom. From here to the skyscraper was not a giant step. Some of these buildings, as noted earlier, seemed aesthetically suited to the steel frame even without it. But the process of discovery took the better part of a decade, culminating in 1890 when he, Frank Lloyd Wright, and maybe even Ellis Wainwright could see that the tulip had finally "broken."

There was no shortage of praise for the Wainwright Building at the time from those who saw it as a new and fitting idea. But its real significance grew in retrospect, especially after Sullivan produced a body of similar work ultimately seen as a style of its own. Sullivan himself writing in 1903, Claude Bragdon fifteen years later, several European architects before and after World War I, Frank Lloyd Wright and architect-historian Thomas Tallmadge in the 1920s, and any number of others by the 1930s understood the Wainwright's importance in skyscraper development. Of those who have recently discussed it, *New York Times* architecture critic Paul Goldberger is among the more perceptive. By the standards of a decade or two later, he pointed out, it was "minuscule. But Sullivan managed to express height in a way no one else could at the time: the Wainwright is not merely tall; it is *about* being tall—it is tall architecturally even more than it is physically."

What Sullivan managed to do, Goldberger explained, was create a facade that could not have existed on a short building. The Wainwright was not a low structure made bigger but was tall in its very essence. Accentuating height was only the most obvious reason for Sullivan's success; even more important was his ability to turn verticality—"taming it almost"—into a coherent composition. Its slightly recessed spandrels anticipated a method of designing still apparent forty years later at Rockefeller Center. Its cornice and base, joined to create a horizontal emphasis, furthermore "offers just the right degree of counterpart to the verticality. Sullivan's ornament, too, has a balancing role": its delicacy, fineness, and natural forms "are played off precisely" against the sleek facades. "The result," Goldberger concluded, "is a nearly perfect composition, in which no element could be removed without seriously damaging the whole."[12] When the Wainwright was restored in the late 1970s for the State of Missouri by architects Hastings and Chivetta, its original "queenly bearing and complexion" helped it begin a "second lifetime," *Progressive Architecture* reported, "as a working landmark." It was also the first time the National Trust for Historic Preservation, which had taken an option to buy if no one else would, "committed itself to saving a major urban commercial structure."[13] After almost a century, the Wainwright was still a pioneer.

The setting now shifts to Chicago, where the next episode in Sullivan's skyscraper saga was acted out. Almost everything important about the Schiller Building changed between March 1890, when it was first announced that Adler & Sullivan would design a new structure on Randolph Street adjacent to their old Borden Block, and July 1891, when the final scheme was approved. At first called the German Theatre, or the German Opera House, it was at one point to be an L-shaped hotel of twelve and fourteen stories, with a number of design features later abandoned. After several client false starts, forcing tedious adjustments on the architects, its basic form was determined by February 1891, but its ultimate size and arrangements were left in doubt until July, when a permit was secured and the principal contracts let. Construction began in July as well, but because of shipment delays, steelwork rose only two or three stories by the end of the year. The Schiller Theatre, one of Adler & Sullivan's best if not most exquisite, was dedicated on September 29, 1892, followed by the opening of the edifice itself around New Year's Day 1893.[14]

The T-shaped building consisted of three major parts. The seventeen-story, forty-four-by-fifty-three-foot tower on Randolph was flanked by nine-story, twenty-by-forty "shoulders" with oriels from the third to the eighth floor, altogether housing ninety-two offices. The second part, the stem of the T, was an eighty-by-eighty-eight-foot rear wing narrowing to fifty-one feet at the seventh story, where the eighty-two offices started, and to forty-one feet from the eighth through the fourteenth floors. The top two stories, for the German Opera Company, were carried by massive fourteenth-floor trusses—one of several Adlerian engineering strokes—hiding storage and mechanical equipment while creating a spacious thirteen-foot dining room one flight down. Company space continued into the foot of the T, the third section of the building, as a vaulted ballroom on the thirteenth floor, kitchens, an internal smokestack, and a freight elevator overhead. Below were thirty offices—for a total of 204—on floors eight through twelve, which were carried by four immense columns supporting brick walls around the theater's stage and rigging loft in the lower seven stories. The auditorium filled most of the central stem as far up as the gallery on the sixth floor, where great bridge trusses took the steel frame above, and as far forward as the tower, where the balcony hall occupied a noncommercial portion of the second floor. With these trusses and columns, Adler demonstrated his engineering brilliance once again, but even though the Schiller Building followed the office-theater precedent of the Auditorium, it was unique in the partnership. Its T-plan (with small crossbars at the foot) and setbacks overcame the confines of a narrow lot by providing outside exposure to every room above the sixth story (the theater did not require natural lighting), even those on the long interior elevations. Necessity and daring made the Schiller Building the first true setback skyscraper.

Like the plan, the foundations were probably conceived by Adler,

X.4 *Schiller Building, 1891.* From *Brickbuilder,* 1894.

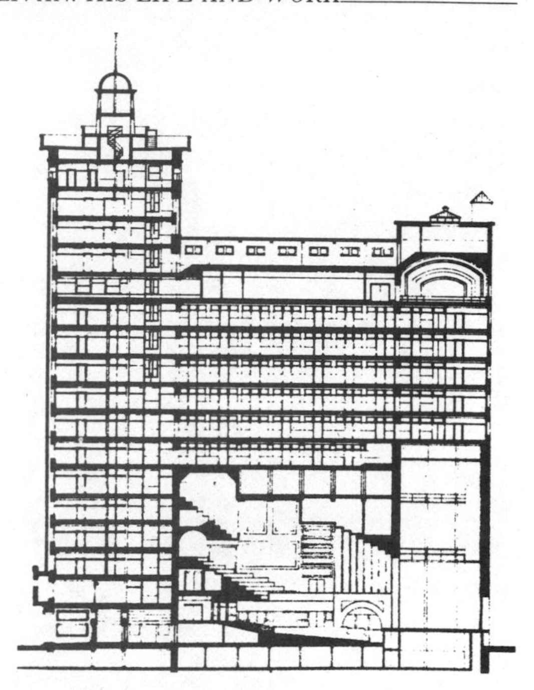

X.5 *Schiller Building section.*

though Sullivan later claimed credit for both. After consulting the highly regarded bridge engineer General William Sooy Smith, Adler decided on concrete rafts laid on huge grilles of oak supported by almost eight hundred sheathed timber piles driven fifty feet to hardpan clay. Though hardly invented by Adler, these pile foundations were among the first in any American city, a step closer to the caissons introduced at Adler & Sullivan's Stock Exchange discussed below. Girders were cantilevered beyond the building's walls to support steel columns and at the sides to carry party walls. Equally innovative was Adler's differential use of the five elevators, all of which went to the ninth floor, with four continuing to the fourteenth, but only two to the tower's top three stories. Adler claimed to have been the first architect to place more than one elevator in a commercial building, two at the 1879 Central Music Hall down the street. It was inevitable in a setback with multiple elevators that someone would arrange them according to traffic density. Adler may have been that someone in the very first setback, in the Schiller Building.

Sullivan's tower facade was in several respects different from, and in some ways an improvement upon, the Wainwright's. The ground floor showed two shop windows, two stairwell openings to the basement, and the spacious three-part entry to the building itself. The second story had an arched and bowed, slightly protruding, ornamented balcony hinting at the theater entrance behind it. Lining up exactly with the second floor of the Borden Block next door, to integrate the two stylistically different structures in an unusually sensitive way that should have been a lesson to other architects, the balcony also referred to the equally rich colonnaded attic under a heavy, far-projecting roof holding an elaborately railed observatory with a small belvedere—recalling the Transportation Building just designed—to shelter a spiral staircase (the only means of approach). From the third to the sixteenth floor, slender ashlar piers wider at the corners rose straight to the attic past inset unornamented spandrels (except at top and bottom) on which sat lightly decorated posts framing even deeper recessed sash windows, one per floor in each of the three bays on a facade. Unlike the Wainwright, all the window tiers were arched on top in the form of concentric rings continuing as layered molding down to the second-floor balcony. The effect of the deep reveals and the bold, strong, shadowed columns on such a nar-

X.6 *Schiller Theatre.* Photo by Richard Nickel.

row tower was to heighten the sense of verticality quite beyond the Wainwright's. The upward sweep was unmatched by any other building, and was certainly "cast in one jet," as Sullivan remarked.

The masterful balance of auxiliary horizontals and relentless verticals, combining to produce the ultimate clean, soaring facade, impressed most critics, some of whom by now recognized Sullivan's new way of doing things. Reluctantly acknowledging its singularity, the New York–based *American Architect* deemed it "successful" inside and out "in the peculiar style of its architects." The *Chicago Tribune* called it "modern and abreast of the times in all its details . . . handsome . . . [and] everywhere attractive and elaborate." But English architect Bannister Fletcher was staggered: as "the best designed tall structure . . . in the United States," it bore "the same relation to the new style of tall buildings as the Parthenon bears to the architecture of Greece." Not to be outdone, perhaps, the perceptive American critic Barr Ferree deemed it "one of the most beautiful and impressive high buildings in the world."[15] And so it might have remained had it not been demolished in the early 1960s.

Also destroyed in the process was the 1286-seat theater, one of Sullivan's most magnificent spaces. Like the Chicago Auditorium, its floor was reached from two levels, directly by stairs from the lower foyer and from another on the second floor overlooking the hall. Corridors along the sides, insulating it from the exterior of the T's stem, connected at various levels with the stage and rear alley. But Schiller Theatre's most striking feature was a majestic series of eight ovalish arches faced with delicate, lacelike, interwoven ornament. The arches diminished in size toward the stage, their lighter-toned soffits separating the darker fascia just enough for the eye to distinguish and revel in their individual glories but at the same time be drawn forward through one of the most compelling vistas in modern theatrical history. Toward the rear of the hall, the plaster ceiling rose past richly framed panels to crown the steel cantilevered balcony and gallery. As usual with Sullivan, the delicate plaster ornament in green, gold, and red referred to the structural requirements while subdividing the space, delighting the eye, and bringing a sense of order to the whole. There were three proscenium boxes on each side, more decorative than useful, with sculpture by Richard Bock of scenes from Schiller's poems, and in the halls there were murals by Sullivan's friends Thomas Healy and Louis Millet depicting, among other things, Schiller riding Pegasus and, with William Shakespeare, being crowned by fame.

Sullivan's ornamental designs were most likely done in the spring of 1892 as the steel framing neared completion. Some, like minor moldings, were probably left to Frank Lloyd Wright and George Elmslie, whose decorative touches can be found on several of the firm's buildings during these busy years, though not to the extent that Wright, for one, claimed. According to the authority for this building, there is no doubt that the major motifs—the balcony face, wall frieze, air grilles, the proscenium, and the arches—were in Sullivan's hand. Popular reaction to the interior was overwhelmingly enthusiastic. "To the taste of many," the *Tribune* reported about the September 29, 1892, theater dedication, it is "the most beautiful in the city. Representatives from the leading old theaters . . . pronounced the place a gem, and gazed about in envy." *The New York Times* called it "one of the most effective and handsome auditoriums in Chicago," with a "particularly beautiful" color scheme. "All who are familiar with the great home of music, art, and oratory on Michigan Avenue," someone else remarked, thought the Schiller Theatre to be the Auditorium "reproduced in miniature . . . but even more striking in magnificence of decorative detail." Impressed by the absence of posts and chandeliers, others decided it was modeled after Adler & Sullivan's Pueblo Opera House, "the first," it was recalled, "to be built without columns supporting the balconies." The stage was not the largest in Chicago, "but there are none with better appointments," another critic concluded, "and none with finer decorations about the arch." No seat in the house was farther than one hundred feet from the apron, and there was nothing but praise for Adler's incomparable acoustics.[16]

Construction on the $750,000 building was still a month away when Adler & Sullivan proposed a conceptually quite different structure for the prestigious Mercantile Club in St. Louis in June 1891. Although it was U-shaped with a skylight over a rear court at ground level something like the Wainwright, its thirteen stories sported a high pyramided attic with dormers capping a very ornate projecting balcony. Ten-story oriels on each facade were linked by lesser balconies on the ninth and tenth floors. Below these elaborate club facilities, a comparatively plain shaft of rental space descended to rectangularly articulated banking and commercial rooms at the street with a richly framed entrance, subsidiary corner doors, and

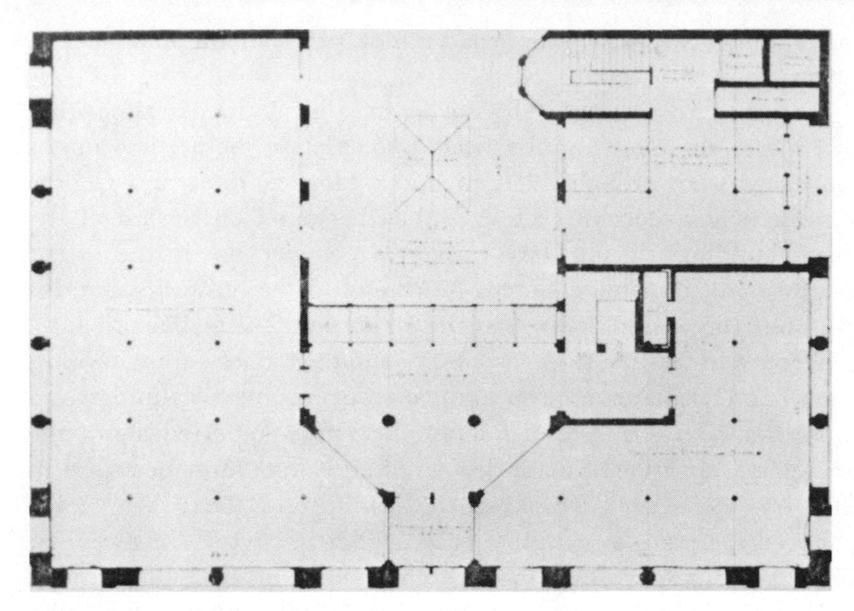

X.7 *Mercantile Club Building project, 1891, main floor plan. From the building's prospectus.* Courtesy St. Louis Mercantile Library Association.

large plate-glass windows. The motive for this bulky, somewhat top-heavy, 91-by-127-foot structure was club need: for space on top, supported by rental income below. The overhanging balcony would have referred to the St. Nicholas Hotel, soon to rise a block away. But the shaft of the building was prophetic in a different way. The oriels with simple windows, framed by taut, skinlike walls, anticipated a similar, more sophisticated facade treatment two years later at the Chicago Stock Exchange, often cited with Sullivan's Schlesinger & Mayer Department Store (1898, 1902–03) as his most literal expression of skeletal construction. The Mercantile's ornament, geometric near the street but leafy higher up, was reserved for portions of the building not devoted to offices. Local observers agreed that this "most magnificent" edifice would far eclipse anything else in town to be "one of the handsomest in the country," but sentiment for hiring a local architect prevented its construction despite considerable interest among club members.[17]

Adler & Sullivan's most spectacular skyscraper was announced in September 1891. The Fraternity Association of the Independent Order of Odd Fellows, Illinois Branch, had been contemplating

X.8 *Mercantile Club Building project, 1891. From the building's prospectus.* Courtesy St. Louis Mercantile Library Association.

a massive new temple since 1886. But nothing happened until in June 1891 it revealed its continuing search for a downtown site on which to erect the tallest building in town at a cost of no less than $3,500,000. Several locations were mentioned by August 20—on Adams Street from State to Dearborn most often, but also Monroe and La Salle, State and Madison, State and Fifth, and Washington and State—when the Order disclosed that the general plans were done. When the rendering was finally released on September 5 to considerable fanfare—and jokes: one wag said that the Temple would probably grow at least another story overnight—the public got a look at what would have been the tallest building in the world.

At 450 feet and more than thirty-six stories, "the most striking skyscraper design of a whole generation," as Hugh Morrison called it, would have towered over everything else in Chicago for years. But that was not its only distinction, for the Odd Fellows (sometimes called the Fraternity) Temple also anticipated by more than two decades and in a quite sophisticated manner the twentieth-century setback made familiar by the New York zoning law of 1916. Its two-story base with rectangularly framed entries like the Golden Doorway occupied an entire 177-by-210-foot block. The tower rose from the center to an arcaded overhanging observation deck at the thirty-fourth floor—serving "as a landmark for the country within a radius of sixty miles . . . visible from Michigan City, La Porte, Aurora, Elgin, Waukegan, and intermediate points," the prospectus said—with two small, steeply pyramided stories on top.[18] Its corners were splayed at forty-five degrees, leaving tiers of single windows to separate the spring points of four twenty-two-story wings forming a cross. From two opposite ends of the cross, four ten-story wings reached the lot lines to make an overall double-H configuration with light wells between the parallel blocks. The ten-story portions recalled the Wainwright Building with third-floor sills, setback spandrels, and richly decorated friezes with porthole windows. Unlike the twenty-two-story wings with two floors of portholes in the attic, they did not have projecting cornices.

Odd Fellows publicity hinted at caisson foundations, which would have been Chicago's first, by mentioning that the architects had again consulted William Sooy Smith on the design of a system to "carry the weight of the building down to the underlying bed rock."

X.9 *Odd Fellows (Fraternity) Temple project, 1891.* From *Industrial Chicago,* II.

X.10 *"The High Building Question," 1891.* From *The Graphic,* 1891.

The superstructure called for riveted steel pillars, girders, and diagonal wind-braces reinforced by masonry on the lower floors, with the ten-story terminal wings acting as additional bracing for their higher counterparts. Had it been built for the $4,000,000 eventually arrived at, the Odd Fellows Temple in addition to five club floors would have had eleven hundred offices in an aggregate of over 350,000 square feet. There would have been 132 prestige offices above the twenty-second floor with another sixty in the tower corners down through the light wells to the third. The entrances and shops along the thirty-foot-high base were clearly delineated by a cornice and would have been readable on a human scale to passersby, despite the giant overall bulk. Although Montgomery Schuyler wrote that the project was "seriously meant" and not a "fancy sketch," three factors prevented construction: lack of funds, inability to secure a downtown site, and a short-lived city ordinance limiting building height to ten stories. Adler & Sullivan's startling proposal nevertheless remains a milestone in setback skyscraper history.[19]

Sullivan knew that his Schiller and Odd Fellows buildings spoke to the future. In December 1891, after both were designed but before he learned the Temple would not go ahead, he developed their implications in a brief but exceptional article called "The High Building Question," published in *The Graphic,* a Chicago pictorial review for general readers. Recognizing the difficulty of preventing American entrepreneurs from doing whatever they wanted, but knowing the public also had its rights, Sullivan proposed a compromise between maximum rentable space and the need for street light and air. His idea was that above a certain specified height limit—twice the width, or 132 feet, for example, on a typical 66-foot thoroughfare—building area should be reduced to 50 percent of the lot. At twice the limit, it would be halved again to 25 percent, and so on indefinitely. In order not to turn the city into a maze of walled canyons, he would apply the restriction to frontage as well as area, and for corners with one wide and one narrow street suggested the distance before setback be the sum of the two. In the New York City zoning law that became a model for the nation in 1916, a variation on this very principle was employed when, to preserve light and air, central Manhattan was divided into districts with setbacks beginning from one and a quarter to twice the widths of their streets.[20]

The principal setbacks and light wells at Schiller were inside the lot, benefiting tenants and neighbors, but not pedestrians, an important consideration nonetheless, as Adler noted in his own November 1892 essay, "Light in Tall Office Buildings." "The experience of real estate agents shows," he admitted candidly, "that high rentals can be obtained only for well lighted offices" like Schiller's, where setbacks allowing "a greater volume of light into the side courts" presumably jacked up the price. The Odd Fellows project, dead by the time he wrote, was guided by similar objectives. Because of its large courts providing "abundant light in every portion . . . and the great distance of the parts carried up to the greater height, disturbing shadows" on the streets and neighboring buildings "would have been avoided."[21] Like Adler, Sullivan was terribly disappointed at losing this commission, not just for the loss of the biggest fee of his life, but also because it would have been "exceedingly picturesque," in Adler's phrase, was a good piece of work, in other words, and represented important design and urban principles. A drawing accompanying Sullivan's *Graphic* essay, entitled "Street View Showing Full Development of the Idea," depicted a fanciful urban vista—no more

X.11 *Union Trust Building, 1892.*

so than Hugh Ferriss's or Corbusier's later on, however—with at least eight setback options. Two were based on the Auditorium tower, but others had onion domes, medieval turrets, conical and pyramidal roofs. The illustration was badly drawn (probably by a commercial engraver), but it revealed Sullivan's concern for preserving those basic human amenities, for the public as well as for tenants, threatened by the very skyscrapers he designed. This drawing alone shows a more advanced social conscience than was usual for architects, including Dankmar Adler. Montgomery Schuyler, for one, was convinced by the embodiment of these principles: one can "imagine a building of the dimensions of the Fraternity Temple at the center of each square mile [shades of *La Ville Radieuse*] or even less, of a crowded city." Had the Temple been built, he believed, it would "have proven an excellent investment."[22]

Adler & Sullivan's next skyscraper was built and was an excellent investment. Contemplating new facilities since 1890, the Union Trust Company of St. Louis found a lot at the northwest corner of Olive and Seventh streets and received the architects' plans by March 1892. Contracts were let in June, when site clearance began, and by November 1893 the fourteen-story, and attic, 128-by-84-foot building was open for business. Union Trust was U-shaped like the Wainwright Building, but its twin towers on a two-story base divided by a *south*-facing front light court was a solar conscious reversal of the scheme. Otherwise it was similar in plan. With the help of a side alley, 254 of its 300 offices (averaging 220 square feet) had outside exposure, and no part of any was more than eighteen feet from external light. The steel skeleton was diagonally braced and covered with hollow clay tiles inside, but on the exterior was encased in masonry envelopes for additional wind and fire resistance. Halls and other public spaces had marble paving and wainscoting over tile floor arches, six elevators went to the rooftop observatory, hot and cold water ran in every office, a barbershop and baths were connected with the toilets, and every room and corridor was equipped with a custom system of shelved moldings to carry conduit, telephone wires, and to facilitate relocation of the electrical outlets serving every desk in the building. Only the mahogany finish in the first story, antique oak office floors, and door and window frames and sash were combustible. In the neighborhood of $750,000, Union Trust was not only pace-setting in terms of equipment, but was also one of the most fire-safe skyscrapers in the country.

At the center of the longer Olive Street base was a two-story, thirty-five-foot wide, rectangularly framed, receding-arch entry, again recalling the Transportation Building, flanked by three plate-glass bays and three large porthole windows in a rich second-floor frieze. Under its slight but emphatic third-story sill, this arrangement continued for six bays around the corner on Seventh Street in buff terra-cotta signaling that the lower levels differed from the superstructure because their banking room, "grand arcade" for "light and elegant merchandise," two additional shops, and "samples" room, and Union Trust's Title Guaranty Department on the second floor, were functionally independent of the facilities above. The next ten stories of offices in buff brick were expressed in continuous arched bays without "false" columns (like Schiller, rather than the Wainwright) containing paired sash windows and the usual recessed spandrels. The overhanging cornice sheltered a less aggressive frieze than Sullivan's previous skyscrapers, but the major departure at Union Trust was a thirteenth-to-fourteenth-floor, vigorously vertical colonnade, severed from the arches by a subsidiary cornice with "bearcat" corners, the building prospectus called them, entertaining little animal faces peering down at passersby. Aside from the large portholes on the base, the other new departure at Union Trust was seven heraldic lions fixed to second-story corners and surmounting the main entrance, huge, slightly grotesque figures eight and one-half feet tall of dubious decorative or artistic merit. Either Sullivan suffered a major lapse or, as seems equally likely, the clients made a demand he could not refuse.[23]

The oversize portholes and lions, but especially the colonnade, compromised the coherence of Union Trust compared with Sullivan's first skyscraper facades. Even so, it surpassed other architectural efforts to deal with the tall office building, and was not without real virtues. An unusually perceptive newspaper columnist detected some of the design subtleties that escaped even the most thoughtful national critics. "It will be seen," he wrote in July 1892, months before the building opened,

> that the ornamentation has been concentrated in such manner as to . . . retain the attention of the passerby. Those who pass near the building will be attracted by the richness of the doorway and by the unique ornamentation of the second story. Those who will see the building from a distance will note the boldness and originality of treatment of the two upper stories and the richness of effect of the main cornice and will be impressed by the twin tower effect consequent upon the use of the external court in the design of this building, which cannot fail to become a point of interest to everyone visiting St. Louis.[24]

Montgomery Schuyler thought the lower stories especially appropriate because the building was not only "erected for rental, but . . . also [as] the abode of a commercial institution [whose quarters Sullivan] signalized in his design." But the top he found "a little bald." Had it been "a more effectual counterpart of the base," had it been as lavish, he implied elsewhere, "Union Trust would have been as successful in execution as it is in conception." Modern tastes might prefer the "capital," as Schuyler called the colonnade and frieze, to be more consistent with the ten stories below. On the other hand, a reviewer for *Builder* magazine concluded in 1893 that "the principle of the design seems right," expressing the architect's contention "that every building . . . should be enclosed within one main idea and should not be a succession of floors piled one above the other without reference to the scheme as a whole."[25] Sullivan might have used the same words had he penned the appraisal himself.

The thirteen-story Portland Building, designed around August 1892 for a site on Chestnut Street in St. Louis, borrowed a good deal from Union Trust. Its three-bay shaft looked like one of the twin towers, with its flat cornice and attic frieze of similar dimensions, its narrow street-to-roof angle piers, its two-floor colonnade on top, and its ornamentally framed base and entry. But its most obvious differences were its attic portholes and arches, and most of all its T- or I-shaped rear wing setback flanked by light wells much akin to the Schiller Building's. The plain brick facade of the second and third floors, reminiscent of the Mercantile Club's skinlike walls, continued up the elevation in the center bay, but on either side was flanked by rather unusual three-sided recessed oriels, of a sort, with windows divided by continuous projecting mullions. (On the side the order was reversed: the seven-story oriel was bordered by plain tiers.) Referring in some way to all the prior skyscrapers except perhaps Odd Fellows, the Portland nevertheless managed to suggest new devices for achieving verticality. Yet at the same time it hinted at another aesthetic objective: revelation by design of the actual nondirectional composition of the steel frame. At a projected $350,000, the 59-by-116-foot-deep Portland Building, with its 175 offices and a ground-floor shop and bank, would have been an important addition to the St. Louis skyline.[26]

Although for unknown reasons it was never built, business prospects looked so good in St. Louis that Adler & Sullivan decided to open a branch office. On the Wainwright job, they had taken on architect and real estate promoter Charles K. Ramsey as an associate, not to assist with design but to handle local authorities and contractors, a common procedure for out-of-town practitioners. When Ramsey moved into the Hauser Building at 509 Chestnut Street, next door to the Portland site, Adler & Sullivan joined him, probably in the same office, in 1891 or 1892. The decision to expand quickly produced results. As the treasurer and a Press Committee member of the American Institute of Architects' local chapter, their new partner helped organize its third annual exhibition in 1895, featuring seven works by "Adler, Sullivan & Ramsey, Chicago and St. Louis," including the Wainwright Tomb, the St. Nicholas Hotel, and the Portland project. The Chicagoans were the only out-of-towners in the show, certainly a measure of their prestige and of high local regard for their work, perhaps an indication of their sagacity in committing themselves to the city, and possibly a reflection of their practical skills: seven of the thirty St. Louis AIA members, including two of the three on the Exhibition and Hanging Committee, had offices in either the Wainwright or Union Trust.[27]

Ramsey may have had a hand in the next two St. Louis skyscrapers, as a promoter, not an architect. Sullivan biographer Hugh Morrison identified them in 1935 as 1892 and 1893 studies for a "Trust and Savings" company, "just across the street from Union Trust." Their renderings show them elsewhere, at two different locations, however, and at no time during the decade was "Trust and Savings" mentioned in local directories or in connection with building ventures. But several entrepreneurs did, in fact, propose new structures for the Olive and Seventh Street intersection during the early 1890s, among them people well known to Charles K. Ramsey. The Mississippi Valley Trust Company held a ninety-nine-year lease at the southeast corner announcing periodically from 1891 to 1893 that plans had been drawn for an edifice "equally if not more handsome than" the Wainwright, Union Trust, and the Mercantile project. In 1894 it sold the lease to another entrepreneur with his own aspirations for "a modern office building on the order of Union Trust." Developer John Hogan intended in 1893 to grace his southwest corner with a "handsome improvement" like Adler & Sullivan's and the eagerly anticipated Mississippi Valley project, while at about the same time a syndicate holding the northeast corner hoped to erect "a fourteen story building to conform with the elegant structure underway" across the street, that is, Union Trust. Adler & Sullivan's skyscrapers had obviously made a big impression, not on "Trust and Savings," but on Mississippi Valley or another of the several speculators.[28]

X.12 *Portland Building project, 1892.* From Third Annual Exhibition Catalogue, St. Louis AIA, 1895.

The first of the still-unidentified proposals was for twelve stories with four large arches in the base and arched tiers of windows something like Schiller's ascending to a shallow attic frieze under a flat incised cornice like the Wainwright's. The especially slender angle piers, now characteristic of Sullivan's St. Louis work, in combination with fluted columns, soared without any interruption whatever from sidewalk to roof. With thin mullions and the familiar inset spandrels, this was Sullivan's sleekest, most aesthetically consistent, and most refined example of "vertical construction" thus far. Drawing on his previous work, but even more streamlined, it was nevertheless surpassed by the second version of sixteen stories, in which he deepened the building from three bays to four, but narrowed it from nine to eight. On its base Sullivan introduced column-encasing display windows slanting back at their tops to form recessed clerestories, an attempt to maximize natural light. The entrance was changed to a rectangle, and large female figures at column tops supported the cornice, a variation and refinement on the lions and bearcats at Union Trust. Like built-in lampposts at base top, triple-shelved corner light stanchions and a string of medallions (both improved from the first version) separated commercial from office space without compromising the elevation's unity. Although it was never built, this project was one of Sullivan's finest contributions to vertical skyscraper form.[29]

Adler & Sullivan's next skyscraper, however, was erected, back in Chicago again. Although they may have designed a major building for the site as early as July 1891, the Chicago Stock Exchange at La Salle and Washington streets took final form on paper during the first half of 1893 under the sponsorship of Auditorium backer Ferdinand Peck. Construction began by July, and on May 1, 1894, it opened for business. At a cost of $1,131,555, the firm's most expensive executed commission since the Auditorium but for the partially constructed Chicago Cold Storage Warehouse, its thirteen stories contained 480 offices plus banking facilities and a magnificent trading room on the second and third floors. Perhaps acknowledging the prestige of this powerful institution, Sullivan increased the height to emphasize the visual impact of the building's base. Over the row of sidewalk shops, he placed a series of bold terra-cotta arches to the top

X.13 *The first version of the so-called "Trust and Savings" project, c. 1892, St. Louis.* From *Western Architect,* 1925.

of the third floor with deep-set reveal and spandrel shadows enhancing an insistent rhythm across the lower facade. The forty-by-thirty-foot portal framed an arched entrance wrapped in a broad smooth stone band bordered by some of Sullivan's best ornament. Above this indication of the trading room's singularity, the facade rose through nine stories of ashlar to a colonnaded attic and a heavily ornamented cornice.[30]

The Stock Exchange was also distinguished by Sullivan's first skyscraper use of "Chicago" windows: the plate-glass center panels flanked by one-over-one sash were arranged in tiers separated by nine-story, three-sided oriels—a variation on the Portland's fenestration—giving the facade a corrugated appearance. Except for these

X.15 *Chicago Stock Exchange, 1893.* From *Inland Architect,* 1893.

X.14 *The second version of the so-called "Trust and Savings" project, c. 1893, St. Louis.* From Hugh Morrison, *Louis Sullivan.*

and very modest moldings, the office portion was entirely unornamented, leading some historians unfamiliar with the Mercantile and Portland projects to conclude that more than any other building, the Exchange not only foreshadowed Sullivan's Schlesinger & Mayer Store a few years later but also anticipated modernism's taut, skin-like envelopes for the steel frame, emphasizing neither horizontals nor verticals. This neutrality of surface direction with its shallow reveals did not particularly symbolize loftiness or become an occasion for ornament, but like the two St. Louis schemes simply suggested that its curtain wall was a thin enclosure for space, a Sullivan insight that some modernists later made a dictum. The oriels may have increased outside exposure, but they also gave texture and rhythm to a facade that could otherwise have looked—except for the base and attic—like an essay about structure, rather than the elegant home of a major institution.

Adler's foundation work also deserves attention. The recurring problem of unequal settlement in heavy buildings on Chicago's watery soil again led him to piles driven to bedrock like the Schiller's, here deployed over most of the 101-by-181-foot lot. But Adler and others feared that on the west side of the Exchange site, pile drivers might damage the presses and weaken the walls of the abutting *Chicago Herald* newspaper building. After another consultation with General Smith, he devised massive footings of waterproof drums packed with concrete to form cylindrical piers, the first caisson foundations in the city. Equally impressive was his solution for carrying ten stories over the thirty-foot-high, sixty-four-by-eighty-one-foot trading room, where there were to be no visual obstructions. Adler transferred the weight to four columns near the room's corners with seven large concealed trusses whose varying locations and depths were indicated on Sullivan's stenciled plaster ceiling. The monumental columns were sheathed in artificial marble and the ceiling and friezes laced with delicate ornament, primarily in greens, reds, and gold. Art glass on the underside of the truss boxes lit from above through skylights with prismatic reflectors and carbon filament lamps provided generous but soft illumination. The space was one of Sullivan's most brilliantly conceived, on a par with the best in the Auditorium Building. After the Exchange was demolished in 1972 despite international opposition, the trading room was reconstructed in the Art Institute, thanks in large part to the efforts and direction of Chicago architect John Vinci.

Note should be made of Sullivan's ornament elsewhere in the building, some of his most elegant ever. Conceived in the spring of 1894, the elevator grilles on the third to thirteenth floors featured oval shapes he later associated with "seed germs," the embryo of the life-force discussed in "Inspiration," his prose-poem of 1886. Fixed to vertical axes and pinned together horizontally, each "germ" had four stamens forming a diagonal cross. On the friezes over elevator doors, circles intersected ovals to form geometric bursts of organic vegetation, similar to the bronze motifs on push- and kickplates. The interwoven geometric and organic forms proceeded linearly in fact, and potentially in all directions in the continuous chains he began to develop around 1885. Limited, of course, by the dimensions of the objects they embellished, they nevertheless suggested the eternal life cycle to which the germs gave birth. The elevators, stairwells, and the lobby in the Stock Exchange showed Sullivan's ornament at its mature best, and though some was saved when the building was razed, most of it was lost.[31]

X.16 *Chicago Stock Exchange elevator grille.* From Southern Illinois University architectural ornament collection.

X.17 *Chicago Stock Exchange, kickplate.* From Southern Illinois University architectural ornament collection.

X.18 *Guaranty Building, 1894–95.* Photo by The Chicago Architectural Photographing Company.

Adler & Sullivan's fifth and last constructed skyscraper is in the minds of many their best, the Guaranty Building at the southwest corner of Pearl and Church streets in Buffalo, designed late in 1894 and 1895, and opened March 1, 1896. In several ways it repeated the themes of the Wainwright Building, partly because the program was so similar. Like the Wainwright, it is U-shaped, on a corner lot with a flat, overhanging cornice, a richly ornamented attic with porthole windows, a two-story base capped with a third-floor sill, mullions made to look like structural piers, and a price tag somewhat over $500,000. But the differences between the two are equally striking. The 93-by-116-foot lot was smaller than in St. Louis, but since the program called for as many offices, it was three stories higher at twelve plus attic. Unlike the Wainwright, the second floor was partially devoted to mercantile use, signaled by the large windows in each bay. The only deviations in plan above the base were a gentlemen's lavatory, a ladies' toilet, and a barbershop on the seventh floor, and a United States weather bureau, fan chambers, storerooms, and larger offices in the attic.[32]

At street level Sullivan revived the slanted-back window tops from the second "Trust and Savings" project to capture more light for display, to free up decorative capitals, and by exposing the entire columns to "float" the building on Corbusier-like *pilotis. These comparatively tall, thin columns encased in broad expanses of glass* gave the base an exceptionally airy quality. By seeming to disappear, they emphasized the nonsupporting curtain wall, albeit in a manner dissimilar from the Stock Exchange, Portland, and Mercantile superstructures. Since the third-story sill dividing multiple functions below from offices above was not as pronounced as the Wainwright's, the Guaranty's upward thrust was cleaner, while at the top, ornament around window arches flowed directly into the attic without molding so that the Buffalo building, even more so than the Schiller, was "cast on one jet."

The principal difference from the Wainwright, however, was the facade ornament. Sullivan had generally followed the convention of decorating only nonstructural elements like spandrels, the attic, the

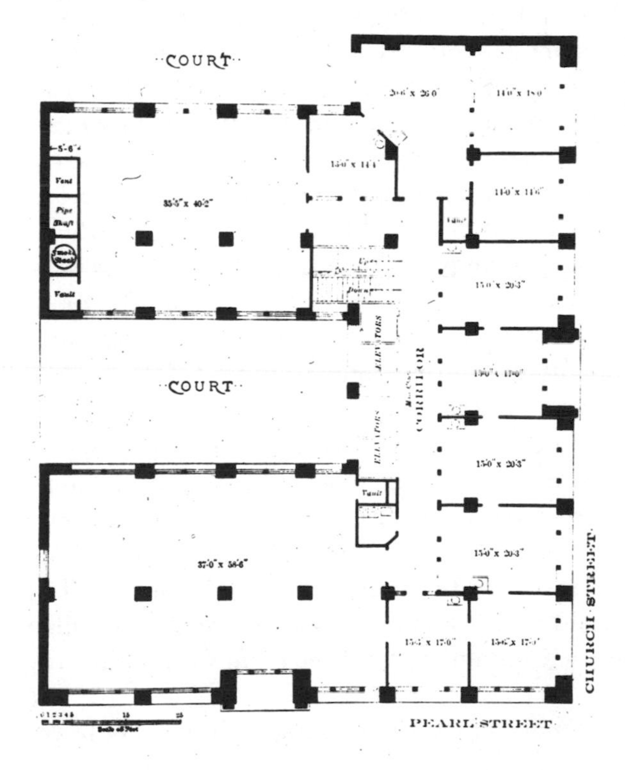

X.19 *Guaranty Building, second-floor plan.* From Guaranty Company prospectus.

cornice, and portals. But at the Guaranty he covered every square inch of nonglazed surface. At the base the ornament was comparatively geometric and flat, on the superstructure it was more organic and three-dimensional, and on the attic was positively *trompe l'oeil.* All of it was delicate and disciplined, but the idea was that the farther up and away the stronger it became. The powerful angle piers, for example, were enriched at the attic by ornament spilling over the cornice fascia at the corresponding corners. And the porthole windows, hooded as the wall curved like coving to the underside of the cornice, appeared to be arch tops from directly below. One result of these ornamental devices was a kind of optical trick: from nearby, the heavier trim on the upper facade appeared similar to that of the lower floors, while from the adjacent sidewalk the false arches suggested the same vertical continuity observers saw from a distance. From farther away, moreover, the ornamental particulars became a rich, textured skin, if anything emphasizing, certainly not contradicting, the steel frame. Like the Parthenon, where unequal spacing of columns seemed to be perfectly equal because of perspective distortion, Sullivan's ornament was a much more subtle way of addressing the public than his ham-handed sculpture at Union Trust.[33]

"Though possibly the most richly decorated commercial building in America," critic Barr Ferree concluded in 1895, "the skill of the artist has produced a design of structural sobriety with great richness of effect." This unity of structure and aesthetics "has been attained," he diagnosed, "by the long vertical lines of the superstructure." Montgomery Schuyler knew of "no steel-framed building in which the metallic construction is more palpably felt through the envelope of baked clay," while a few years later architect Claude Bragdon added that the Guaranty "represents perhaps the highest logical and aesthetic development of the steel-frame office building."[34] If the resolution of the horizontals and verticals at the Wainwright was "nearly perfect," according to Paul Goldberger, at the Guaranty it reached perfection, should such a thing be possible. As a taller, thinner building, it was more a tower than a block, with every other one of its slim verticals visible through its airy base to secure it firmly but delicately to the ground in a kind of unintimidating insistence. If a tall office building should be a "proud and soaring thing," as Sullivan wrote at the time, the Guaranty proved the point with argument to spare.

Although it was their final constructed skyscraper, it may not have been the last the partners designed. Their 1894 project for Cincinnati's Burnet House hotel at Third and Vine streets was not their most successful skyscraper, as Montgomery Schuyler thought, but it certainly added new dimensions to the genre. The scheme called for three buildings in one: L-shaped, eleven-floor corner towers connected by an eight-story mid-block section. Familiar to Sullivan-watchers were the flat incised cornice with ornament bleeding down onto the attic; the recessed spandrels marking the floors horizontally; the narrow angle piers and columns soaring past the spandrels and the thin, nonstructural mullions taken from the Portland project; the triple-shelved lampposts and bent-back display windows seen first at "Trust and Savings"; a projecting colonnaded gallery like Schiller Theatre's placed here atop the central section; and heroic sculptures surmounting doorways and columns.

The most striking new features included the brackets or projecting beams enlivening the attic that Schuyler said was "a suitable counterpart to the richest base," answering his complaint with Union Trust. On the two-story base itself, the entrances to the taller divisions were large arches carrying very similar truncated arched windows on their second-floor shoulders. There were "false piers" in the shorter section but not in the flanking towers, Sullivan's first restriction of nonstructural columns to one portion of a building. And, finally, within each column-spanning arch at the attic, he placed two small arches springing from the mullions and moldings on the tenth floor; a small porthole window bridged the gap between the curvatures, a formulation he revived three years later at the Bayard-Condict Building in New York. With only minor reservations, Schuyler thought the Burnet project one of the "most organically complete and most satisfactory of its author's contributions to the most urgent of the architectural problems [the skyscraper] in this country." Unfortunately for Adler & Sullivan, and perhaps for Cincinnati, the owners decided not to raze the hotel as planned, but to remodel it in 1895 without their assistance.[35]

Also unbuilt and virtually unknown was Adler & Sullivan's eight-story, half-block-long proposal for the Chemical National Bank, adjacent to Union Trust in St. Louis, a design of real theoretical significance. Before the commission for a sixteen-floor tower went to Chicagoan Henry Ives Cobb in April 1895, several developers attempted to build on the site, at least one with Adler & Sullivan. Their scheme called for a high, one-story base, with richly framed fenestration later appearing in different form at Schlesinger & Mayer's Department Store, supporting seven remarkably plain white brick floors. The abbreviated attic was adorned only with a small medallion per bay and a flat projecting cornice. Each pair of broad sash windows were divided by simple mullions in an unusually high glass-to-masonry ratio revealing the walls as mere curtains.

Most striking of all, however, was Sullivan's expression of structure. The columns and spandrels, completely flush with each other to make a directionally neutral facade, stated the steel frame not in terms of height—somewhat beside the point on such a relatively short edifice—but as a cage or network of mutually supporting horizontal and vertical members, a literal revelation of how the structural order actually worked. Hinted at in the Mercantile, Portland, and Stock Exchange facades, the Chemical proposal was a fully matured nonmetaphorical approach to the high-rise. If Sullivan's vertical "system" was, in a sense, a design imposition on construction to exaggerate tallness, the Chemical Building transformed structure into aesthetics without reference to height. Aside from numerous floors, after all, there was nothing about a network of steel girders and columns *per se* to suggest a particular direction. And like tallness, the frame itself begged for its own artistic treatment. The Chemical Building can therefore be seen as Sullivan's conscious attempt to eliminate height from the consideration of a pure structural aesthetic. But for reasons that still remain a mystery, this most "modernist" of all Sullivan's visions, certainly by latter-day standards, was never built.[36]

What happened next was anything but mysterious. Despite repeated assertions of optimism from real estate circles, the 1890s depression was deepening. Its effect on Adler & Sullivan was no less disastrous than on the architectural profession as a whole: in 1894 the partners saw only two new buildings to completion, the $10,000 Herman Braunstein store and flats on North Avenue, designed in May, and in August the $75,000 Chicago Dock Company warehouse on the river at Taylor Street.[37] Their fees did not even cover expenses, and in 1895 nothing came into the office at all. At age fifty-one, with his wife to support and three children still at home, Adler began to feel the pinch more severely than bachelor Sullivan and, bereft of commissions, to the surprise of everyone except his family and partner, quit the architectural profession on July 11. Signing a ten-year contract at "a salary so large it became a difficult task for

X.20 *Chemical National Bank Building project, c., 1894, St. Louis, with Union Trust Building, 1892, in the background.* From Third Annual Exhibition Catalogue, St. Louis AIA, 1895.

him to refuse," one magazine reported—$25,000 per annum according to Frank Lloyd Wright—he became supervising sales manager and consulting architect with an elevator company owned by his friend Richard T. Crane, for whom he and Sullivan had previously designed two buildings. Although pride in his innovative use of elevators might have encouraged him to confront the challenge his need for income had driven him to accept, Adler nevertheless expressed regret at leaving architecture, his first and truest love, in an open letter to his colleagues. Intending to "keep in touch" through the journals, he asked for assistance in his new endeavor, and hoped he could help smooth the traditionally rocky relations between his former profession and contractors. "I have always flattered myself by believing every architect to be my friend," he ended his letter. "I sincerely trust that this pleasant relation may continue."[38]

So after twelve years of partnership with Dankmar Adler, plus two more in close association, Louis Sullivan found himself alone. Frank Lloyd Wright had left under a cloud in 1893, just before the economic downturn, followed involuntarily by others as the climate worsened, reducing the staff of almost fifty in the early nineties to a handful, George Elmslie among the remaining. Sullivan oversaw completion of the Guaranty, visiting Buffalo in August 1895 to learn that steelwork was proceeding more rapidly than expected. With Elmslie carrying out facade ornament and certain indoor details like doorknob plates, Sullivan accelerated interior decoration in the fall, its lavishness undoubtedly keeping him quite busy. But with no new work waiting, the pace in his office slackened further. Only one more commission arrived in 1895, in December, long after Adler left, a $10,000, two-story, sixty-by-eighty-four cooper shop for the National Linseed Oil Company on the South Side. Sullivan could keep the whole fee, but this one was small, and there was nothing else in sight.[39]

Given their close and very successful relationship, Adler must have been reluctant to leave his partner. He must have pondered his decision long and hard, exploring it from every angle, perhaps in wrenching talks with Sullivan, who, for his part, apparently came to accept it as a practical necessity, at least for a time and on a conscious level. But within a few months, he began to interpret the turn of events differently, somewhat bitterly, and not as a business issue. When the Guaranty's rendering first appeared in March 1895, it bore the legend "Adler & Sullivan," but when it was published a second time in November after Adler's departure it read only "Louis H. Sullivan, Architect," a revision of the drawing that could not have been a printer's oversight. In the Guaranty Construction Company's rental prospectus of March 1896, the title page gave both names, but the text ignored Adler to concentrate on "the masterpiece of Louis H.

Sullivan, who is famous on two continents for the beauty, originality and refinement of his conceptions."[40] Since he was solely responsible during the last seven months of construction, Sullivan may have felt justified in taking all the credit, especially if he changed the design in any way, although the renderings do not indicate significant external alterations. Sullivan's seeming dismissal of Adler's contributions to the Guaranty has about it the quality of retaliation, like a headstrong child "punishing" parents for an imagined slight by ignoring them. Adler's understandable pique turned to anger when later in the year Sullivan met his sudden return to architecture with studied indifference.

It did not take Adler long to realize he had made a serious mistake. Although he possessed many of the qualities necessary for public relations success, he was simply not suited to serving someone else's interests, to taking orders, even from a friend, especially one as self-possessed as the successful enterpreneur Richard Crane. Not without reason had Adler been "the Big Chief" in his old Auditorium office. So only six months after signing on, despite the economic climate, he quit the elevator company by mutual agreement with Crane, letting it be known he was again available for architectural work. But this time not with Sullivan. Wright pressed Adler to resume the partnership, but because of the Guaranty matter he refused. "I am going to keep my office in my hat now," he reportedly told Wright, "so far as I can."[41] Sullivan, meanwhile, would not apologize, or approach Adler to set things right, having determined to go it alone up in the Auditorium tower. Had the two proud and stubborn men sat down to discuss their differences, which in point of fact were not so monumental, things might have turned out better for both. Early in 1896 Adler set up shop with his son Abraham, a mechanical engineer, and E. L. Corthell, a civil engineer, in Room 27, a suite on the second floor of the Auditorium Building, Wabash Street side, moving the next year to Suite 64. Adler and Sullivan used different entrances to get to work, but they must have crossed each other's paths quite often.

In years past Sullivan had been a regular guest in the Adler home, bringing toys to the children as they grew up, and sharing all sorts of family activities. He especially liked Adler's wife, Dila, their daughter Sarah remembered many years later, on one occasion making her a copy of a World's Fair tablecloth he had borrowed from Mrs. Potter Palmer. He gave her many beautiful gifts, in fact was rather "extravagant" about it with an "easy come, easy go" attitude toward money, she recalled. It was always "very nice" to have him around, and Sarah remembered that he and her father had a "wonderful friendship."[42]

Perhaps Sullivan's inability to reunite with Adler, to apologize for thoughtlessness, and to move toward reconciliation lay in the very fact that their relationship was so "wonderful." Certainly, it seems to have been more than a simple matter of stubborn pride. As a bachelor, he might have seen himself as a surrogate family member, a kind of benevolent uncle to the children and brother to Dila, possibly even to Adler himself. As his relationship with his own brother and sister-in-law deteriorated, he might have come to depend on the Adlers for more than the normal social intercourse expected of friendly business connections. Because of his own need for family intimacy of the sort he had long ago shed but could have wanted subconsciously, Sullivan may have interpreted the severing of business ties as personal rejection. As a very proper man, expecting order and consistency in things he held dear, he might have been unable to adjust to change. On a more mundane level, he might have even envied Adler's salary at Crane's, or thought with his "easy come, easy go" attitude about money that Adler had compromised his integrity by sacrificing close associations for mere income. If he could hang on through difficult times, in financial sickness as in health, so to speak, then so should Adler, he may have thought. Not to do so could mean that the "wonderful" years had been based on a profound misconception. All this could help explain why Sullivan never attempted to re-form the partnership when it was clearly in his interest to do so, and why he stopped visiting the Adler household.

A comparison with the Wright moonlighting incident is instructive. When Wright, something of a surrogate son to Sullivan, or at least a worshipful admirer, tried to explain his behavior in 1893, Sullivan refused to listen, reportedly saying he could "not tolerate division under any circumstances," that "your sole interest is here." Loyalty—to him and to the firm—was what Wright had violated, and Sullivan could not separate the two, especially when to all practical purposes his life was his work. Two years later, when Adler left him, it was again a matter of loyalty, of "division," in Sullivan's mind. When he learned that Adler was returning to architecture, he would not bend, could not rebuild the old relationship. Unable to forgive, he rejected Adler the man as he imagined Adler had rejected him.

Two months after Adler came back to architecture, just as the Guaranty opened, in March 1896, Sullivan published an important essay for *Lippincott's* magazine, "The Tall Office Building Artistically Considered,"[43] a kind of summation of half a decade's work that turned out to be extraordinarily influential and to open another disheartening rift with his old partner, an additional symptom of their estrangement. Today's architects are face to face "with something new under the sun," Sullivan began, namely, that special grouping of social conditions resulting in "a demand for the erection of tall office buildings." Accepting the social conditions as fact, he recognized the "design of the tall office building . . . [as] a vital problem pressing for a true solution":

> How shall we impart to this sterile pile, this crude, harsh, brutal agglomeration, this stark, staring exclamation of eternal strife, the graciousness of those higher forms of sensibility and culture that rest on the lower and fiercer passions? How shall we proclaim from the dizzy height of this strange, weird, modern housetop the peaceful evangel of sentiment, of beauty, the cult of a higher life?

How, in other words, can we make a spiritual thing of a grubby commercial thing? The answer, Sullivan believed, could be found in "natural law," where "the very essence of every problem . . . contains and suggests its own solution."

The solution to the skyscraper problem was to be found in its essentials. Simple observation had taught him that "every tall office building in the country" required, first of all, a basement for boilers and engines, for power, heating, and lighting apparatus; second, it needed a so-called ground floor for stores, banks, and other establishments with ample area, spacing, light, and freedom of access; third, a related second story easily reached by stairs from the first, usually with large rooms, structural openness, and expansive windows; fourth, "above this an indefinite number of stories of offices piled tier upon tier, one tier just like another, one office just like all the other offices—an office being similar to a cell in a honeycomb, merely a compartment, nothing more"; fifth, an attic, "purely physiological in its nature," where "the circulatory system completes itself and makes its grand turn, ascending and descending," for tanks, pipes, valves, sheaves, and "mechanical etcetera" complementing the "force-originating" power plant hidden below ground in the cellar; and, finally, or perhaps firstly, a main entrance common to all who use the building. This six-part program suggested a solution not 'individual or specific," he insisted, "but for a true normal type," the application to architecture, Sullivan believed, of the "demonstration . . . so broad as to admit of NO EXCEPTION" that his mathematics tutor M. Clopet had insisted upon at the Ecole des Beaux-Arts two decades before.

The floor plan, Sullivan observed, ordinarily took on aesthetic interest only if it had a light court or some other kind of variation. Nevertheless, an office of "comfortable" area and height "naturally" became the standard structural unit determining the approximate size of window openings as well as the true basis for the artistic development of the exterior. Although the first and second floors required larger structural spacings and openings, in the attic they were of no importance whatever. "Hence it follows inevitably, and in the simplest possible way, that if we follow our natural instincts without thought of books, rules, precedents, or any such educational impediments to a spontaneous and 'sensible' result, we will in the following manner design the exterior of our tall office building—to wit": the ground floor with a main entrance attracting the eye should be treated in an expansive, sumptuous way based on the practical necessities already outlined, the second story similarly, but with milder pretensions, since it is a variation on the first. Both constitute the building's base and are considered as a unit. Above this, secondly, the office tiers take their cue from the individual cell requiring a window with its separating pier, sill, and lintel, all cells looking alike because they are alike; and, thirdly, the attic, without offices or a great need for lighting, shows with its broad wall plane and its dominating weight and character that the series of tiers has come to a definite end. A building following this system would not suffer from the "sinister" "speculator-engineer-builder" but would at last show the architect in "the decisive position," not the trained, accomplished architect from the academy, but one responding to instinct "in a direct and simple way." Did Sullivan, by distinguishing between architects and engineers, mean to tweak Adler?

A building like this might certainly seem logical and natural, having skirted the impedimenta of architectural precedent. But, Sullivan continued, a building like this would also "heed the imperative voice of emotion." For what, he asked, "is the chief characteristic of the tall office building?" "It is lofty," he proclaimed, in the first of his memorable answers; this, its most thrilling aspect, is "the very organ-tone in its appeal." Loftiness must be the "dominant chord" in its expression. And "it must be tall," Sullivan continued, "every inch of it tall. . . . It must be every inch a proud and soaring thing, rising in sheer exultation . . . from bottom to top . . . without a single dissenting line." But the tall office building was also "the new, the unexpected, the eloquent peroration of most bald, most sinister, most forbidding conditions." Alluding to the unchecked entrepreneurialism that produced devasting social exploitation and unparalleled urban blight, Sullivan seemed to argue that the architect could somehow ameliorate capitalist brutality: "The man who designs in this spirit and with the sense of responsibility to the generation he lives in must be no coward." He must live life in the fullest, most consummate sense. He must "with the grasp of inspiration" realize "that the problem of the tall office building is one of the most stupendous, one of the most magnificent opportunities that the Lord of Nature in His beneficence has ever offered to the proud spirit of man." If the architect could bring graciousness and culture to the "eternal strife" and "fiercer passions" of the marketplace, he would have advanced the cause of democracy: art for society's sake.

After surveying and dismissing other theories, Sullivan advanced his "final, comprehensive formula" for the solution of the skyscraper problem, indeed, of all architectural problems. All things in nature have shapes, forms, and outward semblances "that tell us what they are, that distinguishes them from ourselves, and from each other," Sullivan asserted. "Unfailingly in nature these shapes express the inner life," and when scrutinized reveal that "the essence of things is taking shape in the matter of things." Life seeks and takes on forms in response to needs, Sullivan argued, in good Darwinian fashion, the life and the form being "absolutely one and inseparable." "Where function does not change," he added, "form does not change," so that it was "the pervading law of all things"—organic, inorganic, physical, metaphysical, human and superhuman—"that form ever follows function. This is the law."

Was it so marvelous, then, "that the shape, form, outward expression, design or whatever we may choose, of the tall office building should in the very nature of things follow the functions of the building, and that where the function does not change, the form is not to change?" Does this not clearly show, he argued, that its bottom one or two stories "will take on a special character suited to the special needs, that the tiers of typical offices, having the same unchanging functions, shall continue in the same unchanging form, and that as to the attic, specific and conclusive as it is in its very nature, its function shall be equally so in force, in significance, in continuity, in conclusiveness of outward expression"? Thus the three-part division of the office building was based on the nature of the species, so to speak, perceived instinctively by the open-minded architect. It was not based on theory, symbol, fancied logic, or history. When "native instinct and sensibility shall govern the exercise of our beloved art," Sullivan concluded, when "form follows function" becomes the law of architecture, "when we know and feel that Nature is our friend," then we will develop a natural and satisfying art that will "live" because it is of, by, and for the people.

Although Sullivan would write and say much more in the years ahead, this paper captured the essence of his architectural philosophy more than any other. By listening to one's instincts and thinking through architectural problems as if they had never been solved before, tossing out assumptions about what once had been correct, American architects could find a native language. Sullivan saw the tall office building as the characteristically American edifice, as the prototypical cultural manifestation of a business civilization, loaded with social meanings, not the least important being entrepreneurial ruthlessness in accumulating the money to build it. But to Sullivan the skyscraper was also an opportunity for cultural salvation. Learning from nature, the architect might unlock the design solution buried in the problem, so that the "higher form of sensibility," the "peaceful evangel of sentiment" that resulted would be a social solution, a spiritual essay about democracy. Through proper form and the process of creating it, worthwhile values could be nurtured. "The Tall Office Building Artistically Considered" set forth Sullivan's clearest thinking about the meaning of his design, but it was also his manifesto on the role of art in social transformation.

By preference and training, Dankmar Adler was less concerned with such lofty issues, especially when addressing a professional audience. But in "The Influence of Steel Construction and Plate Glass Upon the Development of Modern Style,"[44] a paper read in October 1896 to the Thirtieth Annual Convention of the American Institute of Architects, in Nashville, he challenged Sullivan on his own philosophical terrain, something he would not have done publicly before their separation. "The architect is not only an artist," Adler observed—presumably referring to "that clear thinker and brilliant writer [but not architect!], Louis H. Sullivan"—"but also an engineer, a man of science and a man of affairs," who cannot afford to wait until "seized by an irresistible impulse from within," he gives the world the fruits of his studies and musings. Pointedly taking Sullivan's youthful hero as an example, Adler asserted that Michelangelo, "above all, and in all, an artist," would not have been great without knowledge of "science and crafts, the command of which devolves upon the architect." The best design opportunities past and present were generally the result of changes in the environment brought about by human invention. "Natural variations" certainly, but more often "artificial conditions and circumstances," influenced the development of design tools like the beam, the lintel, and more recently the steel frame that in the end helped generate new styles. Taking the essence of architecture to be structure, Adler argued that because steel took up so little space, its fillings and fireproof coverings assumed new importance as "media for artistic treatment." On the facade, he allowed that form could sometimes follow function. But for the *reality* of buildings—the materials and structural arrangements holding them together—Adler concluded that "function and environment [the human-made environment] determined form," a direct rebuke to Sullivan.

As an engineer drawn to structural problems more strongly than Sullivan was, Adler saw architectural art as a kind of dressing, a cladding, for the real building underneath. Sullivan's art was therefore of secondary importance; necessary, to be sure, but auxiliary nonetheless. On this point, representing the division of labor that had made the partnership work, Adler was more "modernist" than Sullivan. It was customary in late-nineteenth-century thinking to separate "architecture" from "building," the former being applied to the latter to make it handsome. A building could or could not have architecture depending on the presence or absence of ornament and the extent of formal composition. Since Sullivan invested these with his own social and metaphysical meanings, he was hardly customary. But neither can he be labeled a modernist, who would more than likely insist that structure and architecture were, if not one, then certainly symbiotic, a position Adler could have endorsed. For Sullivan, just as form followed function, so architecture followed structure while elevating it through art to the level of cultural symbol. The principal difference between Adler and the modernists is that he approached architecture as an engineer, while most of them came at it through design, a professional distinction perhaps more important in form than in fact. As long as Adler and Sullivan worked in tandem, their philosophies were complementary, but once they split up, their ideas became adversarial.

If Adler seemed to belittle Sullivan, turning his hero Michelangelo against him, dismissing him as an architect with the suggestion that facade composition was an incidental art, he did it not from meanness—for Adler was not a petty man—but out of bitterness at Sullivan's claim on the Guaranty, at his distancing himself so resolutely, and at his linking engineers in "The Tall Office Building" to those speculator-builders giving architecture a bad name with unprofessional, indeed downright unethical, conduct. If in his paper Sullivan virtually stripped engineers of a design role, Adler in his appeared to reprimand Sullivan, to hint that without his own expertise in really crucial matters, Sullivan might be out of his depth. Between the lines Adler's paper intimated for those aware of the situation that the acclaimed author of "proud and soaring" buildings was unprepared and too impractical to go it alone.

Chapter XI

NEW BEGINNINGS 1895-1900

LOUIS SULLIVAN may not have had much business in the midst of a national depression, but his press was good. Just two weeks after he removed Dankmar Adler's name from his office door, in July 1895, New York's *American Architect & Building News,* the profession's most influential magazine until *The Architectural Record* usurped its position, reviewed a student exhibition at Chicago's Art Institute school. "Our talented *confrère*" Sullivan, its correspondent disclosed, had hoped for years to found a style but had recently decided he was insufficiently influential to do it. One look at this show, however, would convince anyone that Sullivan's "wildest desire had been realized."

His unique spirit "pervades everything, and in the advanced classes there is absolutely no other spirit shown, from designs for lace-work and wall-paper up to those for wrought-iron work and mosaic." The architectural ornamentation in clay "might well have come from the actual hand of Mr. Sullivan," so faithfully did it convey his geometry and his conventionalized leaf and flower forms. The trouble was that the "whole school" was reduced to a "state of almost servile imitation in which all attempt at originality was lost." The classical, Romanesque, and Gothic styles that any young designer might need to utilize some day had been entirely abandoned. The wrought-iron and illuminated paintings were not all Sullivanesque, to be sure, and the prizewinning drawing for a dowry chest successfully combined his ideals with the classical. But even with these exceptions, the reviewer concluded, his remarks more prophetic than ironic, "if this thing continues there will be a Chicago style resulting in quite different work from that [of] . . . any other art school, and the adjective Sullivanesque will find here many nouns for it to modify."[1]

Undoubtedly flattered by student imitation, Sullivan never encouraged it. The point of his work, he had repeatedly argued, was *not* to copy, *not* to rely on precedent, even his own, except in one sense, namely, to learn from him a *process* of creation: how to find solutions inherent in the very nature of architectural problems. The idea was to approach a design as if it had never been attempted before, to express the raisons d'être for buildings in new forms without relying on history. The real irony of academic recognition was that as Sullivan's style began to permeate the schools, his philosophy remained as difficult for students as ever.

It is nevertheless clear that by the mid-1890s, his influence extended far beyond the Midwestern circles in which it was particularly paramount. At the death of American architecture's "dean," Richard Morris Hunt, on July 31, 1895, Chicago's *Inland Architect* selected Sullivan to draw a border for the memorial portrait in its August commemorative issue. "No more appropriate setting could be devised than an autograph sketch by Louis H. Sullivan," the editors proclaimed. "A pupil of the French school [like Hunt] and yet not of it, with an individuality and genius not only pre-eminent but like [Hunt's] one that has received the recognition of the greatest of French architectural authorities, Mr. Sullivan's tribute is as unique as it is appropriate."[2]

Sullivan celebrated his thirty-ninth birthday on September 3 basking in praise like this but with no new commissions pending. The end of his partnership was probably a factor, but more important was the deepening national depression. *Inland Architect* assessed its impact in grim statistics: from a high of 13,118 worth $63,000,000 in 1892, new Chicago buildings fell to 8265, valued at $28,000,000 in 1893, a dollar loss of well over 50 percent, making for a "pretty trying [year] on the profession," according to *The Economist.* Some observers saw improvement early in 1894, raising hopes for a lasting recovery. But a local building-trades strike beginning in April and a railroad strike in July snuffed out optimism. The 1894 figures of 9736 new constructions costing some $33,000,000 were an improvement over the year before but far below 1892. In April 1895, 1002 structures, estimated at $3,800,000, were started, and everyone took heart, but the April 1896 comparative numbers plummeted to 803 and $2,500,000. Little wonder Sullivan's only 1895 commission after Adler's departure was the $10,000 cooper shop on Seventy-seventh Street in Chicago that after expenses would have netted him considerably less than $1000. "A few architects have done fairly well," *The Economist* reported late in 1894, "but a great majority have not made their living expenses, let alone . . . office rents."[3]

Dankmar Adler certainly found the situation dismal when he returned to architecture on New Year's Day, 1896, a "surprise which was full of pleasure to the entire profession," one magazine exclaimed, for never in its history "has it needed its strong men as now." But, like Sullivan, Adler was powerless to restore prosperity simply by being available. In fact, he got no work for two months, not until he was hired in March as consulting architect for a proposed St. Louis convention hall, and received the commission to convert the top three floors of the four-story National Hotel on South Clark Street to headquarters for the Technical Club, a two-hundred-member association of architects and engineers. At $12,000 to $15,000, the fee for the club was small, but Adler covered his rent by associating in March with civil engineer E. L. Corthell, who was at the time doing preliminary work for a Detroit River bridge and on the Cape Cod Canal. Their new offices were in the Auditorium, but on the second floor, Wabash Street side, away from Sullivan's entrance.[4] The opening that month of the Guaranty Building in Buffalo, plus Montgomery Schuyler's flattering article in *The Record*'s "Great American Architects" series featuring Adler & Sullivan, Daniel H. Burnham, and Henry Ives Cobb, may have helped promote Adler's name.[5]

Sullivan reaped the additional benefit of publishing "The Tall Office Building Artistically Considered" in the March *Lippincott's*. But no new work came along until the first of several 1896 commissions in May from Schlesinger & Mayer's, one of Chicago's prominent department stores. Sullivan's association with the respected dry goods merchants had begun in 1884 on a $20,000 residence for Leopold Schlesinger at 285 South Michigan Avenue. Two years later, with his business partner Daniel Mayer, Schlesinger purchased the W. W. Boyington–designed six-story building they occupied at the corner of State and Madison streets and leased adjacent four-story space on their way to assembling a good deal of the block through to Wabash and south to Monroe. Soon Adler & Sullivan were hired three times: in 1890 and 1891 to design interior alterations, new facades, and two additional stories to bring the four-floor edifice, plus more new leases—running now from 137 to 141 State Street—into conformity with the corner Boyington building. There was also talk of eventually raising the entire complex to ten stories under Adler & Sullivan's direction. The partners were retained again in 1892 to design a forty-foot-wide, fifteen-to-twenty-foot-deep entry and vestibule in mosaic and oak, with six glass doors flanked by seven and one-half feet of windows under a massive clerestory. Most of these alterations were not immediately executed because whenever the merchants expanded their holdings, they revised their building plans, making ongoing architectural work obsolete.[6]

When Schlesinger & Mayer decided on further remodeling in 1896, they turned to Sullivan rather than Adler, possibly because of his well-known facility for "artistic" results. After leasing a four-story building at 141–143 Wabash Avenue, they hired Sullivan to redesign its facade, add two stories, and connect it through the block to their State Street store. But before work began, the clients changed their minds, commissioning Sullivan to work up a completely new $100,000 building for the site. A July drawing in the *Chicago Tribune* showed a very slender two-bay edifice of ten floors, Chicago windows, a high one-story base, and rich spandrel and column ornament. Above the attic with porthole windows, Sullivan indicated an observatory or roof-deck ringed by a balustrade substituting visually for his usual projecting cornice. Since the horizontal members were not noticeably recessed and were wider than the verticals, this proposal was an outgrowth of his Chemical National Bank scheme in St. Louis, where directionally neutral facades explained the frame's structural composition. The Schlesinger & Mayer building would "adhere to the law first announced by Mr. Sullivan," a reporter declared, "that in the true architectural designing the form must always follow the function." Here, where the problem was to give graceful, artistic expression to the fixed demand for abundant light and air, Sullivan completely covered the exceptionally thin frame with delicately ornamented cast iron around broad windows. Since he was led to believe that further acquisitions would result in a property at least four bays long, possibly more,

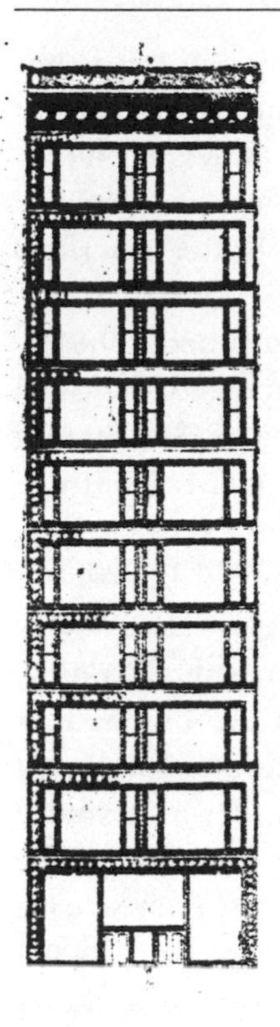

XI.1 *Schlesinger & Mayer Store, ten-story proposal for Wabash Avenue, 1896.* From *Chicago Tribune,* July 5, 1896.

XI.2 *Bridge linking Schlesinger & Mayer Store with Wabash Avenue elevated, 1896.* From *Inland Architect,* 1898.

Sullivan treated the project not as a vertical tower but as the first stage of a horizontal block. According to publicity it would open in September, when yet another Schlesinger & Mayer lease next door at 145–147 Wabash would be remodeled and expanded in exactly the same style.[7]

But the project never came off, probably because when the clients decided to purchase these buildings, they changed their minds again. By September Sullivan had put a new front on the facade at 141–143 Wabash, believing now that six more floors would be added later, and connected its second story to the elevated railroad with an ornate metal bridge. The old masonry facing on the first two floors was ripped off, leaving only thin steel posts set behind broad windows wrapped in geometric metal trim. Higher up, the old-style columns were refaced with painted metal. "The richness of the plate glass and white paint are unquestionably emphasized," *The Economist* announced, "and few people pass without noticing [the] wide contrast with anything else in this vicinity." Schlesinger & Mayer also executed Sullivan's revisions for the two-story addition to 137–143 State Street that he and his partner had first designed in 1890 and 1891, thoroughly remodeled the entire interior, and introduced what quickly became a very popular Paris-style café. When all this work was completed by summer's end, 1897, Schlesinger & Mayer had a Sullivan-altered Boyington-plus building of four bays on Madison Street wrapping around the corner to eight bays on State, as well as the Wabash Avenue properties.[8]

In St. Louis, meanwhile, Sullivan's influence continued. The architect of the Stifel Building on Pine Street, it was reported, designed his facade in Renaissance style, his window mullions in Gothic, and the frieze "in such a manner as would be a credit to Mr. Sullivan himself." More to his credit was his own work on the $250,000 Hippodrome/Colosseum to be inserted within part of the old Exposition Building at the corner of Thirteenth and Locust streets. Hired early in 1897 as consulting architect to work with Charles K. Ramsey, Sullivan reported late in March that his plans for a 112-by-122-foot arena were finished. Normal seating for seven thousand people could be expanded if necessary to over twelve thousand under a "graceful and imposing" arch of clear span from one side of the hall to the other. Purposefully low for acoustical reasons, it was sheltered by a double roof to decrease rain noise. Despite these intriguing features, the Board of Public Improvement at first refused to issue a building permit after determining the roof trusses were insufficiently strong. Although the work later went ahead, Sullivan closed his St. Louis office.[9]

In the two years since breaking with Adler, Sullivan received about six commissions, far less than half the number secured by Adler & Sullivan during the first two depression years. The Hippodrome and Schlesinger & Mayer's ten-story store were the most expensive but one did not go ahead; those that did cost only from $10,000 to approximately $25,000 each. Although he was paid for work on unerected projects, it would be safe to assume that Sullivan earned less than $7500 in fees from July 1895 through the summer of 1897 before paying his staff, office rent, and other business expenses. Forced to change residences by brother Albert and sister-in-law Mary while business was bad, burdened with upkeep and taxes at Ocean Springs, with dues at the prestigious Chicago Club, the Union League, and the Chicago Athletic Club, and not one willing to forgo good food and spirit, Sullivan found himself financially pressed for the first time in almost two decades. On August 23, 1897, he mortgaged his eleven acres of land (but not his home) in Mississippi to

Joseph B. Rose of Chicago to secure a $3000 loan. Despite the fact that Sullivan was virtually a Schlesinger & Mayer in-house architect, probably not on retainer but certainly working regularly, he could not make a living through the practice of architecture, at least not the kind of living to which he had grown comfortably accustomed.

But just after Sullivan sank into debt, his situation suddenly improved when he landed his first major commission actually executed in independent practice. The Bayard Building at 65 Bleecker Street in New York City was financed by the United Loan and Investment Company at some $275,000 to replace a defunct savings bank that burned down in 1895. Sullivan had never built in New York before but may have been drawn to the client's attention by Montgomery Schuyler's essay, by the Guaranty opening, or perhaps by the young New York architect Lyndon P. Smith. Although virtually unknown, Smith was hired by United Loan and may have brought Sullivan into the job, ending up as his nondesigning associate, but without rancor, for the two became good friends. When the plans were finished in October 1897, they were all Sullivan's and, though modified in 1898, remained close to his initial inspiration. Shortly before it opened late in 1899, Emmeline and Silas Condict acquired one-half interest in the building for a year, changing its name to theirs, and forever after Sullivan's only New York City structure has been known as Bayard-Condict.

As originally constructed it was twelve stories high. The two top floors were internally one, surrounded by a gallery and lit by skylight. The next ten were lofts, and the ground floor was divided into two shops and a vestibule. (Later, the top floor was split in two, making thirteen stories total.) The building faced south, with two high, sixty-five-inch-wide windows per bay providing abundant light. An alley at the rear plus offset shafts on either side at the back ensuring ample cross-ventilation and an unexpected northern exposure again demonstrated Sullivan's unflagging concern about the light-and-air problem in tall buildings. On the ground floor he revived the display-case shop windows with slanting clerestories he had introduced in St. Louis and incorporated at the Guaranty Building in Buffalo.

Sullivan's original and revised plans show a confident handling of structural detail for which he has not been given his due. Since Adler had dealt with such matters, it is generally assumed that on his own Sullivan was somewhat at a loss. But the Bayard Building proves otherwise. His original concept called for walls twelve inches thick at the back and sides, fourteen in front, based on the "Gray" system initially developed for bridges. Consisting of square steel columns riveted together vertically with flat tie plates, horizontally with angle seats of varying L-shaped dimensions, the system was speedily assembled. Leaving unusually spacious areas for rental, its nonstructural walls were also suited to the thin terra-cotta cladding Sullivan had used at the Guaranty, his first "Gray" structure. But the conservative municipal Building Department, accustomed to heavy brick or stone walls, would not approve such a radical departure for New York. Sullivan was forced to revise the plans repeatedly, delaying construction for months. When Bayard finally opened, it contained twenty-inch columns and brick walls on the lower five floors, reducing to combinations of sixteen and twelve inches farther up. Even so, the comparatively thin supports and terra-cotta facade were innovations for New York City.[10]

Louis Sullivan reportedly preferred the Bayard to all his other tall buildings.[11] Above the base—his first of only one story in an executed skyscraper—he placed an elaborate arched medallion atop the entrance, reminiscent of the Guaranty and the Burnet Hotel project. But he managed to suggest a two-story base without actually having one by stopping the thin mullions at the top of the second story, where inset ornamented spandrels spanning the entire bay were higher and projected a bit farther than the others and where the only Chicago windows cast darker shadows because they were more recessed. Corner entry was another Sullivan high-rise first. With only a thin sill marking the first floor, the four fluted columns separating paired windows rose directly from their rounded bases sporting ornate capitals, through a broad terra-cotta band dotted with a medallion in each bay, to the elaborately decorated attic, where they divided at window top into arches connecting with adjacent columns. At the spring point of each arch, a sculpture angel with spread wings—similar to the figures on the Transportation Building and at the "Trust and Savings" scheme in St. Louis—seemed to support the five-foot, three-inch overhanging cornice. The cornice and frieze were elaborate, even for Sullivan, but at the same time, the fluted columns were the most insistently vertical of any of his skyscrapers, especially when viewed from a block or two east or west along

XI.3 *Bayard Building, 1897.* From *Brickbuilder,* 1898.

Bleecker Street. From those perspectives it is fascinating to speculate on the origins of Eero Saarinen's 1965 Columbia Broadcasting System Building three miles north.

The Bayard Building was an immediate success, especially the "elaborate scheme of exterior decoration, a speciality for which Mr. Sullivan has a world wide reputation," accord to the *Chicago Tribune.* Columbia University professor A. D. F. Hamlin thought it "simply shows that Mr. Sullivan . . . has been doing 'new art' [Art Nouveau] in American for years wthout making any fuss about it." In "The 'Sky-scraper' Up to Date," Montgomery Schuyler probed more deeply. Echoing his earlier comments on the Transportation Building, he argued that Bayard was a "'very serious attempt" to build "upon the facts of the case." It tells its own story, he said; it "is the thing itself," permitting no convention or tradition to interfere with enclosing the steel frame "in as expressive forms as may be." Reducing the piers to the "mechanically allowable minimum" (Schuyler did not tell the whole story), Sullivan did not simulate masonry construction. The terra-cotta wrapping was so thin, in fact, that it may even have exaggerated the frame.

Never one to mince words, however, or be totally unrestrained with praise, he also said that the horizontals were underemphasized, a denial of their true stabilizing purpose. Citing "form follows function," furthermore, he recalled suggesting to Sullivan that since only the ground floor of a tall office building differed from the rest, his insistence on two- and even three-story bases may have indicated a lingering commitment to traditional proportions. Schuyler stopped short of taking credit for Bayard's single-story base, but felt its facade was Sullivan's best expression of vertical continuity and ground-floor functional singularity. Insisting that it put conventional high-rises "to shame," Schuyler proclaimed it "the nearest approach yet made in New York . . . to solving the problem of the skyscraper," a most promising signal, he concluded, for the few local designers refusing to evade that problem by resorting to historical compromises. This implied dressing down of local architects probably made Schuyler, and Sullivan, few new friends in New York.[12]

Fees from Bayard enabled Sullivan to repay Joseph Rose on March 1, 1898. If his financial situation looked a little healthier as spring approached, everything seemed better as summer neared. In May appeared the first issue of a new Chicago publication called *Forms & Fantasies,* "An Illustrated Monthly Magazine of Decorative

XI.4 *Bayard Building, attic detail.* Photo by Robert Twombly.

Art." Its offices were in Steinway Hall, an eleven-story commercial and theatrical building on Van Buren Street just off the Loop that housed a number of up-and-coming progressive architects including Dwight H. Perkins, Myron Hunt, the building's designer, Robert C. Spencer, Jr., and their office mate Frank Lloyd Wright, who left that year for the Rookery Building. Since many of the tenants were ardent Sullivan admirers, they were quick to pay him tribute in the new publishing venture. The inaugural issue, for example, announced him as the competition judge for the magazine's decorative border, for a brick or terra-cotta mantel, and for the best art photograph. Inside the next month's cover, proudly declaring "Contributions by Louis H. Sullivan," the anonymous editors praised his architectural and decorative work, ran two of his own photographs of Ocean Springs roses, and featured two drawings: an elaborate cover from 1896 for *Music,* a monthly magazine, and a second, much simpler, for another publication, called *Swimming.* If nothing else, the first two issues of short-lived *Forms & Fantasies* showed his elevated status among young progressives in Chicago's designing community.[13]

XI.5 *Schlesinger & Mayer Store, nine-story proposal, 1898.*
From *Architectural Record,* 1899.

More important financially and for his architectural career, however, was Schlesinger & Mayer's announcement in May 1898. Under the headline "Plans $1,000,000 Pile," on the twenty-eighth, the partners described a magnificent bronze and Georgia marble department store, twelve stories tall, that would soon replace their old buildings at State and Madison. The next day a four-column rendering depicted a ten-, not a twelve-, story structure (Sullivan had, in fact, designed two versions, the only major difference being height) that the *Tribune* said would be in construction within a year. The two-story base in highly ornate bronze featured broad display windows all around, punctured by three entries on State Street and two more on

XI.6 *Schlesinger & Mayer Store, twelve-story proposal, 1898.*
From Chicago Architectural Club Catalogue, 1898.

Madison on either side of the sixth and major entrance, a canopied porte-cochere/carriage court. Sullivan turned the corner with large sheets of glass (but no entry) on three sides of an octagon that above the base changed into a vertically articulated half circle of thin continuous mullions, broader spandrels, and five narrow windows per floor. Down both streets he indicated eight identical bays of Chicago fenestration under a shallow attic with decoration and a delicate projecting cornice. The upper walls would be smooth white marble highlighted by bronze window frames.[14]

The superstructure answered Montgomery Schuyler's complaint about the Bayard's horizontals while illuminating another design objective he seems to have missed. On this Schlesinger & Mayer scheme, the horizontals and verticals were flush: no recessed spandrels or projecting columns and mullions. The major facades can therefore be described as neutral in direction, like the metal frame underneath. But the Chicago windows were longer than they were tall and the spandrels were wider than the columns, suggesting an overall horizontal tendency. When the vertically articulated corner is added to the mix, however, it offsets or balances this tendency to a certain extent, meaning that rather than being *neither* vertical *nor* horizontal, the composition is *both* vertical *and* horizontal. And this is quite important because the horizontal impulse pulls the eye down the street along the length of the building, advertising both the store itself and the wares in its windows, a subtle dual marketing device. The vertical corner, on the other hand, acts like a massive stave, pinning the store to its site, which was, and still is, the most important commercial intersection in the city, the symbol of Chicago's downtown, and the point at which the quadrantal street-numbering system originates. Unmistakably identifying Schlesinger & Mayer's with its well-known site, the angled corner, furthermore, returned pedestrian space to the sidewalk, an unusual entrepreneurial give-back for any period. In a single brilliant synthesis, Sullivan combined movement and stasis, permanence and change, private advantage and public amenity with a symbolic and actual resolution of architectural opposites.

The Schlesinger & Mayer facade also illuminates another important design consideration. On tall structures that are essentially shafts or towers, like the Bayard, Schiller, or Guaranty buildings, Sullivan generally emphasized the vertical, soaring qualities of height. But by the mid-1890s, if his projects occupied larger sites, half a city block or more, for example, he drew attention to their breadth even when they were ten or twelve stories tall. Tentatively explored on the chunky Mercantile Club project of 1891 in St. Louis, the multidirectional facade with its implications about the frame was stated more emphatically on that city's Chemical National Bank scheme two or three years later and at the Chicago Stock Exchange in 1893. The telling difference between these and the Schlesinger & Mayer Store was the real and symbolic importance of the corner, occasioning in 1898 a dynamic reconciliation of contending street directions and events, rather than a more passive approach to midblock or consolidated entry.

Press accounts went on to say that the store's cornice would be solid marble, the attic frieze carved marble, and the interior bronze and San Domingo mahogany with twenty-four elevators and widely spaced steel columns with fireproof coverings. Early in June, when the clients announced their contract with Sullivan to supervise the vast construction effort, they completely surprised everyone by announcing a second contract, with none other than Dankmar Adler, to design an immense power plant. Could the former partners "join hands," *The Economist* wondered, to see the project through together? Rumors circulated furiously. One observer questioned the use of marble, since terra-cotta was "largely the medium of Mr. Sullivan." Others were sure that such a mammoth structure would never be built. But *The Brickbuilder* reported that the clients were raising money by selling a $2,000,000 property to Marshall Field, while another magazine asserted that with Adler and Sullivan on board, "those who may doubt the genuineness of their project" will be pleasantly surprised.[15]

The project was indeed genuine but still far from settled. Unable to make up their minds, Schlesinger and Mayer kept Sullivan busy revising plan after plan through the summer. Having contemplated first a twelve-, then a ten-, story store (loosely based on the 1896 scheme for Wabash Street), they decided to scale down even further. On November 2, they secured a permit for a nine-story brick building, 140 feet deep by 182 feet long, that would cost $600,000 and wrap the corner, announcing that work would begin soon but only with three bays on Madison Street. Noting on December 31, 1898, that Sullivan would take estimates within days, *The Economist* proclaimed his working drawings "the most comprehensive of any that have been prepared for this city." Despite all this, on the very next day, the clients released yet another nine-story plan for the entire site, differing in one significant respect from the November proposal. In the new version, Sullivan substituted a gallery doubling as a restaurant for the second-story window display, an imaginative idea that would have considerably enhanced State Street's ambiance. The accompanying news story discussed plans to install Luxfer prism sidewalks, an equally innovative concept that would have brightened the store's basement enough to alter its character and purpose. By now the public was thoroughly confused. No one seemed to know exactly what the building would look like, or what it would offer the city. By the time contracts were awarded, in April 1899, the only certainty was that something was about to go up on Madison Street.[16]

Sullivan had meantime turned out two other projects, noteworthy for different reasons though neither one was built. Shortly after completing the first Schlesinger & Mayer schemes, he was asked by a party still unknown for ideas on a country club. At what was probably a chance meeting away from the office with only his two-by-three-inch business card at hand, Sullivan knocked out all the essentials in a flash of inspiration, in precisely the way his esquisse exercises had trained him twenty years before at the Ecole des Beaux-Arts. His tiny sketch of a three-story elevation included a low arch on the first floor almost the width of the building, a series of rectangular windows making the second floor mostly glass, arched fenestration to the same effect on top, and appropriately placed ornament. A minuscule plan indicated either a skylight or a kind of atrium through the center from bottom to top, suggested by the notation "open 4 sides" jotted in pencil within the arch. This impromptu sketch shows that Sullivan never fundamentally altered his design methodology over the years, as well as the amazing speed with which he could comprehend and solve an architectural problem.[17]

The other project was a vacation house for Albert W. Goodrich at Harbor Springs, Michigan, dated August 10, 1898, on the drawings.

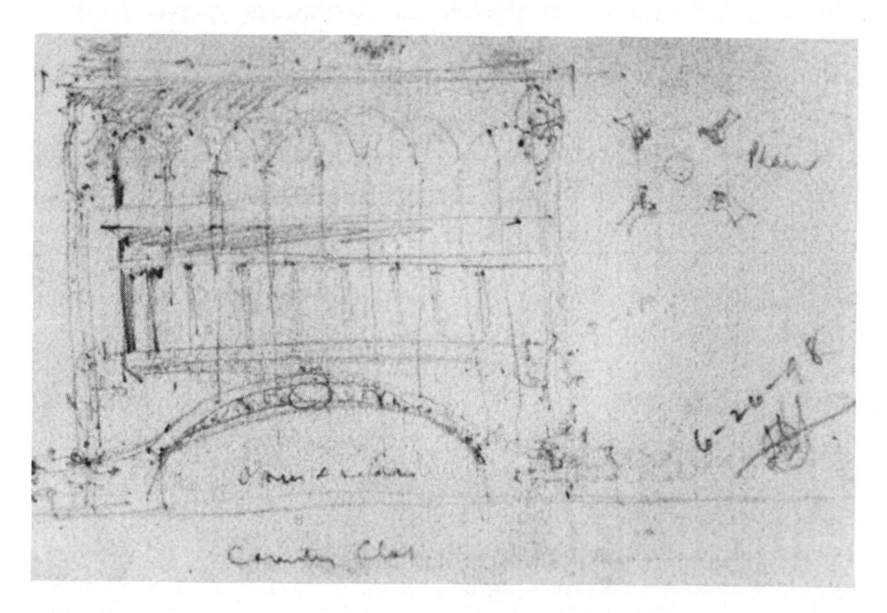

XI.7 *Country club proposal, 1898.* Avery Architectural and Fine Arts Library. Columbia University in the City of New York.

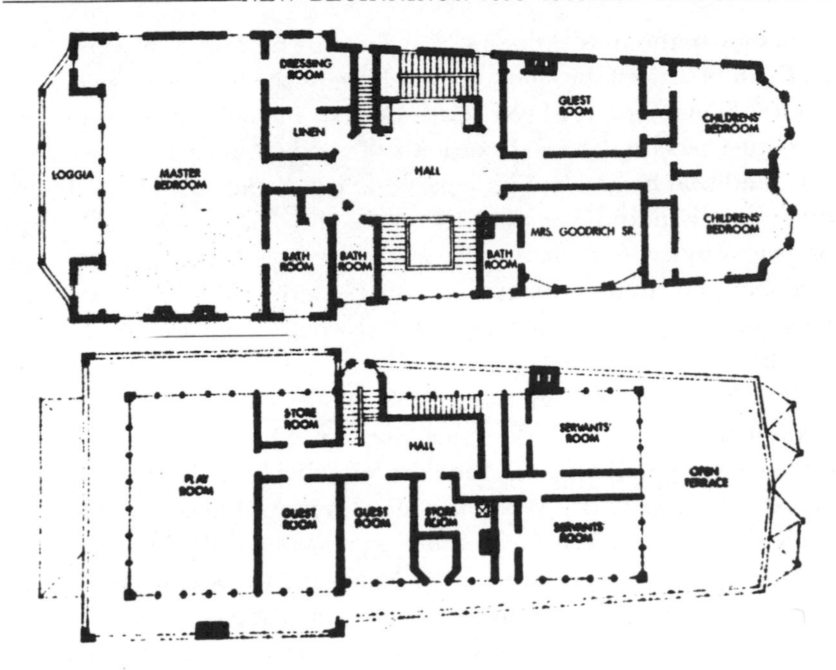

XI.8 *Goodrich residence project, 1898: second-floor plan* (top) *and third-floor plan.*

It would have been massive, three stories over a raised basement with an arcade under hipped roofs. Sullivan devoted most of his energies to the ceremonial aspects of main-floor functions. Entrance was up steps to a terrace, through doors to a vestibule, up again to a sweeping hall where imposing stairs rose to the second floor. To the left was a huge living room the width of the house, a gallery and another terrace, to the right an impressive round dining room. The sweeping vistas within and the dramatic views out would have been breathtaking, although the spaces would have been anything but cozy or relaxed.

Historian Narciso Menocal has creatively critiqued the plan. Pointing out that the excessive cost and formality that probably account for Goodrich's rejection would have been more suitable in Newport than for a family retreat on Lake Michigan, he also noted serious practical flaws: the children's bathroom was forty-five feet away from their bedrooms, the grandmother's bath had no tub and her bedroom no closet, the four servants' rooms and guest rooms had no bathroom at all, while south-facing servants' quarters were given a much more spacious terrace than the colder north-facing children's playroom. Aside from the scatological implications of not being able to design bathrooms properly, it must also be borne in mind that Sullivan produced the Goodrich dwelling in the middle of seemingly endless Schlesinger & Mayer revisions, that he had not done a house in eight years, that he was not fond of residential architecture anyway, and that he had had little personal experience with settled family life. It is nevertheless clear that he did not conceptualize this project as much more than an impressive facade containing dramatic interior opportunities. If anything, the Goodrich project was a shrine for some idealized notion of family that would have been totally unsuitable for real living.[18]

Shortly before Sullivan finished the Goodrich scheme, Chicago entrepreneur Stanley R. McCormick announced his intention to erect three six-story buildings for $800,000 on Michigan Avenue, each to house a millinery firm. When the plans were publicized in October 1898, the cost had been cut to about $300,000 and the heights modified to six, seven, and eight stories. More noteworthy, however, was the unusual designing arrangement: Holabird & Roche would do all three structures except for the tallest and northernmost facade, assigned to Louis Sullivan at the insistence of the Gage Brothers, the prospective tenants, who were willing to pay higher rent to get him. Like Bayard, which Sullivan was revising structurally at the time, the Gage was a loft building of open floors with a scattering of columns, meaning that its architectural interest was all in front. The building permit was issued November 1, the day before Schlesinger & Mayer's, construction began on March 1, 1899, and like the Bayard again, it opened at the end of the year. With three major commercial structures and several lesser projects in various stages of planning and construction, late 1898 and 1899 turned out for Sullivan to be a very busy time.

Although smaller and less heavily ornamented, the Gage Building in white terra-cotta was not unrelated to its New York contemporary. Its one-story base had an off-center entry surmounted by an arched medallion, a decorative border up the terminal piers and across the frieze under the slightly projecting second-story cornice in ornamental cast iron, and a high metallic wall—"with a remarkably beautiful interweaving combination of geometrical and foliated forms," one onlooker said[19]—turning the street windows virtually into clerestories. The second-story cornice, tying into the piers with

XI.9 *Gage Building, 1898.* From *Architectural Record,* 1894.

greater flourish than at Bayard, projected farther, but, like the other building, its fluted columns rose directly to the attic, which at the Gage was plain except for two incredible explosions of decoration at column tops under the flat overhanging cornice. Seeming to take root in the organic forms on the first floor, the columns grew like tree trunks into lush foliage. If the window moldings at Bayard could be read as continuities running up from the second floor over the arches—where angels reach to heaven from the spring points—to return to their source, as Menocal has suggested,[20] a possible dual analogy for the human life cycle and for the circulatory systems inside the walls, then at the Gage Building Sullivan introduced a parallel analogy using similar moldings and columns, this time to support a tree of life.

His three most recent skyscrapers showed continued growth metaphysically, as already noted, and as practical building solutions. Not counting the three Schlesinger & Mayer bays rising on Madison Street as part of a larger structure, his latest work had one-story bases, more literally recognizing "form follows function" in this respect, perhaps, than his earlier high-rises. The unexecuted project for Schlesinger & Mayer at 141–143 Wabash, and the Bayard and Gage buildings, were exceptionally clear statements about structure and height. For reasons already explained, the store project was directionally more neutral, but all three had very thin columns and as much glass as was structurally possible, forthrightly accepting their steel frames as the basis for aesthetic considerations. At the Gage complex, Sullivan revealed the implications of metal construction more literally than Holabird & Roche on their adjacent facades, and at the same time made it ornamentally richer.

His provision for light and air was also superior to Holabird & Roche's. They relied on familiar Chicago windows consisting of large plates with flanking sash: lots of light, but not much ventilation. Sullivan used long strips of casements surmounted by four-foot-high bands of Luxfer Company prisms to reduce the glare of intense morning sun and deflect its rays toward the rear of the building. Since the entire complex was intended for close millinery work, his unusual fenestration was an empirical as well as an aesthetic choice, an improvement on the way he had dealt with similar problems at Bayard. The Gage Building was "one of the rational solutions of the modern building problem," *The Brickbuilder* editorialized, "when treated by an artist of the first ability." And it also demonstrated "how art has its

XI.10 *Gage Building, 1898, street facade detail.* From *Inland Architect,* 1900.

commercial value." Had the Gage Brothers not believed that Sullivan's special facade would benefit their business and been willing to pay higher rent for it, "he would not have been called in."[21]

The last year of the century opened with a flurry of activity. On New Year's Day, 1899, Sullivan announced another new commission, a five-story addition to the Crane Company Foundry on Canal and Twelfth streets, for $112,000. Montgomery Schuyler's flattering assessment of Bayard in "The 'Sky-scraper' Up to Date" appeared in the January *Record.* On the twenty-third Sullivan outlined his "Principles of Architectural Design" to enthusiastic followers at the Chicago Architectural Club.[22] And in *The Artist* that month he responded to a query about American indigenous architecture. Sullivan said that he did indeed see signs of its developing, but more so within the culture of the people than within his profession. Americans were democratic and free, he wrote, self-reliant and resourceful. The trouble was that architects were "feudal" and "monarchic," preferring to design "of the governed for the governing." Consequently, American art forms did not accurately reflect the freedom that made them possible, leaving the public dissatisfied with prevailing modes of design. The solution was for the architect to change, to "himself become indigenous," which was, he thought, the equivalent of "asking him to become a poet, in the sense that he absorb into his heart and brain his own country and his own people." And to Sullivan, it was definitely worth the trouble: "When we open our hearts to nature and to our people as the source of inspiration, . . . the power of imagination and the science of expression become limitless."[23]

As if in response to this essay, Charles H. Caffin praised him in *The Criterion,* a highly regarded cultural journal. Sullivan's tall buildings were "vital embodiments of the colossal energy and aspiring enterprise of American life." Other architects approached the skyscraper as a compromise between practicality and art, but with Sullivan "the aesthetic qualities in each case grow naturally" from pragmatic considerations. He gives the businessman exactly what he wants, and "out of this agglomeration of necessities his artist-mind gets the inspiration for the form." As a decorator, Caffin continued, "no man in the country comes near him," but his ornament always referred to the space it adorned. "His buildings are modern and American. . . . And he never repeats himself. Each problem gets its own separate solution." Caffin saw in the work "the fitness of a thing that has grown out of itself, the inherent dignity of what nobly seems its place in life."[24]

With four major structures under way in April—the Gage, Bayard, Crane, and Schlesinger & Mayer's store—Sullivan added a fifth, for Alexander Euston's Riverside Seed & Cleaning Company, a four-story linseed-oil factory in brick coming in at $40,000. Construction began right away. He also drew plans for alterations and additions to Nettie Fowler McCormick's residence at 135 Rush Street, corner of Erie, on the exclusive North Side Gold Coast. She probably found her architect through Stanley McCormick, owner of the Gage Building, but did not in the end execute Sullivan's ideas, although she hired him later for two other projects.[25]

June opened with Sullivan making his presence felt in Cleveland as part of a new organizational venture, his first in years. The Architectural League of America (ALA) was formed in 1899 largely at the initiative of the Chicago Architectural Club. Composed of ninety-seven delegates from ten local societies and three American Institute of Architects chapters who were generally dissatisfied with established professional thinking, its first convention met June 2 and 3 to increase cooperation among local clubs, especially regarding exhibitions and professional education. The Chicago delegation included

Frank Lloyd Wright and H. Webster Tomlinson, a young designer who read Sullivan's speech, "The Modern Phase of Architecture." (Although he could not attend, Sullivan saw the league as a breath of professional fresh air, and did all he could to support it.) This "ringing paper," one journal called it, "so thoroughly [embodied] the thoughts and feelings of every draftsman present," that "it was the event of the convention."[26] Sullivan professed to see a new era awakening in American architectural thought. He saw in youth—the delegates averaged about thirty-two years of age—a great hope, and urged his audience of admirers to "cast away as worthless the shopworn . . . notion that an architect is an artist . . . and accept my assurance that he is . . . a poet and an interpreter of the national life of his time." If he did not remain faithful to contemporary culture, Sullivan warned, the architect would surely be held accountable by the people.

As you mature, he told his young listeners in particularly pointed prose, you will learn that "a fraudulent and surreptitious use of historical documents, however suavely presented, however cleverly plagiarized, however neatly repacked . . . will be held to be a betrayal of trust. You know well what I mean." You must choose between being fakers and being honest men. "Artistic pretension," he wrote in a portion omitted in publication, "is not a synonym for moral irresponsibility." If you take pains truly to understand your country and its way of life, "you will be understood and sympathetically received in return." The greatest poet—Sullivan meant architect—will be he who shall "grasp and deify the commonplace in our life—those simple, normal feelings which the people . . . will be helpless, otherwise, to express." I truly believe that your coming together will bring serious results, the most important being the regeneration of "an art that should be, may be, and must be, the noblest, the most intimate, the most expressive, the most eloquent of all."[27]

Sullivan closed his strongly worded statement—that must have ruffled feathers in other professional circles—by assuring his followers that though he was not there in person, "I am with you in spirit. . . . Your youth is your most precious heritage from the past," he proclaimed. "I am with you." Several journals rushed the speech into print, with Sullivan contributing a specially drawn decorative border for *Inland Architect.* By all accounts the delegates responded to this stirring articulation of their beliefs with unrestrained enthusiasm. Frank Lloyd Wright, less than a week shy of his thirty-second birthday and in that sense typical of the audience, would later make similar statements. Though still not reconciled with Sullivan six years after their falling out, he, too, must have been moved by his "Master's" words.

Sullivan missed the Cleveland meeting because in June 1899, for the first time in his adult life—as far as anyone knows, that is—he was romantically involved. Stories about his male prowess were once legion, and several still persist, sometimes using Wright and Sullivan interchangeably. One is that during the 1890s his persistent flirtations with a University of Chicago professor's wife was the real cause of his alienation from Albert and Mary. Another is that if all the women Sullivan had loved were placed side by side, the line would stretch from one end of Chicago to the other. This alleged "stud" behavior is in keeping with the view that Sullivan and Wright—sometimes Henry Richardson is included, as well as many nonarchitectural late-nineteenth-century "rugged individualist" males—saw themselves as Nietzschean "supermen" whose talents and achievements sanctioned what amounted to amoral living in conscious defiance of normal conventions. Wright's love affairs, and Sullivan's drinking, athletics, and philandering are often cited as proof. But the facts are that Sullivan did not take Nietzsche's model as his own, that rumors of his rogue male posture cannot be substantiated, and that his romantic interest in women was sporadic enough to be virtually nonexistent. This does not mean he abstained from sex, only that work surpassed sex as his favorite pastime.

But in 1899, presumably, he met the woman who challenged some of this, though how it happened is still unknown. His sometimes unreliable biographer, Willard Connely, wrote in 1960 that strolling down Michigan Avenue one day, Sullivan came upon an exceptionally statuesque woman. Feigning interest in her dog, he stopped to chat, and then to make a date. The woman was "fairly tall," Connely wrote, with dark brown eyes like Sullivan's own, her face a bit rounded and her hair elaborately done up in the prevailing pompadour style. "Slightly less than Junoesque, rather a matured Gibson girl, there was in her figure something voluptuous. . . . [S]he was *bien-soignée.*" On June 29 Sullivan took out a marriage license, and two days later, on July 1, 1899, he and she were married at St. Paul's Reformed Episcopal Church. Sullivan was forty-two.[28]

Born as Mary Azona Hattabaugh in San Francisco on May 29, 1879, this elusive woman was calling herself Margaret by the time she married Sullivan at the age of twenty. Perhaps because of the twenty-two-year difference, she recorded her age as twenty-seven on the license. If Sullivan knew better, he never said. Ironically, however, in an 1899 photograph, Margaret looks even older than her alleged years. Deep lines frame rather full lips on her somewhat soft face; her center-parted hair taken up in a rear bun gives her a middle-aged appearance, although her large dark eyes suggest girlishness. In Sullivan's own photographs, no more than six years later, she is noticeably heavier and more mature but still with thick hair and deep dark eyes. Aside from her physical characteristics, little is known about the mysterious Margaret Sullivan.[29]

Their life together began rather oddly. There was, first of all, no honeymoon. Since Ocean Springs in July was uncomfortably hot, they presumably decided to wait until fall to go south rather than holiday elsewhere in summer. And on the very day he married, furthermore, Sullivan completed and dated "The Master," part three of "Nature and the Poet," a group of prose-poems beginning with "In-

XI.11 *Margaret Sullivan, 1899.*

spiration" (1886) that he had recently returned to writing after a lapse of several years. Even his own wedding was not momentous enough, it seems, to lure him away from work. At least he moved his bride into a new home, at the Windermere Hotel on East Fifty-sixth Street, leaving the Chicago Club, where he had resided since moving from 4853 Kimbark in 1898. The Windermere was one of the finest hotels in town, a third again as expensive as the Auditorium Hotel on a daily basis, for example, and twice as much as the Palmer House or Sherman House. Despite the lavish surroundings Sullivan provided for Margaret, one can certainly speculate about the success of a marriage between a man who completed a writing project on his wedding day and a woman who lied—to her husband?—about her age.

With the founding of the Architectural League of America, Sullivan began to distance himself from AIA. In July 1899 he declined Secretary Glenn Brown's invitation to give a paper at the upcoming annual convention on a legitimate style for skeletal structures, replying he had said it all in "The Tall Office Building Artistically Considered," and in August refused to participate in the discussion of the subject.[30] With the reform-minded league endorsing his principles, he seemed about to spurn the conservative older body, no longer needing it as a platform. By century's end the importance of Sullivan's work was so commonly acknowledged that he had little difficulty finding professional endorsement. The September 1889 *Brickbuilder,* for instance, urged architects to follow Sullivan's lead. His "exquisite and highly organized style," it thought, should spawn "original disciples, able to create and differentiate on similar lines according to their several individualities." If this happened "intelligently," it would give a "strong local character to our architecture."[31]

By October pedestrians could get a sense of what the new Schlesinger & Mayer Store would look like. "The exterior of the three lower floors will be of ornamental iron and plate glass," *The Economist* informed its readers, "the former of an extremely unique design, the windows being broad and low, the whole presenting a very ornate appearance. Above the . . . third story the masons have just begun to set the cut stone which is white. . . . The steel framework is up to the height of eight stories." Passersby, the magazine said, "will at once recognize the work of Louis H. Sullivan." With publicity like this keeping his name in the news and his reputation unassailable, he was invited in December to submit proposals for a new Chicago National

XI.12 *Schlesinger & Mayer Store, Madison Street section, 1899, as built, showing older Adler & Sullivan remodeling to the right.* From *Inland Architect,* 1900.

Bank Building, an offer he declined out of distaste for competitions. But just before the end of the year he accepted a Russian Orthodox congregation's commission for Holy Trinity Cathedral on the North Side, a $20,000 job representing new and different challenges as his first non-Jewish religious edifice. His preliminary plans were done on January 13, 1900—his first project of the new century[32]—less than a month after the Gage, the Bayard, and the Madison Street portion of Schlesinger & Mayer's building all opened in December. Sullivan must have closed out the old century with a good feeling of real accomplishment.

The most revealing event in this half decade of new beginnings was his marriage, which can be read as a classic response to a mid-life crisis. The loss of Adler, of Wright, of Mary and Albert Sullivan, of his home in Chicago, and with them a modicum of family-style connections, coupled with the national depression that struck at his art and almost cost him his Ocean Springs retreat—all these disruptions must have taken their toll. Such devastating blows compressed within a relatively short interval could have easily forced him to reassess his situation, to wonder if his youthful high hopes were as fleeting as the years, to reflect on the tenuousness of his once impregnable position. No amount of fame or former fortune could allay such gnawing misgivings. It is not in the least uncommon for a man with mid-life insecurities to turn to a younger woman. If Margaret—at twenty years old less than half his age, young enough to be his daughter—had allowed him, Sullivan could easily believe that someone of his experience and sophistication might shape their relationship to his liking, which he had been unable to do with others he had cared about, then lost. But since her appearance suggested maturity beyond her years, Sullivan could also convince himself of exactly the opposite: that she was not a child, not a young woman barely out of her teens. Evidence suggests that, in fact, Margaret was self-assured, strong-minded, and demanding, anything but subservient or passive. This meant that Sullivan need not heed the inevitable whispering or face the other meaning of their union.

The considerable age difference also exposes Sullivan's growing inclination to see himself as a kind of father figure. Certainly, the style of his remarks at ALA's inaugural convention, and elsewhere, is instructive. His discovery of youth—his repeated use of the word—and of the importance of young architects with new ideas coincides with his setbacks and perhaps with consciousness of his own aging. (It may also have prompted the forty-year-old to return to boxing, as he did in 1896.) In the late 1890s Sullivan's philosophical position was clear. The entire profession knew his stand against historicism and for new solutions. And now in 1899, as if to underscore the point, he associated himself with the aspirations of youth in a rebellious organization comprised for the most part of a younger generation. Sullivan certainly knew that Frank Lloyd Wright would attend the Cleveland meeting. It might be that his paper was equally a reminder to Wright in particular as to the delegates in general that much of what they stood for had originated with him, that he was in a very real sense their intellectual father, the progenitor of the architectural ideology to which they all subscribed. For years now, Sullivan had seen himself as the titular head of a growing movement demanding progressive architecture, currently embodied in ALA. If his adamance about Wright's 1893 "disloyalty" was a sign he could not forgive the disobedience of a "son," his 1899 speech was an equally uncompromising lesson for all his spiritual children.

If Sullivan saw himself in this relation to his profession, it would have been in character to choose a mate he thought he could lead, instruct, and mold. Impatient with disagreement and compromise, used to having his own way, he may have found in his wife's youth a promise of subservience and loyalty, akin to the malleability of Wright in 1888, when he entered Sullivan's life at about the same tender age as Margaret. But she, of course, appealed to Sullivan in other respects as well. He must have found her intelligent, interesting, and attractive—like Wright, for that matter—for given his preferences he would have had it no other way. Inexperienced with women, lonely away from the office, needing companionship as he entered middle age, Louis Sullivan decided to open the twentieth century with Margaret, believing with good reason that the future would be as kind to him as the best of the past had been.

XII.1 *Louis Sullivan, c. 1900.*

Chapter XII

FRUSTRATED HOPES

1900-1910

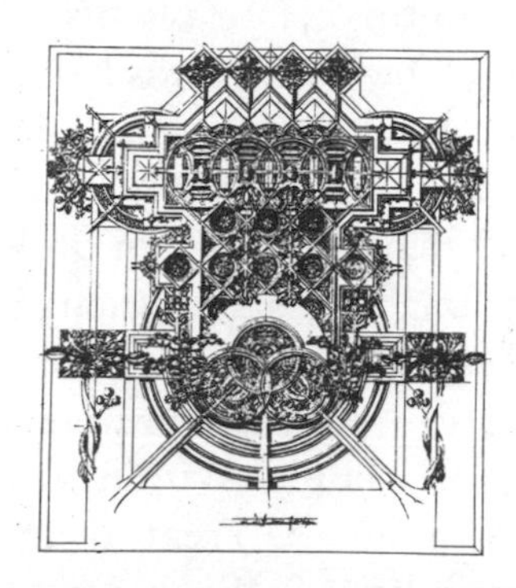

NINETEEN HUNDRED was not particularly kind to Louis Sullivan, at least not financially. There were no new commissions during the year, and work on Schlesinger & Mayer's stalled after the Madison Street section, leaving only revisions on Holy Trinity Cathedral to fill his office hours. But life proceeded normally in other ways. He introduced Margaret to Ocean Springs during the winter—she seemed to love it—then moved her into a flat at 396 North State Street between Kinzie and the Chicago River just beyond the Loop's bustle. Perhaps she wanted an apartment of her own, having experienced the joys of a private home on Biloxi Bay. Neither Sullivan liked hotel living, but the place was probably cheaper than the Windermere, and economy might have been a factor in their thinking.

If anything, professional acclaim increased. Along with architects Daniel H. Burnham and Peter B. Wight, Sullivan began a one-year term in January on the board of directors of the Municipal Art League, devoted to stimulating civic beauty, pride, and artistic improvement. The Bayard and Gage buildings got flattering reviews over the winter, and in April *The Record* made an unusual photographic comparison between Sullivan's "Famous gates at the Getty Tomb" and snowflakes, frost patterns, and other natural forms. Even though his income was down, he contributed time and money to the

Chicago Architectural Club, which responded by designating him an honorary member and patron. At its 1900 competition for a "United States Embassy in a Foreign Capital," Sullivan critiqued the ballroom and grand hall drawings with his decorator friend Louis J. Millet, and with architect Robert C. Spencer, Jr., selected the best bird's-eye view.[1]

Dankmar Adler died unexpectedly on April 16 in his home on Ellis Avenue, three months before his fifty-sixth birthday, from a stroke ten days earlier. The funeral was held at the Kehilath Anshe Ma'ariv Synagogue he and his partner had designed in 1889. Adler's family invited Sullivan to be a pallbearer. What could he have thought as he entered their home again under such circumstances, probably for the first time in years? Although Adler had been hired to do Schlesinger & Mayer's power plant almost two years before, in 1898, repeated changes in program prevented the former partners from actually working together. Within a month Dankmar's son Abraham joined with Samuel A. Treat to carry on his father's business in the Auditorium office.[2] Sullivan drew a decorative border for the memorial portrait in May's *Inland Architect,* perhaps regretting sadly that he and his closest friend had never reunited.

No sooner had he paid his final respects than another estranged colleague made friendly overtures. Though not a member of the Architectural Club, Frank Lloyd Wright exhibited there periodically, probably running into Sullivan during the 1900 show and competition. In May they both answered George R. Dean's query in *The Brickbuilder* about "Progress Before Precedent," a motto proposed for the Architectural League of America. Sullivan wrote that mottoes were neither good nor bad, that talk and the best intentions did not produce good buildings, and that "the advancement of our art . . . lies specifically with the rising generation." Wright agreed that the profession was "hidebound" and that hope for the future lay with "a growing group of young men from the Middle West" plus other "thinking architects who have trifled with the husk sufficiently" to want the kernel. Sullivan had already linked himself to the "rising generation." Was Wright acknowledging Sullivan by his reference to "thinking architects"? Events the next month seemed to indicate he was.

In the first major article about his work, Wright's friend Robert C. Spencer wrote with his approval in the June *Architectural Review* that "no more fortunate circumstances could have befallen him than his schooling with Mr. Sullivan. . . . No one more than he realizes and is grateful for . . . [that] early influence." Mentioning Sullivan half a dozen times, Spencer was probably the first to call him "Wright's master," and to link the two publicly as "master and trusted pupil." Thus far Wright had let Spencer speak for him, but at the second Architectural League convention in Sullivan's own Chicago Auditorium, he paid his own respects.

The entire three days turned out to be a kind of fete to a spiritual leader. At the June 8 working session, with Sullivan unexpectedly in attendance, president Albert Kelsey of Philadelphia reminded the delegates that his 1899 "letter to . . . the Cleveland convention was the corner-stone of our organization." Not to be outdone, perhaps, Elmer Gray of Milwaukee voiced the general sentiment when he spoke of "the man who, above all others, has stimulated us by the most vital thought in architectural expression—Mr. Louis H. Sullivan." The delegates burst into cheers. But "the feature of the morning," one journal reported, "was the ovation to Mr. Sullivan, who was [then] called upon to address the convention. . . . [H]e was greeted with continued and continued applause, which only stopped as he began his extemporaneous remarks." When he finished and Wright rose to give a prepared speech, "The Architect," he said in his own words what Spencer had previously written. "After listening to the master," he declared, perhaps looking out toward Sullivan in the audience, "it hardly seem[s] proper to listen to the disciple." The master must have been pleased.

Sullivan talked that morning about the source of inspiration lying in the inscrutable secrets of nature and mankind. There were two fundamental laws or rhythms beyond which "you will find nothing," he maintained: the rhythms of life and growth, and the rhythms of death and decadence, which progress simultaneously in balance. The origin of this balance is the physical organism, itself a source of inspiration. And "what we find in nature we find precisely in the human mind." If that is degenerate, its work is degenerate, and so is style if it bears no relation to life and environment. A house for New Orleans would therefore be inappropriate in St. Paul, he pointed out, style notwithstanding. So architects must look for inspiration in the needs and wants of people. Style comes from experience, not books, and is the "expression of one idea, solely and organically unfolding itself to the smallest detail." Architecture, he said, "is the true expression of our lives." Sullivan sat down to tumultuous applause.[3]

On June 9, the next day, he was the featured speaker at the convention's closing banquet. The setting was the grand ballroom atop the Auditorium Hotel, one of the most splendid spaces he had ever created. Surrounded by admirers who had already thrilled to his words, who had praised and honored him, and who were enchanted by the room in which they sat, knowing that but for him they might not be there at all, Sullivan was stimulated to oratorical heights. If he secretly wondered why he, the subject of such enthusiastic adulation, had had trouble getting work lately, he held nothing back in "The Young Man in Architecture." His brutal candor was actually one of the reasons for sluggish business.

Reviving the themes of the Cleveland meeting, Sullivan underscored his alliance with the younger generation, and in no uncertain language thumbed his nose at the rest of the profession. "It is my premise," he began, addressing himself to American Institute of Architects sympathizers in the group, "that the Architectural League of America has its being in a sense of discontent with conditions now prevailing in the American malpractice of the architectural art; in a deep . . . sense of conviction that no aid is to be expected from the generation now representing that malpractice; and in the instinctive feeling that, through banding together" something may be done. He confessed a "delightfully cynical sense of shock" at delegate discontent, "and a new-born desire to believe in the good, the true, the beautiful and the young."

American architecture is ninety parts aberration, he declared, eight parts indifference, one part poverty, and one part Little Lord Fauntleroy, a prescription any architectural department store could fill. But he represented the opposing "viewpoint that architecture should be practiced as an art and not strictly as a commercial pursuit." So he would begin at the beginning. The first step in your architectural education, he told his audience, is to learn that the simple observable processes of nature depend on organic complexities that are the basis of rhythm. The second step is to discover with amazement that natural processes and rhythms are the same as those working in your own minds. When you reach the third step, learning with pleasure that the *practical* workings of your own minds and the practical workings of nature around you are also similar, you will have arrived at the basis of organized thinking, ready to start the remainder of your education.

Sullivan then talked about the importance of observing natural things, forming independent judgments, and learning to think *before* studying architectural books and photographs. He urged the development of personal styles because noble past styles may beget ignoble buildings through the agency of ignoble architects. "In truth the American architecture of today is the offspring of an illegitimate commerce with the mongrel styles of the past." Since design schools dwelt on the past, they were educationally worthless. "Ergo, you must educate yourselves." You must train your minds as an athlete trains his body. But since you are young, "you have so much less to unlearn." Today you have a great opportunity, Sullivan assured his audience. "The future is in your hands—will you accept the responsibility or will you evade it? That is the only vital question I have come here today to put to you." Will you become democratic architects, or will you not? "In due time you will doubtless answer in your own way. But I warn you the time left for an answer in the right way is acutely brief. For young as you are, you are not as young as you were yesterday—And tomorrow?"[4]

His listeners were even more challenged and inspired than in 1899, responding with a thundering ovation. *American Architect & Building News* said his speech was "charming, albeit at times quite unintelligible," but *Architecture* reported that Sullivan "sings his song into your ears and, as by the cadence of a lullaby, objection is disarmed and opposition stilled."[5] But Sullivan was not there to lull. He wanted, as he said, to bring "force, discretion and coherence" to ALA's "vague and miscellaneous" discontents. He wanted to challenge the profession, not by the example of his work and writing, but by the power of a new organization. In this sense he put himself farther out on a professional limb than he had ever been before.

If he placed himself at the head of rebellious youngsters in June, in July 1900 he severed his remaining ties with the establishment. Following the pattern of the year before, AIA secretary Glenn Brown contacted Sullivan shortly after the rival meeting, asking him to participate in a discussion of Italian, French, and English gardens scheduled for its next convention. Sullivan answered that such topics originated "in a spirit of dilettantism and self-complacency intended for the edification of the 'superior few,' " about whom "I care nothing. . . . My active sympathies lie with the enlightened solution of problems germane to the development of an American art,—a field of intense and immediate interest demanding virile minds. . . . Learned disquisition as a substitute for creative energy seems to me a feeble occupation for grown men in this time and land."

Refusing to take offense at Sullivan's harsh words, Brown replied that the program committee never intended to confine him to the topic. What it really wanted were his thoughts on "the futility of such sources of inspiration, as well as your views of 'creative energy' as we appreciate so highly [its] products . . . in your work." Would you "criticize" the subject of gardens "along this line?" Brown asked. "I must beg your pardon for the apparent importunity." Ignoring the secretary's placating gesture, Sullivan answered on July 24 that he had exhausted the subject of creativity in "The Tall Office Building," a completely untrue assertion. The truth was he no longer believed AIA capable of creative thought or progressive policy.

Sullivan's second letter would seem to have ended the matter, but on July 25, the very next day, unwilling to let well enough alone, he fired off another: "Until the AIA puts itself squarely on record as an advocate of advanced thinking," he told Brown, "until it indicates clearly that it is alive and stands for realities, not figments, symbols or simulacra,—that it desires to stand not as a lethargic and repressive but as a liberating and upbuilding force,—I choose to take no part in its councils." Until AIA became like the league, Sullivan was saying, he would have nothing more to do with it.[6]

Not satisfied with private indictments, Sullivan went public in an August *Chicago Tribune* interview. American architecture "stands aloof" from the people, closeted in "the musty school," dodging the realities of life in our times. "It is clearly recognized," he said, "that educational methods, hitherto, have been criminally false. . . . The professors of architecture [are] brooding, like blight, over their schools. . . . They extol the artificial, the unreal. They laud symbols and figments. . . . [T]hey repress and pilfer the spontaneity and charm of youth, the sanity, the higher usefulness of the future man." The remedy, of course, was for architects to be honest in their thinking, to interpret true popular feelings in the natural language of their art. Change was imminent, demanded by the younger generation. That is why the recent ALA convention "represented a movement in architectural thought so significant that it may easily be the most important avowal of principles in the architectural history of the country." ALA stood for the encouragement of indigenous, inventive design "as opposed to the imported fashion plates representing the art and lives of nations centuries ago." The demand of our time, he concluded, is for "a new expression of the eternally youthful art of architecture, . . . an art filled with optimism and humanity, . . . a liberation of the creative impulse."[7]

AIA's president interpreted all this as a direct attack. At its annual convention in October 1900, Robert S. Peabody of the Boston firm Peabody & Stearns met Sullivan head on. "It is charged," he said, that as a body "we do not encourage original work, and that architecture" as practiced by our members "is only a repetition of old forms and well worn ornaments." It is said that "most of us produce nothing but imitations." Architecture professors are described as " 'brooding like a blight over their schools,' as lauding 'symbols and figments,' . . . as pilfering 'the spontaneity and charm of youth.' . . . Happily," Peabody added, openly alluding to Sullivan's work, "the horror of adapting to our uses ornamental forms endeared by long association is not widespread. Most of us shudder [at] what our land would be if subjected to 'a liberation of the creative impulse.' " Sullivan responded sarcastically in a magazine article a few months later that he actually knew "a plain public nuisance . . . an architect, yea, an eminent one . . . to smile and shudder at the mere thought of liberating the creative impulse." This man "was none other than the president of the A. I. of A. and he voiced this stupid, paltry sentiment in a presidential address."[8] Sullivan may have fired the last shot in this skirmish, but it was doubtful he could win the war.

His only designing during these literary barrages was Holy Trinity Cathedral. Perhaps lack of work accounts for his strong words, and ALA's force behind him for the courage to say them. In any case, Sullivan took over the Trinity job from another architect in 1899, finished preliminary drawings in January, and revised the plans for both the church and its rectory by November 1900. Immersing himself in orthodox theology and history, he came up with an "octagon-on-square" arrangement deriving from Russian provincial custom. In plan, as tradition demanded, the vestibule, narthex, and sanctuary were square, but the dome and bell tower were octagonal. The interior stenciling, leaded glass, and other decorations were probably Sullivan's interpretations of orthodox imagery filtered through *L'Art Russe* by Viollet-le-Duc, the popular French critic, with assistance from congregation members. While acknowledging orthodox symbolism, the cathedral also incorporated the latest contemporary concepts. Its white stucco-over-brick walls outlined in dark trim and its

XII.2 *Holy Trinity Cathedral, 1899–1900.* Photo by Robert Twombly.

overhanging roofs on church and rectory were visually similar to the pathbreaking houses Frank Lloyd Wright and his colleagues were beginning to design. Sullivan developed bonds of affection with the financially strapped congregation, such close ties, in fact, that in 1903 he donated half his fee—several hundred dollars—to the building fund even though his own income was considerably less than in years past.[9]

At the end of 1900 Sullivan found a new literary platform, albeit a relatively minor one. The ALA convention in Cleveland had apparently captured the interest of the newly founded *Interstate Architect & Builder*, a local publication. In 1900 it covered the Chicago meeting closely, publishing "The Young Man in Architecture," which it said was "a masterpiece. . . . Mr. Sullivan is not only a great architect, but a good writer as well." Its August editorial, "Without a Peer," called him "without question the most popular man in the profession in the United States" whose "hard knock" of "the moss-backed professors of architecture will certainly bring forth good fruit." In December 1900 *Interstate* offered a "rare treat," ten illustrated pages of Sullivan's work. It also ran his "Open Letter" charging the Cleveland firm Tenbusch & Hill with plagiarism. In exceptionally vehement language, Sullivan accused them of "common thievery," "degeneracy of moral tone, a callousness of mental fibre, and a brutish incapacity to respect the rights of others . . . [that could] ruin thc bcauty and the value of my art as such."[10]

Historian Sherman Paul points out that an "intemperate" letter "might have been expected from the former chairman of [AIA's] committee on professional ethics," but not what followed. A two-page spread showed Sullivan's design for a Chicago Athletic Association's swimming certificate opposite Tenbusch & Hull's bronze door for the Cathedral of the Sacred Heart in Duluth. Across the top were dictionary definitions of "plagiarism," "unprincipled," and "turpitude"—words taken from his letter—and below them a biography and photograph only Sullivan could have supplied. Paul remarks that in a moment of vainglory, he must have forgotten what Dwight Perkins said at the league's first meeting: "There is nothing whatever in [Sullivan's] ideas that he does not believe any person, having poetic tendencies, cannot find expression for in building. He is not the only Sullivan." An admirable sentiment, but Perkins was wrong: he was the only Louis Sullivan, and his outburst demonstrated that

XII.3 *Holy Trinity Cathedral interior.* Photo from Historic American Buildings Survey.

whatever his words might imply, he was entirely capable of guarding his own work jealously—recall the McVicker's Theater imbroglio many years before—and of protecting his ego ferociously. The Chicago correspondent for *American Architect* thought that by concentrating on Sullivan's loss of self-control and his ungentlemanly language, Tenbusch & Hill's reply was not satisfactory. But it also wondered why their design, which was "most similar" to his, had generated such wrath since Sullivan never complained when Art Institute students allowed "their thoughts to run in the very mould in which his have run." The "peppery" exchange was "most amusing," he added, but it begged the real issue of how an architect protects his work.[11]

Interstate's interest led to a major literary commitment. In December 1900 Sullivan wrote to Lyndon Smith, his friend in New York from the Bayard job, that "I have arranged to write 52 articles on American architecture for the *Interstate Architect*. . . . [The 52] will constitute *one* argument and will all be interrelated. I have completed two, up to date." Like clockwork each week, *Kindergarten Chats* ran from February 16, 1901, to February 8, 1902. Two days after the first appeared, Sullivan told Smith he wanted the essays circulated widely among "the *laity*," believing "architects will not understand much of what is in them." "It is among the *people* that we want to work." Would Smith please forward a list of everyone interested so E. C. Kelly, *Interstate*'s manager, could send out notices? The series was a "pretty heavy investment" for Kelly, he added a few days later, "and he ought to be backed up with subscriptions." Fired by the possibility of reaching the general public, Sullivan wrote at a furious pace. In only two months he could tell Smith, on February 18, 1901, that he had finished twenty-seven of the fifty-two pieces.[12]

His hopes for *Kindergarten Chats* were soon frustrated. Very little was said in the contemporary press, even in western journals like *Inland Architect* (or eastern ones like *The Brickbuilder*) that generally treated him kindly. Only one reader wrote in, to complain that Sullivan was too hard on architects. Even his league supporters took little notice. Writing about Sullivan in the 1901 *Architectural Annual,* its more or less official publication, A. W. Barker praised *Chats* in three short paragraphs, but that was about it. "What might have been the educational manual of the League and a genuine primer on architecture and society," Sherman Paul concluded, "had for the most part gone unnoticed." Sullivan was hurt. "I am amazed to note how insignificant . . . is the effect produced in comparison to the cost, in vitality, to me," he wrote Claude Bragdon, a young architect, admirer, and friend. "I shall never again make so great a sacrifice for the younger generation."[13]

Sullivan oulined his *Chats* objectives in another letter to Bragdon:

> A young man who has "finished his education" at the architectural schools comes to me for a post-graduate course—hence a free form of dialogue.
>
> I proceed with his education rather by indirection and suggestion than by direct precept. I subject him to certain experiences and allow the impressions they make on him to infiltrate, and, as I note the effect, I gradually use a guiding hand. I supply the yeast, so to speak, and allow the ferment to work. . . .
>
> This is the gist of the whole scheme.

The lad is subjected in logical and psychological sequence to literal, objective, cynical, brutal, and philistine experiences, Sullivan explained. "A little at a time I introduce the subjective, the refined, the altruistic," in an "increasingly intense rhythm of these two opposing themes" until a preliminary crisis comes when the student longs for nobler, purer things. At this point, in Chat 24, "Summer: The Storm," Sullivan takes him to the country for the initial out-door scene, his first real experience with nature, where he learns something of its organic complexity. "Nature's superb drama" affects him deeply. Back in the city he softens, opens up, and begins to think and talk more naturally, more logically. By the second outdoor scene (Chat 36, "Autumn Glory"), he has absorbed his master's philosophy, but when he attempts to apply it to social mores and institutions—democracy, education, culture, architecture, criticism, and so on—he turns deeply pessimistic about the futility of effecting change. "It has to be: Into the depths and darkness we descend, and the work reaches the tragic climax in the third out-of-door scene—Winter" (Chat 47), in which the student experiences the gloom of seasonal slumber. But in winter's death lurk the stirrings of spring. Nature and humanity awake to infinite possibilities. So by the "foreordained climax and optimistic peroration" in the fourth and final outdoor episode (Chat 52, "Spring Song"), he faces life gladly, believing in the "integrity of [his] own thought," in the "art of expression in all things . . . vital to the healthful growth and development of a democratic people." "The *locale* of this closing number is the beautiful spot in the woods, on the shore of Biloxi Bay," Sullivan told Bragdon, "where I am writing this" letter. *Chats* was finished, he wrote to Smith, shortly after January 11, 1902.[14]

It would have been surprising had *Kindergarten Chats* made the sought-for public impact. *Interstate Architect* simply did not have a large-enough audience. But there were other reasons inherent in the work. *Chats* was verbose, dense, esoteric, and ethereal in places, condescending and biting toward the profession throughout, and hard on the eastern United States. It was difficult to see the logic that Sullivan had explained to Bragdon. But *Chats* was also deeply moving in other places, exceptionally insightful on specific buildings and on the social content of architecture, stirring in its call for individual and democratic greatness, and very illuminating when Sullivan linked his metaphysics to design. Edited down, it could indeed have been a primer for young architects, but in its published form, it was too rambling, too poetic, too subjective for most busy professionals, even Sullivan's admirers, and too remote for the public. Yet it remains the single most important avenue to his thinking, an encyclopedia of Sullivaniana for those willing to work through it. Its limited appeal during his lifetime indicated popular frustration with its style, not with him.

The Ocean Springs setting for the closing scene shows how personal *Kindergarten Chats* was, as does its structure. The disciple's intellectual development follows the natural cycle of the seasons, which Sullivan took as an emblem of humanity and the universe eternally regenerating themselves. Chat 28, aptly entitled "On Poetry," stated the essence of Sullivan's philosophy:

> I have taken you to Nature [the Master explains] to show you how our moods parallel her moods; how her problems parallel our problems; and to bring you directly to the one unfailing source, the visible effect of creative energy, that you may find there, now and evermore, the key to solutions; to make plain to you what man may read in Nature's book, to the end that her processes may be our processes; that we may absorb somewhat of her fertility or recourse, her admirable logic, her progression from function into form.

Nature of Sullivan was not merely a showcase of forms architects might adapt to human situations but a model of processes illuminating the human life cycle, out of which came the need to create.

It is said that the dialogue method of *Chats* was inspired by Sullivan's late-night conversations between 1888 and 1893 with Frank Lloyd Wright, to whom the essays may be indirectly addressed. Historians have noted that in his June 1900 article, Robert Spencer argued for "the kindergarten idea in education" since Wright's childhood training with Friedrich Froebel's system was so important to his later development. And in his own speech that month, Wright added that in an architect's education, "the kindergarten circle of sympathetic discernment should be drawn around him when he is born, and he should be brought into contact with nature by prophet and seer until abiding sympathy with her is his." This may have been a reference to Sullivan, who late said himself that *Chats* "was originally written for young architects," most likely the league or, as some think, Wright and his Steinway Hall colleagues.[15] Sullivan may have gotten his title from Spencer and Wright, but the germ of *Chats* can be found in "The Youg Man in Architecture," written before their article and speech appeared, probably in May 1900. Nevertheless, personally educating young architects was one of Sullivan's highest priorities at the turn of the century.

The league's indifference to *Chats,* plus its loss of momentum, affected his relations with it. He did not attend the third convention at Philadelphia in June 1901, contenting himself with a somewhat perfunctory telegram: "Push on with the good work," he wrote. "I am with you in spirit."[16] Nor did he go to the fourth, but feeling more amenable with the passage of time, perhaps, he sent a paper, "Education," read at Toronto in 1902 by Robert Spencer, pretty much recalling familiar themes from previous years. The league had already split into two camps, one urging "deference and respect" toward AIA, which had expressed interest in merging, the other reflecting Sullivan's posture of staunch opposition. The groups tended to divide along regional lines, East versus West, with Chicago members in the western forefront. At the fifth convention, Claude Bragdon did what he could to rally Sullivan's supporters against "the rising tide of Latinism [Classic Revival] which floods the East and flows westward," reminding them of their leader's views. But "a staid conservatism" prevailed in the end, H. Allen Brooks writes. The spirit, enthusiasm, and dissent of the first three or four years succumbed to neoclassicism and the mundane concerns of organizational routine. "Ere long, the League was absorbed by its erstwhile enemy"—AIA.[17] Smarting from the *Chats* debacle, *Interstate Architect* closed its pages to Sullivan, as did *Inland Architect* about three years before folding in 1908. In 1905 he found a new platform at Gustav Stickley's *Craftsman* magazine, but by then his hopes for a progressive organization were quite dead.

Sullivan found respite all the while at Ocean Springs, taking Margaret every winter, to return when the weather improved. Depending on business demands, he occasionally traveled back and forth alone, sometimes using the Chicago Club for urban accommodations. "Am boxing for dear life 3 times a week," he wrote to Smith during one of his bachelor interludes. "Nothing like it." The Sullivans had recently visited the Smiths' Palisades, New York, home. "I look back on our stay with you as a bright spot for sure," but not one devoted entirely to relaxation. Sullivan had sketched out several *Chats* on the banks of the Hudson. Unwilling or unable to buy a house back home, Margaret and Louis found that their Mississippi sojourns made them transients in Chicago. In 1901 they took an apartment at the Virginia Hotel on Rush and Ohio streets—"one of the most exclusive and fashionable . . . in the country," *The Economist* believed, that had "always enjoyed a position of high standing" after opening in 1891—named after Virginia McCormick, whose family owned it and lived nearby. Though not as expensive as the Windermere, it was an impressive address, but the Sullivans objected to "living at the hotel—in durance" between Ocean Springs visits, to living at any hotel, for that matter. Next time back they rented a flat at 135 Lincoln Park Boulevard, a few blocks farther north nearer the water. "We had a most delightful Xmas," he wrote to Smith shortly afterward, "lunch on the gallery, etc.—temp 72—birds singing—water sparkling. . . . Margaret remains in the South for a while and I miss her terribly." In the October past he had reported "business still dull," but in January 1902 said it was "picking up a little."[18]

Business had indeed been dull, only four commissions in 1901 and again in 1902, five of which were not constructed. The McCormick family hired him three times in 1901. In fact, of eleven actual commissions through 1904—not counting imaginative projects—ten were from returning clients. If people did not already know him, it seemed they preferred to go elsewhere. Both Nettie McCormick and Ellis Wainwright asked for houses in 1901. The McCormick project for Lake Forest, Illinois, demonstrated an ability to learn from past mistakes but also Sullivan's dependence on others for house ideas. With its sweeping front porch and symmetrically placed windows sheltered by a broad hip roof, the principal garden facade was similar to George Maher's work and to Wright's 1894 William Winslow house in River Forest, Illinois, published in 1900. The first-floor plan, in addition, may have been based on McKim, Mead & White's 1882 Isaac Bell house in Newport, at least according to Narciso Menocal, who also points out flaws in the way Sullivan handled the living room, really the whole downstairs: directly in sight of callers in the vestibule, it allowed servants no alternative when answering the door but to pass directly through. Nor was the dining room adequately screened off, meaning that after dinner guests had either to look at dirty dishes or watch them being cleared. The main staircase, furthermore, terminated in a living room corner. Sullivan had not thought the program through. But upstairs, he corrected earlier mistakes by giving each of the five bedrooms its own private bath. Plans for the prairie-ish Wainwright house in St. Louis—a hipped roof main mass and separate pavilion connected by a less-formal section—unhappily do not survive.[19]

McCormick rejected the residence but got Sullivan the commission for a women's pavilion at the Presbyterian Hospital in Chicago, a six-story and basement structure that was never built. The final McCormick project was, however: a women's dormitory at Tusculum College in Greeneville, Tennessee, named after Nettie's daughter Virginia, that Sullivan worked on from late winter 1901 until its spring 1902 opening. The brick building was three stories over a raised basement capped by a dormered attic. There were twenty-eight bedrooms approximately fourteen by seventeen feet each and a large, residential-style porch on one narrow end servicing the downstairs public rooms along with an arched porch inset on one side. For a Sullivan design, Virginia Hall was severely plain, its only obvious trim the circular brick courses around porthole windows in the gables, parapet edging and windowsills in white, and corbeling flaring out at the roof corners. At $20,000 there was little money for Sullivan to do his usual magic, but when it opened and McCormick sent her final check, she wrote that the people of east Tennessee admired "their stately and beautiful edifice" and the students "realize that their debt to you for the handsome hall . . . remains, and must ever remain, uncancelled." Hyperbole or not, McCormick also hired Sul-

XII.4 *Virginia Hall, 1901, Tusculum College.* Courtesy Tusculum College.

livan to design residential cottages for the grounds, and to inspect plans she was having another architect do for the College of Wooster in Ohio.[20]

The next year, in May, Sullivan did an eight-room, two-story residence for Arthur Henry Lloyd on Kenesaw Terrace in Chicago, described as a pressed-brick exterior with corners and terraces in common brick and cement with a slate roof, all to cost $12,000. It was not erected.[21] But he did construct a $250,000 linoleum plant for Alexander Euston of St. Louis next door to his 1899 linseed-oil factory on Chicago's near North Side. The new complex included warehousing, heating and boiling houses, and separate rooms for engines, drying and printing machinery, cork grinding, and calendering in stylistically similar brick and stone buildings. Sullivan had trouble when concrete foundations took ten days to set because of a high sulfuric acid content in the site's artesian well, but he improvised a way to pump water in from Lake Michigan.[22] Schlesinger & Mayer returned early in 1902 for a twenty-story tower on their corner, 182 by 145 feet. His preliminary plans for a 280-foot skyscraper were rejected even though the city had rescinded its building-height limitation. When the mayor and the city council's judiciary committee instructed the building commissioner not to allow anything over sixteen stories, or 260 feet, Schlesinger & Mayer secured a writ of mandamus to get their permit. But the restriction stood, leaving Sullivan's tallest building since the Odd Fellows Temple on the drawing boards.[23]

Schlesinger & Mayer went ahead anyway at a much lower scale, although the remainder of their store ended up costing $800,000. Returning to their 1898 twelve-story concept, they hired Sullivan during the summer to add three floors to the nine on Madison Street, then to extend the building at twelve stories farther along State Street than originally intended, that is, through the corner lot and 180 feet down the block, replacing the older structures he had earlier remodeled. It turned out the Madison Street foundations would not support a heavier load, so that portion stayed the same, but in August 1902 Sullivan designed the remainder for construction in three stages: all foundations and basements from October 8, 1902, to January 1, 1903; the corner tower and three bays on either side connecting with the Madison Street section from January 6 through May 11, 1903; and the four southernmost bays on State Street from May 11 through October 12, 1903. Intending to keep the existing store open

XII.5 *Euston & Company factory, 1899, 1902.* Photo by Robert Twombly.

during the 1902 Christmas season, even with new foundations going in underneath the old buildings, the clients hoped to have the whole complex ready for Christmas the following year. Sullivan's ingenious solutions for the inevitable logistical problems were every bit as impressive as his aesthetic finesse, a major personal coup when the undertaking was finished exactly on schedule.

Schlesinger & Mayer insisted Sullivan conceal construction as much as possible. With fifty-nine concrete piers being laid in wells underneath a functioning store in a basement that would be much deeper than the old one, and with no materials to be piled on the sidewalk, Sullivan's methods were adroit. To minimize the debris going out, he crushed as much as possible for the new foundations, removing the leftover and bringing in supplementary pebble gravel through two elevator towers small enough to keep the sidewalk clear and the window displays unobstructed. The older State Street and newer Madison Street sections were connected internally by temporary passageways around the corner construction site. Sullivan hurried the pace by completing demolition in nine sixteen-hour days, using electric lights at night, and when he discovered he could not get delivery of steel columns on schedule, he improvised cast-iron substitutes in the corner tower, reverting to Z-bars elsewhere. The clients spent more than they might have to make the store completely fireproof. Every metal member was encased in terra-cotta, which Sullivan also used in arches to support the floors and act as between-story fire stops. Plaster-and-lath ceilings on steel frameworks were also incombustible. Taking advantage of every opportunity for publicity, Sullivan described previously unknown properties of the subsoil discovered during excavation, as well as his construction innovations, to the Illinois Chapter of AIA (originally the local branch of the Illinois State Association of Architects he had helped organize, hence not an enemy), then published his findings in 1903 and 1904, partly to boost his reputation as a structural architect.

The facade ended up essentially the way he had designed it in 1898 with four major exceptions: the open second-floor gallery was omitted; the highly ornamented base, originally octagonal on the corner, was made circular like the upper floors; the Madison Street portion remained at nine floors, with the rest going to twelve; and in the rest, the top three floors above the Madison Street roof line were reduced in height, possibly to minimize the difference. The cast-iron base was painted bronzed green to imitate oxidation, the superstruc-

XII.6 *Schlesinger & Mayer Store, 1899, 1902–1903, as built.* From *Inland Architect,* 1903.

ture was glazed terra-cotta, and the cornice projected slightly beyond the walls. Sullivan used Chicago windows throughout, except for plate-glass fenestration in the base wrapped with lavish ornament that his assistant George Elmslie later described as a richly flowing picture frame intended to accentuate the merchandise.[24]

In the context of new consuming habits and marketing practices, Sullivan's (and his clients') decorative achievements were brilliant. By the late nineteenth century, department stores were intentionally designed to attract middle- and upper-middle-class women, whose presence downtown was growing rapidly. Freed from many aspects of household routine by laborsaving devices, servants, and new levels of affluence, middle-class women were still barred from professions and other kinds of stimulating employment. With more leisure time, they were "all dressed up with no place to go." As "directors of family consumption," they regarded "the new activity of shopping as a relief from the boredom of family confinement or the drudgery of domestic routine." Shopping in sparkling new retail districts seemed to many a form of emancipation. "The extravagant size of plate-glass display windows also bestowed an aura of security and splendor upon the downtown streets," writes historian Gunther Barth, "making the clean, smooth sidewalks into a woman's world. . . . In the form of a marble palace, a cast-iron showplace, a sprawling grand depot, or a masonry castle, [the department store] emphasized dedication to the ideal of shopping as an endless delight."[25]

Biographer Willard Connely applied this kind of analysis to Schlesinger & Mayer. The boldest innovation was in the bottom two stories, he wrote, where "the most delicate decoration adorned the level at which the passing crowd could see it." Sullivan's aim was to "court unhurried feminity" with a "festive" array of geometrically arranged flowers, vines, and berries, iron garland chains, and great laurel wreaths over the doors. The effect was of a "store permanently bedecked for a permanent commemoration; but the psychology of it was that an individual shopper should feel that her own visit was being celebrated."[26] The compelling sidewalk decoration recalled a series of ornate picture frames around old masters, except that these "old masters" were brand-new commodities. Sullivan's facade demonstrated even more graphically than the Gage Building the commercial value of his art.

The store was a huge success, a landmark of early modern architecture, but Sullivan got precious little work because of it during the next few years. Schlesinger & Mayer hired him one last time, in May 1903, for a $40,000 face-lift and interior remodeling of their Wabash Street store, before selling out to the Carson Pirie Scott Company, one of their main competitors.[27] He added two office buildings at Bridgeport, Connecticut, to the Crane valve company that year, the same Cranes that hired Adler in 1895 but came to Sullivan for subsequent work.[28] In 1904 he gave them "mottled paving brick" offices in Chicago, ninety-three by one hundred feet in five generously windowed stories; continuous sloping sills across each floor balanced strong terminal piers in a clean-cut structure any modernist could easily claim as part of the movement.[29] He also designed an elaborate theater front that George Elmslie reported was purely imaginative, but that William Purcell, hired by Sullivan in 1903 for Schlesinger & Mayer, said was an attempt to land the Orchestra Hall

XII.7 *Schlesinger & Mayer Store, Madison and State streets entry.* From *Inland Architect,* 1903.

job in Chicago that ended up at Daniel Burnham's in 1905. Others say the theater was actually for Atlanta, Georgia. Whatever the case, it was not constructed.[30]

Sullivan made a good deal of money from Schlesinger & Mayer, but by late 1903 was again feeling the pinch. In October he informed Ellis Wainwright he could not repay the $1100 plus interest still outstanding on a $10,000 loan from several years before. To get out from under, and to gain solid financial footing, he tried to market his services in ways he would never have considered earlier, desperate commercial measures he must have thought beneath his dignity. In 1903 and 1904, he sent out letters to various entrepreneurs he knew to be contemplating major construction projects. One was to Joel Hunt in Atlanta, possibly in connection with the theater, enclosing favorable reviews from *The Architectural Record.* Usually, he wrote to businessmen in cities where he already had important buildings. In June 1903, for instance, he reminded Samuel Newhouse that he had designed the Dooly Block in which Newhouse had his offices, asked to be considered for a proposed Salt Lake City venture, and referred him to John E. Dooly, the original client. In August 1904 he sent a similar letter to a Mr. Thatcher in Pueblo, Colorado, where his 1889 Opera House Block stood proudly. None of these solicitations or the dozen or so between brought him any work.

In May 1903, responding to an inquiry from J. M. Henderson of Carson Pirie Scott, Sullivan tried to nail down a warehouse job. "I believe that there is an impression abroad that I deal only with more ornate forms of architectural construction. This is an error," he explained, "for I have had a great deal of work in heavy construction, plain factory buildings, machine shops, etc." Referring Henderson to Messrs. Crane and Euston and "to any officer of Schlesinger & Mayer," Sullivan added that their "drawings and specifications" were "well-nigh perfect" with "every contingency" anticipated. The sad irony was not his failure to get the commission, but that in 1905, a year later, after Carson Pirie Scott absorbed Schlesinger & Mayer, it hired Daniel Burnham to expand the store five bays farther south on State Street. Burnham followed the original design almost exactly. Why the company rejected Sullivan was never explained.

In September 1904 he thought up another moneymaking scheme, a unique investment opportunity, he told several business acquaintances including Lewis Hopkins of Boston. If he moved fast, he could acquire two adjoining lots facing Grant Park between Jackson and Van Buren streets, the only property likely to become available on this stretch of Michigan Avenue. His idea was to replace the present structure with a "thoroughly modern office building at least fifteen stories" tall as a speculative rental venture. Since he did not have the capital himself and did not want to form a stock company, but rather hoped to design the building, he had prepared, he wrote, a twenty-six-page prospectus of "blue-printed sheets" with a financial "discussion." The pamphlet showed a block plan, and a basement, and twenty actual floor plans plus elevations. Unfortunately for Sullivan, no one was interested.[31]

The next year, with only the Chicago Crane Building in construction, Sullivan got no more work at all. To make matters worse, old clients began to go elsewhere. The same Standard Club that hired Adler & Sullivan in 1887 and 1892 turned to Treat & Adler for new six-story quarters. Carson Pirie Scott had passed him by, and now the Brunswick, Balke Company, with Adler & Sullivan buildings from 1881, 1883, and 1891, erected new plants without him at Muskegon, Michigan, and Long Island City, New York: total cost some $700,000.[32] Though his income was declining, he remained an Architectural Club patron, and as he built less, he got more recognition. His contribution to the club's 1902 exhibition was "a positive relief," one reviewer thought, after seeing all that "L'Art Nouveau" stuff.[33]

It was now fashionable, in fact, to compare his work to the new French style. Claims were made for Sullivan that history has since disregarded. In a May 1902 lecture to the Boston Society of Architects, Columbia University's A. D. F. Hamlin said that Art Nouveau was almost as American as French, citing Wilson Eyre, Frank Miles Day, but especially Louis Sullivan. Other reviewers said all sorts of good things, even about his older buildings. *Western Architect* ruminated that "after wandering for a time [through the 1903 Louisiana Purchase Exposition in St. Louis], one needs a relief from classical columns and pediments"; perhaps "Mr. Sullivan's Transportation Building in Chicago was wise" after all. Writers for *The Brickbuilder* praised the new Schlesinger & Mayer Store but reminded readers that the "masterly" Wainwright Building and St. Nicholas Hotel had already made him "famous the world over." Observers were getting a sense of his historic importance but did not yet notice that his career was suffering.[34]

Despite his attacks on the profession's establishment, *The Architectural Record* was particularly friendly to Sullivan. In March 1904 it acknowledged "his highly personal and thoroughly intelligent effort" in skyscraper design to be "very much superior in originality and force to any other productions of the same class." In "Architecture of Ideas" the next month, Arthur C. David argued that the most exciting American work was in Chicago, some of it "absolutely revolutionary" in its break from "stylistic servitude." Chicago "radicals," he wrote, "are seeking for a rational and consistent basis for American design and ornament." The movement "derives its momentum and inspiration chiefly from the work of Mr. Louis Sullivan, and from a very able architect, who issued from Mr. Sullivan's office, Mr. Frank Wright." Barr Ferree applauded Sullivan in the *Record*'s May issue. He alone stated height frankly, giving the tall office building "logical as well as genuinely artistic expression." Later on, Claude Bragdon said he was "the only American architect of eminence who . . . stands for originality" and is a prophet, "if we except the small circle of his disciples and admirers." In back-to-back articles in July

1904—which Sullivan circulated to drum up business—W. H. Desmond examined the significance of his work, while Lyndon Smith explained the Schlesinger & Mayer achievement, following up with a flattering pictorial essay in June 1905 on Sullivan's Ocean Springs estate.[35]

Bragdon meanwhile published a lavishly illustrated article in the January *House & Garden* about his friend, "a man of genius." No longer taking Sullivan's essays, *Inland Architect* nevertheless reported his periodic talks to the Architectural Club, including his February 1905 reading from "Natural Thinking, a Study in Democracy," an in-progress manuscript still growing at forty thousand words. In November it mentioned his presentation from *Kindergarten Chats,* which Sullivan had not shelved, and never would, believing in its importance for young architects. If they would not read it themselves, he would read it to them. In between, *Inland Architect* printed F. W. Fitzpatrick's tribute to his high-rise work, some of which was "really superb."[36]

"Natural Thinking" put Sullivan in touch with Harriet Monroe, poet, playwright, Chicago *Examiner* culture critic, and editor of *Poetry* magazine. Asking her advice on how to ready his manuscript for publication, he also critiqued her plays *Passing Show* and *At the Goal,* which he liked very much, but thought her reviews occasionally too kind, especially of Richard Wagner's opera *Parsifal,* "a fake," he said, with absolutely no bearing on American life, "another imported fraud." He was thinking of changing his title from "Natural Thinking" to "The People," "for whom it will have been written . . . that is to say *all the people.*" The first chapter would be "What Is the Use?" which is, "after all, the fundamental question. 'What is the use?' " he asked Monroe, of struggling always for truth and freedom in art when no one pays attention, least of all publishers, who deceive the public "like feudal barons of old." Reflecting on the fate of *Kindergarten Chats,* perhaps, he felt "sure in advance that no publisher would touch" his new book no matter what he called it.

Sullivan's distrust stemmed from a larger pessimism about his skidding career, which he attributed in a revealing letter to Monroe to the Columbian Exposition and to architects like Daniel H. Burnham. The "tidal wave" of "fool" classic unleashed in 1893 "set back the progress of creative American architecture, up to the present time," Sullivan asserted in 1905, "and for an indefinite time to come." Daniel Burnham's "commercialization of the art," furthermore, "has literally crowded us into the *gutter*." A kind of modern-day "feudalism" permeates everything. "Until the trusts and special privilege are overthrown," he told her in one of his few overtly political passages, "democracy in any work of life will have but little show, and a democratic art least of all." Books like "Natural Thinking" were therefore crucial for countering the general "pessimism."

Curiously enough, Sullivan added, "foreign architects sneer at the classic . . . and without hesitation commend my own [work], as American. But the voice of the foreign men does not reach our people."[37] The irony in this must have escaped his notice: the man determined to create an American art, believing European classicism to be his major obstacle, finds sustenance only from foreign architects. Monroe gave him moral support, praising him in her columns from time to time and publishing "What Is the Use?" in 1915. But Sullivan's cantankerousness hurt him in more influential circles. He reportedly remarked to Cass Gilbert, after inspecting his 1904 West Street Building in New York, that if he (Sullivan) were to critique it he (Gilbert) would not know "what I was talking about." In the June 1905 *Craftsman,* Sullivan took Frederick Stymetz Lamb to task for advocating a "modern use of the Gothic," a perfect example, no doubt, of "our temporary era of insanity" that he bemoaned the next month when he wrote to praise Stickley's editorial policy.[38]

With business at an all-time low, Sullivan borrowed $5000 in August from Gustave Hottinger, a Chicago tile manufacturer, mortgaging his Ocean Springs property against defaulting on repayment in five years at 5 percent annual interest.[39] It must have been devastating again to jeopardize his beloved winter retreat, especially since he had directed Purcell late in 1903 to upgrade the paths and rose gardens, ultimately hiring twelve men for "much needed improvements which I have been postponing from year to year."[40] Still without prospects in December 1905, he took the desperate step, for him, considering his views on the academy, of applying for a lectureship on the same day he learned the University of Michigan planned to establish a school of architecture. "I am . . . taking the liberty to bring myself to your notice," he wrote rather bitterly to president James B. Angell, "because . . . it is perhaps the only means by which you are likely to learn of my existence, (notwithstanding my international reputation as an Architect)." Blasting the worthlessness of existing architecture schools and lecturing Angell on how to proceed may have had something to do with not getting the job.[41]

But in 1906 he found some work, two commissions, in fact. In July old friend Eli B. Felsenthal, relative and next-door neighbor of Dankmar Adler in an Adler & Sullivan house, hired him to design a two-story shop-and-flats building of pressed brick and stone trim at Forty-seventh Street and Langley Avenue. With a flat roof, projecting cornice, huge shop windows, and strip fenestration on the second floor, its clean simplicity was handsome and advanced. Although it did not receive much press attention, it had real architectural merit.[42] The second commission in October eventually made a considerable impression. He and Elmslie worked on the National Farmers' Bank in Owatonna, Minnesota, for more than a year until its opening in the summer of 1908. Elmslie did enough of the ornament, the working drawings, and the overall designing to be considered a project partner, but its spirit and feeling, its great interior space, its colors, and its structural and mechanical systems were all Sullivan's. Elmslie left his own imprint on the final product, to be sure, but Louis Sullivan's inspiration made it a work of art.

Vice-president Carl K. Bennett had seen Sullivan's essay "What Is Architecture?"—reprinted in three 1906 issues of *The Craftsman* from the January *American Contractor*—during a search by the bank's officers for a suitable architect. And they knew just what they wanted: a convenient, modern structure that would also represent the values and tastes of its farmer clientele, objectives Sullivan took to be the essence of democratic architecture. The result was a sixty-eight-foot-square banking room, forty feet high, on Owatonna's most prominent street corner, diminishing to a two-story business building down the block, connected by covered walkway to an "L" for printing and warehousing. Erected for some $80,000, this small, exquisite building turned out to be one of the most memorable Sullivan ever designed.

The facade began with a high, reddish-brown, ashlar sandstone base punctured by deep-set entries and windows. The upper walls in what came to be called "tapestry brick," a Sullivan innovation, consisted of rough units variously tinted to create in combination a richly textured look. All this was handsome enough, but the real showpiece was the gigantic thirty-eight-foot arched window on each street facade divided into vertical strips of green variegated glass with four symmetrically positioned geometric patterns. The art glass was covered by double plate outside to sandwich a hermetically sealed air space, necessary for the wildly fluctuating climate. Each facade was outlined with an inset border of leafy green terra-cotta

XII.8 *National Farmers' Bank, 1906–1907.* Photo by Robert Twombly.

XII.9 *National Farmers' Bank facade detail.* Photo by Robert Twombly.

medallions highlighted by golden balls of fruit, inside of which was an auxiliary border of red, blue, white, and green tiles wrapping brown terra-cotta medallions of the most delicate arrangement in the upper corners. A string of tiny arches was tucked under the slightly overhanging cornice corbeled up to the flat roof. The semicircular windows set within the bank's crisp rectangle accented by carefully chosen colors and forms of locally grown crops was a most successful composition. The vast fenestration addressed the community in a friendly way, yet the sturdy brick walls suggested the safety of a strongbox.

Around the perimeter of the interior walls were spaces for tellers and officers. An entrance medallion rose into the arched window, which was bordered by multicolored stenciling the equal of Sullivan's best theater prosceniums. With a matching rear arch over the clock and elaborate chandeliers hanging near the corners of the stenciled ceiling, the banking room was bright and open but quiet, superbly artful, every bit as monumental as the officers hoped for, but not the least intimidating to provincial customers. Plans for both the banking and commercial areas, furthermore, were exceptionally rational and well organized. Sullivan and Elmslie gave loving attention to every inch of the building, from their choice of Gustav Stickley's furniture to pieces of their own design, from the careful selection of colors and materials to the precise detailing of brickwork, from thoughtful climate control to the orderly layout of multiple functions. All of it demonstrated that Sullivan's genius for making efficiency beautiful had diminished not at all. Reviewers were unusually enthusiastic. Sullivan's friend Louis J. Millet, bank vice-president Bennett, and architect Thomas Tallmadge were among the many to shower it with praise. "Owatonna suddenly found itself famous," Montgomery Schuyler remarked four years later, "and became the Mecca of architectural pilgrimages. At the last report, twenty-five strangers a day were visiting Owatonna expressly to inspect it."[43]

None of the twenty-five pilgrims multiplied over and again went home to hire Sullivan, however. But from 1907 through 1909 he got five new commissions, the two that were built both houses. The first, designed in 1907 for Henry Babson in Riverside, Illinois, showed how closely Sullivan kept tabs on Wright and the "prairie school." Completed in 1909, the $40,000 residence was in the main one hundred by thirty feet, noticeably horizontal on two stories. Its lower walls in tapestry brick terminating at one end with a magnificently arched breakfast porch were straight from National Farmers' Bank. Under a low-pitched, broadly eaved roof, the upper walls were dark-stained board-and-batten cypress with strips of leaded glass casement windows in crisp white frames. Covered porches were flung out from one end, and an arched, roofed-over balcony was cantilevered from the second-floor sitting room. Servants were housed in their own private wing.

The plan mirrored the horizontal exterior, with one downstairs room flowing into the next along a lengthy axis. Upstairs, a gallery on the rear wall connected three bedrooms—two with baths—separated for privacy by a den and the sitting room. Each bedroom

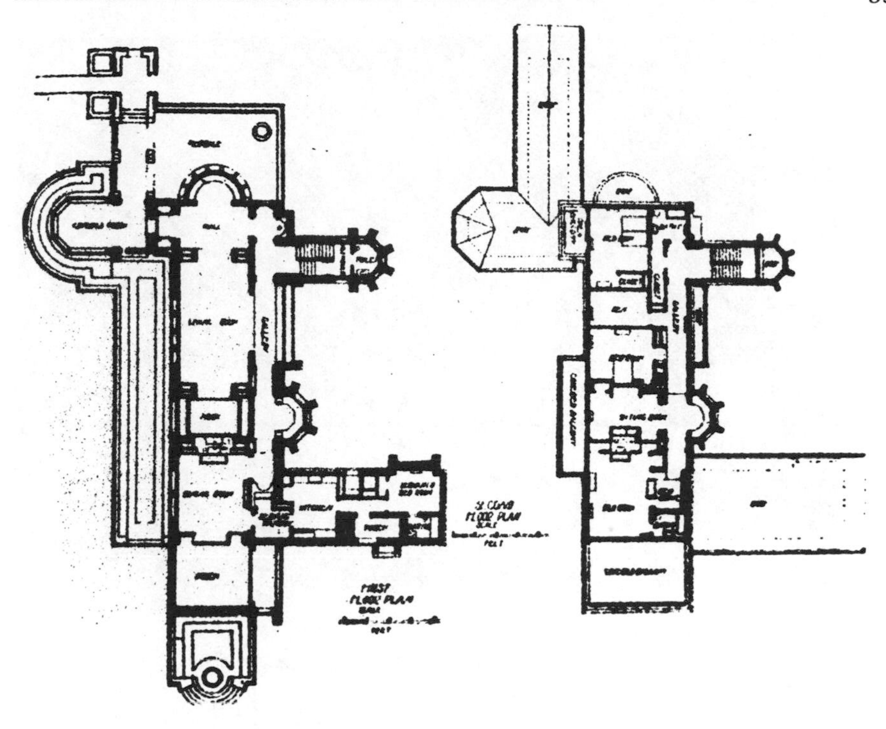

XII.10 *Henry Babson residence plan, 1907.*
From Northwest Architectural Archives.

opened on a balcony, the master bedroom on two. Rooms strung out linearly were distinctly un-Wrightian, but the horizontal lines, the open first-floor plan, the far-flung porches, overhanging roof, and octagonal veranda shaped like Wright's 1895 Oak Park Studio library were all prairie-school-ish. Raised front gardens, three huge elms (one within the terrace perimeter), and stains the colors of nearby landscape gave the Babson house "the appearance of having grown on the spot," one observer noted, a very Wrightian objective. *The Record*'s reviewer thought it better than Wright's 1907 Coonley house—rising simultaneously just a few blocks away—"another illustration . . . of [Sullivan's] genuinely original architectural imagination." Though probably not superior to Wright's acknowledged masterpiece, it was certainly the most handsome dwelling Sullivan ever did.[44]

The other house was the last he built, commissioned by Charles Crane (of the Chicago Cranes) for his daughter and son-in-law, Josephine and Harold Bradley, in Madison, Wisconsin. The first version

XII.11 *Harold Bradley residence, 1909.* Photo by Robert Twombly.

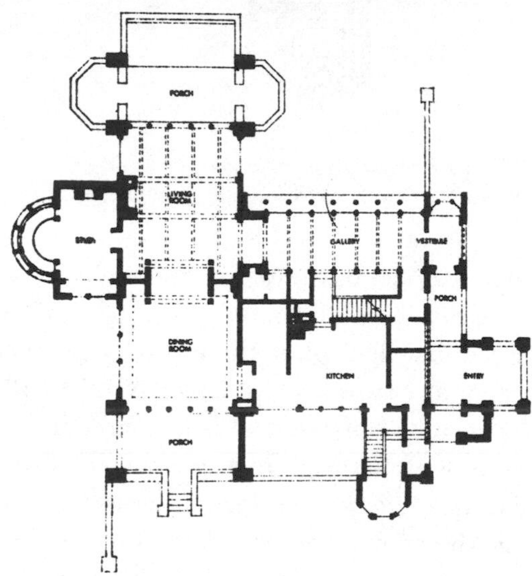

XII.12 *Harold Bradley residence plan, 1909, as built.* From blueprints at State Historical Society of Wisconsin.

in 1908 was rejected as too grandiose, but next year the second was accepted and built, although the Bradleys never liked it. Sullivan initially proposed a cruciform plan with a huge porch and living room on the main axis, and a reception hall at the crossing flanked by a den and the dining room leading to a servants' wing jutting at a forty-five degree angle off the main mass. His revisions from July through December 1909 included plans, elevations, sections, and some details, but from December through March 1910, Elmslie, who had opened his own office the previous fall, teamed up with the Madison firm of Claude & Stark to finish the trim and kitchen. Essentially, the house was Sullivan's and as built for $40,000, it was more compact than the first version. Loosely based on Wright's "Home in a Prairie Town" in the February 1901 *Ladies' Home Journal,* it also drew on the Babson house for its large porches at either end of the main axis, along which room opened into room. The lower brickwork, upper-story board-and-batten, protruding octagonal study, low-pitched overhanging roof, and open plan were well within the prairie-school idiom. But Sullivan's dramatically cantilevered sleeping porches at either end, his white trim around the casements, his powerful brick piers, and Elmslie's decorations gave it a personality all its own. Even if the living room was a bit small, the study somewhat cramped, and the dining room and gallery oversized, the house was perfectly livable, although too large and formal for the Bradleys, who hired Purcell & Elmslie to do them a smaller house elsewhere in Madison in 1914.[45]

None of Sullivan's three other commissions toward decade's end were executed, although they were all quite impressive. As the Babson project got under way in July 1907, he was engaged by a syndicate of Philadelphia and New York capitalists to develop 344-acre Petty's Island in the Delaware River into a massive amusement park. Prepared to spend $1,000,000 on their so-called Island City, John M. Mack and Colonel William P. Donovan, the principal backers, instructed Sullivan to lay out a bathing pavilion, a two-story one-thousand-room hotel with nearby bungalows, an athletic stadium, a marina, theaters, a café and ballroom, a 250-foot tower with six revolving searchlights in different colors, and other lesser facilities. He gave the place a festive spirit, with flapping banners, ornamented pylons, and a broad ceremonial boulevard leading from the docking area past the hotel and other major buildings to the "naval show," a museum of nautical lore. The top of the café was wrapped in a decorative border like the Owatonna bank, on which he was working at the time, while the scenic theater entrance recalled Wright's 1901 village bank scheme for *The Brickbuilder.* Although the Babson project was also in the office in October 1907, Sullivan delivered the preliminary plans on schedule, later showing them at the fourteenth annual Philadelphia T-Square Club exhibition the following April and May. Unfortunately for Sullivan, the backers seem to have had a

XII.13 *Island City (Petty's Island) project, 1907.*
From catalogue of the Fourteenth Annual Architectural Exhibition, Philadelphia.

certain get-rich-quick aura about them. Possibly put off by the financial downturn of late 1907, or by realization of the immense sums Island City was going to cost, they abandoned the project. Sullivan must have been quite distressed. The fees and publicity from a venture on this scale would have been a real boost to his sagging fortunes.[46]

Likewise, the proposed changes in late 1908 and early 1909 to the same Chicago Auditorium that had once established his reputation now promised to resuscitate it. Complaining that the theater had never been profitable, even for vaudeville and musical comedy, management decided to tear it out, hiring Louis Sullivan to redesign the building. His willingness to aid in the demise of his most famous creation was a revelation of financial desperation. Two options were proposed. The first was to convert the entire edifice into a hotel with a grand new entrance on Congress Street. Cafés on either side, and a 70-by-120-foot palm court farther back, would open on a 30-foot-

wide rotunda with lavish fountains, statuary, and paintings leading to Michigan Avenue. Part of the existing tower would be guest rooms with many more in a new twenty-two-story tower on independent foundations replacing the present theater. Around it would be a 30-foot court opening on a mid-block driveway connecting Michigan and Wabash avenues. At $3,000,000, the alterations would be almost as costly as the original building. A cheaper alternative was to convert the entire edifice to offices by adding up to four additional stories for $500,000, the more likely possibility, according to the press. Fortunately for the Auditorium but not for Sullivan's pocketbook, neither design was adopted.[47]

In 1909 Sullivan completed the Babson house, revised the Bradley residence, and began preliminary work on the People's Savings Bank in Cedar Rapids, Iowa. The Island City scheme was revived, only to die a permanent death. Several former clients chose not to hire him for new projects. In one October issue of *The Economist,* he read to his dismay that a new Sinai Temple and another Carson Pirie Scott warehouse had gone to other architects, and that the Auditorium conversion had been permanently shelved.[48] Schlesinger & Mayer, his best money source, was long since out of business, furthermore, and since 1900 ten of his twenty-one projects had not been built. His ten executed buildings from 1903 through 1909 collectively cost some $400,000 to $450,000, seemingly a large sum, but, dividing by six years and a 10 percent fee, left only a $7000 annual income. This, of course, was before expenses (wages, office and apartment rent, Ocean Springs maintenance and taxes, interest on Hottinger's loan, and so on) and was not evenly distributed: he had no commissions in 1905 and erected none from 1908. He probably got additional monies from unexecuted projects, perhaps a small amount from writing and lecturing, but whatever his actual net income, by 1909 it was not enough to support him.

Loyal George Elmslie, Sullivan's right-hand man since Frank Lloyd Wright left, had remained with him for twenty years. But after a prolonged illness in 1909, he decided the time had come to look for greener pastures, forming a partnership that year in Minneapolis with William Purcell. By now, Elmslie could do Sullivan ornament nearly as well as the master himself. He had been patient, dedicated, and more than competent, a good original designer himself, who faithfully did whatever was asked, including sometimes working without pay. His departure was a real loss. But shortly before, Sullivan had hired Parker N. Berry (1888–1918), a talented fledgling from Nebraska via Princeton, Illinois, who had chanced to meet Kristian Schneider of the American Terra Cotta Company, for more than twenty years the modeler for Sullivan's ornament. Schneider introduced the two. At the age of twenty-one, Berry became Sullivan's chief draftsman and in some cases designer until 1917.[49]

Sullivan had hired assistants for Elmslie when business warranted. But in December 1908, when the noted English architect and Arts and Crafts apologist Charles R. Ashbee visited the office, there was only one employee there: "The Soul of the City is sick," Ashbee confided to his still-unpublished "Memoirs," "and she knows it poor thing. . . . The great drafting rooms of the architects are empty. . . . It is more than a temporary check to material development," he thought, alluding to the aftermath of the 1907 financial panic; "it is a growing belief among her finer minds that we are not as certainly on the right lines as eight years ago." Frank Lloyd Wright (and his prairie-school contemporaries) who had been "full of fire and belief . . . has grown bitter, and has drawn in upon himself." And what of Louis Sullivan, that "strange half coherent genius who first struck the light of life into architecture here"? Louis Sullivan "has spent the last three years . . . writing a dreaming chaotic prose epic": "Natural Thinking," completed now as "Democracy, a Man Search!" "He took me up to his office and said 'good God—I'm glad I've got this off my chest! May I read you the first two chapters?' . . . It did not disturb the one draughtsman who was working on bathroom plans . . . nor yet the commercial who dropped in . . . to sell us concrete."[50]

Ashbee was right about the last three years. From 1906 through 1908, Sullivan erected a mere three buildings for under $150,000 total, no more than $5000 a year net to him before expenses. With his income disappearing, he became tightfisted with Margaret, no longer handing her cash to spend but depositing what little he had in their Corn Exchange National Bank account, where it was harder to get at, especially from Ocean Springs. People there thought her somewhat demanding, particularly when she wrote to make arrangements for their visits or was curt to shopkeepers and gardeners when preparations were not exactly to her liking. Sullivan occasionally gave the impression in his own letters that though "Margaret wants" this or "needs" that, he did not approve, signaling the merchants not to comply.[51] Sullivan's economies were surely not her only complaint. Their nomadic existence was equally unsettling. In the ten years since 1899, city directories placed the Sullivans at nine different addresses! Starting out on a Windermere Hotel "honeymoon," they moved to 396 North State Street, the Virginia Hotel, 135 Lincoln Park Boulevard, the Chicago Club, the "strictly modern" Lessing Annex apartments on Surf Street at Evanston Avenue from 1903 to 1907, the Virginia Hotel again, back to the Chicago Club, and finally, when things were quite bad in 1908–1909, to 4300 Ellis Avenue deep on the South Side. If the Chicago Club was merely Sullivan's address during his bachelor business trips to the city, he stayed long enough in 1902 and 1908 to be counted by directory compilers. Assuming Margaret wanted him around, long absences would not have made her happy, but neither would the remaining seven moves in nine years if that was all there were.

There came a point when Margaret may not have wanted her husband around, or wondered at least if his presence was worth the aggravation. With little work and the lengthy "Democracy" finished in 1908, Sullivan had too much time on his hands. Uncomfortable with inactivity and depressed about his career, he fought with Margaret and went out alone at night, presumably to drink. He sometimes returned home difficult to handle. "His wife used to come and see me in the office, and shed tears," Elmslie later said, "not knowing what to do with her Louis. She had to have assistance every night, at times, to help put him to bed."[52] If this was at the Lessing Annex or the Virginia Hotel, it would mean calling in the staff, certainly an embarrassment for all concerned. Several repeat performances and they would be asked to leave. That may have been why they ended up on Ellis Avenue.

To save money, Sullivan quit his clubs, stopped paying dues to AIA (which carried him along, despite everything, for five more years), cut down on business travel, and kept only a skeleton staff. But these meant less to Margaret than moving to a cheaper address, living with his depression, and handling his late-night scenes. The final blow was the worst of all, a sign to Margaret that her marital expectations would never be realized, and to the public that Louis Sullivan was in very dire straits.

On Monday morning, November 29, 1909, almost everything Sullivan owned went up for auction at Williams, Barker & Severn Company showrooms, 185 Wabash Avenue.[53] One hundred thirty household items, including sixteen Oriental rugs, numerous paintings, solid mahogany and mission oak furniture, Japanese and Chinese vases, a twelve-place setting of Haviland china, and many more *objects d'art,* plus a library of 161 titles, including 97 multivolume sets, a number bound in expensive leathers, even his architecture books and journals, 274 titles—all of it went on the block. Things he cherished most—his jade collection, Walt Whitman's letter and his *Leaves of Grass*—that he had carefully carted back and forth from one flat and hotel to another: everything was sold. All the reminders of better days that were icons to a better future—all of them were gone. Margaret had had enough. Unwilling to move to a furnished hotel, especially not the Warner, at Cottage Grove Avenue and Thirty-third Street, a decent-enough place run by the Virginia's owners but too far south and too much of a comedown, Margaret left Louis on December 6, a week after the auction. Sullivan took his few remaining possessions to the Warner, where he lived for the rest of his life.

Margaret went off to New York, to publish a novel in 1914, to serve as a wartime nurse in France, get her divorce from Sullivan in 1916, remarry the next year in London, divorce again in the 1930s, and die in obscurity, where and when no one knows. Sullivan did not realize as much from the auction as he anticipated. Unable to pay some or all of the $5000 loan, he sold Gustave Hottinger six acres at Ocean Springs on January 26, 1910, for $1, hoping against hope he could keep the rest. But with business still moribund, he could not hold out, and on May 1 was forced to sell the last five acres and his house to Hottinger for $8500. Losing his beloved home, his "paradise, the poem of spring, Louis's other self," he remembered years later, was the cruelest hurt of all. Incapable of assuming responsibility, he wrote in his autobiography that the house "was wrecked by a wayward West Indian hurricane."[54] The $8500 meant a lot: it paid the rent and bought him food, almost literally keeping him alive. But in another sense it meant very little, considering that in the past six months he had lost virtually everything. Louis Sullivan appeared to have hit rock bottom.

During their ten years together, Margaret and Louis had no children and may not have wanted any. If she had found in an older man a father substitute to care for her, he might have married her youth out of a need to assume control of his life. Child rearing might not have been part of their individual agendas. As declining income restricted their possibilities, he was increasingly unable to satisfy her needs, while out of necessity or perhaps self-preservation she asserted herself more, much to his distaste. If this is what happened, their marriage was bound to fail. What did or did not go on in their bedroom is also conjectural, of course. But there is a good deal of evidence—some personal, some architectural—to suggest that Louis Sullivan may have been homosexual—a contention not offered here gratuitously, for his sexuality informed and is visible in his work—and that it was so repressed he may not have known it himself.

Sullivan preferred male to female anatomy as the object of study. His few student sketches of women were usually unflattering, but his loving attention to men's bodies, including Bill Curtis's at the Lotus Place Athletic Club, indicates his predilections. He also favored the company of men. His autobiography claimed greater affection for his mother than his father, but the truth may be just the opposite. Throughout his youth he idolized a series of older men, never women, and at the Sistine Chapel learned from Michelangelo the power and possibility of being male, of being *super*-male, in fact, but not of being human. Gender role rigidity in late Victorian America might account for a young man's strong identification with his own sex, but Sullivan's seems to have been especially tenacious. As an adult, all his friends were men, his boxing, his clubs, and architecture were exclusively male preserves, and he showed little interest in women before Margaret, excepting casual encounters with safely married and unavailable Dila Adler, or I. Giles Lewis's wife, for example.

His personal life suggests a male-oriented prudishness uncharacteristic of his architecture. He admired Henry Richardson's Marshall Field Store, he wrote, because of its "virile force": it was "a *man* for you to look at," he told his *Kindergarten Chats* disciple, a man with "red blood; a real man, a manly man . . . an entire male," singing "the song of procreant power" that helped buildings like his own Auditorium be "comely in the nude."[55] But his imagery was never entirely masculine, especially after discovering Emanuel Swedenborg, an eighteenth-century scientist and mystic popular in the 1880s, whom his friend John Root and partner Daniel Burnham admired, and who might have been known to John Edelmann, Sullivan's youthful mentor and pal. Swedenborg taught that God sustained the universe with his most important attributes, love and wisdom, the masculine principle of wisdom or reason balanced with feminine love or emotion. Understanding this and acting on it was the means by which humanity became one with nature.

Sullivan's 1886 essay, "Inspiration," argued that integration of reason and emotion, of the geometric and the organic—in architecture of the classic and the Gothic, he later wrote—was the basis of nature's, hence humanity's, compositional method. He tried to make his work reflect this, at first by uniting these opposites within decorative patterns, then by bonding "male" structural forms to "female" ornament. Even though the "male" rationality of a building's shape provided the occasion for "female" embellishment, he came to believe that, fundamentally, logic was "conscious and secondary," emotion "vital and primary." In his method of designing, inspiration and emotion—the female part of the dichotomy—came first, giving birth to the orderly, logical working out of mass and detail, the male part of the process. "The simple rectangular shape he finally favored for buildings expressed for him, through geometry, the existence of the inorganic as well as the intellectuality of the masculine-rational,"

Narciso Menocal observes. "His ornamentation, on the other hand, represented to him the organic and the lyricism of the feminine-emotional. Linking the two symbolized the heroism of acting like nature."[56]

Menocal's analysis of sexual imagery stops here, but Sullivan seems to have developed to the point where feminine-emotional-organic ornament took over, depriving some of his buildings of the sought-for balance. At first highlighting spatial and structural aspects of skyscrapers, to take one genre as an example, ornament became the entire surface of the Guaranty Building in 1894–95. Two years later the balance tilted further, at Bayard, where the attic was a commanding ornamental outburst, while at the contemporary Gage Building blossoming medallions bore little relation to anything tangible. Their meaning was entirely metaphysical. Both buildings' columns can be read as part of the geometric male form, but when they exploded into huge decorative symbols of femininity at the Gage, the imagery was almost ejaculatory: the male sexual organ emitting a female form. Had Sullivan meant the male to *support* or *give birth* to the female, he would have violated his own reading of universal truths wherein the female was vital and primary. Rather, the Gage imagery was of the male *becoming* female. If this reading is as blatant as the ornament itself, it nevertheless points to the next stage of development at Schlesinger & Mayer, where exceptionally strong ornament—meant to entice *women* customers, remember—supports a comparatively plain upper facade. The sharp contrast between base and superstructure, between ornamental and plain surface, between the female and the male, was unprecedented in his work, with the possible exception of the Chemical Bank project in St. Louis, where the differences were much less striking. Far from simply adorning the masculine, Schlesinger & Mayer's "vital and primary" female base defines the building, explains it visually, and gives it reason for being. The female in Sullivan had become the dominant force.

Later on, in a number of smaller commissions, Sullivan's ornament would be even more powerful. Although simple geometric shapes continued to provide the opportunity, as Menocal noted, ornament was gathered in huge clusters, after Gage, or was otherwise so strong that observers remember it more readily than the structures themselves. Overwhelming ornament did not characterize every late Sullivan building. But it happened often enough to call attention in retrospect to the turn-of-the-century Bayard, Gage, and Schlesinger

& Mayer projects particularly, when the female-emotional appeared to begin its dominance. His labors on *A System of Architectural Ornament* in the early 1920s also indicate the importance he attached to this aspect of design.

Margaret entered Sullivan's life in 1899, while the Gage and Bayard were in construction, during Schlesinger & Mayer's designing, just as the trend emerged. If he sensed that the female side of his sensibility, the female component of his nature, was taking over, he may have tried to repress it through boxing, for one thing, a peculiarly male activity he rediscovered shortly before. In a "macho" environment, it was crucially important that a man be a man. Or it could be that the very act of marrying Margaret was a way of assuring himself that what he suspected was really not true. But if Sullivan married to reclaim his masculinity, the symbol alone would not guarantee success. If one of the several good reasons Margaret left in 1909 was sexual dissatisfaction, the implications of knowing her second husband before her departure are quite intriguing. Journalist Davies Edward Marshall was "a very warm friend of hers and mine," Sullivan told a correspondent early in 1910, "the salt of the earth, never tired of doing for others." If Marshall set out to "assist her in her work," as Sullivan thought, he apparently succeeded well enough to share her New York address. When she began to use Margaret *Davies* Sullivan as a nom de plume around 1912, four years before her divorce and five before remarrying, was she publicly adopting her lover's name or continuing an extramarital affair begun years before? No one may ever know. But the speculation that she had been sexually unfulfilled with Sullivan clarifies her behavior while supporting the contention about his preferences.[57]

Sullivan's emerging homosexuality, if that is what it was, coincides with his marriage and with his fall from popular favor. It is tempting to link his decline to Margaret, to blame her somehow for his increasing inability to get work. But it is more likely that in the male world of architecture doubts about his masculinity would do him greater damage than anything she may have done. His obvious artistic inclinations could have been used to support rumors of lack of manliness. But if there was talk, it cannot be proven and must be left aside. The explanation for Sullivan's decline is nevertheless extremely complicated, with several contributing factors. He blamed it on the Classical Revival stimulated by the 1893 Chicago World's Fair. While it is true that the fair helped legitimize neoclassicism, neither the event nor the style accounts for his situation. For if they had really inhibited progressive architecture, as he and some historians claim, it is difficult to explain the phenomenal success of Frank Lloyd Wright and his prairie-school contemporaries from 1900 to World War I. Their popularity proves that innovative architecture flourished quite splendidly side by side with historicism.

Unlike the prairie architects, Sullivan did not particularly care to do residences, thereby failing to take advantage of their most singular success. To be sure, Wright's generation produced many important nonresidential buildings, some of lasting historical significance. But the public knew its dwellings best. Sullivan's reputation was based on commercial architecture, on theaters and halls, warehouses, and tall office buildings. Only one or two of his few prairie-genre projects were not seriously flawed, and since he erected but two houses, he did not develop a clientele. He may have been the prairie school's patriarch, but potential home buyers had no particular reason to think of him. Had he shifted to residences and been good at it, he might have benefited from the unprecedented suburban movement generated by substantial growth in the turn-of-the-century middle class.

The break with Adler is often cited as the principal reason for his decline. But even if true, it is impossible to demonstrate because of the national depression. From January 1896, when he returned to architecture, through his last commission in 1899, Adler was hired eighteen times as opposed to Sullivan's fifteen. But two or three Sullivan buildings were more costly than any of Adler's, meaning that their careers were financially similar during the four years comparison is possible. When prosperity returned, Sullivan's business improved, to ten jobs in 1898–99, up from five in 1896–97. Exactly the same thing happened to Adler, whose commissions rose from seven in 1896–97 to eleven during his last two working years. Neither returned to pre-1895 affluence, although it is always possible Adler might have had he lived longer. The argument that Sullivan suffered by ending the partnership could just as correctly be applied to Adler. But it is better not to apply it at all.

It is sometimes said that Sullivan did not know enough about construction to attract commercial clients, having been the "artistic" partner for so many years. But the Bayard Building and the 1902–1903 Schlesinger & Mayer Store alone should put that idea to rest. Sullivan nevertheless took pains to prove his nonartistic mettle in business correspondence, speeches, and magazine articles recounting his structural successes. To the limited extent he proved his point, he enhanced his reputation as an exclusively commercial architect, hurting his chances for other kinds of work.

It is also said that Sullivan was inept with client and public relations. Adler had pulled in the business and handled customers, leaving Sullivan to his tower-corner hideaway. Once on his own, the suggestion is that he had neither the experience nor the inclination to "give the client what he wanted." There is a certain truth to this, but it must be carefully stated. There were those to whom Sullivan was friendly and interesting, once they got to know him. But the problem was in the approach. Wrapped in a protective mantle of remoteness, he seemed to suspend judgment until individuals proved themselves. If they agreed with him and his ideas, at least to some extent, or showed some sensitivity to art, he could open a relationship. But if they did not, he could dismiss them quite abruptly, including customers, regardless of the fee involved. When he wanted to, he could deal with the public and with business affairs as well as the next architect, but his reputation for aloofness, even hostility, prevented potential clients from taking the trouble to meet him.

His attitude toward architecture was equally idiosyncratic. Sullivan simply would not design in an alien, historic style, no matter how expensive the commission. If he could not do it his way, he would not do it at all. If this made him dogmatic, that was how he preferred to be. Assuming that no one would come to him without already knowing what a "Louis Sullivan" building would be, he gave the client "what he wanted" only if he wanted him. In another and more fundamental sense, however, he always gave clients exactly what they wanted. His buildings were known to be practical and efficient, solidly based on the program's requirements. In these matters he listened to clients closely. But on questions of style and aesthetics, he would not compromise because the representational side of his art was to him most important. And precisely because he was so "artistic," he was sometimes passed over.

Had his inability to compromise been confined to designing, Sullivan might have survived quite well, but when it affected his relations with architecture's establishment, AIA in particular, it did him considerable damage. Withdrawing from the organization was one thing; even criticizing its policies noisily was not entirely detrimental. But to denounce it repeatedly in the strongest language, to dismiss everything it stood for as "malpractice," and to call its president a "plain public nuisance" with "stupid" ideas were foolhardy invitations to trouble. Retaliation could be subtle but effective. Only a few quiet words in the right places would be enough. From the same social class as most clients, frequenting the same clubs, churches, and other private gathering places, AIA members could easily see to it that Sullivan got his just deserts. The more established the clients, the less they would tolerate controversial connections with troublemakers and firebrands; people who counted were unlikely to hire "ungentlemanly" architects. And when the Architectural League merged with the "enemy," Sullivan lost the buffer between his own outspokenness and AIA's power to punish.

Changing tastes also hurt his career. However mutually different, neoclassicism, the prairie style, and other early twentieth-century design currents shared at least one thing in common: restraint in the use of applied ornament. Neoclassicism was crisp, ordered, sometimes monochromatic, and often deceptively simple. Progressive styles incorporated ornament more organically than the Victorians had, eliminating some of it altogether. Leaded glass, furniture, moldings, balusters, and so on reflected overall design themes, in Frank Lloyd Wright's word, were "integral" with the mass, were functional consequences of the mass itself. Leafy, flowery, intricately sawn, delicately molded appliqués were falling out of favor. The new work was cleaner in line, in many cases conscious articulations of the new machine era. Sullivan accepted cleanliness of outline but not integral ornament. Usually not structure itself, his was generally affixed to it or were comments about it. He seemed to move in the opposite direction, in fact, toward larger and more elaborate patterns, as if consciously bucking the trend. With advanced taste heading toward streamlining, functional detail, and decorative reductionism, Sullivan was left behind.

New design ideas tend to be urban, but Sullivan's late work was not. This is hardly surprising, considering that his first love, high-rise buildings, were exclusively urban at the turn of the century. As the first to articulate a comprehensive theory of skyscraper expression, which, by and large, the profession adopted, Sullivan may have, ironically, hurt himself by "solving" the problem, by making it possible for any architect to do the job properly. For over thirty years after the 1890s, major high-rise buildings did, in fact, incorporate his notions on soaring verticality, even Gothic behemoths like the New

York Woolworth and the Chicago Tribune towers. Traditionalists may have ignored most of Sullivan's other important teachings, but most major architects accepted his ideas on facade organization. With nothing new to offer about skyscrapers while sticking doggedly to increasingly unpopular ornamental notions, Sullivan's commissions after 1908 with only one exception were all for small cities and towns that did not erect tall buildings and had not yet accepted the simpler new look. Newspapers in almost every place he worked described him as if he were still the Louis Sullivan of the mid-1890s, America's foremost architect at the forefront of design. The rural heartland kept the faith precisely because it did not know that Sullivan's once radical ideas had become part of the cultural mainstream.

His genius never failed him. It was not for loss of ability that he got fewer jobs. Sullivan fell from favor because of his assault on the establishment, his lack of institutional support, his standoffish personality, his refusal to compromise, his ill-deserved reputation as an impractical artist, his reluctance to do houses, and because of changing attitudes toward ornament. There was also a bitter irony here: as a proven commercial architect he was not hired for dwellings, and as an established artist and theoretician, he was considered too hightoned for commercial buildings. The result was further withdrawal into himself, so deeply at times that even when he got work, he seemed unable to do it. All these things and probably more in some mysterious combination account for his decline. Neither neoclassicism nor Adler's departure per se was a major factor, although they certainly did not help. The second irony is that Louis Sullivan knew all this very well.

Chapter XIII

LIVING IN HELL 1910-24

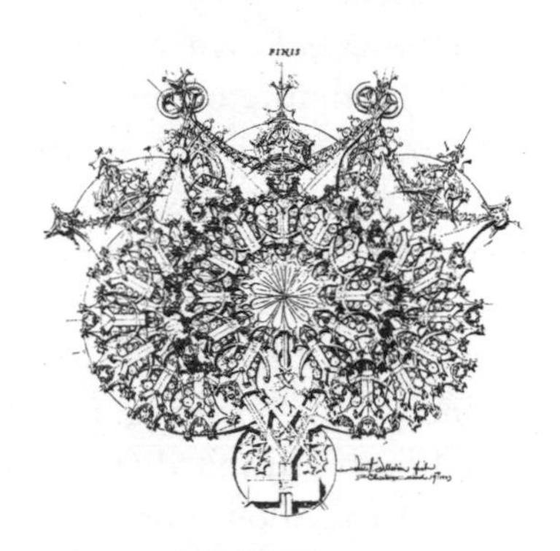

ON JANUARY 4, 1910, Louis Sullivan wrote an extraordinary letter of self-analysis to his friend Carl Bennett, vice-president of the Owatonna, Minnesota, bank. Last November's auction "was a slaughter," he acknowledged. Expecting to realize $2500 from the sale, he came away with a mere $1100, one thousand of which he devoted to Margaret, even though she had left with Davies Edward Marshall for a new life in New York. He had paid her transportation, her life insurance premium through May, and sent the balance to her Manhattan bank. "She has much native talent, as yet untrained and undisciplined. . . . I have made the [financial] sacrifice because I believe in [its] genuineness . . . hop[ing] that the seriousness of the situation will arouse in her the necessary persistence and industry. It is her one chance." The money would keep her "safe for 5 months" and with New York friends she would not be lonely. "So I won't have to worry about her for some time, and I am glad to be left alone to work out my own destiny and start life all over again if I can."

What a telling confession! He was glad to be rid of his wife! Glad to be alone and to start all over again! But what a way to do it: to Bennett, he revealed that insomnia, nervous dyspepsia (indigestion, nausea), poverty, worry, the auction, and the loss of George Elmslie had driven him as if on a whirlwind "to the very verge of insanity or suicide, or nervous collapse." Just as he was at his worst, who should appear in town but "my dear friend Dr. Geo[rge Dute] Arndt [1865–1947] of Mount Vernon, Ohio. . . . He induced me to go home with him. . . . Upon our arrival in [December 1909] I was practically all in. After 3 days of intense suffering, mental, moral and physical, I began to mend and my progress was wonderfully rapid. At the end of 2½ weeks I was practically normal, my courage, strength of nerve body and brain had returned."

Arndt created an atmosphere of love, affection, and mutual congeniality, Sullivan reported. A complete physical examination revealed that he was "absolutely sound, not a sign of organic lesion or degeneration. That my trouble was intestinal putrefication, developing toxins which were disturbing every function in my body. That all that was necessary [was] to eliminate these toxins, which he proceeded to do in his simply scientific and artistic way." Sullivan and Arndt had apparently met in 1908 or 1909, possibly at the Society of Philistines organized by Elbert Hubbard (1856-1915), founder of the William Morris–inspired Roycrofter Press and handicraft shop in East Aurora, New York (near Buffalo), and publisher of *Philistine* and *Fra* magazines, landmarks of the American Arts and Crafts movement. How they met is not entirely clear, but they quickly became fast friends. Arndt practiced homeopathic medicine, the art of curing founded on resemblances, administering minute doses of drugs that would produce in a healthy person symptoms similar to those of the diseased. The particular drugs he prescribed for Sullivan are not known, and probably never will be, since his medical records are gone, but whatever he did seemed to help, lending a sympathetic ear perhaps most of all.

Sullivan returned from Mount Vernon, he told Bennett, "practically flat broke. . . . I am living hand to mouth, on the bounty of a few warm friends who can ill afford the small advances they have made." His financial assets were "an old master" he was trying to sell to the Art Institute for $1000, a few remaining architecture books, and two expensive watches. "Against them I am in a quicksand of petty indebtedness": unpaid bills, rent, and so forth. But "I feel a powerful sense of relief, now that I have survived the crisis. I am prepared to wipe out the past and face reconstruction in whatever it may take, provided only that it furnish an outlet for my long pent-up aggressiveness and productivity. . . . My morbidity has entirely disappeared; and the only thing I fear is a possible return of it in the form of mental depression. But I intend to fight this off for all that is in me."

He had another, more important asset, he believed: "a new outlook on life—I have at last burst the bonds of the prison of self." Heart-to-heart talks with Arndt had shown him that "my crisis, has, with varying fortunes been steadily approaching during the past 17 years [since 1892–93]." The cause of the gathering storm lay "in a flaw in my own character which I, alone, could not discover." But Arndt helped him see that his long-term unhappiness, bitterness, and misery, as well as his recent breakdown, stemmed from "none other than my persistent lack of kindly feeling toward my fellow men." What a devastating revelation this must have been! "He is right," Sullivan concluded, "and I intend to change!" The past few months had been the lowest point in Louis Sullivan's fifty-four years. But believing he had isolated the source of his problem—a personal flaw, not economic circumstances—he faced the future optimistically, eager to get on with the "20 to 30 years of hard work in me yet."[1]

And work he did—hard, at times—but not often enough to reclaim his former standing. In the five years from 1910 through 1914, he designed eleven buildings, none really major, seven of which he saw to completion. The first two in Cedar Rapids, Iowa, gave him trouble, but they were as fresh as anything he had ever done. Sullivan began the People's Savings Bank in the spring of 1909, completing his drawings and specifications by the end of the summer only to have them rejected as too expensive on December 1, the day after the auction, five days before Margaret left. With his only other project the second version of the Bradley house, and that on temporary hold while Elmslie and his Madison, Wisconsin, associates finished it off, Sullivan had ample reason for gloom. The loss of this latest job may have prompted his remark to Bennett in April 1910 that he did not want to do any more small banks. But when the clients reopened negotiations around that time, Sullivan responded with working drawings during the summer. The People's Savings Bank was ready shortly before the end of 1911.

The clients had reportedly noticed his bank at Owatonna, which one might suppose he would have reproduced as nearly as possible on the theory that "nothing succeeds like success." But the Cedar Rapids building was entirely different. "It is, so to speak, grown from its own seed," Montgomery Schuyler said, paying its author an ex-

XIII.1 *People's Savings Bank, 1909–1911.* From *Illuminating Engineer,* 1912.

traordinary tribute when he added that "a new work by Louis Sullivan is the most interesting event which can happen in the American architectural world to-day. There has been nothing like the professional interest which his works inspire since Richardson ceased to produce, a quarter of a century ago." Henry Richardson's appeal was often "selfish and practical" because architects found him easy to copy. "But Mr. Sullivan has few imitators," Schuyler claimed. "There is nothing in [his work] to steal" because "every one of his buildings is the solution of a particular problem, and the result is a highly specialized organism, which is as suitable for its own purposes as it is inapplicable to any other. . . . To go and do likewise would . . . mean to go and do something entirely different." Whereas "the commonplace architect would think that a very slight rehandling of a design already approved in one case would serve perfectly for the other," Sullivan found it impossible to repeat himself, accounting for the clear dissimilarities between the two banks. Schuyler may have put his finger on another reason for Sullivan's declining opportunities: he was simply too individualistic, too unpredictable, for many people to handle.[2]

The People's Savings Bank was a one-story rectangle, fifty by ninety feet in tapestry brick Sullivan said came "from the kiln in about fourteen colors or shades," creating the general effect "of an

XIII.2 *People's Savings Bank interior.* From *Illuminating Engineer,* 1912.

antique Oriental rug." The banking room, roughly twenty-five by fifty feet, rose into a brightly lit clerestory of the same dimensions. Teller and officer space, the vault, and the entry were tucked around the low perimeter, itself amply lit with strips of white-framed windows. Outside, the bank was remarkably simple: above the plinth a belt course of projecting bricks encircled the building at about waist height. The slightly protruding windowsills and flat cornice in terra-cotta were the only other embellishments on the lower walls. The clerestory featured ornately capitaled pilasters and medallioned ventilation stacks rising at the corners to refer to freestanding brick lampposts at curbside. Inside, the lower walls of the clerestory held murals, one depicting the relation of banking to laboring people, the others agricultural scenes typical of Iowa.

Sullivan thought the building " 'democratic,' in that the prospect is open and the offices are in plain view and easily approached," promoting a "feeling of ease, confidence, and friendship between officers, employees, and customers."[3] Schuyler concurred: traditional banks were as "hedged and guarded" as a temple of Isis. You could put your money in and get it out easily, but access to an officer—"the high priest of the temple . . . in some remote and hidden apartment"—involved penetration "only by a series of diplomatic pourparlers." But in Sullivan's scheme "whoever enters . . . can see through it from end to end and from side to side. Even the vault is thrown open to sight during business hours . . . ," enhancing the feeling "of a highly organized and highly specialized machine, in which not only provision is made for every function, but expression given to every provision."

The banking-room floor was green and white tile, the counters statuary-veined Italian marble, the grillework copperplate, the columns cast iron, and the color scheme a multitude of carefully related tints, all creating a rich, inviting atmosphere. In plan the building was the consequence of a thoughtfully developed program, and in elevation the expression of interior space. Sullivan and Schuyler agreed it was designed from inside out, as Frank Lloyd Wright would have put it, with interior space determining outside form. In its simplicity, restrained external ornament (surprising to some Sullivan watchers), its stark, crisp lines, and its uncluttered planes, the People's Bank represented the cutting edge of advanced architecture. Entirely unlike Owatonna in visual respects, it nevertheless accomplished similar practical and aesthetic objectives, remaining an exquisite if underrated landmark of early modern design.

Construction was beginning in October 1910, when Sullivan won the competition among a dozen selected firms, including Purcell & Elmslie, for another Cedar Rapids building, St. Paul's Methodist Episcopal Church, that turned out to be a unique approach to Protestant architecture. His proposal was for a rectangular brick three-story block, 42 by 164 feet, for classrooms and offices running along an alley with a semicircular three-story brick auditorium sixty-five feet in radius affixed to one side. Directly under the square bell tower, the platform and altar occupied the midpoint of the semicircle's spine. Around it was a curved aisle and seven banks containing seven hundred steeply raked seats (there were four hundred more in the gallery) rising to a curved corridor at the outside wall feeding with the aisle into four exits on the spine. There were also two semi-detached stairwells with octagonal ends just outside the front wall. The integration of the two major divisions in style and material symbolically united secular and religious functions, but their differing articulations maintained their independence. By placing a tower at the center of the structure, really at the rear of the religious portion, instead of a steeple at the front as is customary, Sullivan transformed a traditional image of community prominence into an emblem of community service. But that service appeared to be mostly secular,

XIII.3 *St. Paul's Methodist Episcopal Church, 1910–11.* From *Brickbuilder,* 1914.

architecturally speaking, because to the uninformed the church could easily seem to be something else entirely.[4]

It was not for any objection to this that Sullivan resigned in 1912, however. The building committee actually found his scheme to be "exactly fit . . . in a singularly appropriate style of architecture." When it was deemed too expensive, Sullivan modified it, but as it was still beyond the authorized funds, the committee engaged a church architect, W. C. Jones of Chicago, to scale it down even further. Sullivan quit in a huff, as well he might over a serious ethical issue, leaving Jones to change the plans to the extent that George Elmslie was brought to the rescue, although out of respect for Sullivan and his own sense of professionalism, he would not let his name be used. Thanks to Elmslie, St. Paul's Church as built remained Sullivan's in plan, outline, and dimension, but Jones's in minor detail, the attached third-story piers, for example, that Sullivan had intended to be almost free-standing.

Shortly after it opened in May 1914, *Western Architect* protested in an editorial called "A Sullivan Design That Is Not Sullivan's," arguing that "no matter how faithfully his plan and outline may have been adhered to," it was not his building. "What might have been a treasured example of that genius that has been watched with more interest, and founded a more revolutionary departure in architecture than has been known to the profession in modern times," it continued, "is but the first grade pupil's tracing of the master's hand." The general secretary of the Religious Education Association called the school building plan "the very finest, most complete and best adapted . . . I have ever seen." But *Western Architect* lamented that "the loss of an equal rendition of Sullivan's *art* [italics added] in the design is irreparable." Even sadder is that despite encomiums like this, and praise from Schuyler and others, Sullivan could not land a really substantial commission.[5]

His next two projects were for friends, and neither one was built. The Carl Bennett house was mainly designed in 1911, indicated by the February 1912 date on the final drawing. With two Cedar Rapids projects in the office at the time, Sullivan hired Homer Sailor fresh out of the Illinois Institute of Technology as Parker Berry's assistant. Like the Bradley and Babson houses, the Bennett residence sat on a high brick base and, like the first Bradley project, had a huge, cross-axial arrangement. But it was even more "formal, formidable, and non-domestic than its predecessors," writes H. Allen Brooks. Another historian, James Marston Fitch, was "astonished" by the design, claiming it bore no resemblance to anything else Sullivan ever did or to what his contemporaries were doing. The straightforward plan with excellent orientation was surprising enough. "But the sheer severity of the elevations" was totally unlike "all the lyrical flourishes he was using on his bank buildings. It certainly suggests a flare-up of creative energy in 1912 which I'd never expected,"[6] especially from a modernist perspective.

Fitch did not realize that the ground plan was related to the first Bradley project, and that the linear room grouping along the third-floor corridor was similar to the executed Babson house. Nor did he notice that the medallioned chimneys, indeed the "sheer severity of the elevations," were in the manner of People's Savings, designed at almost the same time. Sullivan's so-called "creative flare-up" was really a creative continuation from the Owatonna and Cedar Rapids banks, if not further back.

William Purcell agreed that the Bennett house "is certainly one of the most remarkable buildings that Mr. Sullivan ever conceived": a project of "great originality and vivid imaginative content . . . a tremendous work." But he also understood why the client never built it. It was, first of all, "three times the maximum" he felt he could pay and it was, secondly, "wholly lacking in any feeling for the Bennetts

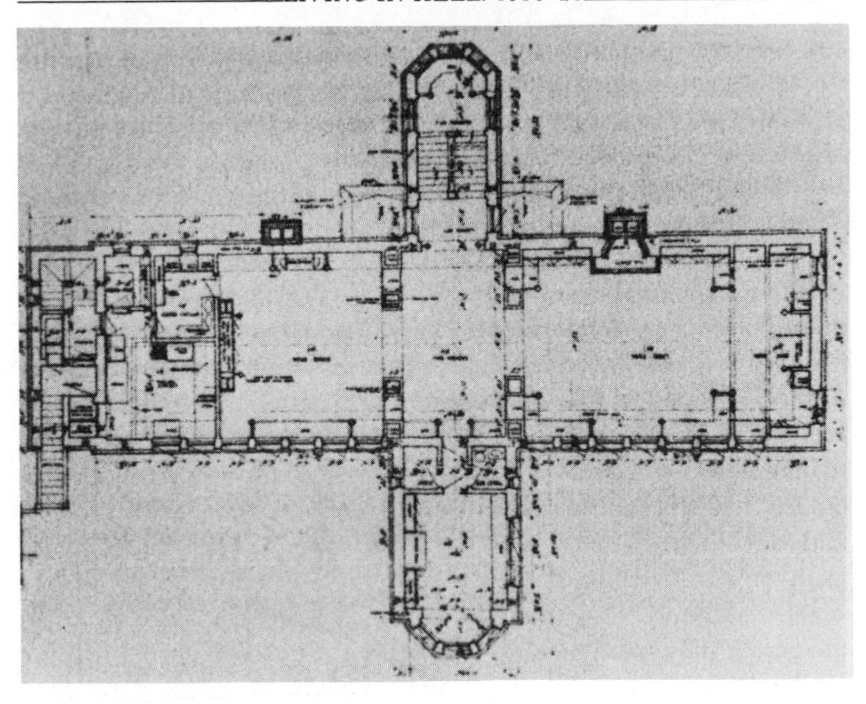

XIII.4 *Carl Bennett residence project plan, 1911.*
From Northwest Architectural Archives.

as a living family, for their relation to the community or . . . of the building to its site in a farmer's village." Elmslie thought it rather like a club suitable for a city lot. "Mr. Sullivan simply had no concept whatever of American family life." The living room was cut off in fact and in spirit from the garden, the great windows—though decoratively beautiful—were a barrier between residents and their world, and the major spaces called for trained servants and a formal social life far beyond the clients' preferences. Although Bennett shelved the house project, he hired Sullivan in September 1913 to landscape his property, but the design was not carried out.[7] During the interval Sullivan drew a garage for his friend Dr. Arndt in Mount Vernon, possibly in return for services rendered, but that, too, was never executed.

Nineteen thirteen was a moderately busy year, at least compared with the way things had been going lately, with four new projects on the boards. The first was an unbuilt museum, published in the Chicago Architectural Club catalogue that year, a surprisingly Beaux-Arts proposal, perfectly symmetrical with a low colonnade entry on the sidewalk underneath an arched, pilastered upper facade: very monumental. A projecting gallery pinned to the plainer flanking bays by huge winged birds just below a classical pediment made it an unusually traditional building for Sullivan.[8]

His plans for Henry C. Adams's Land and Loan Office Building in Algona, Iowa, were accepted in March 1913, eleven months before it opened. Contrary to general belief, it was not a bank, although "the inside is arranged in bank style," a local observer noted, "and may develop into a bank ere long." It was a small corner structure, approximately twenty by seventy feet in one high commercial story dressed in tapestry brick turning into a diapered pattern just below the incised terra-cotta coping flush with the roof. Nine deeply inset, double casement windows separated by wooden friezes from green opalescent leaded glass above were strung down the long elevation and edged in bright white paint, their dividing columns capped with flush terra-cotta capitals, and their sloping continuous sill projecting slightly. Around the corner the entrance was even more recessed, the actual door tucked to the left behind a head-high wall leaping at the opening into flower planters. Overhead, large clerestories flooded the interior with light, supplemented by smaller windows adjacent to the door. The entire entry ensemble outlined in brick courses inset at various depths to form a rich embracing molding was an exceptionally pleasing composition. After passing through a small vestibule, customers entered an open public space flowing past a

XIII.5 *Henry C. Adams Building, 1913.* From *Architectural Record,* 1916.

XIII.6 *Merchants' National Bank, 1913–14.* Photo by Robert Twombly.

huge vault to a work room and lavatories. "A famous Chicago architect named Sullivan," the *Algona Courier* declared, has given us a building "the like of which we never saw before." No "expense was spared to make the offices surpass all others." *The Architectural Record* thought enough of it to let its illustrations speak for themselves. But like other Sullivan buildings, it said, it "can stand the most severe analysis from a structural and practical standpoint, and yet reveal nothing commonplace." The Adams Building was, in fact, a beautiful little gem, hidden away in a tiny prairie town.[9]

As was his next, the much more famous Merchants' National Bank in Grinnell, Iowa. Sullivan finished preliminary planning in November 1913, dated his blueprints in January and February, and saw the building open New Year's Day, 1915. Although slightly wider and taller with spikey little crests atop the terra-cotta coping, the Grinnell bank resembled the Algona Land Office in its materials and side elevation. The most obvious difference was the incredible burst of terra-cotta ornament surrounding the stained-glass oculus over the entrance. At least eight layers of diamond, circular, and square banding, infilled with geometric and organic ornament in brown and green, combined to form a gigantic medallion that has since become a favorite of architectural photographers. The entry has been criticized as too sumptuous for an otherwise austere brick wall and too big for such a small edifice. One authority suggests that Sullivan meant his interlocking forms to represent the mechanisms of a clock or a vault door, elevating time and money—two ready images for banking—to the level of art. The entrance, Kenneth Severns adds, shifting the metaphor slightly, "was designed as a monumental keyhole which unlocked the meaning of the 'jewel box,' Sullivan's own words for his bank buildings."[10] As an isolated fragment, like the 1891 Golden Doorway, it was staggeringly beautiful, a masterpiece of decorative art. But, unlike its predecessor, its tremendous power detached it from the building, throwing the overall composition into a kind of rivalry between detail and mass.

The bank itself was exquisite, inside and out, but did not break new ground in plan or services. Its exterior detail was probably innovation enough. While preparing an *Architectural Record* essay on Sullivan's recent banks including Grinnell, A. N. Rebori interviewed his subject, leaving behind a valuable account of the way he designed, well worth quoting at length. Impressed by the Owatonna bank, the Grinnell directors had invited Sullivan to town to study their requirements firsthand:

> After meeting the committee he set about the customary task of learning the needs of the proposed building . . . in the most detailed manner possible. Judging by the sketches and notes which were made with the aid of an ordinary desk rule on sheets of common yellow paper acquired at a near-by apothecary shop, not a single part of the machinery that was to make up this bank . . . was overlooked. Here we find not only the allotted space to the various departments, but the different desks, cages, and all minor details worked out in an exact scale. For three whole days he talked and drew, rubbing out as changes were made, fitting and adjusting to the satisfaction of all. The dimensions are clearly marked on these original drawings in plan, section and elevation, leaving no doubt as to the exact layout of the building. I asked Mr. Sullivan how it happened that his preliminary sketches were worked out in such a definite manner, and he answered quite simply that "those were the requirements as given, and it only remained to jot them down on paper," which he did.

These notes and preliminary sketches, Rebori added, somewhat in awe, "are the most exquisite bits of architectural memoranda that it has ever been my pleasure to see":

> Every possible element that was to play a part in the future project was fully analyzed and put into architectural form in plan, section and elevation, and what was more, this was all done in a little office adjoining the bank president's room in the old building . . . in full view of and with the aid of the building committee. Before leaving the place, the owner knew from these sketches exactly what his building was going to look like, from the arrangement of the smallest detail to its largest mass, all of which received his approval.[11]

If this account does nothing else, it demonstrates Sullivan's exceptional talents, the persistence of his Ecole des Beaux-Arts training, and his ability to work congenially with sympathetic clients. Unable to land substantial commercial commissions, he was now actively seeking banks. But if Sullivan hoped Rebori's essay would allay certain doubts, making him acceptable to more affluent clients, he was rudely disappointed.

The John D. Van Allen & Sons Dry Goods Store in Clinton, Iowa, was begun late in 1913 and finished early in 1915. Elements of its four brick stories on a corner came from earlier work, but the design is nonetheless unique. Its steel frame was apparent from thin columns, but perhaps because the store was wider than it was high, Sullivan articulated it horizontally by taking sills and window-top ornament clear across the facade around the corners, suggesting Schlesinger & Mayer, but less successfully. There were also thin colonnaded mullions like those as far back as the Wirt Dexter building (1887) projected forward of the wall plane, rising gratuitously—since they had no structural meaning—from elaborate vivid green corbels at the second story to huge terra-cotta bursts of the same color in the attic. Although they resembled their counterparts at the Gage Building, the mullions and ornament seem unnecessary, unless like the Grinnell entry they were uncontrollable outbursts of femininity, as previously discussed, or as H. Allen Brooks suggests, they were intended to turn the six bays into two superbays with flanking shoulders as a way of making the store more monumental. The facade

XIII.7 *Van Allen Store, 1913–15.* Iowa State Historical Society.

would have been better without the heavy ornament, and its potential crispness even sharper without horizontal articulation. Still, the Van Allen Store was obviously Louis Sullivan's, no one else's, and therefore noteworthy even if it did not add much luster to his name.[12]

Three more commissions followed in 1914 during construction on the Grinnell and Clinton buildings. A bank project in Enid, Oklahoma, was not carried out, and little information has survived about it. At $14,600, the Purdue State Bank in West Lafayette, Indiana, was one of his smallest jobs. Plans were accepted in January 1914, a year before it opened on the following New Year's Day. Its triangular form, dictated by a sloping pie-shaped lot at an oddly joined intersection, made the design somewhat tricky, but not for "one of the most noted bank architects in the United States," said the Lafayette paper. Sullivan returned to tapestry brick, incorporating the strong window rows from Algona and Grinnell on the long elevations.

Terra-cotta trim in bright green accented with yellow makes even this tiny building sparkle, although in most respects it was not an opportunity to do anything memorable. His fee of less than $1500 barely covered expenses, but he was grateful to get it.[13]

Like the Purdue State Bank, the $30,000 Home Building Association in Newark, Ohio, has not received much attention, nor should it, given its scale and importance in Sullivan's *oeuvre.* But on its courthouse square, it puts its commonplace neighbors to shame. Its three stories—one for the bank, the upper two for offices—were this time handled in gray terra-cotta, outlined along the edges and around the familiar large side windows with ornamental borders, actually the border-within-a-border arrangement that had long been one of his trademarks. Its color accents were again particularly vivid: on the side, a panel bearing the company's name was executed in gold lettering on bright green tile, while in front a much more elaborate sign put the legend against a background of blue, green, red, brown, and yellow—a ceramic rainbow assembled almost primitively by a local artisan to acknowledge community traditions. Stencils on upstairs

XIII.8 *Purdue State Bank, 1914, with modern sign.* Photo by Robert Twombly.

walls and ceilings as well as wooden venetian blinds cleanly guided to sills in molding channels indicate Sullivan's persistent devotion to detail. The "man who has a national reputation for building," the local paper said, completed preliminary plans in July 1914 and presided over construction until it opened the next spring.[14]

This flurry of activity, seven projects in 1913–14, was the largest since his eight in 1901–1902. In the ten years between, Sullivan had drawn only seventeen buildings, two of them speculative—without client commitments—six others remaining unconstructed. Of twenty-four projects from 1903 through 1914, he erected fourteen, slightly more than one a year on average. And as time passed, on average, his fees got smaller. Yet with the exception of tiny, out-of-the-way Purdue State Bank, every one got national press coverage. *The Record* preferred his Babson house to Wright's Coonley residence when it compared them in October 1911, and *Western Architect* agreed the following month. In *Architecture and Building* a year later, Theodore Starrett called him the only American architect of note. "Genuine Sullivan buildings are beginning to be differentiated from the spurious [copies]," he noted, "and Sullivan's fame is marching on." Next September F. W. Fitzpatrick wrote that the " 'Sullivan School' is growing," while in October 1913 *Western Architect* said "that he has been the recognized leader in the effort of the best and brightest among the profession to 'draw the thing as he sees it for the God of things as they are.' " "Form follows function" and "progress should go before precedent," it concluded, "are now winning popular acceptance."[15] *The Record* reviewed almost every bank and, whether it was Montgomery Schuyler, his successor, A. N. Rebori, or someone else reporting, applauded each one.

The architect received other kinds of encomiums. In 1915 he accepted an invitation from the Australian government to jury an international competition for buildings, at Canberra, which was never held because of World War I. Claude Bragdon extolled him at the Art Institute that year, later maintaining that, sitting in the audience, Sullivan absorbed his remarks like "balm to his bruised spirit." Painter Lawton Parker offered to contribute Sullivan's portrait, the only one of a living architect, to a new "Hall of Fame" at AIA's Illinois Chapter, where he spoke himself when the late Solon S. Beman's portrait was presented in June 1915, returning a year later to pay handsome tribute to Dankmar Adler. Harriet Monroe, meanwhile, published a portion of his manuscript "Democracy, a Man-Search!"

XIII.9 *Home Building Association, 1914, with modern corner entry.*
Photo by Robert Twombly.

under the title "Wherefore the Poet?" "What good does he do?" this poet, Sullivan asked, no doubt speaking autobiographically. He had no answer. In a February 1916 editorial, *Western Architect* said his work was an "inspiration" to "the younger men of his profession," and three months later *The Record* released Rebori's article on the banks that praised him in thirty pages as it praised few others before or since.[16]

But nothing seemed to do any good, to be any help to his sagging career. No matter how carefully critics like Rebori explained the benefits clients might expect from hiring Sullivan, commissions got fewer and further between. The more he was cited for innovation and leadership, the less he was wanted. Perhaps that was part of the problem: perhaps innovation and leadership were not high priorities for people in the second decade of the twentieth century. In 1915 Sullivan got no new work at all, and in 1916 his two projects were not constructed. One of them, together with an Ohio bank he designed in 1917, sheds additional light on his problem.

Because of the National Farmers' Bank and his friendship with

Carl Bennett, he was invited to submit a proposal to the Owatonna, Minnesota, school district. The building he drew with Parker Berry's help was quite remarkable, another indication of his versatility and continuing creativity. The rendering shows an L-shaped, two-story structure of varying heights in a white material, amply windowed. A scattering of column-top ornament on the wing was strong, to be sure, but otherwise the high school was surprisingly similar to the West Coast work of Irving Gill (1870–1936), who had apprenticed with Adler & Sullivan briefly, and to early International Style sallies in the next decade. It was, in other words, a wonderfully fresh and prophetic proposal entirely outside his bank or any other genre. Twenty architects applied for the job, and when the submissions were reduced to four, Sullivan and Berry were invited to Owatonna for an interview with school authorities on April 3, 1917. That was when the trouble began.

XIII.10 *Owatonna High School project, 1916.*
From Homer Sailor Collection.

When Carl Bennett's brother Guy, president of the Owatonna School Board, polled the seven members, he found them lined up four to three in favor of Sullivan. The vote to hire him should have been a mere formality. But before it took place Sullivan got into a dispute with board member F. F. Joestling over some unrelated matter, causing him to throw his support to a local architect. Sullivan and Berry returned to Chicago without the job. With just one other project under way at the time, Berry and Homer Sailor soon quit, leaving only Adolph O. Budina, a recently hired draftsman, to assist in the office. Even though the Owatonna high school would have meant a good deal financially and in other ways, Sullivan let it get away presumably because of his temper and ego.[17]

Plans for a second-story addition to the handsome Adams Building in Algona, Iowa, dated January 16, 1917, were never executed. Margaret got her divorce shortly before that, and in July married Marshall in London, where he operated a news agency. If the information distressed Sullivan further, he did not resolve to curb his stubbornness, as illustrated by his behavior on his only other project, the People's Savings and Loan Association Building in Sidney, Ohio, opened early in 1918. Hired because the bank secretary, L. M. Studevant, heard Sullivan's name everywhere during a 1914 European holiday, he arrived in Sidney, as he had in Grinnell, prepared to give the commission his minutest attention. He "retired to the opposite corner" from the building site, remembered president W. H. Wagner, and

> sat on a curbstone for the better part of two whole days, smoking innumerable cigarettes [a new habit]. Then at the end of that time, he announced to the directors that the design was made—in his head. He proceeded to rapidly draw a sketch for them, and announced an estimate of the cost. One of the directors was somewhat disturbed by the unfamiliarity of the style, and suggested that he rather fancied some classic columns and pilasters for the facade. Sullivan very brusquely rolled up his sketch and started to depart, saying that the directors could get a thousand architects to design a classic bank but only one to get this kind of bank, and that as far as he was concerned it was one or the other.

Despite a desperate financial situation, he was prepared to throw away the job over a matter of principle. But when the directors placated Sullivan and approved the drawing, he returned to Chicago, eventually sending back "meticulously prepared plans," specifying in part:

> glazed center kiln fired brick; polished and crystal plate glass; black Carrara and polished plate mirrors; mosaic tiles selected to create a harmonious effect without patches of color; iron castings free of all blow holes and defects; no joints, screw, bolt or rivet heads exposed in the bronze; skylights to be storm-proof,

> waterproof and air-tight; millwork shall be quarter-sawed white oak of rich grain and figure, matched side-wise and end to end, entirely free from defects and kiln dried; marble shall be selected gray pink Tennessee and selected Vermont Verde-antique of extra rich figure.[18]

The building bore a strong family resemblance, of course, to his other banks, especially Owatonna, with its two-story business room and one floor "tail" for offices. The tapestry brick walls sat on a greenish marble base embellished by a cornice, a belt course, heavy window framing, and decorative "brooches" in terra-cotta. The bright green side panel bearing the bank's name and its blue counterpart in front with "Thrift" emblazoned in bold lettering added just enough color for the edifice to stand out gloriously on its pedestrian corner site. Reviewer Thomas Tallmadge had only glowing words for it in 1918, echoed seventeen years later by biographer Hugh Morrison, who found it "the finest of all the bank buildings designed by Sullivan, and one of the outstanding works of his whole career."[19] Clearly, the master still had the touch.

The Sidney bank is a good example of Sullivan's attention to climate control. Double-glazing and double-thickness walls separated by dead space formed an almost airtight envelope, allowing deployment of a "vapor modulation" heating and ventilating system sustained by a mere four ounces of pressure. Heat came directly from radiators with modulation valves, ventilation from outdoors through a fresh-air shaft connected to preheating coils. The partly warmed air passed through a washer, a second set of coils to raise it to the desired temperature, and was then fan-forced through ducts to various distribution points. Fifty percent of the vitiated air in the main room was recirculated through registers, other ducts, and a main trunk line to the intake chamber, where it was washed and warmed with incoming air. This early system of "air conditioning" has proven to be economical, noiseless, and dust-free, delivering humidity-controlled temperatures ten to fifteen degrees cooler than the summer heat. Posts at the corners of the banking space gathered the vitiated air through registers, while subdividing the room and supporting flower urns, a single-element multiple function for which architects like Wright are often cited, but not usually Sullivan.

People's Savings and Loan was as beautiful inside as out. Sullivan's attention to detail and his finely honed sensitivity to color have

XIII.11 *People's Savings and Loan Association, 1917.*
Photo by Robert Twombly.

XIII.12 *People's Savings and Loan Association facade detail, 1917.*
Photo by Robert Twombly.

already been noted. But this and other banks also reveal his ability to create superbly pleasing and functional interior spaces that can be "read" outside, that were, in other words, designed "from inside out," as he said of his Cedar Rapids building, allowing internal requisites to determine exterior form. Sullivan's best bank facades carried multiple meanings as well; they were legible on several levels.

Their dignified forms elevated banking to the highest standards of gentility in a modern style that was quickly perceived to be appropriate. They strengthened the finest community traditions with new emblems of civic pride. And they preserved the scale of their environments, while at the same time improving the quality of Main Street. Their meticulous detailing, exuberant materials, and exquisite ornament, on the other hand, represented decoration and craftsmanship of the highest level, becoming mini-museums of small town artisan skill. Sullivan's banks can be read as monumentally democratic endorsements of mainstream American life. As macro- and micro-images of architectural and social values, they were as visually successful as they were intellectually complex.

Exemplary as these structures were, Sullivan did so little work he literally could not pay the rent. "I am in excellent health," he wrote to Adolph Budina, no longer working for him in the summer of 1917, "but the bottom has dropped out" of my business affairs. In a desperate effort to find employment, he had opened negotiations with a "party" who knew banking, a salesman to "commercialize" his talents and reputation. If he "is the man he seems to be, he is the man I have been looking for for years, but have never found to my satisfaction." The arrangement did not work out, for at the end of September, he told Budina about his "housecleaning." He was getting rid of old and useless stuff "in case I have to move." On the last day of 1917, he again reported that "the bottom has dropped out—the future is blank." He was looking for a civil service job with the federal government. In February 1918, as the Sidney bank was nearing completion with nothing else in sight, unable to afford his office any longer, Sullivan left the Auditorium for four-room Suite 21 at 431 South Wabash Avenue, second floor front. After twenty-eight years in his beloved tower office, his last touchstone with the good days, he was forced out, certainly amidst much pain.[20]

Shortly afterward he began a lengthy correspondence with Frank Lloyd Wright, a sad and desperate correspondence sometimes, chronicling real misery.[21] "I am not ill, Frank, and have not been recently," he wrote on April 1. "I simply have to 'lay to' every once in a while, from sheer exhaustion due to too much corroding anxiety, and repair my strength as best I can. My worry is of course primarily a money worry, but it is truly awful to one of my nature. With the future blank I am surely living in hell. To think that I should come to this at 61." After describing his affection for landscape architect Jens

Jensen, he went on: "I have much to tell you that I cannot write. . . . I am desperately in need of the right kind of companionship. No doubt you understand." He thanked Wright for the check he had sent. On May 18, 1918, he was still in an awful state of mind, having received "*peremptory* notice" for the month's rent at his new office—fifty dollars he did not have—as well as a warning from his Hotel Warner landlord, whom he had promised to pay the next time Wright came to town.

"Now my dear Frank," he continued, "I fancy you have troubles of your own and I hate to butt in, but I am terribly up in the air and I want to find out where I am." His efforts to raise money had been "most disappointing"; he was trying to sell off his last possessions "but there is still a lot of valuable stuff remaining." Please wire me a night letter on receipt of this (with some money, he did not say, but implied) at the Cliff Dwellers—a writers' club that gave him free space—"as I don't know what these people here [at the South Wabash Avenue office] may do. I hate to write in a panicky tone but I can't help it. It is hell!" In a postscript he added that since his attempts to land a postal department job had failed, he was now trying to get something in the federal government's Construction Division.

Wright sent a check immediately, but it was not enough. "This morning I found my office door locked against me," he wrote on May 21, "followed by a demand for the *cash.* My plan is to raise the other half somehow, pay the rent and *get out* before the 1st." Two days later he revealed to Wright that George Dean had covered the rest of his rent ("I was locked out a second time") but that he still planned to leave by June 1. William Gates of the American Terra Cotta Company gave him enough to put twenty dollars on account at the Warner and pay the telephone and towel bills, "thus cleaning up the office score." He felt a little better without these burdens, apologized for compounding Wright's financial problems, noted that the Cliff Dwellers was now his headquarters and mailing address, but regretted he had no place to store "my stuff." On the last day of May, his "stuff went to [a] warehouse and I turned over my office key. This gives me a sense of relief—and I am foot-loose and ready to jump at whatever my offer: U.S. East-California-Japan [with Wright, he hoped, to work on the Imperial Hotel]-Timbuctoo-anywhere." His health was good and he was not downhearted, but he had heard nothing from Washington about a job.

On June 10, 1918, Sullivan again raised the issue of Japan: "Not having any notion as to what your plans may be I can only trust that my query is not indiscreet." He had resurrected *Kindergarten Chats* because Claude Bragdon thought he might get it published. "I have not found much to change so far. It's good stuff today and I should like to see it in book form." In July he wrote Harriet Monroe that Bragdon had arranged with his own publisher, Alfred A. Knopf, to turn *Chats* into a book if a guaranty fund of $500 to cover expenses could be raised by selling advanced "subscriptions" at three dollars a copy. Would you "send me names and addresses of your friends and acquaintances to whom you believe such a work would make its appeal"?[22] This "skirmish with Knopf the publisher over the K.C.s," he called it in a letter to Wright a week later, gave him the incentive to turn a revised manuscript over to George Dean's secretary on October 6 for typing in her spare time.

Early in November Sullivan received another check from Wright in Japan which "positively paralyzed me, for I was at the very end of my string." With hopes of a bank-remodeling in Manistique, Michigan, still up in the air, he continued to rely on handouts from friends "who have stood by me pretty well, and I can't blame them if they are getting a little poorer every day." The premature death of Parker Berry on December 16 at the age of thirty must certainly have distressed him, but in a letter three days later, he was full of good news: Frank Werner had painted his three-quarter-length portrait; *Kindergarten Chats* had been typed, corrected, bound, and forwarded to Bragdon for Knopf's consideration; and the Michigan bank was still interested. On January 20, 1919, he could happily report that the "remodeling job at Manistique" had at last come through ten days ago. "It doesn't run heavily into money, but will keep the wolf away for a couple of months." He did not mention his other ray of hope: Viennese architect Rudolph Schindler (1887–1953), who three years after his arrival in America entered Wright's office, in 1918, to supervise his California projects during work on the Imperial Hotel, invited Sullivan to dinner at Wright's former Oak Park home, where they discussed a European edition of *Kindergarten Chats.*[23] Sullivan was pleased and excited.

In 1919 he designed another "gem . . . on his chain of brilliants," according to Thomas Tallmadge in *Western Architect,*[24] his final bank commission, the Farmers' and Merchants' in Columbus, Wisconsin. Though different from all the others, the family look was again apparent. The front portal from Sidney was reduced—the new building was smaller—but inset more deeply with a series of concentric arches in brick and ornamented terra-cotta. The side windows were this time expressed as five arches along the lines of his original Elmslie-altered concept for Owatonna, but were not carried into the one-story commercial "tail." Tapestry brick in browns and golden yellows was embellished with mottled green terra-cotta and a polished slab of verde antique marble forming a huge lintel above the entry. The lunette overhead was divided into nine vertical panels of colored glass. Heraldic lions above the door and window, an eagle riding on the cornice, and a slightly battered side wall were new for Sullivan's banks, and did not necessarily add to its clarity. Inside, the long, narrow room—unlike the others—had a dropped ceiling (for tellers' cages) along one wall only, but in several respects was like the Sidney and Grinnell solutions.

Of interest at Columbus were Sullivan's relations with president J. R. Wheeler and his wife, who had discovered him by seeing another of his banks they thought to be like Wright's work, which they admired.[25] With Wright away in Japan, the Wheelers invited Sulli-

XIII.13 *Farmers' and Merchants' Bank, 1919.* Photo by Robert Twombly.

van to their home for a couple of days when he quickly produced preliminary drawings that scared the banker "to death," he remembered. Here he was, a conservative man in a conservative profession "being asked to build a building that looked flamboyantly radical. And I was sure that it would terrify the natives." But Mrs. Wheeler "smoothed my feathers and talked me into going ahead." Knowing Wright's work fairly well and having studied his boyhood Froebelian kindergarten system, she convinced her husband that with Wright away, his master was their only choice.

With that settled, "Sullivan came to Columbus often during construction, and always stayed with us. My admiration for him, and then my liking for him," Wheeler recalled years later, "grew continually stronger." Knowing he could only afford Sullivan because he had fallen on bad days, the banker nevertheless admired his pride and mental independence. In spite of worries about cost, little was changed from the first drawings. A skylight was eliminated, along with large terra-cotta lions on either side of the public writing desk that Wheeler feared might intimidate "our customers . . . [in] their milking clothes," but he later regretted omitting these details. Lingering after breakfast, Sullivan sometimes waxed philosophic with Mrs. Wheeler, who once suggested his ideas were wasted on one who could not fully understand them. "No," he said, "no, I am a gardener. I recognize good ground." He responded to sympathetic companionship, but he never lost his arrogance. When Wheeler asked him if such an original building might not be copied, Sullivan replied simply that "it can't be." And when at one point he thought the project might bankrupt him, the architect turned and said, "Just remember: you will have the only Louis Sullivan bank in the state of Wisconsin." Wheeler thought all this shocking, but in retrospect had to agree that the egotism was entirely justified.

Wheeler hoped that if his bank was a big success, it would generate more work for his architect. But he was sadly disappointed. Sullivan landed only five jobs from 1915 through 1919, of which the Columbus, Sidney, and the Manistique remodeling commissions were eventually completed. After 1919 things got even worse. But he had enough money from Columbus to be surprised by Wright's Christmas check enclosed in a letter from Schindler. "I was not in the least looking for anything of the sort," he told his benefactor, "but it enabled me to do some things for others and for myself that otherwise I could not have done. It certainly was a token of affection on your part which I shall ever cherish." There was other good news that Christmas season: the possibility of a $125,000 chapel at St. John's Military Academy in Delafield, Wisconsin, a library at De Kalb, Illinois, and other bank prospects he was not actively pursuing "until conditions become more settled." He did not explain what that meant. He still wanted to publish "Democracy," and was deeply upset by the death on December 10 of George Dean, "a staunch friend," who helped "pull me through that nightmare year" of 1918.

His little bit of money did not last long and none of the hoped-for commissions came through. He had an office again, at 1808 Prairie Avenue, far south of commercial downtown, but while working on the Manistique bank early in 1920 could not afford proper assistants, settling in the end on two sophomores from the Armour Institute of Technology. The remodeling was far beneath his dignity, a kind of "drudgery," he told Wright. The students thought it a "pleasant novelty," but it was "hell for me." At the end of 1920, his only work was a pedestal for Leonard Crunelle's statue of Governor John Palmer, dedicated in November 1923 in the state capital park in Springfield, Illinois. Its bronze top and sloping granite base with simple ornament at either end were handsome enough, but it was a very small job that could have been done in half a day.[26] He may have accepted it as a favor to Crunelle, but he certainly earned very little from it. As it turned out, there were no prospects for publishing *Kindergarten Chats* in Europe, much to its author's disappointment. And to make matters worse, he also learned that the Austrian architect Adolph Loos (1870–1933), who had been inspired by Sullivan during his 1890s sojourn in America, had decided not to move his Free School of Architecture from Vienna to Paris and consequently not to invite him to be its head, as he had contemplated earlier in the year.[27]

Through it all, praise kept pouring in. Editor Robert Craik McLean wrote in the April 1921 *Western Architect*, which seemed to have taken up Sullivan's cause, that he had "accomplished more than the mere production of things. . . . He has made a younger generation of architects *think*." At its thirty-third annual exhibition a year later, the Chicago Architectural Club gave him an entire wall: "not in years has so considerable a representation of [his] work . . . been brought together," ranging from a painting of the Golden Doorway through illustrations of his skyscrapers to drawings of recent banks. Robert Spencer, who was largely responsible for the exhibition, sold it with Sullivan's consent to the Art Institute. There was critical acclaim for the Columbus bank in July 1920, and on August 3, in a letter to *Western Architect* from Tulsa, young Bruce Goff (1904–1982) wrote of his admiration. The September 1920 issue of the American Terra Cotta Company's *Common Clay* ran Sullivan's portrait plus photos of Farmers' and Merchants'.[28] Some people thought of him as an involuntarily retired elder statesman; others did what they could to keep his name before the public. So he got press coverage, but no work.

In March 1921 he wrote to Schindler that "the architectural situation here, resembles a corpse. . . . There may be a future, but there is no present." By August it was even worse. "Am in trouble," he cabled Wright at the Imperial Hotel. "What can you do in the shortest time?" "The nervous strain has become unbearable," he added in a letter the same day, regretting "we had so little time together here: for there are few people I like or respect sufficiently to care about their personal doings, or esteem enough to take it for granted they have any real object in life." Without knowing it he had restated the analysis given him by Arndt in 1909 when he resolved to change his life. Apparently he had not. Four days later, on the twenty-third of August, he wrote to Wright again: "If you have any money to spare, now is the urgent time to let me have some. . . . I am in a very serious situation: indeed it is now a sheer matter of food and shelter." He clung to the hope of bank prospects in Iowa and Georgia, but "the immediate problem is to keep on earth." Wright authorized Schindler to send $200 within ten days. When the money did not arrive by September 8, Sullivan prodded: "This has been a terrible summer to get through," he reminded Schindler, emphasizing the urgency of his situation a few hours later in a second letter: "In view of the unpleasant fact that every day counts critically now, I suggest and urge that when the money becomes available you have it transmitted to me *by wire.* This will save four days' time."

After Schindler informed him on the thirteenth that nothing had come, Sullivan replied he would "eagerly await further news," even though he had found a small piece of work he could turn out in a few days. "The proceeds will help some, but not much—the rat holes are multiplying." The money arrived on September 27. "Thank you most sincerely for your kindness," he wrote, asking how "Frank is getting on in Japan. . . . I am writing to him by this mail: I simply can't afford to cable."

XIII.14 *Krause Music Store facade, 1922.*

The small piece of work may have been a memorial never built for Mrs. Arthur J. Eddy in a Flint, Michigan, cemetery. It could have been his ornamental platform for a potbellied stove Frederick Wagoner of the American Terra Cotta Company said was designed around this time for a hardware firm. Or it might have been Sullivan's last architectural project, the facade for the Krause Music Store and residence on Lincoln Avenue in Chicago, although the preliminary drawings were dated months earlier, in January and February 1921. In any event, the Krause commission belonged to William C. Presto, a former draftsman for George C. Nimmons, who had sent him to assist Sullivan on the Columbus, Wisconsin, bank. Presto did the plans but asked Sullivan to produce an elevation for the gray terra-cotta facade that came in at $3770. The recessed entry featured an enormous plate-glass piano display window flanked by doors on either side, one to the shop, the other for stairs to the second-floor living quarters. A huge leafy piece of ornament was connected by a protruding pilaster in the center of four upstairs windows to a geometric crest around the letter *K* rising beyond the flat cornice. The color and some details recalled the Home Building Association in Newark, Ohio, eight years before. The feeling about this facade is that while far from Sullivan's finest it is still much more spirited than what most other architects could do.[29]

The store was erected in 1922, when Sullivan began two major projects, both of which turned out happily, for a change. During his search for work he had made amends with the American Institute of Architects, of which he was no longer a member, but from lack of funds, as everyone knew, not from continued ideological opposition. Editor Charles H. Whitaker of AIA's *Journal* approached him toward the end of 1921 to do book reviews, agreeing to read the manuscript of *Kindergarten Chats* with an eye toward publication. Since Sullivan would not consider books he thought unworthy, in the end he never reviewed anything. When Whitaker proposed the alternative of articles on any subject he wanted, Sullivan was lukewarm: he needed larger projects, he said, something he could get his teeth into, like a long thesis he might develop at length. Early in January 1922, A. N. Rebori suggested Sullivan write his autobiography. At first he resisted the idea, but he later got a "flash," and on January 14 told Whitaker what he had in mind:

> Such an autobiography might prove, or be made, an extremely effective medium, in which to carry the vague beginning, the gradual development and the eventual form of my philosophy of architecture. This thought aroused my emotional interest (hitherto lacking) and supplied a dominant idea upon which I could concentrate steadily and about which I could weave a most interesting story of a human trusting to his instincts (a rara avis). The story would lend itself to a free, easy literary treatment, without egotism and without pedantry. Then the plot of sticking to one impulse and idea from the beginning throughout a long intellectual and emotional life has in it the element of drama. As my memory runs back to my second year, you may see that it is a long stretch. At 14 I had fully determined to be an architect. When I look back upon the incessant hard work I have done and the sacrifice I have made—with one end in view, I feel, alas, that the young student of to-day is not capable of it: unless he be given a definite, positive, stimulus, a definite objective:—a star of destiny so to speak. It is precisely this human element that I would cause to permeate the work and radiate from it.[30]

Whitaker was immediately enthusiastic, and told Sullivan so on January 17. The editorial board approved within two weeks and details were quickly settled. Sullivan would be paid $100 for each of at least twelve monthly installments of three thousand to four thousand words. By February 16 a formal agreement was signed, the first two payments were made, Sullivan had finished a draft of chapter 1, had decided to write in the third person, and had found his title: *The Autobiography of an Idea.* He had previously informed Whitaker in January of his arrangement with the Art Institute's Burnham Library to produce twenty sheets of drawings illustrating his system of ornament. He had already written a "prelude" or introduction and now looked forward to doing the drawings and autobiography simultaneously, weaving the two into a kind of personal retrospective. Sullivan approached the projects as a single explanation to the world of what he was all about, a summing up of a lifetime of work and struggle.

When the *Journal* announced the autobiographical series in March 1922, Sullivan had completed the first three chapters and three plates for the library: "This explains my fatigue at times." He had already decided to shortchange certain topics: reactions to French culture during his Ecole days, for example, and experiences at his Biloxi Bay home. Even so, he tended to overwrite, often exceeding his four-thousand-word limit. He worried that he was writing too much about his childhood, all the while regretting each scene he cut. By the time the first chapter appeared in June, Sullivan had finished six in draft. He was amenable to revisions but scrutinized the galleys laboriously, pouncing on errors with a certain editorial glee. He also did his research, telling Whitaker in July, for example, that chapter 7 was delayed because he was awaiting official confirmation from the Boston School Committee of some minor point about his education.

And so the dialogue proceeded between sympathetic editor and eager author. In January 1923, when Sullivan had written and been paid for twelve installments, Whitaker suggested their publication in book form. Discussion had already started about turning the Burnham drawings into another book. When the matter was finally settled, Sullivan threw himself into every aspect of the two productions: from decisions over paper stock and engraving to marketing and pricing. In June he finished the last drawing a month or two before the fifteenth and final chapter of his autobiography, which proved to be so long that Whitaker agreed to print it in two sections—making

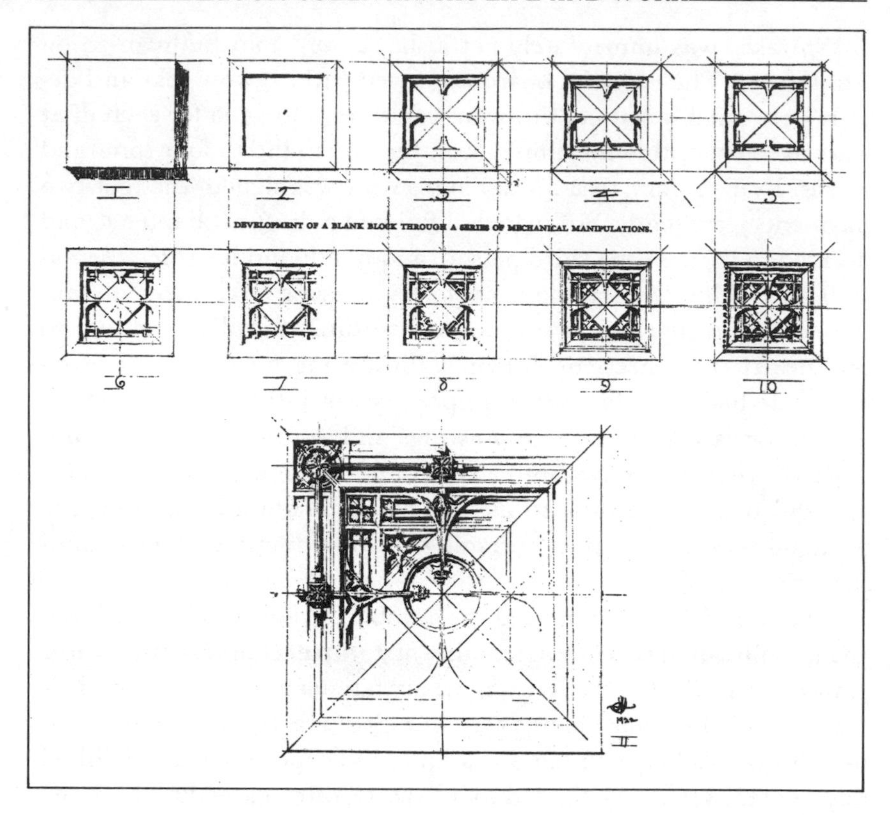
DEVELOPMENT OF A BLANK BLOCK THROUGH A SERIES OF MECHANICAL MANIPULATIONS.
1
2
3
4
5
6
7
8
9
10
11
1922

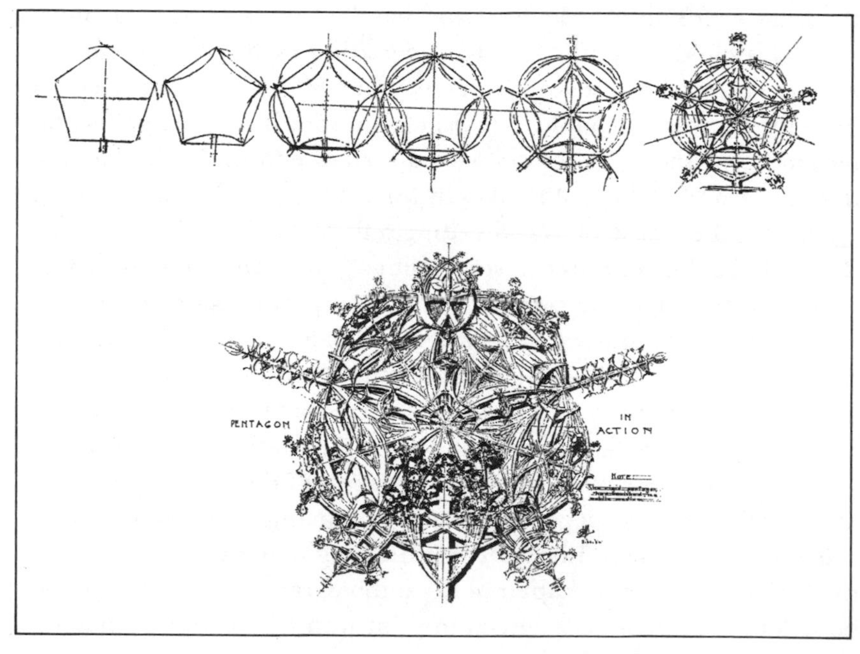
PENTAGON IN ACTION
Note

sixteen in all—and to pay him an additional $100. In the meantime he wrote two important pieces for *The Architectural Record:* in February his assessment of the *Chicago Tribune*'s competition for new headquarters, in which the winning Hood and Howells Gothic Revival entry represented to him a "dying idea." Eliel Saarinen's second-place design, on the other hand, was "resonant and rich, ringing amidst the wealth and joy of life," a "master-edifice." In April he reviewed Wright's Imperial Hotel: it is "so great," he told Whitaker, after poring over the plans with its architect, "that it places Frank head and shoulders above all American architects. That of course is not very high praise. When I place him in the class with Eliel Saarinen and his design for the Tribune building," however, "the idea becomes clearer."

Sullivan described the Imperial—its construction, facilities, and meaning—in far greater detail than he had ever discussed any other building including his own. He approached it philosophically and socially as evidence that the best traditions of architectural art were alive and well, as proof of man's freedom and creative possibilities, as the Michelangelian tour de force he believed he had never achieved. When he compared it with the Chicago Auditorium, he seemed to recognize it as a fulfillment of his own intentions, and when he called Wright a master, he may have been returning the compliment, but he was also more or less officially designating him an heir, an extension of Louis Sullivan into the future. Investing him with his own attributes, he sent Wright out to carry on the struggle. The Imperial Hotel combined vision, imagination, intellect, and sympathy for the

XIII.15 *Two plates from* A System of Architectural Ornament. *Sullivan's own captions read: (top) "No. 11. Represents No. 10 developed with increased freedom, but still largely in the mechanical mode beginning appearance of the imaginative element"; (bottom) "The Awakening of the Pentagon: Rigid geometry here shown progressing, through man's manipulation of a central idea, into plastic, mobile and fluescent phases of expression tending towards culmination in foliate and efflorescent forms. Note: Clearly to grasp the significance of the approaching fusion of the inorganic and the organic into a single impulse and expression of man's will, the idea must steadily be held in mind that the rigid geometric form is considered as a container of energy upon which a germinal, liberating will is imposed by man's free choice, intelligence and skill. The plant organism derives its impulse from the seed-germ, and in its growth develops sub-centers of further growth. The seed-germ may thus be considered also as a container of energy, forming of its own will sub-centers of energy in the course of its functioning development toward the finality of its characteristic form—the expression of its identity."*

human condition in a true vernacular language, he wrote. A poem in stone, it was "the high water mark thus far attained by any modern architect. Superbly beautiful it stands, a noble prophecy." Sullivan's torch had been passed.

In June 1923 he was "much preoccupied just now with a dear friend very seriously ill," possibly the "loyal little henna-haired milliner" Wright said looked after him faithfully. Whoever it was, Sullivan was distressed when that "good friend died suddenly on the 11th."[31] Andrew Rebori, George Nimmons, Max Dunning, and Dankmar's son, Sidney J. Adler, visited him from time to time, occasionally giving him money along with other friends from the American and Northwestern Terra Cotta companies. The Cliff Dwellers kept his desk available for writing. In September he thought he had a bank job in Macon, Georgia, but it did not come through. Later that month and again in December and January he went off to Mount Vernon, Ohio, to see Dr. Arndt about his "tangled nerves which refuse to relax here" in Chicago. Wright recorded his physical deterioration:

> Bad habits engendered by his early life in Paris had gone on and on finally to make havoc with him. Caffeine had added to his distress and now he had come to bromides. His physician said his heart was bulging between his ribs. He had "gone off," as they say, frightfully. . . . Now (years later) his breath was shorter and shorter. After several cups of strong coffee he loved so much (impatient, he would pound the table if coffee was delayed), his breath was so short he would have to take my arm to walk—even very slowly. At the street crossings to step up from the street level to the sidewalk would make him pause for breath.[32]

At year's end he was still worried about *The Autobiography of an Idea* and *A System of Architectural Ornament,* as the Burnham drawings were called. When will they appear? he wanted to know. When will my royalties begin? Anxious about finding someone to introduce his memoirs, at various times he suggested Wright, George Bernard Shaw, John Dewey, and Claude Bragdon, but not without doubt in each case. Wright begged off, saying an architect should not introduce another architect's book. Sullivan accepted that philosophically, but he was disappointed. In January 1924 he visited Professor Emil Lorch at Ann Arbor, spoke to his University of Michigan senior architecture students, and met again with Eliel Saarinen. He had a

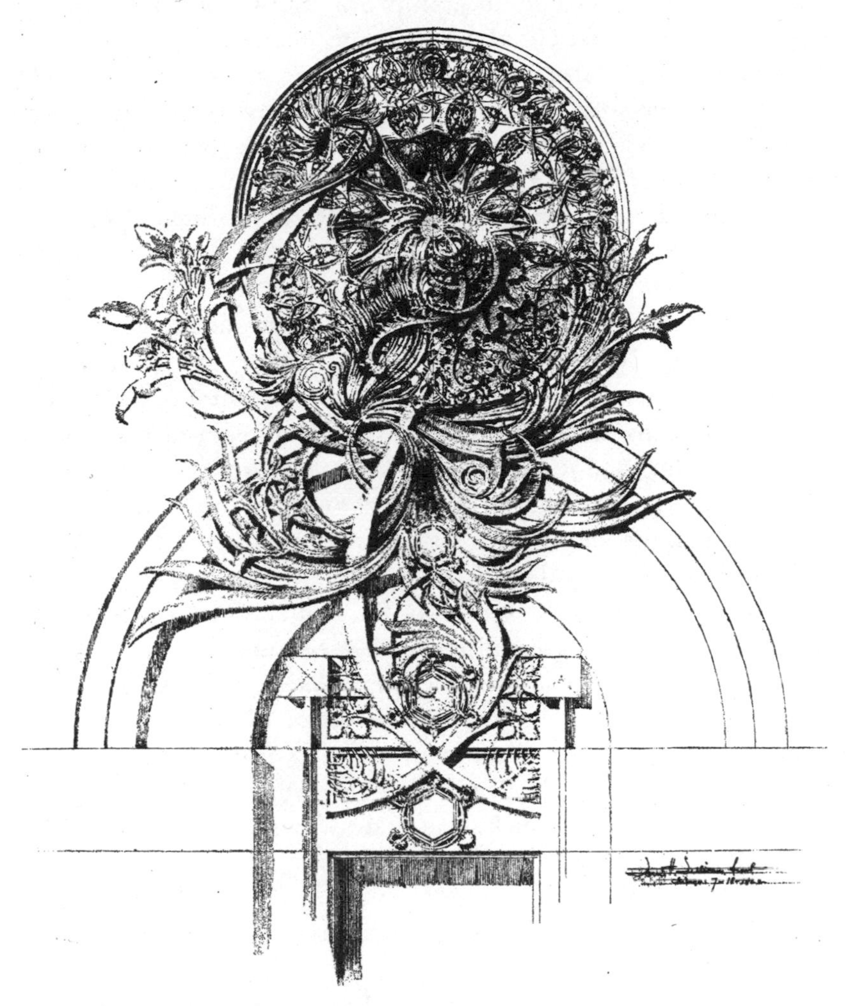

XIII.16 *Another plate from Louis Sullivan's* A System of Architectural Ornament, © 1924 by The American Institute of Architects.

"bully" time, returning home "greatly improved in outlook and in-look," he told his hosts in a letter of thanks.[33]

But that was only talk for friends. Shortly after the first of the year, 1924, Sullivan put himself under the care of Dr. W. Pingree Curtis, who lived within walking distance of the Hotel Warner.[34] By March 1 he was quite ill and about three weeks later asked Sidney Adler to visit. Immediately afterward, Adler went to see Curtis, who told him that Sullivan was suffering from extreme dilation of the heart, that he was very sick and would never improve, that he might go quickly or linger on for years. He also had acute neuritis that was slowly paralyzing his right arm and had already begun to slur his speech. He refused to go to a hospital, but after talking again with Adler allowed his friends to engage a nurse, a Miss Harper, who was in constant attendance by the end of March. Adler, Dunning, and others offered to foot the bills, laying Sullivan's principal concern to rest.

He also asked Adler to inventory his assets. He had no money other than what friends voluntarily deposited in his account at the Corn Exchange National Bank. His few possessions, including a small piece of carved jade he had kept for sentimental reasons, were in his hotel room, and his drawings and architectural equipment were in an office at 1701 Prairie Avenue that the American Terra Cotta Company provided free of charge. Sullivan told Adler the details of his parents' deaths and his lot number in Graceland Cemetery. Early in April Adler deposited $90 in Sullivan's account, bringing the total to $189. Knowing Sullivan's concern, and seeing his rapidly deteriorating condition, either Nimmons or Adler wired the AIA Press to rush bound copies of the *Autobiography* and *A System of Architectural Ornament,* which arrived on or about the eleventh. Wright came to visit on the thirteenth, noting Sullivan's pleasure at having the books in hand. Wright said he gave him his only copy of the memoirs, as well as a thick sheaf of drawings he made him promise to publish someday.[35]

After Wright left, Adler returned for a long chat. Sullivan said he wanted his royalties to go to AIA's educational fund for two reasons: to perpetuate his name in the highest professional circles and because the institute had made it possible to finish his "greatest achievement," the two books. That night Sullivan was almost comatose, and early the next morning, on April 14, 1924, he died in his sleep. He was sixty-seven years old. Dr. Curtis recorded the cause of death as chronic interstitial nephritis (a form of kidney disease), with a contributing factor of myocarditis (inflammation of the cardiac muscles).[36]

During his last three weeks of life, Adler, Dunning, Nimmons, and a few other friends covered all Sullivan's expenses and guaranteed his funeral costs, a little over $600 in all. Sullivan owed the Warner Hotel five or six weeks' rent, amounting to some $54, and a few other small debts. Adler convinced his creditors to forgo payment.

On April 16 he was buried next to his father, Patrick, and his mother, Andrienne, at Graceland Cemetery. Old friend Wallace Rice gave the chapel eulogy at 3:00 p.m. Estranged brother Albert did not attend. "The dean of American architects,"[37] *The New York Times* called him, died without work, penniless, surviving on the largess of a few devoted friends. Within weeks, words of praise laced the pages of major professional magazines, and later on, when history confirmed these admiring essays, he was returned to the heights of his halcyon days. But in his last years Louis Sullivan had fallen about as far as it was possible to fall, to the very brink of living in hell itself.

Appendix A

Louis H. Sullivan's Designs 1876-1923

SULLIVAN'S DESIGNS are grouped as follows:

I Free-lance designer, 1876–81, including jobs for "Dankmar Adler, Architect"
II Partner in "Adler & Company," 1881–83
III Principal in "Adler & Sullivan," 1883–95
IV Independent practice, 1895–1922
V Nonarchitectural designs, 1884–1923

After I compiled these lists, they were reviewed by Tim Barton and Kathleen Roy Cummings, who, with Tim Samuelson and others, have been working under the direction of the Chicago architect John Vinci to complete a project begun in the 1950s by the late historian and photographer Richard Nickel. Tentatively entitled *The Complete Work of Adler and Sullivan,* their book will include documentation and illustrations of all the designs. Anticipating the appearance of this long-awaited compilation, I have omitted detailed information in favor of a simple listing by name and location (Chicago, unless otherwise indicated) according to the year of design.

S: Building was standing in early 1985
PC: Project was partially constructed
P: Project was not constructed

No symbol means the erected commission was since demolished or destroyed.

I *Free-lance designer, 1876 to mid-1881 (nine entries)*

1876

1. Chicago Avenue Church ("Moody's Tabernacle"), interior frescoes, Johnston & Edelmann, architects

2. Sinai Synagogue, interior frescoes, Johnston & Edelmann, Burling & Adler, associated architects

With Dankmar Adler

1879

3. Central Music Hall, interior decorations (?)
4. Sigmund Hyman residence (?), authorship in question

1880

5. John Borden Block
6. John Borden residence
7. Grand Opera House, interior remodeling, decorations
8. Henry Leopold residence (?), authorship in question

1880–81

9. Max M. Rothschild Building

II *Partner in Adler & Company, mid-1881 to April 30, 1883 (fifteen entries)*

1881

10. John M. Brunswick & Julius Balke Factory (S)
11. Levi Rosenfeld flats

1881–82

12. Jewelers' Building (S)
13. Revell Building

1882

14. Academy of Music, Kalamazoo, Michigan
15. John M. Brunswick & Julius Balke Warehouse (S)
16. Frankenthal Building
17. Hammond Library
18. Hooley's Theater remodeling
19. Charles F. Kimball residence
20. Levi Rosenfeld flats and store
21. Max M. Rosenfeld flats
22. Marx Wineman residence

1883

23. F. L. Brand store and flats
24. Wright & Lawther Factory

III *Principal in Adler & Sullivan, May 1, 1883 to June 30, 1895 (158 entries)*

1883

25. Aurora Watch Company (PC, S), Aurora, Illinois
26. John M. Brunswick & Julius Balke lumber-drying plant (P)
27. Ann Halsted residence (S)
28. Ferdinand & William Kauffmann store and flats (S)
29. Frank A. Kennedy Bakery addition
30. Richard Knisely store and flats
31. J. H. McVicker's Theater (P)
32. Max M. Rothschild flats
33. Reuben Rubel store and flats
34. Schoolhouse remodeling, Marengo, Illinois
35. Charles H. Schwab residence
36. Scoville & Towne Factory (P)
37. Morris Selz residence

1884

38. Martin Barbe residence
39. Solomon Blumenfeld flats
40. Louis E. Frank residence
41. Ann Halsted flats (S)
42. J. H. Haverly Theater remodeling
43. Interstate Exposition Building, partial interior remodeling for Democratic National Convention
44. Frank A. Kennedy Bakery
45. Richard Knisely Factory
46. Lakeside Clubhouse (P)
47. Mandel Brothers stable
48. Leon Mannheimer residence
49. Max M. Rothschild flats
50. Reuben Rubel residence
51. Martin A. Ryerson Building
52. Leopold Schlesinger residence
53. B. & S. Schoeneman Factory
54. Sinai Synagogue, interior remodeling and repairs
55. Abraham Strauss residence
56. Leopold Strauss residence
57. A. F. Troescher Building

1885

58. Dankmar Adler residence
59. Chiltenham Improvement Company pavilion
60. Eli B. Felsenthal residence
61. Ann Halsted flats (S), addition to entry 41
62. Interstate Exposition Building, partial interior remodeling for Chicago Opera Festival
63. Fanny Kohn residence
64. Abraham Kuh residence
65. Benjamin Lindauer residence
66. J. H. McVicker Theater remodeling
67. Walter L. Peck double residence
68. J. M. Scoville Factory, additions and alterations
69. M. C. Stearns residence (P)
70. M. C. Stearns residence
71. Henry Stern residence
72. Samuel Stern residence
73. George Watson Warehouse addition
74. Wright & Lawther Factory addition
75. Zion Temple

1886

76. Arthur Block, conversion to flats
77. Chicago Opera House, auditorium remodeling
78. Richard T. Crane Factory
79. Richard T. Crane Factory addition
80. Joseph Deimal residence (S)
81. Dessenberg Building (S), Kalamazoo, Michigan
82. Gustav Eliel residence (S)
83. Levi A. Eliel residence (S)
84. Hugo Goodman residence
85. Hannah Horner residence
86. Illinois Central Railroad Station, Thirty-ninth Street
87. F. M. Jones residence
88. Milwaukee Exposition Building, interior remodeling
89. Edward G. Pauling flats
90. Walter and Clarence Peck Warehouse
91. Ryerson Charities Trust Building
92. Solomon residence (P?)
93. West Chicago Clubhouse

1886–89

94. Auditorium Building (S)

1887

95. Chicago Nursery & Half Orphan Asylum
96. Rudolph Deimal residence (P?)
97. Rudolph Deimal & Bros. Factory and Warehouse
98. Wirt Dexter Building
99. John Krantz Building remodeling
100. Mary M. Lively residence
101. Adolph Loeb Factory
102. Martin Ryerson Building (P, see entry 114)
103. Martin Ryerson Tomb (S)
104. B. & S. Schoeneman Factory addition
105. Selz, Schwab Factory
106. Springer Building remodeling
107. Standard Club

1888

108. Victor Falkenau flats
109. Patrick Farrell flats and barn (P?)
110. Patrick Farrell residence (P?)
111. George M. Harvey residence
112. Illinois Central Railroad Station, Forty-third Street
113. Lazarus Silverman Building addition
114. Walker Warehouse (revision of entry 102)

1889

115. Eliphalet W. Blatchford Warehouse
116. Milan C. Bullock Factory
117. Wirt Dexter residence alterations (P)
118. Eli B. Felsenthal Factory
119. Ira B. Heath residence (P)
120. Inter-Ocean Building, additions and alterations
121. Kehilath Anshe Ma'ariv Synagogue (P, see entry 125)
122. Opera House Block, Pueblo, Colorado
123. Polish and Russian manual training school

1889–90

124. Carnegie Hall, New York City, consultants

125. Kehilath Anshe Ma'ariv Synagogue, revision of entry 121

<u>1890</u>

126. James C. Berry residence (P?)
127. James Charnley residence, Ocean Springs, Mississippi
128. Chicago Cold Storage Exchange Warehouse (PC)
129. Richard T. Crane Factory (addition?)
130. Carrie Elizabeth Getty Tomb (S)
131. Grand Opera House (also known as Das Deutsche Haus, New Stadt Theatre), interior remodeling, Milwaukee, Wisconsin
132. Ontario Hotel (P), Salt Lake City, Utah
133. Opera House Block (P), Seattle, Washington
134. Schlesinger & Mayer Store, additions and alterations, 137–139 State Street
135. Louis H. Sullivan residence (S), Ocean Springs, Mississippi
136. Wainwright Building (S), St. Louis, Missouri
137. Wright, Hill & Co. Factory

<u>1890–91</u>

138. Dooly Block, Salt Lake City, Utah
139. J. H. McVicker's Theater reconstruction

<u>1891</u>

140. C. H. Berry residence
141. John M. Brunswick & Julius Balke Factory addition (S)
142. James Charnley residence (S)
143. Illinois Central Railroad Station, New Orleans, Louisiana
144. Adolph and William Loeb store and flats
145. Mercantile Club Building (P), St. Louis, Missouri
146. Nashville Linoleum Company, Des Plaines, Illinois
147. J. W. Oakley Warehouse
148. Odd Fellows (Fraternity) Temple building (P)
149. Schiller Building
150. Schlesinger & Mayer Store, additions and alterations, 141–143 State Street
151. Shone Ejector Company Factory
152. Sinai Synagogue, additions and alterations
153. Standard Elevator Company Factory
154. Albert W. Sullivan residence
155. Transportation Building
156. Charlotte Dickson Wainwright Tomb (S), St. Louis, Missouri

157. Walker & Oakley Tannery

1892

158. William Mayer Warehouse
159. Portland Building (P), St. Louis, Missouri
160. Schlesinger & Mayer Store entrance, 141–143 State Street
161. Standard Club, additions and alterations
162. St. Nicholas Hotel, St. Louis, Missouri
163. Trust and Savings Building (P), St. Louis, Missouri, name and date are conjectural (see entry 173)
164. Union Trust Building (S), St. Louis, Missouri
165. Victoria Hotel, Chicago Heights, Illinois

1893

166. Eye & Ear Infirmary addition
167. First Regiment Armory conversion to Trocadero Amusement Park
168. Illinois Leather Company tannery
169. Mandel Brothers stable
170. Mandel Brothers Store, roof reconstruction, and remodeling
171. Mandel Brothers Store addition
172. Chicago Stock Exchange Building
173. Trust and Savings Building (P), St. Louis, Missouri, name and date are conjectural (possible revision of entry 163)
174. Wolf, Sayer & Heller Warehouse addition

1893–94

175. J. T. Ball & Company Warehouse

1894

176. Herman Braunstein store and flats (S)
177. Burnet House hotel (P), Cincinnati, Ohio
178. Chemical National Bank Building (P), St. Louis, Missouri, date is conjectural
179. Chicago Dock Company Warehouse
180. Levi A. Eliel apartment building (P)
181. Store building (P), St. Louis, Missouri, date is conjectural and client's name is unknown

1894–95

182. Guaranty Building (S), Buffalo, New York

IV *Independent practice, July 1, 1895 to 1922 (fifty-six entries)*

1895

183. National Linseed Oil Company cooper shop

1896

184. Schlesinger & Mayer storefront and elevated bridge, 141–143 Wabash Avenue
185. Schlesinger & Mayer Store additions and alterations, 137–143 State Street
186. Schlesinger & Mayer Store (P), 141–143 Wabash Avenue

1897

187. Bayard (-Condict) Building (S), New York City
188. Hippodrome, St. Louis, Missouri, consultant

1898

189. Country club (P)
190. Gage Building facade (S)
191. A. W. Goodrich residence (P), Harbor Springs, Michigan
192. Schlesinger & Mayer Store (P), nine-story version
193. Schlesinger & Mayer Store (P), ten-story version
194. Schlesinger & Mayer Store (P), twelve-story version
195. Schlesinger & Mayer Store (S), nine stories, Madison Street

1899

196. Richard T. Crane Company, foundry addition
197. Euston & Company Factory (also known as Riverside Seed & Cleaning Company) (S)
198. Nettie F. McCormick residence alterations (P)

1899–1900

199. Holy Trinity Cathedral (S)

1901

200. Nettie F. McCormick residence (P), Lake Forest, Illinois
201. Presbyterian Hospital women's pavilion (P)
202. Virginia Hall (S), Tusculum College, Greeneville, Tennessee

203. Ellis Wainwright residence (P), St. Louis, Missouri, date is approximate

1902

204. Euston & Company Factory (also known as Riverside Seed & Cleaning Company) (S)
205. Arthur Henry Lloyd residence (P)
206. Schlesinger & Mayer Store (S), twelve stories, State and Madison streets
207. Schlesinger & Mayer Store (P), twenty stories

1903

208. Richard Crane office buildings, Bridgeport, Connecticut
209. Schlesinger & Mayer Store alterations, 143–145 Wabash Avenue

1904

210. Crane Company offices
211. Office building (P)
212. Theater facade (P)

1906

213. Eli B. Felsenthal store and flats
214. National Farmers' Bank (S), Owatonna, Minnesota

1907

215. Henry Babson residence, Riverside, Illinois
216. Island City (Petty's Island) Amusement Park (P), Philadelphia, Pennsylvania

1908

217. Auditorium Building remodeling (P) as hotel
218. Auditorium Building remodeling (P) as offices
219. Josephine Crane Bradley residence (P), Madison, Wisconsin (see entry 220)

1909

220. Josephine Crane Bradley residence (S), Madison, Wisconsin, revision of entry 219

1909–1911

221. People's Savings Bank (S), Cedar Rapids, Iowa

1910–11

222. St. Paul's Methodist Episcopal Church (PC, S), Cedar Rapids, Iowa

1911

223. Carl K. Bennett residence (P), Owatonna, Minnesota

1912–13

224. George Arndt garage (P), Mt. Vernon, Ohio, date is conjectural

1913

225. Henry C. Adams Building (S), Algona, Iowa
226. Museum (P)

1913–14

227. Merchants' National Bank (S), Grinnell, Iowa

1913–15

228. John D. Van Allen & Sons Store (S), Clinton, Iowa

1914

229. Bank (P), Enid, Oklahoma
230. Home Building Association (S), Newark, Ohio
231. Purdue State Bank (S), West Lafayette, Indiana

1916

232. Henry C. Adams Building addition (P), Algona, Iowa
233. Oakland High School (P), Owatonna, Minnesota

1917

234. People's Savings & Loan Association Bank (S), Sidney, Ohio

1919

235. Farmers' & Merchants' Union Bank (S), Columbus, Wisconsin

1919–20

236. Bank remodeling (S), Manistique, Michigan

1921

237. Mrs. Arthur J. Eddy Tomb (P), Flint, Michigan

1922

238. William P. Krause Music Store & residence facade (S)

V *Nonarchitectural designs, 1884 to 1923 (thirteen entries)*

1884

239. Elevator car, Manhattan Bank, New York

1887

240. Catalogue cover for Robert Stevenson & Company, druggists, Chicago

1895

241. Winner's medal, Northern Oratorical League annual competition, University of Michigan Alumni Association
242. Decorative border, Richard Morris Hunt memorial portrait, *Inland Architect,* August

1896

243. Cover for *Music* magazine (Chicago), November, published January 1898

1898

244. Cover (P) for *Swimming* magazine, published in *Forms & Fantasies* magazine (Chicago)

1899

245. Decorative border for Sullivan's "The Modern Phase of Architecture," *Inland Architect,* June

1900

246. Decorative border, Dankmar Adler memorial portrait, ibid., May
247. Swimming certificate, Chicago Athletic Association, date is conjectural

1910

248. Cover for *Gibson's Magazine,* drawn in February, published in March

1913

249. Landscaping for Carl Bennett property (P), Owatonna, Minnesota

1920

250. Pedestal (S) for the Governor John Palmer statue by Leonard Crunelle, Springfield, Illinois

1922

251. Ornamental design in tin for potbellied stove platform, date is approximate

1923

252. "The Christmas Spirit of Joy," drawing for *Common Clay* magazine (Chicago: American Terra Cotta & Ceramic Co.), published in December

Appendix B

Adler & Sullivan and Louis H. Sullivan Buildings Standing in 1985

Chicago (alphabetically)

1. Auditorium Building (1886–89), Congress Parkway, Michigan and Wabash avenues, interior extensively altered but several major rooms restored by Roosevelt University

2–4. Brunswick & Balke Factory, addition, and warehouse (1881, 1882, 1891), Orleans, Huron, Sedgewick, and Superior streets, exterior somewhat disfigured but essentially intact

5. James Charnley residence (1891), 1365 North Astor Street, south porches added

6. Joseph Deimal residence (1886), 3141 Calumet Avenue, considerably altered

7. Wirt Dexter Building (1887), 630 South Wabash Avenue, pediment removed, other minor alterations

8. Gustav Eliel residence (1886), 4122 Ellis Avenue, considerably altered

9–10. Euston & Company linseed oil and linoleum factories (1899, 1902), Kingsbury Street between Blackhawk and Eastman, somewhat disfigured

11. Gage Building (1898), 18 South Michigan Avenue, fire escapes and top four floors added, shop fronts altered

12. Getty Tomb (1890), Graceland Cemetery

13–14. Ann Halsted flats (1884, 1885), 1826–34 Lincoln Park West

15. Ann Halsted residence (1883), 440 West Beldon Street

16. George Harvey residence (1888), 600 West Stratford Place, extensively remodeled inside and out

17. Holy Trinity Cathedral (1899–1900), 1121 North Leavitt Street

18. Jewelers' Building (1881–82), 15–19 South Wabash Avenue, somewhat altered

19. Ferdinand and William Kauffmann store and flats (1883),

2310–2316 Lincoln Avenue, somewhat altered

20. William P. Krause Music Store and residence facade (1922), 4611 Lincoln Avenue, slightly altered
21. Leon Mannheimer residence (1884), 2147 North Cleveland Street
22. Martin Ryerson Tomb (1887), Graceland Cemetery

23–24. Schlesinger & Mayer (now Carson Pirie Scott) Store (1898, 1902–03), State and Madison streets

25–26. Springer/Kranz remodelings (1887), 134–136 North State Street, extensively altered

27. Standard Elevator Company Factory (1891), 1515 West 15th Street, somewhat disfigured

Outside Chicago (east to west)

28. Bayard (-Condict) Building (1897), 65 Bleecker Street, New York City, remodeled as offices, shop fronts altered
29. Carnegie Hall (1889–90), Fifty-seventh Street near Seventh Avenue, New York City, consulting architects
30. Guaranty Building (1894–95), southwest corner, Pearl and Church Streets, Buffalo, New York
31. Home Building Association (1914), West Main and North Third streets, Newark, Ohio, entrance and ground floor altered
32. People's Savings & Loan Association Bank (1917), Court Street and Ohio Avenue, Sidney, Ohio
33. Dessenberg Building (1886), 251 East Michigan Avenue, Kalamazoo, Michigan
34. Bank remodeling (1919–20), Manistique, Michigan
35. Purdue State Bank (1914), State and Vine streets, West Lafayette, Indiana, interior completely altered, disfiguring sign
36. Aurora Watch Company (1883), 603 South La Salle Street, Aurora, Illinois
37. Pedestal (1920), Governor Palmer statue, capital building park, Springfield, Illinois
38. Farmers' & Merchants' Union Bank (1919), James Street and Broadway Avenue, Columbus, Wisconsin
39. Joseph Crane Bradley residence (1909), 106 North Prospect Street, Madison, Wisconsin, somewhat remodeled as fraternity house

40. National Farmers' (now Security) Bank (1906), Broadway and Cedar Street, Owatonna, Minnesota, expanded and remodeled
41. Wainwright Building (1890), northwest corner of Seventh and Chestnut streets, St. Louis, Missouri, remodeled as State Office Building
42. Wainwright Tomb (1891), Bellefontaine Cemetery, St. Louis, Missouri
43. Union Trust (now 705 Olive) Building (1892), northwest corner Seventh and Olive streets, St. Louis, Missouri
44. Henry C. Adams Building (1913), Moore and State streets, Algona, Iowa
45. Merchants' National Bank (1913–14), Fourth Avenue and Broad Street, Grinnell, Iowa
46. People's Savings Bank (1909–1911), Third Avenue SW and First Street SW, Cedar Rapids, Iowa
47. St. Paul's Methodist Episcopal Church (1910–11), Third Avenue SE and Fourteenth Street SE, Cedar Rapids, Iowa
48. John D. Van Allen & Sons Store (1913–15), Fifth Avenue South and Second Street, Clinton, Iowa
49. Virginia Hall (1901), Tusculum College, Greeneville, Tennessee
50. James Charnley residence (1890), Ocean Boulevard, Ocean Springs, Mississippi, side porches added
51. Louis H. Sullivan residence (1890), Ocean Boulevard, Ocean Springs, Mississippi, altered beyond recognition

Appendix C

Unverified Louis H. Sullivan Projects

1. Bank in Ohio, 39.75-by-82-foot lot, mentioned in Sullivan to Adolph Budina, February 23, 1918, Burnham Library, Art Institute, Chicago.
2. Bank in Iowa, two stories, 86-by-132-foot corner lot, mentioned in ibid.
3. Library in De Kalb, Illinois; Sullivan to Wright, December 25, 1919, Bruce Brooks Pfeiffer (ed.), *Frank Lloyd Wright: Letters to Architects* (Fresno: California State University Press, 1984), 16.
4. St. John's Military Academy chapel, Delafield, Wisconsin, $125,000, Sullivan to Wright, ibid.
5. Bank in Iowa, Sullivan to Wright, August 23, 1921, ibid., 20.
6. Bank in Georgia, Sullivan to Wright, ibid., may be same as bank prospect in Macon, Georgia, in Sullivan to Charles Whitaker, August 23, September 6, 1923, American Institute of Architects Archives, Washington, D.C.

Appendix D

Dankmar Adler's Designs 1896-99

1896

1. Convention Hall (P?), St. Louis, Missouri, consultant
2. W. A. Mayer Building
3. Morgan Park Academy dormitory, gymnasium (P)
4. Technical Club, remodeling of National Hotel

1897

5. M. L. Barrett Company addition
6. Chicago Dock Company warehouses
7. Wright & Hill Linseed Oil Company, tank and coke house

1898

8. Auditorium Building roof garden (P)
9. La Crosse Hotel (P), La Crosse, Wisconsin
10. Illinois Leather Company additions
11. Morgan Park Academy dining hall, powerhouse
12. Schlesinger & Mayer Store powerhouse (P)
13. Charles Yondorff Store

1899

14. Ira B. Cook Hotel
15. Isaiah Temple
16. Levi Morgan Building remodeling
17. Selz, Schwab Building fireproofing and new entrance
18. United Hebrew Charities Dispensary

Appendix E

Louis H. Sullivan's Publications and Writings 1882-1924

"Hooley's New Theater," *Daily Inter-Ocean* (Chicago), August 12, 1882, p. 13, interview.

"Characteristics and Tendencies of American Architecture," *Inland Architect* 6 (November 1885): 58–59.

Response to toast, "We Are All Jolly Good Fellows," *Inland Architect* 6 (November 1885): 85–66.

"Essay on Inspiration," *Inland Architect* 8 (December 1886): 61–64, revised and expanded often, and included with other works.

Remarks in discussion, "What Are the Present Tendencies of Architectural Design in America?" *Inland Architect* 9 (March 1887):26.

"What Is the Just Subordination, in Architectural Design, of Detail to Mass?" *Inland Architect* 9 (April 1887):51–52.

"Report of Committee on Standard of Professional Requirement," *Inland Architect* 10 (December 1887): 77.

Letter to the editor, *American Architect & Building News* 23 (February 11, 1888): 70–71, on McVicker's Theater.

"Style," *Inland Architect* 11 (May 1888): 59–60.

Remarks on architects' Protective League, *Inland Architect* 11 (June 1888): 76.

Statement on architects' Protective League, *Building* 9 (August 25, 1888): 64.

Remarks on architects' Code of Ethics, *Inland Architect* 12 (November 1888): 64.

Remarks on merger of Western Association of Architects with the American Institute of Architects, *Inland Architect* 12 (November 1888): 68.

"The Artistic Use of the Imagination," *Inland Architect* 14 (October 1889): 38–39.

"Sub-Contracting: Shall the National Association Recommend That

It Be Encouraged?" *Inland Architect* 15 (February 1890): 18–19.

"Church Spires Must Go," *Chicago Tribune*, November 30, 1890, p. 36, interview.

"Plastic and Color Decoration of the Auditorium," *Industrial Chicago* (Chicago: Goodspeed Publishing Co., 1891), 2: 490–91.

"The High Building Question," *The Graphic* 5 (December 19, 1891): 405.

"Ornament in Architecture," *Engineering Magazine* 3 (August 1892): 633–44.

"The Transportation Building," *Handbook of the World's Columbian Exposition* (Chicago: Rand, McNally & Co., 1893), 30–34, signed by Adler & Sullivan.

"Polychromatic Treatment of Architecture," paper read at World Congress of Architects, Chicago, August 5, 1893, mentioned in *Inland Architect* 22 (August 1893): 11, text lost.

"Emotional Architecture as Compared with Intellectual: A Study in Objective and Subjective," *Inland Architect* 24 (November 1894): 32–34.

"The Tall Office Building Artistically Considered," *Lippincott's* 57 (March 1896): 403–9.

"May Not Architecture Again Become a Living Art?" unpublished manuscript, c. 1897, copy in Burnham Library.

"Opinions on the Use of Burned Clay for Fireproofing," *The Brickbuilder* 7 (September 1898): 189–90.

The Bayard Building (New York: Rost Printing & Publishing Co., n.d.), brochure, copy at Avery Library.

"An Unaffected School of Modern Architecture: Will It Come?" *Artist* 24 (January 1899): xxxiii-iv.

Unpublished address to Chicago Architectural Club, May 1899, copy in Burnham Library.

"The Modern Phase of Architecture," *Inland Architect* 33 (June 1899): 40.

"The Master," unpublished manuscript dated July 1, 1899, in Burnham Library: pt. 3 of "Nature and the Poet," a group of poems beginning with "Inspiration" (1886).

Letter to the editor, *The Brickbuilder* 9 (May 1900): 96.

Remarks at Second Architectural League of America Convention, *Inland Architect* 35 (June 1900): 42–43.

"The Young Man in Architecture," *Inland Architect* 35 (June 1900): 38–40.

"Reality in Architecture," title varies, *Chicago Tribune,* August 1900; reprint, *Inland Architect* 36 (September 1900): 6–7.

"Open Letter," *Interstate Architect & Builder* 2 (December 8, 1900): 7.

Letter to the editor, *Interstate Architect & Builder* 2 (May 18, 1901): 6.

"Kindergarten Chats," *Interstate Architect & Builder* 2–3 (February 16, 1901–February 8, 1902), first published in book form based on Sullivan's 1918 revisions by Claude Bragdon (ed.) and the Scarab Fraternity Press, Lawrence, Kansas, in 1934.

Telegram to Third Architectual League of America Convention, *The Brickbuilder* 10 (June 1901): 112.

"Architectural Style," *Inland Architect* 38 (September 1901): 16.

"Education," *Inland Architect* 39 (June 1902): 41–42.

"Sub-structure at the New Schlesinger & Mayer Store Building," *Engineering Record* 47 (February 21, 1903): 194–96.

"Basements and Sub-basements," *The Economist* 31 (February 20, 1904): 254.

"Reply to Mr. Frederick Stymetz Lamb on 'Modern Use of the Gothic; The Possibility of a New Architectural Style,' " *The Craftsman* 8 (June 1905): 336–38.

Letter to the editor, *The Craftsman* 8 (July 1905): 453.

"What Is Architecture?: A Study in the American People of Today," *American Contractor* 27 (January 6, 1906): 48–54.

"Natural Thinking: A Study in Democracy," title later changed to "Democracy, A Man-Search!" completed in 1908, first published in book form by Wayne State University Press (Detroit, 1961), Ellen Hedges, ed.

Letter to the editor on Gutson Borglum, *The Craftsman* 15 (December 1908): 338.

"Is Our Art a Betrayal Rather Than an Expression of American Life?" *The Craftsman* 15 (January 1909): 402–4.

"Artistic Brick," foreword to *Suggestions in Artistic Brickwork* (St. Louis: Hydraulic-Press Brick Co., n.d.).

"Lighting the People's Savings Bank, Cedar Rapids, Iowa," *Illuminating Engineer* 6 (February 1912): 631–35.

"The People's Savings Bank, Cedar Rapids, Iowa," *Banker's Magazine* 84 (March 1912): 415–26.

Remarks on client-architect cooperation on the occasion of Solon S. Beman's memorial, partially published in *Western Architect* 22 (August 1915): 14.

"Development of Construction," *The Economist* 55 (June 24, 1916): 1252, and 56 (July 1, 1916): 39–40.

Remarks at fifty-fifth AIA convention, 1920, partially reprinted in *Western Architect* 33 (May 1924): 54.

"The Autobiography of an Idea" *AIA Journal,* June 1922–September 1923, and as a book by the AIA Press, New York, 1924.

"The Chicago Tribune Competition," *The Architectural Record* 53 (February 1923): 151–57.

"Concerning the Imperial Hotel, Tokyo, Japan," *The Architectural Record* 53 (April 1923): 333–52.

"Reflections on the Tokyo Disaster," *The Architectural Record* 55 (February 1924): 113–17.

A System of Architectural Ornament According with a Philosophy of Man's Powers (New York: AIA Press, 1924).

Notes

LOUIS SULLIVAN died destitute and without heirs. He left no estate other than anticipated book royalties donated to an American Institute of Architects educational fund. Shortly before his death, he gave over one hundred drawings to Frank Lloyd Wright that ultimately found their way to the Avery Library at Columbia University. Other drawings and his correspondence were privately held.

Over the years Avery Library and the Burnham Library at the Art Institute in Chicago accumulated the largest Louis Sullivan collections of drawings, letters, manuscripts, and memorabilia. The universities of Chicago and Michigan, Tusculum College, the State Historical Society of Wisconsin, and a handful of other institutions have smaller collections. Altogether these holdings amount to some two hundred or more drawings and considerably fewer letters.

Given the dearth of normal biographical material, this book relies heavily on contemporary magazines and newspapers, the remaining physical buildings, photographs of demolished structures, surviving plans and drawings in published and unpublished form, and on nonarchitectural archival material. Secondary literature on Sullivan is also amazingly thin. I have therefore omitted a formal bibliography, leaving it to readers to consult the following notes for specific citations.

The following abbreviations are used for publications frequently repeated in this section:

America Architect & Building News = *AA&BN*
American Institute of Architects Journal = *AIA Journal*
The Architectual Record = *ARec*
The Brickbuilder = *BkB*
Building Budget = *BB*

Chicago Tribune = *CT*
Inland Architect = *IA*
Journal of the Society of Architectural Historians = *JSAH*
The Prarie School Review = *PSR*
Real Estate & Building Journal = *RE&BJ*
Western Architect = *WA*

NOTES FOR CHAPTER I

1. *The Autobiography of an Idea* was first published in sixteen monthly installments between June 1922 and September 1923 by the *American Institute of Architects Journal.* Sullivan was still writing the last chapters when the first appeared. In book form the *Autobiography* was published by the American Institute of Architects Press (New York) in 1924, and with a foreword by architect Claude Bragdon in the W. W. Norton & Company (New York) White Oak Series in 1934. Later reissues were by Peter Smith (New York) in 1949 and by Dover Press (New York) in 1956 and 1980. Quotations in this chapter are taken from the 1956 Dover Press edition, chapters 1–10, pages 9–181, but have not been individually cited except for lengthy excerpts or provocative passages. For a full list of Louis H. Sullivan's writings, see Appendix E.
2. Sullivan, *Autobiography,* 14.
3. Sullivan did not give his grandfather's first name, but Patrick listed it when he married: "Boston Marriages, 1852," August 14, entry no. 1468, stored in the Old City Hall Annex basement, Boston.
4. "Copy of Report and List of Passengers taken on Board the Ship Unicorn of Boston. . . ," September 7, 1847, in "Passenger Lists of Vessels Arriving at Boston, 1820–91," Roll 23, June 1–October 12, 1847, microcopy no. M277, Microtext Division, Boston Public Library.
5. Ibid.
6. Oscar Handlin, *Boston's Immigrants* (Cambridge, Mass.: Harvard University Press, 1959 ed.), 42–49.
7. Ibid., 52.
8. Peter R. Knights, *The Plain People of Boston, 1830–1860* (New York: Oxford University Press, 1971), 33–34.
9. *Unicorn* "List of Passengers," September 7, 1847; see n. 4.
10. Handlin, *Boston's Immigrants,* 77, 250–51.

11. Ibid., 93, and map on page 90.
12. Knights, *Plain People,* 20–21.
13. Willard Connely, *Louis Sullivan* (New York: Horizon Press, 1960), 25; Boston city directories for 1847–51.
14. For the Boston addresses of Sullivan and List, see ibid., 1848 to 1867. On Chapman Hall see its annual catalogues in the Social Sciences Department of the Boston Public Library.
15. Sullivan, *Autobiography,* 16.
16. "Boston Marriages, 1852," entry no. 1468, cited in n. 3.
17. "Register of Births, October 1854–May 1, 1856 [*sic*]," Genealogy Unit, Municipal Archives, Surrogates Building, New York City. The "stillborn" daughter is mentioned in the Sullivan "Family Record," August 26, 1853, Sullivan Collection, Burnham Library, The Art Institute, Chicago.
18. Quoted in Knights, *Plain People,* 101–2.
19. Ibid., 123–24; Stephen Thernstrom, *The Other Bostonians* (Cambridge, Mass.: Harvard University Press, 1973), 97–98.
20. "Suffolk Deeds," v. 699, Document 70, Suffolk County Registry of Deeds, Old Court House, Boston.
21. See ibid., v. 814, Document 184, and v. 832, Document 81; for tax records: Manuscript Street Directories and Manuscript Tax Books, 10th Ward Boston, 1856–62, stored in the Boston Public Library Annex attic; Knights, *Plain People,* 123.
22. "Boston Births, 1856," September 3, entry no. 3882, stored in the Old City Hall Annex basement, Boston.

    The architect's birthplace, commonly given as 22 South Bennet Street, was listed as 22 Bennet Place—essentially an alley—on Patrick Sullivan's deed of purchase. By 1856, school and tax records put the house at 22 Bennet Street and 22 South Bennet Street indiscriminately. Bennet Place and the Sullivan home no longer exist.

    In 1946 the Boston Society of Architects and the Massachusetts Association of Architects placed a commemorative plaque at the site, affixing it to an exterior wall of the New England Medical Center on Bennet Street, a few steps off Harrison Avenue. There is now no South Bennet Street in Boston.

    Municipal birth records establish conclusively that Sullivan's name was not "Louis Henri" as some have thought. In fact, he did not use the gallicized version except informally as a boy in tribute to his grandfather, and he rarely used his full name at all. Grammar school records from 1865 list him as "Louis Henry," but high school records in 1870 shortened his name to "Louis H." Also see Hugh Morrison, letter to the editor, *PSR* 6 (Third Quarter, 1969): 25.

23. See tax records and deed books listed in n. 21; Thernstrom, *The Other Bostonians,* 97–98.
24. Grantee Book no. 877, pp. 420–21, Middlesex County Registry of Deeds, Cambridge, Massachusetts.
25. "Quincy School Records, 1852–1864," Josiah Quincy Community School, Boston. At mid-nineteenth century all Boston primary schools stored their records centrally, hence Quincy School became the repository for Brimmer's archives.
26. No business, hotel, newspaper, or any other public record remains for the Sullivans' several summers in Newburyport.
27. Garry D. Shattuck, Public Archives of Nova Scotia, Halifax, to author, March 20, 1981. A careful search turned up no archival trace of the Sullivans in Halifax.
28. "Quincy School Records, 1852–1864" and "1864–1877," and sketches first published in Paul E. Sprague, *The Drawings of Louis Henry Sullivan* (Princeton, N.J.: Princeton University Press, 1979), figs. 1, 2, confirm the Sullivans' presence in Newburyport in 1865, 1867, and 1868.
29. Rice School records from the 1860s and 1870s were destroyed by fire but see *Expenditures for the Public Schools. School Committee. Report on the Committee on Accounts* (Boston, 1872), 41, 48, 60.

    The chronology of Sullivan's 1862–70 grammar school career, summer and academic-year locations, differing here slightly from what can be reconstructed from his autobiography, conforms to school and municipal records, and other sources listed in the notes. Nineteenth-century records from the West Ward Grammar School in South Reading no longer exist.
30. See Douglass Shand Tucci, *Built in Boston: City & Suburb* (Boston: New York Graphic Society, 1978), 182–83, and fig. 51.
31. Sullivan, *Autobiography,* 118.
32. Anna List, South Reading, to Albert Sullivan, Chicago, November 1869, quoted in Connely, *Louis Sullivan,* 35–36. In this letter Anna mentions that "a year has passed since you left Boston," establishing the Sullivans' departure in 1868, not in 1869, as Louis Sullivan wrote.

33. On the Lists, the Tompsons, and South Reading, see *Wakefield Citizen & Banner,* June 7, 1873; *Directory and Register of Wakefield, Stoneham, Reading* (1882), 94; *Report of the School Committee . . . South Reading, 1866–67* (1867), 18; Grantor Book no. 877, pp. 420–21, Middlesex County Registry of Deeds, Cambridge; Richard Nickel, Park Ridge, Illinois, to Ruth Woodbury, Wakefield, July 30, 1966, and Woodbury to Nickel, August 3, 1966, in the author's possession.
34. Marriage record, August 20, 1862, Town Clerk's Office, Wakefield, Massachusetts.
35. On English High School, see *Catalogue of the Scholars and Teachers of the English High School, Boston, Mass. From 1821 to 1890* (Boston: English High School Association, 1891); *Report on Accounts in Schools, 1869–1872* (Boston, 1872); and *Accounts . . . 1871–1873.*
36. Unnumbered pages from instructors' ledger books, 1870–71, English High School Archives, Boston.
37. Sullivan, *Autobiography,* 168.
38. "Wakefield Deaths, 1848–1890," Town Clerk's Office, Wakefield, Massachusetts; Tax List for 1871, Tax Collector's Office, Wakefield; Grantor Book no. 1189, p. 542, and Grantor Book no. 1294, p. 449, Middlesex County Registry of Deeds, Cambridge, Massachusetts.
39. *Chicago City Directory, 1871,* the first in which Patrick Sullivan was listed.
40. Sullivan, *Autobiography,* 172–73.
41. *Massachusetts Institute of Technology Eighth Annual Catalogue, 1872–1873* (1872), 17, 26, 34–35.

NOTES FOR CHAPTER II

1. On the Massachusetts Institute of Technology and its Architecture School see Walter Muir Whitehill, *Boston: A Topographical History* (Cambridge, Mass.: Harvard University Press, 1968 ed.), 169–70, and Paul R. Baker, *Richard Morris Hunt* (Cambridge, Mass.: The MIT Press, 1980), 105.
2. Douglass Shand Tucci, *Built in Boston: City & Suburb* (Boston: New York Graphic Society, 1978), 23, 43.
3. For biographical information on Ware, see the "Introductory Notes" by Henry Hope Reed to Ware's *The American Vignola*

(New York: W. W. Norton and Company, 1977 ed.), and A. D. F. Hamlin, "William Robert Ware, Organizer of the First American School of Architecture," *Architect and Engineer of California* 42 (July 1915): 100–101.

4. Tucci, *Built in Boston,* 41.
5. Quoted in Baker, *Richard Morris Hunt,* 105.
6. These quotations and his program for MIT can be found in Ware's "On the Condition of Architecture and of Architectural Education in the United States," *Papers of the Royal Institute of British Architects* (1866–1867), 81–90. Also see his *An Outline of a Course of Architectural Instruction* (Boston: John Wilson & Sons, 1866), 36 pp.
7. *The Autobiography of an Idea* (New York: Dover Press, 1956 ed.), 187. In this chapter Sullivan's autobiographical comments are from his chapters 10 and 11, pp. 175–213.
8. "Regulations of the School," *Eighth Annual Catalogue, Massachusetts Institute of Technology, 1872–1873* (1872), n.p.
9. Ware, "Architectural Education in the United States," 87.
10. On MIT policy for special students and military drill, see Samuel C. Prescott, *When M.I.T. was Boston Tech, 1861–1916* (Cambridge, Mass.: The MIT Press, 1954), 52, and *Eighth Annual Catalogue* (1872), 53.
11. Sullivan, *Autobiography,* 181–83; Frank Lloyd Wright, *An Autobiography* (New York: Duell, Sloan, and Pearce, 1943 ed.), 75–76. For the scope of the fire, see the drawing in *Harper's Weekly* supplement, December 14, 1872, and Jane Holtz Kay, *Lost Boston* (Boston: Houghton Mifflin, 1980), 214–19.
12. On Sullivan's curriculum and instructors, see *Eighth Annual Catalogue* (1872), 26, 64–65. His transcript is thus far unavailable for research.
13. This notebook is in the Louis H. Sullivan Collection, Avery Library, Columbia University, New York City.
14. "A Master and His Pupils," *AA&BN* 83 (January 16, 1904): 19–20, an account of a dinner for Ware given by former students and assistants in December 1903.
15. Donald Drew Egbert, *The Beaux-Arts Tradition in French Architecture* (Princeton, N.J.: Princeton University Press, 1980), 184.
16. See the drawings in Paul E. Sprague, ed., *The Drawings of Louis Henry Sullivan* (Princeton, N.J.: Princeton University Press, 1979), pl. 2–4, figs. 8, 9.

17. Photo in the possession of Avery Library. His classmates are listed in *Eighth Annual Catalogue* (1872), 16–17.
18. If he never saw Tompson again, he did keep in touch with George. Many years later, after the Tompsons had moved, Sullivan returned to their home to pay private homage. Ms. Gertrude Stearns, a lifelong resident of Wakefield, remembers seeing Sullivan arrive by taxi one winter night sometime between 1917 and 1922 and enter the barn in which he and George Tompson played as boys. He did not visit the house or the former List residence next door. After a few minutes, he boarded the taxi and left. Interview with Gertrude Stearns, January 21, 1981.
19. Compare Sullivan's *Autobiography,* 190–93, with Wright's *Autobiography,* 65–70, and Robert C. Twombly, *Frank Lloyd Wright: His Life and His Architecture* (New York: John Wiley & Sons, 1979), 17.
20. *Gopsill's Philadelphia City Directory for 1874,* p. 809, and for *1875,* p. 904.
21. James F. O'Gorman, *The Architecture of Frank Furness* (Philadelphia: Philadelphia Museum of Art, 1973), is the principal source for information on Sullivan's first employer. But also see James C. Massey, "Frank Furness in the 1870s: Some Lesser Known Buildings," *Charette* 43 (January 1963): 13–16, and Cervin Robinson, "Furness in '73," *Architecture Plus* 1 (August 1973): 26–33.
22. O'Gorman, *Frank Furness,* 38.
23. *Philadelphia Evening Bulletin,* April 18, 1924, quoted ibid., 33.
24. Henry-Russell Hitchcock, *Architecture: Nineteenth and Twentieth Centuries* (London: Penguin Books, 1958), 331, 333, and Winston Weismann, "Philadelphia Functionalism and Sullivan," *JSAH* 20 (March 1961): 3–19.
25. For discussions of Furness since the appearance of O'Gorman's important book see David Hanks, "Reform in Philadelphia: Frank Furness, Daniel Pabst, and 'Modern Gothic' Furniture," *Art News* 74 (October 1975): 52–54, and David Van Zanten, "Second Empire Architecture in Philadelphia," *Philadelphia Museum of Art Bulletin* 74 (September 1978): 9–24.
26. In *Louis Sullivan: The Shaping of American Architecture* (New York: Horizon Press, 1960), 35, 69, Willard Connely locates the first

Sullivan home in Chicago at 53 Peck Court. Neither the *Autobiography* nor city directories confirm that.

27. *Chicago City Directory,* 1871–77.
28. John W. Reps, *The Making of Urban America: A History of City Planning in the United States* (Princeton: N.J.: Princeton University Press, 1965), 300.
29. Finis Farr, *Chicago: A Personal History* . . . (New Rochelle, N.Y.: Arlington House, 1973), 108; Harold M. Mayer and Richard C. Wade, *Chicago: Growth of a Metropolis* (Chicago: University of Chicago Press, 1969), 94–96, 107–116.
30. On Jenney see work by Theodore Turak: "The Ecole Centrale and Modern Architecture: The Education of William Le Baron Jenney," *JSAH* 29 (March 1980): 40–47; "Jenney's Lesser Works: Prelude to the Prairie Style?" *PSR* 7 (Third Quarter, 1970): 5–20; and "William Le Baron Jenney: Pioneer of Chicago's West Parks," *IA* 24 (March 1980): 39–45. See also Carl W. Condit, "Jenney and the New Structural Technique," chapter 4 in *The Chicago School of Architecture* (Chicago: University of Chicago Press, 1964), 79–94.
31. Donald D. Egbert and Paul E. Sprague, "In Search of John Edelmann: Architect and Anarchist," *AIA Journal* 45 (February 1966): 35–41, remains the most complete account of this elusive figure, who will be discussed further in chapters 3 and 4.
32. The Lotus Club will be examined at greater length in chapter 4. See Sullivan's "Records" book in Avery Library, and Connely, *Louis Sullivan,* 50–53.
33. Turak, "Prelude to the Prairie Style?" 20.
34. See Gwendolyn Wright, *Building the Dream: A Social History of Housing in America* (New York: Pantheon Books, 1981), 106–7, 112–13.
35. *The New York Times,* July 12, 1874, p. 8, listed "L. H. Sullivan" among the *Britannic* passengers sailing for Liverpool via Cork the day before.

NOTES FOR CHAPTER III

1. Louis H. Sullivan, *The Autobiography of an Idea* (New York: Dover Press, 1956 ed.), 213–16. Autobiographical quotations and references in this chapter are from pages 213–40.
2. Except for ground-floor shops and minor interior alterations,

Louis's rue Racine boardinghouse remains much as it was in 1874.

3. A skeletal history of the Ecole des Beaux-Arts can be assembled from Donald Drew Egbert, *The Beaux-Arts Tradition in French Architecture* (Princeton, N.J.: Princeton University Press, 1980), 11–68.
4. On Haussmann's Paris, see David Pinckney, *Napoleon III and the Rebuilding of Paris* (Princeton, N.J.: Princeton University Press, 1958); Norma Evenson, *Paris: A Century of Change, 1878–1978* (New Haven: Yale University Press, 1979), chaps. 1, 2; and Jean Bastie, "Paris: Baroque Elegance and Agglomeration," chap. 3 in H. Wentworth Eldredge, ed., *World Capitals: Toward Guided Urbanization* (Garden City, N.Y.: Doubleday, 1975).
5. For a brief but informative discussion of Second Empire architecture, see Henry-Russell Hitchcock, *The Architecture of H. H. Richardson and His Times* (1936; Cambridge, Mass.: The MIT Press, 1966 ed.), 25–36.
6. Eugene Schulkind, "Introduction" to *The Paris Commune of 1871: The View from the Left* (New York: Grove Press, 1974), 25–57; Karl Marx and V. I. Lenin, *The Civil War in France: The Paris Commune* (New York: International Publishers, 1968).
7. Evenson, *Paris,* 9.
8. Sullivan, *Autobiography,* 220–21.
9. This information provided by David Van Zanten, Northwestern University, Evanston, Illinois.
10. These letters and other documents can be found in Sullivan's Ecole dossier, File AJ^{52} 239, item 2892, and File AJ^{52} 383, items 117–20, housed at the Archives de France, Paris.
11. Paul R. Baker, *Richard Morris Hunt* (Cambridge, Mass.: The MIT Press, 1980), 29–30; Ernest Flagg, "The Ecole des Beaux-Arts," *ARec* 3 (January–March 1894): 306, 308, from which the quotation in the next paragraph is taken.
12. Sullivan's Ecole dossier, item 2892.
13. Sherman Paul, *Louis Sullivan: An Architect in American Thought* (Englewood Cliffs, N.J.: Prentice-Hall, 1962), 19.
14. Louis to Albert Sullivan, December 7, 1874, Sullivan Collection, Burnham Library, The Art Institute, Chicago; or, reprinted, Willard Connely, "New Sullivan Letters," *AIA Journal* 20 (July 1953): 9–11.

15. On Ecole instructional methods, see Egbert, *The Beaux-Arts Tradition,* 115–17; Baker, *Hunt,* 28–36.
16. Illustrated in Egbert, *The Beaux-Arts Tradition,* pl. 12.
17. Frank Lloyd Wright, *Genius and the Mobocracy* (New York: Duell, Sloan and Pearce, 1949), first two captions in the unpaginated "Illustrations" section.
18. Louis to Albert Sullivan, December 7, 1874. The other American students entering the Ecole in 1874 included Henry O. Avery, George R. Shaw, Walter Cook, and Arthur Rotch, Sullivan's MIT classmate: *AA&BN* 22 (September 3, 1887): 113.
19. In his MIT "Records" book, later the Lotus Club notebook, Sullivan on page 190 listed every book he read in 1875: Sullivan Collection, Avery Library, Columbia University, New York.
20. Louis to Albert Sullivan, December 7, 1874.
21. *CT,* April 8, 1876, p. 10; telephone conversation with Charles E. Gregerson, Chicago, July 30, 1982.
22. *CT,* June 2, 1876, p. 8.
23. These drawings are available in Paul E. Sprague, ed., *The Drawings of Louis Henry Sullivan* (Princeton, N.J.: Princeton University Press, 1979), nos. 4–6, figs. 8–10.
24. Chicago *Times,* May 21, 1876, p. 2. For contemporary descriptions, see chapter 4.
25. Sullivan, *Autobiography,* 234–35.
26. His MIT "Records" book lists his reading; his sketches are in the Sullivan Collection, Burnham Library, Chicago.
27. *The New York Times,* May 24, 1875. p. 8; A. T. Andreas, *History of Chicago* (Chicago: A. T. Andreas, Publisher, 1885), 2: 566, puts Sullivan's return home in July, 1875.
28. Architect George Elmslie, for example. See Hugh Morrison, *Louis Sullivan: Prophet of Modern Architecture* (New York: W. W. Norton & Company, 1935), chap. 1, n. 2.
29. Sullivan to Claude Bragdon, July 25, 1904, in Bragdon, "Letters from Louis Sullivan," *Architecture* 6 (July 1931): 8.
30. Sprague, *Drawings,* 11.
31. Sullivan, *Autobiography,* 238.
32. Sullivan to Bragdon, July 25, 1904, op. cit., n. 23.

NOTES FOR CHAPTER IV

1. Quotations in this chapter from *The Autobiography of an Idea* are taken from the 1956 Dover Press (New York) edition, pages 241

to 259, but have not been individually cited except for lengthy or provocative passages.

2. Addresses, occupations, their changes, and other such data in this chapter were taken from the *Chicago City Directory,* 1875 to 1883.
3. Louis to Albert Sullivan, December 7, 1874, Sullivan Collection, Avery Library, Columbia University, New York, will be cited several times in this chapter.
4. Lotus Club activities and Sullivan's reading are chronicled in the "Records" book, Sullivan Collection, Avery Library.
5. Sullivan's annotated copy, inscribed by his father, is in the Avery Library Sullivan Collection.
6. Louis to Albert Sullivan, December 7, 1874, also the source of Sullivan's comments on Edelmann's athletic ability, below.
7. The Lotus Place athletes also called themselves the Chicago Football Club, with William Curtis president, Charles J. Williams treasurer, and a Mr. Cleveland, another Lotus member, its secretary. On July 15, 1876, Williams published an account of its centennial activities, "The Fourth of July at Calumet," in *The New York Sportsman,* mentioning the above three participants as well as John Edelmann and the Sullivan brothers. A Football Club program from May 27, 1876, listed Louis Sullivan's entry in 100-yard and quarter-mile races. These documents are in the Louis Sullivan Collection, Burnham Library, The Art Institute, Chicago.
8. "Madame Girard" is mentioned by Willard Connely, *Louis Sullivan: The Shaping of American Architecture* (New York: Horizon Press, 1960), 87, 92, but like many of Connely's statements has no supporting evidence.
9. Principally in the Burnham Library, The Art Institute, Chicago.
10. Donald D. Egbert and Paul E. Sprague, "In Search of John Edelmann: Architect and Anarchist," *AIA Journal* 45 (February 1966): 39.
11. Louis to Albert Sullivan, December 7, 1874.
12. *CT,* April 8, 1876, p. 10. Also see the *Daily Inter-Ocean,* April 8, 1876, and the Chicago *Times,* April 10, 1876, p. 1, for the consecration sermon.
13. The chalk graffiti was quoted in a long excerpt from an unidentified *Times* article reproduced by Connely, *Louis Sullivan,*

81–82; "Evangelizing Efforts," *Daily Inter-Ocean,* June 2, 1876, p. 2.

14. "The Saint's Rest," Chicago *Times,* May 31, 1876, p. 3.
15. See *Chicago Times,* May 21, p. 2; *Chicago Evening Journal,* May 31; *CT,* June 2, p. 8; and *Daily Inter-Ocean,* June 2, p. 2, all 1876.
16. "D. L. Moody's Church," *CT,* June 2, 1876, p. 8. In *Louis Sullivan,* 83–85, Connely reproduced portions of the May 21 *Times* article, but he changed much of the wording and made other editorial alterations without indication, thereby adding to the overall unreliability of his book.
17. "Artistic Frescoing," Chicago *Times,* May 21, 1876, p. 2; "Moody's Temple," *RE&BJ* 16 (June 3, 1876): 507.
18. Louis H. Sullivan to B. Lowenthal, January 18, 1879; minutes of the board of directors meeting for 1879, in Chicago Sinai Congregation archives. This and other information was made available through the courtesy of Rabbi Howard A. Berman. Ten years after installation, Sullivan's frescoes were destroyed in a fire: *CT,* November 12, 1886, p. 1.
19. So stated by Connely, *Louis Sullivan,* 91.
20. Phone conversation with Charles E. Gregerson, Chicago, July 30, 1982. Also see satyr and urn sketch by Sullivan, April 7, 1880, on Strippelman's letterhead, in the Burnham Library, The Art Institute, Chicago.
21. Sullivan, *Autobiography,* 251.
22. Ibid., 255–57.
23. *RE&BJ* 21 (September 11, 1880): 137.
24. Unpublished "Autobiography of Dankmar Adler," written around 1894 or 1895, copy in author's possession. Other biographical information can be found in Joan W. Saltzstein, "Dankmar Adler: Part One—The Man," *Wisconsin Architect* (July–August 1967): 15–19.
25. The Burling episode, well documented in *CT,* was called to my attention by Charles E. Gregerson in a July 30, 1982, Chicago phone conversation.
26. Adler, "Autobiography," 4; Sullivan, *Autobiography,* 288.
27. John Root, "Architects of Chicago," *IA* 16 (January 1891): 91; Rochelle S. Elstein, "The Architecture of Dankmar Adler," *JSAH* 26 (December 1967): 243, 249.
28. Adler, "Autobiography," 4; *CT,* December 5, 1879, p. 6.

29. Connely, *Louis Sullivan,* 96; Sherman Paul, *Louis Sullivan: An Architect in American Thought* (Englewood Cliffs, N.J.: Prentice-Hall, 1962), 23.
30. Carl W. Condit, *The Chicago School of Architecture* (Chicago: University of Chicago Press, 1964), 31. Also see *CT,* May 11, 1879, p. 8, and December 4, 1879, p. 8. The building was demolished in 1900.
31. *CT,* August 29, 1880, p. 8.
32. "Description of the Decoration and Arrangements of the Grand Opera House," *Daily Inter-Ocean,* September 4, 1880, p. 6; also "The Grand Opera House," ibid., August 28, 1880, p. 7. The building was demolished in 1959.
33. Chicago *Times,* September 5, 1880, p. 4.
34. *Daily Inter-Ocean,* September 4, 1880.
35. *CT,* September 5, 1880, p. 8.
36. Condit, *The Chicago School,* 38; Elstein, "Dankmar Adler," 245. The building was demolished in 1916.
37. The phrase is Hugh Morrison's: *Louis Sullivan: Prophet of Modern Architecture* (New York: W. W. Norton & Company, 1935), 72. In his treatment of the Borden residence in *Old Chicago Houses* (Chicago: University of Chicago Press, 1941), 277, author John Drury perfectly illustrates the way Adler has suffered at historians' hands: "In planning his mansion on Lake Park avenue," Drury incorrectly contends, "John Borden secured the services of Louis Sullivan . . . a partner of Dankmar Adler, another Chicago architect."
38. *RE&BJ* 22 (January 8, 1881), 14, and 22 (June 4, 1881): 250.

NOTES FOR CHAPTER V

1. In his pathbreaking 1935 biography, *Louis Sullivan: Prophet of Modern Architecture,* 294–303, Hugh Morrison cited 103 Adler & Sullivan commissions from 1879 to 1895. Richard Nickel added another seventeen in Edgar Kaufmann, Jr., ed., *Louis Sullivan and the Architecture of Free Enterprise* (Chicago: The Art Institute, exhibition catalogue, 1956), 36–37. Over the years several more surfaced now and again in scattered scholarly monographs. The remaining forty or so were discovered during research for this book. When Chicago architect John Vinci and his associates publish the long-awaited *The Complete Work of Adler and Sullivan,*

they will doubtless add to the 180 (1879–1895) entries in Appendix A.

2. It used to be believed that within the partnership Adler handled business affairs and engineering, Sullivan the architecture. But recent research suggests that Sullivan primarily designed ornament and facades, Adler the rest, in close consultation, of course, with each other. Following this line of thought, I have chosen in this and subsequent chapters on the partnership to treat buildings first of all as visible exteriors, as visual objects, as works of Sullivan the artist, as codes, metaphors, and emblems depending upon his intentions, but not as spatial or technical solutions unless reference is made to Adler. In the chapters on Sullivan's independent practice after 1895, all these approaches will be necessary.
3. Rochelle S. Elstein's unpublished thesis and work by Rachel Baron Heimovich do not attempt complete accounts of Adler's pre- and post-Sullivan careers.
4. John Anderson Miller, *Fares Please! A Popular History of Trolleys, Streetcars, Buses, Elevateds, and Subways* (1941; New York: Dover Press, 1960 ed.), 41–44.
5. Harold M. Meyer and Richard C. Wade, *Chicago: Growth of a Metropolis* (Chicago: University of Chicago Press, 1969), 138, also the source of the Windsor quotation.
6. Ibid., 146.
7. For a survey of these buildings, see John Drury, *Old Chicago Houses* (Chicago: University of Chicago Press, 1941, 1975), pts. 2 and 3.
8. Meyer and Wade, *Chicago,* 145.
9. In the following notes, I have listed the principal primary sources of information for each building. Readers may also refer to Morrison, *Sullivan,* 294–303. All clients have been checked against the Chicago *Lakeside Directory.* I took design dates from the primary sources, thereby correcting errors from previous publications. A list of commissions appears in Appendix A.

   On the Wineman House: *AA&BN* 12 (July 1, 1882): 11; *The Economist* 20 (October 1, 1898): 395; *Industrial Chicago* (Chicago: Goodspeed Publishing Company, 1891), 1: 179.
10. *AA&BN* 11 (June 17, 1882): 290; 12 (October 14, 1882): 188; 14 (September 15, 1883): 131; *Industrial Chicago,* 1: 174; *CT,* October 10, 1882, p. 18.

11. *AA&BN* 14 (July 28, 1883): 47; 14 (September 15, 1883): 141; *IA* 2 (August 1883): 98.
12. Information in the following paragraphs on Adler's family and friends was graciously supplied by his granddaughter, Joan Saltzstein, of Milwaukee.
13. Hugh Morrison, *Sullivan,* 299, thought Levi A. Eliel's house was commissioned by Holzheimer. Chicago city directories for 1887 and subsequent years establish that Eliel lived at that address prior to and during the Holzheimers' period of residence there.

    On the Eliel House, see *IA* 8 (December 1886): 87, and *RE&BJ* 28 (November 27, 1886): 647. On Adler's see *BB* 1 (November 1885): 84, and *CT,* November 15, 1885, p. 18. On all three see *CT,* November 11, 1885, p. 28; November 7, 1886, p. 7; November 21, 1886, p. 7.
14. *BB* 2 (October 1886): 126.
15. *AA&BN* 14 (September 15, 1883): 141. For the Selz house, refer to n. 11.
16. Goodman: *BB* 2 (February 1886): 24; 2 (April 1886): 46; 2 (May 1886): 58; *RE&BJ* 28 (May 1, 1886): 261; *CT,* April 18, 1886, p. 25; *CT,* April 27, 1886. Strauss: *IA* 3 (June 1884): 69.
17. On the Horner residence, see *CT,* May 23, 1886, p. 18, and *BB* 2 (May 1886): 58.
18. Henry Stern: *IA* 5 (February 1884): 14; 5 (June 1885): 79; *AA&BN* 18 (August 15, 1885): 83; *RE&BJ* 27 (February 21, 1885): 89; 27 (July 18, 1885): 383. Samuel Stern: *RE&BJ* 27 (August 22, 1885): 418; *IA* 5 (June 1885): 79; *AA&BN* 18 (August 22, 1885): 95; *CT,* August 7, 1885, p. 9.
19. *IA* 5 (December 1884): 70; *RE&BJ* 27 (July 18, 1885): 363.
20. *RE&BJ* 27 (July 18, 1885): 348; *BB* 1 (July 1885): 45; *IA* 5 (June 1885): 79; *AA&BN* 18 (August 15, 1885): 83; *CT,* July 22, 1885, p. 9; A. T. Andreas, *History of Chicago* (Chicago: A. T. Andreas, Publisher, 1885), 3: 724.
21. Barbe: *IA* 3 (April 1884): 38. Kuh: *CT,* September 2, 1885, p. 9; *AA&BN* 18 (September 12, 1885): 131; *BB* 1 (September 1885): 64; *RE&BJ* 27 (September 19, 1885): 465.
22. Frank: *RE&BJ* 26 (March 8, 1884): 113. M. C. Stearns: *RE&BJ* 27 (July 18, 1885): 348; *AA&BN* 17 (May 9, 1885): 228; *IA* 5 (June 1885): 79; *BB* 1 (July 1885): 45. Joseph Deimal: *BB* 2 (September 1886): 113; *RE&BJ* 28 (October 9, 1886): 509; 29

(May 28, 1887): 297; *CT,* October 10, 1886, p. 17. Rudolph Deimal: 29 (August 13, 1887): 439; 29 (August 20, 1887): 460. Note that Morrison spelled "Deimal" incorrectly. Rubel: *RE&BJ* 27 (July 18, 1885): 363; *IA* 3 (June 1884): 69; *CT,* July 27, 1884, p. 10; August 16, 1884, p. 14.

23. Morrison, *Sullivan,* 74.
24. Much of the work mentioned in the foregoing paragraph is depicted in *Louis H. Sullivan Architectural Ornament Collection* (Edwardsville: Southern Illinois University Office of Cultural Arts and University Museums, 1981).
25. *IA* 3 (March 1884): 23. Morrison misspelled Blumenfeld's name and mistakenly thought his commission to have been a private home, perhaps because its capitals were so similar to those on the Schwab house the year before, although much simplified.
26. *RE&BJ* 26 (March 8, 1884): 245; *AA&BN* 15 (June 7, 1884): 275.
27. *AA&BN* 14 (July 7, 1883): 324; *IA* 1 (July 1883): 84.
28. *RE&BJ* 21 (September 11, 1880): 137; *Industrial Chicago,* 1: 174; Frank A. Randall, *History of the Development of Building Construction in Chicago* (Urbana: University of Illinois Press, 1949), 90, 92; Carl W. Condit, *The Chicago School of Architecture* (Chicago: University of Chicago Press, 1964), 37–38; Morrison, *Sullivan,* 57–58.
29. Morrison, *Sullivan,* 58; Albert Bush-Brown, *Louis Sullivan* (New York: George Braziller Company, 1960), 14. Also see Lewis Mumford, *The Brown Decades* (1931; New York: Dover Press, 1971 ed.), 57; and *RE&BJ* 22 (January 8, 1881): 14.
30. Condit, *Chicago School,* 39; Morrison, *Sullivan,* 60; *Industrial Chicago,* 1: 174.
31. *Industrial Chicago,* 1: 174; *RE&BJ* 22 (August 27, 1881): 381; 25 (December 29, 1883): 665; Condit, *Chicago School,* 39; Morrison, *Sullivan,* 59–60.
32. *Industrial Chicago,* 1: 174; *AA&BN* 14 (September 15, 1883): 131; *RE&BJ* 22 (September 17, 1881): 415.
33. *IA* 2 (August 1883): 98, and materials supplied by Patricia J. Casler, executive director, Aurora Preservation Commission, November 1982. Also see Rochelle S. Elstein, "The Architecture of Dankmar Adler," *JSAH* 27 (December 1967): 246.
34. On the Kennedy Bakery, see *CT,* December 28, 1884, p. 10;

AA&BN 14 (September 15, 1883): 131; 15 (May 3, 1884): 216; *IA* 3 (March 1884): 23, the source of the quotation. On the Knisely Factory, see *IA* 3 (March 1884): 23; Condit, *Chicago School,* 40; Morrison, *Sullivan,* 64–65.

35. *AA&BN* 17 (March 14, 1885): 127.
36. Mumford, *Brown Decades,* 57; Morrison, *Sullivan,* 60–61; Condit, *Chicago School,* 40; *RE&BJ* 27 (July 18, 1885): 363; *AA&BN* 17 (March 14, 1885): 127; *IA* 3 (June 1884): 66; 5 (December 1884): 70; *CT,* July 20, 1884, p. 14; September 14, 1884, p. 18; December 28, 1884, p. 10; "A Fine Structure on Randolph Street," April 12, 1885, p. 7; April 25, 1886, p. 20.
37. *CT,* May 18, 1884, p. 17; July 20, 1884, p. 14; August 31, 1884, p. 19; December 28, 1884, p. 10; Condit, *Chicago School,* 80; Morrison, *Sullivan,* 61–62; *Industrial Chicago,* 1: 183; *IA* 3 (June 1884): 66; *RE&BJ* 26 (March 8, 1884): 113; *AA&BN* 16 (July 5, 1884): 12.
38. Paul E. Sprague, "Sullivan's Scoville Building, a Chronology," *PSR* 11 (Third Quarter, 1974): 23; also *AA&BN* 18 (July 5, 1885): 11; *IA* 3 (June 1884): 69; *RE&BJ* 27 (July 4, 1885): 318; *CT,* June 21, 1885, p. 8; and Nory Miller in the new *IA* 19 (November 1975): 22.
39. The subtitle of Hugh Morrison's 1935 biography.
40. *IA* 6 (November 1885); *Building* 4 (January 23, 1886).
41. Hammond Library: *CT,* August 13, 1882, p. 9; *AA&BN* 11 (May 6, 1882): 216; 12 (August 19, 1882): 91; *IA* 1 (February 1883): 3. Schoolhouse: *AA&BN* 14 (September 15, 1883): 131.
42. Elevator car: *IA* 3 (July 1884): 82. Mandel stable: *IA* 3 (March 1884): 23. Lakeside Club: *IA* 5 (December 1884): 70; 5 (February 1885): 14; *RE&BJ* 27 (February 21, 1885): 89.
43. Zion Temple: *RE&BJ* 27 (July 18, 1885): 363; *IA* 5 (June 1885): 79; *AA&BN* 17 (May 16, 1885): 239; 18 (August 15, 1885): 83; *CT,* April 6, 1885, p. 11; *Industrial Chicago,* 1: 267. Chiltenham pavilion: *IA* 5 (June 1885): 79; *BB* 1 (July 1885): 14; 2 (May 1886): 57.
44. On the Thirty-ninth Street Station, see *CT,* August 5, 1886, p. 6; August 8, 1886, p. 2; and "Our Railway Stations," August 8, 1886, p. 3. It has mistakenly been asserted that Adler & Sullivan designed two stations for the Illinois Central at the same time, but the other, at Forty-third Street, was not announced until 1888. See *CT,* June 17, 1888, p. 31.

45. Patrick Sullivan's certificate of death, dated June 19, 1884, is document number 44234 in the Office of the Coroner of Cook County, Chicago. His obituary appeared in *CT*, June 20, 1884, p. 8. Andrienne's drawing of Anemone Japonica, dated October 1885, in Lyons Falls, establishes her whereabouts, as does her death certificate, document number 24421, dated May 16, 1892, Lewis County, New York.
46. *IA* 6 (November 1885): 86–87.

NOTES FOR CHAPTER VI

1. Louis H. Sullivan, *The Autobiography of an Idea* (1924; New York: Dover Press, 1956 ed.), 258.
2. Sullivan's dates are slightly inaccurate. The Ryerson buildings apparently were: (1) the Jewelers' Building (1881–82) on South Wabash; (2) the Revell Building (1881–83) on the northeast corner of Wabash and Adams; (3) the Ryerson Building (1884) on Randolph across from Central Music Hall; (4) the Ryerson Charities Trust Building (1886) on Market and Adams, completed by Ryerson's son, also named Martin, after his father's 1887 death; (5) another Ryerson Building (1887) redesigned and built as (6) the Walker Warehouse (1888–90) at Adams and Franklin; and (7) the Ryerson Tomb (1887) in Graceland Cemetery.
3. Sullivan, "Development of Construction," *The Economist* 55 (June 24, 1916): 1252. The trusses actually appeared in the 1891 reconstruction: see chapter 9.
4. Carl W. Condit, *The Chicago School of Architecture* (Chicago: University of Chicago Press, 1964), 32; Hugh Morrison, *Louis Sullivan: Prophet of Modern Architecture* (1935; New York: W. W. Norton & Company, 1962 ed.), 288.
5. Dankmar Adler, "Engineering Supervision of Building Operations," *AA&BN* 33 (July 4, 1891): 11, reprinted from *The Economist;* Adler, letter to the editor, *The Economist* 5 (May 9, 1891): 798.
6. *Industrial Chicago* (Chicago: Goodspeed Publishers, 1891), 1: 168; Morrison, *Sullivan,* 287; Condit, *Chicago School,* 32; also see *CT*, May 11, 1879, p. 11; December 4, 1879, p. 8; December 5, 1879, p. 6; January 22, 1888, p. 7.
7. Unpublished "Autobiography of Dankmar Adler," 4, copy in author's possession.

8. *Daily Inter-Ocean,* August 28, 1880, p. 7; September 4, 1880, p. 6.
9. Sullivan, "Development of Construction," 1252.
10. Charles Gregerson, "Early Adler & Sullivan Work in Kalamazoo," *PSR* 11 (Third Quarter, 1974): 5–14.
11. "Wanted—A Music Hall," *RE&BJ* 23 (April 8, 1882): 213.
12. "Hooley's New Theatre," *Daily Inter-Ocean,* August 12, 1882, p. 13, including Sullivan's interview, called to my attention by Charles Gregerson. Also "Hooley's," *CT,* August 13, 1882, p. 6.
13. *RE&BJ* 21 (December 11, 1880): 274; 22 (April 30, 1881): 189; 22 (July 23, 1881): 323–24; *Industrial Chicago,* 1: 173; A. T. Andreas, *History of Chicago* (Chicago: A. T. Andreas, Publisher, 1876), 3: 666.
14. "Haverly's," *CT,* August 23, 1884, p. 8.
15. "Decorations at Haverly's," *CT,* August 24, 1884, p. 8; "The Haverly Theatre as Seen by English Eyes," ibid., December 7, 1884, p. 24.
16. "Haverly's Opening," *CT,* August 26, 1884, p. 5; "Amusements," ibid., August 31, 1884, p. 19.
17. "The Haverly Theatre as Seen by English Eyes," *CT,* December 7, 1884, p. 24; *IA* 4 (September 1884): 28. Also see *CT,* August 3, 1884, pp. 14, 16; August 10, 1884, p. 11; August 16, 1884, p. 8.
18. *CT,* July 8, 1884, p. 9. Adler & Sullivan may have done an even earlier music festival remodeling: *The New York Times,* March 15, 1884, p. 2.
19. Sullivan, *Autobiography,* 293.
20. On the Interstate Building renovation, see Andreas, *Chicago,* 3: 651; Morrison, *Sullivan,* 67–71; "A Mammoth Opera House," *IA* 5 (March 1885): 25; *RE&BJ* 27 (February 21, 1885): 89; 27 (April 4, 1885): 160–61; "The Opera Festival," *CT,* March 1, 1885, p. 7, including a Rand McNally Company floor plan; "The Operatic Festival," ibid., March 28, 1885, p. 12; editorial, "The Opera Festival," ibid., April 5, 1885, p. 4; ibid., April 12, 1885, p. 27.
21. On McVicker's pre–Adler & Sullivan history see Condit, *Chicago School,* 40; Morrison, *Sullivan,* 67; *Industrial Chicago,* 1: 204.
22. The most thorough description is "McVicker's Theatre. A Thespian Temple Worthy of Chicago," *RE&BJ* 27 (July 18, 1885): 347–48.

23. *RE&BJ* 27 (July 18, 1885): 347–48, and G. W. Orear, *Commercial and Architectural Chicago* (Chicago: G. W. Orear, 1887), 55.
24. *RE&BJ* 27 (July 18, 1885): 348.
25. *RE&BJ* 27 (July 18, 1885): 348; Blackall's review is in "Notes of Travel," *AA&BN* 22 (December 24, 1887): 299–300.
26. "McVicker's Opening an Architectural Success and a Dramatic Failure," *CT,* July 2, 1885, p. 5; "McVicker's Theatre," ibid., July 2, 1885, p. 7.
27. *RE&BJ* 27 (July 18, 1885): 348. Also see ibid. 27 (January 24, 1885): 38; 27 (February 21, 1885): 89; *IA* 4 (September 1884): 28; 5 (January 1885): 82; "McVicker and His Tenants," *CT,* April 11, 1885, p. 8; ibid., May 10, 1885, p. 14; "McVicker's Renovated Theatre," ibid., June 19, 1885, p. 6.
28. Joseph Twyman, letter to the editor, *AA&BN* 23 (January 28, 1888): 47; Adler & Sullivan, "The Decoration of McVicker's Theatre" (a letter to the editor), ibid. 23 (February 11, 1888): 70–71; Joseph Twyman, "Decoration of McVicker's Theatre, Chicago" (a letter to the editor), ibid. 23 (March 10, 1888): 118.
29. Arthur Woltersdorf, "Dankmar Adler," *WA* 33 (July 1924): 75.
30. "The Remodeling of the Exposition Interior," *Milwaukee Sentinel,* June 28, 1886, p. 3; *The Milwaukee Daily Journal,* July 13, 1886, p. 1; *CT,* May 16, 1886, p. 17; "The Big Saengerfest," ibid., May 30, 1886, p. 6; "Milwaukee Musical Event," ibid., July 20, 1886, p. 1; *IA* 6 (December 1885): 105.
31. On Cobb and Frost's and Adler & Sullivan's Chicago Opera House, see *CT,* April 4, 1886, p. 7; June 6, 1886, p. 17; August 1, 1886, p. 3; August 15, 1886, pp. 3, 11.

    Two years later a fire caused $20,000 damage to the theater's interior. Although Adler was retained by the Opera House Company to negotiate with insurance adjusters, Sullivan was not hired to redo the decorations: *CT,* December 13, 1888, p. 1; December 14, p. 2; December 24, p. 3.
32. "Subscribers to the Grand Opera-Hall," *CT,* September 26, 1886, p. 7.
33. *IA* 5 (March 1885): 23.
34. Published as "Theatres" in *AA&BN* 22 (October 29, 1887): 206–8, reprinted in *IA* 10 (October 1887): 45–46, and in *BB* 3, (October 1887): 127–29.

NOTES FOR CHAPTER VII

1. The most convenient sources on the Auditorium are Dankmar Adler, "The Chicago Auditorium," *ARec* 1 (April–June 1892): 415–34; Hugh Morrison, *Louis Sullivan: Prophet of Modern Architecture* (1935; New York: W. W. Norton & Co., 1962 ed.), chap. 3; Carl W. Condit, *The Chicago School of Architecture* (Chicago: University of Chicago Press, 1964), 69–79, which follows Morrison closely; and *The Auditorium Building: Its History and Architectural Significance* (Chicago: Roosevelt University, 1976), text by Daniel H. Perlman.
2. *CT*, May 31, 1885, p. 3; January 24, 1886, p. 20.
3. "New Grand-Opera House," *CT*, June 13, 1886, p. 9; "Subscribers to the Grand Opera-Hall," ibid., September 26, 1886, p. 7; "The 'Grand Auditorium,'" ibid., November 28, 1886, p. 7.
4. "The Grand Auditorium," *CT*, December 10, 1886, p. 1; "Chicago Auditorium Association," précis of board of directors' minutes, Chicago Historical Society.
5. Morrison, *Sullivan*, 87.
6. "Chicago Real Estate," *CT*, December 19, 1886, p. 7.
7. Louis to Albert Sullivan, January 20, 1887, Burnham Library, Chicago Art Institute.
8. "The Convention Hall," *CT*, January 30, 1887, p. 17.
9. Adler, "The Chicago Auditorium," 415, 417.
10. Adler to Albert Sullivan, February 12, 1887, Burnham Library, Chicago Art Institute.
11. *CT*, January 30, 1887, p. 17; April 17, 1887, p. 30; May 8, 1887, p. 13; "A New Building-Stone," May 29, 1887, p. 6.
12. *RE&BJ* 29 (April 9, 1887): 191; 29 (October 8, 1887): 539; 30 (January 14, 1888): 26; *BB* 3 (May 1887): 66; *CT*, June 26, 1887, p. 3; October 23, 1887, p. 7; November 30, 1887, p. 8; December 25, 1887, p. 2; "The Auditorium Building," March 11, 1888, p. 7.
13. "The Convention Hall," *CT*, June 9, 1888, p. 1; "The Great Auditorium," June 18, 1888, p. 7; *BB* 4 (June 1888): 61.
14. *CT*, June 9, 1888, p. 1; also see ibid., "The Great Auditorium," June 10, 1888, p. 13, with sketch; "The Decorator at Work," June 12, 1888, p. 1; "The Hall Nearly Ready," June 13, 1888,

p. 1; and large sketch of "Interior of the Great Auditorium," June 17, 1888, p. 9.

15. "Inspecting the Auditorium," *CT,* June 15, 1888, p. 1.
16. *Building* 9 (July 18, 1888): 56; *IA* 12 (August 1888): 1; E. O. Sachs, "The 'Asphaleia' Stage at Buda-Pesth," *AA&BN* 54 (December 10, 1896): 97–100; *CT,* January 20, 1889, p. 17.
17. *CT,* August 19, 1888, p. 18; "The Auditorium Building," September 16, 1888, p. 28; "The Auditorium Hotel," September 22, 1888, p. 1; *IA* 12 (August 1888): 8.
18. "Accident at the Auditorium Building," *CT,* March 29, 1888, p. 8.
19. *CT,* February 5, 1888, p. 6; March 25, 1888, p. 31; May 27, 1888, p. 6; "Another Building Project," August 2, 1888, p. 1; March 3, 1889, p. 5.
20. *The Economist* 2 (February 9, 1889): 97–98, and quoted in "Widening Congress Street," *CT,* February 10, 1889, p. 6.
21. *CT,* August 19, 1888, p. 18.
22. "A Peep at the Auditorium," *CT,* October 18, 1888, p. 1; *The Economist* 1 (October 27, 1888): 10.
23. *CT,* March 24, 1889, p. 30; *The Economist* 2 (April 29, 1889): 314; *Building* 10 (May 11, 1889): 156, on Adler & Sullivan's office moves.
24. "They Visit the Auditorium," *CT,* June 14, 1889, p. 3; "In Their New Quarters," July 14, 1889, p. 25; "The Great Auditorium," September 21, 1889, p. 1; *The Economist* 2 (August 31, 1889): 764, 768, 769.
25. "Blessed by Masons," *CT,* October 3, 1889, pp. 1, 2.
26. "Greatest in the World," *CT,* December 8, 1889, p. 30; "Dedicated to Music and the People," December 10, 1889, pp. 1–3; "Patti on the Auditorium," December 12, 1889, p. 1.
27. Willard Connely, *Louis Sullivan: The Shaping of American Architecture* (New York: Horizon Press, 1960), 121.
28. "A Word for the Architect," *CT,* December 15, 1889, p. 10. "In the eyes of all of the architects and many of the public," *AA&BN*'s Chicago correspondent wrote of the dedication, "there was . . . one thing lacking in all the ceremony and that was that Messrs. Adler and Sullivan, the architects to whose thought, study and conscientious work the whole magnificent pile was due, were not even mentioned by name in the exercises

and received no public recognition whatever": 26 (December 28, 1889): 299.

29. Dankmar Adler, "Foundations of the Auditorium Building, Chicago," *IA* 11 (March 1888): 32.
30. Louis Sullivan, "Development of Building—II," *The Economist* 56 (July 1, 1916): 40.
31. On the foundations, see Adler, "Foundations," 31–32; his letter to the editor, *AA&BN* 32 (April 4, 1891): 15–16; ibid. 31 (March 21, 1891): 189; 26 (November 9, 1889): 223–24; and the sources cited in n. 1.
32. Adler, "Foundations," 32.
33. "New Offices of Adler & Sullivan, Architects, Chicago," *Engineering & Building Record* 22 (June 7, 1890): 5, including floor plans.
34. Paul E. Sprague, "Introduction," *The Drawings of Louis Henry Sullivan* (Princeton, N.J.: Princeton University Press, 1979), 8–12.
35. Morrison, *Sullivan,* 98; Adler, "The Chicago Auditorium," 417, 420.
36. Adler, "The Chicago Auditorium," 421.
37. "The Auditorium Theatre," *Interior Design* 39 (May 1968): 142–45.
38. *AA&BN* 26 (December 28, 1889): 299–300; *Industrial Chicago* (Chicago: Goodspeed Publishers, 1891), 1: 194–96; Moses King and Moses F. Sweetser, *King's Handbook of the United States* (Buffalo: Moses King Corporation, 1891), 215–16; *Daily Inter-Ocean,* September 10, 1889.
39. Montgomery Schuyler, "Architecture in Chicago: Adler & Sullivan," *ARec* special series, 4 (December 1895): 3–48.
40. *The Economist* 20 (October 29, 1898): 509; *RE&BJ* 42 (February 15, 1908): 11; 43 (March 6, 1909): 7.
41. "Sullivan's Auditorium Inducted," *JSAH* 2 (July 1942): 33.

NOTES FOR CHAPTER VIII

1. Louis H. Sullivan, *The Autobiography of an Idea* (1924; New York: Dover Press, 1956 ed.), 294.
2. Willard Connely, *Louis Sullivan: The Shaping of American Architecture* (New York: Horizon Press, 1960), 124.
3. Pueblo Opera House: *RE&BJ* 31 (January 19, 1889): 35;

Wainwright Building: ibid. 4 (April 29, 1890): 900; Seattle Opera House: ibid.; Ontario Hotel: *CT*, May 4, 1890, p. 29; Dooly Block: ibid., November 30, 1890, p. 29.

4. Sullivan's account of his trip and of Ocean Springs is in *Autobiography,* 294–98. A contemporary chronicler of the Pueblo building did not mention a Sullivan visit in his detailed account of its design and construction, but it is clear he did visit Seattle in 1890: see chapter 9, n. 16, 25.
5. New Orleans *Daily Picayune,* July 24, 1892, p. 12, brought to my attention by James Stevens of Biloxi. On Alto Park see Jackson County Mississippi Deed Record Book, 39, pp. 272–73, at the county court house, Pascagoula, Mississippi. On Ocean Springs and Sullivan's work there: Thomas Ewing Dabney, *Ocean Springs: The Land Where Dreams Come True* (c. 1915; reprinted Ocean Springs: 1699 Historical Committee, 1974); Regina B. Hines, *Ocean Springs, 1892* (Pascagoula: Regina B. Hines, 1974); Mary Wallace Crocker, *Historic Architecture in Mississippi* (Jackson: University of Mississippi Press, 1973), 96–99; Kenneth Severns, *Southern Architecture* (New York: E. P. Dutton, 1981).
6. Jackson County Mississippi Warranty Deed Book, 11, p. 13 (March 1, 1890); 11, p. 44 (March 7, 1890); 14, pp. 461–62 (December 22, 1892).

    In *An Autobiography* (New York: Duell, Sloan and Pearce, 1943 ed.), 110, and in *Genius and the Mobocracy* (New York: Duell, Sloan and Pearce, 1949), 51, Frank Lloyd Wright claimed to have designed both houses. But Sullivan wrote (*Autobiography,* 297) that "he [Sullivan] planned for two shacks or bungalows, 300 feet apart, with stables far back; also a system of development requiring years for fulfillment. . . . The building work was let to a local carpenter." Given Wright's propensity for exaggeration and for claiming credit for most everything, plus the visual evidence of the Charnley house—the Sullivan residence is altered almost beyond recognition—including its local pine paneling, its siting, and its semitropical climate controls that only someone on the scene could have devised, Sullivan's account seems the more reliable.

    Willard Connely and many local residents believe that Sullivan also designed the Ocean Springs St. John's Episcopal Church. But the church's "Book of [Ladies'] Guild Minutes,"

October 11, 1891, states that the plans were "drawn from illustrations in the 'Churchman' of July 11th." The Episcopal publication *The Churchman* (64 [July 11, 1891]: 52–53) does in fact show a rendering and plan by New York City architect Manly N. Cutter for the Church of the Ascension, Rockville Center, Long Island, corresponding in all essentials to St. John's. Access to the "Minutes" was arranged and considerable other help provided by Ms. Courtney Blossman of Ocean Springs, a member of St. John's and a Sullivan aficionado.

7. Jackson County, Mississippi, Deed Records, 11, p. 97; 13, p. 425; 14, pp. 79, 262. *The Biloxi Herald,* February 7, 1891, p. 1; April 4, 1891, p. 1.
8. *The Biloxi Herald,* April 25, 1891, p. 1; "Where the Palmettos Grow," *IA* 19 (February 1892): 13.
9. Sullivan's friend and occasional colleague, Lyndon P. Smith, a Palisades, New York, architect, wrote a detailed account of the Ocean Springs residence in "The Home of an Artist-Architect," *ARec* 17 (June 1905): 471–91, including illustrations and a site plan. Some of Sullivan's own rose photographs are here and in *Forms & Fantasies* 1 (June 1898).
10. April 1983 interviews with J. K. Lemon, Bobby Davidson Smith, and Charles E. Schmidt of Ocean Springs, and with James Stevens of Biloxi.
11. On I. Giles Lewis, see the Chicago *City Directory* and the *Chicago Blue Book* 1890 to 1900; Paul E. Sprague, *The Drawings of Louis Henry Sullivan* (Princeton, N.J.: Princeton University Press, 1979), 32, 53; Dankmar Adler to Albert Sullivan, February 12, 1887, Burnham Library, Chicago Art Institute; Lewis's certificate of death no. 24209, filed September 19, 1918, Bureau of Vital Statistics, State Board of Health, Chicago.
12. *The Economist* 6 (November 7, 1891): 800; *CT,* November 8, 1891, p. 27.
13. On Albert Sullivan and family: *Daily Picayune,* September 3, 1891, p. 2; February 12, 1893, p. 4; *Railroad Gazette* 37 (July 8, 1904): 123 in "General News Section"; *Railway Age Gazette* 52 (February 9, 1912): 257; his obituary in *Poughkeepsie Eagle-News,* March 29, 1938; *Poughkeepsie Journal,* October 2, 1974, on the death of his daughter Andrienne; and John E. Stover, *History of the Illinois Central Railroad* (New York: Macmillan, 1975), 301.

Even after he left Chicago, Albert continued to dabble in local real estate: *The Economist* 34 (July 29, 1905): 166. When he sold the Sullivan house, it was featured in the realtor's advertising: ibid. 33 (March 18, 1905): 383.

14. Daniel Wogan to author, October 29, 1982; Jackson County Mississippi Deed Record, 18, pp. 550–52; 23, p. 310.
15. Wright's principal recollections are in *An Autobiography,* 89–110, and in *Genius and the Mobocracy, passim.* Elmslie is quoted by Hugh Morrison, *Louis Sullivan: Prophet of Modern Architecture* (1935; New York: W. W. Norton & Co., 1962 ed.), 82–83; Purcell in his "Recollections," *Northwest Architect* 8 (July 1944): *passim,* and "Sullivan at Work," ibid. 8 (January–February 1944): 11; and William L. Steele in Morrison, *Sullivan,* 237–38, and Connely, *Sullivan,* 207–8.
16. John Root, "Architects of Chicago," *IA* 16 (January 1891): 92; Karl to Marie Bitter, August 6, 1903, quoted in James M. Dennis, *Karl Bitter: Architectural Sculptor, 1867–1915* (Madison: University of Wisconsin Press, 1967), 277–78.
17. Copies of the 1909 inventory and the 1887 letter to Whitman are in the American Institute of Architects Archives, Washington, D.C. On Sullivan and Whitman, see Sherman Paul, *Louis Sullivan: An Architect in American Thought* (Englewood Cliffs, N.J.: Prentice-Hall, 1962), 1–3.

    In February 1887, when Sullivan wrote to Whitman and also met Professor William R. Ware in New York to get his final approval of the Auditorium renderings, the poet was living in Camden, New Jersey, a short rail trip away. One wonders if the two actually met.
18. On Sullivan's clubs see the *Chicago Blue Book* from 1890 on and "The Chicago Clubs," *RE&BJ* 32 (1890 supplement). The quote is William Steele's in Connely, *Sullivan,* 208.
19. On the Chicago Architectural Club, see H. Allen Brooks, *The Prairie School: Frank Lloyd Wright and His Midwest Contemporaries* (Toronto: University of Toronto Press, 1972), 37–38; Mark L. Peisch, *The Chicago School of Architecture: Early Followers of Sullivan and Wright* (New York: Random House, 1964), 32–33.
20. *Northwest Architect & Building Budget,* 10 (December 1892): 96; and *BkB* 5 (December 1896): 223.
21. *BB* 5 (March 1889): 44; *IA* 7 (April 1886): 46; 10 (January

1888): 101; 13 (June 1889): 89; *Building* 9 (July 28, 1888): 31; 11 (September 14, 1889): 90; *Industrial Chicago* (Chicago: Goodspeed Publishers, 1891), 1: 306; *The Economist* 2 (July 13, 1889): 598.

22. *IA* 12 (December 1888): 80.
23. "Style," *IA* 11 (May 1888): 59–60.
24. "Artistic Use of the Imagination," *Building* 11 (October 19, 1889): 129–30, comment in *IA* 14 (October 1889): 42. Here and in the following pages on Sullivan's speeches and organizational affiliations, I use male gender terminology when paraphrasing his references to artists, since he did so and to correct him in light of modern sensibilities would be presumptuous, and in reference to architects, for the same reasons and because professional organizations in his day were exclusively male.
25. *IA* 6 (October 1885): 43; 7 (June 1886): 82; 7 (July 1886): 98; 8 (August 1886): 8; 8 (September 1886): 24; 9 (March 1887): 23; *BB* 1 (October 1885): 68; 3 (March 1887): 32; *RE&BJ* 27 (January 31, 1885): 52. Sullivan's remarks are in *IA* 5 (February 1885): 5–8.
26. *BB* 4 (June 1888): 73, 76; 4 (November 1888): 156; *IA* 10 (October 1887): 35; 10 (November 1887): 66; 10 (February 1888): 9; 12 (December 1888): 81, 86–88; 13 (March 1889): 42; 14 (January 1890): 96; *AA&BN* 22 (October 8, 1887): 175; 22 (December 10, 1887): 273; *Building* 9 (December 22, 1888): 228; 9 (December 29, 1888): 236; 11 (December 21, 1889): 225–26. *Industrial Chicago,* 1: 304–5, has a brief organizational history.
27. Sullivan's letter is in *Building* 9 (August 25, 1888): 64.
28. *BB* 4 (December 1888): 167–68.
29. *BB* 3 (November 1887): 152; *AA&BN* 20 (December 4, 1886): 267; 22 (November 26, 1887): 252–53; *IA* 4 (November 1884): 3, 8, 12 (extra number); 6 (November 1885): 71–87, source of the impromptu exchange; 10 (December 1887): 77, for Sullivan's quote. Also *Industrial Chicago,* 1: 300.

    Also a founding member, Adler was elected president of the Western Architects in November 1885: *AA&BN* 18 (November 28, 1885): 253.
30. Sullivan is quoted in *IA* 12 (November 1888): 64, 68. Also see "Architects in Council," *CT,* November 22, 1888, p. 2; *Build-*

ing 9 (December 1, 1888): 196–203; *BB* 4 (November 1888): 150–56; and *IA* 11 (April 1888): 53, showing that between conventions Sullivan tried to generate momentum on the code of ethics issue.

31. Membership ledgers, AIA Archives, Washington, D.C. Sullivan became a member of the Western Association at its founding, November 17, 1884. On October 21, 1887, he was elected an associate in AIA. At the twenty-third AIA convention in November 1889, consolidating the two organizations, it was determined that all WAA members would be "fellows" of AIA retroactive to the date they joined WAA. Sullivan was henceforth listed as an AIA member beginning November 17, 1884, causing some confusion for later observers, including Sullivan himself who in 1893, replying to a letter from Alfred Stone, AIA's secretary, wrote "I am unable to [tell you] whether I was elected a member of AIA in 1887 or 1884. I cannot find any records." Sullivan to Stone, November 9, 1893, AIA Archives. Also see *Annuary of the American Institute of Architects for 1907 and 1908,* 16, 23.
32. *IA* 12 (November 1888): 68.
33. *IA* 16 (September 1890): 13; George C. Nimmons to Sullivan, February 13, 1890, AIA Archives.
34. *IA* 22 (August 1893): 11; supplement, "The World's Congress of Architects," *AIA Proceedings* (1893), 131; Sullivan to Alfred Stone, December 27, 1893, AIA Archives.
35. Stone to Sullivan, October 22, 1894; January 14, 1895 (two letters that day); May 29, 1895; July 27, 1895, AIA archives; *IA* 24 (November 1894): 39; 24 (January 1895): 54; 25 (July 1895): 60; *AA&BN* 50 (October 19, 1895): 34.
36. AIA membership ledgers, AIA Archives; *IA* 14 (January 1890): 96.
37. "Essay on Inspiration," *IA* 8 (December 1886): 61–64; Paul, *Sullivan,* 36–40; Lauren S. Weingarten, "Louis H. Sullivan: Investigation of a Second French Connection," *JSAH* 39 (December 1980): 297–303.

    Most of Sullivan's early speeches were published in *IA,* where he, Adler, and several others were listed on the masthead during the 1890s as "special contributors."

    Commentary on "Inspiration" was in *AA&BN* 20 (November 27, 1886): 254, and in *CT,* November 18, 1886. On its change in title, see Sullivan to John Root, WAA secretary, October 20, November 3, 1886, AIA Archives.

38. *IA* 9 (March 1887): 26.
39. "What Is the Just Subordination, in Architectural Design, of Detail to Mass?" *IA* 9 (April 1887): 51–52, additional comments on pp. 52–53; also in *BB* 3 (April 1887): 62–64.
40. This was Sullivan's original title as proposed by AIA secretary Alfred Stone in letters to Sullivan, June 4, August 21, 1894, AIA Archives. The title was later changed to "Emotional Architecture as Compared with Intellectual" for publication in *IA* 24 (November 1894): 32–34.

NOTES FOR CHAPTER IX

1. Grant Manson, "Sullivan and Wright: An Uneasy Union of Celts," *ARec* 118 (November 1955): 297–300.
2. Frank Lloyd Wright, *An Autobiography* (New York: Duell, Sloan and Pearce, 1943 ed.), 110.
3. *BB* 4 (February 1888): x.
4. Wright, *An Autobiography*, 110.
5. Frank Lloyd Wright, "Form and Function," a review of Hugh Morrison's *Louis Sullivan,* in *Saturday Review of Literature* 13 (December 14, 1935).
6. Wright claimed to have designed "the broad paneled wooden tablet to be put in the foyer" and the Auditorium bar: *Genius and the Mobocracy* (New York: Duell, Sloan and Pearce, 1949), 48.
7. On Charnley, see *CT,* June 21, 1891, p. 9, and July 5, 1891, p. 14.
8. *An Autobiography,* 110–11. In 1892 Wright was listed in the Chicago *City Directory* at 1600 Auditorium Building, Adler & Sullivan's, but in 1893 he was at 1501 Schiller Building, his own office. When his drawings for municipal boathouses won a city-sponsored competition in May 1893, Wright was described as "a former Madison boy, now a Chicago architect": *Wisconsin State Journal* (Madison), May 12, 1893.
9. Henry-Russell Hitchcock, *In the Nature of Materials: The Buildings of Frank Lloyd Wright, 1887–1941* (New York: Duell, Sloan and Pearce, 1942), 18–22; Grant Manson, *Frank Lloyd Wright to 1910: The First Golden Age* (New York: Reinhold Publishing Corporation, 1958), 33–44, 44–60 *passim.*

Probably not bootlegs were the houses for W. S. MacHarg (1890, Chicago), who was well known to Adler and Sullivan; Henry N. Cooper (1890, La Grange), an unbuilt project Hitchcock says Wright drew before he joined Adler & Sullivan; Walter Gale (1893, Oak Park), which Wright designed after opening his own office: *The Economist* 10 (October 28, 1893): 466; and for W. Irving Clark, now known to have been designed by and publicly attributed to Wright in 1894: Wayne Michael Charney, "The W. I. Clark House, La Grange, Illinois," *The Frank Lloyd Wright Newsletter* 1 (May–June 1978): 4–8.

10. *The Economist* 6 (July 11, 1891): 92; 7 (June 18, 1892): 933; and *CT,* July 12, 1891, p. 14.
11. "Louis H. Sullivan: Beloved Master," *WA* 33 (June 1924), and "Louis H. Sullivan — His Work," *ARec* 56 (July 1924).

    Years later, in a letter never meant for publication, George Elmslie recalled this episode bitterly: "I happen to have first hand knowledge from the Master himself," he reminded Wright, "as to your behavior on your agreement with the firm [his contract with Adler & Sullivan]. It is not a pleasant story for your friends to hear and need not be told by me. [Sullivan's] vitriolic comments on your ways and means will remain unsaid." Elmslie to Wright, June 12, 1936, in *JSAH* 20 (October 1961): 140–41.
12. *CT,* April 14, 1886, p. 10; January 1, 1887, p. 14; July 7, 1887, p. 7; "A Club House Warming," February 22, 1889, p. 3; *RE&BJ* 29 (May 28, 1887): 297; 29 (June 25, 1887): 355; "The Standard Club's New Building," *AA&BN* 25 (March 23, 1889): 137.

    An adjacent six-story, $50,000 addition with a three-story southside wing to its rear was quite nicely blended by Adler & Sullivan into the original structure in 1892: *The Economist* 2 (June 29, 1889): 549; 8 (July 23, 1892): 148; and *RE&BJ* 34 (August 6, 1892): 1009.
13. On the Dexter Building, see *RE&BJ* 29 (May 28, 1887): 297; 29 (June 25, 1887): 355; *CT,* July 17, 1887, p. 7; Morrison, *Sullivan,* 62–63; Carl Condit, *The Chicago School of Architecture* (Chicago: University of Chicago Press, 1964), 41.

    Two years later Adler & Sullivan designed a $25,000 alteration for Dexter's home at 1721 Prairie Avenue consisting of a three-story, fifty-by-twenty, front addition of rough stone, and an interior remodeling of the original structure: *IA* 14 (September 1889): 27; *CT,* July 14, 1889, p. 2; August 25, 1889, p. 6.

On Selz, Schwab see Morrison, *Sullivan,* 65; Condit, *Chicago School,* 42, n. 20; Albert Bush-Brown, *Louis Sullivan* (New York: George Braziller, Inc., 1960), 15; *RE&BJ* 29 (May 28, 1887): 297; 29 (June 25, 1887): 355.

14. *BB* 3 (November 30, 1887): supplement p. 2; Montgomery Schuyler, "Architecture in Chicago: Adler & Sullivan," *ARec,* Great American Architects Series, no. 2 (December 1895): 45; Morrison, *Sullivan,* 128.
15. *Industrial Chicago* (Chicago: Goodspeed Publishers, 1891), 1: 191; *CT,* January 2, 1887, p. 14; April 17, 1887, p. 30; February 19, 1888, p. 7; July 22, 1888, p. 3; "The New Wholesale District," November 4, 1888, p. 24; *RE&BJ* 29 (January 8, 1887): 19; 30 (April 14, 1888): 183; *BB* 4 (February 1888): x; Condit, *Chicago School,* 41–42; Morrison, *Sullivan,* 114–16.
16. *RE&BJ* 21 (January 19, 1889): 35. My thanks to Norman Kaufmann of Pueblo, Colorado, for sending me *The Pueblo Chieftain,* October 10, 1890, which had three stories on the Opera House Block in two editions the morning after its opening, including a detailed history and description. Its several illustrations consisted of a first-floor plan, the architects' rendering, and sketches of the main entrance, the stage from the dress circle, a side view from a stage corner, and a view from the stage toward the rear.
17. *BB* 5 (March 1889): xi; *IA* 15 (March 1890): 38; *The Economist* 3 (May 3, 1890): 560; *RE&BJ* 32 (March 15, 1890): 203; *CT,* May 4, 1890, p. 29; *Industrial Chicago,* 1: 271; Morrison, *Sullivan,* 124–25; Lauren Weingarden Rader, *Faith & Form: Synagogue Architecture in Illinois* (Chicago: Spertus Collection Press, 1976), 40, 43, quoting *Reform Advocate* 1 (June 12, 1891): 284–86.
18. Quoted in "Accounting for Carnegie Hall Acoustics," an undated Carnegie Hall brochure. Also see *CT,* July 28, 1889, p. 17; *Architect & Building* 12 (June 14, 1890): 278, 281; Donald Henahau, "The Sound of Carnegie Hall," *The New York Times,* May 3, 1981, Arts & Leisure section; and "The Building of Carnegie Hall," undated Carnegie Hall publication.

It has never been demonstrated that Louis Sullivan was consulted on Carnegie Hall, even though his name appeared with Adler's on its published drawings. But an early description suggests that, at the least, architect Tuthill drew on Sullivan's theatrical expertise:

> [The] arch is defined by a continuous row of electric lights at the back, while on the soffits the lights are arranged so as to punctuate the patterns of the decoration. In fact, one of the most admirable novelties of the interior is the manner in which the lights are made an integral part of the scheme of architectural decoration. . . . Groups of lights are arranged in the coves of [the] ceiling at the sides so as to bring out the ornament in relief with which they are encrusted. Two concentric rings of lights, the inner continuous, perform the same office for the central decorations, in the spandrils [*sic*] of which are also clusters of incandescent lights.

"It Stood the Test Well," *The New York Times,* May 16, 1891, p. 5, also described acoustical features — the elliptical proscenium arch, the coved auditorium ceiling, and the "carefully varied" curves of the stage ceiling — that, allowing for a different architectural style, could easily have been Adler's.

19. *The Economist* 3 (March 29, 1890): 361; 3 (April 5, 1890): 397; 4 (November 15, 1890): 792; 4 (December 20, 1890): 966; *IA* 15 (April 1890): 51; *RE&BJ* 33 (July 11, 1890): 992; 33 (August 16, 1890): 693; 33 (November 15, 1890): 1099; *CT,* May 25, 1890, p. 28; "It Will Be a Big One," ibid., August 9, 1890, p. 8; "Biggest in the World," ibid., November 14, 1890, p. 6; *Industrial Chicago,* 1: 207–8.
20. Three floor plans and a section were published by Dankmar Adler in "Theater-Building for American Cities," *Engineering Magazine* 7 (August–September 1894). See also *CT,* May 4, 1890, p. 29; and the Milwaukee *Journal,* February 7, 1890, p. 1; August 7, 1890, p. 8; September 13, 1890, p. 2; September 18, 1890, p. 4, the source of the quote.

    There is a certain confusion about the name of this building. Originally called the Grand Opera House, it was locally known after Pabst's purchase as the Stadt or New Stadt Theatre, although the old name continued in use. Adler published it as the

Deutsches Stadt Theatre in 1894 and in 1935 Morrison (in *Sullivan,* 301) listed it as Das Deutsche Haus.

Remodeling of the entire building was discussed in the *Journal,* November 15, 1890, p. 7, and in the *Sentinel,* same date, by R. C. Spencer, possibly the architect Robert C. Spencer, Jr., later, or perhaps even then, a friend of Frank Lloyd Wright: Thomas Beckman, formerly the Milwaukee Art Museum registrar, to author, September 21, 1982.

21. Wright, *An Autobiography,* 103. Also see *IA* 15 (May 1890): 63; 16 (December 1890): 81; *The Economist* 4 (November 29, 1890): 900; *CT,* May 4, 1890, p. 29; November 30, 1890, p. 29; "Sullivan in the West," *Western Architect & Engineering News* 218 (November 1959): 34–37.
22. "Story of a Theater Watchman," *CT,* August 4, 1890, p. 3; "McVicker's Is in Ruins," ibid., August 26, 1890, p. 1; "Was It Incendiarism?" ibid., August 27, 1890, pp. 1–2.
23. "Enter–New McVicker's," *CT,* March 22, 1891, p. 9.
24. *RE&BJ* 33 (September 27, 1890): 872; *BB* 6 (September 1890): ix. Also see "To Rebuild McVicker's," *CT,* September 23, 1890, p. 3; "McVicker's Theatre Subscription," ibid., September 5, 1890, p. 3; "The New McVicker's," ibid., October 5, 1890, p. 37; *RE&BJ* 33 (February 14, 1891); *Industrial Chicago,* 1: 204.
25. *Seattle Telegraph,* August 16 and September 14, 1890. Also: *RE&BJ* 33 (October 18, 1890): 969; *CT,* November 30, 1890, p. 29; *The Economist* 4 (November 29, 1890): 900; *IA* 16 (December 1890): 81.
26. "Sullivan in the West," *Western Architect & Engineering News,* 34–37; *IA* 16 (December 1890): 81; *The Economist* 4 (November 29, 1890): 900; 6 (August 15, 1891): 312; *CT,* November 30, 1890, p. 29; Morrison, *Sullivan,* 116.
27. Schuyler, "Adler & Sullivan," 44–45; Narciso Menocal, *Architecture as Nature: The Transcendentalist Idea of Louis Sullivan* (Madison: University of Wisconsin Press, 1981), 34–36.
28. For concise introductions to this historic event, see *The Chicago World's Fair of 1893* (New York: Dover Publications, 1980), text by Stanley Appelbaum; and Thomas S. Hines, "The Make-Believe City," chap. 5 of *Burnham of Chicago: Architect and Planner* (New York: Oxford University Press, 1974), 92–124. For data on the Transportation Building, see David H. Crook, "Louis Sullivan and the Golden Doorway," *JSAH* 26 (December

1967): 250–58, and *CT,* February 4, 1891, p. 6; February 11, 1891, p. 2; July 25, 1891, p. 12; February 21, 1892, p. 6.

All the fair architects received their travel and drawing expenses, plus $10,000: $3,000 when preliminary sketches were accepted, $6,000 when the drawings were completed, and $1,000 when the building was constructed: *AA&BN* 31 (February 21, 1891): 122.

29. This oft-quoted letter can be found in Crook, "Golden Doorway," p. 256, and Hines, *Burnham of Chicago,* 100–101, cited in n. 8.
30. "The Transportation Building" was originally published in *Handbook of the World's Columbian Exposition* (Chicago: Rand McNally & Company, 1893), 30–34.
31. Frank Lloyd Wright, "Louis H. Sullivan — His Work," *The Architectural Record* 56 (July 1924): 29; George Davis in *CT,* October 21, 1892, p. 22; for a structural critique see Dimitri Tselos, "The Chicago Fair and the Myth of the 'Lost Cause,' " *JSAH* 26 (December 1967): 259–68.
32. Montgomery Schuyler, "Last Words About the World's Fair," *ARec* 3 (January–March 1894): 271–301; Peter B. Wight, "The Great Exhibition Reviewed — I," *AA&BN* 42 (October 7, 1893): 8; Henry Van Brunt quoted by Appelbaum, *Chicago World's Fair* (1980), 58; Gustave Kobbe quoted in ibid.; Denton Snider, *World's Fair Studies* (Chicago: Sigma Publishing, 1895), 154–58; Halsey C. Ives, introduction to *The Dream City* (St. Louis: N. D. Thompson Publishing Company, 1893), n.p.
33. *AA&BN* 37 (July 30, 1892): 71–72.
34. Reprinted in *AA&BN* 42 (November 11, 1893): 76.
35. "France Honors Louis H. Sullivan," *IA* 25 (March 1895): 20–21; Crook, "Golden Doorway," 250–52; and Lauren S. Weingarten, "Louis H. Sullivan: Investigation of a Second French Connection," *JSAH* 39 (December 1980): 297–303.
36. Wright, "Sullivan — His Work," 29.
37. Payment vouchers and correspondence for the 1884 and 1891 commissions are in the archives of Temple Sinai, Chicago. Also see Rader, *Faith & Form,* 40–41, and *The Economist* 5 (June 20, 1891): 1124.
38. The design and construction of the station can be traced in the New Orleans *Daily Picayune,* August 26, 1891, p. 8; September 1, p. 15; September 12, p. 3; October 6, p. 8; November 22, p. 2;

December 3, p. 8; January 6, 1892, p. 4; "The Illinois Central's New Depot," April 4, 1892, p. 7; April 13, p. 2; April 20, p. 6; May 17, p. 2; June 1, p. 9; June 2, p. 6. Also see "A Modern Depot," *Times Democrat,* April 3, 1892; "City Depot Era Ends But Ghosts Linger," *New Orleans States,* January 9, 1954, p. 1; Walter G. Berg, *Buildings and Structures of American Railroads* (New York: Wiley, 1893), 422; and a student paper, "I. C. Passenger Terminal" (1954) by James P. Mueller, Tulane University School of Architecture.

39. Morrison, *Sullivan,* 168–69; Condit, *Chicago School,* 136–37; *CT,* February 21, 1892, p. 28; June 12, 1892, p. 26; July 12, 1892, p. 14; *The Economist* 7 (April 9, 1892): 554; *IA* 19 (April 1892): 41, in the issue that published the original two-page rendering.
40. Morrison, *Sullivan,* 122, 124; Condit, *Chicago Schoool,* 135; *CT,* September 18, 1892, p. 30; *The Economist* 8 (September 24, 1892): 454.
41. "The St. Nicholas Hotel," *St. Louis Post-Dispatch,* December 11, 1892, p. 10.
42. Schuyler, "Adler & Sullivan," 35–36. Also see Morrison, *Sullivan,* 122–23, and the *Post-Dispatch:* "A New Hotel Project," October 1, 1892, p. 3; October 28, 1892, p. 2; November 4, 1892, p. 2; January 15, 1893, p. 11; February 20, 1893, p. 2; June 13, 1893, p. 1; August 20, 1893, p. 22; and "New Buildings," December 31, 1893, p. 26.
43. Morrison, *Sullivan,* 129–30; Schuyler, "Adler & Sullivan," 45, 47; Tselos, " 'Lost Cause,' " 264–67; Menocal, *Architecture as Nature,* 36–42; and "Grand Memorials," *Post-Dispatch,* January 14, 1894, p. 28.
44. Schuyler, "Adler & Sullivan," 48.

NOTES FOR CHAPTER X

1. Paul Goldberger, *The Skyscraper* (New York: Alfred A. Knopf, 1981).
2. Barr Ferree, "The High Building and Its Art," *Scribner's* 15 (March 1894): 297.
3. Winston Weisman, "A New View of Skyscraper History," in Edgar Kaufmann, Jr., ed., *The Rise of an American Architecture* (New York: Praeger Publishers, 1970), 115–60.
4. Sullivan to Bragdon, November 8, 1903, in his "Letters from Louis Sullivan," *Architecture* 64 (July 1931): 9.

5. "The Tulip," reprinted in *Kindergarten Chats and Other Writings* (New York: George Wittenborn, Inc., 1947 ed.), 74–75.
6. Willard Connely, *Louis Sullivan: The Shaping of American Architecture* (New York: Horizon Press, 1960), 129–30; Frank Lloyd Wright, "Louis H. Sullivan—His Work," *ARec* 56 (July 1924): 29.
7. *St. Louis Post-Dispatch,* May 29, 1890, p. 2; May 30, 1890, p. 2; May 31, 1890, p. 5.
8. *Post-Dispatch,* September 18, 1890, p. 3; November 7, 1890, p. 5; for history and particulars see Hugh Morrison, *Louis Sullivan: Prophet of Modern Architecture* (1935; New York: W. W. Norton & Company, 1962 ed.), 144–56, and Carl W. Condit, *The Chicago School of Architecture* (Chicago: University of Chicago Press, 1964), 135–40.
9. "Cubic-Foot Cost of Building," *CT*, May 6, 1894, p. 30.
10. "The Wainwright," *St. Louis Post-Dispatch,* January 18, 1893, p. 8.
11. "Is Sullivan the Father of Functionalism?" *Art News* 55 (December 1956): 56.
12. Goldberger, *The Skyscraper,* 19.
13. George McCue, "Spirit from St. Louis," *Progressive Architecture* 62 (November 1981): 102–6.
14. Paul Sprague, "Adler & Sullivan's Schiller Building," *PSR* 2 (Second Quarter, 1965): 5–20, is the best single source, but also see Morrison, *Sullivan,* 156–62, and Condit, *Chicago School,* 128–33. The theater dedication was reported in *CT,* September 30, 1892, p. 1.
15. *AA&BN* 39 (February 4, 1893): 72; *CT,* September 30, 1892, p. 2; Bannister Fletcher, "American Architecture Through English Spectacles," *Engineering Magazine* 7 (June 1894): 318; Ferree, "The High Building," 312.
16. Various reports in *CT,* September 30, 1892, p. 1. On construction history, in addition to secondary sources cited above, see ibid., April 6, 1890, p. 29; April 13, 1890, p. 31; May 25, 1890, p. 28; "The German Opera-House," August 3, 1890, p. 28; April 19, 1891, p. 9; April 26, 1891, p. 9; May 10, 1891, p. 15; "Home for the Germans," May 3, 1891, p. 2; July 5, 1891, p. 14; July 12, 1891, p. 14; "The Effect of One Pile Foundation," July 19, 1891, p. 29; "The German Opera House Building," *The Economist* 5 (February 14, 1891): 253; G. Twose, "Steel and

Terra Cotta Buildings in Chicago, and Some Deductions," *BkB* 3 (January 1894): 4; *Industrial Chicago* (Chicago: Goodspeed Publishers, 1891) 1: 223–24; *The New York Times,* September 30, 1892, p. 4.

17. On the Mercantile Club proposal, see W. A. and A. E. Wells, "To the Members of the Mercantile Club," a prospectus dated June 1, 1891, with plans and a rendering, on file at the Mercantile Library Association, St. Louis; *St. Louis Post-Dispatch,* February 23, 1891, p. 3; "Angry Architects," June 12, 1891, p. 3; "St. Louis Gets It," June 13, 1891, p. 4; June 17, 1891, p. 2; June 20, 1891, p. 6; June 25, 1891, p. 8; July 7, 1891, p. 3, showing Isaac S. Taylor's rendering of the accepted design.
18. William C. McClintock, J. P. Ellacott, and Norman Totten, "Fraternity Temple: An Announcement to the Independent Order of Odd Fellows of Chicago and the State of Illinois" (September 1891), a brochure partially reproduced in *Industrial Chicago* (1891) 2: 593–95, and "Plans for the Odd-Fellows Temple," *CT,* September 6, 1891, p. 29.
19. On its design history, see *CT,* February 13, 1886, p. 8; June 21, 1891, p. 9; August 30, 1891, p. 26; "Higher Than Others," September 5, 1891, p. 1; "Will Build the Temple," September 19, 1891, p. 2; "The Odd Fellows Temple," *RE&BJ* 33 (August 20, 1891): 1247; *The Economist* 5 (June 20, 1891): 1093; 6 (September 12, 1891): 453–54.
20. "The High Building Question," *The Graphic* 5 (December 19, 1891): 405, reprinted, Donald Hoffmann, "The Setback Skyscraper of 1891: An Unknown Essay by Louis H. Sullivan," *JSAH* 29 (May 1970): 181–87.
21. "Light in Tall Office Buildings," *Engineering Magazine* 4 November 1892): 171–86.
22. Montgomery Schuyler, "Architecture in Chicago: Adler & Sullivan," *ARec,* Great American Architects Series, no. 2 (December 1895), 24.
23. On Union Trust construction history: Morrison, *Sullivan,* 165–66; *St. Louis Post-Dispatch,* December 14, 1890, p. 21; March 24, 1892, p. 11; May 26, 1892, p. 7; June 3, 1892, p. 4; July 1, 1892, p. 4; August 20, 1893, p. 22; "Art & Architecture," August 27, 1893, p. 18; "The Great Buildings of St. Louis Completed," December 10, 1893, pp. 33–34; December 30,

1893, p. 2; *The Economist* 7 (May 28, 1892): 826; 7 (June 25, 1892): 965.

24. "The Union Trust Building," *St. Louis Post-Dispatch,* July 8, 1892, p. 3, is an unusually perceptive account.
25. Schuyler, "Adler & Sullivan," 31–33; *Builder,* reprinted in *AA&BN* 41 (September 30, 1893): 194.
26. On the Portland project see *The Economist* 8 (September 24, 1892): 454, or *RE&BJ* 34 (October 8, 1892): 1294. The rendering in the *Catalogue of the Third Annual Exhibition of the St. Louis Chapter of the American Institute of Architects* (March 1–20, 1895), republished here for the first time, shows it next door to what is clearly the Hauser Building (509 Chestnut Street) as depicted in A. C. Shewey, *Pictorial St. Louis* (St. Louis: A. C. Shewey, 1892), 133.
27. Shewey, *St. Louis,* 133, *Gould's St. Louis Directory,* and *Gould's Commercial Register* for the 1890s. Sullivan apparently closed the office in late 1896 or early 1897, well over a year after his partnership dissolved.
28. The various Mississippi Valley Trust Company proposals for the Olive and Seventh intersection were discussed in the *St. Louis Post-Dispatch,* September 18, 1890, p. 3; October 22, 1891, p. 8; and April 18, 1893, p. 2. For the others, see October 20, 1892, p. 6; May 12, 1893, p. 7; and July 1, 1894.
29. Morrison, *Sullivan*, 166, 168, published what he called the 1893 version (pl. 52) but gave no documentation. Neither scheme was published at the time, but the other, identified as "Study for a Skyscraper," appeared in *WA* 34 (January 1925).
30. General descriptions of the Stock Exchange are in Morrison, *Sullivan,* 169–72; Condit, *Chicago School,* 136–38; and also: Twose, "Buildings in Chicago," 4–5; *AA&BN* 43 (January 20, 1894): 31; D. Everett Waid, "Recent Brick and Terra-Cotta Work in American Cities," *BkB* 4 (January 1895): 132; *The Economist* 10 (July 22, 1893): 80; 10 (August 5, 1893): 137; 10 (October 28, 1893): 459; 11 (January 20, 1894): 71; *CT,* July 23, 1894, p. 14; "Warming the House: Chicago's New Stock Exchange Building Is Dedicated," May 1, 1894, p. 12.
31. On the trading room and ornament, see John Vinci, *The Art Institute of Chicago: The Stock Exchange Trading Room* (Chicago: The Art Institute, 1977), and *Louis H. Sullivan Architectural Ornament*

Collection, Southern Illinois University at Edwardsville (Edwardsville, Ill.: Office of Cultural Arts and University Museums, Southern Illinois University, 1981), 18.

32. Guaranty Construction Company, *The Guaranty Building* (Chicago: Guaranty Construction Company, 1896).
33. Morrison, *Sullivan,* 172–74; Condit, *Chicago School,* 138–41; "Two Buffalo Buildings," *The Economist* 13 (March 16, 1895): 300; *IA* 25 (June 1895): 48; "Buffalo's Finest Office Building," *CT,* March 8, 1896, p. 30; and "Balconies for a Sullivan Facade?" *ARec* 18 (September 1905): 238–39, wherein it was suggested that balconies would carry the eye along the street better than the powerful vertical columns that allegedly impeded lateral vision.
34. Barr Ferree, "The Modern Office Building," *IA* 27 (June 1896): 45; Schuyler, "Adler & Sullivan," 33; Claude Bragdon, "Architecture in the United States. III: The Skyscraper," *ARec* 26 (August 1909): 92.
35. Schuyler, "Adler & Sullivan," 33, 35. A copy of the only known and never published rendering of the Burnet House hotel is in the Sullivan Collection, Burnham Library, Chicago Art Institute, which will not permit its reproduction.
36. On the Chemical project, see the *St. Louis Post-Dispatch,* October 20, 1892, p. 6; November 11, 1892, p. 2; "Another Skyscraper," April 20, 1893, p. 15; November 13, 1894, p. 11; April 1, 1895, p. 2; April 14, 1895, pp. 30, 34.
37. *The Economist* 11 (May 5, 1894): 506; 12 (August 25, 1894): 206.
38. "An Important Letter from Mr. Dankmar Adler," July 11, 1895, *IA* 25 (July 1895): 61, was published "with surprise, regret, and still with a considerable degree of congratulation." Also see *AA&BN* 49 (August 24, 1895): 77, and *BkB* 4 (August 1895): 178.
39. *IA* 26 (August 1895): 9, on Sullivan's trip to Buffalo; *CT,* December 29, 1895, p. 29, on the National Linseed Oil commission.
40. *BkB* 4 (November 1895): 243; Guaranty Construction Company prospectus: first page of text.
41. Frank Lloyd Wright, *Genius and the Mobocracy* (New York: Duell, Sloan and Pearce, 1949), 70–71.

42. Hugh Duncan, Richard Nickel, Aaron Siskind, and Hugh Goldstein, taped interview with Adler's daughter, Sarah Adler Weil, December 26, 1961, copy in possession of her daughter, Joan Saltzstein, Milwaukee.
43. "The Tall Office Building Artistically Considered," *Lippincott's* 57 (March 1896): 403–9, has often been reprinted, including in *Kindergarten Chats and Other Writings* (1947 ed.), 202–13.
44. "The Influence of Steel Construction. . . ," *IA* 28 (November 1896): 34–47, has often been reprinted, including as "Function and Environment" in Lewis Mumford, ed., *Roots of Contemporary American Architecture* (1952; New York: Dover Press, 1972 ed.), 243–50.

NOTES FOR CHAPTER XI

1. *AA&BN* 49 (July 27, 1895): 39.
2. *IA* 26 (August 1895): 5.
3. "Business of the Architects," *The Economist* 12 (September 15, 1894): 287; *IA* 25 (February 1895): 7; *CT*, May 3, 1896, p. 42.
4. *IA* 26 (January 1896): 55. Adler's partnership was described in *The Economist* 15 (March 28, 1896): 400; by the end of the year, he had moved to the Auditorium's sixth floor: ibid. 16 (December 31, 1896), back cover of special number. On the Technical Club, see ibid. 15 (March 28, 1896): 385.
5. The special issue on local architects "accords to Chicago designers an exalted position among the profession in the country," according to the March 8, 1896, *CT* (p. 31), "and gives them credit for great originality and artistic insight."
6. On Adler & Sullivan's early work for Schlesinger & Mayer, see *RE&BJ* 32 (March 15, 1890): 203; *CT,* March 9, 1890, p. 28; May 4, 1890, p. 26, with sketch; July 21, 1891, p. 3; July 26, 1891, p. 10; July 3, 1892, p. 22; *Industrial Chicago* (Chicago: Goodspeed Publishing Company, 1891), 1: 230; and Narciso G. Menocal, *Architecture as Nature: The Transcendentalist Idea of Louis Sullivan* (Madison: University of Wisconsin Press, 1981), 168.
7. *CT,* May 31, 1896, p. 43. On the ten-story project, see ibid., July 5, 1896, p. 18 (story) and p. 38 (sketch).
8. On the 1896–97 work, see *CT,* August 30, 1896, p. 34; June 10, 1897, p. 7 in supplement (sketch); *The Economist* 15 (May 30,

1896): 666–67; 15 (June 13, 1896): 728–29; 15 (June 27, 1896): 789; 16 (August 8, 1896): 161; 16 (September 19, 1896): 310; 18 (September 4, 1897): 263; 18 (September 18, 1897): 319–20; Menocal, *Architecture as Nature,* 169.

9. *BkB* 5 (September 1896): 177, on the Stifel Building; on the Hippodrome, see *CT,* March 28, 1897, p. 35; *IA* 29 (April 1897): 30; *St. Louis Post-Dispatch,* March 18, 1897, p. 9; March 19, 1897, p. 2; April 1, 1897, p. 11; "The St. Louis Coliseum," *The Engineering Record* 38 (October 1, 1898): 383–85.
10. *BB* 7 (June 1898): 127; *The Economist* 18 (October 9, 1897): 407; and Joseph Pell Lombardi, *The Bayard (Condict) Building* (New York: privately published, n.d.).
11. According to Frank Lloyd Wright in *Saturday Review* 13 (December 14, 1935).
12. *CT,* October 10, 1897, p. 30; A. D. F. Hamlin, "L'Art Nouveau, Its Origin and Development," *The Craftsman* 3 (December 1902): 138; Schuyler, "The 'Sky-scraper' Up To Date," *ARec* 8 (January–March 1899): 255–56.
13. The cover for *Music* was reproduced in Paul E. Sprague, ed., *The Drawings of Louis Henry Sullivan* (Princeton, N.J.: Princeton University Press, 1979), no. 105 and fig. 48. The *Swimming* cover was never again published. Before it expired, *Forms & Fantasies* also published Sullivan's pencil drawing of the southwest corner of the Bayard Building showing the entrance, two bays, and part of the second floor in 1 (November 1898): pl. 76, actually the October issue; his ink drawing of a mantel corner in 1 (December 1898): pl. 102; and a photo of Stock Exchange elevator grilles in 1 (February 1899): pl. 150.
14. *CT,* May 28, 1898, p. 13; May 29, 1898, p. 30 (sketch); *BkB* 7 (June 1898): 129.
15. *BkB* 7 (June 1898): 171; *The Economist* 19 (June 4, 1898): 645; 20 (July 16, 1898): 78; *CT,* June 5, 1898, p. 38.
16. *CT,* November 1, 1899, p. 36; *The Economist* 20 (December 31, 1898): 772; permit number 1093, November 2, 1898, file copy at University of Illinois, Chicago Circle campus.
17. Depicted in Sprague, ed., *Drawings,* no. 106, dated June 26, 1898.
18. Depicted and discussed in Menocal, *Architecture as Nature,* 106–11.
19. *BkB* 8 (April 1899): 81.

20. Menocal, *Architecture as Nature,* 62–69, figs. 38–39.
21. *BkB* 8 (December 1899): 253–54. For further information on the Gage (McCormick) Building, see ibid. 8 (April 1899): 81; 9 (February 1900): 36; *AA&BN* 62 (November 19, 1898): 67; *IA* 33 (March 1899): 20; 34 (January 1900): 46–47; *The Economist* 20 (July 9, 1898): 49; 20 (October 8, 1898): 421; *CT,* July 10, 1898, p. 15; October 16, 1898, p. 34; December 31, 1899, p. 38.

    The Economist discussed the later, non-Sullivan, addition: 25 (March 30, 1901): 371, and 40 (August 8, 1908): 217. Architect Thomas Tallmadge years later thought the Gage Building still stood "as one of the best expressions of the skeleton steel commercial skyscraper . . . the high point of Louis Sullivan's material achievement": *The Story of Architecture in America* (New York: W. W. Norton & Company, 1936 ed.), 224.
22. *CT,* January 1, 1899, p. 17; *BkB* 8 (January 1899): 22 mentioned "The Principles of Architectural Design."
23. "An Unaffected School of Modern Architecture: Will It Come?" *The Artist* 24 (January 1899): xxxiii–xxxiv.
24. "Louis H. Sullivan: Artist Among Architects, American Among Americans," *The Criterion* 20 (January 28, 1899): 20, reprinted in *The Architectural Annual* 2 (1901): 67–68.
25. Euston Factory: *The Economist* 21 (April 8, 1899): 423; 21 (May 27, 1899): 658; McCormick residence: the State Historical Society of Wisconsin has blueprints and drawings.
26. H. Allen Brooks, *The Prairie School: Frank Lloyd Wright and His Midwest Contemporaries* (Toronto: University of Toronto Press, 1972), 37–38, quoting *BkB* and *IA.*
27. "The Modern Phase of Architecture," *IA* 33 (June 1899): 40.
28. Willard Connely, *Louis Sullivan: The Shaping of American Architecture* (New York: Horizon Press, 1960), 210; Marriage License no. 294275, filed July 5, 1899, Cook County, Illinois.
29. Alan K. Lathrop to author, June 12, 1981; Sullivan's photographs are in Lyndon P. Smith, "The Home of an Artist-Architect," *ARec* 17 (June 1905).
30. Brown to Sullivan, July 7, 22, 27, August 12, 24, 1899; Sullivan to Brown, July 24, 1899, AIA Archives, Washington, D.C.
31. *BkB* 8 (September 1899): 187–88.
32. *The Economist* 22 (October 7, 1899): 419; see also ibid. 22 (December 9, 1899): 685, on opening. On the Chicago National Bank: ibid. 22 (November 4, 1899): 538, and 22 (December 16,

1899): 719. On Holy Trinity: ibid. 23 (January 13, 1900): 59; *CT*, January 14, 1900, p. 39, and November 18, 1900, p. 34.

NOTES FOR CHAPTER XII

1. *BkB* 9 (January 1900): 18; "Nature as an Ornamentalist," *ARec* 9 (April 1900): n.p.; annual catalogues of the Chicago Architectural Club, 1900, 1901.
2. Adler's April 17 obituaries in *The New York Times*, p. 9, and *CT*, p. 7; also see *The Economist* 23 (May 26, 1900): 641.
3. *IA* 25 (June 1900): 42–43, includes Sullivan's extemporaneous remarks; *AA&BN* 68 (June 16, 1900): 87.
4. "The Young Man in Architecture," *IA* 25 (June 1900): 38–40; and in *BkB* 9 (June 1900): 115–19.
5. Both quoted in H. Allen Brooks, *The Prairie School: Frank Lloyd Wright and His Midwest Contemporaries* (Toronto: University of Toronto Press, 1972), 39.
6. Brown to Sullivan, July 6, 12, 1900; Sullivan to Brown, July 10, 24, 25, 1900, American Institute of Architects Archives, Washington, D.C.
7. "Reality in Architecture," *IA* 36 (September 1900): 116, reprinted from *CT*, August 1900.
8. Peabody's remarks are reprinted in Louis Sullivan, *Kindergarten Chats and Other Writings*, Isabella Athey, ed. (New York: George Wittenborn, Inc., 1947), 238, as is Sullivan's reply, which originally appeared in Kindergarten Chat 40, "On Scholarship," *IAB* in 1901. He deleted the reply from his manuscript revision in 1918.
9. *CT*, January 14, 1900, p. 39; November 18, 1900, p. 34; Theodore Turak, "A Celt Among Slavs: Louis Sullivan's Holy Trinity Cathedral," *PSR* 9 (Fourth Quarter, 1972): 5–22; and *Holy Trinity Orthodox Cathedral and Rectory* (Chicago: Commission on Chicago Historical and Architectural Landmarks, 1978).
10. *IAB* 2 (June 23, 1900): 1; 2 (August 11, 1900): 1; 2 (December 22, 1900): 11–20; "Open Letter," 2 (December 8, 1900): 7.
11. Sherman Paul, *Louis Sullivan: An Architect in American Thought* (Englewood Cliffs, N.J.: Prentice-Hall, 1962), 57–58; Perkins in *IA* 33 (June 1899): 40; *AA&BN* 71 (March 9, 1901): 75–76.
12. Sullivan to Smith, December 13, 1900; February 18, 22, 1901;

reprinted in *Kindergarten Chats* (1947 ed.), 243–44, with other letters to Smith cited in this chapter.

13. Paul, *Sullivan,* 58.
14. Sullivan to Bragdon and Sullivan to Smith, January 11, 1902, in *Kindergarten Chats,* 244–45.
15. This matter is discussed in Kenneth W. Severns, "The Reunion of Louis Sullivan and Frank Lloyd Wright," *PSR* 12 (Second Quarter, 1975): 10–11.
16. Published in *BkB* 10 (June 1901): 112.
17. Brooks, *PSR,* 4; Paul, *Sullivan,* 58–59.
18. Sullivan to Smith, October 1, 1901, quoted in Willard Connely, *Louis Sullivan: The Shaping of American Architecture* (New York: Horizon Press, 1960), 224–25; Sullivan to Smith, January 11, 1902, in *Kindergarten Chats,* 244; *The Economist* 40 (July 8, 1908): 104.
19. Narciso G. Menocal, *Architecture as Nature: The Transcendentalist Idea of Louis Sullivan* (Madison: University of Wisconsin Press, 1981), 111, 116. The Wainwright residence was illustrated in the 1902 Chicago Architectural Club catalogue.
20. N. F. McCormick to Sullivan, May 29, 1902, McCormick Collection, State Historical Society of Wisconsin, Madison, which holds other material on both the Greeneville and the Presbyterian Hospital projects. Additional information was furnished by Wayne W. Dobson, Tusculum College archivist.
21. *The Economist* 27 (May 31, 1902): 719.
22. "A Big Linoleum Plant," *The Economist* 28 (October 25, 1902): 554; ibid. 28 (December 6, 1902): 769.
23. *The Economist* 27 (March 1, 1902): 264; 27 (April 5, 1902): 435; *CT,* February 23, 1902, p. 29.
24. Menocal, "A Chronology of the Construction of the Schlesinger and Mayer Building (Carson-Pirie-Scott)," *Architecture as Nature,* 168–78, can be supplemented by "The New Schlesinger and Mayer Building, Chicago," *BkB* 12 (May 1903): 101–4; and *The Economist* 28 (August 23, 1902): 249; 28 (December 6, 1902): 768; 29 (April 18, 1903): 516; and 31 (June 18, 1904): 860.

    Sullivan's findings from the work are in "Sub-structure at the New Schlesinger & Mayer Store Building," *Engineering Record* 47 (February 21, 1903): 194–96; and "Basements and Sub-basements," *The Economist* 31 (February 20, 1904): 254.

25. Gunther Barth, *City People: The Rise of Modern City Culture in Nineteenth-Century America* (New York: Oxford University Press, 1980), 111, 129, 130, and chapter 4 generally.
26. Connely, *Sullivan,* 235.
27. *The Economist* 29 (May 23, 1903): 702.
28. Sullivan to George K. Harper, May 7, 8, 1903, and to J. Caldwell, May 12, 1903, Burnham Library, The Art Institute, Chicago.
29. *The Economist* 32 (November 12, 1904): 652; 32 (November 26, 1904): 721.
30. "Sullivan's Theatre-Front Design: A Mystery Set to Music," *IA* 13 (October 1969): 18–19.
31. Sullivan to Wainwright, October 17, 1903; to Joel Hunt, August 8, 1904; to Samuel Newhouse, June 17, 1903; to Thatcher, August 8, 1904; to J. M. Henderson, May 23, 1903; to Lewis Hopkins, September 22, 1904, and to other correspondents, in the Burnham Library, The Art Institute, Chicago.
32. *The Economist* 25 (June 8, 1901): 690; 32 (December 31, 1904): 871; 34 (September 30, 1905): 514.
33. *AA&BN* 76 (April 26, 1902): 29.
34. *WA* 2 (October 1903): 18; *BkB* 11 (May 1902): 106, 108; 12 (April 1903): 75. Also see Claude Bragdon, "L'Art Nouveau in American Architecture," *IA* 42 (October 1903): 19–20.
35. *ARec:* "A Rational Skyscraper," 15 (March 1904): 276; Arthur C. David, "The Architecture of Ideas," 15 (April 1904): 361–84; Barr Ferree, "The Art of the High Building," 15 (May 1904): 463; Claude Bragdon, "'Made in France' Architecture," 16 (December 1904): 566–67; Lyndon P. Smith, "The Schlesinger & Mayer Building: An Attempt to Give Functional Expression to the Architecture of a Department Store," 16 (July 1904): 53–60; W. H. Desmond, "Another View: What Mr. Louis Sullivan Stands For," 16 (July 1904): 61–67.
36. Bragdon, "An American Architect," *House & Garden* 7 (January 1905): 47–55; *IA* 45 (February 1905): 8; 45 (March 1905): 20; 45 (June 1905): 46; 46 (November 1905): 48.
37. Sullivan to Monroe, April 5, 10, July 20, 1905, Monroe Collection, University of Chicago Library.
38. *The Craftsman* 8 (June 1905): 336–38; 8 (July 1905): 458.
39. Jackson County, Mississippi, *Records of Mortgages and Deeds of*

Trust on Land, vol. 2, pp. 143–44, Pascagoula, Mississippi, county courthouse.

40. Sullivan to Bragdon, November 8, 1903, in Bragdon, "Letters from Louis Sullivan," *Architecture* 64 (July 1931): 9.
41. Sullivan to Angell, December 15, 1905, in Edward J. Vaughn, "Sullivan and the University of Michigan," *PSR* 6 (First Quarter, 1969): 22.
42. *The Economist* 36 (July 14, 1906): 74.
43. On National Farmers' Bank the principal sources are: *The Economist* 36 (October 27, 1906): 662; Carl K. Bennett, "A Bank Built for Farmers," *The Craftsman* 15 (November 1908): 176–85; Louis J. Millet, "The National Farmers' Bank of Owatonna, Minn.," *ARec* 24 (October 1908): 249–54; and Paul E. Sprague, "The National Farmers' Bank, Owatonna, Minnesota," *PSR* 4 (Second Quarter, 1967): 5–21. The quotation is from Montgomery Schuyler, "The People's Savings Bank of Cedar Rapids, Iowa," *ARec* 31 (January 1912): 46.
44. *The Economist* 37 (April 27, 1907): 799; "Beautiful New House at Riverside," ibid. 41 (April 24, 1909): 760; "A Departure from Classic Tradition: Two Unusual Houses by Louis Sullivan & Frank Lloyd Wright, Architects," *ARec* 30 (October 1911): 327–38.
45. Gordon Orr, "The Collaboration of Claude and Stark with Chicago Architectural Firms," *PSR* 12 (Fourth Quarter, 1975): 5–12; Harold C. Bradley to James V. Edsell, October 14, 1965, copy in author's possession.
46. *The Philadelphia Press,* July 14, October 14, 1907; *IA* 52 (October 1908): illustration section; *Catalogue of the Fourteenth Annual Architectural Exhibition* (Philadelphia T-Square Club, 1908).
47. "Big Auditorium Theater Doomed," *CT,* February 14, 1908, p. 1; *RE&BJ* 42 (February 15, 1908): 11; ibid. 43 (March 6, 1909): 7.
48. *The Economist* 42 (October 9, 1909): 540–41.
49. Donald L. Hoffmann, "The Brief Career of a Sullivan Apprentice: Parker N. Berry," *PSR* 4 (First Quarter, 1967): 7–15.
50. Charles R. Ashbee, "Memoirs" (typescript), vol. 3, pp. 72–73, Victoria and Albert Museum Library, London.
51. Interviews with Ocean Springs residents, Sullivan letters in the possession of J. K. Lemon, Ocean Springs, Mississippi.

52. Quoted in Connely, *Sullivan,* 244.
53. Copies of the auction catalogue are at the Burnham Library and the American Institute of Architects Archives.
54. Summaries of the scanty information on Margaret Sullivan's life were provided by Alan K. Lathrop, curator of the Northwest Architectural Archives in Minneapolis, who is continuing the research of the late Robert Warn.

    On Sullivan's property see: Jackson County, Mississippi, *Records of Mortgages and Deeds. . . ,* vol. 2, pp. 143–44; *Deed Records,* vol. 35, pp. 600–602; Mary Wallace Crocker, *Historic Architecture in Mississippi* (Jackson: University of Mississippi Press, 1973), 96–99; Louis H. Sullivan, *The Autobiography of an Idea* (1924; New York: Dover Press, 1956 ed.), 297.
55. Kindergarten Chat 6, "An Oasis," is about the Marshall Field Store; Sullivan, "Ornament in Architecture," *Engineering Magazine* 2 (August 1892).
56. Menocal, *Architecture as Nature,* 31, and the chapter called "Geometry and Ornamentation," *passim.*
57. Sullivan to Carl Bennett, January 4, 1910, in Robert R. Warn, "Bennett & Sullivan, Client & Creator," *PSR* 10 (Third Quarter, 1973): 14. In the New York city directory of 1913/14, Margaret Davies Sullivan (the name she used in her first, 1912, entry) resided at 250 West Eighty-fourth Street. Marshall was not listed at all until 1916/17, compiled the year before their marriage, giving his residence as Eighty-fourth Street and Broadway, the same building as number 250.

NOTES FOR CHAPTER XIII

1. Sullivan to Bennett in Robert R. Warn, "Bennett & Sullivan, Client & Creator," *PSR* 10 (Third Quarter, 1973): 14–15.
2. Montgomery Schuyler, "The People's Savings Bank of Cedar Rapids, Iowa," *ARec* 31 (January 1912): 45–56.
3. Louis Sullivan, "Lighting the People's Savings Bank, Cedar Rapids, Iowa," *The Illuminating Engineer* 6 (February 1912): 631–35; Hugh Morrison, *Louis Sullivan: Prophet of Modern Architecture* (1935; New York: W. W. Norton & Sons, 1962 ed.), 211–13.
4. Morrison, *Louis Sullivan,* 213–16; "St. Paul's M. E. Church," *WA* 20 (August 1914): 87–88.

5. "A Sullivan Design That Is Not Sullivan's," *WA* 20 (August 1914): 85.
6. H. Allen Brooks, *The Prairie School: Frank Lloyd Wright and His Midwest Contemporaries* (Toronto: University of Toronto Press, 1972), 228–29; Fitch to author Robert R. Warn in his "Louis H. Sullivan, '. . . an air of finality,' " *PSR* 10 (Fourth Quarter, 1973): 9.
7. Quoted in *PSR* 10 (Fourth Quarter, 1973): 10, which depicts the landscaping plan.
8. The sketch is reproduced in "Sullivan Seen by His Contemporaries: In His Centennial Year, Another Look," *ARec* 120 (September 1956): 18.
9. *Algona* (Iowa) *Courier,* March 14, 1913; February 14, 1914; A. N. Rebori, "An Architecture of Democracy: Three Examples from the Work of Louis H. Sullivan," *ARec* 29 (May 1916); Morrison, *Sullivan,* 217.
10. Kenneth W. Severns, "Louis Sullivan Builds a Small-Town Bank," *AIA Journal* 65 (May 1976): 68–71.
11. Rebori, "Architecture of Democracy," 438; Morrison, *Sullivan,* 217–19.
12. Morrison, *Sullivan,* 216–17; Brooks, *The Prairie School,* 233–34.
13. *Lafayette* (Indiana) *Daily Courier,* January 29, December 25, 29, 31, 1914; January 1, 1915; *Weekly Courier,* January 29, February 20, July 3, December 11, 1914.
14. *Newark* (Ohio) *Daily Advocate,* March 30, July 14, August 10, 1914; Rebori, "Architecture of Democracy," 441–53; Morrison, *Sullivan,* 219–20.
15. "A Departure from Classic Tradition: Two Unusual Houses by Louis Sullivan & Frank Lloyd Wright, Architects," *ARec* 30 (October 1911): 327–38; "Comparison of Master and Pupil Seen in Two Houses," *WA* 17 (November 1911): 95; Theodore Starrett, "The Architecture of Louis H. Sullivan," *Architecture and Building* 44 (December 1912): 469–75; F. W. Fitzpatrick, "American Architecture," *WA* 20 (September 1913): 76–77; " 'Rebels' in Architecture Discovered by the Daily Press," ibid. 20 (October 1913): 85.
16. Mark L. Peisch, *The Chicago School of Architecture: Early Followers of Sullivan and Wright* (New York: Random House, 1964), 120; Claude Bragdon, *More Lives Than One* (New York: Alfred A. Knopf, 1938), 108; "Plan 'Hall of Fame' for Chicago Archi-

tects," *CT*, June 9, 1915, p. 6; "Mr. Sullivan on Client-Architect Co-operation" and on Solon Beman, *WA* 22 (August 1915): 14; *The Economist* 55 (June 10, 1916): 1166, and 55 (June 17, 1916): 1207, on Adler; Sullivan, "Wherefore the Poet?" *Poetry: A Magazine of Verse* 7 (March 1916): 305–7; "The Works of Sullivan an Inspiration Rather than a Model," *WA* 23 (February 1916): 13.

17. Warn, " '. . . an air of finality,' " 16–18.
18. Quoted in *Historical Sketches of People's Federal Savings and Loan Association* (Sidney, Ohio, n.d.), n.p.
19. Thomas E. Tallmadge, "The People's Savings & Loan Association Building of Sidney, Ohio," *The American Architect* 114 (October 23, 1918): 477–82; also Morrison, *Sullivan,* 220–23.
20. Sullivan to Budina, August 10, September 27, December 31, 1917; February 23, 1918, Sullivan Collection, Burnham Library, The Art Institute, Chicago.
21. Sullivan's letters to Wright from 1918 to 1923 quoted here and in the following pages were published in Bruce Brooks Pfeiffer, ed., *Frank Lloyd Wright: Letters to Architects* (Fresno: California State University Press, 1984), 5–37.
22. Sullivan to Monroe, July 18, 1918, Monroe Collection, University of Chicago Library.
23. Esther McCoy, ed., "Letters from Louis H. Sullivan to R. M. Schindler," *JSAH* 20 (December 1961): 179–84, is the source of Sullivan-Schindler correspondence here and below.
24. Thomas E. Tallmadge, "The Farmers' and Merchants' Bank of Columbus, Wisconsin," *WA* 29 (July 1920): 63–65; also Morrison, *Sullivan,* 223–24.
25. On the Wheelers and the Columbus project see John Szarkowski, *The Idea of Louis Sullivan* (Minneapolis: University of Minnesota Press, 1956), 3–14.
26. Special thanks to Mark Heyman of Springfield, Illinois, for photographs, research, and commentary on the Palmer pedestal.
27. McCoy, ed., "Sullivan to R. M. Schindler," 180.
28. Robert Craik McLean, "Louis H. Sullivan: An Appreciation," *WA* 28 (April 1919): 32; "The Thirty-third Annual Chicago Architectural Exhibition," ibid. 29 (April 1920): 33–34; exchange with Goff quoted in Willard Connely, *Louis Sullivan: The Shaping of American Architecture* (New York: Horizon Press, 1960), 279; *Common Clay* 1 (September 1920): iv–vii.

29. Sullivan, *Morrison,* 224; Bernard C. Greengard, "Sullivan/Presto/The Krause Music Store," *PSR* 6 (Third Quarter, 1969): 5–10.
30. Sullivan to Whitaker, January 14, 1922, together with numerous other letters between the two in the American Institute of Architects Archives, Washington, D.C. The publishing story has been told by George E. Pettengill in "The Biography of a Book: Correspondence Between Sullivan and The Journal," *AIA Journal* 63 (June 1975): 42–45, and " 'A System of Architectural Ornament . . .': Further Sullivan-Journal Correspondence," ibid. 63 (September 1975): 28–30.
31. Frank Lloyd Wright, *Genius and the Mobocracy* (New York: Duell, Sloan and Pearce, 1949), 72; Sullivan to Whitaker, June 5, 20, 1923.
32. Wright, *Genius,* 71, 74.
33. Sullivan to Mr. and Mrs. Pickell, January 31, 1924, Emil Lorch Collection, University of Michigan Library, Ann Arbor.
34. This account of Sullivan's last weeks is based in small part on Wright's *Genius,* 70–77, and in large part on a memorandum from N. Max Dunning to Sidney J. Adler, April 28, 1924, Sullivan Collection, Burnham Library, The Art Institute, Chicago.
35. Wright did publish the drawings, but not until 1949, as part of his "biography," *Genius and the Mobocracy.* Years later, the Frank Lloyd Wright Foundation at Scottsdale, Arizona, sold the collection to Avery Library at Columbia University.
36. Standard Certificate of Death no. 10575, dated and filed April 16, 1924, Cook County Clerk's Office, Chicago.
37. *The New York Times,* April 16, 1924, p. 23; also see *CT,* April 15, 1924, p. 10, and April 16, 1924, p. 10.

Index

Boldface indicates pages on which illustrations appear.

Sources of Illustrations

American Architect & Building News: IX.24
The Architectural Record: VII.6, 7, 11, 12, 13, 16, 17; VIII.2, 3, 5, 6, 7; X.3; XI.5, 9; XIII.5.
The Art Institute, Chicago: I.3, 6; IV.4.
The Auditorium Building: VII.2.
Avery Architectural and Fine Arts Library: I.1, 2, 4, 7; II.2, 4; III.4, 5; IV.1, 2; VIII.1; XI.7.
Barron, Joseph: V.9, 11.
Bostonian Society: I.5; II.1.
The Brickbuilder: X.4; XI.3; XIII.3.
Building Budget: V.1.
Bunk and McFetridge: II.6.
Chicago Architectural Club catalogue: XI.6.
Chicago Architectural Photographing Company: VIII.4, 7; IX.5, 20; X.18.
Chicago Daily News: IV.7.
Chicago Historical Society: IV.6; V.14.
Chicago Tribune: XI.1.
Engineering & Building Record: VII.10.
Engineering Magazine: VI.1; VII.14, 15.
Engineering Record: VI.2.
Furness, George Woods: II.3, 5.
The Graphic: X.10.
Guaranty Company Building Prospectus: X.19.
Guerinet, Armand, *Les Grand Prix de Rome d'architecture:* III.3.
Historic American Buildings Survey: XII.3.
Illuminating Engineer: XIII.1, 2.
Industrial Chicago: X.9.
Inland Architect: V.16, 17; VI.4, 5; VIII.9; IX.1, 10, 12, 13, 14, 15, 18, 19, 21, 22, 23, 25; X.15; XI.2, 10, 12; XII.6, 7.

Iowa State Historical Society: XIII.7.
Kaufman & Fabry: V.13; IX.6.
King's Handbook of the United States: VI.3.
Line, R. M.: V.3.
Lotus Club Notebook: II.9; III.3.
Mercantile Building prospectus: X.7, 8.
Michigan Historical Collections: III.6.
Morrison, Hugh, *Louis Sullivan:* V.12; IX.16; X.14.
Nickel, Richard: X.6.
Northwest Architectural Archives: XII.10; XIII.4.
Philadelphia Architectural Exhibition Catalogue: XII.13.
Pueblo Chieftain: IX.11.
Riverside magazine: II.10.
Roger-Viollet: III.2.
Homer Sailor Collection: XIII.10.
Joan Saltzstein: IV.5.
Southern Illinois University Architectural Ornament Collection: V.4, 5, 6, 7; X.16, 17.
State Historical Society of Wisconsin: XII.12.
Stearns, Gertrude: I.8.
St. Louis Chapter, AIA, catalogue: X.12, 20.
Louis H. Sullivan, *A System of Architectural Ornament:* XIII.15, 16.
Taylor, J. W.: VII.9.
Tusculum College Archives: XII.4.
Twombly, Robert: III.1; IV.2, 10, 15; VII.1, 8; IX.4, 8; XI.4; XII.2, 5, 8, 9, 11; XIII.6, 8, 9, 11, 12, 13.
Western Architect: VIII.4; X.13.
Woodbury, Ruth: I.9.
Frank Lloyd Wright Home and Studio Foundation: IX.2.